MW00358391

LYING IN EARLY MODERN ENGLISH CULTURE

Lying in Early Modern English Culture

From the Oath of Supremacy to
the Oath of Allegiance

ANDREW HADFIELD

OXFORD
UNIVERSITY PRESS

OXFORD

UNIVERSITY PRESS

Great Clarendon Street, Oxford, OX2 6DP,
United Kingdom

Oxford University Press is a department of the University of Oxford.
It furthers the University's objective of excellence in research, scholarship,
and education by publishing worldwide. Oxford is a registered trade mark of
Oxford University Press in the UK and in certain other countries

© Andrew Hadfield 2017

The moral rights of the author have been asserted

First Edition published in 2017

Impression: 1

Published in the United States of America by Oxford University Press
198 Madison Avenue, New York, NY 10016, United States of America

British Library Cataloguing in Publication Data
Data available

Library of Congress Control Number: 2017935046

ISBN 978–0–19–878946–8

Printed and bound by
CPI Group (UK) Ltd, Croydon, CR0 4YY

For

Lucy Eleanor Hadfield
Neil Rhodes
Jennifer Richards

Acknowledgements

I am extremely grateful to All Souls College, Oxford, where I spent a very happy visiting fellowship, Hilary term 2015. The project had been started before but that was where it really began. I am indebted to so many fellows who made time to discuss ideas with me and who provided me with stimulating advice which moved the project on considerably, in particular Robin Briggs, Vincent Crawford, Ian McLean, Sir Noel Malcolm, Sir Keith Thomas, Marina Warner, and Frederick Wilmot-Smith, and to my fellow visitors for being such an agreeable and intellectually demanding cohort, in particular Annalise Acorn. For help and advice about the law I am grateful to Paul Brand and Michael McNair; on John Payne Collier, Arthur and Janet Ing Freeman; Colin Burrow suggested I think more about Thomas More; John Kerrigan and Richard McCabe have both provided me with especially valuable suggestions. The Leverhulme Trust awarded me a research fellowship to work on the project (2015–16), which enabled me to build on institutional leave provided by The School of English, University of Sussex. I am extremely grateful to both.

Over the course of writing the book I have benefited from many conversations with colleagues and friends, who have helped the project in ways they may and may not have realized: in particular I learned from Peter Boxall, Rebecca Stott, and Matthew Woodcock. Sections have been read by many kind and helpful friends, whose incisive comments have vastly improved earlier versions: I am grateful to the generosity and critical acumen of Shanyn Altman, Angela Andreani, Matthew Dimmock, José Maria Pérez Fernández, Duncan Fraser, Paul Hammond, Lana Harper, John Kerrigan, Chloe Porter, Neil Rhodes, Jennifer Richards, Jim Shapiro, Cathy Shrank, and Greg Walker. The anonymous readers at OUP have provided incisive and helpful criticism, saved me from making some foolish errors, and improved the book immensely. All remaining faults are my responsibility.

Colleagues at Sussex have been congenial as always and I am fortunate to have been able to work with such an intellectually vigorous and socially amenable team of medieval and early modern scholars: Shanyn Altman, Angela Andreani, Matthew Dimmock, Duncan Fraser, Lana Harper, Margaret and Tom Healy, Nicole Mennell, Charles Nicholl, Chloe Porter, Paul Quinn, Maria Shymgol, and Katie Walter. Research was carried out in The Bodleian Library; The British Library; The Codrington Library, All Souls College; The Folger Shakespeare Library; The National Library of Wales; and Sussex University Library. I am extremely grateful to the help I received from so many kind and diligent expert librarians.

Papers based on research in the book have been given at All Souls College, Oxford; Brighton University; Cardiff University; The University of East Anglia; Glasgow University; The University of Granada; Justus Liebig University, Giessen; The Oxford English Faculty Graduate Seminar; Reading University; Sheffield University; The 44th Annual Shakespeare Association of America Conference,

New Orleans (2016); Sussex University; and The University of Westminster. Earlier versions of sections of the introduction and Chapters 3 and 6 appeared as 'Lying in Early Modern Culture', *Textual Practice* 28 (2014), 339–64; sections of the Introduction, and Chapters 2, 5, and 6 as 'Literature and the Culture of Lying Before the Enlightenment', *Studia Neophilologica* 85 (2013), 133–47; sections of Chapter 6 as 'Truth and Lies in *The Unfortunate Traveller*', *Critical Imprints* 1 (2017), 70–8, and 'A Red Herring?', *English Literary Renaissance* 45 (2015), 231–54; and sections of Chapter 7 as 'Jonson and Shakespeare in an Age of Lying', *Ben Jonson Journal* 23 (2016), 52–74. I am grateful to Edinburgh University Press, Taylor and Francis, and Wiley-Blackwell for permission to reproduce the material included here.

My love and thanks, as ever, to my family, Alison, Lucy, Patrick, Maud, and Daisy, who always help to make writing a far more enjoyable and much less lonely experience than it can be. This book is for Lucy, who is brave and truthful, and two wonderful friends, Neil and Jenny, who have been there for the whole journey.

Contents

List of Figures

List of Abbreviations

AJLH	*The American Journal of Legal History*
Bacon, ed. Spedding	*The Works of Francis Bacon*, ed. James Spedding, Robert Leslie Ellis, and Douglas Denon Heath, 7 vols (London: Longman, 1857–61)
BSRS	*Bulletin of the Society for Renaissance Studies*
C16J	*The Sixteenth-Century Journal*
Calvin, *Commentaries*	John Calvin, *Commentaries*, ed. Rev. John King, 22 vols (Grand Rapids, MI: Baker House Books, 1989)
CD	*Comparative Drama*
CH	*Church History*
CHR	*Catholic Historical Review*
Christian Church	F. L. Cross and E. A. Livingstone, eds, *The Oxford Dictionary of the Christian Church* (3rd edn, Oxford: Oxford University Press, 2005)
CL	*Comparative Literature*
CR	*Contemporary Review*
CRS	Catholic Record Society
CSPSp.	*Calendar of State Papers, Spanish, 1485–1558*, ed. Royall Tyler et al., 20 vols (London: HMSO, 1862–1954)
CSSH	*Comparative Studies in Society and History*
CUA	The Catholic University of America
Dyer, *Reports*	Sir James Dyer, *Reports of Cases in the Reigns of Henry VIII, Edward VI, Queen Mary, and Queen Elizabeth*, 3 vols (Dublin, 1794)
Ec.HR	*Economic History Review*
EETS	Early English Text Society
EHR	*English Historical Review*
ELH	*English Literary History*
Ellis, ed., *Letters*	Sir Henry Ellis, ed., *Original Letters Illustrative of English History*, 11 vols (London, 1824–6)
ELR	*English Literary Renaissance*
Erasmus, *Collected Works*	*The Collected Works of Erasmus* (Toronto: Toronto University Press, 1975–)
GR	*Greece & Rome*
HJ	*Historical Journal*
HLQ	*Huntington Library Quarterly*
HMSO	Her Majesty's Stationary Office
HTR	*Harvard Theological Review*
JCLC	*The Journal of Criminal Law and Criminology*
JEH	*Journal of Ecclesiastical History*
JEMCS	*The Journal of Early Modern Cultural Studies*
JHI	*Journal of the History of Ideas*
JHP	*Journal of the History of Philosophy*

JMEMS	*Journal of Medieval and Early Modern Studies*
Jonson	*The Cambridge Edition of the Works of Ben Jonson*, ed. David Bevington, Martin Butler, and Ian Donaldson, 7 vols (Cambridge: Cambridge University Press, 2012)
JPE	*Journal of Political Economy*
JWCI	*Journal of the Warburg and Courtauld Institutes*
KJV	Authorised (King James) Bible (1606)
Law and Hum.	*Law and Humanities*
LC	*Literature Compass*
Lemprière	J. Lemprière, *Lemprière's Classical Dictionary* (1865) (London: Bracken Books, 1984)
Letters and Papers	*Letters and Papers, Foreign and Domestic, Henry VIII*, ed. J. S. Brewer, James Gairdner, and R. H. Brodie, 28 vols (London: PRO, 1862–1932)
LHB	*Law and Human Behaviour*
LQR	*Law Quarterly Review*
MHRA	Modern Humanities Research Association
MLQ	*Modern Language Quarterly*
MLR	*Modern Language Review*
More, *CW*	Thomas More, *The Yale Edition of the Complete Works of St. Thomas More*, 15 vols (New Haven: Yale University Press, 1963–97)
MP	*Modern Philology*
MRTS	Medieval and Renaissance Text Society
N. & Q.	*Notes and Queries*
Narrative and Dramatic Sources	Geoffrey Bullough, ed., *Narrative and Dramatic Sources of Shakespeare*, 8 vols (London: Routledge, 2000, rpt of 1962)
Nashe, *Works*	Thomas Nashe, *The Works of Thomas Nashe*, ed. Ronald B. McKerrow, rev. F. P. Wilson, 5 vols (Oxford: Blackwell, 1966)
NLH	*New Literary History*
ODNB	*Oxford Dictionary of National Biography*
OED	*Oxford English Dictionary*
OJLS	*Oxford Journal of Legal Studies*
P. & P.	*Past and Present*
PAPS	*Proceedings of the American Philosophical Society*
Partridge, *Bawdy*	Eric Partridge, *Shakespeare's Bawdy* (London: Routledge, 2001)
PI	*Philosophers' Imprint*
PIMS	Pontifical Institute of Mediaeval Studies
PMLA	*Publications of the Modern Language Association of America*
Popes	J. N. D. Kelly, ed., *The Oxford Dictionary of Popes* (Oxford: Oxford University Press, 1986)
PRO	Public Record Office
PT	*Political Theory*
Quintilian, *Institutes*	Quintilian, *The Orator's Education*, ed. and trans. Donald A. Russell, 5 vols (Cambridge, MA: Harvard University Press, 2001)

R. & R.	*Renaissance and Reformation*
RES	*The Review of English Studies*
RESS	*Review of Ecumenical Studies Sibiu*
RETS	Renaissance English Text Society
RH	*Recusant History*
RQ	*Renaissance Quarterly*
RS	*Renaissance Studies*
Saints	David Hugh Farmer, ed., *The Oxford Dictionary of Saints* (2nd edn, Oxford: Oxford University Press, 1987)
SB	*Studies in Bibliography*
SCJ	*Sixteenth-Century Journal*
SEL	*Studies in English Literature, 1500–1900*
SHPS	*Studies in the History and Philosophy of Science*
Sh. Sur.	*Shakespeare Survey*
SJT	*Scottish Journal of Theology*
Smith, ed., *Worlds of Shakespeare*	Bruce R. Smith, ed., *The Cambridge Guide to the Worlds of Shakespeare*, 2 vols (Cambridge: Cambridge University Press, 2016)
SP	*Studies in Philology*
SPCK	Society for the Promotion of Christian Knowledge
Sp. Enc.	*The Spenser Encyclopedia*, ed. A. C. Hamilton (Toronto and London: University of Toronto Press and Routledge, 1990)
Spenser, *Variorum*	*The Works of Edmund Spenser: A Variorum Edition*, ed. Edwin Greenlaw, Charles Grosvenor Osgood, Frederick Morgan Padelford, and Ray Heffner, 11 vols (Baltimore: Johns Hopkins Press, 1932–45)
Sp. St.	*Spenser Studies*
SQ	*Shakespeare Quarterly*
SR	*Studies in the Renaissance*
State Trials	*Cobbett's Complete Collection of State Trials and Proceedings for High Treason and Other Crimes and Misdemeanors from the Earliest Period to the Present Time*, 21 vols (London, 1821)
Statutes	*The Statutes of the Realm*
STC	Katharine F. Pantzer, A. W. Pollard, G. R. Redgrave, eds, *A Short-Title Catalogue of Books Printed in England, Scotland, and Ireland and of English Books Printed Abroad, 1475–1640*, 3 vols (London: The Bibliographical Society, 1976–91).
Stuart Royal Proclamations	James F. Larkin and Paul L. Hughes, eds, *Stuart Royal Proclamations, Volume I: Royal Proclamations of King James I, 1603–1625* (Oxford: Oxford University Press, 1973)
Summa Theologica	St Thomas Aquinas, *Summa Theologica*, trans. Fathers of the Dominican Province, 5 vols (Notre Dame: Christian Classics, 1948)
TCBS	*Transactions of the Cambridge Bibliographical Society*
Tilley, *Proverbs*	Maurice Palmer Tilley, *A Dictionary of the Proverbs in England in the Sixteenth and Seventeenth Centuries: A Collection of the Proverbs Found in English Literature and the Dictionaries of the Period* (Ann Arbor: University of Michigan Press, 1950)

TP	*Textual Practice*
TRHS	*Transactions of the Royal Historical Society*
TS	*Theological Studies*
Tudor Constitution	G. R. Elton, ed., *The Tudor Constitution: Documents and Commentary* (Cambridge: Cambridge University Press, 1972)
Tudor England: An Encyclopedia	Arthur F. Kinney and David W. Swain, eds, *Tudor England: An Encyclopedia* (London: Routledge, 2000)
UTQ	*University of Toronto Quarterly*
Venn	J. and J. A. Venn, eds, *Alumni Cantabrigienes: a biographical list of all known students, graduates and holders of office at the University of Cambridge, from the earliest times to 1900: Part One From the earliest times to 1751*, 4 vols (Cambridge: Cambridge University Press, 1922–7)
YJLH	*Yale Journal of Law and Humanities*
YSPSR	*Yearbook of the Spanish and Portuguese Society for English Renaissance Studies*
YWM	*The Year's Work in Medievalism*

Introduction
Being Economical with the Truth in Early Modern England

I

There were few subjects that animated people in early modern Europe more than lying. The subject is endlessly represented and discussed in literature; treatises on rhetoric and courtiership; theology, philosophy, and jurisprudence; travel writing; pamphlets and news books; science and empirical observation; popular culture, especially books about strange, unexplained phenomena; and, of course, legal discourse. For many, lying could be controlled and limited even if not eradicated; for others, lying was a necessary element of a casuistical tradition, liars balancing complicated issues and short-term pragmatic considerations in the expectation of solving more problems than they caused through their deceit.

This study explores forms, modes, and significance of lying—and debates about lying—from the Oath of Supremacy (1535) to the Oath of Allegiance (1606). I do not especially like so vague a term but this book is therefore a cultural, rather than a philosophical, theological, or political, history of lying, even though, of course, it touches upon all these subjects.[1] The Oath of Supremacy marked the decisive break with Rome and the establishment of the English monarch as sovereign within his dominions, head of the Church, and answerable to no foreign authority (i.e. the Pope).[2] In its wake came religious division: no one can be sure how many people were converted to the new faith and how many continued to think and practise their devotions as they always had done.[3] As the religious nature of the Tudor regime changed with bewildering speed and with differing forms of brutality and tolerance, the parameters of lying became a central question. Could one avoid

---

[1] On the problems of defining the subject see Peter Burke, *What is Cultural History?* (Cambridge: Polity, 2004).

[2] John Guy, *Tudor England* (Oxford: Oxford University Press, 1988), ch. 5; *Tudor Constitution*, p. 358.

[3] For differing assessments of the evidence in what is now becoming an ever more complicated debate, see Eamon Duffy, *The Stripping of the Altars: Traditional Religion in England, 1400–1580* (New Haven: Yale University Press, 1992); Alexandra Walsham, *The Reformation of the Landscape: Religion, Identity, and Memory in Early Modern Britain and Ireland* (Oxford: Oxford University Press, 2011); Alec Ryrie, *The Age of Reformation: The Tudor and Stewart Realms, 1485–1603* (Harlow: Pearson, 2009).

taking oaths?[4] How permissible was it to bend the truth? Was what passed for truth now the same as it had been a year or two ago? What would God tolerate? He might not approve of lying but did he want his faithful flock to be destroyed?

In his public defence of the Oath of Allegiance, *Triplici Nodo*, written in answer to attacks by Pope Paul V and Cardinal Robert Bellarmine, James I acknowledged the significance of the Oath of Supremacy, explained how and why his new oath followed in its predecessor's footsteps, and acknowledged a significant development in the nature of a subject's declaration of loyalty to the crown: 'For as the Oath of Supremacie was devised for putting a difference betweene Papists, and them of our profession: so was this Oath, which hee would seeme to impugne, ordained for making a difference betweene the civilly obedient Papists, and the perverse disciples of the Powder-Treason.'[5] James was acutely aware of the historical relationship between the two oaths, arguing that the Oath of Allegiance completed the work of the Oath of Supremacy in controlling and flushing out subversion, lying, and deception that led directly to the Gunpowder Plot. Times had changed and the government needed to root out deceitful subjects who avoided the spirit of the oath through their cunning and duplicitousness, a strategy that the state had to counteract. Accordingly, the Oath of Allegiance forms a logical *terminus ad quem* for this study.

Lying, as the Bible tells us, began almost at the very beginning, with the serpent telling Eve that she would not die if she ate the fruit of the Tree of Knowledge, a narrative that was soon intertwined with the story of Satan's fall from heaven and desire to corrupt mankind.[6] It has a history that shows no signs of ending. However, my opening contention is that studying a particular body of evidence will provide most obvious insight into the nature and history of lying, rather than an overarching work that aims to be comprehensive. Exploring the cultural significance of lying in early modern England from the late 1520s to the early 1600s provides a large enough sample and a long enough period to enable me to undertake a proper comparative study without losing focus on a coherent period. This coherence is provided by two crucial moments in English/British history which forced individuals to choose allegiance and decide where their loyalties really lay, the one the logical consequence of the other. I want to try to understand why and how people lied in that period. What pressures were placed upon individuals to tell the truth or to lie? How did they think about lying? Were conceptions of lying

---

[4] Jonathan Michael Gray, *Oaths and the English Reformation* (Cambridge: Cambridge University Press, 2013), ch. 1. Catholics were told that they could break oaths they were forced to make to heretics: Peter Holmes, ed., *Elizabethan Casuistry* (London: CRS, 1981), p. 52.

[5] King James VI and I, *Triplici Nodo, Triplex Cuneus. Or, An Apologie for the Oath of Allegiance* in *Political Writings*, ed. Johann P. Sommerville (Cambridge: Cambridge University Press, 1994), pp. 85–13, at p. 103. On James's quarrel with Cardinal Bellarmine, see David Harris Willson, *King James VI and I* (London: Cape, 1956), pp. 231–6; W. B. Patterson, *King James VI and I and the Reunion of Christendom* (Cambridge: Cambridge University Press, 1997), ch. 3; Rebecca Lemon, *Treason by Words: Literature, Law, and Rebellion in Shakespeare's England* (Ithaca: Cornell University Press, 2006), pp. 118–23.

[6] Dallas G. Denery II, *The Devil Wins: A History of Lying from the Garden of Eden to the Enlightenment* (Princeton: Princeton University Press, 2014), pp. 21–61.

very different from what we experience now? And if definitions of lying did not change a great deal, did the ways in which it was imagined and represented change? Put another way, did changes in the vocabulary of lying transform specific and possible forms of lying?

The book actually originated in a very specific fear about trust and evidence, which then developed into a wider study: what if much of the information we use when constructing any history is not actually true? When writing a history of anything what you do not know is often as important as what you do know. Research will reveal that things that you thought you knew are not actually as clear cut as you imagined, and far more of what seemed once to be evidence is really conjecture, hearsay, retrospective reconstruction, or simply falsification. Far too much apparent information falls into the category of 'unknown unknowns', to use Donald Rumsfeld's felicitous phrase, and it would help matters if we could transform as many of these as possible into 'known knowns' and 'known unknowns'.[7] In order to achieve this task we have to start thinking about modes of untruth as well as truth: fictions, errors, falsifications, misunderstandings, misreadings, distortions, and, of course, lies, because our understanding of what these are and can be orders our comprehension of the truth. Sometimes the truth is not properly recorded because it has been shaped in a particular way; sometimes because it is inaccessible; and sometimes because it is deliberately hidden. We operate on the understanding that we know what the truth is—more or less—even if we do not have an explicitly articulated theory of what it might be unless we are professional philosophers. Accordingly, most historians of every stripe are in broad agreement about what it is possible to achieve through their researches and reading of texts, standards that guide how we all then read the evidence, at first and second hand.[8] As Paul Ricoeur put it, 'We expect history to have a certain objectivity.'[9]

We certainly do not have concomitant theories of lying, although the word has been with us since Anglo-Saxon times: 'lygen', a noun meaning 'A lie, falsehood', derived from Old High German.[10] Historians base their work on the search for archival evidence, on the gold standard of finding a document that provides hitherto unknown evidence that solves a particular conundrum, so it is perhaps not surprising that the history of great discoveries is littered with stories of forgeries and fakes: The Donation of Constantine, which purported to show that the Emperor had handed over authority in Rome to the Pope; *The Protocols of the Elders of Zion*, first published in 1903, which showed how the Jews had secretly

[7] Slavov Zizek, 'What Rumsfeld Doesn't Know that he Knows about Abu Ghraib', 'In These Times', 21 May 2004 (http://www.lacan.com/zizekrumsfeld.htm) (accessed 28 May 2015).

[8] Steven Shapin, *A Social History of Truth: Civility and Science in Seventeenth-Century England* (Chicago: University of Chicago Press, 1994), pp. 409–18. Two representative recent guides to historiography are Ludmilla Jordanova, *History in Practice* (2nd edn, London: Arnold, 2006); Gabrielle M. Spiegel, ed., *Practicing History: New Directions in Historical Writing after the Linguistic Turn* (London: Routledge, 2005).

[9] Paul Ricoeur, *History and Truth*, trans. Charles A. Kelbley (2nd edn, Chicago: Northwestern University Press, 1965), p. 21.

[10] Bosworth-Toller Anglo-Saxon Dictionary (http://bosworth.ff.cuni.cz/054878) (accessed 6 July 2015).

planned to take over the world; the Piltdown Man, a fake skull planted in a gravel pit in Sussex which provided evidence of early man's existence in the British Isles; and the Hitler Diaries.[11] And, of course, there are numerous fakes and forgeries of artworks.[12] Forgery can be a mode of lying, and it should not surprise us that in 1597 when two goldsmiths were accused of this crime they were tried under the 1563 perjury statute because they 'had sworn not to commit forgery'.[13] A similar point can be made about impostors.[14] Or, indeed, plagiarists.[15] As Natalie Zemon Davis pointed out in a justly influential article based on her study of French pardon trials, there is all too often fiction in the archives when there is assumed to be fact, an insight the implications of which have yet to be fully thought through. Many testimonies that are thought to be simply factual evidence are based on existing literary models. They should not be read as unmediated modes of truth-telling, but in terms of widely understood forms of storytelling and any historian examining them as evidence needs to be alert to this issue.[16] Postmodernist historians assumed that the close relationship between fact and fiction meant that there was no such thing as truth and, therefore, that narratives determined what reality was. In doing so they collapsed any distinction between fact and fiction, a dangerous move away from the equally problematic assumptions of a confident historiography which imagined that 'known knowns' were easier to uncover than they were.[17]

My contention in this book is that we need to question the ways in which certain historical events are known to us through documents full of lies—such as the trial of Anne Boleyn—but also to try to understand how a culture of lying, and thinking about truth and lies, characterized life for most people in early modern England, and therefore determines what we uncover in the written records left behind that enable us to recover what we can of that era. As Bernard Capp has rightly argued, there may well have been 'fiction in the archives' but this does not mean that we

---

[11] Only *The Protocols of the Elders of Zion* has its believers today, as a variety of anti-Semitic websites demonstrate, e.g. http://www.biblebelievers.org.au/przion1.htm; http://www.jewwatch.com/jew-references-protocols-full-text-folder.html; http://www.threeworldwars.com/protocols.htm (all unfortunately accessed 28 May 2015).

[12] See Brian Innes, *Fakes and Forgeries: The True Crime Stories of History's Greatest Deceptions: The Criminals, the Scams, and the Victims* (London: Reader's Digest, 2005).

[13] Michael D. Gordon, 'The Invention of a Common Law Crime: Perjury in Elizabethan Courts', *AJLH* 24 (1980), 145–70, p. 152.

[14] See Miriam Eliav-Feldon, *Renaissance Impostors and Proofs of Identity* (Basingstoke: Palgrave Macmillan, 2012), a study inspired by Natalie Zemon Davis, *The Return of Martin Guerre* (Cambridge, MA: Harvard University Press, 1984).

[15] Lambert Ennis, 'Anthony Nixon: Jacobean Plagiarist and Hack', *HLQ* 4 (1940), 377–401; Paulina Kewes, ed., *Plagiarism in Early Modern England* (Basingstoke: Palgrave Macmillan, 2003).

[16] Natalie Zemon Davis, *Fiction in the Archives: Pardon Tales and their Tellers in Sixteenth Century France* (Stanford: Stanford University Press, 1987). The objection by Stuart Carroll that the stories are also factual, not just fiction, misses the mark and assumes a rigid distinction between fact and fiction that Davis's work is challenging: *Blood and Violence in Early Modern France* (Oxford: Oxford University Press, 2006), pp. 23–4. See also Barbara J. Shapiro, *A Culture of Fact: England, 1550–1720* (Ithaca, NY: Cornell University Press, 2000), p. 42.

[17] See, for example, Beverley Southgate, *Postmodernism in History: Fear or Freedom?* (London: Routledge, 2003); Alun Munslow and Robert A. Rosenstone, eds, *Experiments in Rethinking History* (London: Routledge, 2004); Ann Curthoys and John Docker, *Is History Fiction?* (Ann Arbor: University of Michigan Press, 2005).

cannot 'establish at least a core of agreed fact'.[18] On the one hand this is a practical problem that needs to be addressed. There is surely a significant difference between telling a crafted tale that shapes a story in a particular manner according to established models and an outright lie, a distinction crucial when asking to be judged, acquitted, and pardoned. A false document sets in train a series of problems that cannot be solved by an appeal to the inherently fictional nature of narrative, disabling the historian's belief that an authentic archival source always takes evidential precedence. On the other, it is a matter of uncovering a mentality that understood that lies were a part of everyday life—as they surely always are—and that they structured reality, especially after the Reformation when the confessional divide led each side to label their opponents as liars. As Perez Zagorin noted, 'with the Reformation, the problem of dissimulation acquired new urgency and importance'.[19]

II

In 1578–9 the young Englishman Anthony Munday (1560?–1633) travelled through France and Italy until he arrived in Rome. For three months (February to May) he stayed at the English College, making him the only significant English literary author between Sir Thomas Wyatt (1503–42), who went as a member of Sir John Russell's diplomatic mission to the Pope in 1527, and John Milton (1608–74), whose grand tour took place in 1638–9, to travel to the ancient city.[20] Rome featured a great deal in the English imagination but no one apart from Munday witnessed it first-hand until well after the Reformation.[21] Munday was also one of the very few Englishmen in this period to meet the Pope and he described his encounter in vivid detail when he published his account of his travels in 1582. The students of the English College are told by their rector, Alfonso the Jesuit, that the Pope has sent for them:

> Then we went with him to the Pope's Palace, where coming into the Pope's chamber, and having everyone kissed his foot, we stayed to attend what was his pleasure. But before he spake any word, with a dissembling and hypocritical countenance, he fell into tears, which trickled down his white beard, and began in Latin with these, or the very like words.

[18] Bernard Capp, *When Gossips Meet: Women, Family, and Neighbourhood in Early Modern England* (Oxford: Oxford University Press, 2003), p. 3.

[19] Perez Zagorin, *Ways of Lying: Dissimulation and Conformity in Early Modern Europe* (Cambridge, MA: Harvard University Press, 1990), p. 68. See also Perez Zagorin, 'The Historical Significance of Lying and Dissimulation', *Social Research* 63 (1996), 863–912.

[20] Susan Brigden, *Thomas Wyatt: The Heart's Forest* (London: Faber, 2012), pp. 103–30; Gordon Campbell and Thomas N. Corns, *John Milton: Life, Work, and Thought* (Oxford: Oxford University Press, 2008), pp. 116–19, 122–3. On Munday's presence at the English College, see Anthony Kenny, 'Antony Munday in Rome', *RH* 6 (1962), 158–62.

[21] On Rome in the English imagination see Andrew Hadfield, 'Renaissance England's Views of Rome', *BSRS* vol. xxxii, 2 (Oct. 2015), 9–12.

'O you Englishmen, to whom my love is such as I can no way utter, considering that for me you have left your prince, which was your duty, and come so far to me, which is more than I can deserve, yet as I am your refuge when persecution dealeth straitly with you in your country by reason of the heretical religion there used, so will I be your bulwark to defend you, your guide to protect you, your Father to nourish you, and your friend with my heart-blood to do you any profit.'

Behold what deceits the Devil hath to accomplish his desire: tears, smooth speeches, liberality, and a thousand means to make a man careless of God, disobedient to his prince, and more, to violate utterly the faith of a subject. These tears that he shed, these words that he spake, made divers of them say within themselves, as one of them for example presently to me said, 'O singular saint, whose life, love, and liberality may be a spectacle to the whole world. Who would live in England, under the government of so vile a Jezebel, and may rest in safety under the perfect image of Jesus? Who would not forsake father, mother, friends, goods, yea, and the life itself, to have the bountiful blessing of such a provident Father?' The Pope recovering his health again from his weeping, caused this devout fellow to stay his talk, because he began again as thus:

'What is the cause that you will depart from me, that have so well provided for you, to thrust yourselves on the rock of your own destruction?'[22]

This is an extraordinary passage, the one eyewitness account by someone outside the diplomatic circles of the Pope, who was from 1534 with the passing of the Act for the submission of the clergy to the King's Majesty, the sworn enemy of the English monarch as supreme head of the Church of England.[23] Munday acknowledges that there may be some anxiety about his representation of the pontiff, Gregory XIII, a keen supporter of the missionary work of the Jesuits, and confirms that he has reproduced the exact—or almost exact—words that he spoke to the assembled young Englishmen.[24] The words in Munday's text are certainly plausible and represent the Pope as he was seen in England: hypocritical and self-serving, eager to persuade generations of zealots to do his bidding at the expense of the truth, breaking their bonds of loyalty to their princes and their nations in the process.[25] Gregory was, after all, well known as a Counter-Reformation Pope who, as soon as he had been elected, had celebrated news of the St Bartholomew's Day Massacre, a traumatic event for Protestants which terrified many into renouncing their faith, with *Te Deums* and a thanksgiving service.[26] Here we witness him 'dissembling', as he pretends to cry for the young Englishmen who have sacrificed their security and happiness for his cause whereas, so Munday implies, he feels no such strong emotion. Such practice might be acceptable in a politician—although Munday does not actually state this—but it marks the Pope out as a moral

[22] Anthony Munday, *The English Roman Life*, ed. Philip J. Ayres (Oxford: Clarendon Press, 1980), pp. 91–2.

[23] *Tudor Constitution*, pp. 339–41.   [24] On Gregory, see *Popes*, pp. 269–71.

[25] See Anon., *Certain Sermons Appointed by the Queen's Majesty To be Declared and Read By All Parsons, Vicars, and Curates, Every Sunday and Holiday in Their Churches; And By her Grace's Advice Perused and Overseen For The Better Understanding Of The Simple People* (1574) (Cambridge: Parker, 1850), pp. 469–70, 588–9, 596, *passim*.

[26] Robert M. Kingdon, *Myths about the St. Bartholomew's Day Massacres, 1572–1576* (Cambridge, MA: Harvard University Press, 1988), p. 42; Zagorin, *Ways of Lying*, pp. 107–8.

impostor, a sly worldly politician masquerading as a spiritual authority. Justus Lipsius's edition of Tacitus's histories (1574) had made stories of the horrifying regimes of the first Roman imperial family, the Julio-Claudians, easily available to European readers.[27] Most literate readers understood the dishonesty and disguise that characterized the reigns of Tiberius, Caligula, Claudius, and Nero, and it is surely this comparison that Munday, who was a skilful linguist and energetic translator, and who certainly knew Latin well, intended his readers to make. The hopeful young Catholics eager to restore their faith are being used by a cynical, self-serving figure familiar to literate readers with more experience.

The Pope is a liar, the incarnation of the Devil on earth, luring the unwary away from their duties to prince and country with false promises that will lead to their destruction, not the salvation of lost souls.[28] For Munday, the Pope is skilled in the rhetorical arts and his performance is a clever self-presentation designed to attract those already predisposed towards martyrdom, as the speech of the scholar indicates.[29] The Pope opens his speech with the familiar rhetorical figure of *ecphonesis*, the 'exclamation of extreme emotion', which he also performs with his dissembling actions, another practice available to the student of oratory and rhetoric.[30] He expresses his apparent concern for the English students and represents himself as their 'bulwark', a *prosopopoeia* signalling that he is the rock on which Christ built his Church, but at the same time he alludes cunningly to their potential martyrdom in pledging that he is their friend and will use his 'heart-blood' to do them profit whereas the truth is that he will be advantaged by their sacrifice.[31] The Pope is following Quintilian's dictum that 'The life and soul of oratory... is in the emotions.'[32] Such 'smooth speech' is complemented by the insincere rhetorical question—*interrogatio*—wondering out loud why the students would ever leave the safety of life in Rome for the hazardous probability of martyrdom in the lands of the vile Jezebel who rules England, when all know the answer.[33] In posing the question and affecting to be musing aloud because he is so overcome with emotion the Pope is also enacting the figure, *occupatio*, drawing attention to what he is pretending to pass over, that is, martyrdom and its attendant rewards in heaven.[34]

[27] Jon R. Snyder, *Dissimulation and the Culture of Secrecy in Early Modern Europe* (Berkeley: University of California Press, 2009), p. 15; Peter Burke, 'Tacitism', in T. A. Dorey, ed., *Tacitus* (London: Routledge, 1969), pp. 149–71; David Womersley, 'Sir Henry Saville's Translation of Tacitus and the Political Interpretation of Elizabethan Texts', *RES* 42 (1991), 313–42.

[28] On the Pope as the Devil, see Nathan Johnstone, *The Devil and Demonism in Early Modern England* (Cambridge: Cambridge University Press, 2006), ch. 2.

[29] Susannah Brietz Monta, *Martyrdom and Literature in Early Modern England* (Cambridge: Cambridge University Press, 2005), ch. 5; John Donne, *Pseudo-Martyr*, ed. Anthony Raspa (Montreal and Kingston: McGill-Queen's University Press, 1993); Shanyn Altman, 'John Donne and Martyrdom', PhD Thesis, University of Sussex, 2016, ch. 5.

[30] Brian Vickers, *In Defence of Rhetoric* (Oxford: Clarendon Press, 1988), p. 493; Quintilian, *Institutes*, 9.1.34.

[31] Vickers, *Rhetoric*, p. 498.

[32] Quintilian, *Institutes*, 6.2.7; Coppélia Kahn, 'Reading Faces in *Hamlet*', in Panja, ed., *Shakespeare and the Art of Lying*, pp. 37–58, at p. 48.

[33] Quintilian, *Institutes*, 9.2.6.

[34] Quintilian, *Institutes*, 9.3.98; Vickers, *Rhetoric*, p. 496; Lee A. Sonnino, *A Handbook to Sixteenth-Century Rhetoric* (London: Routledge, 1968), p. 135.

Munday's book would appear to have been timed to appear after the first Jesuit campaign and the execution of Edmund Campion and his fellow Jesuits in 1581, providing an eager and anxious English readership with a wealth of insights into the world that sent hostile missionaries prepared to die for their cause to their shores.[35] However, the passage may not be quite what it seems to be and the author may be just as dissembling as he claims the Pope is. No one knows why Munday made a sudden decision to abandon his apprenticeship to the printer and bookseller John Allde and travel to Rome (coincidentally, at the same time that Henry Garnet abandoned his apprenticeship with Richard Tottel to become a Jesuit).[36] Munday's text places the author's anxiety on display. He claims that he travelled to Rome through the natural curiosity of a traveller: 'Whenas desire to see strange countries, as also affection to learn the languages, had persuaded me to leave my native country, and not any other intent or cause, God is my record.'[37] The need to make a public declaration that his intentions were entirely innocent, in the form of an oath, suggests that either Munday has been challenged about his motives in travelling to Rome, or he anticipates that readers are likely to be suspicious of his reasons for going there.[38] Munday's journey is an unusual one for a loyal Protestant to have made and his account has been questioned by commentators ever since. For Tracey Hill, Munday was responding to critics who had questioned his religious allegiance affirming his loyalty in order to allay suspicions; but for Donna Hamilton, Munday's title, *The English Roman Life*, is studied in its ambiguity, the author declaring that he maintains his Catholic loyalty in describing the life of an English Roman Catholic who has refused martyrdom, reassuring the authorities and explaining his actions to his co-religionists.[39]

However we read Munday's words it is clear that he is eager to persuade his readers that he is telling the truth and not lying, even if he is. The dedicatory epistle to the Privy Council—which names the Lord Chancellor, Sir Thomas Bromley, Lord Burghley, and the Earl of Leicester for good measure—states that the author has been honest and faithful in his account: 'I have been careful to note down nothing in it that might impeach me either with error or untruth, malice or affection to any, but even have ordered the same according to certainty and knowledge.'[40] This declaration, like the oath on the first page of the work itself, is conspicuously legalistic in its language and reads like a formal defence in court in

[35] On Campion, see below, pp. 74–9.

[36] *ODNB* entry on Munday; on Garnet, see below, p. 87. Celeste Turner Wright suggests that Allde had Catholic sympathies: 'Young Anthony Munday Again', *SP* 56 (1959), 150–68, p. 154.

[37] Munday, *English Roman Life*, p. 5. Munday's editor, Philip J. Ayres, takes his statement of motives as read, adding that 'boredom with his life as an apprentice no doubt provided the spur' ('Introduction', p. xiv).

[38] 'God is my record' was a familiar form of oath: see John Tillotson, 'Sermon Twenty Two: The Lawfulness and Obligation of Oaths', in *The Works of the Most Reverend Dr. John Tillotson* (London, 1720), pp. 209–19, at p. 214.

[39] Tracey Hill, *Anthony Munday and Civic Culture: Theatre, History and Power in Early Modern London, 1580–1633* (Manchester: Manchester University Press, 2004), p. 85; Donna B. Hamilton, *Anthony Munday and the Catholics, 1560–1633* (Farnham: Ashgate, 2005), pp. 47–9.

[40] Munday, *English Roman Life*, p. 1.

a treason trial, perhaps even like Edmund Campion's defence at his trial two years earlier with its careful description of what the Jesuits were and were not doing: 'We are dead men to the world, we only travelled for souls; we touched neither state nor policy, we had no such commission.'[41] Munday, unlike Campion, was not expecting to die, but his language suggests that he knew that he had to defend himself effectively. The *OED*, recognizing the tenor of Munday's language, cites his use of 'impeach' (verb) as one of its examples of definition 4a., 'To bring a charge or accusation against; to accuse of, charge with'. 'Malice' was the key term used in the majority of treason trials that dealt with words rather than actions: it was the duty of the defendant to prove that he or she had not uttered the potentially treasonable words with malice, but honestly, openly, and innocently, a perilous enterprise for any defendant and a difficult task to achieve.[42]

Munday's claim is that the testimony of *The English Roman Life* should be enough to exonerate him, as it is definitely true and was not written to please a patron. Munday had written a number of works for Edward de Vere, Earl of Oxford, who acted as his patron in the late 1570s and early 1580s, a peer who confessed to the Queen in 1580 that he had been a Catholic since 1576.[43] Dedicating the work to the Privy Council may have been an act of sensible, pragmatic good sense, or more desperate self-preservation, as it is possible that Munday was interviewed by the Privy Council on his return from Italy, just as Ben Jonson was interviewed on various occasions in his life about his confessional allegiance and loyalty.[44] But it is most likely that Munday dedicated the work to the Privy Council because he was already a spy, as Cardinal William Allen, head of the English Catholics in Rome, recognized.[45]

The English Roman Life is a slippery and complicated work that professes to tell the truth, and in doing so dissimulates and tells lies. It is likely that Munday's account of the Pope's words and actions is accurate as witnesses corroborate other aspects of his account of his time in Rome.[46] What is noticeable is that it is Munday's comments surrounding the speeches of the Pope and the unnamed English student which cast those speeches in a negative light. The judgements could easily be reversed and the Pope's words praised as the sincere rhetoric and emotions of a pontiff concerned for the salvation of the English, much like the desire to convert that distant people expressed by the Pope's predecessor and namesake, Gregory the Great. Gregory encountered the English boys in the market at Rome and sent Augustine of Canterbury to convert the English, a well-known

---

[41] *State Trials*, I, p. 1054.   [42] See below, pp. 44–6.

[43] Hill, *Munday and Civic Culture*, pp. 84–5; Alan H. Nelson, *Monstrous Adversity: The Life of Edward de Vere, 17th Earl of Oxford* (Liverpool: Liverpool University Press, 2003), pp. 80–1, 238–9, 381–4, *passim*; Turner Wright, 'Young Anthony Munday', p. 156.

[44] David Riggs, *Ben Jonson: A Life* (Cambridge, MA: Harvard University Press, 1989), pp. 32–3, 127–30; Richard Dutton, *Ben Jonson, Volpone, and the Gunpowder Plot* (Cambridge: Cambridge University Press, 2008), ch. 1.

[45] Stephen Alford, *The Watchers: A Secret History of the Reign of Elizabeth I* (London: Penguin, 2012), p. 68. Celeste Turner Wright argues that Munday was a sincere convert: 'Young Anthony Munday', p. 155. On Allen (1532–94), see the *ODNB* entry.

[46] Munday, *English Roman Life*, Introduction, pp. xix–xx; *ODNB* entry.

story that Munday might have had in mind when telling his.[47] The question is not really whether Munday is telling the truth about the Pope's words, but whether he has recorded his reactions honestly, or framed the story of his visit to Rome in a recognizable manner that supports what would have been expected of a loyal Protestant in the Pope's city. Munday reminds the reader throughout of his good faith and behaviour: 'And this I may say boldly, for that it is true, as God is my witness, that in all that time I was amongst them I neither offered moiety of misordered or undecent speech, either of Her Majesty, or any nobleman in the Court,' and that rumours of his treachery are unfounded:

> And because my adversaries object against me, that I went to mass, and helped the priest myself to say mass: so that (say they) who is worst, I am as evil as he. I answer, I did indeed, for he that is in Rome, especially in the College among the scholars, must live as he may, not as he will; favour comes by conformity, and death by obstinacy.[48]

This passage would seem to raise as many questions as it answers and it is hard to take Munday's words at face value. Was he really just in Italy because he wanted to learn the language and see the eternal city? Perhaps he was simply bolder or more foolish than the rest of his countrymen and women. The final clause hints at a different explanation, and the dictum that success depends on toeing the line, and that the penalty for deviance is death, leaves the reader to make up his or her own mind about Munday. Is he saying this about Rome in particular and so affirming the loyal identity he asserts throughout the book? Or pointing out that in the post-Reformation world it is dangerous to tell the truth to power whether in England or in Rome and in so doing cleverly undermining his protestations of loyalty? It is hard to believe that Munday is not lying but equally difficult to pinpoint exactly which way his lies direct us.

Once a language—or a particular set of skills—exists it can be learned and it was not difficult for those trained in the art of rhetoric to acquire new skills: after all, that is what people did at school, learning how to use a language and its particular features to persuade an audience to believe one's argument, exactly as Munday claims the Pope behaves.[49] But his analysis could equally well be applied to his own text, and its representation of the superstitious, idolatrous, and ignorant nature of Catholic worship, which fits into a well-established pattern of Protestant rhetoric.[50] It is never clear throughout Munday's text when he is protesting too much and

---

[47] *Popes*, p. 67. For other writers the story had a much more sinister significance: Allen J. Frantzen, 'Bede and Bawdy Bale: Gregory the Great, Angels and the "Angli"', in Allen J. Frantzen and John D. Niles, eds, *Anglo-Saxonism and the Construction of Social Identity* (Gainsville: University Press of Florida, 1997), pp. 17–39, at p. 37; Benedict Scott Robinson, 'John Foxe and the Anglo-Saxons', in Highley and King, eds, *Foxe and His World*, pp. 54–72.

[48] Munday, *English Roman Life*, p. 66.

[49] Peter Mack, *Elizabethan Rhetoric: Theory and Practice* (Cambridge: Cambridge University Press, 2002), chs 1–2.

[50] Peter Lake, 'Anti-Popery: The Structure of a Prejudice', in Richard Cust and Ann Hughes, eds, *Conflict in Early Stuart England: Studies in Religion and Politics, 1603–1642* (Harlow: Longman, 1989), pp. 72–106; Paul Quinn, 'Anti-Papistry and the English Stage, 1580–1642', PhD Thesis, University of Sussex, 2006.

performing sincerity and when he might actually be sincere. Munday reproduces details of Catholic worship of saints' relics, a common Protestant target, but his descriptions are often surprisingly sparing in critical comment, certainly when compared to accounts of other English travellers.[51] For example, his account of the pilgrimage to Santiago de Compostela, which, under the guise of informing the English reader more fully about the English Roman life, reads less as a critique and more as a means of informing Catholics in England about the religious practices of their co-religionists:

> it is a thing that is usually frequented all the year, by such a number of people as you would scantly judge, among whom, divers of our Englishmen be so holy that they will not stick to bear them company. There, they say, lieth the body of St. James the apostle; and there is the cock that crowed when Peter denied Christ; some of the hair of Our Lady's head; certain of the thorns of the crown of thorn; the napkin that was about Christ's head in the grave; certain drops of his blood; a piece of the cross whereon he was crucified; and a number suchlike relics, which are honoured and worshipped, as if they were God himself.[52]

Again, this could read as criticism of the English Romanists; but, perhaps not coincidentally, it provides a great deal of information about Catholic practices which might well attract a sympathetic reader who can discard the ostensibly critical context. We learn that vast crowds flock to these pilgrimages but that the English are 'so holy that they will not stick to bear them company'. This suggests that they are among the most pious on the pilgrimage who do not wish to be tainted by the frivolous, carnivalesque aspects of the practice, which either serves to condemn them or celebrates them as the particularly devoted.[53]

Munday's representation of the English Roman life might be compared to Sir Lewis Lewkenor's description of the life of English exiles in Spain (1595).[54] Lewkenor's account purports to be a long letter sent by the author, 'a Gentleman entertained by the King of Spaine in pension' to 'a yong Gentleman his Kinsman in England'. Lewkenor, like Munday, protests his patriotic devotion to the Queen, claiming that he has written his work 'chiefly in respecte of the sincere, faythfull, reverent, and loyall fidelitye and regarde' he has 'to the person of our sacred, renowned, and most gracious Soveraigne the Queenes most excellent Majestie, and to my native Countrie and Country-men', of his long and painful experience fighting for Spain in the Low Countries.[55] Lewkenor argues that he

---

[51] Compare Fynes Moryson, *An Itinerary Containing His Ten Yeeres Travell* (1617), 4 vols (Glasgow: MacLehose, 1907), I, pp. 287–8.

[52] Munday, *English Roman Life*, p. 70.

[53] For the variety of behaviour on pilgrimages see Norbert Ohler, *The Medieval Traveller*, trans. Caroline Hillier (Woodbridge: Boydell, 1989), pp. 56–73.

[54] For analysis of the significance of Lewkenor's text in terms of Elizabethan politics see Peter Lake, *Bad Queen Bess? Libels, Secret Histories, and the Politics of Publicity in the Reign of Queen Elizabeth I* (Oxford: Oxford University Press, 2016), pp. 434–48.

[55] Lewis Lewkenor, *A Discourse of the Usage of the English Fugitives, by the Spaniard* (London, 1595), sig. A4r. For a related case see Anthony Copley, *A Fig for Fortune: A Catholic Response to* The Faerie Queene, ed. Susannah Brietz Monta (Manchester: Manchester University Press, 2016), Introduction, pp. 4–6, 10–11.

hopes to persuade naive young soldiers not to be tempted into serving Spain as the terms and conditions in the Spanish armies are awful. More importantly, he is targeting 'Our credulous Papistes at home, upon whose grosnes and simplicitie, our rebellious traitors here abroade doo build their chiefest foundations of all their villanies, whom while they entertaine with vaine expectations, in the meane time with spies, Priests, and traitours, which they daily send over, they abuse with treacherous practises, to the irrepiable [irreparable] ruine and overthrowe of them and theirs.'[56] Lewkenor attacks the 'tyrannical government of the Spanish tyrant, his cruell and inhumane usage of his miserable subjects', and urges his fellow countrymen not to choose a life that will be characterized by 'a perpetuall grudging and remorse of conscience, scandalized with infinite and innumerable examples of ill lyfe, impietie, sodomie, blasphemie, defamation, and perjurie', a checklist of Protestant complaints of life under Catholic rule.[57] He outlines a familiar description of the evils of Catholicism. In answer to those who might be tempted to choose the Spanish English life, Lewkenor responds:

> I doubte not but you would be of another opinion, especially the woful slaverie considered in which the cleargie, or rather the ravening multitude of Jesuites, Friers, Monkes, and priests doo keepe their minde subjected. It is not sufficient that they holde their mindes in a perpetuall despair, pronouncing upon everie frivolous point damnation unto them: but withal, they compel them perforce to offerings, to buying of pardons and indulgences, to give them money towards the reparation of their Churches, pictures, images, and waxe candles, always having one device or other in hand to robbe them, and to drawe from them their substance: for whosoever yeeldeth not to everie of these demands, is presentlie an heretike.[58]

Such a description of Catholic bad faith, devious and self-interested oppression of the people could have appeared in any number of vociferous Protestant works by John Bale, John Ponet, or Bernardino Ochino.[59]

As with Munday, however, things are not quite what they seem to be. Lewkenor was from a well-established Sussex Catholic family and, as his account suggests, had served in the Spanish army in the Low Countries.[60] As Marco Nievergelt has pointed out, the much reprinted *Discourse of the Usage of the English Fugitives* (also entitled *The Estate of English Fugitives*) served as a 'manifesto of Catholic loyalism', binding together Catholics in the service of the Queen in opposition to 'the seditious resistance theory advocated by such works as Robert Parsons' *Conference*

---

[56] Lewkenor, *English Fugitives*, sig. B2r.
[57] Lewkenor, *English Fugitives*, sigs B2v, E4r–v.   [58] Lewkenor, *English Fugitives*, sig. F3r.
[59] John Ponet, *A Defence for Mariage of Priestes by Scripture and Aunciente Wryters* (London, 1549); Bernardino Ochino, *A Tragoedie or Dialoge of the Vniuste Vsurped Primacie of the Bishop of Rome, and of all the iust abolishyng of the same*, trans. John Ponet (London, 1549); John Bale, *The Pageant of Popes, contayninge the lyues of all the bishops of Rome, from the beginninge of them to the yeare of grace 1555* (London, 1574).
[60] See the *ODNB* entry on Lewkenor; Albert J. Loomie, S.J., *The Spanish Elizabethans: The English Exiles at the Court of Philip II* (New York: Fordham University Press, 1963), pp. 10–11; Caroline Adams, 'Elizabeth I's Progresses into Sussex', in Matthew Dimmock, Andrew Hadfield, and Paul Quinn, eds, *Art, Literature and Religion in Early Modern Sussex* (Farnham; Ashgate, 2014), pp. 15–40.

About The Succession of the Crowne of Ingland'.[61] Lewkenor's text is undoubtedly 'an urgent personal apology and confession of youthful folly', but can we read it as sincere, especially with its declarations of hostility to the superstitious and oppressive nature of the Catholic faith?[62] There is no evidence that Lewkenor remained anything other than faithful to the Church, providing in his later writings a 'distinctively Catholic loyalist insistence on the queen's need for counsel and advice', a hope that she would listen to her faithful Catholic subjects.[63]

III

Neither Munday nor Lewkenor were telling the truth—or, at least, the whole truth. Their protestations about their fidelity and loyalty should alert us to an unease and an anxiety that they would be challenged, and perhaps labelled as liars. Accusing someone of lying or of being a liar in early modern England was a grievous charge, then, as now, which shamed the accused.[64] Sir Walter Ralegh, a man who was eventually executed for treason as a result of his involvement in the rather ludicrous Bye Plot, which 'aimed to kidnap the King and to hold him hostage against promises of wholesale changes in government and an openly acknowledged toleration of Catholicism in England', spent much of his life at court balanced between conspicuous success and the risk of imprisonment and execution.[65] An earlier work, already circulating widely in various forms in the early 1590s after Ralegh's banishment from court resulting from his relationship with his future wife, Elizabeth Throckmorton, and his notorious quarrel with Robert Devereux, second Earl of Essex, was his most famous poem, 'The Lie'.[66] The poem, which belongs to the wealth of satirical material produced in the early 1590s aimed at urban and ecclesiastical targets, lists a variety of forms of abuse that must be countered by the good, honest citizen:

> Go sowll the boddies guest
> uppon a thanckles errant
> fear not to towche the best
> the trewthe shalbe thy warrant
> go synce I needs must Dye
> and gyve the world the lye

[61] Marco Nievergelt, *Allegorical Quests: From Deguiville to Spenser* (Woodbridge: D. S. Brewer, 2012), p. 143; Robert Parsons, *A Conference About The Next Succession of the Crowne of Ingland* (London, 1594).
[62] Nievergelt, *Allegorical Quests*, p. 143. [63] Nievergelt, *Allegorical Quests*, p. 164.
[64] Adam Eric Greenberg, Paul Smeets, and Lilia Zhurakhovska, 'Lying, Guilt and Shame' file:// smbhome.uscs.susx.ac.uk/ah55/Downloads/LyingGuiltAndShame_preview.pdf (accessed 7 March 2017).
[65] Mark Nicholls and Penry Williams, *Sir Walter Raleigh in Life and Legend* (London: Continuum, 2011), p. 194.
[66] For discussion of the poem's origins and circulation, see Sir Walter Ralegh, *The Poems of Sir Walter Ralegh: A Historical Edition*, ed. Michael Rudick (Tempe, AZ: MRTS, 1999), Introduction, pp. xlii–xlvii; Nicholls and Williams, *Raleigh*, pp. 147–9; Stephen Greenblatt, *Sir Walter Raleigh: The Renaissance Man and His Roles* (New Haven: Yale University Press, 1973), pp. 70–4.

Say to the cowrtt it glowes
and shynes lyke rotten wood
say to the churche it shewes
whattes god yet doothe no good
If cowrtt and churce replye
Gyve cowrtt and churche the lye

Tell potentates they lyve
acttyng but others actions
not loved unles they gyve
not strong but by affections
If potenattes replye
Gyve potentatttes the lye[67]

'To give the lie' had, of course, the meaning 'make an accusation of lying', but what is important about the phrase and its significance in Ralegh's poem is the notion of a public challenge, a facing down of one's enemies, as the opening stanza suggests.[68] The poem recounts hypocrisy and failure to live up to the required standards—the Church shows what is good but does not actually do anything good; potentates (absolute monarchs, often biblical tyrants) rely on others to do their dirty work— problems that need to be confronted but which can only be challenged by a condemned man who has nothing left to lose. The poem is curiously not about lying at all, but about publicly shaming one's enemies in order to expose their failures and dishonesty and asserting one's own virtue in contrast, the familiar position of the satirist as the proud man apart.[69] We might read Ralegh's poem alongside Sir Philip Sidney's discussion of the issue of fictionality in his *Apology for Poetry*, where he argues that if children realize that they are not seeing the real Thebes when they watch a play set there then surely adults will make the same assumptions and 'never give the lie to things not affirmatively but allegorically and figuratively written'.[70] Again, the main issue is that of challenging a series of assumptions which masquerade as the truth rather than actually pointing out that someone is lying.

Ralegh's poem shows that lying was a public phenomenon as much as a technically defined problem—honour dictated that accusations of lying required

[67] Ralegh, *Poems*, 20A, lines 1–18 (p. 30). On ecclesiastical satire, see Patrick Collinson, 'Ecclesiastical Vitriol: Religious Satire in the 1590s and the Invention of Puritanism', in Guy, ed., *Reign of Elizabeth I*, pp. 150–70; on urban London satire, see Lawrence Manley, *Literature and Culture in Early Modern London* (Cambridge: Cambridge University Press, 1995), ch. 7.

[68] See William Haughton, *Englishmen For My Money* (1598), in Lloyd Edward Kermode, ed., *Three Renaissance Usury Plays* (Manchester: Manchester University Press, 2009), 3.2.line 129 (p. 230), 'Frisco. Hoo, hoo, hoo! Do you give the gentleman the lie?' *OED*, 'lie, n.1', 2a., dates the first usage to 1593. See also Hubert Languet to Sir Philip Sidney, 14 October 1579, in *The Correspondence of Sir Philip Sidney*, ed. Roger Kuin, 2 vols (Oxford: Oxford University Press, 2012), II, p. 923; Carroll, *Blood and Violence*, pp. 87, 90.

[69] Alvin Kernan, *The Cankered Muse: Satire of the English Renaissance* (New Haven: Yale University Press, 1959), p. 18.

[70] Sir Philip Sidney, *An Apology for Poetry*, ed. Geoffrey Shepherd, rev. and expanded by R. W. Maslen (Manchester: Manchester University Press, 2002), p. 103.

a riposte and perhaps even the offer to fight a duel—and that accusing someone of lying and making that accusation stick was more important than a discussion about what actually constituted a lie.[71] Hannah Arendt has argued, 'The liar, who may get away with any number of single falsehoods, will find it impossible to get away with lying on principle.'[72] We can tell lies but being called a liar spells danger: casual lying, as Arendt points out, is in the nature of political life, but lying cannot become an accepted principle of public behaviour. As is well known, it is still the case that members of the House of Commons cannot call each other liars, whatever the truth of such allegations.[73] Notions about lying vary between different groups of people, as anthropologists and sociologists have long recognized, some societies believing that what other societies consider a lie to be merely the sort of understandable exaggeration that characterizes social and public life. In fact, according to Georg Simmel, the relative tolerance of lying can be used to measure the difference between societies: 'Sociological structures differ profoundly according to the measure of lying which operates in them.'[74] The anthropologist Peter Metcalf, reflecting on his experience among the Upriver People in northern Borneo, points out that the lack of privacy in the longhouses generates a much greater tolerance of lying than exists in a culture in which people experience and value their individual space as a routine part of everyday life.[75]

In early modern England, primarily because of the difficulty of heating separate rooms before the widespread advent of chimney flues, private rooms (closets) were a rarity for the rich only, and people lived most of their lives in the company of others.[76] Accordingly, we should expect there to have been a somewhat different understanding of the significance of lying than there is in modern Britain, and perhaps a more robust toleration of falsification in everyday life, although a pervasive Christian culture which condemned lying as an abuse of God's gift of language clearly complicates such a straightforward comparison.[77] For Francis Bacon, lying could give pleasure—or, at least, many following Greek philosophy thought so—and not making allowance for 'Vaine Opinions, Flattering Hopes, False valuations, Imaginations . . . and the like . . . would leave the Mindes, of a

---

[71] Richard Jones, *The Booke of Honor and Armes* (London, 1590), pp. 1–18.

[72] Hannah Arendt, 'Lying in Politics', in *Crises of the Republic* (Harmondsworth: Penguin, 1973), pp. 9–42, at p. 12.

[73] 'House of Commons Information Office: Some Traditions and Customs of the House', p. 5 (http://www.parliament.uk/documents/commons-information-office/g07.pdf) (accessed 10 March 2016).

[74] Quoted in J. A. Barnes, *A Pack of Lies: Towards a Sociology of Lying* (Cambridge: Cambridge University Press, 1994), p. 22.

[75] Peter Metcalf, *They Lie, We Lie: Getting On with Anthropology* (London: Routledge, 2002), pp. 4–5. I owe this reference to David Parkin.

[76] Lena Cowen Orlin, *Locating Privacy in Tudor London* (Oxford: Oxford University Press, 2007), pp. 182–3; Alan Stewart, 'Epistemologies of the Early Modern Closet', in *Close Readers: Humanism and Sodomy in Early Modern England* (Princeton: Princeton University Press, 1997), pp. 161–87; Laura Gowing, *Domestic Dangers: Women, Words, and Sex in Early Modern London* (Oxford: Clarendon Press, 1998), pp. 70–2, 98–9, *passim*

[77] Zagorin, *Ways of Lying*, ch. 1.

Number of Men, poore shrunken Things; full of Melancholy, and Indisposition, and unpleasing to themselves'.[78] Such lies, however, are relatively trivial: 'it is not the *Lie*, that passeth through the Minde, but the *Lie* that sinketh in, and setleth in it, that doth the hurt'.[79] Bacon recognizes that lies are of different types and different orders, arguing that it is important to recognize that lying has a public significance but is most deadly and corrosive when it has theological import, and can cut men off from God:

> There is no Vice, that doth so cover a Man with Shame, as to be found false, and perfidious. And therefore *Mountaigny* saith prettily, when he enquired the reason, why the word of the *Lie*, should be such a Disgrace, and such an Odious Charge? Saith he, *If it be well weighted, To say a man lieth, is as much to say, as that he is brave towards God, and a Coward towards men*, For a *Lie* faces God, and shrinkes from Man. Surely the Wickednesse of Falshood, and Breach of Faith, cannot possibly be so highly expressed, as in that it shall be the last Peale, to call the Judgements of God, upon the Generations of Men, It being foretold, that when Christ commeth, *He shall not finde Faith upon the Earth*.[80]

Bacon moves with apparent effortlessness from a discussion of trivial forms of deception to the Day of Judgement. In doing so he raises the question of whether the first type of lie leads, in the end, to the second, while maintaining the distinction between the two, the first leaving the mind after it has provided a brief moment of illicit pleasure, the second forcing the individual to face God with their soul in mortal peril as Christ returns to earth to find no one possessing true faith. Bacon cites Montaigne's essay, 'Of Giving the Lie', in John Florio's translation (1603).[81] Like Montaigne, Bacon condemns those who abuse speech by lying, the thrust of the argument being that one can get away with lying as a public act but that, in the end, one has to face one's maker when the truth will be revealed. Bacon wonders whether Christ, when he returns to earth, will find any honest and faithful Christians.

Ralegh's poem ends with lines of bitter invective that might be compared to Bacon's disdain of the casual nature of public lying in contrast to the fidelity of the true Christian:

> So when thou hast as I
> commanded thee doon blabbing
> althoughe to gyve the lye
> deserves no les then stabbing
> stab at thee he that wyll
> no stab the sowll can kyll[.][82]

---

[78] Francis Bacon, 'Of Truth', in *The Oxford Francis Bacon, Vol. XV: The Essayes or Counsels, Civill and Morall*, ed. Michael Kiernan (Oxford: Clarendon Press, 1985), pp. 7–9, at p. 7.

[79] Bacon, 'Of Truth', p. 7.   [80] Bacon, 'Of Truth', p. 9.

[81] Michel de Montaigne, 'Of Giving the Lie', in *The Essayes of Michael, Lord of Montaigne*, trans. John Florio (London, 1603), 3 vols (London: Everyman, 1910), II, pp. 390–4, at p. 394.

[82] Ralegh, *Poems*, 20A, lines 73–8 (p. 33).

The poet adopts a Stoic stance challenging the world to do its worst, because what matters is the integrity of the individual whatever overwhelming odds he or she faces. At his trial for treason (17 November 1603) Ralegh adopted exactly this pose, pleading his innocence, claiming ignorance of the charges against him, and scornfully refusing to answer questions put to him by the prosecution. When accused of having an English face but a Spanish heart and having been the figure who persuaded Henry Brook, eleventh Baron Cobham to instigate the Bye Plot, Ralegh simply blocked the questions of the Attorney General, Edward Coke: 'You tell me news, Mr. Attorney.'[83] Ralegh was giving the lie, and the public were largely on his side and unimpressed by Coke's aggressive performance.[84]

Accordingly lying had a distinct social significance. As Montaigne stated, 'Our intelligence being onely conducted by the way of the Word: Who so falsifieth the same, betrayeth public society.'[85] Thomas Lupton, thinking more about an individual's situation, has one character advise another that it 'were better tel truth & to auoide the danger of lying, than to tell a lye, & neuerthelesse the truth be knowen'.[86] But the really serious problem of lying for Ralegh, Bacon, and Montaigne, whose essay deals with great men who stand apart, was the abuse of God's word and the personal risk to the soul, which is why all three value the concept of the man who can rise above society's dissimulation and dishonesty: '*whosoever lieth, witnesseth that he contemneth God and therewithal feareth men*'.[87] Lying involved breaking a contract with God, undermining a fundamental oath that one would tell the truth. The confirmation service for children in the 1559 Book of Common Prayer made children promise to honour a series of duties towards their neighbours: 'To beare no malice, nor hatred in my harte. To kepe my hands from pickyng and stealyng, and my tongue from evil speaking, liyng and slaunderyng,' a reference to the ninth commandment.[88] Breaking this promise to govern one's tongue, body, and heart was to dishonour a fundamental contract with God, as every child in England was expected to make this public promise when they were ready to enter the congregation of the Church of England.[89] Bacon's conception of lying in terms of the Last Judgement foregrounds an understanding of lying as the breaking of a religious oath, a violation that will always have future consequences.

Lying broke two of the Ten Commandments: the third, 'Thou shalt not take the name of the LORD thy God in vain: for the LORD will not hold him guiltless that taketh his name in vain' (Exodus 20:7) and the ninth, 'Thou shalt not bear false witness against thy neighbour' (16), the translations being identical in the Geneva and Authorized versions. After the Reformation the Ten Commandments replaced

---

[83] *State Trials*, II, pp. 1–60, at p. 8; Nicholls and Williams, *Ralegh*, pp. 205–19.

[84] Nicholls and Williams, *Ralegh*, pp. 205–6.   [85] Montaigne, *Essayes*, II, p. 394.

[86] Thomas Lupton, *The Second Part and Knitting vp of the Boke Entituled Too Good to be True Wherin is Continued the Discourse of the Wonderfull Lawes, Commendable Customes, [and] Strange Manners of the People of Mauqsun* (London, 1581), sig. H2r.

[87] Montaigne, *Essayes*, II, p. 394.

[88] *The Book of Common Prayer: The Texts of 1549, 1559, and 1662*, ed. Brian Cummings (Oxford: Oxford University Press, 2011), p. 153.

[89] William P. Haugaard, *Elizabeth and the English Reformation: The Struggle for a Stable Settlement of Religion* (Cambridge: Cambridge University Press, 1968), p. 113.

the Seven Deadly Sins as 'the staple of Protestant teaching'.[90] This change inspired greater concentration on individual responsibility rather than a more public understanding of morality in terms of an ideal of neighbourliness, a transformation in Christian behaviour that perhaps inaugurated a more widespread understanding of the significance of concepts such as lying.[91] Certainly the two commandments are linked in the mind of Peter Martire Vermigli in his commentary on oaths and forswearing:

> An other thing that is to be blamed in an oth, is, if a man do not sweare, but forsweare. Which sinne is so graeuous, as of that onelie, among the ten commandments, you find written, *Lo Linke*, He will not forgive him, He will not hold him guiltlesse. For God is highlie offended when we abuse his name to confirme our lies. But if so be the basest sort of men manie times cannot abide, that they should be accounted witnesses of a lie; how much lesse will God suffer a lie? Besides, our neighbor taketh verie great hurt, not of the bodie, substance, or name; but of the mind, that is to wit, of reason: for he that is a forswearer, doth alwaies beguile and deceiue; which is to seduce the reason of man. Politicke gouernements, and common-weales also are overthrowne, unlesse we stand unto our oths & couenants. And this the Hebrues, in a certaine Apollogie of theirs doo declare; who write, that when the tables were given upon mount *Sina*, so soone as the lawe was made concerning periurie, the whole world was shaken.[92]

The author is providing a commentary on Exodus 20:7, as the marginal note informs us, linking the two commandments as God's pronouncements on lying and perjury. A lie, when confirmed with a forsworn oath using God's name as a guarantee of its truthfulness, becomes a crime that God cannot easily forgive, raising the possibility that, like despair, such a sin leads directly to damnation.[93] It destroys the relationship between the liar and his or her neighbours, which is why, thinking on a larger scale, lying undermines human reason and, therefore, co-operation and interaction, probably leading to catastrophic political consequences. Peter Martire's comment that the whole world was shaken as soon as the law against perjury was given on Mount Sinai is, presumably, an interpretation of Exodus 20:18: 'And all the people saw the thunderings, and the lightnings, and the noise of the trumpet, and the mountain smoking: and when the people saw *it*, they removed, and stood far off' (emphasis in original). In this reading the key sin that threatens to undermine individuals, society, and the relationship between God and mankind, is lying.

---

[90] Naomi Tadmor, *The Social Universe of the English Bible: Scripture, Society, and Culture in Early Modern England* (Cambridge: Cambridge University Press, 2010), p. 48; John Bossy, 'Moral Arithmetic: Seven Sins into Ten Commandments', in Leites, ed., *Conscience and Casuistry*, pp. 214–34; William Tyndale, *An Exposicion Upon The V. VI. VII. Chapters of Mathewe* (Antwerp?, 1533?), fo. xxxi.

[91] Tadmor, *Social Universe*, p. 36.

[92] Pietro Martire Vermigli, *The Common Places of . . . Doctor Peter Martyr diuided into foure principall parts*, trans. Anthony Marten (London, 1583), Part 2, ch. 6 (p. 371): see John Kerrigan, *Shakespeare's Binding Language* (Oxford: Oxford University Press, 2016), pp. 181–4. On Pietro Martire Vermigli see Zagorin, *Ways of Lying*, pp. 109–11.

[93] Paola Baseotto, '*Disdeining Life, Desiring Leaue To Die*': Spenser and the Psychology of Despair* (Stuttgart: Ibidem-Verlag, 2008), pp. 39–43.

IV

How, then, should we think about lying, and, in particular, about lying in the early modern period? Modern debates about lying invariably look back to Immanuel Kant (1724–1804), who famously argued that lying was always wrong. Even if you are faced with a murderer at the door asking for your friend, your duty is to tell the truth no matter what the consequences. For Kant, truth-telling is a categorical imperative, a fundamental sign of our shared humanity, and something that can never be violated. To lie is to diminish one's status as a human being.[94] Kant was reacting against the long and well-established tradition of casuistry, the belief that every moral dilemma requires individual treatment so that ethical reasoning should proceed on a case-by-case basis and not be bound by a series of abstract rules.[95] Of course, casuists accept that some principles have to be upheld, and it is rarely acceptable to lie, just as it is hardly ever morally beneficial to kill somebody. However, when faced with insoluble dilemmas and aggressively hostile enemies morally upright individuals have the right to protect themselves by dealing cleverly and creatively with the truth, as long as they do not actually tell outright lies.[96] Casuistical thinking, adopted by Catholics and Puritans alike, often precipitated a cat and mouse game between authorities and individuals.[97] A much-cited example was that of the Church Father St Athanasius (*c.*296–373) who was ordered to leave his bishopric in Alexandria by the Emperor Julian during his persecution of the Christians. Fleeing in a rowing boat up the Nile, Athanasius was overtaken and asked by his pursuers if he knew whether Athanasius was 'close at hand'. The wily bishop replied, 'He is not far from here', and so made good his escape, as no one there knew what he looked like.[98] Kant's strictures were uttered in direct opposition to such casuistry and this may have been an example that he had in mind when formulating his philosophical principle.

[94] Immanuel Kant, 'On a Supposed Right to Lie from Altruistic Motives', (http://www.unc.edu/courses/2009spring/plcy/240/001/Kant.pdf) (accessed 9 June 2015); Christine Korsgaard, 'The Right to Lie: Kant on Dealing with Evil', *Philosophy and Public Affairs* 15 (1986), 325–49.

[95] Although Kant owed much to the casuistic tradition in establishing the categorical imperative: see H. D. Kittsteiner, 'Kant and Casuistry', in Leites, ed., *Conscience and Casuistry*, pp. 185–213. I owe this reference to John Kerrigan.

[96] See Edmund Leites, ed., *Conscience and Casuistry in Early Modern Europe* (Cambridge: Cambridge University Press, 1988); Harald Braun and Edward Vallance, eds, *Contexts of Conscience in Early Modern Europe, 1500–1700* (Basingstoke: Palgrave Macmillan, 2004); George L. Mosse, *The Holy Pretence: A Study in Christianity and Reason of State from William Perkins to John Winthrop* (New York: Howard Fertig, 1968, rpt of 1957).

[97] Elliot Rose, *Cases of Conscience: Alternatives Open to Recusants and Puritans Under Elizabeth I and James I* (Cambridge: Cambridge University Press, 1975), pp. 71–102, 185–205; Patrick Collinson, *The Elizabethan Puritan Movement* (Oxford: Clarendon Press, 1967), pp. 435–7; Zagorin, *Ways of Lying*, chs 8–10.

[98] Cited in Jennifer Saul, *Lying, Misleading, and What is Not Said: An Exploration in Philosophy of Language and in Ethics* (Oxford: Oxford University Press, 2012), p. 2; see also Alasdair MacIntyre, 'Truthfulness, Lies, and Moral Philosophers: What Can We Learn from Mill and Kant?', *Tanner Lectures on Human Values*, pp. 309–69 (Princeton University) (tannerlectures.utah.edu/_documents/a-to-z/m/macintyre_1994.pdf) (accessed 9 June 2015).

We can surely never eliminate lying from human experience, and, *pace* Kant, it might be a disaster if this utopian goal was ever achieved. While for some commentators lying can and should be eliminated if we value free speech and the benefits of a properly functioning public sphere, for many others lying is part of what makes us human.[99] Perceptions of lying vary from culture to culture and for many thinkers learning to lie is a crucial marker of the passage from childhood to adulthood.[100] Surely this is something we should consider even if lying does not actually take place. As Jon Snyder has pointed out, the expectation that one would be misled in virtually every significant aspect of one's life defined how people behaved in early modern Europe. Snyder identifies a series of important areas in which 'legitimacy of dissimulation was an issue': '(i) civility or good manners, (ii) the court, (iii) the prince and reason-of-state politics, (iv) moral philosophy, and (v) religious dissent'.[101] Issues of dissimulation were not limited to these areas, of course, but characterized the nature of everyday life in early modern Europe. The anticipation of untruthfulness defined people's conceptions of how they should live and we need to understand this expectation when we try to reconstruct their lives and explore the records they left behind. A culture of untruthfulness provides a lot of misleading information in the texts and archives it leaves behind.

We may not think that the difference between what is a lie and what is a form of deception matters all that much now, and that there is no meaningful distinction between falsification and concealment as strategies of avoiding telling the truth, especially when there are so many techniques for exposing unconscious betrayals of deceit.[102] As Bernard Williams has argued, 'if deceit is justified at all, as in defending the innocent fugitive, something is wrong if one thinks that it is more honourable to find some weasel words than to tell a lie'.[103] In terms of philosophical arguments this makes good sense, and would seem to be a sensible guide in societies where relatively few people believe in a higher controlling power. However, Thomas Carson is careful not to conflate lying with deception. Lying

[99] For the first argument see Dorothy Rowe, *Why We Lie: The Source of Our Disasters* (London: Fourth Estate, 2011), on individual behaviour; Peter Oborne, *The Rise of Political Lying* (London: Simon & Schuster, 2005), on public ethics; and Adrienne Rich, 'Women and Honour: Some Notes on Lying', in *On Lies, Secrets, and Silence: Selected Prose, 1966–1978* (New York: Norton, 1979), pp. 185–94, on how a culture of lying invariably advantages men at the expense of women. For the second, see Ian Leslie, *Born Liars: Why We Can't Live Without Deceit* (London: Quercus, 2011), pp. 5–22; Michael Lewis and Carolyn Saarni, 'Deceit and Illusion in Human Affairs', in Lewis and Saarni, eds, *Lying and Deception in Everyday Life* (New York: Guilford Press, 1993), pp. 1–29. The comic possibility of a world without lies was exploited in Ricky Gervais and Matthew Robinson's film, *The Invention of Lying* (2009).
[100] Barnes, *Pack of Lies*, p. 75; Michael Lewis, 'The Development of Deception', in Lewis and Saarni, eds, *Lying and Deception*, pp. 90–105.
[101] Snyder, *Dissimulation*, p. 19.
[102] See Paul Ekman's influential *Telling Lies: Clues to Deceit in the Marketplace, Politics, and Marriage* (rev. edn, New York: Norton, 2001), pp. 28–9; Sigmund Freud, *The Psychopathology of Everyday Life*, trans. Alan Tyson (Harmondsworth: Penguin, 1975), chs 6–7.
[103] Bernard Williams, *Truth and Truthfulness* (Princeton: Princeton University Press, 2002), p. 107. I owe this reference to Paul Davies.

involves the production of a false statement, whereas deception can be achieved through the production of a true statement that does not adequately reveal the truth. Moreover, Carson points out, deception presumes success, whereas lying can, and often does, fail, which suggests that we should be able to excavate a history of lying if we can establish a series of meaningful categories.[104] Carson also points out that not everything that looks like a lie actually is a lie. Some apparently wilfully false statements are simply the result of faulty memory, and some were never intended to mislead the interlocutor, as Augustine argued: 'If I say something that is clearly false as a joke that is not intended to be taken seriously, I am not lying.'[105] Definitions still matter.

However, there is still a heavy weight attached to accusations of lying, as even the most basic Internet search will demonstrate, showing how significant is the claim that a liar has been exposed.[106] One notorious modern case of a clever but visible lie/deception may further clarify matters. Stuart Green has analysed the precise nature of the physical relationship between President Bill Clinton and Monica Lewinsky to determine whether the President's statement that he had never had 'sexual relations with that woman' was a lie and therefore perjury.[107] Green concludes that Clinton did not actually lie in drawing a distinction between sexual relations as penetrative intercourse and fellatio. The difference between what Clinton said and the nature of his transgression in court is indeed a fine one, but Green's point, based on the leading case concerning literal truth in the US, *Bronston v United States*, is that such close distinctions are precisely what we need to consider: 'evasive answers are not perjurous: if a witness evades, it is the lawyer's responsibility to recognize the evasion and to bring the witness back to the mark, to flush out the whole truth with the tools of adversary examination'.[108] Clinton was undoubtedly evasive and misleading in his testimony, but did not actually commit perjury. The clever witness always stays the right side of the truth/lying divide because accusations of lying still matter. Indeed, this distinction, part of a much older legal tradition, is central to our understanding of early modern conceptions of truth and lies. As Debora Shuger has pointed out, '[i]t was precisely to give witnesses and defendants a way out of the perjury trap that theologians distinguished between

[104] Thomas L. Carson, *Lying and Deception: Theory and Practice* (Oxford: Oxford University Press, 2010), pp. 46–64.
[105] Carson, *Lying and Deception*, p. 17; Supriya Chaudhuri, 'Being True to Yourself: Lying in *Hamlet*', in Panja, ed., *Shakespeare and the Art of Lying*, pp. 59–76, at p. 70.
[106] For a recent cluster, many of which even provide numbers, see https://www.theguardian.com/us-news/series/lyin-trump-a-weekly-fact-check; http://www.forbes.com/forbes/welcome/?toURL=http://www.forbes.com/sites/emilywillingham/2016/09/27/why-does-donald-trump-lie-so-much/&refURL=https://www.google.co.uk/&referrer=https://www.google.co.uk/; http://www.vox.com/2016/10/26/13417532/donald-trump-lies; http://www.vanityfair.com/news/2016/02/politics-media-gaffes-lies; http://www.nytimes.com/2016/09/27/opinion/campaign-stops/the-lies-trump-told.html?_r=0 (all accessed 7 March 2017).
[107] Stuart P. Green, *Lying, Cheating, and Stealing: A Moral Theory of White-Collar Crime* (Oxford: Oxford University Press, 2006), pp. 140–7. See also Roelf Bolt, *The Encyclopaedia of Liars and Deceivers* (London: Reaktion, 2014), p. 16.
[108] *Bronston*, 409 US, at 358–9, cited in Green, *Lying, Cheating*, p. 142.

a lie and a misleading or equivocal statement'.[109] Perjury requires lying: the balance was established in favour of a strong definition of lying so that it was possible for defendants and witnesses to evade its boundaries; a witness who made an 'evasive or unresponsive, but literally true, statement, has not lied', and therefore not committed perjury, however morally culpable observers may feel them to be.[110]

But, of course, if lying is prohibited by a higher decree, then efforts must be made to avoid lying, which is why so much intellectual energy was dedicated to defining the boundaries between truth and lies. In his study of interpretation and meaning in Renaissance jurisprudence, Ian Maclean shows how arguments in civil law were directly related to fundamental theological and linguistic issues. The seventeenth-century German doctoral student Christophorus Bremerus argued that it was possible 'to tell the truth logically, but lie ethically, and to lie logically, but tell the truth ethically'.[111] He cites the example of a Jew declaring that Christ is the Messiah, who is telling the logical truth but lying ethically. If he denied that Christ was the Messiah he would be telling the truth ethically but lying logically. It is a fascinating case, one that could easily be applied by Protestants or Catholics eager to catch out opponents who do not wish to be ensnared by the authorities into declaring a false allegiance nor to tell lies. In obvious ways it is the equivalent of the 'bloody question'—whether one would admit one knew where the Queen was to an invading Catholic army—used to gauge the loyalty of Catholics after the Pope had declared Elizabeth excommunicate (February 1570).[112] Bremerus's comments do not constitute a new definition of lying, but they might well indicate a transformation in the ways in which lying had to be conceived, exposed, and prevented. In short, if they have a particular significance it is because they either reproduce a commonly held belief about lying that enables us to understand what contemporaries considered important about mendacity; or, they denote a departure in ideas about lying that can be recorded and understood.

William Perkins's treatise, *A Direction for the Government of the Tongue* (1593), provides a common and uncontroversial definition of lying. Perkins selects a relatively minimalist, common-sense description that might not pass muster with modern analytical philosophers, or, indeed, with trained canon lawyers such as Bremerus. Perkins argues that 'Lying is when a man speaketh otherwise then the trueth is, with a purpose to deceive.'[113] Even so, Perkins is not very far away from

---

[109] Debora Shuger, 'Sins of the Tongue', *Slate Magazine*, 15 Sept. 1999 (accessed 9 June 2015); Green, *Lying, Cheating*, p. 137.

[110] Green, *Lying, Cheating*, p. 137.

[111] Ian Maclean, *Interpretation and Meaning in the Renaissance: The Case of Law* (Cambridge: Cambridge University Press, 1992), p. 160.

[112] Patrick MacGrath, 'The Bloody Question Reconsidered', *RH* 20 (1991), 415–35. See below, p. 91.

[113] William Perkins, *A Direction for the Government of the Tongue According To Gods Word* (London, 1593), p. 19.

the definition of lying provided by a modern analytical philosopher, Seana Valentine Shiffrin. According to Shiffrin, a lie is:

An intentional assertion by A to B of a proposition P such that
1. A does not believe P, and
2. A is aware that A does not believe P, and
3. A intentionally presents P in a manner or context that objectively manifests A's intention that B is to take and treat P as an accurate representation of A's belief.[114]

For lying to take place there has to be an intention to deceive.[115] According to Shiffrin, the important point about lying is that it is 'a falsification presented in a context that objectively conveys that the statement is represented as a *true* representation of the speaker's beliefs' and not merely something that is true.[116] Lying has to be distinguished from deception: it is important that the speaker does not believe what he or she says, according to Shiffrin. Hence Athanasius of Alexandria's reply to his pursuers was cunningly deceptive but not actually lying.

Shiffrin's is an important distinction, and other philosophers, such as Jennifer Saul and Stuart Green, argue that we need to separate lying from misleading, which is 'morally better than lying' in many situations, such as 'an adversarial context like a courtroom', and draw a distinction between 'asserting what one believes is literally false' and 'leading the listener to believe something false by saying something that is either true or has no truth value'.[117] But did such distinctions actually matter outside a courtroom—and they may not have always mattered there, of course—if accusations of lying were understood in terms of the violation of public promises, especially the binding force of oaths, rather than subtle distinctions? The truth is that popular and philosophical definitions of lying, then as now, existed side by side.

As Perkins's definition indicates, early modern analysis of lying was often rough and ready and based on a popular understanding of truth/falsehood. It is no surprise that Perkins includes a large number of anecdotes and stories of divine punishment in his treatise, showing how God will reveal the liar who suffers justifiable agonies *pour encourager les autres*.[118] Other writers told similar tales: Thomas Lupton concludes a long story by having three false witnesses, exposed by the just ruler, experience a horrible swelling of the tongue, made lame, and struck blind, three appropriate punishments (although the ruler has them pulled apart by horses and

[114] Seana Valentine Shiffrin, *Speech Matters: On Lying, Morality, and the Law* (Princeton: Princeton University Press, 2014), p. 12.
[115] Paul J. Griffiths, *Lying: An Augustinian Theology of Duplicity* (Grand Rapids, MI: Brazos Press, 2004), pp. 27–8; Jacques Derrida, 'History of the Lie: Prolegomena', in *Without Alibi*, ed. and trans. Peggy Kamuf (Stanford: Stanford University Press, 2002), pp. 28–70, at p. 35; Bart D. Ehrman, *Forgery and Counter-forgery: The Use of Literary Deceit in Early Christian Polemics* (Oxford: Oxford University Press, 2013), pp. 128–32.
[116] Shiffrin, *Speech Matters*, p. 15. See also Lionel Bentley, 'Identity and the Law', in Walker and Leedham-Green, eds, *Identity*, pp. 26–58, at p. 49.
[117] Saul, *Lying, Misleading*, p. 99; Green, *Lying, Cheating*, p. 78.
[118] On this phenomenon see Alexandra Walsham, *Providence in Early Modern England* (Oxford: Oxford University Press, 1999), chs 2–3.

their lands and goods given to the relief of the poor for good measure).[119] In early modern England lying is more often condemned than defined: the two major treatises on lying, Matthieu Coignet's *Politique Discourses upon Truth and Lying* (1586), translated by Sir Edward Hoby, and Henry Mason's *The New Art of Lying* (1624) are long on exposition and short on definition.[120] Coignet's treatise is an anti-realpolitik work, very much like Innocent Gentillet's *Contra-Machiavel*; Mason's is an exposure of the Jesuits and their practices of mental reservation and equivocation. Mason is clear about the difference between ambiguity and equivocation. When Jesus says that Lazarus is sleeping he is not lying but being figurative and so helping his audience understand that death is not as bad as they fear it to be.[121] This serves as a pointed contrast to a Jesuit saying that he is not a priest but then silently adding 'So as I am bound to tell you'.[122] According to Mason, the second form of equivocation is a lie, which enables him to distinguish between 'logicall equivocation', which results from ambiguity and which requires explanation, and 'Jesuiticall Equivocation', which is simply a cunning form of lying.[123] Jesuitical equivocation has the same relationship to the truth as a thief who claims that he had no intention of actually stealing, but that he simply plans to make use of the money he has obtained.[124] Mason argues that if we allow equivocation to be true then no man can ever be a liar.[125] His claim would appear to have had even greater force in the later seventeenth century as many thinkers acknowledged that what had once seemed admirable clever practice had become simply self-serving duplicity.[126]

Coignet, like Mason, is concerned to show how pernicious a culture which tolerates lying will inevitably become and to make the case that a prince should be concerned to establish the truth through listening to proper counsel.[127] He includes poetry as a form of untruthful writing that has to be condemned, one of the many deceptive practices, like flattery, that need to be swept aside.[128] Coignet argues that truthful speech imitates the word of God: 'for so much as there is nothing more proper to man, being formed according to the image of God, than in his words and manners to approche him the nearest that he is able, & to make his

---

[119] Thomas Lupton, *Siuqila. Too Good, to be true…Herein is Shewed by waye of dialogue, the wonderful maners of the people of Mauqsun, with other talke not friuolous* (London, 1580), sigs N2v–N3r. I owe this reference to Cathy Shrank.

[120] Mathieu [Martin] Coignet, *A Politique Discourse Upon Trueth and Lying An instruction to princes to keepe their faith and promise: containing the summe of Christian and morall philosophie, and the duetie of a good man in sundrie politike discourses vpon the trueth and lying*, trans. Edward Hoby (London, 1586); Henry Mason, *The New Art of Lying, Covered by Jesuits Under the Vale of Equivocation* (London, 1624). For comment see Zagorin, *Ways of Lying*, pp. 204–5.

[121] Mason, *Lying*, p. 21.   [122] Mason, *Lying*, pp. 31, 39.

[123] Mason, *Lying*, p. 10. For a related discussion see John March, *Actions For Slaunder, or, A Methodicall Collection Under Certain Grounds and Heads of What Words Are Actionable in the Law* (London, 1647), pp. 35–6.

[124] Mason, *Lying*, p. 40.   [125] Mason, *Lying*, p. 25.

[126] Thomas Wood, *English Casuistical Divinity During the Seventeenth Century with Special Reference to Jeremy Taylor* (London: SPCK, 1952), pp. 107–8.

[127] Joanne Paul, 'The Best Counsellors are Dead: Counsel and Shakespeare's *Hamlet*', *RQ* 30 (2016), 646–65, p. 652.

[128] Peter C. Herman, *Squitter-wits and Muse-haters: Sidney, Spenser, Milton, and Renaissance Antipoetic Sentiment* (Detroit: Wayne State University Press, 1996), pp. 51–2.

words serue for no other ende, than to declare his good intent & meaning, whereby
he may be better able to informe his neighbour'.[129] Conversely, lying, as Coignet
recognizes, is the opposite of truth, but a precise definition proves elusive: 'So haue
we of purpose discoursed of the trueth, before we com to shew the vice of lying, the
which we may define by a contrary signification vnto the truth when one speaketh
of things vncertain, contrarie to that which one knoweth, making them seeme other
then they are. S. Augustin writeth to Consentius, that it is a false signification of
spech, with a wil to deceiue.'[130] Coignet, as he acknowledges, is following the
foremost authority on truth and lying from the early Middle Ages onwards,
St Augustine.[131]

Augustine's Neoplatonic theology was based on his belief that a clear separation
of good and evil was both possible and desirable, a distinction Coignet recognizes
and adopts. Augustine, whose diverse comments on lying were well known in
Elizabethan England, returns time and again to the distinction between truth and
lies in his voluminous writings, but the works that were most frequently cited, to
which Coignet is referring, are the short treatises, *De Mendacio* (*On Lying*) and
Contra Mendacium ad Consentium (*To Consentius, Against Lying*).[132] Augustine
acknowledges that there are differences of opinion about lying: as Bart D. Ehrman
points out, 'Augustine needed to argue so vociferously for his position on lying
precisely because most Christians took a different view.'[133] Some Church Fathers
accept that it is 'sometimes useful to utter a falsehood with will to deceive', citing
Abraham stating that Sarah was his sister while neglecting to mention that she was
his wife (she was his half-sister); Sarah denying that she laughed when told she
would have a child in old age (Calvin argued that this was because she was terrified
of displeasing God); Jacob deceiving Isaac by covering his forearm with goatskin to
imitate his older brother, Esau; and the Hebrew midwives in Egypt misleading
Pharaoh to stop him slaughtering the Hebrew infants.[134] In January 1602 the
lawyer and diarist John Manningham (*c*.1575–1622) attended a sermon by the
controversial Henoch Clapham (*fl.* 1585–1618), on the murder of Cain, another
favourite biblical text for theologians discussing lying, and a work which was clearly
inspired by Augustine.[135] For Augustine the murder divided the earthly city of man
from the heavenly city of God, through the two lines of descent from Cain and

[129] Coignet, *Politique Discourse*, p. 1.　　[130] Coignet, *Politique Discourse*, p. 127.
[131] For commentary, see Denery, *The Devil Wins*, pp. 105–19, *passim*; Albert R. Jonsen and
Stephen Toulmin, *The Abuse of Casuistry: A History of Moral Reasoning* (Berkeley: University of
California Press, 1988), pp. 196–7; Sissela Bok, *Lying: Moral Choices in Public and Private Life*
(Hassocks: Harvester Press, 1978), pp. 33–7, *passim*; Kenneth E. Kirk, *Conscience and Its Problems:
An Introduction to Casuistry* (London: Longmans, 1927), pp. 188–92.
[132] On Augustine on lying in early modern England see Lupton, *Siuqila*, sig. M1r.
[133] Ehrman, *Forgery and Counter-forgery*, p. 537.
[134] Augustine, 'On Lying', trans. H. Browne (http://www.newadvent.org/fathers/1312.htm),
(accessed 23 June 2015), section 5. For the stories of Abraham and Sarah, see Genesis 12:10–20,
18:1–15, 20:1–18, and 26:6–11; Calvin, *Commentaries*, I, pp. 476–7; Zagorin, *Ways of Lying*, p. 172;
and Griffiths, *Lying*, pp. 33–4; on Jacob deceiving Isaac, see Genesis 27:1–45 (and below, pp. 29,
109); on the Hebrew midwives, see Exodus 1:15–22; Zagorin, *Ways of Lying*, pp. 238–9.
[135] See Calvin, *Commentaries*, I, pp. 205–6. On Manningham and Clapham see the *ODNB* entries.

Abel's replacement, Seth.[136] Clapham provides a distinctive Augustinian reading of Genesis 4:9:

'Where is Habel thy brother?' The Lord careth for the righteous.

Whoe answered, 'I cannot tell' He slaps God in the mouth with a ly at the first word; a general rule that after murder lying followeth, they are links together, and commonly noe syn committed but a lye runnes after; for none is soe impudent to confesse it, every one would have the face of virtue.[137]

Lying is intimately connected in Manningham's imagination with the first murder, an insolent and petty assault on God in a futile attempt to disguise a grave crime.[138] Lying creates division in the fallen world, separating man from God.

Augustine acknowledges that others have argued that the Ten Commandments and a series of biblical verses forbid lying. Accordingly, he argues that while the Old Testament does contain some episodes that appear to condone lying, the New Testament strictly prohibits it.[139] Calvin accepts Augustine's interpretation of the Hebrew midwives episode, claiming that while 'some argue that this kind of lie...is not reprehensible...whatever is opposed to the nature of God is sinful'.[140] Augustine also accepts that lying is not always easy to define and that sometimes lying might not seem very different nor less morally culpable than other forms of deception; that one can tell the truth for harmful purposes; and that one can deceive people without meaning to do so. However, his fundamental definition of lying will seem familiar enough: 'none doubts that it is a lie when a person willingly utters a falsehood for the purpose of deceiving: wherefore a falsehood put forth with will to deceive is manifestly a lie'.[141] As Jacques Derrida has pointed out in his essay, 'History of the Lie: Prolegomena', Augustine's definition 'seems to exclude the lie to oneself, the "being-mistaken" as "lie to oneself"'.[142] Lying to oneself is, strictly speaking, impossible, whatever assumptions are made in colloquial usage now.[143] It is not a concept with any particular currency in the early modern period, although Erasmus does write of 'some men so inured to lying that they believe themselves to be telling the truth even when they lie most shamelessly'.[144]

[136] Augustine, *City of God*, trans. Henry Bettenson (Harmondsworth: Penguin, 1984), Book 15, ch. 15 (p. 621).

[137] *The Diary of John Manningham of the Middle Temple, 1602–3*, ed. Robert Parker Sorlien (Hanover: University Press of New England, 1976), p. 170 (fo. 89b). I am grateful to Mat Dimmock for this reference.

[138] Manningham, or Clapham, is probably following Calvin, who described Cain's act as a 'kick against God' (Calvin, *Commentaries*, I, p. 206).

[139] Augustine, 'On Lying', 6, 8.   [140] Calvin, *Commentaries*, II, pp. 34–5.

[141] Augustine, 'On Lying', 5.   [142] Derrida, 'History of the Lie', p. 31.

[143] F. M. Barnard, *Reason and Self-Enactment in History and Politics: Themes and Voices of Modernity* (Montreal: McGill-Queen's Press, 2006), p. 64; Roy F. Baumeister, 'Lying to Yourself: The Enigma of Self-Deception', in Lewis and Saarni, eds, *Lying and Deception*, pp. 166–83.

[144] Erasmus, *Collected Works*, 29, p. 326.

Moreover, Psalm 115 acknowledges that 'All men are lyers' (115:11, Geneva translation), which would seem to blur any distinction between truth-tellers and liars and suggest that lying happens whatever we try to do.[145] On the contrary, Augustine argues, a lie is always wrong, is forbidden by scripture, and even telling a lie for the safety of another risks committing another iniquity for the sake of preventing one, because two wrongs do not make a right.[146] Augustine asserts that the mind must never be corrupted for the sake of the body, which is why he condemned Lucrece for her suicide after she was raped by Tarquin, and why lying to prevent physical harm could never be condoned by God.[147] Lying, like lust, corrupts the mind and 'who will say that the mind of him who tells a lie has its integrity?'[148] Good men can never tell lies, and if we 'once break, or but slightly diminish the authority of truth . . . all things will remain doubtful: which unless they be believed true, cannot be held as certain'.[149] Small lies will eventually lead to far more serious deceptions. It is easy for Augustine to dismiss lies that are told for pleasure by a habitual liar who 'loves to lie, and inhabits in his mind the delight of lying', as well as those that may seem harmless—that one's father or grandfather was a good man when he was not—but which corrode the value of truth because they are told to 'please people better than the truth'.[150] But, as Augustine acknowledges, 'the whole dispute turns' when one considers more marginal cases, 'whether that person does harm to himself, who benefits another in such sort as to act contrary to the truth'.[151]

Augustine, who often sounds very much like Kant and who makes a similar—though not identical, given his other pronouncements—case about truth-telling and murder, establishes a classification of eight types of lie in descending order of culpability.[152] He starts with the capital lie about religious doctrine, 'to which lie a man ought by no consideration to be induced', followed by lies that hurt someone unjustly, down to the two which have generated controversy, which hurt no one and help some. There is a sliding scale of lying and sin: 'a man sins less when he tells a lie, in proportion as he emerges to the eighth: more in proportion as he diverges to the first'.[153] But the really problematic lie is one that hurts no one 'and does good in the preserving somebody from corporal defilement'.[154] Here a more delicate moral balancing act is required so that we are no longer considering lying alone as an ethical problem but performing utilitarian calculations: 'here the question is no longer about lying, but it is asked whether an injury ought to be done to any man, even otherwise than by a lie, that the said defilement may be warded off from another'.[155] This is the one exception to the general prohibition of lying. Augustine

---

[145] See Harald Weinrich, *The Linguistics of Lying and Other Essays*, trans. Jane K. Brown and Marshall Brown (Seattle: University of Washington Press, 2005), pp. 8–9.

[146] Augustine, 'On Lying', 9.

[147] Augustine, 'On Lying', 10. On Lucrece, see Augustine, *City of God*, pp. 28–31.

[148] Augustine, 'On Lying', 10.   [149] Augustine, 'On Lying', 11, 17.

[150] Augustine, 'On Lying', 18.   [151] Augustine, 'On Lying', 19.

[152] Augustine, 'On Lying', 14.   [153] Augustine, 'On Lying', 42.

[154] Augustine, 'On Lying', 25.   [155] Augustine, 'On Lying', 25.

refs again to the example of the Hebrew midwives in Egypt who, the Bible makes clear, behaved properly and virtuously in lying:

> And he [the king of Egypt] said, When ye do the office of a midwife to the Hebrew women, and see *them* upon the stools; if it *be* a son, then ye shall kill him; but if it *be* a daughter, then she shall live.
>
> But the midwives feared God, and did not as the king of Egypt commanded them, but saved the men children alive.
>
> And the king of Egypt called for the midwives, and said unto them, Why have ye done this thing, and have saved the men children alive?
>
> And the midwives said unto Pharaoh, Because the Hebrew women *are* not as the Egyptian women; for they *are* lively, and are delivered ere the midwives come in unto them.
>
> Therefore God dealt well with the midwives: and the people multiplied, and waxed very mighty.   (Exodus 1:16-20: KJV)

The text seems to endorse the behaviour of the midwives whose virtuous actions in saving the Hebrew infants are rewarded by God who oversees the powerful growth of the people, although their actions were criticized by some Church Fathers, such as Gregory the Great, who argued, like Augustine, that the New Testament set a 'higher standard' than the Old.[156] The passage is also surely humorous, with Pharaoh falling for such an obvious lie, one that reveals his lamentable lack of understanding of how women give birth, enabling the midwives to mock him and the Egyptians as they aggrandize the reproductive achievements of their fellow women (either they are much more 'lively' than the Egyptians, or, as is the case, they are cleverer).[157] It is the growth, the liveliness, which inspires Augustine's approval 'because it is some step towards loving the true and eternal saving of the soul, when a person does mercifully for the saving of any man's albeit mortal life even tell a lie'.[158] God will never approve of lying, but in a few rare circumstances it has to be endorsed because it prevents mankind from being defiled by a greater sin. The moral imperative is to please God not mankind so that it is possible to hate lies yet to have to tell them in extreme circumstances, if lying prevents something worse happening.[159] Accordingly, 'a lie which does not violate the doctrine of piety, not piety itself, nor innocence, nor benevolence, may on behalf of pudicity of body be admitted'.[160] Although a defence of lying has done a great deal of harm in corrupting mankind, it is still possible to lie on rare occasions, even though all forms of lying are sin and whoever imagines otherwise 'will deceive himself foully'.[161]

As Coignet's comments demonstrate, Augustine was an authority on lying but not necessarily read in a scrupulously philosophical manner and his name could be invoked to perform little more than a condemnation of dissimulation and

---

[156] Kirk, *Conscience and Its Problems*, p. 192.

[157] On the frequent humour in the Old Testament, see Gabriel Josipovici, *The Book of God: A Response to the Bible* (New Haven: Yale University Press, 1988).

[158] Augustine, 'On Lying', 34.   [159] Augustine, 'On Lying', 38.

[160] Augustine, 'On Lying', 41.

[161] Augustine, 'On Lying', 43, 42. See also Augustine, 'To Consentius, Against Lying', trans. H. Browne (http://www.newadvent.org/fathers/1313.htm) (accessed 23 June 2015), section 2.

mendacity.[162] The way that his writings were read, responded to, and appropriated in early modern England provides a nice illustration of the basic argument of this book: that in a time when there was a great pressure on individuals to make difficult choices about whether to tell the truth or to lie, authorities who provided sophisticated arguments about truth/falsehood and lying were sometimes carefully read and sometimes simply invoked. In such periods there is always a simple response to set beside the complicated one, the two frequently intermingled, overlapping and even confused.

V

This study has been based on a series of case studies, which have to be outlined at some length. I am sceptical about how much a history of lying as a concept on its own will really tell us, although I admire many attempts to tell this particular story, and have, of course, learned a great deal from them.[163] Lies are informed by ideas, perceptions, and definitions, but, as so many books of moral philosophy and ordinary language philosophy have (quite rightly) assumed, working definitions of lying do not obviously change over the millennia.[164] They may not be quite the same, but is there a fundamental difference between the debates surrounding Jacob's deception of Isaac, when he pretended to be Esau and said to allay his father's suspicions, 'I *am* Esau thy firstborn' (Genesis 27:19), and Bill Clinton's declaration that he 'did not have sexual relations with that woman'?[165] Two comments by distinguished commentators on lying would seem to provide a more helpful way of thinking about lying than one based on the history of its definitions. The anthropologist J. L. Barnes, in his study of the different types of lies and the different attitudes towards them in various communities, dismissed one notion of a history of lying with good-natured exasperation: 'Whether lies are in fact told more often nowadays than previously is anyone's guess, but at least there is a greater awareness of the prevalence of lying.'[166] Hannah Arendt, responding to the release of *The Pentagon Papers* in 1967 charting the 'History of U.S. Decision-Making on Vietnam Policy' argued that 'To the many genres in the art of lying developed in the past, we must now add two more recent examples', those of the 'public-relations managers in government who learned their trade from the inventiveness of Madison Avenue' and

---

[162] Although this is not to deny that some writers read Augustine with scrupulous attention: see Katrin Ettenhuber, *Donne's Augustine: Renaissance Cultures of Interpretation* (Oxford: Oxford University Press, 2011); Harold L. Weatherby, *Mirrors of Celestial Grace: Patristic Theology in Spenser's Allegory* (Toronto: University of Toronto Press, 1994), pp. 156–80, *passim*.

[163] See Denery, *The Devil Wins*, for the most recent history, and my review, *TP* 29 (2015), 773–80.

[164] See, for example, Williams, *Truth and Truthfulness*, pp. 96–7; Shiffrin, *Speech Matters*, ch. 1; J. L. Austin, *How to Do Things with Words*, ed. J. O. Urmson and Marina Sbisà (Oxford: Oxford University Press, 1976), pp. 11, 20.

[165] Kirk, *Conscience and Its Problems*, p. 185; Green, *Lying, Cheating*, pp. 140–7; Carson, *Lying and Deception*, p. 16; Saul, *Lying, Misleading*, pp. 42–8, 118–26. On Esau, see also Philip Kerr, ed., *The Penguin Book of Lies* (Harmondsworth: Penguin, 1990), pp. 9–10.

[166] Barnes, *Pack of Lies*, p. 1.

those of the 'professional "problem-solvers"', university-trained men who were employed by think tanks, 'some of them equipped with game theories and systems analyses'.[167] What is implicit in the arguments of both writers is that the contexts in which lies are uttered and received change, which transforms our understanding of lying, even if the basic concept of the lie remains the same.[168] Barnes suggests that we might possibly understand lying better now because there is a greater awareness of the ubiquity of the phenomenon—he may, of course, be mistaken and I am not sure he is right, especially if we consider the evidence from sixteenth-century England. Arendt argues that we need to think about new genres of lying: strictly speaking she means types of people who produce lies, but the point is the same, that the contexts in which lies are articulated have changed, not the nature and character of lies and the act of lying. The point can be illustrated via the toxic libel case when Lillian Hellman took Arendt's friend Mary McCarthy to task for her notorious statement, 'every word that she wrote was a lie, including "and" and "the"'. As Alan Ackerman has argued in his meticulous study of the case, what might seem obvious at first sight—surely it would be easy enough to decide if Hellman really was a habitual liar and whether McCarthy had defamed her in her statement—turned out to be a conflict about the understanding of the personal and the political which exposed a fault line central to American life in the twentieth century, complicating a straightforward understanding of truth, falsehood, and lying.[169]

Accordingly, studying how lies are produced, how they are imagined, analysed, and understood, and in which contexts they are articulated, is as important as noting the ways in which philosophers, theologians, and moralists have written about lying. Literature must be a central part of this story, not simply because literary authors reflect on lies and lying in their work—which, of course, they do—but because literature was often a testing ground for ideas about lying. Literature was dismissed by hostile authorities, like Stephen Gosson, the former playwright, as an excuse for lying, which is the substance of Plato's suspicion of the literary arts, one that frequently recurs.[170] Philip Stubbes in *The Anatomie of Abuses* (1583) attacked the theatre as a place where dangerous and addictive vice is on display and where the foolish play-goer can 'learne to deceive . . . to playe the hypocrite . . . to cog, to lie and falsify'.[171] For Plato art and literature produce words and images that are 'three removes from the truth', and so are at best useless, and, at worst, misleading, duplicitous, and even outright lies.[172] Authors of literary works are

---

[167] Arendt, *Crises*, pp. 13–14.

[168] I am very grateful to Vincent Crawford for illuminating conversations on this issue.

[169] Alan Ackerman, *Just Words: Lillian Hellman, Mary McCarthy, and the Failure of Public Conversation in America* (New Haven: Yale University Press, 2011).

[170] On Gosson, see Jean E. Howard, 'Renaissance Antitheatricality and the Politics of Gender and Rank in *Much Ado About Nothing*', in Jean E. Howard and Marion O'Connor, eds, *Shakespeare Reproduced: The Text in History and Ideology* (London: Routledge, 1987), pp. 163–87, at p. 168.

[171] Philip Stubbes, *The Anatomie of Abuses*, ed. Margaret Jane Kidnie (Tempe, AZ: RETS, 2002), p. 204.

[172] D. A. Russell and M. Winterbottom, eds, *Classical Literary Criticism* (Oxford: Oxford University Press, 1989), p. 44.

invariably concerned with lying as a subject about which they need to write. They are writing at one remove from the literal truth, as Sidney and Ralegh demonstrate, and so can represent controversial subjects more safely than authors of factual works, and because the nature of what they do requires them to think about what knowledge their work produces. Furthermore, literature as an art of representation has to push the boundaries of what it can possibly achieve, and in its striving to produce new forms of writing, writers have to worry about the truthfulness of their work, which makes them especially sensitive to the issue of lying.

So much thinking about lying involves how to deal with lies as they are told, which is what concerns Augustine in his two major studies of lying. But this only tells part of the story of lying and the anxieties about why lies are told. We also need to think about the lie as the breaking of a future promise, the most important form of which is the oath. An oath is a (public) promise that one will remain faithful to the person or institution to whom or which one had sworn loyalty.[173] Violating that oath was a form of lying, the lie taking place when one broke the oath, even if it may have been a lie all along. If I promise to pay you £5 next week and do not do so only I can know whether I lied when I made the promise, changed my mind, or believed that I would pay the sum but was too weak-willed or forgetful to do so when the time came.[174] Thomas Lupton acknowledges that, in the end, no one but the liar and God know the truth of the matter:

> Onely GOD whiche is witnesse good inough, and wyll be founde true in hys witnessing when all other shall be founde lyars : and though you may now escape the worldly punishment for lying, because wee haue no worldly witnesses against you, yet assure you, you cannot escape the punishment in Hell without repentaunce for lying, if GOD bee a witnesse against you, (who sayeth) that Lyars shall haue their postion in the Lake that burnes with fire and Brimstone.[175]

The matter is a crucial one when oaths and promises conflict, as they did after the Reformation with the monarch eager to secure the loyalty of his subjects and abjure their promises to the Church, as he had done.[176] Could promises be kept? How serious a sin was it to violate such contracts? Or was a change of mind simply a case of having one's eyes opened, an understanding that another oath or promise took precedence over the one sworn previously when circumstances changed and new evidence came to light? People rarely agreed about the consequences of breaking a promise, as the first

---

[173] Oath, n., *OED* definition 1a: 'A solemn or formal declaration invoking God (or a god, or other object of reverence) as witness to the truth of a statement, or to the binding nature of a promise or undertaking; an act of making such a declaration'. The definition is dated to Anglo-Saxon England.

[174] For relevant discussion, see Bernard Gert Stone, *Morality: Its Nature and Justification* (Oxford: Oxford University Press, 1998), pp. 191–2. Stone points out that not all broken promises involve lying.

[175] Lupton, *Siuqila*, sig. P2r.

[176] G. R. Evans, *Problems of Authority in the Reformation Debates* (Cambridge: Cambridge University Press, 1992), ch. 11; Claire Cross, *Church and People: England 1450–1660* (2nd edn, Oxford: Blackwell, 1999), pp. 50–1; Norman Jones, *The English Reformation: Religion and Cultural Adaptation* (Oxford: Blackwell, 2002), p. 151.

chapter demonstrates, and, in the period in question, the relationship between oaths and promises that were not kept and lies was a corrosive issue.

Religious belief was undoubtedly the central concern in debates about lying, the common culture that connected everyone whatever their differences. As Debora Shuger has expressed it, 'whatever the orthodoxies or dominant ideologies of the period might be, they could not be divorced from theocentric concerns'.[177] But a study of lying in early modern England cannot be limited to religious belief: its central role in determining the culture means that other subjects, other institutional forms and modes of thinking, writing, and speaking need to be considered as well as religion. Habits of thought are connected, directly and indirectly, and the ubiquitous existence of religion in the world means that there is a symbiotic relationship between religion and other modes of thinking: the law, philosophy, politics, rhetoric, polite behaviour and courtesy, empirical observation, travel writing, and literature. Although nothing is ever isolated and self-contained, each particular context produces its own logic of truth/lies.

This book has two parts and seven chapters. Part I, 'Lying and the Culture of Oaths', consists of two chapters. The first explores the impact of the Oath of Supremacy, looking at two trials, those of Thomas More and Anne Boleyn, which resulted from the astonishing changes precipitated by Henry's decision to divorce Catherine of Aragon, forcing English men and women to wonder how honest they could be about their loyalties and precipitating a crisis concerning the nature of speech and language in public culture. The chapter explores these two important trials in terms of the Reformation, showing how arguments about truth and lying became particularly significant as the King assumed the right to rule the Church as well as the state. Uncovering the truth of each trial may be less important than understanding that they are about truth and whose right it is to declare what is truth and what lies. Chapter 2 explores the slow progress from the excommunication of Elizabeth by Pope Pius V in 1570 to the Oath of Allegiance in the wake of the Gunpowder Plot. That oath has been seen as a tolerant act by some, a hostile one by others, designed to flush out Catholics and force a loyalty that silenced dissent. However it is read, the oath marks another transformation in English public culture, one that crystallized religious divisions. The chapter shows how significant the change was through the study of another trial that has not always been seen in terms of the culture of the oath, the Essex divorce trial. Both, as I have already suggested, are particular pressure points in English history, moments when questions of truth and lies became even more significant than usual as monarchs sought to impose oaths on their reluctant subjects.[178]

Part II, 'Modes of Lying in Early Modern England', consists of five chapters. Chapter 3 discusses the varieties of religious belief and religious debates about the

[177] Debora Kuller Shuger, *Habits of Thought in the English Renaissance: Religion, Politics, and the Dominant Culture* (Berkeley: University of California Press, 1990), p. 251.

[178] For a discussion of the emphasis placed on such unique, particular historical moments in relation to the need to take action and seize the day see Joanne Paul, 'The Use of *Kairos* in Renaissance Political Philosophy', *RQ* 67 (2014), 43–78.

nature of lying, in particular whether there was a need to declare religious belief to hostile authorities or whether it was possible to equivocate or practise 'mental reservation' even if one could not actually lie. The chapter explores discourses of martyrdom and arguments about the limits of testifying one's faith, as well as how authorities were to be obeyed or disobeyed. It outlines the implications of the beliefs of a variety of diverse religious groups such as the Jesuits, varieties of Protestants, and those whom Calvin labelled 'Nicodemites'. Chapter 4 examines a variety of treatises and debates about rhetoric and its value and whether the art of persuasion could be a dangerous tool in the hands of the unscrupulous or even whether it was a skill that risked corrupting the user, dangers that were identified by Quintilian, whose *Institutio Oratoria* (The Orator's Education) shaped so much rhetorical theory and practice in the Renaissance. The chapter analyses the practice of commonplacing, noting down particular maxims which could then serve as the basis for explorations of particular issues, a practice that, like rhetoric, generated anxiety about truth, falsehood, and lying. Chapter 5 contains a discussion of courtesy books and political conduct manuals and whether the behaviour they recommend could or should be divorced from moral conduct, and, if so, what implications this had for truthfulness and whether courtiers were ever permitted to tell lies in the name of a greater good. Political speech has always been calculated, and it is rare to encounter 'naïve communication—where a speaker states literally all that he thinks, and/or an audience accepts his representation at face value'.[179] The chapter examines the question of whether small lies led to big lies or whether they could be contained, a central question asked in Edmund Spenser's *Faerie Queene*. Chapter 6 explores the issues of eyewitness accounts and testimony. In both legal disputes and for information about foreign countries great reliance was placed on the accounts of eyewitnesses. But how could anyone be sure that those who provided testimony were telling the truth? Reliable, honest testimony was central to questions of truth and lying and so features heavily in discussion in this period. Chapter 7, concentrating on a particular literary work, *Othello*, looks at evidence, apparently miraculous events and phenomena, and travel writing, asking whether such writings were really an excuse to delude and dupe a public, suspending ordinary standards of truthfulness, and to tell a series of lies. The chapter shows how Shakespeare is alive to the wide variety of forms of lying identified by commentators, placing diverse types of falsehood together in order to ask many of the main questions posed by debates about lying in this period: did small lies lead to big lies? How could one tell when someone was lying? Could one ever be permitted to lie and, if so, what might the consequences be? And, why do people tell lies?

---

[179] Glenn C. Loury, 'Self-Censorship in Public Discourse: A Theory of "Political Correctness" and Related Phenomena', *Rationality and Society* 6 (1994), 428–61, p. 431. See also Stephen Morris, 'Political Correctness', *JPE* 109 (2001), 231–65, at p. 249. I owe these references to Vincent Crawford.

PART I

LYING AND THE CULTURE
OF OATHS

1

The Oath of Supremacy

I

After he had been imprisoned in the Tower for some months for refusing to take the Oath of Supremacy Thomas More was visited by the King's solicitor, Richard Rich, who was accompanied by Sir Richard Southwell, principal secretary to the Privy Council, and his servant, Master Palmer.[1] Their brief was to remove More's books. While Southwell and Palmer set about their task, Rich 'pretending friendly talk' with More asked him a hypothetical question:

'Forasmuch as it is well known, Master More, that you are a man both wise and well-learned, as well in the laws of the realm as otherwise, I pray you therefore, sir, let me be so bold as of good will to put unto you this case. Admit there were, sir,' quoth he, 'an act of Parliament that all the realm should take me for king. Would not you, Master More, take me for King?'

'Yes, sir', quoth Sir Thomas More, 'that would I.'

'I put case further,' quoth Master Rich, 'that there were an act of Parliament that all the realm should take me for Pope. Would not you, then, Master More, take me for Pope?'

'For answer, sir,' quoth Sir Thomas More, 'to your first case. The Parliament may well, Master Rich, meddle with the state of temporal princes. But to make answer to your other case, I will put you this case: Suppose the Parliament would make a law that God should not be God. Would you, then, Master Rich, say that God were not God?'

'No, sir,' quoth he, 'that would I not, since no Parliament may make any such law.'

'No more,' said Sir Thomas More, as Master Rich reported of him, 'could the Parliament make the King supreme head of the Church.'[2]

The conversation, also recorded in the formal legal documents, is crucial to our understanding of More's fate because it was upon Rich's 'only [single] report' that 'Sir Thomas More [was] indicted of treason upon the statute whereby it was made treason to deny the King to be supreme head of the Church'.[3] As William Roper

---

[1] On Rich (1496/7–1567), Palmer (1502/3–64), and Southwell (1502/3–64) see the respective *ODNB* entries.

[2] William Roper, *The Life of Sir Thomas More*, in R. S. Sylvester and D. P. Harding, eds, *Two Early Tudor Lives* (New Haven: Yale University Press, 1962), pp. 244–5. Subsequent references to the text to this edition in parentheses in the text.

[3] Duncan M. Derrett, 'The Trial of Sir Thomas More', *EHR* 79 (1964), 449–77, p. 462. For the relevant documents and translations see Henry Ansgar Kelly, Louis W. Karlin, and Gerard B. Wegemer, eds, *Thomas More's Trial by Jury: A Procedural and Legal Review with a Collection of Documents* (Woodbridge: Boydell, 2011), pp. 175–85.

points out in his sympathetic and partisan life of More, More's indictment further claimed that More had uttered these words 'Maliciously, traitorously, and diabolically' (p. 245).[4]

Roper (1495/8–1578), More's son-in-law and a 'conservative lawyer', makes his opinion clear in adding his own gloss, describing the prosecution's words as 'heinous'.[5] When More is confronted by Rich's evidence at the trial in the Court of King's Bench in Westminster Hall, Roper indicates that he speaks with carefully controlled fury:

> If I were a man, my lords, that did not regard an oath, I needed not, as it is well known, in this place at this time nor in this case, to stand here as an accused person. And if this oath of yours, Master Rich, be true, then pray I never see God in the face, which I would not say, were it otherwise, to win the whole world . . . In good faith, Master Rich, I am sorrier for your perjury than for my own peril . . . And I, as you know, of no small while have been acquainted with you and your conversation, who have known you from your youth hitherto. For we long dwelled both in one parish together where, as yourself tell (I am sorry you compel me to say) you were esteemed very light of your tongue, a great dicer and of no commendable fame. (pp. 245–6)[6]

More then asks the jury of his peers whether he would ever 'in so weighty a cause, so unadvisedly overshoot myself, as to trust Master Rich, a man of me always reputed for one of so little truth as your lordships have heard'. In a trial in which the nature, substance, and intention of words is the key to the outcome, More makes it clear that, although he did speak the words that Rich reported, he did not utter them as Rich claimed: 'And yet if I had so done indeed, my lords, as master Rich hath sworn, seeing it was spoken but in familiar secret talk, nothing affirming, and only in putting of cases without other displeasant circumstances, it cannot justly be taken to be spoken "maliciously". And where there is no malice, there can be no offense' (p. 246).[7] According to Roper, Rich, 'seeing himself so disproved and his credit foully defaced', appealed to Southwell and Palmer to support his story, but they, in their depositions (i.e. under oath), claim that they took no notice of the exchange because they were 'so busy about the trussing-up of Sir Thomas More's books in a sack' (p. 248). Southwell's reticence stands in marked contrast to the outspoken boldness of his grandson, the Jesuit, Robert Southwell, when he was accused of treason in 1595.[8]

---

[4] John Bellamy, *The Tudor Law of Treason: An Introduction* (London: Routledge, 1979), pp. 32–3.

[5] *ODNB* entry.

[6] On the court see E. E. Reynolds, *The Trial of St. Thomas More* (London: Burns & Oates, 1964), p. 72.

[7] On the nature and procedure of the trial, see Derrett, 'Trial'. The significance of identical words uttered in different contexts is famously explored in Borges's short story 'Pierre Menard, Author of the *Quixote*': see Adrian Poole, 'Identity of Meaning', in Walker and Leedham-Green, eds, *Identity*, pp. 9–25, at p. 10.

[8] Christopher Devlin, *The Life of Robert Southwell: Poet and Martyr* (London: Longmans, 1956), pp. 1–2. On Robert Southwell, see below, pp. 79–81, 84–7.

Roper's version of More's trial has More, rather like Socrates at his, holding centre stage and running rings around his accusers.[9] Even so, More is found guilty and condemned to death, a verdict he accepts with good grace as he has known all along that this will be the inevitable outcome of the trial. Rich, the perjurer, is a villain, but the real villain is the King who has created conditions under which such creatures can thrive and whose desires cannot, in the end, be thwarted. More and Roper are in agreement that the nature of More's utterances is more important than its substance. More made his defence clear, pointing out that 'if those only odious terms—"Maliciously, traitorously, and diabolically"—were put out, he saw therein nothing justly to charge him' (p. 245).

Roper's version of the trial reproduces only the speeches of More and Rich, making it clear that the trial hinges on the truthful word of More against the perjury of Rich, a version of the event that has been generally accepted, enshrined in Robert Bolt's influential play, *A Man for All Seasons* (1960).[10] Nicholas Harpsfield's more substantial account of the trial reproduces a practically identical account of Rich's testimony and More's defence to that of Roper.[11] The *Expositio Fidelis* (1535), the earliest account of the trial based on an unknown eyewitness account, immediately translated from Latin into French as *The Paris Newsletter* and then circulated throughout Europe, does not even mention the Rich–More exchange.[12] Accusations of perjury were relatively rare as the crime is difficult to prove because it involves the proof of an intention to deceive and so pervert the course of justice and an admission of guilt or proof beyond a reasonable level of doubt when only testimony is involved. To compensate it was sometimes imagined that God, who could see what humans could not, would inflict terrible punishments on perjurers as in the case of one who was driven to suicide and eternal damnation.[13] Even today, accusations of and convictions for perjury are few and far between.[14] Perjury was only properly instituted as a common law crime in the statute of 1563, with the passing of 'An Act for the Punishment of Such Persons as Shall Procure or Commit any Willful Perjury', which increased penalties for the crime and centralized prosecution, ensuring that more cases were tried by Star Chamber, giving the

---

[9] Plato, *Apology*, in *The Last Days of Socrates*, trans. Hugh Tredennick (Harmondsworth: Penguin, 1954), pp. 43–76.

[10] Louis L. Martz, *Thomas More: The Search for the Inner Man* (New Haven: Yale University Press, 1990), p. 3; Brian Cummings, *Mortal Thoughts: Religion, Secularity, and Identity in Shakespeare and Early Modern Culture* (Oxford: Oxford University Press, 2013), pp. 67–70.

[11] Nicholas Harpsfield, *The Life and Death of Sr Thomas Moore, knight*, ed. E. V. Hitchcock (Oxford: Oxford University Press, 1936), EETS, original ser., 186 (1932), pp. 181–93. For an argument—to me, unpersuasive—that the accounts of More's trial differ, see Henry Ansgar Kelly, 'A Procedural Review of Thomas More's Trial', in Kelly, Karlin, and Wegemer, eds, *Thomas More's Trial by Jury*, pp. 1–52, at pp. 36–8.

[12] *Humanistica Lovaniensia: Acta Thomae Mori: History of the Reports of His Trial and Death with an Unedited Contemporary Narrative*, ed. Henry De Vocht (Louvain: Publications of the Institute for Economics of the University, 1947), pp. 142–63, 254–7; Thomas More, *The Correspondence of Sir Thomas More*, ed. Elizabeth Frances Rogers (Princeton: Princeton University Press, 1947), pp. 368–78; Harpsfield, *Life*, appendix 2. There is no record of Rich's testimony in the account of the trial in *Letters and Papers*, VIII, 996 (pp. 394–5). See also *State Trials*, I, pp. 385–96.

[13] Anon., *The Fearefull Example of God Showed on Perjured Person* (London, 1591).

[14] Anon., 'Perjury: The Forgotten Offense', *JCLC* 65 (1974), 361–72.

central authorities greater control over this legal abuse.[15] Perjury assumed its modern understanding after the watershed ruling of Justice Popham in Slade's Case (1596–1602), which restricted fraudulent claims in contract disputes, and made the legal action for a breach of promise (assumpsit) a central feature of contract law.[16] Before then perjury was broadly defined as a lie under oath rather than its more modern and specific definition as 'a wilful assertion made by a witness in a judicial proceeding upon oath and known by such witness to be false'.[17] Accordingly perjury was often seen as an ecclesiastical crime, 'an offence which pertains to the dishonour of God', that could be prosecuted in various courts, especially Star Chamber which dealt with cases that the common law was not thought to be able to solve.[18] False swearing and perjury are intertwined in the 'Sermon Against Swearing and Perjury' included in the *Book of Homilies* (1547, 1562, 1571), which were read out in church services as a way of explaining the Thirty-Nine Articles to a wider population struggling to comprehend the changes inaugurated by the Reformation.[19] In William Bullein's popular and influential *Dialogue Against the Fever Pestilence* (1564, 1573, 1578), the lying traveller Mendax claims to have visited the famous city of antiquity, Metonoyae, or Tareg Natrib, 'the best reformed Citie of this woorlde', where crimes against true religion are properly and severely punished.[20] The common swearer loses his tongue but punishment is even worse for the 'wilfull periurie', who 'is stoned to death, with tongue cut out', the fictional punishments suggesting that sins of the tongue were seen as severe offences against God.[21]

More's accusation is, presumably, something of a gamble by a man who knows that the game is probably already up and that only by discrediting a hostile witness has he any chance of success, probably in salvaging his reputation rather than in saving his life.[22] If so, then to a significant extent More has succeeded in damning Rich and, as P. R. N. Carter acknowledges, nothing has been able to 'efface the

[15] Norman Jones, *Governing by Virtue: Lord Burghley and the Management of Elizabethan England* (Oxford: Oxford University Press, 2015), p. 83; Michael D. Gordon, 'The Perjury Statute of 1563: A Case History of Confusion', *PAPS* 124 (1980), 438–54.

[16] Michael Ibbotson, 'Sixteenth-Century Contract Law: Slade's Case in Context', *OJLS* 4 (1984), 295–317, p. 313; Paul Raffield, 'The Trials of Shakespeare: Courtroom Drama and Early Modern English Law', *Law & Hum.* 8 (2014), 53–76, p. 61. See also Hannah Crawforth, Sarah Dustagheer, and Jennifer Young, *Shakespeare in London* (London: Bloomsbury, 2015), p. 107.

[17] Gordon, 'Invention', p. 150. See also Lupton, *Siuqila*, sig. M1v.

[18] Gordon, 'Invention', p. 151; Cora L. Scofield, *A Study of the Court of Star Chamber* (Chicago: The University of Chicago Press, 1900), p. xxviii. See also John A. Guy, *The Cardinal's Court: The Impact of Thomas Wolsey in Star Chamber* (Harvester: Hassocks, 1977), pp. 18–19. Aquinas defines perjury as 'a falsehood confirmed by an oath': *Summa Theologica*, II.ii.qu.98 (III, pp. 1610–13).

[19] Anon., *Certain Sermons*, pp. 69–77. See also James Morice, *A Briefe Treatise of Oathes Exacted by Ordinaries and Ecclesiasticall Iudges* (London, 1590), sig. A2r.

[20] William Bullein, *A Dialogue Against the Fever Pestilence*, ed. Mark W. Bullein and A. H. Bullein (London: EETS, 1888), p. 103. On Bullein's originality and influence see R. W. Maslen, 'The Healing Dialogues of Doctor Bullein', *YES* 38 (2008), 119–35.

[21] Bullein, *Pestilence*, p. 109. See also Lupton, *Siuqila*, sig. L3r.

[22] As Sir Geoffrey Elton noted, More's case was 'very special . . . pursued to death by a vengeful King': *Policy and Police: The Enforcement of the Reformation in the Age of Thomas Cromwell* (Cambridge: Cambridge University Press, 1972), p. 307.

stain upon his [Rich's] character resulting from his possible perjury in 1535'.[23] Evidence from John Foxe and other Protestant martyrologists indicates that, having supported Somerset's reforming regime, Rich's vigorous pursuit of heresy in Mary's reign led to accusations of hypocrisy, which were surely justified as he had been responsible for illegally racking Anne Askew in 1546.[24] However, there is no corroborating evidence of Rich's youthful behaviour or his reputation as a liar beyond More's testimony.[25]

But however we read More's accusation of perjury there is no real dispute over the words spoken. The written report of them, the basis for the indictment, has a slightly different conclusion with More answering Rich's question why he does not obey the King who has been declared head of the Church, whether that were Henry VIII or Rich himself:

> To which the said Thomas More, falsely, traitorously and maliciously by words persisted in his treason and malice, and wishing to propose and defend his aforesaid treacherous and malicious intent and purpose, then and there replied according to the said Richard Rich, namely 'that those cases are not like, because a King can be made by Parliament and can be deprived by Parliament, to which Act any subject being at the Parliament may give his consent, but to the case of a primacy the subject cannot be bound because he cannot give his consent from him in Parliament, and although the King were accepted as such in England, yet most outer parts do not affirm the same'.[26]

Even so, if this version is correct More is still denying the monarch's supremacy over the clergy within his realms, a statement that the statute defined as treason.[27] Rich's version of More's words appears to have been accepted by More, and by later commentators, all of whom are either sympathetic to More or neutral, none sympathizing with Rich. The significant issue, therefore, is how the words were actually spoken and whether More was guilty of treason in speaking as he did.[28] Did he actually intend the words 'maliciously, traitorously, and diabolically', as his indictment claimed, but which he denied? If questioning the King's supremacy, even in the most hypothetical manner, is treason then More was surely guilty and Rich right to report his words, as not reporting a crime made the witness guilty by failing to declare a crime, an issue that was central to the Anne Boleyn trial.[29] If Rich was making a private and inconsequential conversation seem like an act of treason then he was guilty as More charged him; if he was acting properly in

---

[23] *ODNB* entry.

[24] *ODNB* entry. On the racking of Anne Askew see Alec Ryrie, *The Gospel and Henry VIII: Evangelicals in the Early English Reformation* (Cambridge: Cambridge University Press, 2003), p. 55.

[25] More's account of Rich's character is widely accepted: see Cummings, *Mortal Thoughts*, who refers to Rich as 'a habitual liar' (p. 146). See also Derrett, 'Trial', p. 465.

[26] Brian Byron, 'The Fourth Count of the Indictment of St. Thomas More', *Moreana* 10 (1966), 33–46, p. 35.

[27] J. Duncan M. Derrett, 'The "New" Document on Thomas More's Trial', *Moreana* 3 (1964), 5–22. Derrett argues that More was quibbling at his trial, accepted contemporary legal practice (pp. 5, 16–17).

[28] R. W. Chambers, *Thomas More* (Harmondsworth: Penguin, 1963, rpt of 1935), pp. 304–6.

[29] See below, pp. 64–6.

accordance with the law then it is More who is the guilty party, especially if we bear in mind the long-lasting effect of More's words on our understanding of the trial.

More is accusing Rich of defaming him, using hostile words to undermine his reputation, perjury and defamation being closely related crimes in early modern England.[30] English courts—ecclesiastical, local, and common law—had long dealt with defamation cases, a crime that depended on the purpose and actions of the speaker and their harmful effects: the truth of the speaker's words was not always a sound defence if the words in question had had harmful effects on the accuser intentionally caused by the defendant.[31] The burden was on the accuser to prove that they had been defamed, which is why More's words are so unusual as well as a sign of his perilous situation: Rich was unlikely to have been able to counter-accuse More of defamation in a separate trial, as More was unlikely to be alive to face the accusation. There were strict rules about defamation: a woman who said to a priest 'I do not know how to piss holy water as you do' was acquitted as her words were abuse not defamation.[32] Ensuring that verbal crimes could be properly recounted as evidence was also important: a 1585 perjury case against a lawyer's bad practice was dismissed as the charges were too vague to be substantiated.[33] Almost all treason trials after the 1534 Treason Act were based on words spoken rather than actions, which were extremely rare, so that the words and intentions of speakers were examined with scrupulous care.[34] The most significant issue in treason trials was the motivation of the speaker: were the words uttered with malice?[35] More had been accused of speaking with malice and he fought back by accusing the witness of an identical crime. As a common law lawyer More surely knew exactly what he was doing: the penalty for maliciously imputing a crime to someone else had invariably been excommunication.[36]

The Act of Attainder against More accused him of treason in failing to swear the Oath of Supremacy:

> The said Thomas More contrary to the truste and confidence aforesaid beyng lawfully and dewly required, syns the firste day of May [1534] last past unnaturally and contrary to his dutie of alleggaunce, entendying to sowe and make sedycion murmour and gruge within this Kynges Realme amongst the true obedeyent and faythfull Subiectes of the same, hath obstynatly forwardly and contemptuously refused to

---

[30] Sir John Baker, *The Oxford History of the Laws of England, Volume VI: 1483–1558* (Oxford: Oxford University Press, 2003), pp. 782–99; Robert Zaller, *The Discourse of Legitimacy in Early Modern England* (Stanford: Stanford University Press, 2007), pp. 277–8.

[31] R. H. Helmholz, ed., *Select Cases on Defamation to 1600* (London: Selden Society, 1985), introduction, p. xix. See also David Cressy, *Dangerous Talk: Scandalous, Seditious, and Treasonable Speech in Pre-Modern England* (Oxford: Oxford University Press, 2010), pp. 23–7.

[32] Helmholz, ed., *Defamation*, introduction, p. xxvii.

[33] Sir John Baker and S. F. C. Milsom, eds, *Sources of English Legal History: Private Law to 1750* (Oxford: Oxford University Press, 2010), pp. 701–2.

[34] Lemon, *Treason by Words*, pp. 2, 5–10; Christopher W. Brooks, *Law, Politics and Society in Early Modern England* (Cambridge: Cambridge University Press, 2008), p. 48; Ethan H. Shagan, *Popular Politics and the English Reformation* (Cambridge: Cambridge University Press, 2003), pp. 51–2; Brigden, *Wyatt*, p. 35; Cressy, *Dangerous Talk*, pp. 54–60.

[35] Helmholz, ed., *Defamation*, introduction, p. xxxiii.

[36] Helmholz, ed., *Defamation*, introduction, p. xiv.

make and receive such corporell othe as was ordeyned to be accepted of every Subjecte of the Realme . . . the said Sir Thomas More, by his obstinate refusell of the said othe hath committed and done misprision of High Treason.[37]

Again, it is the purpose and effects of More's words and actions that are crucial: More's defence had been that he had not sought to discuss his refusal to take the oath with anyone so his actions were merely private not public, and that he had no desire to persuade Henry's subjects not to take the oath because his silence was dictated by his conscience.[38] Rich was a perjurer, according to More, because he had made a private conversation public and so deliberately misrepresented the nature and purpose of what had been said, acting maliciously in doing so. In beginning a conversation that More thought was familiar—and private—Rich had trapped More and, in the act of making his words public, he had distorted what had been intended. More's accusation of perjury is, therefore, a claim that in intending to deceive him all along, Rich was lying.[39] However, Rich's evidence, read another way, was simply the report of a loyal subject acting in accordance with the Act of Supremacy and the accompanying Treason Act of 1534.

The Act of Supremacy, as More acknowledged in his exchange with Rich, made Henry the head of the Church of England and gave the King

> Full power and authority from time to time to visit, repress, redress, reform, order, correct, restrain and amend all such errors, heresies, abuses, offences, contempts and enormities, whatsoever they be, which by any manner spiritual authority or jurisdiction ought or may lawfully be reformed, repressed, ordered, redressed, corrected, restrained or amended, most to the pleasure of Almighty God, the increase of virtue in Christ's religion, and for the conservation of the peace, unity and tranquillity of this realm: any usage, custom, foreign laws, foreign authority, prescription or any other thing or things to the contrary hereof notwithstanding.[40]

Henry's control over his realm and power to determine the policy of his Church and the religious life of his people is clear enough, the words here ensuring that no exceptions are possible. As Alec Ryrie has pointed out, distinctions in religious belief and doctrine were relatively unimportant in the years immediately after the Reformation because 'the driving force behind Henry VIII's religious policies during the last decade of his life was the Royal Supremacy and his insistence on maintaining it'.[41] More could hardly have been ignorant of this transformation in

---

[37] *Statutes*, 26 Henry VIII.23, 'An Acte conteynyng the Attaynder of Syr Thomas More Knyght'. On More's silence see Katharine Eisaman Maus, 'Proof and Consequences: Inwardness and its Exposure in the English Renaissance', *Representations* 34 (1991), 29–52, p. 35.

[38] Harpsfield, *Life*, pp. 184–5; R. H. Helmholz, 'Natural Law and the Trial of Thomas More', in Kelly et al., eds, *Thomas More's Trial by Jury*, pp. 53–70, at pp. 63–5; Kelly, 'Procedural Review', pp. 18–26; Cummings, *Mortal Thoughts*, ch. 2; Peter Ackroyd, *The Life of Thomas More* (London: Vintage, 1999), pp. 351–6.

[39] Roderick M. Chisholm and Thomas D. Fehan, 'The Intent to Deceive', *The Journal of Philosophy* 74 (1977), 143–59, p. 148.

[40] *Tudor Constitution*, p. 356.

[41] Ryrie, *Gospel*, p. 39. See also Alec Ryrie, 'Divine Kingship and Royal Theology in Henry VIII's Reformation', *Reformation* 7 (2002), 49–77.

monarchical power as his dispute with the lawyer Christopher Saint German had centred on Henry's right to change church doctrine and the supremacy of the common law over canon law, changes Saint German had been instrumental in introducing with Thomas Cromwell, and which More had opposed.[42] It is a potent irony that Saint German was eager to assert the supremacy of the common law courts over the ecclesiastical courts, move from an inquisitorial system of justice to an accusatorial one, and so remove the reliance on the *de veritate dicenda* oath which denied the suspect any right to silence, whereas More, who defended what Saint German opposed, now asserted his right to silence when forced to swear the Oath of Supremacy.[43] The final section repudiates the right of the papacy to undermine the authority of the English King, exactly what Rich had successfully led More to deny in their conversation. Before the final steps that resulted in the secession of the English Church from the rule of the papacy, Henry had been eager to limit papal influence in England, and Thomas More's predecessor as Lord Chancellor, Cardinal Wolsey, was accused of praemunire, supporting the rights of the papacy, a foreign or imperial power, or any other alien laws which contradicted or undermined those of the legitimate English monarch, dying before his trial (1530).[44] Now, on Rich's testimony, More was acting in the same way, supporting the authority of the papacy against the monarch. Like More, Rich had chosen his words and the nature of his accusation with great care.

The Act, which revised earlier treason Acts to ensure that Henry and his new queen would be safe from every form of attack, places particular emphasis on the use of words.[45] The Act made it treason for the King's subjects to

> Maliciously wish, will, or desire by words or writing, or by craft imagine, invent, practise or attempt any bodily harm to be done or committed to the King's most royal person, the Queen's or their heir's apparent, or to deprive them or any of them of the dignity, title or name of their royal estates, or slanderously and maliciously publish and pronounce, by express writing or words that the King our sovereign lord should be heretic, schismatic, tyrant, infidel or usurper of the crown . . . every such person and persons so offending . . . their aiders, counsellors, consenters, and abettors, being thereof lawfully convict according to the laws and customs of this realm, shall be adjudged traitors[.][46]

---

[42] Alistair Fox, *Thomas More: History and Providence* (Oxford: Blackwell, 1982), pp. 187–91; *ODNB* entry on Saint German. See also R. S. White, *Natural Law in English Renaissance Literature* (Cambridge: Cambridge University Press, 1996), pp. 50–4.

[43] Gregory W. O'Reilly, 'England Limits the Right to Silence and Moves towards an Inquisitorial System of Justice', *JCLC* 85 (1994), 402–52, at pp. 411–12.

[44] John Guy, 'Henry VIII and the Praemunire Manoeuvres of 1530–1531', *EHR* 97 (1982), 481–503; Stanford E. Lehmberg, *The Reformation Parliament, 1529–1536* (Cambridge: Cambridge University Press, 1970), pp. 107–16.

[45] The Act was then used against Queen Anne, who it was actually designed to protect, an irony that is surely understood in Nicholas Harpsfield's record of More's comment to his daughter, Meg, when told that the Queen was 'never better' that 'it pitieth me to remember into what misery, poor soul, she shall shortly come' (Roper, *More*, p. 38).

[46] *Tudor Constitution*, p. 62. See also Kelly, 'Procedural Review', p. 12; D. Alan Orr, *Treason and the State: Law, Politics and Ideology in the English Civil War* (Cambridge: Cambridge University Press, 2002), pp. 18–19.

It is hard to see how More was not guilty of treason in his conversation. He had not imagined any bodily harm of the monarch, the Queen or their heirs, nor had he tried to deprive them of the right to their estates, but he had denied the King the sole right to be head of the Church and so had, implicitly, defined him as a heretic, usurper, and, most obviously, a schismatic. In refusing to take the oath and in being known to have refused to take it he was also denying the King's right to his full authority.[47] If Rich did not report the conversation he would be guilty of being More's counsellor, perhaps even his aider or abettor, so he was duty bound to declare More's words to the authorities or face similar penalties himself. But, of course, the conversation was undoubtedly designed to produce this outcome.

The 1534 Treason Act was not a major departure in English legal history and it was by no means comprehensive, failing to close a number of loopholes, issues that were later rectified.[48] The notion that planning to harm or plotting against and so imagining ('compassing') the death of the monarch was a treasonable offence that dated back to the statute of 1352 (25 Edward III st. 5 *c.* 2) and was to play an important role in English legal history well into the eighteenth century.[49] The specific legal developments of Henry's reign cannot be confined to changes in the law—although ensuring that all cases of treason were tried under the common law was a major element of Cromwell's centralizing reforms.[50] What matters is the significance placed on words in the immediate aftermath of the break with the Church of Rome when heavy emphasis was placed on loyalty to the monarch with the concomitant fear of heresy as a corrosive force that could undermine legitimate authority. This was a period in which there was an imperative to translate religious works into the vernacular alongside a fear that inaccurate or dubious wording could lead to accusations of heresy.[51] But in a time of bewildering religious change no one could ever be entirely sure what the difference between true religion and heresy really was, especially as Henry sought to curtail the spread of the Reformation at different points in his terrifying last years.[52] The wording of the Act and the Oath of Supremacy and the Treason Statute confirms that the monarch now had the authority to distinguish between proper and improper words. Treason by words was already an occupational hazard of taking high office, an issue implicitly acknowledged in More's *Utopia*.[53] But in the early 1530s language became an especially dangerous activity and even silence could be constituted an offence: our modern understanding of the 'right to silence' is a later development, in place in

---

[47] Ways of trying to avoid swearing the oath continued throughout the century, especially in the universities: see Gerard Kilroy, *Edmund Campion: A Scholarly Life* (Farnham: Ashgate, 2015), p. 56.

[48] Bellamy, *Treason*, pp. 34–6.

[49] Bellamy, *Treason*, p. 9; John Barrell, *Imagining the King's Death: Figurative Treason, Fantasies of Regicide, 1793–1796* (Oxford: Oxford University Press, 2000).

[50] Elton, *Policy and Police*, p. 292.

[51] Brian Cummings, *The Literary Culture of the Reformation: Grammar and Grace* (Oxford: Oxford University Press, 2002), ch. 5.

[52] Greg Walker, *Writing Under Tyranny: English Literature and the Henrician Reformation* (Oxford: Oxford University Press, 2005), ch. 10.

[53] See below, p. 174.

1688, resulting in part from legal struggles precipitated by the passing of the Oath of Supremacy, the *terminus post quem* of this book.[54]

In the deadly verbal battle between More and Rich we witness accusations of two of the most serious crimes involving words: More counters Rich's evidence of his treason with a counter-accusation of perjury. The later stages of More's writing career show him to be intimately concerned with the problem of perjury and lying. He reflected on the issue in his *Dialogue Concerning Heresies* (1528–9), which defended the authority of the Church against the heresy of *sola scriptura*.[55] More's principal target is William Tyndale but the work also contains a discussion of Thomas Bilney (*c.*1495–1531), who was burned at the stake for heresy, having originally recanted and then repented of his cowardice.[56] More takes an Augustinian line, arguing forcefully that whatever the dangers facing the accused they should never perjure themselves.[57] In his protracted and vicious argument with Tyndale, More provides further reflections on perjury when he uses the word to define the act of breaking a solemn religious oath or promise, targeting Protestants who had broken away from the Church, the first such usage recorded in the *OED*.[58] More lists a catalogue of equally abhorrent sins that are now ignored to provide the reader with a clear sense of the serious nature of oath-breaking. The list provides a series of analogies to give the reader a proper understanding of the crime, and the scandal of contemporary indifference: 'That... runnynge out of relygyon in apostacy, brekyng of vowys, & frerys weddyng nonnys, & periury were no synne at all.'[59]

While imprisoned in the Tower (April 1534–July 1535) More returned to the subject and produced a fragment of a work on perjury, as well as more extended discussion in his final work, the *Dialogue of Comfort Against Tribulation* (1534). The short Latin work is More's most sustained analysis of lying and we will undoubtedly never know whether it predates and so informs his decision to accuse Rich publicly of perjury, or whether it was written as a result of their encounter in court. Perjury is defined as 'a violation of a lawful oath' and whoever commits perjury is guilty of a mortal sin: violating an unlawful oath does not count, 'Otherwise, he who swears to kill someone, would sin if he did not kill.'[60] More's discussion is a defence of the binding nature of oaths, a lawyer's reflection

---

[54] J. Duncan M. Derrett suggests that the framers of the Treason Statute had civil law in mind in making silence a crime, as it was 'no crime by common law', but precedents could be found in civil law: 'More's Silence and His Trial', *Moreana* 22 (1985), 87–8. On the right to silence see O'Reilly, 'England Limits the Right to Silence', pp. 414–19.

[55] Louis Karlin, 'More's Dialogue Concerning Heresies and the Idea of the Church', *More Studies* 3 (2008), 32–40.

[56] On Bilney, see the *ODNB* entry; Susan Wabuda, *Preaching During the English Reformation* (Cambridge: Cambridge University Press, 2002), pp. 83–5, *passim*.

[57] More, *CW*, VI, pp. 275–81, *passim*.   [58] 'perjury', *OED* 1b.

[59] More, *CW*, VIII, p. 28. For the wider significance of such disputes after the Reformation see Jonathan Michael Gray, 'Vows, Oaths, and the Propagation of a Subversive Discourse', *C16J* 41 (2010), 731–56.

[60] More, *CW*, 'More's Discussion of Perjury', VI, pp. 764–9, at p. 765; Shapiro, *Culture of Fact*, p. 42.

on the vows and promises that create a properly religious society.[61] He argues that it is sometimes permissible to lie and to keep secrets:

> If therefore any lawful secret is entrusted to anyone outside of confession, and if it is of such a kind that the revelation of it might harm the person who entrusted it, then he is bound by a double bond to conceal it: both because the thing was entrusted to him for safekeeping as a deposit, and because he is bound to conceal everything which, if it were not concealed, would harm his neighbour, no matter how it came to his knowledge, provided it is not a misdeed which it would benefit the state to reveal.
>
> (More, *CW*, VI, p. 765)

The final clause resembles Augustine's qualification of his elaborate taxonomy outlining his belief in an absolute injunction against lying because it is an abuse of God's word: lying to prevent harm to others could be permissible. If they were written before his exchange with Rich then More's words might be seen to support Rich's actions; if they were written after, then they might well be read as an acknowledgement that Rich had a duty to act as he did. However, given More's understanding of the significance of oaths, as well as his belief that breaking a binding oath is perjury, then, in his eyes, the court had surely been assembled by perjurers and was not fit to judge his case.[62] More had resigned as Lord Chancellor on 16 May 1532, the day after the English clergy had surrendered to Henry and pledged loyalty to the King of England and not the Pope, after the King declared to a delegation from the House of Commons that until that moment the clergy had been only half his subjects.[63] More, presumably in the light of his thoughts about perjury and the violation of oaths, considered the King and the English Church to be guilty of perjury, exactly what he had always feared that heresy would eventually cause.[64]

More's concern in his brief excursus on the crime of perjury is whether it is ever lawful to force people to reveal secrets 'as can and should be kept hidden'. More claims to be following Augustine in concluding that the duty to keep a lawful oath secret overcomes the injunction not to lie. He imagines the trials and tribulations of a man of conscience who has sworn such an oath to keep a secret:

> If, overcome by force, he swears, nevertheless he is not bound to discharge what he has sworn, but on the contrary he is bound not to discharge it. So where are we then? Will

[61] On the binding nature of oaths, see John Spurr, '"The Strongest Bond of Conscience": Oaths and the Limits of Tolerance in Early Modern England', in Braun and Vallance, eds, *Contexts of Conscience*, pp. 151–65, at p. 159; Christopher Saint German, *Hereafter Foloweth A Dyalogue in Englysshe, Betwyxt A Doctoure Of Dyuynyte, And A Student In The Lawes of Englande* (London, 1530), Dialogue II, ch. 24; Angela McShane, 'Material Culture and "Political Drinking" in Seventeenth-Century England', in Withington and McShane, eds, *Cultures of Intoxication*, pp. 247–76, at p. 261.

[62] See also Henry de Bracton, *On the Laws and Customs of England*, trans. Samuel E. Thorne, 4 vols (Cambridge, MA: Harvard University Press, 1977), III, p. 346, and his description of the fate of oath-breakers: 'They incur perpetual infamy and lose the *lex terrae*, so that they will never afterwards by [*sic*] admitted to an oath, for they will not henceforth be oathworthy, nor be received as witnesses, because it is presumed that he who is once convicted of perjury will perjure himself again.'

[63] Chambers, *More*, pp. 240–1.

[64] David Loewenstein, *Treacherous Faith: The Specter of Heresy in Early Modern English Literature and Culture* (Oxford: Oxford University Press, 2013), pp. 33–47.

it be lawful for him to lie? I shall deny this if I follow Augustine's opinion; if I follow Jerome's, I won't deny it; for their opinions regarding the 'officious' lie do not agree. But in the meanwhile I decide as follows: should he lie, he is not guilty of perjury because he is not violating a lawful oath . . . And I say 'according to Augustine,' not because I remember that he said this in so many words, but because it seems to me clearly to follow from the way his thought develops. For I have satisfied myself that Augustine, even though he is unwilling that anyone should lie to preserve either his own or another's life, does not, nevertheless, want anyone, rather than he should lie, either to kill himself or someone else, or to bring that killing about by what he had said. Neither could he, therefore, betray a lawful secret entrusted to him, if the revelation of it might harm whoever entrusted it to him. (pp. 765–6)

More's need to rely on his own conscience is undoubtedly a sign of the changes that were taking place in conceptions of an individual's rights, duties, and relationship to institutions. More can no longer depend on the advice of the Church to resolve his dilemma but has to work alone in conversation with God: his writings constantly warn his readers how fundamental and how dangerous this change will be. Broadly speaking, the Reformation transformed an understanding of conscience as objective in nature, subject to the dictates of the Church, to subjective, as individuals had to rely on their own understanding of how to behave morally.[65] Here, More articulates the difficulties of adapting to the new regime of truth that he dreaded.[66]

More has recast Augustine in terms of his own thinking, making the oath the central concept around which all other moral issues—including the right to lie and to kill—revolve. While Augustine wrote in general terms about lies as speech acts, More places emphasis on the oath as a binding promise. More undoubtedly has canon law in mind in making his distinctions, as canon lawyers considered perjury a worse sin than homicide because 'homicide killed only the body while perjury murdered the soul'.[67] More's definition of perjury means that the crime is about a fundamental verbal contract that cannot be broken, one which unites speaker and addressee in the eyes of God. An oath is a future promise that these sacred words cannot be undermined, 'to commit oneself not to be affected by time, to remain the same at moment B, whatever may happen, as the one who swears previously, at

[65] On the change in notions of conscience see Carol Loar, ' "Under Felt Hats and Worsted Stockings": The Uses of Conscience in Early Modern English Coroners' Inquests', *C16J* 41 (2010), 393–414; Keith Thomas, 'Cases of Conscience in Seventeenth-Century England', in John Morrill, Paul Slack, and Daniel Woolf, eds, *Public Duty and Private Conscience in Seventeenth-Century England: Essays Presented to G. E. Aylmer* (Oxford: Clarendon Press, 1993), pp. 29–56. See also Ceri Sullivan, 'Conscience as Syllogism', in *The Rhetoric of Conscience in Donne, Herbert, and Vaughan* (Oxford: Oxford University Press, 2008), pp. 11–38. On More's conscience see Brian Cummings, 'Conscience and the Law in Thomas More', *RS* 23 (2009), 463–85; Paul Strohm, *Conscience: A Very Short Introduction* (Oxford: Oxford University Press, 2011), pp. 17–23.

[66] See also Elizabeth Young, arrested in 1558 for importing Reformed books who answered her accusers that she refused to attend mass because 'my conscience will not suffer me: for I had rather all the world should accuse mee, then mine own conscience' (cited in Marsha S. Robinson, 'Doctors, Silly Poor Women, and Rebel Whores: The Gendering of Conscience in Foxe's *Acts and Monuments*', in Highley and King, eds, *Foxe and His World*, pp. 235–48, at p. 242.

[67] Gray, *Oaths*, p. 36.

moment A'.[68] Therefore, lying under oath or about an oath one has undertaken is a mortal sin and a crime that cannot easily be forgiven.[69] More's strong definition of oath-taking enables him to argue that other lies told to protect the oath are not, therefore, perjury because that crime is violating the legally binding oath made with the Church.[70] He is following the generally agreed position that 'binding words need only be kept if they are not overruled by a higher power': in this case the Church has to come before the state.[71]

How does More's accusation of Rich's crime relate to his thinking about perjury in his writings? The representation we have of More's defence is that Rich is a perjurer because he has violated and abused More's speech in misrepresenting its nature and purpose. More was articulating a hypothetical case based on certain unlikely possibilities—that Rich would be made king, or, even more implausibly, pope—which have no significant purchase on reality. However, the key to the issue is surely in the assertion that Parliament did not have the power to make the King supreme head of the Church. More may well have said this, which would make him guilty of denying the Act of Supremacy (1534: 26 Henry VIII, c 1), even if his words were uttered in jest. The Act declared that the Kings of England 'shall be taken, accepted and reputed the only supreme head in earth of the Church of England called *Anglicana Ecclesia*, and shall have annexed and united to the imperial crown of this realm as well the title and style thereof, as all honours, dignities, preeminences, jurisductions, privileges, authorities, immunities, profits and commodities', which makes it clear that the English monarch's right to the throne is based on his or her spiritual authority as supreme head of the Church.[72] Furthermore, the monarch has the right 'to repress and extirp all errors, heresies and other enormities and abuses', which coupled with the Treason Act's declaration that a subject could be punished for declaring that the King was 'heretic, schismatic, tyrant, infidel or usurper of the crown', makes it clear that More's purported statement, whether hypothetical or not, must surely be treason according to the recently established laws. More is caught in a cleft stick: either he did utter these words—and at no point does he deny that he did—in which case his only possible defence is to destroy the credibility of the witness; or, he is right that Rich is lying and his words have been deliberately falsified or distorted. Making this defence would not have saved More because he would then have been asked whether he held such an opinion. He would either have had to admit that he did, in which case he was guilty, or deny that he did, which would have made him a liar, forced him to agree to sign the oath, and negated the purpose of the principled stand that he had made which had led to the trial. More's defence that he did not seek to influence anyone by trying to persuade them to oppose the King's will could no longer be

---

[68] Jacques Derrida, '"*Le Parjure*," *Perhaps*: Storytelling and Lying', in *Without Alibi*, pp. 161–201, at p. 173; Kerrigan, *Shakespeare's Binding Language*, p. 9.

[69] Norman Doe, *Fundamental Authority in Late Medieval English Law* (Cambridge: Cambridge University Press, 1990), p. 152. Augustine acknowledged that lying under oath was a worse sin than simply lying: Gray, *Oaths*, p. 44.

[70] See also Edmund Bicknoll, *A Sword Against Swearing* (London, 1579), sig. C1v.

[71] Kerrigan, *Shakespeare's Binding Language*, p. 3.   [72] *Tudor Constitution*, p. 355.

made as he had to either declare that Rich was telling the truth, or debate the matter in court, which would amount to the same thing, as he would have broken his silence and tried to influence his interlocutors. Either way his accusers would declare that his words were 'malicious' in seeking to undermine Henry's authority as supreme head of the Church and hence legitimate king.

More's thinking about lying and perjury has a more fundamental basis, that is, the issue of violating an oath to the Church and God. More could, as his writings make clear, tell lies in order to protect an oath made to God.[73] But that strategy would not work in this case and his attempt to preserve a right of silence had been exposed by Rich's careful machinations. More accuses Rich of perjury not simply because he has lied and repeated the lie in court and so distorted More's words or wrenched them out of context, but because he has violated a fundamental oath in obeying the secular authority of the English King and Parliament rather than the Church: he took a similar line over clerical marriage and the breaking of a vow of chastity.[74] More's writings on perjury in the Tower, along with his other discussions of the subject, make it clear that More thought that breaking an oath to a legitimate authority was a worse crime than treason to a secular authority which had violated its own bond to the Church and dismissed its own need to abide by the oaths that had been sworn. Of course, this could not be the basis of a successful defence in a court established by that secular authority and More's logical position had to be that those trying him, along with Rich, were perjurers and liars in refusing to acknowledge the words they had sworn to God. One of the great ironies of More's trial, however, may be that Richard Rich, the man who has endured a reputation as a liar, whatever we think about his actions and the cunning entrapment he instigated, was probably telling the truth. More had little chance to save himself, but in damning the reputation of Rich so carefully and so successfully he illustrated how significant the violation of an oath could be and what terrible effects the accusation of perjury and lying would inevitably have on an individual's subsequent place in the historical record.

II

Why was Anne Boleyn executed? The anonymous author of *The Spanish Chronicle* comments after Anne has been beheaded, 'And so ended this lady, who would never admit or confess the truth.'[75] John Foxe, source of so much of our understanding of the executions of the period, as Thomas Freeman has pointed out, is

---

[73] The Douai-Rheims cases, written about 1575, make More's logic explicit: e.g. 'It seems to be . . . a sin to break one's word . . . Faith should be kept . . . unless other more serious matters persuade to the contrary' (Holmes, ed., *Elizabethan Casuistry*, p. 55).

[74] Helen L. Parish, *Clerical Marriage and the English Reformation: Precedent, Policy and Practice* (Farnham: Ashgate, 2000), p. 13.

[75] *A Chronicle of King Henry VIII of England, Being a Contemporary Record of Some of the Principal Events of the Reigns of Henry VIII and Edward VI. Written in Spanish by an Unknown Hand* [*The Spanish Chronicle*], ed. Martin A. Sharp Hume (London: George Bell & Sons, 1889), p. 71.

'terse' on Anne's fall.[76] Modern historians have also been at a loss to explain exactly why Anne fell when she did. Suggestions fall into three broad categories: the most frequently made claim is that she was the victim of a plot inaugurated by Cromwell who had turned against the Queen when he realized that she was unlikely to serve the Reformed cause well in the future; others suggest that a deformed still birth convinced Henry that their marriage was cursed and Anne was a witch; and there is a third explanation, which has surfaced again relatively recently, that Anne was quite probably guilty of at least some of the crimes of which she was accused and that she did indeed commit multiple adulteries.[77]

Anne was executed on 19 May 1536, about ten months after Thomas More (6 July 1535). Her fall, as has long been recognized, was sudden and dramatic.[78] There are some signs that Henry was tiring of Anne, notably in the correspondence of Eustache Chapuys, the Spanish ambassador to England (not always a reliable source), to his master, Emperor Charles V. On 1 April 1536 Chapuys reports Cromwell as saying that 'he believed that he [the King] would henceforth live honourably and chastely, continuing in his marriage' while uttering the words 'so coldly as to make me suspect the contrary', and then assuring the Spanish ambassador that 'if the King his master were to take another wife, he would not seek her among them [i.e. the French, as Anne had come to England from their court]'.[79] Furthermore, as Greg Walker has pointed out, it is possible that the appointment of commissions of oyer and terminer to investigate 'unspecified treasons' in Middlesex and Kent on 24 April 1536, and the summoning of Parliament on 27 April, may indicate that the first machinations against her had begun, but there is no compelling reason to assume that these developments had anything to do with the case against the Queen.[80] The first proper evidence that survives is the arrest and interrogation of Mark Smeaton on 30 April.[81] This means that from the first

[76] Thomas S. Freeman, 'Hands Defiled with Blood: Henry VIII in Foxe's "Book of Martyrs"', in Betteridge and Freeman, eds, *Henry VIII and History*, pp. 87–118.
[77] The literature on Anne Boleyn's fall is substantial. The key works are E. W. Ives, 'Faction at the Court of Henry VIII: The Fall of Anne Boleyn', *History* 57 (1972), 169–88; Reitha M. Warnicke, 'The Fall of Anne Boleyn: A Reassessment', *History* 70 (1985), 1–15; Reitha M. Warnicke, *The Rise and Fall of Anne Boleyn: Family Politics at the Court of Henry VIII* (Cambridge: Cambridge University Press, 1989); G. W. Bernard, 'The Fall of Anne Boleyn', *EHR* 106 (1991), 584–610; E. W. Ives, 'The Fall of Anne Boleyn Reconsidered', *EHR* 107 (1992), 651–64; G. W. Bernard, 'The Fall of Anne Boleyn: A Rejoinder', *EHR* 107 (1992), 665–74; Reitha M. Warnicke, 'The Fall of Anne Boleyn Revisited', *EHR* 108 (1993), 653–65; Greg Walker, 'Rethinking the Fall of Anne Boleyn', *HJ* 45 (2002), 1–29; Eric Ives, *The Life and Death of Anne Boleyn* (Oxford: Blackwell, 2004); G. W. Bernard, *Anne Boleyn: Fatal Attractions* (New Haven: Yale University Press, 2010).
[78] See, most recently, Brigden, *Wyatt*, pp. 278–83. See also Warnicke, *Rise and Fall*, p. 187.
[79] *Letters and Papers*, IX, 601 (p. 244).   [80] Walker, 'Rethinking', pp. 3–4.
[81] George Constantyne, 'A Memorial from George Constantyne to Thomas, Lord Cromwell', ed. Thomas Amyot, *Archaeologia* 23 (1831), 50–78, p. 64. In a work on lying it would be remiss not to note that there is something odd about this source. It was passed on to Amyot by his younger friend, John Payne Collier (1789–1883), later to become infamous as a forger: see Arthur Freeman and Janet Ing Freeman, *John Payne Collier: Scholarship and Forgery in the Nineteenth Century*, 2 vols (New Haven: Yale University Press, 2004). The Freemans suggest, however, that the letter, which has disappeared, would be a 'very unlikely Collier forgery', as he did not undertake such ambitious imitations at this early stage of his life, and, because he liked and respected Amyot, was unlikely to have wanted to abuse his trust. It is more likely that the document 'is . . . a genuine document, which had "strayed" from its

public awareness of Anne's crimes to her execution was under three weeks, an astonishingly rapid denouement: it is hard to compare cases easily but it is worth noting that from accusation to execution took three months in the case of Thomas More (although events were in progress a long time before), and over six months in the case of Thomas Howard, 4th Duke of Norfolk.[82] The indictment read out at her trial on 15 May 1536 at the King's Bench in Westminster Palace, the same location where More had been tried and condemned, accused the Queen of instigating a series of adulterous liaisons with various men:

> She, despising her marriage, and entertaining malice against the King, and following daily her frail and carnal lust, did falsely and traitorously procure by base conversations and kisses, touchings, gifts, and other infamous incitations, divers of the King's daily and familiar servants to be her adulterers and concubines, so that several of the King's servants yielded to her vile provocations[.][83]

The details are quite clear and explicit, notably the description of the Queen's unnatural intimacy with her brother. The indictment states that she

> Procured and incited her own natural brother, Geo. Boleyn, lord Rocheford, gentleman of the privy chamber, to violate her, alluring him with her tongue in the said George's mouth, and the said George's tongue in hers, and also with kisses, presents, and jewels; whereby he, despising the commands of God, and all human laws, 5 Nov. 27 Hen. VIII [1535], violated and carnally knew the said Queen, his own sister, at Westminster; which he also did on divers other days before and after at the same place, sometimes by his own procurement and sometimes by the Queen's.[84]

The Queen is alleged to have procured Henry Norris 'by sweet words, kisses, touches, and otherwise' on 12 October 1533 (25 Hen. VIII); William Brereton is alleged to have violated the Queen at Hampton Court on 8 December 1533, and on other days before and afterwards, sometimes at her procurement, sometimes at his; the Queen procured Sir Francis Weston on 8 and 20 May 1534; and Mark Smeaton on 12 April 1534 and 26 April 1535.[85] The crimes are said to have taken place over a period of eighteen months, beginning with that of Henry Norris (a detail that may well be important), the last of which took place before the summoning of Parliament and only four days before the arrest of Mark Smeaton, who had allegedly begun his sexual relations with the Queen over a year earlier.

The indictment continues that a rivalry developed between the Queen's suitors: 'lord Rocheford, Norreys [Norris], Bryreton, Weston, and Smeton, being thus inflamed with carnal love of the Queen, and having become very jealous of each other, gave her secret gifts and pledges while carrying on this illicit intercourse', and the Queen cannot bear any of them to look at other women, so on 27 November 1535 'she gave them great gifts to encourage them in their crimes'. However, a

---

original home and ended up with Collier' (personal correspondence of the author and the Freemans, March 2015).

[82] See the respective *ODNB* entries.   [83] *Letters and Papers*, IX, 876 (p. 361).
[84] *Letters and Papers*, IX, 876 (p. 362).
[85] *Letters and Papers*, IX, 876 (pp. 361–2); *State Trials*, I, p. 417.

month earlier an even greater crime had been planned, as on 31 October, together they 'conspired the death and destruction of the King', the Queen 'often saying she would marry one of them as soon as the King died, and affirming that she would never love the King in her heart'. The King had only realized Anne's treasons 'a short time since . . . took such inward displeasure and heaviness, especially from his said Queen's malice and adultery, that certain harms and perils have befallen his body'. The witnesses, who provide evidence under oath, are named: 'Giles Heron, Roger More, Ric. Awnsham, Thos. Byllyngton, Gregory Lovell, Jo. Worsop, Will. Goddard, Will. Blakwall, Jo. Wylford, Will. Berd, Hen. Hubblythorn, Will. Hunyung, Rob. Walys, John England, Hen. Lodysman, and John Avery', all presumably servants in the royal household. No aristocrats or courtiers are named.[86]

The indictment requires some interpretation, as it is distinctly unusual. John Bellamy, in his study of Tudor treason trials, concludes that throughout the dynasty 'the essential accuracy of the vast majority of descriptions of traitorous crimes contained in the indictments cannot be denied'.[87] Anne's trial is unusual in another way, because the details of most significant trials in the period are 'largely wanting', making 'the true legal history of treason . . . remarkably elusive'.[88] In contrast, the charges against Anne Boleyn and her co-conspirators are notably precise, with times, dates, and motives provided in fine detail (although the indictment entered at Deptford on 11 May differs with regard to times and places).[89] It is hardly surprising that at least one modern historian has suggested that Anne may well have been guilty of the crimes of which she was accused, and another has suggested that the extent of the Queen's alleged depravity would have served to convince some that she was justly condemned.[90] The details in the indictment of her liaison with her brother are provided in vivid, specific, and graphic detail; the motives are given throughout; the evidence is provided; and there are numerous witnesses. Indeed, the accusation was so well known that it reappeared in William Thomas's account of his defence of Henry VIII before a hostile audience while he was resident in Italy, which he produced for Edward VI in the late 1540s. Thomas, who would have been at least ten when Anne was executed (he was married by 1540), justifies the punishment meted out to Henry's second wife because her 'liberall lyfe were shamefull to rehearse'.[91] Thomas's testimony is

[86] *Letters and Papers*, IX, 876 (p. 362).

[87] Bellamy, *Treason*, p. 129. See also Lacey Baldwin Smith, *Treason in Tudor England: Politics and Paranoia* (London: Pimlico, 2006, rpt of 1986), pp. 3–4. The opposite view is provided in Margery S. Schauer and Frederick Schauer, 'Law as the Engine of State: The Trial of Anne Boleyn', *William & Mary Law Review* 22 (1980), 49–84.

[88] Baker, *Laws of England, Volume VI*, p. 581. See also Kelly, 'Procedural Review', p. 5.

[89] *Letters and Papers*, IX, 876 (p. 362).

[90] Bernard, *Anne Boleyn*, ch. 12; David Starkey, *Six Wives: The Queens of Henry VIII* (London: Vintage, 2004), p. 576.

[91] William Thomas, *The Works of William Thomas, clerk of the privy council in the year 1549*, ed. Abraham D'Aubant (London, 1774), pp. 90–1. For analysis see Cathy Shrank, *Writing the Nation in Reformation England, 1530–1580* (Oxford: Oxford University Press, 2004), pp. 105–10; Kevin Sharpe, *Selling the Tudor Monarchy: Authority and Image in Sixteenth-Century England* (New Haven: Yale University Press, 2009), pp. 182–3; Sydney Anglo, *Machiavelli—the First Century: Studies in Enthusiasm, Hostility, and Irrelevance* (Oxford: Oxford University Press, 2005), pp. 102–9; Brett

important because, while it is by no means a smoking gun proving the crime, the fact that he could state such views to the King demonstrates that the accounts of Anne's behaviour were widely accepted at court and that Thomas could assume that they would not have offended the young Edward (his successful career was certainly not affected). The contrast to the trial of Thomas More is pointed; the judgement in that case hinged on the interpretation of one conversation, whereas here we have a multitude of events, apparent eyewitness accounts, and motives of the perpetrators.

In some respects the trial was a success. Already possessing a problematic reputation, after her execution Anne became a byword for inconstancy and female lust throughout Catholic Europe, starting with the poem by Lancelot de Carles, the French diplomat who was probably a witness to the trial and execution.[92] Throughout her short reign she was referred to with scathing contempt in the lengthy correspondence of Chapuys and Charles V, as the 'concubine' and the 'whore', a promiscuous upstart who had displaced the lawful queen and forced Henry to declare her daughter, Mary, illegitimate.[93] In a letter to the king's secretary, Stephen Gardiner, and Sir Robert Wallop, written the day before her trial, Cromwell claimed that 'The Queen's incontinent living was so rank and common that the ladies of her privy chamber could not conceal it,' adding that investigations had led to the discovery of 'a certain conspiracy of the King's death, which extended so far that all we that had examination of it quaked at the danger his Grace was in'.[94] He later claimed to Chapuys that he had engineered the downfall of Anne, which has led to the conclusion by some modern historians that Cromwell was the puppet master behind the scenes.[95]

Most later sixteenth-century accounts accept this hostile assessment of Anne's character, invariably adding further details to embellish the crimes. The relatively sober—and early—*Wriothesley's Chronicle* repeats the evidence provided at the trial, accusing the five men of 'fornication with Queene Anne' and 'conspiracie of the Kinges death' and Anne of 'committinge treason against his person'.[96] The anonymous author of *The Spanish Chronicle* describes Anne's fall as an inevitable consequence of her lascivious character. Emboldened by the death of the true

Foster, 'Harry's Peregrinations: An Italianate Defence of Henry VIII', in Betteridge and Freeman, eds, *Henry VIII and History*, pp. 21–50. On Thomas's life, see the *ODNB* entry.

[92] Lancelot de Carles, 'Poème sur la mort d'Anne Boleyn', in Georges Ascoli, ed., *La Grande-Bretagne devant l'opinion française, depuis la Guerre de Cent Ans jusqu'à la fin du XVIe siècle* (Paris: Gamber, 1927), pp. 231–73, especially pp. 242–6 (lines 339–444). There is a translation in Susan Walter Schmid, 'Anne Boleyn, Lancelot de Carle, and the Uses of Documentary Evidence', PhD Thesis, Arizona State University, 2009, pp. 110–75. On Carles see Bernard, *Anne Boleyn*, pp. 152–60.

[93] *CSPSp.*, V, ii, pp. 39–40, 59, 108, *passim*; Ives, *Boleyn*, pp. 191–6, *passim*. On Chapuys's methods and his use of spies to obtain information, see Garrett Mattingly, *Renaissance Diplomacy* (Harmondsworth: Penguin, 1964, rpt of 1955), pp. 210–12.

[94] *Letters and Papers*, IX, 875 (pp. 360–1).

[95] *CSPSp.*, V, p. 137; Ives, *Boleyn*, pp. 316–29; Bernard, *Anne Boleyn*, pp. 135–50.

[96] Charles Wriothesley, *A Chronicle of England during the Reigns of the Tudors, from A.D. 1485 to 1559, by Charles Wriothesley*, ed. W. D. Hamilton, 2 vols (London: Camden Society, 1875–7), I, pp. 36, 38. On Wriothesley (1508–62), see the *ODNB* entry.

queen, Catherine of Aragon, Anne, 'who ostentatiously tried to attract to her service the best-looking men and best dancers to be found', hears that Mark Smeaton, a poor carpenter's son, 'was one of the prettiest monochord players and deftest dancers in the land'.[97] She assembles her minions, Norris and Brereton, and has him play and dance, which leads to her falling in love with him, beginning a long-standing affair after she persuades Henry to employ him as a musician on the extremely generous salary of £100 a year. An intricate plot involving an elderly maidservant, Margaret, who acts as a pander, has Mark enter the Queen's bed-chamber naked with Margaret carrying a pot of marmalade, requested by the Queen. Once admitted, Margaret cries out that she has brought the marmalade, Anne asks her to leave, and she proceeds to seduce the trembling young man.[98] Mark, nervous at first, 'soon lost his bashfulness, and remained that night and many others', and he foolishly begins to flaunt his success at court 'to such an extent that there was not a gentleman at court who was so fine, and Anne never dined without having Mark to serve her'.[99] Anne plays her minions off against each other while favouring Mark, but he eventually crosses Thomas Percy, leading him to inform Cromwell who then plots the Queen's downfall. When the Archbishop of Canter-bury is sent to arrest her, Anne initially denies any wrongdoing, claiming that Henry is simply tired of her as he was of 'the good lady Katherine'. But when pushed, her denials simply confirm her guilt:

[T]he Bishop continued: 'Say no such thing, Madam, for your evil courses have been clearly seen; and if you desire to read the confession which Mark has made, it will be shown to you.' Anne, in a great rage, replied, 'Go to! It has all been done as I say, because the King has fallen in love, as I know, with Jane Seymour, and does not know how to get rid of me. Well, let him do as he likes, he will get nothing more out of me; and any confession that has been made is false.[100]

---

[97] *Spanish Chronicle*, p. 55.

[98] Mark, therefore, acts as the Queen's marmalade. 'Marmelada/marmellata' was a generic term for jam in this period, as it is in most of Europe now. In England it had a much more specific meaning and was a rich, sweet, and luxurious confection, often made of quinces, which had 'a special venereal connotation' (prostitutes in the later seventeenth century being known as 'marmalade madams') and which was often consumed as an aid to pregnancy, a strategy adopted by Mary Tudor: Jennifer Stead, '"Bowers of Bliss": The Banquet Setting', in C. Anne Wilson, ed., *'Banquetting stuffe': The Fare and Social Background of the Tudor and Stuart Banquet* (Edinburgh: Edinburgh University Press, 1991), pp. 115–57, at p. 151; C. Anne Wilson, *The Book of Marmalade* (Totnes: Prospect Books, 1999), pp. 41–2. See also Gillian Riley, 'Food in Painting', in Fabio Parasecoli and Peter Scholliers, eds, *A Cultural History of Food*, 6 vols (London: Bloomsbury, 2013), III, pp. 171–82, at p. 177; Joan Fitzpatrick, *Shakespeare and the Language of Food: A Dictionary* (London: Bloomsbury, 2010), p. 349. The chronicle's author certainly knew English and English customs well, which suggests that he understood the culture of marmalade and, as the account was written later in the century, may perhaps have known of Mary's use of marmalade (although the chronicle was probably largely written in 1550 before Mary became queen). Anne's demand for marmalade here suggests that her desire for sexual gratification and pregnancy are closely related; that her servants are knowing and complicit in her deception of the King, so that her household is run like a brothel; and that her expensive tastes dictate that she consumes men as she does luxurious food, for which she pays a heavy price. I am grateful to Marina Warner for her advice on marmalade.

[99] *Spanish Chronicle*, pp. 57–8.   [100] *Spanish Chronicle*, p. 65.

Anne goes to her death maintaining her lies, claiming that her only fault was her pride, which enabled her to seduce the King away from Queen Catherine, but that 'everything they have accused me of is false'.[101]

The Spanish Chronicle builds on existing details in order to produce a damning picture not just of Anne, but of a court ruled by a weak and stupid king who can easily be duped by his malicious queen. There is no proper respect for order or hierarchy, and truth is a casualty when false appearances matter more than real values. Anne is wicked and guilty but the *Chronicle* makes it clear that her rise is the consequence of England being severed from its true allies and natural destiny— union with a Catholic Europe dominated by Spain, a desirable prospect foolishly discarded as a consequence of the Reformation.

In his account of the Anglican schism, the Catholic priest and polemicist Nicholas Sander (*c.*1530–81) takes the representation of the degeneration of the English court a few stages further.[102] Referring to the debates about the annulment of the marriage between Henry and Catherine and the issues of consanguinity and proximity, Sander argues that it was Anne who was too close to Henry, not Catherine.[103] Anne was in fact very close to Henry indeed, because not only had he had a well-known relationship with her sister, Mary, but her mother too, Anne being the result of their union.[104] With the schism England has become a land cut off from God's law with only a 'holy remnant left in the land, which had utterly refused to bend the knee before Baal', the most prominent of whom was Thomas More.[105] Anne parades in a yellow dress when she hears of Catherine's death—a story common to nearly all the chronicles—and appears to be invincible.[106] But God's justice will not enable her triumph to continue and she is delivered of 'a shapeless mass of flesh' rather than the male heir that the King desires.[107] Although this statement has been taken as evidence by one historian, providing a reason why Henry would have wanted to divorce Anne, the detail of the dead premature baby is surely meant to be read as a punishment from God for Henry's incestuous relations.[108] The failure also helps to explain why Anne then tries to have a son with her brother: once a sin like incest has started it tends not to stop and events

[101] *Spanish Chronicle*, p. 70.
[102] On the impact of Sander's account on Catholic perceptions of Henry VIII see Victor Houliston, 'Fallen Prince and Pretender of the Faith: Henry VIII as Seen by Sander and Persons', in Betteridge and Freeman, eds, *Henry VIII and History*, pp. 119–34. See also Lake, *Bad Queen Bess?*, pp. 258–62.
[103] For details see Philip Campbell, 'The Canon Law of the Henry VIII Divorce Case', senior thesis, Social Studies Department, Madonna University, Livonia, MI, 2009.
[104] Nicholas Sander, *Rise and Growth of the Anglican Schism*, ed. David Lewis and Edward Rishton (London: Burns & Oates, 1877), p. 98.
[105] Sander, *Anglican Schism*, p. 116. Sander died in Ireland trying to lead a crusade to overthrow English Protestantism: *ODNB* entry.
[106] Warnicke, *Rise and Fall*, p. 188.
[107] Sander, *Anglican Schism*, p. 132; Julie Crawford, *Marvelous Protestantism: Monstrous Births in Post-Reformation England* (Baltimore: Johns Hopkins University Press, 2005), shows how the mother's religious belief was thought to influence her baby (p. 18).
[108] Warnicke, *Rise and Fall*, ch. 8; Virginia Murphy, 'The Literature and Propaganda of Henry VIII's First Divorce', in Diarmaid MacCulloch, ed., *The Reign of Henry VIII: Politics, Policy and Piety* (Basingstoke: Palgrave, 1995), pp. 135–58.

spiral out of control.[109] Furthermore, Anne, 'a woman excessively given to pride and to self-love', wanted the next king to be a Boleyn come what may. When her 'incest prospered not', she naturally fell into the promiscuity that caused her downfall.[110]

Sander's account (1585) builds on that of *The Spanish Chronicle* to reveal a court in the grip of moral turpitude and chaos resulting from the schism. This became received wisdom about Henry's reign, although there were some exceptions defending Anne's virtue which appear to have been written for her daughter, Elizabeth I.[111] The problem that this particular case poses is that only Mark Smeaton actually confessed to his crime—and his confession may have been extracted under torture.[112] The others all maintained their innocence. In a letter to Henry written on 6 May 1536, Anne declared not simply her innocence but her bemusement at Henry's treatment of her, offering to confess if it would satisfy him: 'Your Grace's displeasure and my imprisonment are things so strange unto me as what to write or what to excuse I am altogether ignorant. Whereas you sent unto me, willing to confess a truth and so to obtain your favour, by such a one whom you know to be my ancient professed enemy [Cromwell], I no sooner received this message by him than I rightly conceived your meaning; and if, as you say, confessing a truth indeed may procure my safety, I shall with all willingness and duty perform your command.'[113] Anne studiously avoids confessing anything in this sentence, declaring her loyalty to the King as a means of eliding a statement of what she might or might not have done, a pointed contrast to Thomas More. She then professes her innocence, something that will be made clear on the Day of Judgement, while acknowledging the King's right to punish her as an unfaithful wife, and accusing her enemies of slander.[114] In her widely reported scaffold speech Anne was equally adept at avoiding a declaration of guilt or innocence, accepting instead that the law had run its course: 'I here humblye submit me to the lawe as the lawe hath judged me, and as for myne offences, I here accuse no man, God knoweth them; I remit them to God, beseeching him to have mercye on my sowle.'[115] George Boleyn in his scaffold speech two days earlier had also been careful to accept his fate in terms of a general understanding of the precarious nature of human existence: 'to the lawe I submit me, desiring you all, and speciallie you my maisters of the Courte, that you will trust on God speciallie, and not on the vanities of the worlde, for if I had so

---

[109] Frank Whigham, *Seizures of the Will in Early Modern English Drama* (Cambridge: Cambridge University Press, 1996), pp. 189–96; Richard A. McCabe, *Incest, Drama, and Nature's Law 1550–1700* (Cambridge: Cambridge University Press, 1993), pp. 248–54.

[110] On the providential signs of deformed births, see Walsham, *Providence*, pp. 194–203; David Cressy, *Agnes Bowker's Cat: Travesties and Transgressions in Tudor and Stuart England* (Oxford: Oxford University Press, 2000), pp. 29–50.

[111] William Latimer, 'William Latymer's Chronickille of Anne Bulleyne', ed. Maria Dowling, *Camden Miscellany* 30 (1990), pp. 23–65; George Wyatt, 'Some Particulars of the Life of Queen Anne Boleigne', in George Cavendish, *The Life of Cardinal Wolsey*, ed. Samuel Weller Singer (London, 1827), pp. 421–49, at p. 447.

[112] Constantyne, 'Memorial', p. 64, states that Smeaton was racked; Wriothesley, *Chronicle*, p. 61, that a rope was twisted around his head.

[113] *Letters and Papers*, IX, 808 (p. 341).   [114] *Letters and Papers*, IX, 808 (pp. 341–2).

[115] Wriothesley, *Chronicle*, pp. 41–2.

done, I thincke I had bene alive as yee be now', his penitence at odds with his demeanour at his trial when he had been openly defiant to his accusers (although his words are a reflection on the vicissitudes of life and definitely not a declaration of his guilt).[116] While performing the expected role of the penitent sinner on the scaffold and warning of the vanity of human wishes, neither Boleyn had actually confessed to any crime.[117]

It is clear that the Boleyn case is determined by lies and deception: the problem is knowing who was actually telling the truth. Were the final speeches of Anne and George Boleyn proof of their innocence or evidence that they were lying? Were any of the accounts of the trials based on anything other than rumour and gossip? Was anyone in control of the situation as Chapuys claimed Cromwell told him he was? Is it likely that Anne committed some or all of the crimes of which she was accused? Or were these all fabricated by Cromwell and his spies? Two other courtiers, Sir Thomas Wyatt and Richard Page, were initially accused of treasonable crimes connected with the Queen, but these were then dropped. The accusation against Page is especially mystifying and seems to have had no effect on his later, rather unremarkable, career as a successful crown functionary in the provinces who was well rewarded for his loyal service.[118]

Wyatt wrote poems based on his experiences that have served as the best descriptions of the terror experienced at court by the rapid demise of the Boleyns, 'Who list his wealth and ease retain' and 'In mourning wise since daily I increase'.[119] In the first poem Wyatt points out the dangers of staying at court in such times and of the frightening and arbitrary judicial process:

> These bloody days have broken my heart:
> My lust, my youth did them depart,
> And blind desire of estate.
> Who hastes to climb seeks to revert:
> Of truth, *circa Regna tonat.*

---

[116] Wriothesley, *Chronicle*, pp. 39–40. At his trial Lord Rochford had been asked to read his sister's description of Henry's impotence, and told not to read it aloud, but that is what he did: Ives, *Boleyn*, pp. 341–2. Chapuys noted in a letter to Antoine Perrenot de Granvelle, a Habsburg minister, that Henry 'has neither vigour nor virtue' based on Anne's account: 18 May 1536, *Letters and Papers*, IX, 901 (pp. 373–4).

[117] On the formulaic nature of the scaffold speech in sixteenth-century England see Elizabeth Bouldin, '"Dying Men's Wordes": Treason, Heresy, and Scaffold Performances in Sixteenth-Century England', MA thesis, North Carolina State University, 2005; Lacey Baldwin Smith, 'English Treason Trials and Confessions in the Sixteenth Century', *JHI* 15 (1954), 471–98. As J. A. Sharpe points out, the 'insistence that the condemned should be brought to a state of penitence and contrition before their death . . . seems to have been a sixteenth-century innovation': '"Last Dying Speeches": Religion, Ideology and Public Execution in Seventeenth-Century England', *P. & P.* 107 (May 1985), 144–67, at p. 165. One example of an exemplary death is Anon., *The Manner of the Death and Execution of Arnold Cosbie, for Murthering the Lord Boorke* (London, 1591).

[118] On Page (d.1548) see the *ODNB* entry. He served as sheriff of Surrey and Sussex, lieutenant of the gentlemen pensioners and chamberlain at Hampton Court to Edward VI, acquiring former monastic property in Buckinghamshire and Hertfordshire.

[119] For analysis, see Walker, *Writing Under Tyranny*, pp. 289–95.

> The bell-tower showed me such sight
> That in my head sticks day and night:
> There did I learn out of a grate,
> For all favour, glory or might,
> That yet *circa Regna tonat.*
>
> By proof, I say, there did I learn
> Wit helpeth not defence to earn,
> Of innocency to plead or prate:
> Bear low, therefore, give God the stern.
> For sure, *circa Regna tonat.*[120]

Wyatt, like Anne and George Boleyn, represents himself as a humble supplicant to a merciless and arbitrary king. Proof of his innocence does not help his case; nor does the ability to argue in clever ways; nor does a simple truthful plea.[121] Instead the poet has to watch the events unfold with his head poking from his prison grate, lines that helped create the story that Wyatt was forced to witness the execution of his ex-lover, Anne, from his cell.[122] This is a poem about language failing to work in the expected ways.

Wyatt's elegy for the executed struggles with the issue of writing a lament for those who have perished because of their treachery. Without denying the *possibility* of treason, Wyatt's lines, although not attributing any direct blame to the King, could be read to suggest that Henry was at fault in killing so many:

> What though to death desert be now their call,
> As by their faults it doth appear right plain?
> Of force I must lament that such a fall
> Should light on those so wealthily did reign,
> Though some perchance will say, of cruel heart,
> A traitor's death why should we thus bemoan?
> But I alas, set this offence apart,
> Must needs bewail the death of some be gone.[123]

The stanza is an exercise in studied ambiguity and non-commitment, exactly right for the times Wyatt is attempting to represent.[124] The deaths of the traitors might seem appropriate because their 'faults' (not their crimes) are 'right plain', but this is also a tautology: their faults are obvious because they have been found guilty and—presumably—the sight of the body parts of the dead criminals serves to remind onlookers of their guilt. The concomitant point is made in Sir John Harington's famous epigram: 'Treason doth never prosper? What's the Reason? / for if it prosper

---

[120] Thomas Wyatt, *Collected Poems*, ed. Joost Daalder (Oxford: Oxford University Press, 1975), CXLIII (pp. 185–6).

[121] Baldwin Smith, 'English Treason Trials', p. 473.

[122] See, for example, *Spanish Chronicle*, p. 68, where Wyatt watches the executions of Norris, Brereton, Smeaton, and George Boleyn, before writing a letter to the King which secures his pardon.

[123] Wyatt, *Poems*, CXLIX, lines 9–16 (p. 191).

[124] On Wyatt's slippery rhetoric and its effects on readers, see Chris Stamatakis, *Sir Thomas Wyatt and the Rhetoric of Rewriting: Turning the Word* (Oxford: Oxford University Press, 2012), pp. 1–36.

none dare call it treason.'[125] The next two lines of Wyatt's verse seem as if the poet is compelled to note their fall—because they were his friends, because he almost shared their fate—and the use of the adverb 'wealthily' summons the familiar subject of medieval tragedy recounting the rise and fall of overmighty subjects whose story serves as a warning, exactly as George Boleyn announced to the crowd on the scaffold.[126] However, the next two lines make explicit what was implicit in the opening lines, that such traitors should die unlamented and be remembered only for their crimes. The poet, however, sows seeds of doubt in the reader's mind in suggesting that such views are only held by those who might be described—he does not state by whom—'of cruel heart'. Some readers will surely conclude that those 'of cruel heart' are the King, Cromwell, and those loyal to them. In the final two lines the narrator confesses that he cannot view their fate as everyone else does but must 'set this offence apart', the last line indicating that he has to do this because of his loyalty to the dead, but before that line is read the possibility is opened up that he is objecting to their fate because they are not actually guilty. Wyatt has not confirmed their guilt, asserted their innocence, or accepted the judicial process other than comparing their fates to a tragedy, looking backwards to the *de casibus* tradition of Boccaccio and Lydgate.[127]

In the next five stanzas before he concludes the poem Wyatt reflects on each victim of Henry's justice, reiterating that he is acting out of compulsion, bound by 'right reason' (18) and 'by force of mourning mind' (20). George Boleyn/Rochford is described in terms of unattributed rumour, 'Some say "Rochford, haddst thou been not so proud, / For thy great wit each man would thee bemoan"' (21–2), a witty tribute to the dead man. The sentence can either be read to mean that if Rochford's pride had not obscured his wit then he would be mourned properly for his virtues; or that Rochford should be mourned because pride has brought his downfall so early in his life and prevented him from achieving what he might have done, a sad case from which others should learn. Either way, it is pride that has obscured and distorted Rochford's virtues: instead of Rochford's wit we have Wyatt's few lines. Norris is admonished in ways that express Wyatt's bemusement at the course that events have just taken: 'To think what hap did thee so lead or guide / Whereby thou hast both thee and thine undone' (26–7). Does this mean that Wyatt thinks that Norris has undone himself and his family because he is guilty? Or is he a tragic victim, a man who rose too high and who was too close to the unstable seat of power, another character in a late medieval tragedy? 'Hap' could refer to an event or to the unplanned intervention of fortune: again, Wyatt is studiously ambiguous in his judgement, as Norris may have been unlucky or actually responsible for his own downfall.[128] The lines 'In place also where thou

---

[125] Sir John Harington, *The Epigrams of Sir John Harington*, ed. Gerard Kilroy (Farnham: Ashgate, 2009), III.43 (p. 185).

[126] Geoffrey Chaucer, *The Riverside Chaucer*, ed. Larry D. Benson et al. (Oxford: Oxford University Press, 1988, rpt of 1987), pp. 929–30; Raymond Williams, *Modern Tragedy* (London: Verso, 1979, rpt of 1966), pp. 19–23.

[127] D. W. Robertson, Jr, 'Chaucerian Tragedy', *ELH* 19 (1952), 1–37.

[128] *OED*, 'hap', n., 1 and 2.

hast never been / Both man and child doth piteously thee moan' (29–30) suggest that Norris will now be remembered as a victim of fortune, either because he is genuinely admired and mourned, or because he has become a literary type whose story can easily be told and recognized. The poem seems to be arguing that Norris has lost the right to be remembered as a character whose end will instruct others, when he should have been remembered as an individual who was widely loved and respected. Weston suffers a similar verbal fate, as Wyatt tells us that 'thy faults we daily hear so rife', another elusive line that does not commit the poet to believing the stories he often hears about his dead friend.

Wyatt's description of Mark Smeaton is conspicuously different from the rest and he is lamented far more begrudgingly:

> Ah! Mark, what moan should I for thee make more,
> Since that thy death thou hast deserved best,
> Save only that mine eye is forced sore
> With piteous plaint to moan thee with the rest?
> A time thou haddst above thy poor degree,
> The fall whereof thy friends may well bemoan:
> A rotten twig upon so high a tree
> Hath slipped thy hold, and thou art dead and gone. (49–56)

Smeaton has deserved his death 'best', perhaps because he was the only one to confess to his crime.[129] Wyatt's lines might suggest that he believed that Smeaton was guilty, especially valuable testimony if Wyatt had indeed been Anne's lover and knew her character and what she might have been prepared to do.[130] But as the stanza continues, this reading becomes less secure: Mark's real crime is to rise too high above his station, imagining that he has a place among aristocratic society. If Rochford, Norris, Weston, and Brereton are guilty of pride in climbing too high then Mark—he is always Mark in the indictments, a sign of his status as a familiar servant, because his family name does not matter—is the guiltiest of all and the most deserving of his fate. The time he has spent raised above his 'poor degree' might have seemed exciting to him, although it led not just to his premature death, but that of the others accused of adultery with the Queen. Was this because he was guilty? On the scaffold he appeared to confirm his confession, in marked contrast to the others: 'Master I pray you all pray for me for I have deserved the death.'[131]

However, Anne's reported reaction to Mark's words was 'Alas! I fear that his soul will suffer punishment for his false confession.'[132] Like Wyatt, Anne had made reference to Mark's social status as a key factor in the unfolding of events,

---

[129] Edward Baynton to the Treasurer; Cavendish, *Wolsey*, pp. 61–2.

[130] The purported relationship between Anne and Wyatt is based on inference not evidence and his imprisonment in 1536 may well have been the result of his allegiance to the Boleyns. Colin Burrow argues that 'neither Wyatt's imprisonment nor his poetry indicates that he was a lover of Anne Boleyn': *ODNB* entry.

[131] Ives, *Boleyn*, p. 343; Walker, 'Rethinking', pp. 8–9.

[132] *State Trials*, I, p. 429; Ives, *Boleyn*, p. 343.

referring to him as 'no gentleman' in her conversations with her gaoler, the constable of the Tower, Sir William Kingston, and claiming that he only ever came into her chamber once to play the virginals, when she was lodged above the King at Winchester.[133] Anne, as reported by Kingston, is clearly horrified that she has been accused of adultery with a servant, and her words suggest that there is a further shame in not being believed, of being accused of lying about a sexual act with a social inferior, which was simply unthinkable. The last lines of Wyatt's stanza surely allude to a hanging, even though Mark was beheaded. Beheading was an unusual fate for a commoner and probably a sign that he co-operated with the authorities—or, at least, was believed to have co-operated—and so enabled them to prosecute others of higher status.[134] The 'rotten twig' on the high tree which causes Mark's downfall in the poem is therefore both the small flaw that brings everything crashing to earth and Mark himself, whom Wyatt blames for causing the deaths of his (Wyatt's) friends. Does this mean that Wyatt thought that it was the servant who was lying, or, if not, had placed himself in a perilous position which would have catastrophic implications for all concerned? Mark and the Boleyn circle were executed in the same way, but Wyatt's poem suggests that this should not have been the case, that Mark did not deserve such gracious treatment, and that he should have been strung up not beheaded (hence the image of the 'high tree'?). Truth-telling and rank are simultaneously equated and confused, so that it is not clear whether the real issue for Wyatt is lying or social status, as the two are intertwined.

The downfall of the Boleyns was a catastrophe that surprised and shocked observers throughout Europe. Even Chapuys and the Spanish faction, who had a significant vested interest in Anne's downfall, did not see it coming as rapidly as it did. In a long letter to Charles V written on 21 April Chapuys observes far more conflict between the King and Cromwell than disdain of Anne. He writes that she dines with Henry after mass and treats the ambassador with proper courtesy in front of the large gathering of courtiers who have come 'partly to see how the concubine and I behaved to each other'.[135] However, by 28 April he was reporting to his master that 'the King was already as sick and tired of the concubine as could be', but this was only three weeks before her execution.[136] On 3 May Cranmer, whose rise to prominence was aided by the support of the Boleyns, made a cautious attempt to defend the Queen in a letter to Henry, which is clearly also an act of self-protection:

> If the reports of the Queen be true, they are only to her dishonour not yours. I am clean amazed, for I had never better opinion of woman; but I think your Highness would not have gone so far if she had not been culpable. I was most bound to her of all creatures living, and therefore beg that I may, with your Grace's favour, wish and pray

---

[133] Sir William Kingston to Cromwell, May 1536, *Letters and Papers*, IX, 798 (p. 338). On Kingston (*c.*1476–1540), see the *ODNB* entry.
[134] K. J. Kesselring, *Mercy and Authority in the Tudor State* (Cambridge: Cambridge University Press, 2003), p. 25.
[135] Chapuys to Charles V, 21 April, *Letters and Papers*, IX, 699 (pp. 287–95, at pp. 290–1).
[136] Chapuys to Charles V, 29 April, *Letters and Papers*, IX, 752 (pp. 315–16).

that she may declare herself innocent. Yet if she be found guilty, I repute him not as a faithful subject who would not wish her punished without mercy.[137]

George Bernard argues that these words show that Cranmer 'accepted the truth of the charges against Anne', but the conditional nature of his acceptance indicates that a more natural reading is that the letter was an attempt to make Henry think carefully about what he was about to do and whether he was actually sure that he was right, so incredible did the Queen's alleged behaviour seem.[138] John Husee writing to Lady Lisle on 13 May adopts a similar logic to that of Cranmer, commenting that 'if all the books and chronicles were totally revolved, and to the uttermost persecuted and tried, which against women hath been penned, contrived, and written since Adam and Eve, those same were, I think, verily nothing in comparison of that which hath been done and committed by Anne the Queen'.[139] Husee does think that Anne has confessed to some crimes and has a stronger sense of Anne's guilt than Cranmer; but the shock expressed is similar. Anne was not a popular queen with many—Sir John Russell wrote to Lord Lisle immediately after Henry's hastily arranged marriage to Jane Seymour that 'The King hath come out of hell into heaven, for the gentleness in this [i.e. Jane's behaviour], and the cursedness and the unhappiness in the other'—but few at court found it easy to understand why she had fallen so swiftly or believe that she had been guilty of all the crimes of which she was accused.[140] Even Chapuys, who was as eager as anyone to witness the fall of Anne and the restoration of Mary as Henry's heir, was sceptical of the legal process used to condemn the Queen. He informed Charles V that her supposed lovers were 'condemned upon presumption and certain indications, without valid proof or confession'.[141]

It is surely for similar reasons that Catholic Europe tended to exaggerate Anne's crimes and her inherent wickedness: no one could easily believe that Anne had committed so many dangerous and random acts and, to make the case against her credible, she had to be transformed into a monster, as John Husee's letter suggests. Either Anne was a truly terrible woman who had managed to dupe her husband in extremely unusual ways, or the accusations made against her were fictitious; either Anne went to her grave maintaining a false innocence or the Henrician court was

---

[137] Cranmer to Henry VIII, 3 May 1536, *Letters and Papers*, IX, pp. 333–4. On Cranmer and the Boleyns, see Diarmaid MacCulloch, *Thomas Cranmer: A Life* (New Haven: Yale University Press, 1996), pp. 82–3, 157–9.

[138] Bernard, *Anne Boleyn*, p. 171. See also Rowan Williams, 'The Martyrdom of Thomas Cranmer: Sermon at Service to Commemorate the 450th Anniversary' Tuesday 21 March 2006 (http://rowanwilliams.archbishopofcanterbury.org/articles.php/1599/the-martyrdom-of-thomas-cranmer-sermon-at-service-to-commemorate-the-450th-anniversary) (accessed 20 April 2015). Williams's description of Cranmer struggling with a belief in Anne's innocence or guilt is also slightly wide of the mark in a letter designed to advise a notoriously difficult king. On the genre of letters of advice, see Peter Mack, *A History of Renaissance Rhetoric, 1380–1620* (Oxford: Oxford University Press, 2011), p. 249.

[139] John Husee to Lady Lisle, 13 May 1536, *Letters and Papers*, IX, 866 (p. 357); Walker, 'Rethinking', p. 5.

[140] Sir John Russell to Lord Lisle, 3 June 1536, in *The Lisle Letters*, ed. Muriel St. Clare Byrne, 6 vols (Chicago: University of Chicago Press, 1981), III, 713 (pp. 395–6).

[141] Chapuys to Charles V, 19 May 1536, *Letters and Papers*, IX, 908 (pp. 376–80, at p. 377).

spectacularly dysfunctional in ways that exceeded the belief of its most hostile critics. One or both sides were lying in ways that were unusual, as the horrified and bemused reactions demonstrate.

As already noted, according to Chapuys, Cromwell had boasted of masterminding the downfall of Anne as Henry began to tire of her and she became ever more dangerous:

> Et que [a] luy auoit este lauctorite de descouvrir et parachever les affaires diçelle concubine, en quoy il avoit eu une merveilleuse pene, et que sur le desplesir et courroux quil avoit eu sur la reponce que le roy son maistre mauvoit donnee le tires iour de pasques il se mist a fantasier et conspirer le dict affaire.
>
> He himself had been authorised and commissioned by the King to prosecute and bring to an end the mistress's trial, to do which he had taken considerable trouble. It was he who, in consequence of the disappointment and anger he had felt on hearing the King's answer to me on the third day of Easter, had planned and brought about the whole affair.[142]

However, it was also clearly in Cromwell's interest to make this boast to the most powerful ambassador at Henry's court who already had a somewhat jaundiced view of the King, and the more Cromwell appeared to be in control the more both Henry and Chapuys were likely to rely on him.[143] Cromwell, like so many others involved in the case, may well have been lying.

While we have some chance of uncovering the truth of Thomas More's accusation that he was perjured by Richard Rich, it is unlikely that we will ever get through the wealth of lies that characterize the story of Anne Boleyn's downfall, one reason why she continues to fascinate academic and non-academic readers alike.[144] Whatever the extent of plotting and counter-plotting behind the scenes at court, and whether her fall can be explained by factional conflict at court or Henry's disappointment at his queen not producing the promised son, one particular conversation, perhaps even one sentence within it, appears to have sealed Anne's fate. Sir William Kingston, whose conversations may have helped to convict Anne—although he was notably courteous towards her—reports a series of desperate conversations with the terrified and traumatized Queen on 3 May, the day after her incarceration. Anne veers from weeping to laughing, at one point in her first conversation with Kingston asking him if he knows why she is in the Tower before concluding the exchange in a manner that could be read as a confirmation of guilt: 'I [hear say, sai]d she, that I shuld be accused with iii. men; and I can say [no more but] nay withyowt I shuld open my body. And ther with opynd her gown. O, No[res], hast thow accused me? Thow ar in the Towre with me, [and thow and

---

[142] Chapuys to the Emperor, 6 June 1536, *CSPSp.*, V, Pt. 2 (Henry VIII, 1536–8), 61 (pp. 137–62, at p. 137).

[143] Walker, 'Rethinking', p. 10.

[144] For a useful overview of popular perceptions see Susan Bordo, *The Creation of Anne Boleyn: A New Look at England's Most Notorious Queen* (New York: Houghton, Mifflin, Harcourt, 2014).

I shall] dy together; and, Marke, thow art here to.'[145] The gesture of opening her dress to expose her body as a sacrifice suggests that Anne represents herself as a martyr, as well as the harlot her accusers imagine her to be.[146] However, the anxiety about whether Norris has accused her suggests that Anne has a suspicion that she knows what is probably the root cause of her trouble. Kingston shows how Anne's unstable state may well reveal the truth for his political master, and a conversation recorded between the Queen and one of her ladies in waiting, Mrs Cofyn, would seem to provide the key:

[And she (Anne) said, Mr. Norr]es dyd say on Sunday last unto the Quenes am[ner that he would s]vere for the Quene that she was a gud woman. [And then said Mrs.] Cofyn, Madam, Why shuld ther be hony seche maters [spoken of? Marry,] sayd she, I bad hym do so: for I asked hym why he [did not go through with] hys maryage, and he made ansure he wold tary [a time. Then I said, Y]ou loke for ded men's showys, for yf owth ca]m to the King but good], you would loke to have me. And he sayd yf he [should have any such thought] he wold hys hed war of. And then she sayd [she could undo him if she wou]ld; and ther with thay felle yowt[.][147]

The significance of these words is obvious enough: Norris distances himself from her joke about him wanting to marry her if anything happened to the King; Norris then returns later that day to swear to the Queen's almoner (the official who oversees the charity and good deeds performed by their employer) that she is a good woman, clearly nervous that the conversation has been overheard; and Anne later asks whether Norris is in the Tower. Anne's last comment suggests that she knows that the conversation could well be construed as treason ('compassing' the King's death) in terms of the 1534 Act that, ironically, was designed to protect her from malicious gossip.[148] Sir Edward Bainton, writing the same day to the Lord Treasurer, had spoken to the almoner and was clearly expecting a confession soon based on what he had heard.[149]

Kingston provides an elaborate account of how he acquired the information, explaining that he has made sure that all conversations with the Queen have been recorded. Although he cannot hear everything that she says because he sleeps next to his wife in an adjoining chamber he makes sure that Mrs Cofyn lies next to Anne and he has 'everye thynge told me by Mestres Cofyn that she thinks met for you

[145] Sir William Kingston to [Cromwell], 3 May 1536, *Letters and Papers*, IX, 793 (pp. 334–5, at p. 334); Ellis, ed., *Letters*, I (ii), pp. 54–6. Walker, 'Rethinking', pp. 21–2. My interpretation of events is much indebted to Walker's excellent article.

[146] Anne M. Ashton, 'Interpreting Breast Iconography in Italian Art, 1250–1600', PhD thesis, University of St Andrews, 2006, ch. 3.

[147] *Letters and Papers*, IX, 793 (pp. 334–5, at p. 334).

[148] Dale Hoak, 'Booby, Baby or Classical Monster? Henry VIII in the Writings of G. R. Elton and J. J. Scarisbrick', in Betteridge and Freeman, eds, *Henry VIII and History*, pp. 241–59, at pp. 247–8.

[149] Baynton (c.1495–1544) was a client of Cromwell's and a noted Protestant. In his letter he notes that although 'There is much communication that no man will confess anything against her', he also places great importance on the conversation with Norris: 'I think much of the communication which took place on the last occasion between the Queen and Master Norres', evidence that it was circulating at court because of its explosive nature: Sir Edward Baynton to Mr Treasurer [Fitzwilliam?], 3 May 1536, *Letters and Papers*, IX, 799 (p. 338).

[Cromwell] to know'.[150] Anne has also realized that what she says is passed on for the letter concludes with an afterword in which she tries to explain another incriminating conversation:

> Sir, syns the makynge of thys letter the Quene spake of Wes[ton saying that she] had spoke to hym bycause he did love hyr kynswoman [Mrs. Skelton, and] sayd he loved not hys wyf, and he made ansere to hyr [again that h]e loved wone in hyr howse better then them bothe. And [the Queen said, Who is] that? It ys yourself. And then she defeyed hym, as [she said to me].[151]

This second episode suggests that words were used in careless and dangerous ways in the Boleyn household and that the flirtatious relationship between the Queen and her courtiers was getting out of hand and they were exposing themselves to the hostile attention of their enemies: a further conversation with Mark Smeaton provides yet more evidence of aggressively sexualized behaviour beneath a veneer of courtesy.[152] Kingston's letter to Cromwell further indicates that the case against Anne would be based on the close scrutiny of her words. Thomas Wyatt's poem on the executed implicitly acknowledges the danger of speech at Henry's court in the 1530s. Obedience to the crown was based on the Oath of Supremacy and the attendant Treason Act, declarations of loyalty whereby inappropriate speech or the wrong kind of silence could be fatal errors, as in More's case: 'Never before had a spiritual instrument of commitment been used as a political test.'[153] The case that had enabled Anne to become Queen had witnessed her predecessor being forced to tell the truth about her relationship with Prince Arthur and whether they had actually experienced sexual relations, which she denied, but others confirmed.[154] The public humiliation of Catherine of Aragon was only a small part of the febrile culture which placed intense pressure on subjects to tell the truth that had developed by the time that Anne was tried. Once the subject had broken a sacred oath of loyalty to the crown in ways that only the monarch could define in accordance with the collection of Acts passed after the Reformation Parliament, s/he effectively surrendered all rights to defence and protection. The case against Anne stands in pointed contrast to that against Mary Stuart fifty years later, as Cathy Shrank has demonstrated.[155] Anne was subjected to the circulation of rumour, which still affects her ambiguous reputation today, and it is extremely difficult to reconstruct the events leading to her downfall. Mary, an equally controversial figure who also has her supporters and detractors, was condemned by a

---

[150] *Letters and Papers*, IX, 793 (pp. 334–5, at p. 335).

[151] *Letters and Papers*, IX, 793 (pp. 334–5, at p. 335).

[152] Bernard, *Anne Boleyn*, p. 162. See also Warnicke, 'Reassessment', pp. 10–11.

[153] Susan Brigden, *London and the Reformation* (Oxford: Clarendon Press, 1989), p. 223.

[154] The most widely reported testimony is that of Sir Anthony Willoughby, a gentleman in the service of Prince Arthur, who claimed that the Prince had said to him on the morning after his first night as a married man, 'Willoughby, bring me a cup of ale, for I have been this night in the midst of Spain': 'A set of depositions as to Katharine's marriage with prince Arthur', 3, 12 July 1529, *Letters and Papers*, IV, part III, 5774(2) (p. 2575).

[155] Cathy Shrank, 'Manuscript, Authenticity and "evident proofs" against the Scottish Queen', in A. S. G. Edwards, ed., *Tudor Manuscripts 1485–1603* (English Manuscript Studies, 1100–1700, vol. 15) (London: British Library, 2010), pp. 198–218. On Mary Stuart see below, pp. 66–7.

legal system which increasingly relied on the discovery of 'fact', and the 'sustained endeavour to influence those beyond a political elite'.[156] Accordingly, her case has been somewhat easier to reconstruct than Anne's, as far more paper trails have been left for historians to follow.[157] In 1534 the royal propaganda machine was still in its infancy: by the end of the century it worked in far more sophisticated ways, and was prepared to disseminate lies in print.[158]

Anne may not have been guilty of the crimes of which she was accused at her trial but she seems to have been acutely aware of what caused her downfall, even if we are not. If she was not lying about her relationships with her brother, Norris, Weston, Brereton, and Mark Smeaton, then perhaps she was being economical with the truth, and her concern for their fate might be read to indicate a guilty conscience.[159] Of course, if Anne was innocent of at least some of the crimes then the case against her involved a significant amount of perjured testimony and false confession, as has long been received wisdom.[160] The Boleyn trial was evidently a departure from understood judicial practices, but it is not best viewed as an isolated incident resulting from the whim of an increasingly despotic and deranged monarch. The trial emerged out of a context of oath-breaking, perjury, and lying precipitated by the Reformation, which placed heavy emphasis on the power and rights of the monarch and the duty of his subjects to him.[161] The More and Boleyn trials are therefore more intimately linked than has generally been assumed. More's case against Rich, and, by implication, the crown, was that a sacred oath to the Church had been broken which resulted in perjury and a series of lies based on broken future promises. The crown's case against the Queen was that she and her co-conspirators had broken oaths they had made to the crown in speaking so casually about the King, loose speech being an indication of uncontrolled, transgressive behaviour, usually associated with women.[162] Once such oaths had been broken, as More had recognized two years previously, the contract between sovereign power and subject no longer held good and almost anything could be justified. The Oath of Supremacy encouraged the proliferation of lies and lying.

[156] Shrank, 'Manuscript', p. 214. For differing assessments of Mary Stuart see Jenny Wormald, *Mary Queen of Scots: A Study in Failure* (London: Collins & Brown, 1991); James Mackay, *In My End is My Beginning: A Life of Mary Queen of Scots* (Edinburgh: Mainstream, 1999).

[157] See John Guy, *'My Heart is My Own': The Life of Mary Queen of Scots* (London: HarperCollins, 2004), pp. 396–417.

[158] Sharpe, *Selling the Tudor Monarchy*, ch. 2; Cathy Shrank, '"This fatall Medea," "this Clytemnestra": Reading and the Detection of Mary Queen of Scots', *HLQ* 73 (2010), 523–41.

[159] Ives, *Boleyn*, p. 349. See also Warnicke, *Rise and Fall*, p. 226; Schauer and Schauer, 'Law as the Engine of State', p. 75.

[160] Although condemned in many accounts, there were a number of defences of Anne in the sixteenth century based on witness accounts: see Freeman, 'Hands Defiled with Blood'.

[161] Franklin Le Van Baumer, *The Early Tudor Theory of Kingship* (New Haven: Yale University Press, 1940); Quentin Skinner, *The Foundations of Modern Political Thought*, 2 vols (Cambridge: Cambridge University Press, 1978), II, pp. 65–73.

[162] Andy Wood, *The 1549 Rebellions and the Making of Early Modern England* (Cambridge: Cambridge University Press, 2007), p. 113; Keith M. Botelho, *Renaissance Earwitnesses: Rumor and Early Modern Masculinity* (Basingstoke: Palgrave Macmillan, 2009).

Those who supported it had to root out enemies by fair means and foul; those who opposed it were forced to disguise what they really thought if they did not wish to come out into the open. And then there were those who were caught in the inevitable crossfire, who may have been victims or perpetrators of lies, and most probably both.

2

The Oath of Allegiance

I

The execution of Father Henry Garnet on 3 May 1606 was a distinctly odd affair. His last moments and words were recorded in meticulous detail, and a piece of straw splashed with his blood produced a perfect likeness of the martyr, which became a celebrated miracle throughout Catholic Europe.[1] As he climbed onto the scaffold Garnet 'stood much amazed', which according to an anonymous eyewitness, showed 'feare, and guiltinesse appearing in his face'.[2] Although the deans of St Paul's, John Overall, and Winchester, George Abbot, 'exhorted him to a true and liuely faith to God-ward, a free and plaine acknowledgement to the world of his offence; and if any further Treason lay in his knowledge, to vnburthen his conscience, and shew a sorrow and detestation of it', Garnet refused. Garnet was 'impatient of perswasions, and ill pleased to be exhorted by them', as he had come properly resolved to die. The Recorder of London, the chief criminal judge in the city, Henry Montagu, then asked Garnet if he had anything to say as a final speech, warning him that 'It was no time to dissemble, and now his Treasons were too manifest to bee dissembled', so he should censure himself for his crimes.[3] Garnet, exhausted and afraid that his voice would not carry to the crowd, separated himself from the crime of which he was accused, helping to plan and instigate the Gunpowder Plot, in a first response to those around him on the scaffold: 'The intention [of the plotters] was wicked, and the fact would haue been cruell, and from his soule he should haue abhorred it, had it effected. But he said, he oneley had a general knowledge of it by M. *Catesby*, which in that he disclosed not, nor

---

[1] Alison Shell, *Oral Culture and Catholicism in Early Modern England* (Cambridge: Cambridge University Press, 2007), pp. 134–7; Monta, *Martyrdom and Literature*, pp. 69–70; Philip Caraman, *Henry Garnet, 1555–1606, and the Gunpowder Plot* (London: Longmans, 1964), pp. 443–7; Jonathan Bate and Dora Thornton, *Staging the World: Shakespeare* (London: British Museum, 2012), pp. 194–5. Garnet's last words were set to music by Catholic sympathizers: see Emilie K. M. Murphy, 'Musical Self-Fashioning and the "Theatre of Death" in Late Elizabethan and Jacobean England', *RS* 30 (2016), 410–30, p. 425.

[2] Anon., *A True and Perfect Relation of the Whole Proceedings Against the Late Most Barbarous Traitor, Garnet, A Iesuite, and His Confederats* (London, 1606), sig. Fff1r. For analysis see Frances E. Dolan, *True Relations: Reading, Literature, and Evidence in Seventeenth-Century England* (Philadelphia: University of Pennsylvania Press, 2013), pp. 29–51.

[3] Anon., *Perfect Relation*, sig. Fff1v. On recorders, see Baker, *Laws of England, Volume VI*, pp. 307–8.

vsed meanes to preuent it, Herein he had offended; What he knew in particulars was in Confession, as hee said.'[4]

Garnet's distancing of himself from the crime inspired a vociferous response from Montagu, who carefully outlined to Garnet and the crown the precise evidence of his guilt based on the testimony of Oswald Tesimond (alias Oswald Greenway), the Jesuit who revealed details of the Gunpowder Plot to Garnet.[5] Montagu provided four pieces of evidence to condemn Garnet: that Greenway told Garnet of the plot and consulted with him about it; that Garnet was approached by both Robert Catesby and Greenway; that there was later sustained discussion between Garnet and Greenway about the plot; and that Greenway had asked Garnet who would be the protector once the King was dead, but that Garnet had replied 'That was to be referred till the blow was past.'[6] Garnet agreed that he had not disclosed everything to the King and for that 'He confessed himselfe iustly condemned; and for this did aske forgiuenes of his Maiestie.'

Garnet was then allowed to address the crowd, which he did, ignoring Montagu's words and reiterating his original position:

> Good countrymen, I am come hither this blessed day of *The inuention of the holy Crosse*, to end all my crosses in this life; The cause of my suffering is not vnknowen to you: I confesse I haue offended the King, and am sory for it, so farre as I was guiltie, Which was in concealing it, and for that I aske pardon of his Maiestie; The treason intended against the King and State was bloody, My selfe should haue detersted it, had it taken effect. And I am heartily sorry, that any Catholickes euer had so cruell a designe.[7]

This looks like an admission of guilt as is required, but it is not. Like the Boleyn siblings, Garnet simply confesses that he is sorry for having offended the King, not that the King is right to take offence, in doing so turning his apology against his accusers by suggesting that he is sorry that the King is offended. In projecting the effects of the thwarted treason into a future that will never happen, Garnet constructs a future unreal conditional sentence, enabling him to express regret for something that did not and will not take place and so, by implication, minimize any connection between him and the non-event. In expressing his regret that any Catholics planned such an event he is speaking the truth, as he had always advised the conspirators to abandon the plot, and he had earlier condemned the Bye Plot hatched as soon as James became King.[8] And, in opening his speech with a

---

[4] Anon., *Perfect Relation*, sig. Ffflv. Protestants frequently complained about 'auricular confession' which undermined the authority of the secular authorities in binding a priest to silence: see Adrian Streete, *Protestantism and Drama in Early Modern England* (Cambridge: Cambridge University Press, 2009), p. 116. Catholics made confession a central issue of their faith: Diarmaid MacCulloch, *Reformation: Europe's House Divided, 1490–1700* (London: Penguin, 2004), pp. 411–13, *passim*.
[5] On Tesimond see the *ODNB* entry. On his role in the plot see *The Gunpowder Plot: The Narrative of Oswald Tesimond alias Greenway* (London: Folio Society, 1973); Antonia Fraser, *The Gunpowder Plot: Terror and Faith in 1605* (London: Weidenfeld & Nicolson, 1996), *passim*. On his role in Garnet's trial and conviction, see Caraman, *Garnet*, pp. 242–4, 399–401, *passim*.
[6] Anon., *Perfect Relation*, sigs Ffflv–Fff2r.   [7] Anon., *Perfect Relation*, sig. Fff2r–v.
[8] Fraser, *Gunpowder Plot*, pp. 130, 64. On the Bye Plot, see Mark Nicholls, 'Treason's Reward: The Punishment of Conspirators in the Bye Plot of 1603', *HJ* 38 (1995), 821–42.

reference to the Day of the Invention of the Holy Cross, the day when the supposedly British St Helena, mother of Constantine the Great, rediscovered the Cross (3 May *c.*309), Garnet was surely reminding his listeners of his continued adherence to the Church's ancient traditions and the refusal of their monarch to allow them to celebrate these sacred rituals.[9] In doing so he was confirming his role as spiritual leader of the Catholics, repeating publicly his frequent claim that he disapproved of the actions of those who wanted to stage a bloody *coup d'état*, and reinforcing the division of Church and state which his accusers wished to collapse.[10]

Garnet concludes his speech with a defence of Anne Vaux, the widow with whom he had been linked, and referring those interested back to his own confession: 'whatsoever is vnder my hand in any of my Confessions, said he, is true', which, again, looks like an admission of guilt but which is really a confirmation of the power of confession.[11] Garnet is carefully distinguishing between sacramental confession, which confirms the power of the Church to absolve the sinner before God, and legal confession, whereby the accused does not have a duty to incriminate himself, especially not when dealing with heretical authorities.[12] Garnet then requests that he can pray before his death. He is told to limit his prayers and that no one should interrupt him. The anonymous eyewitness narrates this passage in ways that show Garnet in a strangely ambivalent light:

> It appeared he could not constantly or deuoutly pray; feare of death, or hope of Pardon euen then so distracted him: For oft in those prayers he would breake off, turne and looke about him, and answere to what he ouer-heard, while he seemed to be praying. When he stood vp, the Recorder finding in his behauiour as it were an expectation of a Pardon, wished him not to deceiue himselfe, nor beguile his owne soule, he was come to die, and must die; requiring him not to Equivocate with his last breath, if he knew any thing that might bee danger to the King or State, he should now vtter it. *Garnet* sayd, It is no time now to Equiuocate: how it was lawfull, and when, he had shewed his mind elsewhere. But sayth hee, I doe not now Equivocate, and more than I haue confessed, I doe not know.[13]

This is an extraordinary passage which balances contempt for the condemned with his own fierce voice of defiance. The author represents Garnet as fearful, delaying his execution as long as he can in the futile hope of a pardon; or unable to pray, presumably because of the guilt he bears, in part because he was well known as one

---

[9] *Christian Church*, p. 847. Helena was actually from Bithynia (now part of Turkey), but Geoffrey of Monmouth claimed she was the daughter of Coel, King of Colchester: *Saints*, pp. 201–2.

[10] Garnet had long argued for the separation of secular and spiritual authority: see Thomas M. McCoog, *'And Touching Our Society': Fashioning Jesuit Identity in Elizabethan England* (Toronto: PIMS, 2013), p. 318.

[11] Anon., *Perfect Relation*, sig. Fff2v.

[12] On confession see Lawrence S. Cunningham, *An Introduction to Catholicism* (Cambridge: Cambridge University Press, 2009), pp. 112–14. Confession was assuming greater importance for Catholics in the later sixteenth century with Cardinal Carlo Borromeo (1538–84) in particular 'convinced that confession had a crucial role in regulating the lives of the faithful' (MacCulloch, *Reformation*, pp. 411–12).

[13] Anon., *Perfect Relation*, sigs Fff2v–Fff3r.

of the chief opponents of Catholic compromise and conformity.[14] Garnet had admitted on several occasions that he was afraid of pain so the interpretation is by no means implausible.[15] The most resonant passage is Montagu's challenge to Garnet, reminding him that the hour of one's death was no time to equivocate when one had to meet God with as clean a conscience as possible.[16] Does Garnet's response that he had no intention of equivocating at this moment, as he had laid out when it was possible to quibble with double meanings elsewhere, make him admirable or treacherous? It is hard for a reader to decide one way or the other. Garnet again reminds observers of the significance of confession, something few of them can experience, suggesting that in his mind he knows the boundaries between different speech acts and their contexts, and, indeed, in a letter to the Jesuit Father General Claudio Acquaviva he acknowledges that English law understands Catholic confession to be an act hostile to state security.[17] A more critical reading would see Garnet's statements as admissions of guilt, that he had equivocated before but had now run out of opportunities as he could no longer save himself. Furthermore, English law did not recognize 'the inviolability of confession' which made Garnet's defence irrelevant in legal terms.[18]

Finally Garnet ascended the steps to the gibbet, commending himself to all good Catholics, and asking God to preserve the King and the Privy Council, before finally admitting—or getting close to admitting—his guilt: 'I am sorie that did dissemble with them [i.e. the King and Council]: I did not thinke they had had such proofe against me, till it was shewed mee; But when that was proued, I held it more honour for me at that time to confess, then before, to haue accused.'[19] Does this mean that Garnet has accepted that he misled his accusers about what he knew about the Gunpowder Plot? Is he admitting that he should not have withheld information that he knew? Or is he still holding the sacrament of confession sacred, admitting what he knows only in his final moments as a last confession?

However we read the words of the witness—and we cannot be sure that his account is not without its distortions—the last actions of Father Garnet are characterized by ambiguity and anxiety, the hallmarks of equivocation, the policy of verbal trickery associated in English minds with the Jesuits.[20] Did Garnet

---

[14] Zagorin, *Ways of Lying*, pp. 146–52.

[15] Caraman, *Garnet*, pp. 152–3.

[16] Philippe Ariès, *The Hour of Our Death*, trans. Helen Weaver (New York: Knopf, 1981), pt 2.

[17] Paul D. Stegner, *Confession and Memory in Early Modern English Literature: Penitential Remains* (Basingstoke: Palgrave Macmillan, 2015), p. 156.

[18] Mark Nicholls, *Investigating Gunpowder Plot* (Manchester: Manchester University Press, 1991), pp. 71–2.

[19] Anon., *Perfect Relation*, sig. Fff3r–v; John Gerard, *The History of the Catholics Under James I: Father Gerard's Narrative of the Gunpowder Plot*, ed. John Morris (London: Longmans, 1871), p. 292. On Gerard's non-involvement in the plot, see A. F. Allison, 'John Gerard and the Gunpowder Plot', *RH* 5 (1959), 43–63.

[20] See below, pp. 110–1. Equivocation had a venerable history in philosophy, especially logic: Paul Vincent Spade, 'Synonymy and Equivocation in Ockham's Mental Language', *JHP* 18 (1980), 9–22. It had appeared earlier in theological debates as a means of avoiding accusations of heresy: Loewenstein, *Treacherous Faith*, pp. 82–3; James Shapiro, *1606: William Shakespeare and the Year of Lear* (London: Faber, 2015), chs 9–10.

imagine that he might be saved by a pardon at the last minute?[21] Or was this a subterfuge to enable him to say more before his death? Or, perhaps he was hesitating and delaying his fate, genuinely frightened of pain, an issue which he admitted elsewhere influenced his actions?[22] Was there actually more to confess, as the Recorder asks? Was Garnet telling the whole truth or, even in his last words, was he lying?

Garnet's defence of equivocation at his trial was, as he rightly pointed out, a long-established practice that went back to the Church Fathers. After the prosecution launched a series of attacks on the Jesuits as equivocators who taught everyone in their charge to be duplicitous, Garnet argued that, on the contrary, the Church, following Augustine, did indeed condemn lying with regard to matters of faith. In words that predicted events on the scaffold, he conceded that equivocation should be avoided at times when it was the individual's duty to tell the truth such as the Day of Judgement. Garnet's argument was that it was permissible to tell August-ine's lowest form of lie when necessary, that is, in order to prevent harm to somebody.[23] In making this case Garnet's position was fundamentally the same as that of Thomas More, that is, that certain forms of promise made before God— oaths—could not be broken and that it was legitimate to deceive authorities that sought to violate such oaths because they had broken their contract with the Church. The crown produced evidence from one of the Gunpowder plotters, Francis Tresham, who had died in prison.[24] Tresham confessed that Garnet had been informed of the plot, then, implored by his wife, wrote a letter claiming that he had lied and that he had not seen Garnet for sixteen years. However, from Garnet's own examinations and other evidence it was known that 'His protestation and oath . . . were proved to be untrue.' When asked about this discrepancy Garnet answered evasively: 'It might be he meant to equivocate,' pretending not to be able to remember the nature of the conversation, a further act of equivocation.[25] Garnet was presumably using the term as he had defined it earlier in the trial, as a small lie designed to protect a larger truth, analogous to Thomas More's distinction between lying and perjury. He defended Tresham as honest in his usage but misconceived, especially as he had committed a 'manifest treason'. Garnet added that while it was rarely a good idea to equivocate in confession, it was permissible if harm to others might be prevented.[26]

[21] As Pedringano hopes in *The Spanish Tragedy*, only to be 'turned off' without reprieve: Thomas Kyd, *The Spanish Tragedy*, ed. Philip Edwards (Manchester: Manchester University Press, 1977, rpt of 1959), III, vi; Lukas Erne, *Beyond The Spanish Tragedy: A Study of the Works of Thomas Kyd* (Manchester: Manchester University Press, 2001), p. 88.

[22] Caraman, *Garnet*, p. 191; Thomas More also admitted that he feared pain, a natural reaction: Seymour Baker House, '"the field is won": An Introduction to the Tower Works', in A. D. Cousins and Damian Grace, eds, *A Companion to Thomas More* (Madison: Farleigh Dickinson Press, 2009), pp. 225–42, at p. 237.

[23] *State Trials*, I, pp. 238–9; Gerard, *History*, p. 244.

[24] On Tresham (1567?–1605), see the *ODNB* entry.

[25] *State Trials*, I, p. 256; Nicholls, *Investigating Gunpowder Plot*, p. 71.

[26] Gerard, *History*, p. ccxx.

The vocabulary with which it was possible to describe lying changed in the last years of Elizabeth's reign with the advent of the Jesuit crusade and Garnet's own particular contribution, which defined a new way of imagining truth and lies. The major event in the history of Elizabethan Catholicism was Pope Pius V's bull issued in February 1570 excommunicating Elizabeth as a heretic and declaring that her subjects had a duty to depose her.[27] A decade later the first Jesuit mission to England was dispatched.[28] Debates among Catholics were lively and complicated, but the community was divided between those, led by the Jesuits, who wished to carry out the Pope's demands one way or another, and the 'Appellants', who were far more eager to reach a compromise with the secular authorities.[29]

The first wave of Jesuit missionaries to England began in June 1580, and soon led to the well-publicized trial of Edmund Campion.[30] Campion and Robert Parsons were the first two Jesuits to be sent to England, their presence precipitating a carefully organized hunt for the priests in the midlands and north of England, which further intensified after the circulation of Campion's challenge to the Protestant authorities offering to debate the fundamental principles of theology and ecclesiology with his opponents.[31] Campion's work was answered in forceful style by Meredith Hanmer (1543–1604), who warned English readers to 'Beware of false Prophets' and 'trust not in false lying words'. Hanmer quibbled on Campion's name as 'Champion' and gave the letter its subsequent colloquial title, Campion's 'brag'.[32] Campion was eventually betrayed by the Catholic informer

---

[27] Text in *Tudor Constitution*, pp. 414–18. For comment see Adrian Morey, *The Catholic Subjects of Elizabeth I* (London: George Allen and Unwin, 1978), pp. 55–9; Peter Holmes, *Resistance and Compromise: The Political Thought of the Elizabethan Catholics* (Cambridge: Cambridge University Press, 1982), p. 26; Michael C. Questier, 'Elizabeth and the Catholics', in Ethan H. Shagan, ed., *Catholics and the 'Protestant Nation': Religious Politics and Identity in Early Modern England* (Manchester: Manchester University Press, 2005), pp. 69–94; Kilroy, *Campion: A Scholarly Life*, pp. 155–6.

[28] Carolyn Vinnicombe, 'Recusancy and Regicide: The Flawed Strategy of the Jesuit Mission in Elizabethan England', *Penn History Review* 19 (2012), 25–43; John Bossy, *The English Catholic Community, 1570–1850* (London: Darton, Longman & Todd, 1975), pp. 36–48; Alexandra Walsham, *Catholic Reformation in Protestant Britain* (Farnham: Ashgate, 2014), p. 89.

[29] Arnold Pritchard, *Catholic Loyalism in Elizabethan England* (London: Scolar Press, 1979); Michael C. Questier, *Catholicism and Community in Early Modern England: Politics, Aristocratic Patronage and Religion, c.1550–1640* (Cambridge: Cambridge University Press, 2006), pp. 288–314; Victor Houliston, 'Filling in the Blanks: Catholic Hopes for the English Succession', *YSPSR* 25 (2015), 77–104. For one complex case see Stefania Tutino, 'Thomas Preston and English Catholic Loyalism: Elements of an International Affair', *C16J* 41 (2010), 91–109.

[30] Holmes, *Resistance and Compromise*, pp. 35–6; Anglo, *Machiavelli*, p. 396.

[31] For details see the *ODNB* entries on Campion and Parsons. The text of Campion's challenge is reproduced in *Campian Englished. Or a translation of the ten reasons in which E. Campian insisted in his challenge, to the universities of Oxford and Cambridge. By a priest of the catholicke and Roman church* (Rouen?, 1632), a translation of *Rationes Decem: Quibus Fretus, Certamen Aduersarius Obtultit in Causa Fidei* (Henley-on-Thomas, 1581). See also Evelyn Waugh, *Edmund Campion: Scholar, Priest, Hero, and Martyr* (Oxford: Oxford University Press, 1980, rpt of 1935), pp. 200–3; Kilroy, *Campion: A Scholarly Life*, pp. 173–6.

[32] Meredith Hanmer, *The Great Brag and Challenge of M. Champion A Iesuite* (London, 1581); Kilroy, *Campion: A Scholarly Life*, p. 190. For analysis see Angela Andreani, 'Between Theological Debate and Political Subversion: Meredith Hanmer's Confutation of Edmund Campion's *Letter to the Privy Council*', *Aevum* 3 (2016), 557–73.

George Eliot, on 17 July 1581, captured and sent to London for interrogation and trial.[33]

Campion's trial was a landmark that was to establish the nature of religious trials in the second half of Elizabeth's reign, as the authorities sought to classify religious opposition in terms of treason rather than heresy, to counter the papacy's claim that it had a duty to bring the heretic nation back into the Catholic fold.[34] Proclamations declared the need to arrest all Jesuits and those who harboured them.[35] For each side of the religious divide the Jesuit mission was a major turning point that transformed an understanding of religious identity, community, and belonging.[36] The authorities represented the Jesuits as subversive, self-interested hypocrites, eager to destroy the progress of the Reformation and return England to an era of superstition and ignorance in thrall to the tyrannical authority of the Church of Rome. The Jesuits were 'seditious slanderers' working to undermine the legitimate authority of the queen, their primary loyalty being to the Pope, the head of an international conspiracy which targeted England in particular. This interpretation of loyalties was a logical application of the Oath of Supremacy, demonstrating how well Thomas More's understanding of it had been.[37] Particular emphasis was placed on the papal bull excommunicating Elizabeth, with claims that the Pope's words inspired the opposition to the monarch: 'the later rebellion in the North was manifestly by lyke meanes put in execution'.[38]

Accordingly, Jesuits were frequently represented as inspired by Satan, the father of lies. Anthony Munday in his response to pamphlets defending Campion argued that these Catholic missionaries had been schooled in lying which had therefore become a way of life: 'The Father of lyes hath made his Children so prompt in his

---

[33] Even the facts of Campion's capture were disputed, resulting in another controversy in print: Anthony Munday, *A Discouerie of Edmund Campion, and his confederates* (London, 1581); George Elyot, *A Very True Report of the Apprehension and Taking of That Arch Papist Edmond Campion* (London, 1581); Alford, *Watchers*, p. 106.

[34] 'The Arraignment of Campion, Sherwin, Bosgrave, Cottam, Johnson, Bristow, Kirbie, and Orton for High Treason', *State Trials*, I, pp. 1049–87. See also Walsham, *Catholic Reformation*, pp. 347–8. On the nature of Elizabeth's later reign see John Guy, 'Introduction: The 1590s: The Second Reign of Elizabeth I?', in John Guy, ed., *The Reign of Elizabeth I: Court and Culture in the Last Decade* (Cambridge: Cambridge University Press, 1995), pp. 1–19; on Mary's heresy laws, see Eamon Duffy, *Fires of Faith: Catholic England Under Mary Tudor* (New Haven: Yale University Press, 2009), pp. 89–92; Guy, *Tudor England*, pp. 235–8.

[35] Jones, *Governing by Virtue*, pp. 106–7.

[36] Walsham, *Catholic Reformation*, ch. 10; Peter Lake and Michael Questier, 'Puritans, Papists, and the "Public Sphere": The Edmund Campion Affair in Context', *JMH* 72 (2000), 587–627.

[37] Anon., *A Particular Declaration Or Testimony Of The Undutifull and Traiterous Affection Borne Against Her Maiestie By Edmund Campion Iesuite* (London, 1582), sig. A3v; Patrick Collinson, *Richard Bancroft and Elizabethan Anti-Puritanism* (Cambridge: Cambridge University Press, 2013), p. 5.

[38] Anon., *An Advertisment and Defence for Trueth Against Her Backbiters, and Specially Against The Whispering Fauourers, and Colourers of Campions* (London, 1581), sig. A3v. The Pope had blessed the rebels but the bull was issued later: K. J. Kesselring, *The Northern Rebellion of 1569: Faith, Politics, and Protest in Elizabethan England* (Basingstoke: Palgrave Macmillan, 2007), pp. 34–5. A translation is reproduced in Robert S. Miola, ed., *Early Modern Catholicism: An Anthology of Primary Sources* (Oxford: Oxford University Press, 2007), pp. 486–8.

Art, that they cannot chuse but make knowledge thereof.'[39] In his description of Campion's trial Munday attempts to turn the priest's good qualities against him to make the same point: 'the Judges dyd admire, that a man as he was, professing learning and lawe in outward appearance, shoulde be so ouercome by the Deuil, as to seeke the spoyle and ruine of his Princesse and Countrey'.[40] It was believed, therefore, that the Jesuits would not be able to resist telling lies and so would always incriminate themselves. A compilation of the interrogation of Jesuits tried alongside Campion published in 1582 was designed to show how they would condemn themselves out of their own mouths when they were finally run to ground. Asked 'Whether the Queenes Maiestie be a lawfull Queene, and ought to be obeyed by the subiects of England, notwithstanding the Bull of *Pius quintus*', Luke Kirby answered that he 'thinketh that in some cases . . . her Maiestie is not to be obeyed against the Popes Bul and sentence, for so hee saith he hath read, that the Pope hath so done, *de facto*, against other princes'.[41] Asked whether the Pope 'had the power to authorize the Earles of Northumberlande and Westmerland . . . to rebell or take armes against her Maiestie', Kirby replied simply 'he cannot answere it', which was taken as proof of his support.[42]

The case against Campion was made in terms of familiar notions of true and false argument. Jesuits, when tried in the 1580s, were always accused of sophistry, shorthand for the cunning abuse of rhetoric, use of impressive but insubstantial and misleading arguments and chop logic.[43] Sophistry, in common as well as academic parlance, signified a commitment to outmoded forms of thinking and argument, a refusal to understand that learning—and religion—had been reborn.[44] In his account of the capture of Campion, Anthony Munday labels the attempts of Jesuits to distinguish between their spiritual allegiance to the Pope and their secular allegiance to the Queen as sophistry, warning the authorities not to be taken in by practised, cunning answers and so be mistakenly lenient to men whose treachery is easily visible:

> For this consideration they cary with them, that if by their showe of humilitiye and deuised order of craftye aunsweringe, they might moue our Maiestrates to haue a good opinion of them and not to deale so strictlye, as lawe and their deseruinge dooth worthily merit: then they might with lesse suspect goe about their holy Fathers busines, in that their Sophisticall aunswers, couered so foule an abuse.[45]

---

[39] Anthony Munday, *A Breefe Aunswer Made Unto Two Seditious Pamphlets . . . Contayning a Defence of Edmund Campion* (London, 1582), sig. B6r. Donna B. Hamilton argues that Munday was covering his true Catholic allegiance and protecting himself in writing these works: *Munday and the Catholics*, pp. 40–3. For Tracey Hill, the pamphlets show that 'Munday's youthful anti-Catholicism persisted': *Munday and Civic Culture*, p. 34.

[40] Munday, *Breefe Aunswer*, sig. C2r.

[41] Anon., *Particular Declaration*, sig. C2r–v. On Kirby's trial, see Bellamy, *Treason*, pp. 70–1, *passim*.

[42] Anon., *Particular Declaration*, sigs C2r, C3r.

[43] *OED* 1a.

[44] E. J. Ashworth, 'Traditional Logic', in Schmitt and Skinner, eds, *Cambridge History of Renaissance Philosophy*, pp. 143–72, at pp. 164–6.

[45] Munday, *Discouerie*, sigs C4v–C5r.

Munday's description of Campion's behaviour on the scaffold sought to further discredit the martyred Jesuit.[46]

A detailed narrative of the four days of Campion's interrogations was published by two of his interrogators, Alexander Nowell (*c.*1516/17–1602), Dean of St Paul's, and William Day (1529–96), Bishop of Winchester.[47] The account reproduces the dialogues about the fundamental nature of the Christian Church and its faith in painstaking detail, evidently trusting its readers to understand the difference between the true Protestant and the false Catholic Church, the latter exposing its falsehood through its malicious sophistry. On the third day the divines argue about the nature of the sacraments and whether Christ's blood is really present when the wine and bread are consumed by the true believer (transubstantiation, the doctrine of the Catholic Church), or whether the bread and wine continue to exist with the blood and body of Christ appearing miraculously beside them (sacramental union, the belief of Luther, adopted by Cranmer and adapted for English Protestant liturgy).[48] William Fulke, theologian and master of Pembroke College, Cambridge, engages Campion in dispute:

CAMPION. I say there is really present in the Sacrament, the naturall body and blood of Christ vnder that bread and cup.

FULKE. What meane you by these wordes vnder the bread and cup, that we may agree of termes?

CAMPION. You knowe in the bread is whitenes, & c. that is not in his body: make your argument.

FULKE. So I will. The cup is not the naturall blood of Christ: Ergo the other parte is not his naturall body.

CAMPION. There is present in the cup, the naturall blood of Christ. Go to my wordes.

FULKE. Well. The naturall blood of Christ is not present in the cup: Ergo the naturall body is not present in the other part.

CAMPION. The naturall blood of Christ is present in the cup.

FULKE. Thus I disproue it. The wordes of Christes institution be these: This cup is the new testament in my blood: But the naturall blood of Christ is not the newe testament in his blood: Ergo the naturall blood of Christ is not in the cup.[49]

---

[46] Scott Pilarz, '"Campion Dead Bites with his Friends' Teeth": Representations of an Early Modern Catholic Martyr', in Highley and King, eds, *Foxe and His World*, pp. 216–31, at p. 220.

[47] On Day and Nowell, see the *ODNB* entries. However, as Gerard Kilroy has demonstrated, their report 'differs significantly in substance and tone from the manuscript accounts' of Thomas Tresham and others: *Campion: A Scholarly Life*, p. 273.

[48] William R. Crockett, 'Holy Communion', in Stephen Sykes and John Booty, eds, *The Study of Anglicanism* (London: SPCK, 1988), pp. 272–84; MacCulloch, *Cranmer*, pp. 180–4; Martin Luther, 'The Lord's Supper', *Sermons on the Catechism* (1528), in John Dillenberger, ed., *Martin Luther: Selections from His Writings* (New York: Anchor Books, 1961), pp. 234–9.

[49] Alexander Nowell and William Day, *A True Report of the Disputation or Rather Priuate Conference had in the Tower of London, with Ed. Campion Iesuite, the last of August. 1581* (London, 1583), sig. P2r. On Fulke (1536/7–89), see the *ODNB* entry.

This mode of reasoning and argument based on syllogisms results in frequent stalemates and it is hard to see that a Catholic or a Protestant reader would have been convinced that their opponents had won the day.[50] As Gerard Kilroy has argued, the later debates, designed to trap Campion, descend into a 'horrible parody of disputation'.[51] Furious arguments over the Eucharist were central to the confessional division for much of the sixteenth century, as is indicated by the number of Protestant martyrs in John Foxe's *Acts and Monuments* who are prepared to die for their cause because of their understanding of the nature of the sacraments.[52] In places, if the seriousness of the debate was not so obvious, the protagonists sound as though they have simply returned to the schoolroom and are arguing like precocious children:

CAMPION: Make your argument.
FULKE: I haue made it already.
    The substance of the bread and wine remaineth:
ERGO there is no transubstantiation.
CAMPION: I denie your *Antecedent*.
FULKE: The words of *Gelasius* proveth it.
    The substance of bread and wine departeth not.
ERGO it remaineth.[53]

Unsurprisingly, the debate ends inconclusively with a discussion of man's inherent sinfulness or goodness between Campion and William Charke, a lecturer at Lincoln's Inn, who, like Hanmer, had written an answer to Campion's *Brag*.[54] It concludes with a prayer in which Charke repeats his belief in man's inherent sinfulness and the need for Christ's salvation, thanking God that he has given his children the right knowledge to repel hostile forces:

Also wee thanke thee for the inestimable treasure and armour of thy holy worde, whereby thou makest thy children rich in all spirituall and heauenly wisdome, inhabling them, euen the weakest of them, to triumphe against proud and bold ignorance, against the deceitfull and lying spirits gone out into the world in these last times, to deceiue those that receiue not the knowledge and loue of thy trueth.[55]

Here we have one of only two references to 'lying' in the work: Charke began the fourth day's interrogation with a prayer—which Campion obviously refused to join—celebrating those who had understood God's true word and asking that those who failed to hear His word 'may yeelde either to the manifest trueth, if they

[50] Lake and Questier, 'Public Sphere', p. 606.
[51] Kilroy, *Campion: A Scholarly Life*, p. 290.
[52] Loewenstein, *Treacherous Faith*, pp. 72–93; David Aers and Sarah Beckwith, 'The Eucharist', in Brian Cummings and James Simpson, eds, *Cultural Reformations: Medieval and Renaissance in Literary History* (Oxford: Oxford University Press, 2010), pp. 153–65; Alec Ryrie, *Being Protestant in Reformation Britain* (Oxford: Oxford University Press, 2013), pp. 336–51, *passim*.
[53] Nowell and Day, *True Report*, sig. P3v.
[54] On Charke (d.1617), see the *ODNB* entry. Charke's reply is *An Answere to a Seditious Pamphlet Lately Cast Abroade by a Jesuite, with a Discouerie of that Blasphemous Sect* (London, 1580).
[55] Nowell and Day, *True Report*, sig. Gg1v.

appertayne to thy holy election: or being none of thine, that they may appeare guyltie and conuicted of a lying spirite, such as is gone out into the worlde to deceyue those that will not receyue the loue of thy trueth, but delight in darkenesse'.[56]

It is easy to see why the Campion trial was such a significant watershed in terms of hardening England's religious divisions. Protestant England secured its safety through the execution of a dangerous subversive Jesuit; Catholicism had a martyr who had held his own in debates with the authorities and whose example would galvanize the faith and inspire future generations.[57] The works printed in England did little to counter the Jesuit claim that their priests were sent to England to provide spiritual guidance only, as they simply confronted one assertion with a counterclaim rather than providing evidence of a more obviously political purpose.[58] Meredith Hanmer's response to Campion's *Brag* is notably ineffective in refuting Campion, simply bombarding his opponent's straightforward statements with an aggressive Protestant sermon taunting his opponent:

The Jesuit
My charge is free to preach the Gospell, to minister the Sacraments, to instruct the simple, to reforme sinners, to confute errors, and in briefe to trie all armoure spirituall agaynst foule vice and proude ignoraunce, wherewith many of my deare Countreymen are abused.

The aunswere.
Now ye publish your commission, is your calling ordinarye or extraordinary? extreame ordinary. who made you a Preacher? youre Prouost of Rome. Are ye a preacher of the Gospell? I pray ye of what Gospel? there haue bene many heretikes that reiected the true gospel (that is) of Iesus Christ, and deliuered into the world the Gospels of Peter, Thomas, Mathias, Andreve, and yet would they be counted preachers of the Gospell.[59]

It is hard to see how Hanmer's assertions that Campion is a heretic who has no right to preach the gospel would have persuaded readers that he had the better of the argument even if the reader in question were predisposed to sympathize with his position, because there is no real argument here that can be won or lost.

The most significant event that changed the nature of religious and legal debate was the trial and execution of Robert Southwell (21 February 1595).[60] In response,

---

[56] Nowell and Day, *True Report*, sig. R3v.   [57] Waugh, *Campion*, pp. 198–9.

[58] An issue reproduced at times in the historiography: see Christopher Haigh, 'The Continuity of Catholicism in the English Reformation', in Christopher Haigh, ed., *The English Reformation Revised* (Cambridge: Cambridge University Press, 1987), pp. 176–208, at p. 195; Lake and Questier, 'Public Sphere', pp. 588, 600–1. While Campion was clear that his mission was a spiritual one, other Jesuits such as Nicholas Sander and Robert Parsons were eager to transform the spiritual crusade into a political one: Kilroy, *Campion: A Scholarly Life*, p. 184.

[59] Hanmer, *Great Brag*, pp. 13–14. On Protestant preaching styles, see Peter Lake with Michael Questier, *The Antichrist's Lewd Hat: Protestants, Papists and Players in Post-Reformation England* (New Haven: Yale University Press, 2002), pp. 335–76; Wabuda, *Preaching*; Arnold Hunt, *The Art of Hearing: English Preachers and their Audiences, 1590–1640* (Cambridge: Cambridge University Press, 2010), ch. 1.

[60] See Zagorin, *Ways of Lying*, pp. 186–93. Southwell had written on equivocation, but his treatise has been lost: A. E. Malloch, 'Father Henry Garnet's Treatise of Equivocation', *RH* 15 (1981), 387–95, p. 394 n. 9.

Henry Garnet produced his instruction manual for besieged Jesuits, *A Treatise of Equivocation* (*c*.1595), written to prepare priests sent on missions to England.[61] The *Treatise* was also designed to defend the reputation of his executed co-religionist, and to counsel other Jesuits how to evade the hostile enquiries of the authorities without actually lying.[62] Southwell had established this precedent at his trial in February 1595 as he had advised the woman who eventually betrayed him, Anne Bellamy, that it was possible for her to deny that there was a priest in her house if asked by the authorities, on the grounds that answering 'No' really meant 'No, you have no right to know', however her interrogators might interpret her words. The point was to protect the householder, as the officer would search the house anyway, but if the priest could not be found then no crime would have been uncovered.[63] Southwell had then claimed that he did not know her at the trial, defending his actions in terms of a need to protect those he knew from harm.[64] In response to accusations that he was defending perjury, Southwell produced his own version of the 'bloody question'. He asked Sir Edward Coke, the Attorney General, if he would tell the truth if the King of France invaded and asked to know where the Queen was and only he, Coke, knew where she was, and that his silence would be read as evidence that she was in the house, an intervention which appears to have discomforted Coke.[65]

Southwell argued at his trial that, as a general principle, a Christian should avoid equivocation 'except in the case when something is asked him, either actually or virtually, which the questioner has no right to ask, and the declaration of which will turn to his own hurt if he answers according to the intention of the questioner', a defence in line with Augustine's comments on lying.[66] According to Southwell this was the practice Christ had adopted when stating that no one knew when the Day of Judgement was to be, as well as when he denied that he was going to Jerusalem when he had planned to go, an argument repeated later by Henry Garnet at his trial.[67] For Southwell, the issue came down, as with other Catholic martyrs, to oaths to the Church and he lamented the unfortunate fate of the true English Catholics who found themselves in the same position as the persecuted Christ. Catholics, according to Southwell,

> Are in peril of their liberty, their fortunes, and their lives, if they should have a Priest in their houses. How can it be forbidden them to escape these evils by an equivocal answer, and to confirm this answer, if necessary, by an oath? For in such a case, three

[61] Janet E. Halley, 'Equivocation and the Legal Conflict over Religious Identity in Early Modern England', *YJLH* 3 (2013), 33–52, p. 34.

[62] Henry Garnet, *A Treatise of Equivocation*, ed. David Jardine (London: Longman, 1851).

[63] Devlin, *Southwell*, p. 301.

[64] Caraman, *Garnet*, pp. 253–4; Gerard, *History*, p. ccxiv.

[65] Devlin, *Southwell*, p. 313. On the 'bloody question', see below, p. 91.

[66] Gerard, *History*, p. ccxvi. See also Malloch, 'Garnet's Treatise of Equivocation', pp. 387–8. Southwell's sacrifice was in marked contrast to the actions of his grandfather, who enjoyed a successful and lengthy career at court (see above, pp. 37–8).

[67] Gerard, *History*, pp. ccxvi, 245.

things must be remembered: first, that a wrong is done unless you swear; secondly, that no one is obliged to answer everybody's questions about everything; thirdly, that an oath is always lawful, if made with truth, with judgement, and with justice, all which are found in this case.[68]

For Southwell swearing a misleading oath based on equivocation to the secular authorities was simply what Christ and the saints had done when necessary to protect the faith: fully truthful oaths could only be sworn to religious authorities.

Garnet, anxious to avoid the suffering that he had witnessed at Southwell's trial, advised a Catholic reader that God would permit them to mislead hostile authorities 'if he cannot otherwise auoide such inconueniences as may ofte insew to himself or to his neighbour' because 'this was that Blessed father Southwell his doctrine'.[69] A copy of the treatise was discovered at the Inner Temple, then endorsed by Coke on 5 December 1605, who notes 'This boke consisting 62 pages I founde in a chamber in the Inner Temple wherein Sir Thomas Tresham used to lye, and whiche he obteyned for his two younger sonnes.'[70] The manuscript, now in the Bodleian Library, shows signs of being altered in a desperate attempt to disguise the true nature of its contents.[71] The original title, 'A Treatise of Equivocation wherein is largely discussed the question whether a Catholicke or any other person before a magistrate beying demaunded upon his oath whether a Prieste were in such a place, may (notwithstanding his perfect knowledge to the contrary) without Perjury and securely in conscience answere No, with this secreat meaning reserued in his mynde, That he was not there so that any man is bounde to detect it', covers all bases and makes it clear to a reader that the treatise will deal with oaths, perjury, conscience, and mental reservation, issues associated with lying that can now be dealt with by 'equivocation'.[72] The manuscript title is altered to 'A Treatise Against Lying and Equivocation', as though the treatise was used by the Treshams, an established Catholic family who were prepared to suffer greatly for their faith, as a means of supporting their loyal attempts to root out heresy, not a means of forestalling interrogation.[73] In fact, Francis Tresham, the eldest son of Sir Thomas, was one of the Gunpowder Plot conspirators, providing a direct link between the treatise and the plot.[74] Protestant authors gleefully seized on this change of the title as a further sign of the desperate guilt of underground Catholics.[75] As Johann P. Sommerville comments: 'Hitherto

---

[68] Gerard, *History*, p. ccxix. [69] Garnet, *Equivocation*, p. 46.

[70] See the *ODNB* entry for Coke.

[71] 'A Treatise of Equivocation', Bodleian MS Laud Misc. 655.

[72] Garnet, *Equivocation*, p. i. For discussion, see Lowell Gallagher, *Medusa's Gaze: Casuistry and Conscience in the Renaissance* (Stanford: Stanford University Press, 1991), pp. 64–7; Zagorin, *Ways of Lying*, pp. 163–220.

[73] On the Treshams, see Kilroy, *Campion: A Scholarly Life*, ch. 5.

[74] On Francis Tresham (1567?–1605) and his role in the plot, see the *ODNB* entry; Tesimond, *Gunpowder Plot*, pp. 124–6, 231–46; Kilroy, *Campion: A Scholarly Life*, p. 135.

[75] Rose, *Cases of Conscience*, pp. 92–3; Anon., *Perfect Relation*, sigs I1v–I2r.

most laymen, Catholic as well as Protestant, had been ignorant of mental reservation. Now they reacted to it with horror.'[76]

The work was designed to perform a neat trick: how to prevent Catholic readers, their friends, and allies from being tortured and executed by hostile authorities, without imperilling any souls through telling lies. Garnet attempts to show how direct lies can be avoided in extreme situations through the utterance of a duplicitous statement that read in a particular way would actually be truthful. Like More he acknowledges that in swearing an oath, and making a future promise, one must tell the truth. Like More, he also acknowledges that swearing such an oath releases the swearer from having to tell the truth to those who would violate it:

> Thou shalt swear (sayeth the Prophett Hieremy) our Lord liveth, in trewth and in iudgement, and in justice. Uppon wch place the holy doctor St. Hierom noteth that there must be three companions of euery oath, truth, iudgement, and justice. Of whome all the deuines have learned the same, requiring these three conditions in every lawfull oath, and condemning all oaths wch are made without all or any one of them. The reason heareof is, for that an oath beying an invocation of the soueraigne ma^{tie} of God for testimony of that wch is sworne, wee ought always in such invocations to vse judgement or discretion to see that wee do nothinge rashly, or wthout dew reverence, devotion, and faith, towards so great a ma^{tie}. But we must especially regard that wee make not hym, who is the chiefe and soveraigne veritye and inflexible justice, a witnesse of that wch eyther is false or an uniust promise; for otherwise an oath wanting Judgement or discretion, and wisedome, is a rashe oath; that wch wanteth justice is called an vniust oath; and that finally, where there is not truthe is *adiudged a false or lyinge oathe, and is more properly then all the rest called Periurye.* (My emphasis)[77]

Garnet argues that swearing a false oath is such a heinous crime that any methods possible must be adopted in order to preserve the sanctity of the original promise. Catholics forced to swear a false oath can adopt any casuistical weapons they have in their armoury to avoid committing perjury: ambiguity, equivocation, mental reservation, and so on, precisely the argument that More had employed in his notes on perjury, and, unsurprisingly, forcefully attacked as hypocrisy by Protestant opponents.[78] Garnet declares his belief in the value of oaths at length and with unquestionable sincerity: oaths can only be sworn if the speaker intends to keep them so that swearing a false oath that one has no intention of adopting is much worse than not swearing one, meaning that individuals placed in such an unfair position are justified in using any means necessary to thwart the illegitimate actions of unjust authorities who try to impose their will unreasonably and against God's injunctions. It is the very truthfulness of the properly sworn oath which leads to an argument in defence of lying. The stronger the need for the truth, the more clear its

---

[76] Johann P. Sommerville, 'The "New Art of Lying": Equivocation, Mental Reservation, and Casuistry', in Leites, ed., *Conscience and Casuistry*, pp. 159–84, at p. 177. See also Halley, 'Equivocation', p. 42; Wood, *English Casuistical Divinity*, pp. 113–15.

[77] Garnet, *Equivocation*, pp. 6–7.

[78] Thomas Morton, *An Exact Discoverie of Romish Doctrine in the Case of Conspiracie and Rebellion by Pregnant Obseruations* (London, 1605), pp. 13, 44–5. For comment see Zagorin, *Ways of Lying*, pp. 200–1.

definition, the more excusable will be the subterfuge—which will be called a lie by Protestant opponents. For Garnet, the importance of truth leads directly to the necessity of lying.

Equivocation is a development of a loophole that Augustine had established, 'mental reservation', 'having one thing in one's heart and uttering another', a doctrine designed to prevent the twin evils of telling the truth in dangerous situations and lying.[79] Nor was it exclusive to one confessional faith. Very few English Protestants chose to lie outright to hostile authorities, although some briefly considered this option.[80] Rather, many took advantage of a 'long tradition of dissembling inherited from Lollardy', and some divines counselled others to submit to the authorities in order to save their lives and so help further the faith, as well as to give them a chance to explain and defend some version of their beliefs.[81] The aim was for the speaker to be able to preserve his or her status as a truth-teller before God, while deliberately misleading the authorities, keeping the Cokes of this world at bay. In the end God would know that you had tried to do the right thing, as long as you took some precautions to avoid the sort of barefaced lies that troubled Augustine. Garnet clearly enjoys sailing close to the wind as this cunning and punning example demonstrates:

> [W]e may use some quivocall word wch hath many significations, and we vnderstand it in one sense, wch is trewe, although the hearer conceive the other, wch is false. So did Abraham and Isaac say, that theire wives were theire sisters, wch. was not trewe as the hearers vnderstood it, or in the proper meaning, whereby a sister signifyeth one borne of the same father or mother, or of both, but in a general signification, whereby a brother or sister signifyeth one neere of kynred, as Abraham called Lott his brother, who was but his brother's sonne; and our Lord is sayed to haue had brothers and sisters, whereas properly he had neyther. The like vnto this were if one should be asked whether such a straunger lodgeth in my howse, and I should aunswere, 'he lyeth not in my howse,' meaning that he doth not tell a lye there, althoughe he lodge there.[82]

As before, this is an excellent and witty piece of writing, which illuminates and deceives at the same time, making a serious point if you are sharp enough to read the words correctly. The two examples are not, of course, the same. The first example is a piece of shorthand, whereby a relationship is used to characterize a series of different ones for ease of reference, as the term 'cousin' or 'kinsman' was used ubiquitously in this period, in the form of a synecdoche, a practice which makes it hard to establish early modern family groups with any confidence. Garnet then provides the real example which may be of use to those harbouring priests, a

---

[79] Bok, *Lying*, p. 35; Saul, *Lying, Misleading*, pp. 101–9; Leslie, *Born Liars*, pp. 303–10.

[80] Susan Wabuda, 'Equivocation and Recantation During the English Reformation: The "Subtle Shadows" of Dr. Edward Crome', *JEH* 44 (1993), 224–42, pp. 228–9.

[81] Andrew Pettegree, *Marian Protestantism: Six Studies* (Aldershot: Scolar, 1996), p. 97; Wabuda, 'Equivocation and Recantation', pp. 228–9, 239–42. See also Ryrie, *Gospel*, pp. 78–81; John F. McDiarmid, '"To Content God Quietlie": The Troubles of Sir John Cheke under Queen Mary', in Elizabeth Evenden and Vivienne Westbrook, eds, *Catholic Renewal and Protestant Resistance in Marian England* (Farnham: Ashgate, 2015), pp. 185–27, at p. 219.

[82] Garnet, *Equivocation*, pp. 48–9.

homonym that joins two entirely different meanings: lying, meaning not to tell the truth, and lying, meaning 'lodging' (perhaps also meaning not standing or sitting up), signifying in turn, as a synecdoche, staying. Garnet cannot have written this passage innocently as if the disparity of the examples had not occurred to him, and he would have been aware of the sleight of hand he was performing. The choice of the word 'lying', placed next to three biblical examples, two well-known sibling relationships from the Old Testament, and one involving God himself, suggests a certain brio, a sparkling confidence demonstrated to help inspire readers who surely felt themselves under serious threat. The passage suggests that if a Jesuit, a man who faced the severest possible dangers, could write with such insouciance, then surely Catholics could survive anything and all will eventually be well.

It is possible that the spirit of the treatise inspired Coke to indulge in a related quibble when he wrote on the first page of the manuscript that Thomas Tresham and his sons 'used to lye' in the chamber where the treatise was discovered. Was he continuing the joke in a grim vein, yet another case of Protestants and Catholics sharing a common language?[83] Coke, in his role as Attorney General, had been instrumental in prosecuting Catholics, as the legal records demonstrate, and had made systematic efforts to discover recusant literature.[84] Like his Jesuit opponents Coke placed great value on the sanctity of oaths, which is why he was so hostile to the use of equivocation as a means of undermining the need to make public promises of loyalty by eliding and abusing their language.[85] In Garnet's treatise Coke also wrote 'the mouth which lies kills the spirit', quoting Wisdom 1:11 ('the mouth that speaketh lyes, slayreth the soule'), equating the Jesuits with false preachers and abusers of God's word.[86]

II

Coke had been the crown's chief prosecutor in the trial of Robert Southwell and had attacked Southwell 'most bitterly on the question of his advocacy of equivocation'.[87] Southwell was a distinguished and adept poet, writing a large number of lyrics while on his mission in England (1586–92). Southwell's poetry, which may well have had a significant influence on the development of an English poetic tradition, is characterized by startling juxtapositions, striking metaphors which connect apparently unrelated phenomena, irony, and wordplay.[88] 'New Prince, new pompe', for example, stresses the contrast between the vulnerable infant Jesus:

---

[83] Alison Shell, *Catholicism, Controversy and the English Literary Imagination, 1558–1660* (Cambridge: Cambridge University Press, 1999), ch. 2; Cummings, *Literary Culture*, p. 332.

[84] Kilroy, *Campion: A Scholarly Life*, p. 57; Allen D. Boyer, *Sir Edward Coke and the Elizabethan Age* (Stanford: Stanford University Press, 2003), pp. 242–71.

[85] See also William Barlow, *An Answer to a Catholike English-man* (London, 1609), p. 224.

[86] David Chan Smith, *Sir Edward Coke and the Reformation of the Laws: Religion, Politics and Jurisprudence, 1578–1616* (Cambridge: Cambridge University Press, 2014), p. 186.

[87] Robert Southwell, *The Poems of Robert Southwell*, ed. James H. McDonald and Nancy Pollard Brown (Oxford: Clarendon Press, 1967), introduction, p. xxxiii.

[88] Shell, *Catholicism, Controversy*, pp. 66–77; Cummings, *Literary Culture*, p. 364.

> Behold a silly tender Babe,
> In freesing Winter night;
> In homely manger trembling lies,
> Alas a piteous sight

and his majestic power as king of heaven, signs of which can be seen in his humble surroundings if read properly by the true Christian:

> This stable is a Princes Court,
> The Crib his chaire of state:
> The beasts are parcel of his pompe,
> The wooden dish his plate.
>
> The persons in that poore attire,
> His royall livories weare,
> The Prince himselfe is come from heaven,
> This pompe is prized there.
>
> With joy approach o Christian wight,
> Doe homage to thy King;
> And highly prise this humble pompe,
> Which he from heaven dooth bring.[89]

It would not take a terribly sophisticated contemporary reader long to understand that the contrast between the situation of Jesus is now manifested in the plight of his most faithful followers, the Society of Jesus, sent abroad to live a dangerous hand-to-mouth existence before, like Christ, suffering an agonizing death on behalf of mankind. The spiritually blind reader will not understand the proper meaning of the poem, impeded by their indifference or hostility to the truly faithful, whereas the loyal Catholic will realize that they need to support the mission of the humble, disguised priests because they represent God's holy Church on earth.[90]

Much of Southwell's poetry explores similarly spiritually charged paradoxes contrasting the undeserved fate of the faithful. 'I dye without desert'—a poem which prefigures George Herbert's lyric 'Life', a work long acknowledged as a response to Jesuit practices of meditation—describes innocent and unfortunate creatures who should inspire pity: an 'orphane Childe enwrapt in swathing bands', a 'Relinquisht Lamb in solitarye wood'.[91] Southwell compares his own innocent state to that of these suffering beings, claiming that he has been 'A frend to truth, a foe was I to vice, / And loe, alas, nowe Innocente I dye, / A case that might even make the stones to crye'. In the end it is God's will: 'God doth sometimes first cropp the sweetest floure, / And leaves the weede till tyme do it devoure.' As in 'New Prince, new pompe', there is a striking contrast between the nature of the

---

[89] Southwell, *Poems*, pp. 16–17.
[90] On Jesuit attire, see McCoog, *'And Touching Our Society'*, ch. 8; Gillian Woods, *Shakespeare's Unreformed Fictions* (Oxford: Oxford University Press, 2013), pp. 93–4.
[91] George Herbert, 'Life', in *The English Poems of George Herbert*, ed. Helen Wilcox (Cambridge: Cambridge University Press, 2007), pp. 341–2; Louis L. Martz, *The Poetry of Meditation: A Study in English Religious Literature of the Seventeenth Century* (rev. edn, New Haven: Yale University Press, 1962), pp. 58–9; Southwell, *Poems*, pp. 48–9.

world and the proper spiritual order created by God and understood by the faithful. For many non-believers the death of the child, lamb, and Jesuit may seem sad and meaningless but a more insightful reading inspired by true faith will realize that there is an order and purpose that can be understood, however hard the message might appear.

For Southwell, a binding oath could only be sworn to the Church not to the secular authorities. It was the failure to honour this oath that made people liars, exactly as More had argued sixty years earlier. Before undertaking his mission Southwell had written to either Claudio Acquaviva or Alfonso Agazzari, both senior Jesuits, of the bad faith of the Protestant authorities: 'Liars must in the first place strengthen and confirm by lies what they have achieved by lies. Only in one area is there consistency: the harassment and ill-treatment of Catholics.'[92] It is a relatively small step from the poetry showing how the truth can be understood by the faithful if they are guided to read signs, metaphors, and allegorical representations to a belief that ambiguous, even misleading, speech to hostile authorities is justified by God. The words and actions of the faithful can only be properly understood by fellow believers who have accepted the authority of God's Church.

Southwell's series of poems about St Peter's suffering after he had betrayed Christ three times are directly relevant to his own dilemma as a Jesuit as he wrestled with the burden of truth. St Peter was an obvious figure for Southwell to choose as the central figure in his poetry, as his experiences most directly resembled those of the Jesuit mission in England. Not only was he the rock on which the papacy was built, but he denied Christ three times, equivocating about his knowledge of the messiah. Never is this more clear than in Peter's third and final denial just before the cock crows when he states 'Man, I know not what thou sayest' (Luke 22:59 (Geneva translation) after he has been linked to Jesus because both come from Galilee, Peter's words quibbling on the various forms of the verb 'to know' (most significantly 'recognize' and 'understand').[93] An early version of his longest poem, 'Saint Peter's Complaint', demonstrates how closely Southwell compared his spiritual burden to that of the chief apostle.[94] Throughout the poem St Peter asks a series of rhetorical questions to chide himself (epiplexis) because of his feeble support for Christ:

> If tyrans bloody thretts had me dismay'd:
> Or smart of cruell torments made me yelde,
> There had bene some pretence to be afray'de,
> I should have fought before I lost the feilde.
> But o infamous foyle: a maydens breathe
> Did blowe me downe and blast my soule to death.
>
> Was I to stay the Churche a Chosen rocke
> That with so soft a gale was overthrowen?

[92] McCoog, *'And Touching Our Society'*, p. 152.

[93] I owe this point to John Kerrigan.

[94] For recent comment on the two versions of the poem see Stegner, *Confession and Memory*, pp. 167–72.

> Was I chief pastour of the faithful flocke,
> To guide their soules that murdred this my owne?[95]

St Peter's failings—in particular denying that he knew Christ to a young woman—should serve as a source of inspiration to Catholic missionaries. If the rock on which the Church was built could have such setbacks and yet achieve so much before his own crucifixion, then surely they could endure equal torment and learn from the agony of his failure? Or, perhaps, they could become more subtle and elusive in order to escape the tyrants who would torment them into betraying the faith? Peter is shown cursing the power of speech, after he has betrayed Christ:

> O impious tongue, no tongue but vipers stinge,
> That could with cursinge othes forsweare thy kinge.
>
> O tongue, the first that did his godhedd sounde,
> How couldst thow utter such detesting wordes,
> That every word was to his hart a wounde,
> And lawncd him deeper then a thowsand swordes?
> What Jewish rage, yea what infernall sprite,
> Could have disgor'gd against him greater spite? (lines 59–66)

Yet again oaths play the fundamental role in establishing the culture in which lying operates. Peter has broken his promise to Christ who had told him that he would deny him three times before the cock crowed in the morning (Luke 22:34). He has betrayed Christ because he is not yet brave enough to stand up to his enemies and so has violated an oath which he is too weak to keep. There are only two ways of avoiding the agony that St Peter experienced: either one needs to tell the truth to the authorities or find a way to circumvent and frustrate their demands without denying God, which means equivocating.

If anyone was in a good position to appreciate such verbal strategies it was Southwell's superior Jesuit on their mission to England, Henry Garnet. On leaving school in 1570 Garnet had been apprenticed to Richard Tottel (c.1528–93), one of the most prominent printers in England who had made his name publishing legal works as well as the manuscript sonnets and lyrics of Wyatt, Surrey, and others so that they could reach the relatively wide audience who had access to print.[96] *Tottel's Miscellany*, as it became known, was printed eight times before 1600 and helped to secure the publisher's fortune. Tottel, 'primarily a legal printer' who was probably also a Catholic, was canny enough to work with writers either side of the religious division.[97] In the same year (1557) that he first published his anthology, Tottel also published the first edition of the works of Thomas More; later he published Richard Grafton's *Chronicle*, which had emerged out of the Protestant political climate of Edward VI's reign (1568).[98] Garnet would have been aware of the

[95] Southwell, *Poems*, pp. 29–31, lines 13–22.
[96] On Tottel see the *ODNB* entry.
[97] Matthew Zarnowiecki, *Fair Copies: Reproducing the English Lyric from Tottel to Shakespeare* (Toronto: Toronto University Press, 2014), p. 22.
[98] Sir Thomas More, *The Workes of Sir T. More . . . written by him in the English Tongue* (London, 1557); Richard Grafton, *A Chronicle at Large . . . of the Affairs of Englande* (London, 1568). On

complicated and divided nature of writing and allegiance after the Reformation, and in *Tottel's Miscellany* he would have witnessed writing that emphasized the ambiguous possibilities of language. Titles given by the printer to manuscript verse highlighted the unstable and perilous state of the lover, often employing legalistic terms. A sequence towards the end of the longer first part in the 1557 edition contains poems with the titles: 'The wounded louer determineth to make sure to his lady for his recure'; 'The louer shewing of the continuall paines that abide within his brest determineth to die because he can haue no redresse'; 'The power of loue ouer gods them selues'; 'Of the sutteltye of craytye louers'; most significantly, 'Of the dissembling louer'; 'The promise of a constant louer'; and 'Against him that had slaundered a gentlewoman with him selfe'. Another verse, two leaves later, has the title 'Of one vniustly defamed'.[99]

'Of the dissembling louer', which may be by Surrey, is in the tradition of female complaint.[100] A longer manuscript version compares the situation of the female speaker to Susannah abused by the lying Elders, a popular biblical story for poets and artists in the sixteenth and seventeenth centuries, especially during the Counter-Reformation. The story is a later addition to the Bible, added to Daniel 13, and was considered Apocryphal by Protestants and so excised from Reformed Bibles, which helps to explain why it assumed significance for Catholics, as a part of the true Bible which the heretics failed to understand.[101] But its appeal was also surely because it was a tale of underhand deception and duplicity created by the abuse of religious power for discreditable motives, with virtue winning out in the end. The female narrator opens the poem describing her ability, finally, to see the truth: 'Girt in my giltlesse gowne as I sit here and sow, / I see that thynges are not in dede as to the outward show'.[102] A striking simile expresses her understanding that people do not always accept responsibility for their actions: 'For with indifferent eyes my self can well discerne, / How some to guide a ship in stormes seke for to take the sterne' (lines 5–6). Some fail to speak out when they could have done so (lines 9–10), and some understand well what is taking place, but the more they know the less they do (lines 11–12). The speaker,

Grafton, see E. J. Devereux, 'Empty Tuns and Unfruitful Grafts: Richard Grafton's Historical Publications', *The Sixteenth Century Journal* 21 (1990), 33–56; David Womersley, *Divinity and State* (Oxford: Oxford University Press, 2010), pp. 71–94.

[99] Richard Tottel, *Songes and Sonettes, written by the ryght honourable Lorde Henry Howard late Earle of Surrey, and other* (London, 1557) (Menston: Scolar, 1970), sigs Aa1v–Bb1r–v; *Tottel's Miscellany*, ed. Hyder Edward Rollins, 2 vols (Cambridge, MA: Harvard University Press, 1965, rpt of 1928), I, pp. 186–93.

[100] On the authorship question see Henry Howard, Earl of Surrey, *Poems*, ed. Emrys Jones (Oxford: Clarendon Press, 1964), pp. 19–20, 128; W. A. Sessions, *Henry Howard, the Poet Earl of Surrey: A Life* (Oxford: Oxford University Press, 1999), p. 197, n. 24. On female complaint see John Kerrigan, ed., *Motives of Woe: Shakespeare and 'Female Complaint': A Critical Anthology* (Oxford: Clarendon Press, 1990).

[101] On the significance of the story of Susannah and the Elders see Dan W. Clanton, *The Good, the Bold, and the Beautiful: The Story of Susanna and Its Renaissance Interpretations* (London: T. & T. Clark, 2006), p. 145.

[102] *Tottel's Miscellany*, ed. Rollins, I, pp. 189–90, no. 243, lines 1–2.

however, can easily make sense of what has happened by lining up current actions against past words:

> But I can beare full well in minde the songe now sounge and past.
> The author whereof came wrapt in a craftye cloke:
> With will to force a flaming fire where he could raise no smoke.
> If power and will had ioynde as it appeareth plaine,
> The truth nor right had tane no place their vertues had ben vain.
> So that you may perceiue, and I may safely se,
> The innocent that giltlesse is, condemned should haue be. (lines 14–20)

Just as Wyatt's love poems were often written with a diction and in a style that connoted political and legal oppression, representing the lover as a subject adrift in a malign world, so is this poem of a 'dissembling lover'.[103] *Tottel's Miscellany* represents and expresses the political and religious anxieties of living through the catastrophic and bewildering changes of the mid-Tudor period.[104] The poem reads, as Bill Sessions has suggested, as if it had been written by a 'good lawyer' who is able to take 'her defensive case to the highest canon of communal myth', which emphasizes the intimate link between law and literature in Tottel's business.[105] She has been assaulted with words from a powerful agent whose desire is to impose his will, and had his plan worked, the twin virtues of truth and right would have been unable to resist him. But, now that she has uncovered the truth her innocence is made plain for all to see. In a world swirling with confusing cross-currents of deception, duplicity, and lies, her words stand apart as the truth, the poem as it was printed in the 1557 edition ending with a bold statement of support for the innocent in a hostile world.[106] The surviving manuscript version concludes with another eighteen lines which ends with an exhortation to trust in God to reveal the truth: 'And he that her preserv'd and let them of their lust / Hath me defendyd hitherto and will do still I trust.'[107] Amanda Holton and Tom McFaul suggest that these last eighteen lines may have been omitted because of the Protestant sensibilities of the scribe or editor, eager not to dwell too much on the story of Susannah and the Elders because of its Catholic associations.[108] This explanation may well be right, but the excision could equally be the result of an editor wanting to show that, in perilous times, and in line with the surrounding poems, truth needs to be represented cunningly.

[103] Stephen Greenblatt's powerful reading remains relevant: *Renaissance Self-Fashioning: From More to Shakespeare* (Chicago: University of Chicago Press, 1980), ch. 3.

[104] Andrew Hadfield, *Literature, Politics and National Identity: Reformation to Renaissance* (Cambridge: Cambridge University Press, 1994), ch. 3; John N. King, *English Reformation Literature: The Tudor Origins of the Protestant Tradition* (Princeton: Princeton University Press, 1982). See below.

[105] Sessions, *Surrey*, p. 198.

[106] Editors have expressed surprise at the omission of the eighteen lines in the manuscript, but the poem makes clear sense in terms of the miscellany as it stands: see *Tottel's Miscellany*, ed. Rollins, II, p. 300.

[107] Cited in *Tottel's Miscellany: Songs and Sonnets of Henry Howard, Earl of Surrey, Sir Thomas Wyatt and Others*, ed. Amanda Holton and Tom McFaul (Harmondsworth: Penguin, 2011), p. 377.

[108] *Tottel's Miscellany*, ed. Holton and McFaul, p. 377.

In such a malign world truth needs allies and to be supported by some of the craftiness of the practised lawyer if it is to survive. The poet demonstrates an awareness that truth will not simply appear of its own accord and that the guardians of the truth need to adopt some of the weapons used by their adversaries. It is not a huge leap from the songs and sonnets of *Tottel's Miscellany* to Garnet's justification of equivocation, especially as Garnet was working in Tottel's printshop as the 1574 edition of the poems was being set, immediately before he sailed for Portugal in 1575 to become a Jesuit for 'reasons unknown'.[109] And, as Stephen Hamrick has argued, 'some writers encoded a Catholic poetics within that text, which both preceded English Jesuit discourse and existed independently of the highly popular Catholic hagiographic tradition', a point that is perhaps even more significant than he suggests.[110]

In supporting a policy of equivocation in his writings and at his trial for his role in the Gunpowder Plot, Garnet was established as the public voice of the Jesuits, duplicitous and underhand, prepared to lie in order to further the Catholic cause of supporting a papal revolution that would overthrow the Protestant regime.[111] Claims that Garnet was a martyr, his face miraculously preserved on an ear of corn, were ridiculed by Protestant authorities as further evidence of Catholic duplicity, whereby lies were deployed to disguise lies and so maintain the excessive power of the Pope.[112] Garnet's defence that he was duty bound to equivocate because he heard about the plot in a confession and that he had no real part in the plans but had actually tried to stop them in some ways made matters worse for Catholics as it exposed the fault line of their loyalties.[113] Confession was a central issue that divided Catholics and Protestants in parishes after the Reformation, making religious conflict visible.[114] For Catholics it was a sacrament and one of the principal functions of the priests hidden throughout England was to hear the confessions of the faithful as a means of establishing the authority of the true Church in a land of heresy; for Protestants, confession was a sign of the Church's overarching power, a challenge to the legitimate authority of the individual and the state.[115] It is at least possible that Shakespeare's joke against equivocation in the Porter's speech in *Macbeth* acknowledges Garnet's situation and his defence of his actions: 'Knock, knock. Who's there in th'other devil's name? Faith, here's an equivocator, that could swear in both the scales against either scale, who committed treason enough for God's sake, yet could not equivocate to Heaven: O come in, equivocator.'[116] The

---

[109] *ODNB* entry.

[110] Stephen Hamrick, '*Tottel's Miscellany* and the English Reformation', *Criticism* 44 (2004), 329–61, p. 330. Hamrick does not mention Garnet in his suggestive essay.

[111] *State Trials*, I, pp. 217–358, at p. 223; Caraman, *Garnet*, pp. 348–419. On Jesuit defences of the plot see Robert Appelbaum, *Terrorism Before the Letter: Mythography and Political Violence in England, Scotland, and France, 1559–1642* (Oxford: Oxford University Press, 2015), pp. 142–6.

[112] Robert Pricket, *The Iesuits Miracles, Or New Popish Wonders* (London, 1607), sigs A4v–B3r.

[113] *State Trials*, I, pp. 245–6; Caraman, *Garnet*, pp. 415–16.

[114] A. G. Dickens, *Lollards and Protestants in the Diocese of York, 1509–1558* (London: Hambledon, 1982, rpt of 1959), pp. 28–9, 47–9, *passim*.

[115] Cummings, *Literary Culture*, pp. 338–55.

[116] William Shakespeare, *Macbeth*, ed. Nicholas Brooke (Oxford: Oxford University Press, 1990), 2.2.7–11; Zagorin, *Ways of Lying*, pp. 193–4.

audience witness the secrecy of sacramental confession brought out into the open for all to see, and the equivocator has to be identified as Garnet given the proximity of the first performances of the play to the trial. Garnet's defence is exposed as treason by the porter, and, for all his clever eloquence, he cannot save himself from descending to Hell, because his words, like those of the witches, are equivocal. There is a definite—albeit tangential—relationship between the treason of the equivocator and the plot of the play, just as there was between Garnet and the course of the Gunpowder Plot.[117]

The result of the plot and the subsequent trials was that James sought to force the hand of Catholics through the imposition of the Oath of Allegiance, which known recusants and those who had not attended church for a year were made to swear.[118] As I have already indicated, in many ways the imposition of the oath of 1606 was the logical outcome of the Oath of Supremacy.[119] Imprisoned Catholics had been forced to answer the 'bloody question' since the late 1570s, which placed them in an impossible dilemma.[120] They would be asked what they would do if the Pope, claiming that it was his duty to bring England back into the fold, stated that the only way he could achieve this was by sending over an invasion force. Would they be loyal to the Queen or their spiritual leader? If the accused said the Pope he or she would be condemned as a traitor as well as providing an 'answer that no Catholic Prince of that day would have countenanced if turned against himself'. If the answer was the Queen then the Church was betrayed—like Peter denying Christ—and the suffering of the priests in vain.[121] Now this dilemma would have to be faced by ordinary subjects who would be required to declare their loyalty as a matter of course. The subsequent struggle between the inquisitorial practices demanded by those administering the oath and the accusatorial nature of the common law courts eventually led to the triumph of the latter and the establishment of the 'right to silence' by the end of the century.[122]

The Oath, following on from the 'bloody question', made law on 22 June 1606, less than two months after Henry Garnet had been hanged, drawn, and quartered in St Paul's Churchyard (3 May), gave subjects the same stark choice. The loyal subject had to acknowledge James as the 'lawful and rightful King of this realm' and publicly declare that the Pope had no power to depose the King or to 'discharge any of his Subjects of their allegiance and obedience to his Majesty', a confrontational formula.[123] In addition, the loyal subject had to state that the Pope had no right to excommunicate the King or to grant 'any absolution of the said subjects from their obedience', and to inform the authorities of any knowledge of 'all treasons and

---

[117] Fraser, *Gunpowder Plot*, pp. 181, 286; Tesimond, *Gunpowder Plot*, pp. 191–2; Gerard, *History*, p. ccxxxv.

[118] Nicholls, *Investigating Gunpowder Plot*, p. 49; Clarence J. Ryan, 'The Jacobean Oath of Allegiance and English Lay Catholics', *CHR* 28 (1942), 159–83, p. 161.

[119] Kerrigan, *Shakespeare's Binding Language*, pp. 417–18.

[120] Zagorin, *Ways of Lying*, pp. 192–3; Shapiro, *1606*, p. 230.

[121] Devlin, *Southwell*, p. 166; A. D. Nuttall, *Shakespeare the Thinker* (New Haven: Yale University Press, 2007), pp. 16–17.

[122] O'Reilly, 'England Limits the Right to Silence', pp. 418–19. See above, p. 22.

[123] Ryan, 'Jacobean Oath', p. 162.

traitorous conspiracies'. The most significant sections required the subject to denounce the claims of the papacy without reservation:

> And I do believe and in conscience am resolved, that neither the Pope nor any person whatsoever, hath power to absolve me of this oath, or any part thereof, which I acknowledge by good and full authority to bee lawfully ministered unto me, and do renounce all pardons and dispensations to the contrary: And all these things I do plainly and sincerely acknowledge and swear, according to these express words by me spoken, and according to the plain and common sense and understanding of the same words, without any Equivocation, or mental evasion, or secret reservation whatsoever: And I doe make this recognition and acknowledgement heartily, willingly, and truly, upon the true faith of a Christian: So help me God.[124]

The Act was explicitly designed to close any possible loopholes so that the act of swearing the oath meant that it had to take precedence over other oaths (such as those to the Church). Thomas Morton in his response to the Gunpowder Plot had already argued that Catholics were subject to the will of the Pope and that an oath to the pontiff invalidated any oath to temporal powers.[125] The loyal subject now had to swear that he or she had not equivocated or applied mental reservation in declaring their loyalty, removing the possibility of ambiguity and deception. The oath was disseminated widely in various proclamations as numerous anti-recusancy laws were passed in order to force the hand of subjects who might be wavering in their loyalty.[126] Catholics, who had eagerly anticipated James's reign, hoping that it would herald a new age of toleration, were dismayed.[127] Many had to pay exorbitant fines which helped fund James's generosity towards his favourites, and the oath was widely viewed as a cynical way of supporting James's munificent style of rule.[128] The Catholic community was now divided even more widely than before, as Michael Questier has argued. The authorities claimed that the oath was a moderate demand, demanding temporal not spiritual obedience to the crown. In practice, however, it ensured that a specifically Protestant public sphere would emerge. In effect it turned 'a denial of the deposing power into what could plausibly be regarded as a rejection of the papal primacy', and was, therefore, 'the ideological equivalent of the oath of supremacy'.[129] Conversey, it undoubtedly helped unite loyal Protestants against the fear of the enemy within. According to W. B. Patterson, one of 'James's conspicuous achievements was to bring English Protestants together

---

[124] *Statutes*, 3 James I, c 4.

[125] Morton, *Exact Discoverie*, p. 45; Matthew Sutcliffe, *A Challenge Concerning the Romish Church, her Doctrine & Practises* (London, 1602), p. 228.

[126] *Stuart Royal Proclamations*, 84, 96, 111, 118.

[127] Tesimond, *Gunpowder Plot*, pp. 21–9; Nicholls, *Investigating Gunpowder Plot*, Pt II.

[128] John J. La Rocca, 'James I and his Catholic Subjects, 1606–1612: Some Financial Implications', *RH* 18 (1987), 251–62.

[129] Michael C. Questier, 'Loyalty, Religion and State Power in Early Modern England: English Romanism and the Jacobean Oath of Allegiance', *HJ* 40 (1997), 311–29, pp. 320–1. See also Lemon, *Treason by Words*, pp. 110–11; Glenn Burgess, *Absolute Monarchy and the Stuart Constitution* (New Haven: Yale University Press, 1996), pp. 101–2; Roger Lockyer, *The Early Stuarts: A Political History of England, 1603–1642* (London: Longman, 1989), pp. 285–6; Stefania Tutino, *Law and Conscience: Catholicism in Early Modern England, 1570–1625* (Farnham: Ashgate, 2007), ch. 5.

in a common front which, for the moment at least, obscured the theological and ecclesiological differences among them'.[130] Therefore, it is hardly surprising that the establishment of the oath led to a pamphlet war between the British King and Catholic Europe, nor that it has been a source of controversy ever since, some seeing the oath as a first indication of tolerant secularism, others as a cunning sectarian manoeuvre.[131]

III

Certainly, concern with lying and duplicity was rife in 1606. Thomas Dekker's *The Seuen Deadly Sinnes of London*, published that year, is a work directly concerned with the aftermath of the Gunpowder Plot, as the author links the evil behaviour which has engulfed the capital to that which caused the plague in 1603, the subject of his earlier *The Wonderful Year* (1603).[132] London needs to awake from its slumbers and combat the seven-headed beast of the Apocalypse that threatens to overwhelm it.[133] After the initial entrance of the chariots carrying the sins and their attendant figures on the first day, the first sin to be paraded on the second is lying, indicating that Dekker saw this as the chief means of London's downfall in 1606. Once established, lying proliferates and overwhelms the life of the city:

> How quickly after the Art of *Lying* was once publiquely profest, were false *Weights* and false *Measures* inuented! and they haue since done as much hurt to the inhabitants of Cities, as the inuention of *Gunnes* hath done to their walles: for though a *Lye* haue but short legs (like a Dwarfes) yet it goes farre in a little time, . . . the reason is, that *Truth* had euer but one *Father*, but *Lyes* are a thousand mens *Bastards*, and are begotten euery where.[134]

Lying undermines the basic social building blocks, the family and commerce, until what was once based on truth is now defined by falsehood. Lying, founded on false oaths ('*Crutches*, vpon which *Lyes* (like lame soldiers) go, & neede no other pasport'), leads to a series of interrelated crimes: '*Lying* is Father to *Falshood*, and Grandsire to *Periury: Frawd* (with two faces) is his Daughter, a very Monster:

---

[130] Patterson, *James VI and I*, pp. 75–123.

[131] Willson, *King James*, p. 228; Lemon, *Treason by Words*, pp. 110–11; Questier, 'Loyalty', p. 329; Alexandra Walsham, *Church Papists: Catholicism, Conformity and Confessional Polemic in Early Modern England* (Woodbridge: Boydell and Brewer, 1993), pp. 84–5; Marcy L. North, 'Anonymity's Subject: James I and the Debate over the Oath of Allegiance', *NLH* 33 (2002), 215–33.

[132] Thomas Dekker, *The Seuen Deadly Sinnes of London Drawne in Seuen Seuerall Coaches, Through the Seuen Seuerall Gates of the Citie Bringing the Plague with them* (London, 1606), sig. A3r; Thomas Dekker, *The Wonderfull Yeare, Wherein is shewed the Picture of London, Lying Sicke of the Plague* (1603). The link between plague and bad behaviour was a familiar one: see also Bullein, *Pestilence*, p. 37. On *The Seven Deadly Sinnnes of London* see Manley, *Literature and Culture in Early Modern London*, pp. 362–3; J. F. Merritt, 'Introduction: Perceptions and Portrayals of London, 1598–1720', in J. F. Merritt, ed., *Imagining Early Modern London: Perceptions and Portrayals of the City from Stow to Strype, 1598–1720* (Cambridge: Cambridge University Press, 2001), pp. 1–24, at pp. 16–17.

[133] Dekker, *Seuen Deadly Sinnes*, sig. A4r.   [134] Dekker, *Seuen Deadly Sinnes*, sig. C4r.

Treason (with haires like Snakes) is his kinseman'.[135] Dekker combines two
startling images, that of crippled soldiers using oaths for crutches which also then
serve as passports enabling them to roam freely through the land, to show that the
Gunpowder Plot has enveloped London in lies and treason, just as beggars are
engulfing England.[136] Dekker addresses a loaded question to the city: 'Haue so
many *Triple-pointed* darts of *Treason* bin shot at the heads of thy *Princes,* because
they would not take *Truth* out of thy *Temples...*?'[137] The triple treason would
appear to be a reference to the plan to blow up the Houses of Parliament; the
attempt to lead a wider uprising; and the trial of Father Garnet for spreading the
doctrine of equivocation. Religion is the key and now lying is everywhere. Dekker
exploits the obvious pun on lying to show how promiscuous lying has become and
how hard it is to control once moral restraints have been removed: 'for thou
sufferest *Religion* to lye with *Hipocrisie: Charity* to lye with *Ostentation: Friendship*
to lye with *Hollow-heartednes:* the *Churle* to lye with *Simony: Iustice* to lye with
Bribery, and last of all, *Conscience* to lye with euerie one'.[138] Conscience is now
infected, as lying has spread like the pox to undermine the healthy body politic.[139]

Dekker was probably the most committed Protestant writer of pamphlets and
plays in early Jacobean England.[140] He was eager to expose the danger of the subtle
Catholics and he had already written *The Whore of Babylon* (1605), to demonstrate
the ever present threat of the assassination of the monarch, reminding his audiences
of attempts on Elizabeth's life, before he turned to the sinfulness of London as a
cause of the Gunpowder Plot.[141] There the Empress of Babylon (the Whore),
'vnder whom is figured Rome', boasts to her satellite kings that 'From our mouth
flow riuers of blasphemy / And lies'.[142]

For many Catholics equivocation was a legitimate strategy for the truly faithful to
adopt under illegitimate pressure from hostile heretics; for the Protestant authorities
it was simply another means of peddling lies to undermine the true Church.[143] Ben
Jonson's epigram 'On Inviting a Friend to Supper', first published in the volume of
Epigrams (1616), may have been written in the wake of his imprisonment in 1597
after his part in the scandalous lost play *The Isle of Dogs,* written with Thomas
Nashe.[144] But it is also surely a reflection on his subsequent interrogation in front of

---

[135] Dekker, *Seuen Deadly Sinnes,* sig. C4r. For a sophisticated analysis of the relationship between
Protestantism and ideas of the monstrous see Crawford, *Marvelous Protestantism,* pp. 1–27.

[136] On attitudes to crippled soldiers and passports see A. L. Beier, *Masterless Men: The Vagrancy
Problem in England, 1560–1640* (London: Methuen, 1985), pp. 75–6, 142–4.

[137] Dekker, *Seuen Deadly Sinnes,* sig. C4r. Oaths and promises were frequently associated with the
number three, and the trinity: see Kerrigan, *Shakespeare's Binding Language,* ch. 12.

[138] Dekker, *Seuen Deadly Sinnes,* sig. D1r.

[139] On the cultural and political significance of the pox see Margaret Healy, *Fictions of Disease:
Bodies, Plagues and Politics* (Basingstoke: Macmillan, 2001), ch. 5.

[140] Curtis Perry, *The Making of Jacobean Culture* (Cambridge: Cambridge University Press, 1997),
pp. 179–82.

[141] Susan E. Krantz, 'Thomas Dekker's Political Commentary in *The Whore of Babylon'*, *SEL* 35
(1995), 271–91.

[142] Thomas Dekker, *The Whore of Babylon* (London, 1607), sigs A2r, B1r.

[143] Sommerville, 'New Art of Lying', p. 180; Kilroy, *Campion: A Scholarly Life,* p. 156.

[144] Ian Donaldson, *Ben Jonson: A Life* (Oxford: Oxford University Press, 2011), pp. 113–14.

the Privy Council after he had supper with some of the Gunpowder Plotters at the Irish Boy on 9 October 1605, just under a month before the plot was exposed.[145] Jonson praised the man who uncovered the plot, Sir William Parker, Lord Monteagle, in another epigram, arguing that the country should 'have raised / An obelisk of column to thy name', but, in the absence of a stone monument, the poet is glad that he can write a poem in praise of the 'saver of my country'.[146] 'On Inviting a Friend to Supper', however, is a defence of liberty that places the pleasures of the exchanges possible when friends can hold all things in common against the brutal realpolitik of an age in which duplicity, untruthfulness, and lying have become the norm.[147] Jonson extols the virtues of truth-telling as he explains the course of the evening to his unnamed friend: the long list of expensive foodstuffs that make up the numerous courses that they will consume has its origins in three Martial invitation poems.[148] The poem is also a serious joke about Jonson's gluttony and his desire to be honest, at least on this social occasion. While Jonson's servant reads from Virgil, Tacitus, or Livy, the two men will be able to talk openly about the significance of such writing and, presumably, its contemporary application: 'Of which we'll speak our minds amidst our meat'.[149] Jonson draws attention to his fondness for drink and its inspirational qualities: 'But that which most doth take my muse and me / Is a pure cup of rich Canary wine, / Which is the Mermaid's now, but shall be mine' (lines 28–30), which seems straightforward enough given John Aubrey's description of Jonson as a man who 'would many times exceed in drinke: Canarie was his beloved liquour'.[150] But the key detail may be the movement from the public space of the tavern, where Jonson was known to hold court to his friends and admirers from some time before 1611 onwards, to the private space of his own house.[151] In doing so the poem gestures towards a personal time and place where the truth can be told. Jonson leaves behind the sociable nature of a culture of intoxication, restricting the convivial intellectual symposium to a conversation between two friends, because the private space will permit them to speak more truthfully.[152]

---

[145] Donaldson, *Jonson*, p. 223.

[146] *Jonson*, V, p. 141 (lines 1–2, 10); Donaldson, *Jonson*, p. 219.

[147] 'Friends Hold All Things in Common' is one of Erasmus's adages: for its significance see Kathy Eden, *Friends Hold All Things in Common: Tradition, Intellectual Property, and the* Adages *of Erasmus* (New Haven: Yale University Press, 2001).

[148] Victoria Moul, *Jonson, Horace and the Classical Tradition* (Cambridge: Cambridge University Press, 2010), pp. 54–63. For the broader significance of the classical references in the poem see Susanna Braund, 'Complaint, Epigram and Satire', in Patrick Cheney and Philip Hardie, eds, *The Oxford History of Classical Reception in English Literature, 1558–1660* (Oxford: Oxford University Press, 2015), pp. 345–72, at pp. 365–6.

[149] *Jonson*, V, p. 167 (line 23). On the political significance of Roman history, see Blair Worden, 'Ben Jonson among the Historians', in Peter Lake and Kevin Sharpe, eds, *Culture and Politics in Early Stuart England* (Basingstoke: Macmillan, 1994), pp. 67–89.

[150] John Aubrey, *Brief Lives with An Apparatus for the Lives of our English Mathematical Writers*, ed. Kate Bennett, 2 vols (Oxford: Oxford University Press, 2015), I, p. 363.

[151] On Jonson at the Mermaid see Donaldson, *Jonson*, pp. 262–5; Michelle O'Callaghan, *The English Wits: Literature and Sociability in Early Modern England* (Cambridge: Cambridge University Press, 2007), pp. 1, 76–9.

[152] See Phil Withington, 'Introduction: Cultures of Intoxication', in Phil Withington and Angela McShane, eds, *Cultures of Intoxication* (Oxford: Oxford University Press, 2014), pp. 9–33.

Accordingly, he suggests that even this poem, which is honest in its use of autobio-graphical detail, may not be without its deceptions and duplicities, and withholding of the whole truth: 'Tobacco, nectar, or the Thespian spring / Are all but Luther's beer to this I sing' (lines 33–4). Jonson contrasts the canary wine that they have brought to their private dinner to other, baser pleasures which might be enjoyed elsewhere, comparing them to ordinary fare, Luther's beer. Beer was often associated with the Reformed faith and with Puritans.[153] Canary wine is therefore implicitly associated with Spain and Catholicism, suggesting that the dinner of friends could have a religious significance, even if it is not as foolish and dangerous as the supper in the Irish Boy, a possibility made more explicit in the closing lines:

> And we shall have no Poley or Parrot by,
> Nor shall our cups make any guilty men:
>   But, at our parting, we will be as when
> We innocently met. No simple word
> That shall be uttered at our mirthful board
> Shall make us sad next morning, or affright
> The liberty that we'll enjoy tonight. (lines 36–42)

We will never learn what these simple words were or what they might have been, but the poem suggests that it is better for the interlocutors that they remain secret.[154] Robert Poley and Henry Parrot were government informers: Poley, of whom more evidence survives, had played a significant role in the Babington Plot which led to the execution of Mary Stuart in 1587, and been involved in the tavern brawl that led to the death of Christopher Marlowe in 1593; Parrot appears in government records as a spy in 1600.[155]

It is possible—indeed likely—that Jonson was being economical with the truth in the poem, as he may have acted as an informer himself after the Gunpowder Plot in exchange for his liberty, publicly representing himself as one of the persecuted, which adds a further layer to this nuanced representation of the complicated relationship between truth-telling and lying.[156] The reference to Poley and Parrot takes us back to Jonson's imprisonment in 1597, when he appears to have resisted interrogation successfully, something he proudly advertised in his work, boasting to William Drummond that his 'judges could get nothing of him' even though 'They placed two damned Villains to catch advantage of him'.[157] Whatever the truth, and however cunning, duplicitous, and equivocal Jonson was being in representing

[153] *Jonson*, V, p. 168.
[154] See O'Callaghan, *English Wits*, p. 78; Colin Burrow, 'Ben Jonson', in Claude Rawson, ed., *The Cambridge Companion to English Poets* (Cambridge: Cambridge University Press, 2011), pp. 122–39, at p. 129.
[155] Charles Nicholl, *The Reckoning: The Murder of Christopher Marlowe* (London: Picador, 1993, rpt of 1992), pp. 133–46, *passim*; Alford, *Watchers*, pp. 198, 224–7, 317; Mark Eccles, 'Jonson and the Spies', *RES* 13 (1937), 385–97; *ODNB* entry on Henry Parrot.
[156] Donaldson, *Jonson*, p. 223.
[157] *Jonson*, V, p. 373. Jonson has the knaves and rogues land on the Isle of Dogs in the co-authored comedy *Eastward Ho* (*c.*1605), a reference to the play that led to his imprisonment in the Marshalsea; Donaldson, *Jonson*, p. 117.

himself, 'On Inviting a Friend to Supper' is a poem published in the aftermath of the Oath of Allegiance. The speaker longs for a time and a place where he is not forced to declare his hand; where he can overindulge and no one will mind what he says; and he has no reason to worry that his words will return to haunt him. This is a space where liberty flourishes—albeit briefly—and the duplicities of the outside world, to which the poem draws attention, are irrelevant. In conversation the two men are not bound by the burden of truth and lying, but can articulate their opinions without consequences as they will leave the meal as innocent as when they came.

Jonson's plays written in the early years after the accession of James are, hardly surprisingly, intimately concerned with issues of truth and lying, responses to the frequent plots that were hatched to force the new King's hand to improve the conditions of his Catholic subjects.[158] Jonson represents a world of conspiracy in which it is not clear who is telling the truth and who is lying: the conspirators and their supporters or the government under Sir Robert Cecil.[159] *Volpone* can be read as central to Jonson's subtle, paranoid art, written in the wake of the Gunpowder Plot.[160] As Richard Dutton has argued, the protagonist stands for both Robert Cecil, commonly identified as a fox, especially after Edmund Spenser's *Mother Hubberd's Tale* (published 1591) represented Cecil's father, William, Lord Burghley, this way.[161] Jonson's annotated copy of Spenser's *Works* survives: *Mother Hubberd's Tale* is the only one of Spenser's shorter poems with significant underlinings and notes, demonstrating that Jonson read it carefully.[162] In making the comparison of his protagonist to the fox, Jonson is also suggesting that he too is a cunning beast, more cunning than Cecil even in outwitting his enemies and critics.

The play is set in a world in which no one can be sure what is really true and what is fictitious, constructed by liars. Volpone's lies are indiscriminate, being both small and large, and, in the end, he is unable to tell the difference between the two, nor how much the consequences matter, one reason why the play unsettles so many readers eager to discover a moral core and unable to locate one.[163] When the elderly, deaf Corbaccio pronounces Mosca, Volpone's servant, to be honest, in front of his apparently supine, dying master, Mosca responds, 'You do lie, sir', knowing that Corbaccio cannot hear what he is saying, but Volpone can.[164] There may, of course, be a further joke based on the use of 'lying' in the 'Treatise of Equivocation', which Jonson would surely have known given his connections, because Volpone, the only one who hears Mosca's words, is both supine and

---

[158] See, in particular, Worden, 'Ben Jonson among the Historians'; Blair Worden, 'Politics in *Catiline*: Jonson and His Sources', in Martin Butler, ed., *Re-Presenting Ben Jonson: Text, History, Performance* (Basingstoke: Macmillan, 1999), pp. 152–73.

[159] Dutton, *Jonson*, pp. 66–72, 110–15, *passim*.

[160] For the influence of the plot on literary works see Appelbaum, *Terrorism*, pp. 64–5.

[161] Dutton, *Jonson*, pp. 75–82.

[162] James A. Riddell and Stanley Stewart, *Jonson's Spenser: Evidence and Historical Criticism* (Pittsburgh: Duquesne University Press, 1995), pp. 52–4, 147.

[163] See the neat overview in James Loxley, *The Complete Critical Guide to Ben Jonson* (London: Routledge, 2002), pp. 69–74.

[164] *Volpone* 1.4.124 (*Jonson*, III, p. 66).

being duplicitous. Corbaccio, a self-interested fortune hunter, as are all who come to see the 'dying' Volpone, does not know what honesty is and so cannot recognize its lack in the devious Mosca; is genuinely deceived by Mosca's appearance of honesty into assuming that he has encountered a straightforward servant; or, most likely, is flattering Mosca, not knowing that he will not get what he wants by doing so because the joke is really on him. Volpone and Mosca can enjoy this jest together, but they will soon be at odds as no one can be trusted in the obsessively devious world of the early modern city, whether Venice or London.[165]

Of course, in such a context people are most easily fooled if they deal in lies and deception themselves and there is an obvious and satisfying irony in Corvino prostituting his virtuous and resistant wife, Celia, whom he jealously guards in normal circumstances, in the hope of future gain. Volpone's attempt to woo her with his *carpe diem* lyric, 'Song, To Celia', makes the game of lying in the play considerably more problematic still. The poem, reprinted as the fifth poem in *The Forest* in the folio of Jonson's *Works* (1616), is included in the play to present the reader with a moral conundrum, one that can be related to issues of spying and conspiracy as well as sexual behaviour. 'Song, To Celia' is an imitation of Catullus's poem to Lesbia, a breathless verse urging the speaker's sweetheart to abandon everything and imagine a future of the delights of endless 'kissing'.[166] Jonson's controlled and elegant adaptation, 'Come, my Celia, let us prove, / While we can, the sports of love', in contrast, 'precedes an attempted rape'.[167] Art is put in the service of deception, a means to a bad end, which does not discredit the poem itself, but the motives of the speaker. The audience witnesses something that should be true and beautiful transformed into base and evil desires. The subsequent debate between Volpone and Celia shows that Volpone has taken writers such as Catullus rather too seriously and believes that the sensual pleasure of sex and money can be permanent and so he cannot hear or understand her moral discourse. Jonson makes a related point in *Timber, or Discoveries*, Jonson's 'commonplace book', which further demonstrates how literature and politics were closely intertwined in Jonson's imagination.[168] Glossing *'Stare a partibus'* ('To stand by one's party'), Jonson comments:

> Some actions, be they never so beautiful and generous, are often obscured by base and vile misconstructions, either out of envy or ill nature, that judgeth of others as of itself. Nay, the times are so wholly grown to be either partial, or malicious, that if he be a friend, all sits well about him, his very vices shall be virtues; if an enemy or of the contrary faction, nothing is good or tolerable in him; insomuch that we care not to discredit and shame our judgements to soothe our passions.[169]

[165] On Venice and London in Jonson see Richard Dutton, '*Volpone*: Venice in London, London in Venice', in Andrew Hiscock, ed., *Mighty Europe 1400–1700: Writing an Early Modern Continent* (Frankfurt: Peter Lang, 2007), pp. 133–51; David C. McPherson, *Shakespeare, Jonson and the Myth of Venice* (Newark: University of Delaware Press, 1990), pp. 91–116.
[166] *The Poems of Catullus*, trans. Peter Whigham (Harmondsworth: Penguin, 1966), 5 (p. 55).
[167] *Jonson*, V, p. 222.   [168] *Jonson*, VII, p. 438.
[169] *Discoveries*, 370–6 (*Jonson*, VII, p. 517).

Significant words that define debates in religion, philosophy, and art characterize this judgement on the dominance of factions and factional politics in Jacobean England. Beauty and generosity have become irrelevant as mankind debases itself and passion triumphs over reason, transforming vices into virtues and virtues into vices, depending on one's allegiance, ending all hope of toleration.[170] The truth has been lost in a welter of lies, and it is the poet's duty to point this problem out and so help the public better understand the forces that assail proper values.

Celia exhorts Volpone to understand that there are higher spiritual values, using explicitly Catholic language:

> If you have ears that will be pierced—or eyes,
> That can be opened—a heart, may be touched—
> Or any part that yet sounds man about you—
> If you have touch of holy saints—or heaven—
> Do me the grace to let me 'scape.—If not,
> Be bountiful and kill me.[171]

Celia pleads to God and the saints and, if mercy cannot be granted her, asks to be martyred, replicating the dilemma that Catholics like Jonson felt after the Gunpowder Plot and the imposition of the Oath of Allegiance. And there is surely an allusion to the failed—or invented—coup in Celia's lament that her beauty was the cause of Volpone's desire: 'flay my face, / Or poison it with ointments, for seducing / Your blood to this rebellion'.[172] Her shocked incredulity that something so good could have such bad effects would appear to explain the terrible situation of English Catholics, who were sure that they were in possession of the truth, but dismayed that this should cause them such harm, which is why so many hoped that James would eventually see the light.[173] Furthermore, the seduction of beauty that leads to rebellion distances Jonson, as a Catholic loyal to the crown, from the plotters whose response to the true and the beautiful was ugly, wrong, and destructive. Volpone cannot hear this language and brings us back to comedy with his misunderstanding of her words as an attack on his manliness: 'Think me cold, / Frozen, and impotent'.[174] But he is no longer in control of the action as Mosca has started to plot against his master, hiding Bonario in the bedroom, who now leaps out and confronts Volpone. In the same way the audience is no longer under Volpone's spell, realizing his moral and practical limitations, just as in Shakespeare's history play any enjoyment of Richard III's antics surely vanish when he plans to murder the two princes.[175]

[170] For the significance of these issues see Christopher Tilmouth, *Passion's Triumph over Reason: A History of the Moral Imagination from Spenser to Rochester* (Oxford: Oxford University Press, 2007), ch. 1; Alexandra Walsham, 'Cultures of Coexistence in Early Modern England: History, Literature and Religious Toleration', *The Seventeenth Century* 28 (2013), 115–37; Quentin Skinner, *Visions of Politics*, 3 vols (Cambridge: Cambridge University Press, 2002), III, ch. 4.
[171] *Volpone* 3.7.239–44 (*Jonson*, III, p. 123).   [172] *Volpone* 3.7.251–3 (*Jonson*, III, p. 124).
[173] Shell, *Catholicism, Controversy*, p. 142. See also Monta, *Martyrdom and Literature*, p. 210, on the gendering of martyrdom.
[174] *Volpone* 3.7.259–60 (*Jonson*, III, p. 124).
[175] Andrew Hadfield, *Shakespeare and Republicanism* (Cambridge: Cambridge University Press, 2005), pp. 124–9.

The connection between these two famous liars may be more than coincidence as Richard Burbage played both roles, which could well have been written with his acting style in mind.[176]

Until he tries to rape Celia, Volpone has lived in a world of people who have debased themselves and become beasts like him, unable to understand the language of reason or of religion, their lies and deceptions transforming them into animals. But now he encounters a different world of beauty and truth which he misrecognizes as unmanning him whereas, in fact, it gives him the opportunity to regain his humanity. For Jonson, however, the world is so confused and inverted that values are no longer clear and truth and lies have often changed places. In many ways it is better if people cannot understand Celia's language, as the profession of true religion in England is a dangerous activity. Jonson himself may be the clever fox who has outwitted the authorities and been prepared to swear the Oath of Allegiance, even if he stopped short at taking communion.[177] The price he paid, as he acknowledges in the play, is his spirituality, and, therefore, the ability to distinguish truth from lies.

IV

Jonson was not alone in having to reimagine his relationship to truth and lies by the events that led from the first Jesuit missions of the 1580s to the widespread adoption of the practice of equivocation, the Gunpowder Plot and the Oath of Allegiance. At times, however, the relationship between those events and their significance is difficult to uncover. One series of events in particular, that culminated in the two trials of Robert Carr, Earl of Somerset, and his wife, Frances Howard, played a significant role in defining the understanding of lying and its relationship to justice and the monarchy in the early seventeenth century. And, of course, such a fascinating scandal also helped establish the character of Jacobean public literature in its wake, as has often been noted.[178] Interest in the two court cases has continued and still remains strong, as a wealth of popular histories, novels, and television programmes indicates.[179]

---

[176] Stanley Wells, *Great Shakespeare Actors: Burbage to Branagh* (Oxford: Oxford University Press, 2015), pp. 17–20; Bart Van Es, *Shakespeare in Company* (Oxford: Oxford University Press, 2013), p. 234.

[177] Donaldson, *Jonson*, pp. 258–9.

[178] See the two excellent studies: David Lindley, *The Trials of Frances Howard: Fact and Fiction at the Court of King James* (London: Routledge, 1993); Alastair Bellany, *The Politics of Court Scandal in Early Modern England: News Culture and the Overbury Affair, 1603–1660* (Cambridge: Cambridge University Press, 2002). See also Johanna Rickman, *Love, Lust, and License in Early Modern England: Illicit Sex and the Nobility* (Farnham: Ashgate, 2008), pp. 74–5.

[179] See, for example, Philip Gibbs, *King's Favourite: The Love Story of Robert Carr and Lady Essex* (London: Hutchinson, 1909); Brian Harris, *Passion, Poison, and Power: The Mysterious Death of Sir Thomas Overbury* (London: Wildy, Simmonds & Hill, 2010); Jean Plaidy, *The Murder in the Tower: The Story of Frances, Countess of Essex* (New York: Random House, 2012, rpt of 1964). An episode of the BBC genealogy series, 'Who Do You Think You Are?', which featured the actor Celia Imrie, a

Frances Howard (1592/3–1632) was the daughter of Thomas Howard, the first Earl of Suffolk; granddaughter of Thomas Howard, fourth Duke of Norfolk who was executed for his part in the Ridolfi Plot in 1572; and great-granddaughter of Henry Howard, the Earl of Surrey, author of poems published in *Tottel's Miscellany* and the last aristocrat to be executed by Henry VIII.[180] On 5 January 1606 at the age of fourteen she was married to the thirteen-year-old Robert Devereux, third Earl of Essex, son of the second Earl who had been executed in 1601, the ceremony including a masque specially written by Ben Jonson, *The Hymenaei, or The Masque of Hymen*. From 1607 to 1609 he went on a European tour, the marriage apparently not having been consummated. By the time Essex returned his wife had started an affair with Robert Carr, favourite of James I, and was eager to have the marriage annulled. Essex appears initially to have agreed to this course of action and a plan to argue for a divorce on the grounds of his temporary impotence, caused by witchcraft, which rendered him helpless in front of his wife, but did not affect him on other occasions, a convenient solution which would not affect his chances of making a desirable second marriage.[181] The case, which had no exact legal precedent, came before a special commission headed by George Abbot (1562–1633), Archbishop of Canterbury from 1611 until his death, who had attended Garnet on the scaffold as Dean of Winchester. The commission consisted of three other bishops, and six civilian lawyers and judges. After much argument the annulment was eventually agreed on 25 September 1613, largely through the intervention of the King, despite the strong opposition of the Archbishop. Carr, now Earl of Somerset, and Howard were married in a lavish ceremony on 26 December 1613, with another masque written by Ben Jonson, *The Irish Masque at Court*.[182] Things soon took a turn for the worse. A friend of Carr's, Sir Thomas Overbury, who strongly opposed the match and advised Carr against marrying the Countess of Essex, was imprisoned in the Tower in April 1613, where he started to become seriously ill with stomach problems, after he refused to act as ambassador to Russia, much to the anger of the King. Overbury may have declined the office for a number of reasons: perhaps he felt that his prior duty was to his friend in London; perhaps he was already ill; or perhaps he realized that he was being excluded as a threat to the King's plans.[183] He died during the annulment proceedings on 14 September 1613.

Rumours soon spread that Overbury's death was the result of foul play (his corpse had been particularly foul smelling) and, by autumn 1615, as James was replacing Somerset with a new favourite, George Villiers, later to be created first Duke of Buckingham, evidence emerged that Overbury had been poisoned in the Tower. Despite the efforts of James to remain neutral a new trial had to be held at which it became clear that Overbury had been poisoned by a Mrs Turner who had

---

descendant of Frances Howard, was broadcast in 2012 (http://www.bbc.co.uk/programmes/b01n7m49) (accessed 12 May 2015).

[180] *ODNB* entry.   [181] *State Trials*, II, p. 800.
[182] David Lindley, 'Embarrassing Ben: The Masques for Frances Howard', *ELR* 16 (1986), 434–59.
[183] Lindley, *Howard*, p. 146.

given him lots of jellies and tarts with (probably) sulphuric acid in them. Mrs Turner also introduced Frances Howard, now Countess of Somerset, to the notorious astrologer Simon Forman, who died before the trial so was not required to give evidence.[184] Even so, his association with the Countess did her no favours, and encouraged further speculation about her dubious associations.[185] The Countess eventually confessed that she was guilty of ordering Overbury's murder. The Earl and Countess were condemned to death but this was transmuted to life imprisonment and they remained in the Tower until pardoned and freed in 1622, living in relative obscurity until Frances Howard died in 1632 and Carr in 1645.[186]

The scandal was immense and it had a significant impact on public culture and, in particular, literature. Thomas Middleton and Thomas Rowley's play *The Changeling* (1622), with its murderous heroine and hideously absurd virginity test, owes much to the two interrelated cases.[187] More immediately a not very subtle play, *The Insatiate Countess*, first performed in 1608, was published in 1613 and 1616 in what looks like an attempt to cash in on the interest in the scandal, the text probably revised for publication.[188] The play's opening line is 'What should we do in this Countess's dark hole?', and the jokes, with their images of open doors and falling into ditches, are in a similar vein to those in many plays performed at the Whitefriars Theatre.[189] Throughout the seventeenth century the case inspired strong opinions and feelings. Frances Howard became notorious as a scarlet woman from the time of the case onwards and she has been subjected to the most appalling misogynist representation, notably in the gossipy pro-parliamentarian histories of Arthur Wilson and Anthony Weldon.[190] Arthur Wilson made great

[184] *State Trials*, II, p. 961; Lindley, *Howard*, pp. 71–3; A. L. Rowse, *Simon Forman: Sex and Society in Shakespeare's Age* (London: Weidenfeld and Nicolson, 1974), pp. 255–8. Mrs Turner's repentance and death was the subject of a number of pamphlets: see Anon., *Mistress Turners Repentance, Who, About the Poisoning of That Ho: Knight Sir Thomas Overbury, was executed the fourteenth of November, last* (London, 1615); Anon., *Mistress Turners Teares, for the Murder of Sir Thomas Ouerbury* (London, 1615). For discussion of the case and the links made between Mrs Turner and malign Catholic influence at court see Alastair Bellany, 'Mistress Turner's Deadly Sins: Sartorial Transgression, Court Scandal, and Politics in Early Stuart England', *HLQ* 58 (1995), 179–210.

[185] Rickman, *Love, Lust, and License*, p. 81.

[186] See the *ODNB* entries for Carr and Howard.

[187] Frances E. Dolan, 'Re-reading Rape in *The Changeling*', *JEMCS* 11 (2011), 4–29; Lisa Jardine, *Reading Shakespeare Historically* (London: Routledge, 1996), p. 122.

[188] D. J. Lake, '*The Insatiate Countess*: Linguistic Evidence for Authorship', *N. & Q.* 28 (1981), 166–70; Jeanne Addison Roberts, 'Marriage and Divorce in 1613: Elizabeth Cary, Frances Howard and Others', in Laurie E. Maguire and Thomas L. Berger, eds, *Textual Formations and Reformations* (Cranbury, NJ: Associated University Press, 1998), pp. 161–78, at pp. 170–1.

[189] John Marston and Others, *The Insatiate Countess*, ed. Giorgio Melchiri (Manchester: Manchester University Press, 1984), I.i.1. On the humour of the Whitefriars Theatre see Mary Bly, *Queer Virgins and Virgin Queans on the Early Modern Stage* (Oxford: Oxford University Press, 2000); Duncan Fraser, 'An Annotated Edition of Lordling Barry's *Ram Alley*', PhD thesis, University of Sussex, 2013.

[190] Arthur Wilson, *The History of Great Britain, being the Life and Reign of King James I* (London, 1653); Anthony Weldon, *The Court and Character of King James* (London, 1650); Anon., *Truth Brought To Light By Time*, in *Somers Tracts*, ed. Walter Scott (1809), pp. 304–63; Cynthia B. Herrup, *A House in Gross Disorder: Sex, Law and the 2nd. Earl of Castlehaven* (New York: Oxford University Press, 1999), pp. 80, 89; Rickman, *Love, Lust, and License*, pp. 85–6.

capital out of the divine punishment meted out by God when she died from what appears to have been ovarian cancer in his fanciful reconstruction of her death:

> For that part of her Body which had been the *receptacle* of most of her *sin*, grown rotten (though she never had but one *Child*) the *ligaments* failing, it fell down, and was cut away in *flakes*, with a most *nauseous* and putrid *savour*, which to augment, she would roul her self in her own *ordure* in her bed, took delight in it.[191]

Given the long tradition of pious judgements—the principal authority on Stuart history of the Victorian Age described Frances Howard, with no real evidence, as 'Headstrong and impetuous by nature, she had received an evil training at the hands of her coarse-minded and avaricious mother'—it is easy to see why recent historians such as Alastair Bellany and David Lindley have sought to redress the balance by re-examining the evidence.[192]

However, the problem may be as much conceptual as factual and it is unlikely that looking at the episode in terms of a romance or a scandal tells the whole story.[193] Furthermore, it can be argued that too much emphasis is placed on the second case, the poisoning of Sir Thomas Overbury, as though the first case, the Essex divorce, were simply a prelude to the real event of an evil woman's crime.[194] What has been lost in both versions is the question of truth and lying and the divorce case forces us to ask serious questions about its progress and outcome because there surely are right and wrong answers that can be determined based on the surviving evidence.

The most significant account of the first case is the extraordinary testimony left by George Abbot. Abbot has long been regarded as one of the least successful primates, his tenure surrounded by strong personalities who left their mark on the Church: Parker, Grindal, Bancroft, and Laud. Although it is generally accepted that Abbot was a man of 'moral courage', the few historians who have written about him usually claim that he was 'not strong enough' to prevent Arminians and Calvinists 'from becoming more antagonistic'.[195] Overall he is seen as 'a far better man than he was an archbishop'.[196] It may be that this is too neat a distinction and that Abbot's lack of influence for most of his relatively long tenure—he was the longest

---

[191] Wilson, *History of Great Britain*, p. 83. Compare the description of the death of Sir Francis Walsingham in a Catholic libel cited in Lake, *Bad Queen Bess?*, p. 342. Wilson may have the fate of Overbury in mind.

[192] S. R. Gardiner, *History of England from the Accession of James I to the Outbreak of the Civil War, 1603–1642*, 10 vols (London: Longman, 1883–4), II, p. 167. See also John Ford, *The Collected Works of John Ford, Volume I*, ed. Gilles Monsarrat, Brian Vickers, and R. J. C. Watt (Oxford: Clarendon Press, 2012), pp. 670–6.

[193] Bellany is convinced that Frances Howard probably did poison Overbury (*Court Scandal*, p. 56); Lindley argues that such questions are irrelevant for his purpose (*Howard*, p. 6).

[194] On poison as a woman's weapon, see Thomas Kyd [?], *The Trueth of the Most Wicked and Secret Murthering of Iohn Brewen, goldsmith of London committed by his owne wife* (London, 1592), sig. A3r; Rickman, *Love, Lust and License*, p. 192; Randall Martin, ed., *Women and Murder in Early Modern News Pamphlets and Broadside Ballads, 1573–1697* (Farnham: Ashgate, 2005), introduction, p. xiv. The attribution of the first pamphlet to Kyd is extremely doubtful: see Freeman and Freeman, *Collier*, II, pp. 859–61.

[195] Paul A. Welsby, *George Abbot: The Unwanted Archbishop, 1562–1633* (London: SPCK, 1962), pp. 150–1, 154.

[196] Hugh Trevor-Roper, *Archbishop Laud* (London: Macmillan, 1940), p. 42.

serving Archbishop from the accession of Elizabeth to the end of the seventeenth century—stems from his strong intervention in the Essex divorce case in the first two years of his primacy.[197]

Abbot's manuscript account of the annulment case—published in the early eighteenth century by the unscrupulous bookseller Edmund Curll, as *The Case of Impotency as Debated in England: In that Remarkable Tryal, 1613, Between Robert Earl of Essex, and the Lady Frances Howard* (1715), and in the volumes of State trials—makes it very clear throughout that what troubles him is the fact that the proposed action is based on a series of lies.[198] At the time of the trial the only way that a woman could annul her marriage was on the grounds of her husband's failure to provide children, as had long been the case in canon law, and what Abbot clearly objected to was that in the Essex case the evidence had then been made to manufacture the result.[199] Abbot is deeply suspicious of the midwives who find Frances Howard to be still a virgin and he is further worried by the failure to test Essex for his potency, as he has not seen any proof that the Earl is actually impotent. He is also unprepared to rely on the Countess's oath that she is a virgin—presumably because he knew that the affair with Robert Carr was already underway.[200]

Abbot's account shows that he thinks that the case for annulment is fraudulent throughout. He begins by recalling his own private interview with Essex: 'Having private speech with him, only about the Ability of his Body, and nothing else, I found him generally much reserv'd in Talk, but only avowing the Ability of himself for Generation; and that he was resolv'd never to lay any Blemish upon himself that Way.'[201] Abbot shows that the evidence that he has uncovered in the most straightforward manner is at odds with that presented by the Commission, a

---

[197] Abbot was not wholly ineffective: he did play a role in the establishment of the Virginia Company and acted as the patron of Samuel Purchas: see Andrew Fitzmaurice, *Humanism and America: An Intellectual History of English Colonisation, 1500–1625* (Cambridge: Cambridge University Press, 2003), p. 63.

[198] George Abbot, *The Case of Impotency as Debated in England: in that remarkable trial an. 1613* (London, 1715), a transcript of George Abbot, 'James I of England: Narrative of the divorce between Lord Essex and his wife in 1613, written by Archbishop Abbot', BL Sloane MS 3828. The manuscript is in a seventeenth-century hand, not that of Abbot, so the genesis, purpose, intended readership, and circulation of the document remain obscure. It was owned by the Whig statesman John Somers, first Baron Somers (1651–1716). On Curll and his plans see Paul Baines and Pat Rogers, *Edmund Curll, Bookseller* (Oxford: Oxford University Press, 2007), p. 35; on its impact see Herrup, *House in Gross Disorder*, pp. 136–8.

[199] The literature on impotence and divorce is ever expanding. See, for example, R. M. Helmholz, *Marriage Litigation in Medieval England* (Cambridge: Cambridge University Press, 1975); James A. Brundage, 'Impotence, Frigidity, and Marital Nullity in the Decretists and the Early Decretalists', in P. Linehan, ed., *Proceedings of the Seventh International Conference on Medieval Canon Law* (Vatican City: Biblioteca Apostolica Vaticana, 1988), pp. 407–23; James A. Brundage, *Medieval Canon Law* (London: Longman, 1995), p. 73; Bronach Kane, *Impotence and Virginity in the Late Medieval Ecclesiastical Court of York* (York: University of York, 2008), Borthwick Paper No. 114; Jacqueline Murray, 'On the Origins and Role of "Wise Women" in Causes for Annulment on the Grounds of Male Impotence', *Journal of Medieval History* 16 (1990), 235–49; Edward J. Behrend-Martínez, *Unfit for Marriage: Impotent Spouses on Trial in the Basque Region of Spain, 1650–1750* (Reno: University of Nevada Press, 2007), pp. 58–62, 100–8.

[200] Abbot, *Impotency*, p. 9. On the virginity tests see also Rickman, *Love, Lust, and License*, pp. 85–6.

[201] Abbot, *Impotency*, p. 3.

sign that the proceedings are not so much a distortion or cunning cover-up, as a lie. Essex's wry answer to the Commission suggests that he had the same understanding of matters as the Archbishop:

> He gave the Reason of his having no Motions to know his Lady carnally, and of his thinking that he never should. When I came out of France I lov'd her; I do not so now, neither ever shall I. When he was to answer to the Article, that she was Virgo incorrupta; he smil'd, and said, She saith so, and she is so for me.[202]

Abbot, taking Essex's side, obviously thinks that there is no case to answer and that the investigations of the Commission are deceitful and corrupt, dictated by a higher (royal) authority who has decided the outcome in advance. Essex suggests that he was prepared to make the marriage work when he returned from France and was fully expecting to treat the Countess as his wife, but her desire for another man had rendered sexual relations between them impossible either because she refused his advances or because her lack of desire for him rendered him impotent. Either way, for a man schooled in canon law like Abbot, this is no reason to accede to a divorce.

Abbot, a man known for his literary taste, whose library contained many works of English literature as well as material more usually in the possession of bishops, uses his verbal skills to represent a vivid image designed to demolish the findings of the Commission:

> The Sunday I spent at Croydon [the Archbishop's summer palace], and preach'd on that Text of Christ's raising the Widow's Son of Naim, to the great Comfort of mine own Heart. That Day I conferr'd with a Friend, and settled some Courses, if any Trouble should befall unto me. I was also by a good Friend inform'd, that my Lord of Essex, on that Sunday Morning, having five or six Captains, and Gentlemen of Worth in his Chamber, and Speech being made of his Inability, rose out of his Bed, and taking up his Shirt, did shew to them all, so able, and extraordinarily sufficient Matter, that they all cry'd out Shame of his Lady, and said, That if the Ladies of the Court knew as much as they knew, they would tread her to Death.[203]

One wonders for whom this saucy and cunning anecdote—designed to stick in the reader's mind—might have been written. Is Abbot admiring the Earl's boldness and celebrating his potency defending his suitability for marriage? Or condemning the lax morals of the Jacobean court which had already become notorious, satirized frequently on the public stage, and which the Essex/Howard/Overbury scandals simply confirmed?[204] There is surely a pointed contrast between the biblical story of raising the dead and the Earl's proof that what is thought to be dead is really very much alive. And should the reader side with the court ladies whom the gentlemen claim would be incensed if they knew what the Countess was rejecting, or is this a further sign of the lascivious nature of Jacobean court life, as the men represent the

---

[202] Abbot, *Impotency*, p. 8.

[203] Abbot, *Impotency*, p. 15. On Abbot's library, se Ann Cox-Johnson, 'Lambeth Palace Library, 1610–1664', *TCBS* 11 (1954–8), 105–26.

[204] Rickman, *Love, Lust, and License*, p. 70; Sandra Clark, *Renaissance Drama* (Cambridge: Polity, 2007), p. 145.

women in terms of their real or imagined lustiness? The careful use of the ambiguous verb 'tread' in the last sentence further suggests that this is a passage that combines moral condemnation and satirical wit. The verb could mean trample, dance, or have intercourse with (as in *The Nun's Priest's Tale*), and indicates that the ladies in question might be angry with the Countess for either moral reasons or questions of jealousy, or that they might simply be rather eager to reach the potent Earl and would create a stampede to do so.[205]

Abbot refers throughout his account to his conscience, an indication of the anxiety he feels about what he has to do and what consequences it might have.[206] What disturbs him most is the role the King plays in trying to gain a divorce for his favourite. Abbot never uses the word but it is clear that he thinks the King is lying, a bitter irony given James's own well-publicized belief in his ability to expose fraudulence in cases of witchcraft, part of the deadly battle between the forces of truth and the father of lies.[207] It is equally clear that James knows exactly what he is being accused of and he does all he can to put pressure on Abbot to grant the annulment. The King and the Archbishop argue about the merits of the case and Abbot tells James that he can be persuaded to end his opposition only if he is presented with sufficient reason to believe that the Earl really is impotent. They discuss the law, with Abbot claiming that he cannot 'give Sentence where [he sees] no proof' and that he cannot vote against his conscience, telling James that he will argue against all of England 'on the Peril of my Head', a sign of his commitment to telling the truth. James replies that Abbot 'would have no lawyers' but the Archbishop responds that 'There is not an honest Lawyer in England that would not be on my Side', yet another sly dig that pits embattled truth against worldly values (one of the lawyers Abbot clearly has in mind is one of the civil lawyers on the Commission, Dr Daniel Dun of All Souls College, Oxford, whom he regards as a time-serving lickspittle who will do whatever the King bids).[208] James, never really an enthusiast for the common law, counters with a possible precedent, that of Bury's case.[209] Bury's case concerned a man who was kicked in the testicles by a horse and whose wife then divorced him for impotence.[210] The problem proved temporary and when Bury remarried he produced a son who inherited his property which was then disputed by 'one Webber, next in line to Bury's inheritance' on the grounds that the Church had been deceived when making its first judgement and so Bury's son was a bastard.[211] However, Bury's son won the case on appeal on the grounds that, even though the first marriage should not have been annulled, the

---

[205] Chaucer, 'Nun's Priest's Tale', Fragment B, line 3178 (*Riverside Chaucer*, p. 258); *OED* 8a–c.

[206] Abbot, *Impotency*, pp. 52, 56, 87, 92, *passim*.

[207] Willson, *King James*, pp. 103–6, 308–12. On James's authority called into question during the Overbury case, see *Bacon*, ed. Spedding, V, p. 284.

[208] Abbot, *Impotency*, pp. 50–1. On Dun (1544/5–1617), see the *ODNB* entry.

[209] James fought a long-running battle with Coke about the relationship of the law to the monarch's prerogative: R. G. Usher, 'James I and Sir Edward Coke', *EHR* 18 (1903), 664–75; Smith, *Coke*, pp. 176–9.

[210] Dyer, *Reports*, II, pp. 178b–179a; Katharine Eisaman Maus, *Inwardness and Theater in the English Renaissance* (Chicago: University of Chicago Press, 1995), pp. 134–5.

[211] Maus, *Inwardness*, p. 134.

second marriage was conducted in good faith, and so had the blessing of the Church and the law. Abbot does not accept the connection between the cases and reports that he said to the King 'if he would pardon me, it should not be long before that I would shew, that his separation was for Lack of his Stones', emphasizing that Essex is not thought to be impotent, unlike Bury.[212]

Abbot is also not persuaded that connections can usefully be made to other cases, such as that of Anne of Cleves, whose marriage to Henry VIII was never consummated, or those of Edward the Confessor and Pulcheria, sister of the Emperor Theodosius, both of whom chose virginity within marriage. Accordingly, Abbot argues, there is no precedent for divorce in the Howard–Essex case, just as there is no logic to the arguments for it.[213] Discussing the theory that witchcraft caused the Earl's impotence, Abbot is even more sceptical and demands proof and evidence 'least the World should say, that wilfully we shut our Eyes against the Truth'.[214] Abbot is prepared to put his head above the parapet because he knows that the trial is based on a straightforward lie, one that cannot be obscured by any number of historical precedents. Abbot rather piously defends his actions to himself stating that he is 'afraid of God, least he should be angry with me if in this Case I be silent', a pointed contrast to a Justice, 'who sitteth in the Place of God' and who will be 'worthy to lye in the flames of Hell, for abusing of the Trust which is committed unto him'.[215]

Abbot's desire to seek out the truth and his assumption that if there is a lack of love between the parties seeking a divorce then they can sort it out in the future is at odds with the assumptions of the King, as well as other members of the Committee. Abbot is especially eager to challenge the arguments of the commissioner, Daniel Dun, because, insincere sycophant and time-server that he is in Abbot's eyes, he is persuaded by the precedents of the annulment of Anne of Cleves's marriage and Bury's case, and claims that he believes that the dispute between the couple is based on 'want of ability' rather than 'lack of love'.[216] However, despite Abbot's principled opposition, James granted the divorce anyway, and in an angry letter he accused Abbot of making his stand because of a personal animus to Carr and Howard ('the Prejudice you have of the Persons') and warned the Archbishop about his future conduct, suggesting that he would not be fit to judge future cases if he did not become more impartial.[217] The King counselled the Archbishop not to trust in dubious external principles but to follow the King's judgement in such matters as he knows best, the letter concluding:

It should become you rather, to have a kind of Faith implicit, in my Judgement, as well as in respect of some Skill I have in Divinity; as also that I hope no honest Man doubts

---

[212] Abbot, *Impotency*, pp. 17–18.

[213] Abbot, *Impotency*, pp. 9, 118. On the divorce of Anne of Cleves, see J. J. Scarisbrick, *Henry VIII* (London: Methuen, 1988, rpt of 1981), pp. 271–3; on the chastity of Edward the Confessor see Dyan Elliott, *Spiritual Marriage: Sexual Abstinence in Medieval Wedlock* (Princeton: Princeton University Press, 1995), pp. 120–2; on Pulcheria see Dragoş Boicu, 'Marian Devotion as a Form of Legitimization of the Imperial Authority', *RESS* 6 (2014), 102–20.

[214] Abbot, *Impotency*, p. 40.   [215] Abbot, *Impotency*, p. 32.

[216] Abbot, *Impotency*, p. 22.   [217] Abbot, *Impotency*, pp. 132–5.

of the uprightness of my Conscience; and the best of thankfulness that you that are so far my Creature, can use towards me, is, to reverence, and follow my Judgement, and not to contradict it, except where you may demonstrate unto me that I am mistaken, or wrong imformed, and so farewell.[218]

James bristles because his integrity and conscience have been called into question by his premier ecclesiastic, whom he believes should support him. He understands that he has been accused of lying, and it is clear that relations between the two men were never the same again after this dispute and 'from this point begins the slow drift of this already isolated Primate into the political and ecclesiastical wilderness'.[219] The Archbishop outlived James, eventually dying in 1633, but he was unable to prevent the rise of a man he frequently argued would endanger the fragile Calvinist-inspired unity of the Church, the Arminian, William Laud.[220]

It is clear that Abbot thought that a king who was prepared to lie poisoned the body politic, as John Webster represented in especially striking lines in the opening scene of *The Duchess of Malfi* which was first performed (1613–14) while the divorce case was proceeding.[221] Antonio argues in the first substantial speech in the play that:

> Considering duly that a prince's court
> Is like a common fountain whence should flow
> Pure silver drops in general, but if't chance
> Some curs'd example poison't near the head,
> Death and diseases through the whole land spread.[222]

Webster's lines would suggest that he (and perhaps many of his audience) would probably have sympathized with Abbot—had they known of his stand—and would have seen the King's actions as verging on tyranny. Certainly the link between the poisoning of Overbury and the image of poison spreading throughout the realm in Antonio's lines has frequently been made.[223] Even so, James's claim that Abbot took the stand he did through self-interest and an animus against Carr and Howard has often been taken at face value by historians. David Lindley argues that Abbot's antipathy to the family 'evidently fuelled his moral indignation at the proposed divorce and the news that Frances was likely to marry Carr further increased anxiety as he saw the favourite being captured by his opponents'.[224]

---

[218] Abbot, *Impotency*, p. 135.   [219] Welsby, *Abbot*, p. 71.

[220] See the discussions in Nicholas Tyacke, ed., *England's Long Reformation, 1500–1800* (London: Routledge, 1998).

[221] John Webster, *The Duchess of Malfi*, in *The Works of John Webster: An Old-Spelling Critical Edition*, ed. David Gunby, David Carnegie, Antony Hammond, and Doreen Delvecchio, 2 vols (Cambridge: Cambridge University Press, 1995), I, pp. 379–80.

[222] Webster, *Duchess of Malfi* I.i.lines 11–15. See the discussion in Bellany, *Court Scandal*, pp. 1–4; Curtis Perry, *Literature and Favoritism in Early Modern England* (Cambridge: Cambridge University Press, 2006), p. 108.

[223] Lindley, *Howard*, p. 166; Catherine E. Thomas, 'Toxic Encounters: Poisoning in Early Modern English Literature and Culture', *LC* 9 (2012), 48–55, p. 50.

[224] Lindley, *Howard*, pp. 83–4. See also Andrew W. Foster, 'A Biography of Archbishop Richard Neile (1562–1640)', DPhil thesis, University of Oxford, 1978, pp. 168–9. Neile, Bishop of Lichfield, was a member of the Commission, and was heavily criticized by Abbot.

Perhaps by coincidence in 1616 Abbot's *Explicatio Sex Illustram Quaestionum* was republished, nineteen years after it first appeared as a thesis for his doctorate of divinity at Oxford.[225] The first question Abbot answered was 'De Mendacio', 'Of Lying', taking as his text Genesis 27:24, the verse in which Jacob lies to Isaac, claiming that he is Esau, which leads to the question of whether God was condoning lying in paving the way for Jacob to usurp his elder brother and become patriarch of the Jews.[226] Abbot, following Augustine's ingenious interpretation of Jacob's words, concludes that Jacob was not lying but speaking beyond his immediate context in acknowledging his future role as Jewish patriarch, fulfilling God's plan.[227] John Calvin, probably the most influential theologian in late Elizabethan and Jacobean England, provided a more obvious reading: 'At first Jacob was timid and anxious; now, having dismissed his fear, he confidently and audaciously lies...when Jacob pretended that God was the author of a benefit which had not been granted to himself, and that, too, as a cloak for his deception, his fault was not free from perjury.'[228]

Abbot was concerned to counter the casuistry of the Jesuits and their attempts to avoid capture when undertaking their missionary work in Protestant territory. What they regarded as equivocation and mental reservation, vital aspects of the true Christian's armour in the crusade for truth, Abbot, like most other Protestants, saw as duplicity and lying.[229] Abbot was well aware of the sets of questions and answers that Jesuits used to prepare priests in seminaries for the ordeals that lay ahead for them, instructing them how to reconcile what they had to do with their consciences and understanding of doctrine.[230] Novices were instructed which customs they could obey, what practices they had to avoid, how far they could participate in religious life, and whether they could equivocate when answering the intrusive questions of heretical authorities (answers in the Douai-Rheims and Allen-Parsons manuals differed, the former suggesting that it is better to serve the

[225] Welsby, *Abbot*, pp. 5–6.
[226] See above, p. 25. George Abbot, *Explicatio Sex Illustram Quaestionum: De Mendacio, De Circumcisione Et Baptismo, De Astrologia, De Praesentia In Cultu Idololatrico, De Fuga In Persequutione Et Peste, An Deus Sit Author Peccati* (Frankfurt, 1616).
[227] Augustine, *Against Lying*, in *Treatises on Various Subjects*, ed. Roy J. Deferrari (Washington, DC: CUA Press, 1952), pp. 111–79, at p. 155; Denery, *The Devil Wins*, p. 118. Gratian also defended Jacob: Kirk, *Conscience and Its Problems*, pp. 192–3. Other commentators on the Old Testament were more prepared to accept that the patriarchs might have lied and simply cautioned Christians against their example: Perkins, *Government of the Tongue*, p. 20: '*Object. II*: The holy Scriptures have mentioned the lyes of the Patriarches. *Answ*: We must not live by examples against rules of Gods worde'. For the wider context of the debate, see Roland H. Bainton, 'The Immoralities of the Patriarchs According to the Exegesis of the Late Middle Ages and of the Reformation', *HTR* 33 (1990), 39–49.
[228] Calvin, *Commentaries*, Genesis, II, pp. 88–9. On the spread and influence of Calvinism, see R. T. Kendall, *Calvin and English Calvinism to 1649* (Oxford: Oxford University Press, 1979); Andrew Pettegree, 'The Spread of Calvin's Thought', in Donald McGinn, ed., *The Cambridge Companion to Calvin* (Cambridge: Cambridge University Press, 2004), pp. 207–24; Nicholas Tyacke, *Anti-Calvinists: The Rise of English Arminianism, c.1590–1640* (Oxford: Clarendon Press, 1987), pp. 1–8.
[229] See below, pp. 152–7.
[230] Máté Vince, 'From "Aequivocatio" to the "Jesuitical Equivocation": The Changing Concepts of Ambiguity in Early Modern England', PhD thesis, University of Warwick, 2013, pp. 71–2.

faith by becoming a martyr).[231] *Explicatio Sex Illustram Quaestionum* is one of a number of works designed to counter such texts.[232] A work in Latin would reach a wide international audience of scholars, theologians, and English Catholic exiles preparing to return to their homeland. Abbot is unequivocal in his condemnation of Jesuit practices, regarding all failures to provide straightforward, honest answers as lies, which were mortal sins. Discussing a variety of examples taken from the Catholic instruction manuals, including the question of whether a priest was permitted to disguise himself to avoid capture and whether equivocal answers could be given to judges who had no authority (all judges in England), Abbot counters in two ways. He defends the authority of the Church and judiciary in England and dismisses the interpretations of the biblical examples cited by Catholic theologians.[233] Abbot argues that Jesus 'spoke plainly to his judges', teaching that 'lying is not allowed even in the direst situations'.[234] The Jesuits are therefore at odds with Christian teaching in their defence of lying, because 'in serious matters and those that pertain to God, [the Jesuits] swear and respond falsely and sophistically, therefore as liars and disseminators of perjury, [and] should be expurged from the register of true Christians'.[235]

Abbot was a theologian with an international reputation, and was especially prominent in discussions of truth and lies, in particular equivocation. Henry Mason's *New Art of Lying* was dedicated to Abbot, a sign that if he did not have influence in high places he did command respect among many of the clergy who did not necessarily share all his views.[236] While Abbot was firmly within the established Calvinist orthodoxy of the Church in James's reign, Mason was a controversial and outspoken Arminian.[237] Moreover, Abbot and Mason have no obvious personal connection (although, of course, there may have been one). Mason, who is particularly concerned to counter the claims of Garnet about the justifiable use of equivocation, sees Abbot as a powerful ally, and cites his work on mendacity as the definitive rebuttal of Garnet's treatise on equivocation:

> In *Queene Elizabeths* time, there was a Treatise found out, which before was in the secret keeping of Jesuits or Priests: in which . . . were contained sundry instructions given by *Sixtus Quintus*, for the practising of this mysterie of *Equivocation*. Which, if the Reader be desirous to know more fully, he may reade a Relation thereof set downe by a most reverend and learned *Prelate*.[238]

[231] Holmes, ed., *Elizabethan Casuistry*, p. 52. See also Zagorin, *Ways of Lying*, p. 108.
[232] See Morton, *Exact Discoverie*; Sutcliffe, *Challenge*.
[233] Vince, 'From "Aequivocatio" to the "Jesuitical Equivocation"', p. 80.
[234] Vince, 'From "Aequivocatio" to the "Jesuitical Equivocation"', p. 82.
[235] Cited in Vince, 'From "Aequivocatio" to the "Jesuitical Equivocation"', p. 83 [Vince's translation].
[236] Abbot also receives fulsome praise in William Vaughan's eccentric treatise, *The Spirit of Detraction, Coniured and Conuicted in Seuen Circles* (London, 1611), pp. 106–7.
[237] See the *ODNB* entry on Mason; Peter Lake, 'Calvinism and the English Church 1570–1635', *P. & P.* 114 (1987), 32–76; Peter Lake, *Moderate Puritans and the Elizabethan Church* (Cambridge: Cambridge University Press, 1982).
[238] Mason, *Lying*, p. 108.

Mason also repeats the story of Robert Southwell's instruction to his 'Woman-Disciple' that 'if she shulde be examined, whether himselfe were or had bin in that house, she should upon her oath utterly deny it', using the art of equivocation, citing Abbot as the chief authority on the significance of the case.[239] The story is immediately followed by the story of Francis Tresham's deathbed confession and Garnet's admission that Tresham 'meant to Equivocat'.[240] For Mason—and surely for many others—there was a direct link between the Jesuit trials of Elizabeth's last years and the Gunpowder Plot, which had necessitated the passing of the Oath of Allegiance.[241] The principal crusader in England against the lies told by the unscrupulous Jesuits was George Abbot.[242] Abbot may never have recovered his political influence after he acted as a whistleblower pointing out just what lies were told at court and how important it was to speak the truth, but he enjoyed a powerful reputation as a champion for those determined to speak the truth at all costs—probably because of his principled opposition to the monarch. When Abbot objected to James near the end of his reign (1623) he was silenced by the King and, although he enjoyed some 'restoration to favour' in the early years of Charles's reign, he was 'still eclipsed by Laud'.[243] Can we really believe that self-interest provides the key to Abbot's actions during the Essex divorce case?

Accusations of lying are relatively rare, which should not surprise us, given the gravity of the accusation and the social stigma attached to being labelled a liar. It should therefore not seem odd that what went on in the Essex divorce case seems rather less straightforward than it has sometimes been represented: this sad affair is a good example of why we need to look in less obvious places if we are to understand the real story of truth and lies. Significant cases of lying always emerge from a context: people lie all the time but only on specific occasions does a specific lie really matter.[244] Abbot's opposition to the Essex divorce perhaps stemmed from a personal squeamishness, but it was clear that he objected because he was steeped in canon law and understood that robust legal practices had been developed to deal with cases when married partners fell out. Most likely it stemmed from his conviction, after the influence of the Jesuits and their defence of equivocation, that the truth had to be told and that any form of deception or duplicity would lead to disaster. George Abbot, as is probably right in an Archbishop of Canterbury, was a warrior for truth, but this is obscured because he chose a case that few people in modern Britain now would support and which became buried in the other more sensational issues that came later (poisoning, murder). The Howard divorce trial shows us why it is so hard to get at the truth and expose lies and how, paradoxically,

---

[239] Mason, *Lying*, p. 181.   [240] Mason, *Lying*, p. 183.

[241] Mason, *Lying*, p. 167.

[242] For another example of Abbot's indignant response when confronted by lies see Nicholas S. Davidson, '"Le Plus Beau Meschant Esprit Que Ie Aye Cogneu": Science and Religion in the Writings of Giulio Cesare Vanini, 1585–1619', in Brooke and Maclean, eds, *Heterodoxy in Early Modern Science and Religion*, pp. 59–79, at p. 64.

[243] Willson, *King James*, p. 439; Welsby, *Abbot*, pp. 136–7.

[244] Compare E. H. Carr on crossing the Rubicon: E. H. Carr, *What is History?* (Harmondsworth: Penguin, 1964), p. 11.

the truth/lying issue is often the least interesting aspect of any such case even when our subject is lying. What matters more is why certain lies are significant at that particular historical moment. These two cases, the divorce and the Overbury murder, as has often been recognized, played a significant role in the fractious history of the seventeenth century. They marginalized the influence of the mainstream Archbishop and so helped to pave the way for the rise of the Arminian faction led by William Laud, as well as helping to accentuate the division between a court enveloped in self-regard, scandal, and popery, and the opposition.[245] The Oath of Allegiance was designed to force the truth into the light but, as its opponents duly noted, too much pressure to tell the truth often leads to the proliferation of lies.

[245] Tyacke, *Anti-Calvinists*, p. 68; Christopher Hill, *Milton and the English Revolution* (London: Faber, 1977), p. 18; Lawrence Stone, *The Crisis of the Aristocracy, 1558–1641* (Oxford: Clarendon Press, 1979, rpt of 1967), p. 667; Bellany, 'Mistress Turner's Deadly Sins', pp. 180, 209–10.

PART II

MODES OF LYING IN EARLY MODERN ENGLAND

3

The Religious Culture of Lying

I

William Tyndale was quite clear. Lying was acceptable to God if the lie was uttered in the right circumstances. In his analysis of the Sermon on the Mount, published in 1533 shortly before his imprisonment and death, Tyndale stated that 'To lye also and to dissemble is not alwaye synne.'[1] Tyndale uses the example of David escaping from Achish, King of Gath when he pretends to be insane, as he 'scrabbled on the doors of the gate, and let his spittle fall down upon his beard', an example of the just employing nefarious means for good purposes.[2]

Tyndale was commenting on Matthew, chapter 5, which he cited in his own translation, the only English version available at the time:

> Agayne ye haue harde how it was sayd to them of olde tyme / forsweare not thy selfe / but paye thyne othes unto the lorde. But I saye unto you / that ye sweare not at all / neyther be heauen / for it is the seate of God / nether by the earthe / for it is his fotestole / nether by Jerusalem / for it is the cety of the great kynge nether thou shalte swere by thyne heed / for thou canst not make a whyte here or blacke. But your communicacyon shalbe ye ye / nay naye. For yf ought be aboue that / it procedeth of euell.[3]

Tyndale's statement, therefore, has to be read in terms of promises or oaths, when these can be lawfully demanded and when they are actually binding.[4] Tyndale's translation of Jesus's words makes them a warning against false swearing, not simply against those who make insincere promises but against those who impose false oaths. Promises made to earthly powers are not binding and run the risk of having an evil origin so language should be kept as simple as possible. The only valid promises are those made to God, which should involve nothing more than a simple yes or no, the contract being sealed by the power of the deity's omniscience. Tyndale interprets the gospel to mean that a culture of oaths is at best unnecessary, as ordinary words should suffice: 'Wherefore our dealing ought to be so substancyal that our words might be beleued without an othe' because 'Our words are the signes

---

[1] Tyndale, *Exposicion*, fo. xlvir. For analysis see Ryrie, *Gospel*, pp. 74–5; David Daniell, *William Tyndale: A Biography* (New Haven: Yale University Press, 1994), p. 220.

[2] 1 Samuel 21:13.

[3] Tyndale, *Exposicion*, fo. xlvir; William Tyndale, *New Testament*, ed. Priscilla Martin (Ware: Wordsworth, 2002), p. 27.

[4] Cummings, *Mortal Thoughts*, pp. 83, 144.

of the truth of our hartes.'[5] For Tyndale the gospel demands that we use the ordinary speech that God gave us and do not add extra layers which will always introduce worldly sin and obscure God's gifts to us. He is thinking, of course, of the complexities added by the Church which had 'broken God's covenant, and had replaced it with man's own ideas'.[6] The demand for the use of free, ordinary speech is integral to his project to rely on the word of God and make it comprehensible to the ploughboy and so to create a just and fair society of all men equal before God.[7]

Tyndale is elsewhere clear that lying is a deadly sin and the perpetrator should expect no mercy from God: 'And when thou sweare by the gospel boke or bible, the meaning is, that God yf thou lye, shall not fulfyll vnto the, the promyses of mercye therein wrytten.'[8] But the real villains are those who impose their power on ordinary people and force them to aspire to unobtainable standards. Tyndale's comment on Leviticus 19:11–12, when God tells Moses that lying to each other as well as to God is forbidden, is especially revealing in its analysis of the problems caused by the imposition of false oaths and their effect on an ability to distinguish between truth and lies:

> And thoughe Moyses say Leuitici. xix. Lye not nor deceyue any man hys neyghboure or one another, yet they interpreted it but good councell / yf a man desired to be perfecte. But no precept to bynde vnder payne of synne. And so by that meanes not onelye they that spake true / but also they that lyed to deceyue, were compelled to swere and to confyrme theyr words with othes, yf they wolde be beleued.[9]

The imposition of false oaths by the Church leads to chaos and sin, as people are forced to swear oaths that render the truthfulness of their speech irrelevant. In Tyndale's eyes, the desire to establish unattainable standards and the failure to recognize the inherently sinful nature of mankind has been a major factor in destroying the social fabric and has undermined the authority of God who simply demanded that we tell the truth in everyday speech.

The truth is that 'the inferior ought rather to dye then to swere' an oath that dishonours God.[10] Therefore, one either has to sacrifice one's life, or find some means of avoiding swearing the false oath if one is to honour God properly, which is why it is sometimes permissible to deceive the authorities because 'to sweare to do euel is dampnable, and to performe that is double dampnable'.[11] It is better to act duplicitously than to make false promises that one either cannot or should not keep, which is why it may be possible to lie in certain circumstances. Moreover, there is an ambiguity about the status of all earthly authorities and all actions on

---

[5] Tyndale, *Exposicion*, fo. xlvr.
[6] Ralph S. Werrell, *The Theology of William Tyndale* (Cambridge: James Clark, 2006), p. 171.
[7] Thomas Betteridge, 'William Tyndale and Religious Debate', *JMEMS* 40 (2010), 439–61; Werrell, *Theology*, p. 20; Daniell, *Tyndale*, pp. 1, 18. Although invoking the ploughboy was a literary trope, linking the comment to a long tradition of anti-ecclesiastical satire: Andrew Hadfield, 'Foresters, Ploughmen and Shepherds: Versions of Tudor Pastoral', in Mike Pincombe and Cathy Shrank, eds, *The Oxford Handbook of Tudor Literature, 1485–1603* (Oxford: Oxford University Press, 2009), pp. 537–53.
[8] Tyndale, *Exposicion*, fo. xlvr. [9] Tyndale, *Exposicion*, fo. xlivr.
[10] Tyndale, *Exposicion*, fo. xlvr. [11] Tyndale, *Exposicion*, fo. xlvir.

earth. Tyndale argued strongly for the need to obey the secular authorities in *The Obedience of a Christian Man* (1528), arguing that vengeance was God's prerogative and that he 'had all tyrants in his hand and letteth them not do whatsoever they would, but as much only as he appointeth them to do and as farforth it is necessary for us' because 'Evil rulers . . . are a sign that God is angry and wroth with us.'[12] Even so, there is a limit to the power of rulers who should only be obeyed when they act in accordance with God's truth: 'when men saye, a kynges worde muste stande / that is trouth, yf his othe or promise be lawfull and expedyent'.[13] Tyndale himself, although his work at times pleased Henry VIII, did not act in accord with his monarch's wishes.[14]

Tyndale's position about the possibility of lying in extreme circumstances is easy to understand but set a dangerous precedent for Reformers, as his admission that lying was permissible meant that, in Alec Ryrie's words, 'it became impossible to find a coherent and defensible position'.[15] Lying is properly condemned throughout his writings but the strong belief in the power of ordinary language which naturally establishes a contract between the godly individual and the deity also establishes an ambiguous relationship with authorities that are accepted as legitimate.[16] The issue is exposed in Tyndale's vitriolic exchange with Thomas More in the early 1530s.[17] The controversy established the pattern for subsequent debates in print, religious and otherwise, and as late as 1589–90, more than fifty years after the works were published, the 'colloquial directness and linguistically inventive style, language, and polemical approach' of Tyndale had a major influence on the nature of the Martinist pamphlets.[18]

The polemical battle between More and Tyndale was the first case of a religious debate between a member of the established Church and a Reformer in print in England.[19] Each party, acutely conscious of the success of Luther's demotic writings and the propaganda campaign that made him the most recognizable figure outside

---

[12] William Tyndale, *The Obedience of a Christian Man*, ed. David Daniell (Harmondsworth: Penguin, 2000), pp. 12, 54–5; Greenblatt, *Renaissance Self-Fashioning*, pp. 88–93.

[13] Tyndale, *Exposicion*, fo. xlvir.

[14] Scarisbrick, *Henry VIII*, pp. 247, 400; Daniell, *Tyndale*, pp. 361–84.

[15] Ryrie, *Gospel*, p. 75.   [16] Skinner, *Foundations*, II, pp. 67–70.

[17] For analysis see John N. King, ed., *Voices of the English Reformation: A Sourcebook* (Philadelphia: University of Pennsylvania Press, 2004), pp. 37–48; Rainer Pineas, 'William Tyndale: Controversialist', *SP* 60 (1963), 117–32; Rainer Pineas, 'Thomas More's Use of Humor as a Weapon of Religious Controversy', *SP* 58 (1961), 97–114; Rainer Pineas, 'More Versus Tyndale: A Study of Controversial Technique', *MLQ* 24 (1963), 144–50; C. S. Lewis, *English Literature in the Sixteenth Century Excluding Drama* (Oxford: Oxford University Press, 1973, rpt of 1954), pp. 173–6, 191–2.

[18] Joseph L. Black, ed., *The Martin Marprelate Tracts: A Modernised and Annotated Edition* (Cambridge: Cambridge University Press, 2008), introduction, p. xxx.

[19] Jamey Hecht, 'Limitations of Textuality in Thomas More's Confutation of Tyndale's Answer', *SCJ* 26 (1995), 823–8. For the wider impact of Tyndale on print culture see John N. King, '"The Light of Printing": William Tyndale, John Day, and Early Modern Print Culture', *RQ* 54 (2001), 52–85. Jesse Lander argues that 'what distinguishes polemic from earlier forms of contentious writing is its connection to print', but does not discuss the More–Tyndale exchange: *Inventing Polemic: Religion, Print, and Literary Culture in Early Modern England* (Cambridge: Cambridge University Press, 2006), p. 14.

aristocratic circles in Europe, wrote in a forceful and aggressive manner that was designed to appeal to a popular understanding of the dramatic nature of a heated exchange about fundamental values.[20] One of the consequences of the nature of the debate was that subtle theological and ecclesiological distinctions were inevitably obscured. Accusing the other party of being a liar is a central feature of both Tyndale's *An Answer to More's Dialogue* (1531) and More's extensive reply, *The Confutation of Tyndale's Answer* (1532). While each author used their wide-ranging knowledge of the Church Fathers, Christian history, philosophy, and classical rhetoric elsewhere in their writings, in the heat of battle the terms 'liar', 'lie', and 'lying', liberally sprinkled throughout the texts, assume a far more popular significance.

Tyndale's *Answer* opens with his forceful insistence that scriptural authority supports the reading that the words 'church' and 'congregation' are interchangeable. The essence of the Church is not the corrupt institution that has ruled Christendom since the early Middle Ages, as More believes, but the faithful worshippers of God who form his Church on earth.[21] For Tyndale the words matter only in so far as they describe the honest contract between men and their God, not as signifiers of fundamentally created structures that men can administer in God's name:

> And when M. More saith, that this word *church* is known well enough, I report me unto the consciences of all the land, whether he say truth or otherwise; or whether the lay-people understand by *church* the whole institution of all that profess Christ, or the juggling spirits only. And when he saith that *congregation* is a more general term; if it were, it hurteth not: for the circumstance doth ever tell what congregation is meant. Nevertheless yet saith he not the truth. For wheresoever I may say a *congregation*, there may I say a *church* also; as the church of the devil, the church of Satan, the church of wretches, the church of wicked men, the church of liars, and a church of Turks thereto.[22]

Tyndale uses irony and sarcasm to good effect, his syntax reading as if he is conceding some details to his opponent ('it hurteth not'), before producing a long list of examples that support his own position (if we are careless in the ways that we use 'church' and 'congregation' we can use the word 'church' to describe a whole series of false churches). Tyndale's argument is based on his understanding that God has given mankind speech which provides all the necessary meanings. There is no need to add extra details and layers of significance, or to insist that certain words have special meanings, as to do so risks undermining and obscuring the relationship of men and women with God. One could substitute 'congregation' for 'church' in the final list of real and imagined institutions; but that would be

---

[20] Cummings, *Literary Culture*, pp. 68–88; Andrew Pettegree, *The Invention of News: How the World Came to Know about Itself* (New Haven: Yale University Press, 2014), pp. 67–72.

[21] On the clash between Church and scripture see Brad S. Gregory, 'Tyndale and More, in Life and in Death', *Reformation* 8 (2003), 173–97.

[22] William Tyndale, *An Answer to Sir Thomas More's Dialogue*, ed. Henry Walter (Cambridge: Parker Society, 1850), pp. 14–15.

counter-intuitive, would distort the natural meaning of ordinary language, and would make no sense to the speaker or the listener, unless both were deluded. Or were liars.

Tyndale's aim is to demonstrate that More's argument that the Church possesses a secular authority is pernicious and stems either from More's stupidity or, more likely, from his duplicity, a manoeuvre that becomes clear in the following paragraph, when he speculates on why More might have made his errors and what he needs to do to correct his errors:

> Howbeit, M. More hath so long used his figures of poetry, that (I suppose) when he erreth most, he now, by the reason of a long custom, believeth himself that he saith most true . . . So blind he counteth all other men, in comparison of his great understanding . . . But charitably I exhort him in Christ to take heed; for though Judas were wilier than his fellows to get lucre, yet he proved not most wise at the last end . . . Let, therefore, M. More and his company awake by times, ere ever their sin be ripe; lest the voice of their wickedness ascend up, and awake God out of his sleep, to look upon them, and to bow his ears unto their cursed blasphemies against the open truth, and to send his harvestmen and mowers of vengeance to reap it.[23]

This is another well-conceived polemical passage and it is easy to see why Tyndale had such a profound influence on later satirical writing. Tyndale moves easily from a relatively benign comment about More's commitment to poetry, part of the long-standing debate about whether the beauties of secular poetry were good or bad for sacred verse; to an arch comparison of More to Judas, taking money to undermine religious truth; and concludes with a judgement about the impending Apocalypse which More and his fellow Catholics are ignoring, because they cannot see how much Christendom needs to change, having lost sight of God. The artfulness of the argument, the obvious result of profound rhetorical training, establishes a context for the comment about More's overcommitment to his own poetry. Tyndale is again employing sarcasm, contrasting his own proper use of rhetoric in the service of God to More's self-regarding and therefore sinful writing.[24]

Tyndale's point is surely even more wide-ranging and judicious. In suggesting that More's sin may be the result of the careless pursuit of his own pleasure, Tyndale is employing the Augustinian distinction between two forms of deception, *fallax* and *mendax*. *Fallax* was a lie intended to deceive the hearer, while *mendax* was 'a fabulous kind of falsehood, to please rather than deceive'.[25] Tyndale is ostensibly suggesting that More is guilty of *mendax*, an overindulgence in pleasure. But it is clear that caring too much about such earthly matters cannot simply be a minor sin, especially when a serious matter such as the nature and authority of the Church is at stake. More's error, in Tyndale's eyes, would be a grave sin if it were the fault of an ordinary member of the congregation; but when committed by a leading churchman it reveals his own lack of spiritual health and explains why the Church is 'the

[23] Tyndale, *Answer*, p. 15.
[24] For Tyndale's use of rhetoric, see Betteridge, 'Tyndale and Religious Debate', p. 454.
[25] Subha Mukherji, *Law and Representation in Early Modern Drama* (Cambridge: Cambridge University Press, 2006), p. 153. See also Maclean, *Interpretation*, pp. 140–2.

church of liars', why it is full of Judases, and why God will soon call time on the people of earth. Augustine, as he makes clear in his *Confessions*, was rather too addicted to the pleasures of the world—including poetry and rhetoric—before his conversion, renouncing his former life once he had realized the errors of his ways. Tyndale is baiting More with the comparison, urging him to repent, like Augustine, and admit the truth.[26]

Tyndale is also putting into practice his belief that dissembling is not always a sin. He clearly does not imagine that More is simply guilty of a minor sin but sees him as instrumental in deceiving the English people through his support for the papacy. Like a good lawyer, he pretends that he thinks this in order to add 'colour' to his case, a practice related to the invention of legal fictions to secure the truth, a common legal practice in sixteenth-century England.[27] Tyndale can then build an increasingly serious critique of More, and persuade the reader/hearer exactly what is at stake over disputes about the meaning of words. In doing so Tyndale is reminding the alert reader that More was a lawyer, the first common lawyer to occupy the position of Lord Chancellor at the time that Tyndale was writing, and about to enter into another significant—though less violent—dispute about the relationship between canon and common law and the King's ability to fix the interpretation of scripture with Christopher Saint German, author of the standard legal textbook, *Doctor and Student* (1528).[28] Here, the tables are turned and More comes under the sort of scrutiny to which he was more used to exposing others.

More's reply, the *Confutation*, although it preserves the appearance of a learned treatise, paying particular attention to countering Tyndale's interpretations of the Church Fathers, is largely a sustained exercise in abuse. In this way More abandoned the playful rhetoric of his earlier works and ceased to adopt masks and voices.[29] His eagerness to dismantle Tyndale's arguments brings out 'the absolutist' in More and his meandering polemic destroys 'any vestige of form'.[30] Nowhere is this issue more obvious than in More's frequent accusations that Tyndale is lying. As in his opponent's text, 'lying', a term he uses with care elsewhere, is employed as a portmanteau insult, damning Tyndale as a wilful abuser of true belief, a heretic who cannot be permitted to live for his own sake as well as that of others. In contemporary

---

[26] Augustine, *Confessions*, trans. R. S. Pine-Coffin (Harmondsworth: Penguin, 1961), pp. 43–4; Molly Murray, *The Poetics of Conversion in Early Modern English Literature: Verse and Change from Donne to Dryden* (Cambridge: Cambridge University Press, 2009), pp. 9–10.

[27] Mukherji, *Law and Representation*, p. 149; White, *Natural Law*, p. 89; Lon L. Fuller, *Legal Fictions* (Stanford: Stanford University Press, 1967); Luke Wilson, *Theaters of Intention: Drama and the Law in Early Modern England* (Stanford: Stanford University Press, 2000), pp. 217–18. For a hostile assessment of the practice see Jeremy Bentham, 'Judicial Fictions', in Kerr, ed., *Penguin Book of Lies*, pp. 204–8.

[28] For discussion of the significance of this debate and its impact on literary texts see John Guy, 'Thomas More and Christopher St. German: The Battle of the Books', in Fox and Guy, *Reassessing*, pp. 95–120; Lorna Hutson, *The Invention of Suspicion: Law and Mimesis in Shakespeare and Renaissance Drama* (Oxford: Oxford University Press, 2007), pp. 50–63; James Simpson, 'The Psalms and Threat in Sixteenth-Century English Culture', *RS* 29 (2015), 576–94, pp. 592–3.

[29] James Simpson, 'Rhetoric, Conscience, and the Playful Positions of Sir Thomas More', in Pincombe and Shrank, eds, *Oxford Handbook of Tudor Literature*, pp. 121–36, at p. 134.

[30] Fox, *Thomas More*, p. 124.

morality plays and interludes, such as Henry Medwall's *Fulgens and Lucres* (1515), John Heywood's *The Play of the Wether* (1533), and John Redford's *Wit and Science* (c.1535), to accuse someone of lying, or to call them a liar, was to engage in abuse and to signal the level of their depravity: moreover, the dialogue in such plays was characterized by verbal echoes and chiasmic reversals of previous statements, rhetorical ploys derived from the schoolroom.[31] For David Loewenstein, More represents Tyndale as a theatrical fraud, his 'evangelical guile' falsifying not just More's words but Christ's.[32] In the preface More claims that 'any good crysten men' who read Tyndale's *Answer* 'shall not onely be well able to perceyue hym for a folysshe heretyke, & his arguments easy to answere / but shall also se y^t he sheweth hym selfe a false lyar'.[33] At first glance the statement might look like an impassioned affirmation of More's faith in the truth of the Church but it is, of course, carefully crafted to provide this impression. More puts pressure on the reader to agree with him, suggesting that only someone as stupid as Tyndale could follow his example, or, someone who is not really a Christian. Tyndale is not simply a 'foolish heretic'—and More was writing as an authority having just written *A Dialogue Concerning Heresies* (1531)—but a 'false lyar', the tautology serving as rhetorical reinforcement. The point is that, just as there are two levels of lying so there are two types of heretics, the foolish and the dangerously stubborn, Tyndale showing himself to belong to the latter category, like his spiritual mentor, Martin Luther. Both damage the authority of the Church, which should be the arbiter in any dispute over the meaning of scripture: if heretics are able to argue using scripture it is because the Church has taught them what they know and they ought to recognize its authority.[34] The reader is therefore given the opportunity to continue following Tyndale and so become a 'false lyar', or admit their foolish heretical errors and submit to the authority of the Church.

There is a consistency in More's thought about lying even if the style of accusation varies according to the situation. As in his trial, More conceives the liar as someone who breaks their oath to the Church.[35] Later in the preface More analyses the case of George Constantine, whose support for Tyndale led him to import his books illegally. When his actions were exposed, Constantine admitted his guilt, confessed, and informed on his companions, Robert Necton and Johan Byrte.[36] More, as Lord Chancellor, had been in charge of the investigation, and was able to quote from letters exchanged between the guilty parties to make his case against Tyndale.[37] Citing a letter in which Byrte advises Constantine to 'go forth in your matter boldly and put them to theyr proues', More interprets this to mean that

[31] Peter Happé, ed., *Tudor Interludes* (Harmondsworth: Penguin, 1972), pp. 93, 172, 196, 282, 299.
[32] Loewenstein, *Treacherous Faith*, p. 48.
[33] Thomas More, *The Confutation of Tyndale's Answer*, ed. Louis A. Schuster, Richard C. Marius, James P. Lusardi, and Richard J. Schoeck, More, *CW*, VIII (1973), p. 8.
[34] Thomas More, *A Dialogue Concerning Heresies*, ed. Thomas M. C. Lawler, German Marc'hadour, and Richard C. Marius; More, *CW*, VI (1981), pp. 162–6; Parish, *Clerical Marriage*, pp. 44–5.
[35] See above, pp. 48–50.   [36] More, *CW*, VIII, introduction, p. 1248.
[37] Ackroyd, *Life of More*, p. 297; Gray, *Oaths*, p. 172.

mendacity and lying are acceptable tactics for the Reformers dealing with the authorities they think of as tyrants.[38] More refers sarcastically to the letter as 'an apostolycal pystle', and then imagines how Byrte would justify his advice to Constantine:

> Here wyll Byrt peraduenture preche, and brynge vs in the mydwyves of Egypt that saued the chyldren of Israell from Pharo, for which god gaue them new howses. Wherein Byrt and I wyll not myche dispute. For all be it that god hath given hym no howse yet, nor it is not all one wyth a lye to saue a Yonge innocent babe, and wyth periurye to defende an olde pestilent heretycke / and though saynt Austayn sayth that it is not lawfull to lye for nothing: yet I tell not my tale to lay a lye so highly to any suche mennes charge as these folke be, whose hole secte is nothing els but lyes / but I reherse you his letter bycause ye shold se what trewth there is in suche folks wordes.[39]

The passage provides further proof that, cut off from the wise, godly advice of the Church apparently pious men will behave in the most immoral ways and will rapidly lose sight of the truth. More cites one of the limit cases of lying in the Old Testament, the example of the virtuous Hebrew midwives, which appeared to provide most justification for lying in extreme circumstances in order to create more good than harm. More's example is carefully chosen and his argument designed to be even more persuasive to the learned—who would therefore be flattered at being drawn into the author's confidence—than to those reading the text with no real knowledge of the debates of the Church Fathers. Augustine cited the example of the Hebrew midwives in both *De Mendacio* and *Contra Mendacium* as the case most likely to persuade Christians that God might reward lying in exceptional circumstances. But he was careful to distinguish between the actions of people and God's understanding of them: 'it was not their deception that was rewarded, but their benevolence'.[40] For Augustine God always condemns lying even when he does not punish it, and this awareness colours More's discussion.

According to More, the Reformers are far worse than the midwives, which enables More to imply that their actions can never be justified. While the midwives defended innocent children giving them a chance of obtaining salvation as adults and so avoiding limbo, the Reformers are more eager to defend corrupt old heretics.[41] More begins his passage—much as Tyndale begins his by accusing More of a minor sin—with an apparent agreement with his opponent. But the accord is far less significant than would at first appear because More is not agreeing that lying may be possible in some situations, as the sentence suggests. Rather, as the following sentence makes clear, they are agreeing that God did grant the midwives houses ('he made them houses' (Exodus 1:21)) not that this was a reward for lying to save the babies. More then escalates his attack, accusing Byrte of perjury, just as he was to accuse Richard Rich three years later.[42] As a result

[38] More, *Confutation*, p. 19.   [39] More, *Confutation*, pp. 19–20.
[40] Augustine, *Treatises on Various Subjects*, p. 165.
[41] On limbo see Cunningham, *Introduction to Catholicism*, p. 104. The theology of Old Testament salvation has never been entirely clear.
[42] See above, pp. 37–50.

the Reformers' 'hole secte' (a pun on its emptiness masquerading as a return to fundamental Christian values) is 'nothing els but lyes', a direct result of their refusal to be part of the established Church, which involves telling a lie (breaking a solemn promise to keep an oath) in order to exist and then producing ever more lies as a result.

More consciously resorts to demotic language to insult Tyndale, a sign of the low level of debate that the Reformer has inaugurated and which More is therefore forced to adopt in return. Commenting on Tyndale's accusation that many in the Church are time-serving sinners who obey simply because it suits them, More responds with 'All this gere is but a fardel full of lyes / and that woteth Tyndale hym selfe well inough', a sign that to dignify such observations with serious argument would simply magnify the sin.[43] Commenting on Tyndale's attack on the delusory powers of priests, More repeats his words, 'Thys is another ferdell full of lyes, and that he woteth well inough', the repetition serving to articulate the boredom that More feels in having to refute such manifest nonsense.[44] Answering Tyndale's charge that he and others care too much about poetry, More cites Paul's epistle to Titus (1:12) to show that God would use poets to condemn liars like Tyndale: 'One being of themselves, which was a poet of their own, said: The Cretans are always liars, evil beasts, and slow bellies.'[45] For More, Tyndale's accusations about poetry are 'blynde malyce', which makes them akin to a capital crime such as treasonable words which had to be uttered with malice.[46] More is especially keen to refute this particular point and demonstrate that he knows how poetry works and when to use it.[47] To do so More confronts Tyndale's use of a conspicuously poetic conceit, designed to humiliate the distinguished lawyer: 'Tyndale telleth me, yt I haue ben so longe vsed in my fygures of poetry / that when I erre most, I do now as he supposeth by reason of a long custume, byleue my self yᵗ I say most trew / or ellys as wise people when they daunce naked in a net, byleue yᵗ no man can spie them.'[48] More's use of the conceit turns the tables on his opponent:

> Now yf I be by custome of poetrye so blynded, that I can not se myne errours but wene that my lyes were trew: yet yf I fynde any that can shewe them me, I shall sone amende the fawte. But I haue one good lyklyhad that I do not erre or lye after suche fashion as Tyndale tellth me / in that yf it were so, Tyndale than that pryeth there vppon so narrowly, and wyth suche egles eyen as he hath, were very likely to spye it / namely syth I go so bare dawnsyng naked in a net.[49]

---

[43] More, *Confutation*, p. 125.   [44] More, *Confutation*, p. 128.

[45] More, *Confutation*, pp. 150–1; Tyndale, *New Testament*, p. 381.

[46] Richard Marius, *Thomas More: A Biography* (New Haven: Yale University Press, 1984), p. 481; Baldwin Smith, *Treason in Tudor England*, p. 179; Elton, *Policy and Police*, p. 350.

[47] Herman, *Squitter-wits*, pp. 35–7.

[48] More, *Confutation*, p. 176; Tyndale, *Answer*, p. 15. More is quoting Tyndale verbatim. For discussion see Neil Rhodes, with Gordon Kendal and Louise Wilson, *English Renaissance Translation Theory* (London: MHRA, 2013), pp. 84–108, at p. 99; Ruth Ahnert, *The Rise of Prison Literature in the Sixteenth Century* (Cambridge: Cambridge University Press, 2013), p. 123.

[49] More, *Confutation*, p. 176.

More makes a careful appeal to a wider community of readers through his stated desire to correct any errors in his writings, which serves to emphasize Tyndale's isolation beyond the reach of the Church as he attacks the faithful from his position as the proud man apart. It is a reminder of—and variant on—the familiar Catholic taunt to Protestants, where was your church before Luther?[50] Catholic political thinkers argued that while they have the Church to guide them when they worry about whether they are obliged to resist the secular authorities, Protestants have to rely on their own conscience, a terrifying prospect which opens the way for madmen to act unchecked.[51] More insults Tyndale as a reader, claiming that he is no match for him, either because he is not able to see any errors in More's writings or because he is lying in claiming to find any. Tyndale, according to More, has no idea when to use figurative language, a sign that he is a poor rhetorician, unable to read or write with the requisite skill to argue in public, and, therefore, translate the word of God. More knows how to sort truth from fiction and so can understand when a lie is being told, while for Tyndale such distinctions are shrouded in confusion, which is why his arguments are characterized by 'blynde malyce', and why his translation of the Bible should be banned because it makes 'the blessed worde of god, to serue hym for an instrument to dryue men to yᵉ deuell'.[52]

More complains of Tyndale's 'lowde lye' in claiming the Pope permits and encourages immoral behaviour (the Church forbids it); he asks how any 'honest eare' can listen to Tyndale's 'abomynable filthy lyes' about the number of brothels established in Rome (Tyndale is probably inflating the truth somewhat in claiming there are 20,000–30,000 whores in Rome, as the population was severely reduced after the sack of Rome in 1527 and probably stood at only 30,000 or so in the years afterwards, and it is unlikely that even the most vigorous and depraved metropolis could support a ratio of one to one); and he repeats the saying that men who have been to Jerusalem once may 'lye by authoryte' to show that Tyndale lies 'without controllment'.[53] Accusations of lying are central to this debate about the authority of the Church, its relationship to scripture, and whether individuals have the right to form their own judgement about the word of God.[54] Given its influence on later

[50] S. J. Barnett, 'Where Was Your Church Before Luther? Claims for Antiquity of Protestantism Examined', *CH* 68 (1999), 14–41.

[51] See, for example, William Allen, *A true, sincere and modest defence, of English Catholiques that suffer for their faith both at home and abrode* (Rouen, 1584), pp. 84–5; Anne Dillon, *The Construction of Martyrdom in the English Catholic Community, 1535–1603* (Farnham: Ashgate, 2002), p. 354. For an analysis of the context in which debates about conscience developed see Andrew Pettegree, 'The Politics of Toleration in the Free Netherlands', in Grell and Scribner, eds, *Tolerance and Intolerance*, pp. 182–98; Edward G. Andrew, *Conscience and its Critics: Protestant Conscience, Enlightenment Reason, and Modern Subjectivity* (Toronto: Toronto University Press, 2001), pp. 16–26.

[52] More, *Confutation*, p. 176.

[53] More, *Confutation*, pp. 481, 596, 812. On the traumatic effects of the sack of Rome, not least on its population, see Peter Partner, *Renaissance Rome, 1500–1559: A Portrait of a Society* (Berkeley: University of California Press, 1976), pp. 30–3. Tyndale was the first prominent Protestant commentator to equate the Pope with the Antichrist: Diarmaid MacCulloch, 'Archbishop Cranmer: Concord and Tolerance in a Changing Church', in Grell and Scribner, eds, *Tolerance and Intolerance*, pp. 199–215, at p. 202.

[54] John Guy, 'Scripture as Authority: Problems of Interpretation in the 1530's', in Fox and Guy, *Reassessing*, pp. 188–220.

print exchanges such as the debate about the theatres inaugurated by Stephen Gosson's *School of Abuse* (1579), as well as the Marprelate tracts and the Nashe–Harvey quarrel in the late 1580s and 1590s, the importance of lying as a concept and an insult needs to play a central role in our understanding of the polemical culture of Renaissance England.[55] Furthermore, the tone and style of debates was set by religious polemic. Debates needed to reach a wide audience after the Reformation had embraced the concept of the priesthood of all believers in the age of print.[56]

II

Both Tyndale and More frequently invoke the authority of Augustine to support their arguments, as his reputation as the pre-eminent Church Father meant that both Catholics and Protestants habitually looked back to his writings to anchor their positions.[57] Of course, elevating the authority of Augustine marginalised a series of other church fathers and Medieval authorities who had written on lying even though other aspects of their writings were frequently cited elsewhere.[58] They also cite Thomas Aquinas, the dominant theologian of the late medieval Church, at key points in their arguments, and, while not read as widely in the post-Reformation world as Augustine, he had an important influence on many Protestant as well as Catholic thinkers in the post-Reformation world, including the influential Anglican divine Richard Hooker.[59] Aquinas also largely took his cue for his extensive discussion of lying from Augustine, using the same set of examples. He accepts that every lie is a sin and that God never rewards sinful behaviour, even though that might seem to be the case, as with the Hebrew midwives.[60] Aquinas follows Augustine in arguing that we should follow biblical figures of virtue and that 'If . . . any of their statements appear to be untruthful, we must understand such statements to have been figurative and prophetic.'[61] However, he argues for far more exceptions than Augustine. Aquinas claims that some Old Testament figures 'are commended . . . not on account of perfect virtue, but for a certain

---

[55] On Gosson and the More–Tyndale dialogue, see Herman, *Squitter-wits*, ch. 1. On the polemical tradition of prose in the sixteenth century see Dermot Cavanagh, 'Modes of Satire', in Andrew Hadfield, ed., *The Oxford Handbook of English Prose, 1500–1640* (Oxford: Oxford University Press, 2013), pp. 380–95.

[56] Euan Cameron, *The European Reformation* (Oxford: Oxford University Press, 1991), p. 176; Andrew Hadfield, 'John Ponet and the People', in Elizabeth Evenden and Vivienne Westbrook, eds, *Catholic Renewal and Protestant Resistance in Marian England* (Farnham: Ashgate, 2015), pp. 229–50, pp. 236–7.

[57] Arnoud S. Q. Visser, *Reading Augustine in the Reformation: The Flexibility of Intellectual Authority in Europe, 1500–1620* (Oxford: Oxford University Press, 2011).

[58] For an overview see Denery, *Devil Wins*.

[59] Charles H. Lohr, 'Metaphysics', in Schmitt and Skinner, eds, *Cambridge History of Renaissance Philosophy*, pp. 537–638, at pp. 560–3, 597–600, *passim*; Shuger, *Habits of Thought*, pp. 42–3.

[60] *Summa Theologica*, p. 1660. Aquinas discusses lying at II.ii.110–11 (pp. 1657–66).

[61] *Summa Theologica*, II.ii.110, article 3, Reply Obj. 3 (p. 1660).

virtuous disposition', citing the example of Judith, slayer of the tyrant Holofernes, because she exposed herself to danger in her 'desire to save the people'.[62] Aquinas is presumably referring to Judith's promise at the Assyrian camp that when she appears before Holofernes she will 'declare him true thinges, & I will shewe him the way whereby he shal goe and winne all the mountains, without losing the body or life of any of his men'.[63] Judith, of course, had no intention of doing so and planned to cut off Holofernes's head, so Aquinas's judgement that 'one might also say that her words contain truth in some mystical sense' is a rather creative act of interpretation.[64]

It is particularly interesting that Aquinas places the statement that 'every lie is a mortal sin' as one of the objections that he has to counter.[65] His fictitious objector cites Psalm 6:5, 'Thou shalt destroy them that speak in lyes' (Geneva translation), but Aquinas counters that the lie uttered is a 'mischievous lie' (i.e. one designed to harm another person), and so the quotation from the Psalms is not to be taken at face value, as it is hyperbolic, a figure of speech in poetry, and refers only to pernicious lies not every form of lying.[66] In doing so he is directly contradicting Augustine who cited the same verse to quash speculation that some of the Bible could be interpreted as figurative speech, citing Matthew 5:37: 'our divine Lord said with His own lips: "Let your speech be 'Yes, Yes;' 'No, No'"'.[67] Aquinas, among the least obviously poetic of writers, is here defending the scriptural use of figurative writing against the literal-minded Augustine, who was known for his skilful use of rhetoric.[68] Aquinas offers a further hostage to fortune in the series of answers to the next question, 'Of Dissimulation and Hypocrisy'. Answering an objection as to whether hiding a sin is identical to dissimulation, Aquinas disagrees and carefully distinguishes between dissembling 'when by outward signs of deeds or things [a man] signifies that which he is not', and not declaring something: 'one may hide one's sin without being guilty of dissimulation'.[69] Furthermore, he establishes an elaborate taxonomy of lies with different levels of seriousness: 'One lie is more grievous than another, sometimes on account of the matter which it is about—thus a lie about a matter of religious doctrine is most grievous—and sometimes on account of the motive for sinning; thus a mischievous lie is more grievous than an officious or jocose lie.'[70] Aquinas's threefold distinction between officious, jocose, and mischievous and malicious lies—the last two could be further distinguished—which is still influential today, qualifies and rethinks the taxonomy

---

[62] *Summa Theologica*, II.ii.110, article 3, Reply Obj. 3 (p. 1661).
[63] Judith 10:13 (Geneva translation).   [64] *Summa Theologica*, p. 1661.
[65] *Summa Theologica*, II.ii.110, article 4, Obj. 1 (p. 1661).
[66] *Summa Theologica*, II.ii.110, article 4, Reply Obj. 1 (p. 1662).
[67] Augustine, *Treatises on Various Subjects*, p. 61. See also Griffiths, *Lying*, p. 173.
[68] Griffiths, *Lying*, p. 172.
[69] *Summa Theologica*, II.ii.111, article 4, Reply Obj. 4 (p. 1664). See also the discussion in Sissela A. Bok, *Secrets: Concealment and Revelation* (Oxford: Oxford University Press, 1986), chs 2, 4.
[70] *Summa Theologica*, II.ii.113, article 2, Reply Obj. 3 (p. 1669). On Aquinas's classification of lies see Timothy R. Levine, ed., *Encyclopedia of Deception* (New York: Sage, 2014), pp. 31–3.

that Augustine had established in *De Mendacio*.[71] Augustine provided an eightfold hierarchy of lies:

1. Lies in teaching religion.
2. Lies which hurt someone and help nobody.
3. Lies which hurt someone but benefit someone else.
4. Lies told for the pleasure of deceiving someone.
5. Lies told to please others in conversation.
6. Lies which hurt nobody and benefit someone.
7. Lies which hurt nobody and benefit someone by keeping open the possibility of their repentance.
8. Lies which hurt nobody and protect a person from physical defilement.[72]

Even so, Augustine was absolutely clear that lying was always a sin, an issue that is less obvious in Aquinas, who provides more exceptions and qualifications, rather like Augustine's intellectual opponent, Jerome. Augustine's two works spend most time discussing the difficult limit cases of when a lie might be thought to do some good, not in distinguishing between the modes of lying that all agree are sinful: 'There are many kinds of lies, all of which, indeed, we should detest uniformly. There is no lie which is not contrary to truth.'[73] Aquinas is cited, albeit sparingly, by both More and Tyndale, but not his discussion of lying, a sign that their thought about lying may have been informed by Aquinas, but took its cue from Augustine.[74]

Church Fathers who had other significant discussions of the ethics of lying were also ignored, an indication that popular and philosophical perceptions of lying did not necessarily overlap, which is why a history of lying cannot just refer to academic debates. Jerome and Augustine argued about lying, 'one of the fiercest exchanges between any two church fathers'.[75] However, as Dallas Denery points out, 'their disagreements had little traction'.[76] Jerome was also prepared to accept that God might tolerate lying more often than Augustine imagined, and that in fact life on earth was characterized by deception, lies, and falsehood, returning time and again to the theme in his writings. His homily on Psalm 115, hardly an obvious source for material on lying, begins with a Neoplatonic proposition that as 'There is no truth in our substance; there is only shadow and in a certain sense a lie,' every man is a lie. The Psalm is interpreted to mean that 'I shall please the Lord in the land of the living; still, as I reflect upon human life and ponder over all the different species of

---

[71] Bok, *Lying*, p. 34; Denery, *The Devil Wins*, p. 115.

[72] Leslie, *Born Liars*, p. 300; Augustine, *On Lying*, ch. 14 (*Treatises on Various Subjects*, pp. 86–8).

[73] Augustine, *Against Lying*, ch. 3 (*Treatises on Various Subjects*, p. 129).

[74] Brian Gogan, *The Common Corps of Christendom: Ecclesiological Themes in the Writings of Sir Thomas More* (Leiden: Brill, 1982), pp. 76–7; Werrell, *Theology*, p. 175.

[75] Jason A. Myers, 'Law, Lies and Letter Writing: An Analysis of Jerome and Augustine on the Antioch Incident (Galatians 2: 11–14)', *SJT* 66 (2013), 127–39, p. 138. See also Snyder, *Dissimulation*, pp. 16–17; Denery *The Devil Wins*, pp. 107–8.

[76] Denery, *The Devil Wins*, p. 107. Some philosophers cited Jerome: see Kerr, ed., *Penguin Book of Lies*, p. 111.

error, I do not find truth in this world.'[77] This observation leads Jerome to the Cretan liar paradox, which was cited in the Renaissance as a 'classic example of perfect equivocation':

> If you are lying and in your very fact of lying are speaking true to form, you are, therefore, lying... O you, who are speaking with me, if you lie and speak truly by lying, by the very fact you are lying, and in the same proposition one may be speaking truly and lying at the same time... By their clever art and deception, philosophers have made the great discovery of how in the same utterance one may be speaking truly and telling a lie.[78]

Jerome's position is fundamentally at odds with that of Augustine. While Augustine argued that the mind could separate spiritual truth from earthly lies, Jerome argued that the world was so immersed in sinful deception that the two could hardly ever be prised apart successfully. It was true that the 'man of holiness' could see the difference because he had become a god 'and when he is a god, he ceases to be a man and no longer utters lies'.[79]

For Jerome the recognition of our sinfulness was likely to inspire humility and an acceptance of the glory of God.[80] It is hardly surprising that Jerome and Augustine clashed so forcefully over the interpretation of Paul's Letter to the Galatians 2:11–14.[81] Paul explains how he upbraided Peter for withdrawing from eating with the Gentiles in Antioch when a group of Jewish Christians arrived. Paul accuses Peter of hypocrisy as he is acting not out of conviction but out of fear. Furthermore, Peter had no need to separate himself from Gentile Christians and return to the Jews who wanted to preserve their distinction from non-Jews: in doing so he was undermining Christ's message of universal salvation: 'If thou being a Jewe, liuest as the Gentiles, and not like the Jewes, why constrainest thou the Gentiles to doe like the Jewes?' (Galatians 2:14 (Geneva translation)). For Jerome this was a staged argument as Paul knew that Peter was trying to avoid offence in sitting with the strict Jews and only rebuked him in public because he was concerned not to cause equal offence to the Gentile Christians. Both Peter and Paul, like Jerome, had the unity of the Church at heart and were doing all they could to prevent dangerous division. For Jerome, Peter is labelled a hypocrite only as a 'tactical rhetorical device', the passage requiring careful decoding by the faithful who need to be alert to the complex nature of truth in the Bible.[82]

---

[77] Jerome, *Homilies: I (1–59 On The Psalms)*, trans. Sister Marie Liguori Eward (Washington, DC: The Catholic University of America Press, 1964), Homily 40 (On Psalm 115), pp. 293–9, at pp. 293–4.
[78] Jerome, *Homilies*, pp. 294–5. On the Cretan paradox as classic equivocation see Mitchell B. Merback, 'Nobody Dares: Freedom, Dissent, Self-Knowing, and Other Possibilities in Sebald Beham's *Impossible*', *RQ* 63 (2010), 1037–105, p. 1055. See also Wolfgang Künne, 'On Liars, "Liars", and Harmless Self-Reference', in Anne Reboul, ed., *Mind, Values, and Metaphysics: Philosophical Essays in Honor of Kevin Mulligan* (New York: Springer, 2014), pp. 355–431.
[79] Jerome, *Homilies*, p. 295.   [80] Jerome, *Homilies*, p. 296.
[81] For an analysis of this dispute, to which I am indebted, see Griffiths, *Lying*, pp. 145–53.
[82] Griffiths, *Lying*, p. 147.

Augustine has little time for such a complicated explanation which reads the Bible as a subtle and nuanced text demanding, at times, counter-intuitive interpretation. A far more serious error, according to Augustine, is that Jerome has interpreted scripture to contain a number of lies, exactly what Augustine had been eager to avoid through his own ingenious readings of challenging passages, notably his interpretation of Jacob's deception of his father as 'not a lie but a mystery'.[83] For Augustine, Jerome had introduced the 'useful lie' into scripture which would open the floodgates for all sorts of disingenuous arguments and deceptive behaviour in the name of furthering the truth: 'Once any useful lie is admitted into such a high authority, no part of these [scriptural] books that seems to anyone difficult with respect to conduct or incredible with respect to faith will escape being referred by this same most pernicious rule to the stratagems or compassionate politeness of a lying author.'[84] Augustine's strictures would have a prophetic resonance down the ages and variations of his argument were used throughout the sixteenth century to combat the phenomenon of 'Nicodemism', which flourished throughout Europe after the Reformation.[85] Galatians was central to debates about the declaration of faith after the Reformation, with Paul declaring that there was now no difference between identities under one faith ('Now there is neither Jew, neither gentile' (Tyndale translation)), and was the subject of one of Luther's most influential treatises, especially widely read in England, in which he outlined his understanding that the Bible demanded that all Christians are equal before God ('the priesthood of all believers').[86] He attacked Jerome's commentary in particular, for not recognizing clearly enough that Christ had made the Old Law obsolete, and that it was vital that Christians make an open profession of faith not that they live to protect the Church.[87] In his commentary, Calvin, the central opponent of Nicodemism, was quite clear that Peter was wrong to hide his faith and Paul was right to insist that every Christian stand up and be counted and not risk being a hypocrite or a liar, and he upbraids the apologists of Peter:

> There are some who apologize for Peter . . . because, being the apostle of the circumcision, he was bound to take a peculiar concern in the salvation of the Jews; while they at the same time admit that Paul did right in pleading the cause of the Gentiles. But it is foolish to defend what the Holy Spirit by the mouth of Paul has condemned. This was no affair of men, but involved the purity of the gospel, which was in danger of being contaminated by Jewish leaven.[88]

For Calvin this episode provides a clear message and urges Christians to follow Paul's example and proclaim their faith: 'It was particularly advantageous, that the

---

[83] Augustine, *Against Lying*, ch. 10 (*Treatises on Various Subjects*, p. 152).

[84] Griffiths, *Lying*, p. 147.   [85] See below, pp. 141–4.

[86] Tyndale, *New Testament*, p. 332; Robert Kolb, 'The Influence of Luther's Galatians Commentary of 1535 on Later Sixteenth-Century Lutheran Commentaries on Galatians', *Archiv für Reformationsgeschichte* 84 (1993), 156–84.

[87] Martin Luther, *Commentary on Galatians*, in Luther, *Selections*, pp. 99–165; Jerome, *Commentary on Galatians*, ed. Andrew Cain (Washington, DC: The Catholic University of America Press, 1964).

[88] Calvin, *Commentaries*, XXI, p. 64.

good cause, in which all had an interest, should be openly defended in the presence of the people, that Paul might have a better opportunity of shewing that he did not shrink from the broad light of day.'[89]

Other voices which were more in line with Jerome's position than Augustine's were not hard to find. St John Chrysostom, whose work, like that of Augustine and Jerome and unlike Aquinas, was translated into English in the sixteenth century, also argues in favour of occasional duplicity in order to further the gospel. In *De Sacerdotio* (*Six Books on the Priesthood*) Chrysostom represents himself as a worldly young man debating how to live life with his close friend, the ascetic and morally upstanding Basil. Basil tries to persuade Chrysostom to enter the priesthood, but before ordination Chrysostom plans to escape. Basil, upset and affected by what he sees as his friend's betrayal, points out that he has put him in an unenviable position, especially if he has to lie to deny knowledge of Chrysostom's plans. Chrysostom replies that he has indeed deceived Basil, but he has done this for his friend's benefit, which leads to a reflection on the problem of deception:

> For if the evil of deception is absolute, and it is never right to make use of it, I am prepared to pay any penalty you please... If the thing is not always harmful, but becomes good or bad according to the intention of those who practise it, you must desist from complaining of deceit, and prove that it has been devised against you for a bad purpose... A well-timed deception, undertaken with an upright intention, has such advantages, that many persons have often had to undergo punishment for abstaining from fraud.[90]

For Chrysostom, such deceit is vital to existence in the world, as many modern secular students of lying have argued, and he argues that deception is vital in warfare, in marriage, between friends, and parents and children.[91] Deceit 'is beneficial not only to the deceivers, but also to those who are deceived', as physicians well know.[92] Only those with malign intentions are sinners: 'For that man would fairly deserve to be called a deceiver who made an unrighteous use of the practice, not one who did so with a salutary purpose.'[93]

Chrysostom, like Jerome, argues that the intention of the deceiver or liar is crucial in evaluating the nature of the particular speech act. Tyndale would seem to be following suit, urging Reformers to preserve their faith using devious means if necessary, not proclaiming the truth at all costs. However, although the argument may be the same, Tyndale does not cite either authority on the subject of truth and lying. He does cite Jerome elsewhere in the *Apology* to support particular points, claiming that Jerome would have allowed clerical marriage and that there is nothing in his writings to suggest that he supported the practice of confession.[94] And

---

[89] Calvin, *Commentaries*, XXI, pp. 64–5.

[90] Saint John Chrysostom, *Six Books on the Priesthood*, trans. W. R. W. Stevens and T. P. Brandram, in Saint Chrysostom, *On the Priesthood; Ascetic Treatises; Select Homilies and Letters; Homilies on the Statues* (Edinburgh: T. & T. Clark, 1996), pp. 33–83, at p. 37; Griffiths, *Lying*, pp. 137–8.

[91] Chrysostom, *Priesthood*, p. 37.

[92] Chrysostom, *Priesthood*, p. 38. Augustine argues the opposite case: *Treatises on Various Subjects*, p. 67.

[93] Chrysostom, *Priesthood*, p. 38.   [94] Tyndale, *Answer*, pp. 152, 213–14.

Chrysostom is further cited to prove that he was not a believer in the doctrine of transubstantiation, contrary to what More had claimed.[95] Like More, Tyndale cites Augustine frequently to support his case, arguing that Augustine, as Chrysostom, did not believe in transubstantiation, and claiming that when he wrote that Chrysostom had been converted to Christianity by the 'authority of the church' he really meant 'holy conversation' with godly men, not the institution and its practices.[96]

Given the significance of the More–Tyndale debate, the importance that truthfulness assumes in the exchange, and the frequency with which the terms 'lies', 'liar', and 'lying' are bandied about, it is important to note the lack of a substantial exchange about the nature of lying. More cites Augustine on lying, a passing reference to the case of the Hebrew midwives, but Tyndale, versed as he was in the works of the Church Fathers, does not provide any reasoned opposition with counter-examples, or a different interpretation of More's polemical citation. It is most probable, therefore, that his advice to Reformers that they could resist hostile authorities in devious ways in order to further the faith is his own judgement—based in part, of course, on his reading of the Church Fathers and his own contemporary theologians, in addition to the translation of the Bible. The result was that in the anglophone world Augustine was invariably the sole authority on questions of lying and that when debates took place they either followed his line of reasoning that lying was always a sin and never acceptable in the eyes of God, or they took the opposite approach, and sought to find loopholes that admitted that untruthfulness could occasionally be sanctioned in the name of a higher cause.

The More–Tyndale debate serves as a prelude to the post-Reformation arguments about truth and lying, and how to interpret Mark 12:17, 'Then give to Caesar that which belongeth to Caesar; and to God, that which pertaineth to God' (Tyndale translation).[97] For Tyndale this meant that one had a duty to obey secular rulers and make sure that one had a clear idea about the spiritual realm which belonged to God so that this could be protected when the secular authorities exceeded their rights (i.e. one could lie). This was a complicated task that placed great demands on the individual Christian to be able to make the right choice under pressing circumstances. For Catholics, the failure to adhere to a sacred authority would inevitably lead to a cacophony of voices, all claiming to tell the truth, but all inspired by Satan, the father of lies.[98]

III

William Baldwin (d.1563), probably the most significant English writer to emerge during the reign of Edward VI, and therefore a writer who had lived through the

[95] Tyndale, *Answer*, pp. 260–1.
[96] Tyndale, *Answer*, pp. 259–60, 49–50.   [97] Tyndale, *New Testament*, p. 93.
[98] Evans, *Problems of Authority*; Haigh, 'Continuity of Catholicism'; MacCulloch, *Reformation*, pp. 172–9.

bewildering religious changes in England in the mid-sixteenth century, captures this issue in an extended description in his prose fiction, *Beware the Cat* (*c.*1552, published 1570).[99] The narrator, Master Streamer, takes a magic potion which will enable him to listen to the voices of the cats on the roof of the house of the Protestant printer John Day, where he is staying.[100] The problem is that the drugs work rather too successfully and enable him to hear everything taking place within a wide radius of London's city walls:

> While I harkened to this broil, laboring to discern both voices and noises asunder, I heard such a mixture as I think was never in Chaucer's House of Fame; for there was nothing within an hundred mile of me done on any side, (for from so far but no farther, the air may come because of obliquation) but I heard it as well as if I had been by it, and could discern all voices, but by means of noises understand none. Lord what ado women made in their beds—some scolding; some laughing, some weeping; some singing to their sucking children, which made a woeful noise with their continual crying. And one shrewd wife a great way off (I think at St. Albans) called her husband 'cuckold' so loud and shrilly that I heard that plain; and would fain have heard the rest, but could not by means of barking of dogs, grunting of hogs wawling of cats, rumbling of rats, gaggling of geese, humming of bees, rousing of bucks, gaggling of ducks, singing of swans, ringing of pans, crowing of cocks, sewing of socks, cackling of hens, scrabbling of pens, peeping of mice, trulling of dice, curling of frogs, and toads in the bogs, chirping of crickets, shutting of wickets, shriking of owls, flittering of fowls, routing of knaves, snorting of slaves, farting of churls, fizzling of girls, with many things else—as ringing of bells, counting of coins, mounting of groins, whispering of lovers, springling of plovers, groaning and sewing, baking and brewing, scratching and rubbing, watching and shrugging, with such a sort of commixed noises as would a-deaf anybody to have heard[.][101]

This long description of the noises that Streamer hears is not easy to interpret with any certainty, which is surely the point. Streamer plans to listen to the cats, who can be seen to stand as the shadowy state of Catholics, able to communicate with each other and feed off the official state by creating their own news network which functions with remarkable success.[102] The problem is that not only are the Cats not straightforwardly Catholics and distinguishable from the rest of society, but that trying to discover who they are proves impossible owing to the cacophony of noises that Streamer is able to hear when he takes the potion. As he looks out of his window at the gate the night before he takes the medicines, Streamer sees the

[99] On Baldwin and his significance, see King, *English Reformation Literature*, pp. 358–406; Stephen Gresham, 'William Baldwin: Literary Voice of the Reign of Edward VI', *HLQ* 44 (1981), 101–16; Harriet Archer and Andrew Hadfield, eds, A Mirror for Magistrates *in Context: Literature, History and Politics before the Age of Shakespeare* (Cambridge: Cambridge University Press, 2016).

[100] On Day, see the *ODNB* entry; Elizabeth Evenden, *Patents, Pictures and Patronage: John Day and the Tudor Book Trade* (Aldershot: Ashgate, 2008).

[101] William Baldwin, *Beware the Cat: The First English Novel*, ed. William A. Ringler, Jr, and William Flachmann (San Marino: Huntington Library, 1988), pp. 31–2; Paul M. Gaudet, 'William Baldwin's *A Treatise of Moral Philosophy* (1564): A Variorum Edition with Introduction', PhD dissertation, Princeton University, 1972, pp. 21–2.

[102] Andrew Hadfield, 'Grimalkin and Other Shakespearean Celts', *YSPSR* 25 (2015), 55–76, at pp. 56–9.

'quarters of men' impaled on the gate spikes.[103] These are the remains of men executed for treason, most probably those dispatched after the Prayer Book Rebellion in the south-west (1547–9) and Kett's Rebellion (1549), the former desiring a return to the practices of the late medieval Church, the latter alleviation for economic distress.[104] The authorities' actions in identifying and executing traitors suggest that they have a confidence in being able to uncover the truth that is at odds with the reality that Streamer experiences when his senses are artificially heightened: the different reasons for the revolts suggesting that Streamer's experience reflects the complicated reality of Edwardian England.

It has often been assumed that Baldwin was a relatively hot Protestant, eager to foster the Reformation under Edward VI.[105] *Beware the Cat* would appear to provide a more complicated and nuanced picture of his religious position, and suggest that he was acutely aware that religion could never be isolated from other aspects of life. Streamer experiences a wall of sound when he is able to hear what is happening in England, the comic variety of the description suggesting that life goes on whatever religious policy might be imagined or imposed by the government. Mouse-Slayer's story of her picaresque adventures in various households, recounted in part three as her defence against accusations that she has broken cat law, demonstrates that few people in England have any idea that the old Catholic faith has been replaced by Protestantism. Mouse-Slayer's story culminates in an episode in a household where a young woman believes that the cat is really the incarnation of a child of an old bawd. The cat is tormented by 'an ungracious fellow' who finds it amusing to shoe the cat by sticking walnut shells to her feet. When she tries to catch a mouse she wakes her master who thinks she is the devil and a priest is called to exorcize the house. The priest arrives with a 'holy candle he had kept two year' and 'a holy water sprinkle'—clearly after the religious reforms of 1548 banned them—and Mouse-Slayer, little realizing that she is about to be the subject of an exorcism, imagines that she will 'have seen some Mass that night', as she had 'many nights before in other places'.[106] However, the episode ends in farce: when the priest sees the cat, he collapses in fear and his candle singes the clothes of another priest. The priest falls so that 'his face lay upon a boy's bare arse, which belike was fallen headlong under him, was so astonished that, when the boy, which for fear had beshit himself, had all to-rayed his face, he neither felt nor smelt it, nor

---

[103] Baldwin, *Beware the Cat*, p. 10.

[104] Anthony Fletcher, *Tudor Rebellions* (London: Longman, 1983), chs 5–6; Wood, *1549 Rebellions*; Robert W. Maslen, *Elizabethan Fictions: Espionage, Counter-Espionage, and the Duplicity of Fiction in Early Elizabethan Prose Narratives* (Oxford: Clarendon Press, 1997), pp. 78–9. On executions, see Bellamy, *Treason*, ch. 5.

[105] Scott Lucas describes him as 'zealously evangelical': A Mirror for Magistrates *and the Politics of the English Reformation* (Amherst: University of Massachusetts Press, 2009), p. 36. John King sees him as a more ecumenical figure, writing 'in the tradition of Protestantized Erasmianism' (*English Reformation Literature*, p. 361).

[106] Baldwin, *Beware the Cat*, p. 48. On the significance of Edward's religious reforms, see Jennifer Loach, *Edward VI*, ed. George Bernard and Penry Williams (New Haven: Yale University Press, 1999), pp. 49–50; Felicity Heal, *Reformation in Britain and Ireland* (Oxford: Oxford University Press, 2003), pp. 164–5.

removed from him'. Mouse-Slayer makes her way to her young mistress, the mistaken identity is revealed, and the perpetrator of the crime takes the candle to see the cat and laughs. The others curse him, hot water is used to remove the pitch that had held the shells on Mouse-Slayer's feet, and the company retire to bed.[107]

The description contains many of the elements of anti-Catholic satire: gullible superstition, the fetishization of holy objects, fear and cowardice, and a concentration on the anus.[108] But is that what we are witnessing here? The people are represented as foolish and silly, but not particularly unusual or reprehensible, and more lost and confused than wilful and wicked. Furthermore, Mouse-Slayer had been looking forward to a mass and she is quite clear that it was easy to experience one in the early 1550s. If the cats are Catholics—and it is an allegorical representation the reader is invited to make—then they appear no different from the people in whose houses they live. *Beware the Cat* shows us a nation of Catholics, a not-so-secret state that is, in fact, easy to uncover. For contemporary readers, especially those who were committed Protestants—and there would have been a higher percentage of Reformers among the literate—Baldwin's text would have made uncomfortable reading, revealing the nation to be almost exclusively Catholic and, worse still perhaps, indifferent to the dramatic religious changes taking place in London.[109] Rebels could be executed and their body parts displayed on the capital's walls *pour encourager les autres*, but life would probably go on as before.

The series of deafening noises that Streamer hears are, on the one hand, an innocent mixture of good, bad, and indifferent sounds emanating from any population that could be found in contemporary Europe, as the structures of everday life continue whatever political changes take place.[110] But, on the other, they are a sign of the diverse nature of human religious experience, one that needs to be controlled and ordered if anarchy is not to become a serious danger, precisely what Catholics warned Protestants they were in danger of doing in removing the unified authority of the Church. As Norman Jones has pointed out, while there could be a calm belief that, in the words of the Earl of Derby writing in 1539, the English had 'forsaken Satan, his satellites and all the works of darkness and dedicated themselves to Christ's words and faith', fifty years later they 'were happily calling one another heretics, schismatics, infidels, Anabaptists, Puritans, Papists, and other divisive terms'.[111] After the cat has been identified and the company calmed down, the priest who has been singed gets up, 'took heart a grace, and before he was spied rose up and took the candle in his hand, and looked upon me and all the company, and fell a-laughing at the handsome lying of his fellow's face'.

[107] Baldwin, *Beware the Cat*, p. 49.
[108] Tessa Watt, *Cheap Print and Popular Piety, 1550–1640* (Cambridge: Cambridge University Press, 1993), pp. 88–9; R. W. Scribner, *Popular Culture and Popular Movements in Reformation Germany* (London: A. C. Black, 1987), ch. 13.
[109] On literacy and Protestantism, see David Cressy, *Literacy and the Social Order: Reading and Writing in Tudor and Stuart England* (Cambridge: Cambridge University Press, 1980), ch. 4.
[110] Fernand Braudel, *Civilization and Capitalism, 15th–18th Century*, 3 vols, *Volume I: The Structures of Everyday Life: The Limits of the Possible*, trans. Siân Reynolds (London: Collins, 1986, rpt of 1981).
[111] Jones, *English Reformation*, p. 97.

The priest's face is covered in shit and lying on an arse, so the 'handsome lying' works as a description of its uncomfortable position, but it is also a sign of his duplicity and his failure to tell the truth. Yet again, this looks very like anti-Catholic satire. However, it is notable that another priest, not a figure who might be allied to the Reform movement, observes this unsavoury image and laughs, and that it is the cat, eager to hear mass, who records the exchange. This chain of events may be a sign that the faults of the Church were recognized by its clergy. Perhaps they were complacently ignored and the problem could only be solved by splitting the Church as Reformers claimed; or perhaps this is an indication that reform could have come from within and that the really serious problem is the break with authority creating an insecure and terrifying future as one and a half millennia of Christian history came to an end with no one really sure what would come next as power was devolved to the competing voices of the people.[112]

IV

Beware the Cat reveals men and women caught between a series of competing authorities: Catholicism and Protestantism; the state and the shadowy state of the cats; writing and speech; print and oral culture.[113] In this complicated world it is not clear who tells the truth and who lies, either through claiming a false authority or by committing a series of falsehoods and perjuries.[114] Of course, it was not long before attempts were made to stabilize Protestant authority and establish a tradition that would secure the truth and explain to Catholics that the Protestant Church did indeed predate Luther, enabling Reformers to reveal that it was their opponents who were the liars who had abused and distorted the message of Christ with their false traditions.[115] John Foxe's *Acts and Monuments of the Christian Church* (1563) was the work which performed this task throughout the whole Elizabethan period. Conceived originally in exile during the reign of Mary as an international history of Protestant martyrs, the brainchild of John Day as well as John Foxe, *Acts and Monuments* developed into a historical defence of the Church of England.[116]

---

[112] For a related argument see Andrew Hadfield, 'Spenser and Religion—Yet Again', *SEL* 51 (2011), 21–46.

[113] For relevant analysis, see Terence N. Bowers, 'The Production and Communication of Knowledge in William Baldwin's *Beware the Cat*: Toward a Typographic Culture', *Criticism* 33 (1991), 1–29; Jennifer Richards, 'Reading and Listening to William Baldwin', in Archer and Hadfield, eds, Mirror for Magistrates *in Context*, pp. 71–88; Rachel Stenner, 'The Act of Penning in William Baldwin's *Beware the Cat*', *RS* 30 (2016), 334–49.

[114] A marginal note labels the 'ungracious fellow' 'a liar and a doer of shrewd turns' when, on recognizing the cat, he pretends to call 'to mind that erst he had forgot' (Baldwin, *Beware the Cat*, p. 49).

[115] For a recent version of the history see Andrew Escobedo, *Nationalism and Historical Loss in Renaissance England: Foxe, Dee, Spenser, Milton* (Ithaca, NY: Cornell University Press, 2004), pp. 25–44.

[116] Elizabeth Evenden and Thomas S. Freeman, *Religion and the Book in Early Modern England: The Making of John Foxe's 'Book of Martyrs'* (Cambridge: Cambridge University Press, 2011), pp. 56–60.

Eventually, in 1632, when the Church was firmly established as the national Church, a new section detailing the histories of martyrs reverted to 'an earlier form of protestant identity' based on the sacrifice of the faithful, which 'effectively destroyed Foxe's painfully constructed justification for an established protestant church'.[117]

For Foxe, unlike Baldwin, lying was a straightforward issue: Protestants told the truth and Catholics tried to stop them by telling lies.[118] The true villain of papal history was Gregory VII (Hildebrand of Sovana) (1073–85) who had the power to excommunicate and depose the Emperor Henry IV and replace him with Duke Rudolf of Swabia in 1077.[119] For Foxe he is guilty of a double lie, as the marginal note signals to the reader. Duke Rudolf was sent

> a crowne from the Pope wt this verse.
> Petra dedit petro, Petrus diadema Rodolopho.
> The rocke gaue the crowne to Peter,
> Peter geueth it to Rodolph.

> Here by the way of digressyon, to make a litle glose, vpon this barbarous verse, two notable lies are to be noted. One, where he lieth vppon Christ, the other where he lieth vpon S. Peter. First that Christ gaue any temporal diadem to Peter it is a most manifest lie, and agaynst the scriptures, whan as he would not take it, being geuen to him self, and saith his kingdome is not of this world. Again where he saith that Peter geueth it to Rodulh. Here he playeth the Poet, for nether had Peter any such thing to geue, & if had, yet he wold not haue geuen it to Rodulph, from the right heir. Nether is it true that Peter did geue it, because Hildebrand gaue it. For it is no good argument Hildebrand did geue it. Ergo Peter did geue it, except ye wil say, Hildebrand stirred vp great warres and bloudshed in Germany.[120]

Foxe's sarcastic and exasperated prose bears many resemblances to the language of the More–Tyndale exchange, not least in its contemptuous use of the word 'poet' to describe the invention of an authority that does not exist, and so abusing the fundamental division between Christ's kingdom in heaven and secular authority on earth established in Jesus's debate with Pilate in John 18.[121] Foxe mimics the syllogistic style of argument of late medieval schoolmen in order to ridicule and undermine his Catholic opponents: their desire to lie and so bully people into

[117] David Loades, 'The Early Reception', 'John Foxe's Acts and Monuments Online' (http://www.johnfoxe.org/index.php?realm=more&gototype=modern&type=essay&book=essay7) (accessed 18 August 2015).

[118] As Patrick Collinson points out 'For Foxe's Catholic detractors, his book was not some curate's egg, good and bad in parts. It was all bad, consisting entirely of lies, "as full of lies as lines"': 'Truth, Lies and Fiction in Sixteenth-century Protestant Historiography', in Donald R. Kelley and David Harris Sacks, eds, *The Historical Imagination in Early Modern Britain: History, Rhetoric and Fiction, 1500–1800* (Cambridge: Cambridge University Press, 1997), pp. 37–68, at p. 48.

[119] See *Popes*, pp. 154–6; F. Donald Logan, *A History of the Church in the Middle Ages* (2nd edn, London: Routledge, 2013), pp. 105–7; Christopher Brooke, *Europe in the Central Middle Ages, 962–1154* (2nd edn, London: Longman, 1987), pp. 354–69.

[120] John Foxe, *Acts and Monuments of the Church* (London, 1563), p. 42, 'John Foxe's Acts and Monuments Online' (http://www.johnfoxe.org/index.php?realm=text&gototype=modern&edition=1563&pageid=42&anchor=lies#kw) (accessed 19 August 2015).

[121] Francis Oakley, 'Christian Obedience and Authority, 1520–1550', in Burns and Goldie, eds, *Cambridge History of Political Thought*, pp. 160–92, at p. 183; Skinner, *Foundations*, II, pp. 15–19.

acquiescing to their demands needs to be exposed in ordinary language so that the extent of their duplicity can be widely recognized. The verse—which may or may not be authentic—neatly encapsulates Foxe's case against the papacy.[122] Popes claimed a false power over the other Churches, and in order to do so they resorted to a fictitious history. Gregory/Hildebrand's rule was a particular turning point for Protestant historians, the dawn of the fourth stage of the Apocalypse, 'The Time of Antichrist', as the Pope humiliated the Emperor and provided the forces of Satan with a temporarily unassailable power.[123] Christ did not give a secular crown to Peter so he could not have passed down this power to his successors in the papacy, a double falsehood that obscures and distorts the significance of the Church and its history. The final sentence cited here illustrates as it mimics the chop logic that Foxe thought had increasingly dominated the Church before the Reformation. To argue that Hildebrand acted on his own authority in giving Rudolf the crown would expose the Church to the eyes of the world, so a lie has to be invented, that Peter provided the authority for the Pope to transfer the power from one emperor to another, in order to hide the truth that is obvious to all parties that 'Hildebrand stirred vp great warres and bloudshed in Germany.' Foxe is placing his (suppressed) truthful syllogism,

> Hildebrand caused war and bloodshed.
> Hildebrand did this as Pope.
> Therefore, the Pope caused war and bloodshed

against the lying logic of the Catholic Church. Only a true history of the Church and the martyrs who were the witnesses of the faith can combat this level of institutional duplicity.

Foxe frequently represents clergy attempting to undermine secular authority resorting to lies, a sign of Satan's rule in 'The Time of Antichrist'. His account of the reign of King John (1199–1216), just over a hundred years after Gregory's papacy, was influential in creating a widespread understanding of John as a flawed monarch of a precariously independent England eventually succumbing to overwhelming odds as he is poisoned by monks, and informed the two important plays about John performed in the 1590s.[124] Foxe makes much of Peter of Wakefield, a hermit who was executed in 1213 for his prophecy that John would die before the

---

[122] The story was reproduced in eighteenth-century histories of the papacy, but may have reached authors from Foxe: Jean-Henri-Samuel Formey, *An Ecclesiastical History: From the Birth of Christ, to the Present Time*, 2 vols (London, 1766), I, p. 189.

[123] John N. King, *Foxe's 'Book of Martyrs' and Early Modern Print Culture* (Cambridge: Cambridge University Press, 2006), pp. 38–9. V. N. Olsen, *John Foxe and the Elizabethan Church* (Berkeley: University of California Press, 1973), pp. 70, 113, 164, *passim*. John Bale had earlier placed great significance on Hildebrand's actions in his apocalyptic scheme of ecclesiastical history: Hadfield, *Literature, Politics and National Identity*, p. 63. The two plays are George Peele (?), *The Troublesome Reign of King John*, ed. Charles R. Forker (Manchester: Manchester University Press, 2011); and William Shakespeare, *King John*, ed. E. A. J. Honigmann (London: Methuen, 1954). For Foxe's influence see Peele (?), *Troublesome Reign*, pp. 47–50; *Narrative and Dramatic Sources*, IV, pp. 49–54.

[124] Dermot Cavanagh, *Language and Politics in the Sixteenth-Century History Play* (Basingstoke: Palgrave Macmillan, 2003), pp. 82–3; Willy Maley, '"And bloody England into England gone": Empire, Monarchy, and Nation in *King John*', in Willy Maley and Margaret Tudeau-Clayton, eds, *This*

next Ascension Day (23 May 1213).[125] He describes Peter as 'an idell gadder about, and pratling marchaunt', who is then thrust onto the bigger stage when his potential to inspire opposition in the credulous people is recognized by the self-interested and untrustworthy clergy:

> This Peter they made to prophecie lies, rumoring his prophecies abrode to bring the king out of al credit with his people. They noysed it dayly among the commons of the realme, that Christe had twyse appeared to this prophet of theirs, in shape of a childe be-twene the priestes handes, once at Yorke, another time at Ponfret: and that he had breathed vpon him thrise, saying: peace, peace, peace, and teaching many thinges which he anone after declared to the byshops, and bid people amend their noughty liuing. Being rapt also in spirite (they say) he beheld the ioyse of heauen, and sorowes of hell. For skant were there three sayth the Chronicle, among a thousand that liued christianly.[126]

John, being a relatively sane monarch, laughs at Peter's prophecies and makes sure that he is visible to all in his royal tent on Ascension Day with his counsellors, while musical festivities take place all around. Afterwards 'his enemies being confused, tourned all to an allegoricall vnderstandyng, to make the prophet good, & said: he is no longer king. for the Pope reigneth and not he', which is such a creative/poetic explanation of matters that it cannot be counted true: 'yet reigned he still & his sonne after him, to proue that Prophet a lyar'.[127] Foxe again appeals to the Protestant dichotomy of plain, truthful speech and elaborate, false Catholic circumlocution. However, the clergy's words persuade many of the King's foolish subjects and, although he does not want to, John is eventually forced to have the false prophet executed because his words 'had troubled all the realme, peruerted the harts of the people, & raised the commens against him'.[128]

The case of Peter of Wakefield illustrates the dangers of living in a superstitious time when so few people were really Christians, exactly as William Baldwin had represented England in the reign of Edward VI in *Beware the Cat*.[129] So few people have a proper religious sensibility and understanding that they do not have a strong enough faith to recognize the threat of a concerted enemy such as the medieval clergy, or the ability to expose even the most straightforward lies. Duplicity, falsehood, and lying inevitably flourish if the true faith is hidden, not properly supported and made visible. Foxe is at pains to show that not only did the shadowy, anonymous clergy put the foolish hermit up to the job, but that they were able to expand and develop their evil plan, spreading false rumours of the Christ-child appearing to Peter which he—or, more likely, the bishops—interpreted to mean that God was angry with the behaviour of the people. Protestants believed that false miracles were cynically used, like relics, to enhance the Church's power among the

England, that Shakespeare: New Angles on Englishness and the Bard (Farnham: Ashgate, 2010), pp. 49–61, at pp. 50, 52.

[125] W. L. Warren, *King John* (2nd edn, London: Eyre Methuen, 1978), p. 201.

[126] Foxe, *Acts and Monuments*, p. 115.   [127] Foxe, *Acts and Monuments*, p. 116.

[128] Foxe, *Acts and Monuments*, p. 116.

[129] See Bowers, 'Production and Communication of Knowledge', p. 22.

credulous people who did not have the knowledge to tell truth from lies.[130] Providential signs from God were a different matter.[131]

The martyrs serve as witness to the true Church during the ages of intense persecution, especially after the dawn of the fourth age. Thomas Bilney (1495– 1531) is an important figure in Foxe's history, worthy of a woodcut of him 'in an inn on the way to his execution' placing his finger in a candle flame to test his resolution to endure martyrdom, an image that prefigures that of Thomas Cranmer thrusting his hand into the flames as penance for signing a document renouncing his faith.[132] Bilney was a predominantly orthodox priest who was frequently in trouble with the authorities for his vociferous opposition to the veneration of saints and relics. He was imprisoned for heresy and forced to recant, but, repenting of his weakness, he continued to denounce what he saw as idolatry, before he was arrested and burned at the stake in Norwich in 1531.[133] Bilney's case was notorious and he was singled out by Thomas More and John Skelton as one of the chief perpetrators of heresy, Skelton referring to Bilney and the other 'yong scolars' who supported him as half-educated, eager 'to prate and to preche proudly and leudly, and loudly to lye'.[134] But, for John Foxe, Bilney was one of the central figures who helped the true faith to re-emerge in the last years of Henry VIII's reign.

Theologically Bilney is unusual and unorthodox in his beliefs and his approach to the nature of belief. Writing to the Bishop of London, Cuthbert Tunstall (1474–1559), who was presiding over his trial, Bilney outlined his objections to the practices of the Church. Although he had denied being a Lutheran, Bilney's opposition to what he had heard from the pulpit sounds remarkably similar to Luther's belief in the liberating effects of understanding the depravity of our sin and the nature of Christ's grace in *The Bondage of the Will*, his riposte to Erasmus.[135] Bilney, according to Foxe, singles out an unnamed eminent preacher who berated his congregation with the claim that they have been 'lien rottinge in thine own lustes, by the space of these lx. yeres euen as a beast in his fylth and carnalitye',

---

[130] Heal, *Reformation*, pp. 479–80; Evans, *Problems of Authority*, pp. 5, 12, 13; Helen L. Parish, *Monks, Miracles and Magic: Reformation Representations of the Medieval Church* (London: Routledge, 2005); Bolt, *Encyclopeadia of Liars and Deceivers*, pp. 189–92; Kerr, ed., *Penguin Book of Lies*, pp. 88–91; Felicity Heal, 'Readership and Reception', in Paulina Kewes, Ian Archer, and Felicity Heal, eds, *The Oxford Handbook of Holinshed's* Chronicles (Oxford: Oxford University Press, 2013), pp. 355–72, at p. 370.

[131] See below, pp. 255–63, 273.

[132] Evenden and Freeman, *Religion and the Book*, p. 214; Brian Cummings, 'Images in Books: Foxe *Eikonoklastes*', in Tara Hamling and Richard L. Williams, eds, *Art Re-Formed: Re-assessing the Impact of the Reformation on the Visual Arts* (Newcastle: Cambridge Scholars Press, 2007), pp. 183–200.

[133] On Bilney, see the *ODNB* entry; Margaret Aston, *England's Iconoclasts, Volume I: Laws Against Images* (Oxford: Clarendon Press, 1988), pp. 164–9.

[134] John Skelton, 'A Replycacion Agaynst Certayne Yong Scolers Abjured of Late, Etc', in John Skelton, *The Complete English Poems*, ed. John Scattergood (Harmondsworth: Penguin, 1983), pp. 373–86, at p. 374; More, *CW*, VI (1981), pp. 255–79. See also Thomas Betteridge, *Literature and Politics in the English Reformation* (Manchester: Manchester University Press, 2004), pp. 17–19.

[135] Luther, *Selections*, pp. 166–203.

without providing any solace to inspire them to repent. This is to negate the purpose of the Gospels and to transform the apostles into liars:

> is this the preaching of penaunce in the name Iesus? or rather to tread downe Christ with Antichrist? for what other thing did he speake in effect, then that Christe died in vaine for thee. He wil not be they Iesus or sauioure, thou muste make satisfaction for thy selfe, or els thou shall pearishe eternallye. Then doth S. Ihon lie which sayeth: behold the Lambe of God which taketh away the sinnes of the world. And in a nother place, his bloude hath cleansed vs from al our sinnes. And again he is the propitiation for the sinnes of th^e whole world, beside an infinite nombre of other lies, what other thing is this then that which was spoken by the holy ghost, by the mouth of Peter, sayinge. There shall be false teachers that shall deny the Lord Iesus which hath redemed them, and what foloweth vpon the doctrin of such deuils speaking lies throughe hipocrisye, but onlye the conscience troden downe in despaire, geuing him selfe ouer vnto his owne lustes, according to the saying of S. Paule. After that they be come to this poynte that they sorow no more, they geue them selues ouer vnto wantonnesse, to commit all kinde of fylthinesse, euen with a gredy desire, seing that it is impossyble for them to make satisfactyon.[136]

Bilney's argument is that he has to speak out against the Church because it is corrupted by liars and lying. As a result the ordinary congregation have to work even harder than they would do to overcome a state of sinfulness, which leaves them cut off from God, a wicked perversion of the Gospels and the role of the Church perpetrated by devils in the guise of Christian preachers. Luther's argument that 'the Christian's chief and only comfort in every adversity lies in knowing that God does not lie, but brings all things to pass immutably, and that His will cannot be resisted, altered or impeded', surely informs Bilney's taunts that if we accept what the unnamed preacher says about the state of mankind then John was lying in representing Christ as the lamb of God who takes away our sins (John 1:29).[137] Bilney fits easily into Foxe's schema of apocalyptic history, preaching a simple message of truth against falsehood, Christians against worldly hypocrites, and witnesses of the gospel against liars who will lead mankind to damnation (2 Peter 2:1). The message of *sola scriptura*, originating from Luther and popularized in English by Tyndale, enables Foxe to establish the religious battleground with a force and clarity that had an enormous influence on the culture of early modern Europe.[138] Richard Verstegan's *Theatrum Crudelitatum Haereticorum Nostri Temporis* (*Theatre of the Cruelties of the Heretics in our own Times* (1592)) was a response to the success of Protestant martyrologies in determining a discourse of truth and falsehood as the basis for religious divisions in England and his work 'appears to follow John Foxe's editorial plan' and it is clear that, as in other matters, the same 'cultural and religious sources influenced both Catholic and Protestant constructions of martyrdom'.[139]

---

[136] Foxe, *Acts and Monuments*, p. 525.
[137] Luther, *Selections*, p. 185. See also Loewenstein, *Treacherous Faith*, pp. 49–50, 55; *ODNB* entry.
[138] Daniell, *Tyndale*, p. 255; Orlaith O'Sullivan, 'Introduction', in Orlaith O'Sullivan, ed., *The Bible as Book: The Reformation* (London: British Library/Oak Knoll Press, 2000), pp. 1–7, at pp. 1–2.
[139] Dillon, *Construction of Martyrdom*, pp. 254, 6.

Verstegan produced an elaborate Counter-Reformation work that employed terrifying graphic images of intense cruelty to counter Foxe's emphasis on the truth of scripture. Foxe provided a series of well-informed Protestants besting their Catholic oppressors in debate, woodcuts accompanying the text showing their heroic suffering. Verstegan made the visual central, clearly planning to reach a wider audience by carefully inverting Foxe's narrative, and adapting his style and values for a Catholic audience.[140] The *Theatrum Crudelitatum* represented Protestants at work oppressing and slaughtering Catholics: 'The images cry out to readers to take immediate action against the further bloodletting of innocent Catholics.'[141] Words might confuse and dissemble but pictures would not lie.

V

Of course matters were not quite so simple as these two stark histories outlined, and Bilney's procrastination and backtracking were more characteristic of the behaviour of most people at odds with the authorities than his decision to risk or embrace martyrdom.[142] For Calvin a Christian's duty was to stand firm by their faith, and he fulminated against Nicodemites, named after Nicodemus, the Pharisee who was converted by Jesus and who helped Joseph of Arimathaea prepare Jesus's body for burial after the crucifixion, but who failed to declare himself a Christian (John 3:1–21; 7:50–1; 19:39–42). If a Nicodemite was a person who did not honestly declare their confessional identity for fear of the consequences, and Nicodemism can be characterized as an 'attitude rather than a movement', then it is likely that Nicodemites could have been the largest category of religious believers in early modern Europe.[143] Certainly the number of Nicodemites would have dwarfed the number of convinced Protestants.[144] There were specific groups who could be considered Nicodemites such as the antinomian Family of Love, whose founder, the visionary Hendrik Niclaes, argued that as the sect had access to the truth they had no obligation to declare their knowledge to non-believers, an extreme version of the argument that oaths made to authorities which exceeded their boundaries were

[140] Christopher Highley, 'Richard Verstegan's Book of Martyrs' and Richard Williams, '"Libels and Payntinges": Elizabethan Catholics and the International Campaign of Visual Propaganda', in Highley and King, eds, *Foxe and His World*, pp. 183–97, pp. 198–215. See also Donna B. Hamilton, 'Richard Verstegan's *A Restitution of Decayed Intelligence* (1605): A Catholic Antiquarian Replies to John Foxe, Thomas Cooper, and Jean Bodin', *Prose Studies* 22 (1999), 1–38.

[141] Christopher Highley, *Catholics Writing the Nation in Early Modern Britain and Ireland* (Oxford: Oxford University Press, 2008), p. 71.

[142] Greg Walker, 'Saint or Schemer? The 1527 Heresy Trial of Thomas Bilney Reconsidered', in *Persuasive Fictions: Faction, Faith and Political Culture in the Reign of Henry VIII* (Aldershot: Scolar Press, 1996), pp. 143–65.

[143] Carlos M. N. Eire, *War Against the Idols: The Reformation of Worship from Erasmus to Calvin* (Cambridge: Cambridge University Press, 1986), p. 253. See also Carlos M. N. Eire, 'Calvin and Nicodemism: A Reappraisal', *C16J* 10 (1979), 44–69; Eliav-Feldon, *Renaissance Impostors*, pp. 44–7.

[144] Pettegree, *Marian Protestantism*, p. 89; Karl Gunther, *Reformation Unbound: Protestant Visions of Reform in England, 1525–1590* (Cambridge: Cambridge University Press, 2014), ch. 2.

not binding.[145] Most Nicodemites, however, were simply people who refused to declare their hand, and evidence is often emerging that many figures once thought to have had distinct religious positions should really be classified as Nicodemites.[146]

For Calvin this refusal to stand up and be counted was lying, and an abuse of God's gifts to mankind that was every bit as heinous as Augustine had argued. Calvin, to the dismay of erstwhile friends and supporters such as Gérard Rousel, 'refused to make a single concession', urging Christians to be consistent at any cost.[147] In contrast to some theologians who argued that dissimulation was permitted when Christians lived in hostile territories such as those ruled by Islam, Calvin argued that Christians had to leave the places where they were persecuted so that they could profess the gospel freely, as they could in Geneva.[148] It was vital to eschew all forms of idolatry, that is, all forms of false worship that hindered the pure message of the scriptures.[149] His treatise *Excuse A Messieurs Les Nicodemites* (1544) argued forcefully that 'un homme fidele conversant entre les papistes ne peut communiquer à superstitions, sans offenser Dieu' (a faithful man talking to papists cannot communicate about superstitions, without offending God).[150] Calvin adopts the language of the debates about lying among the Church Fathers in condemning those 'qui cognoissent en leurs cueurs et confessant de bouche leur povreté' (who know in their hearts and with their mouths confess their weakness).[151] Failure to admit one's faith in public 'est aussi bien un blaspheme oblique, avec ce qu'il n'y a qu'hypocrisie et mensonge' (is the same as indirect blasphemy with nothing less than hypocrisy and lying) and Calvin asks sarcastically, 'Comment? Ne pouvons nous server à Dieu, et suyvre sa parole, sans souffrir persecution?' (What? Can we not serve God and follow his word, without suffering persecution?).[152] To emphasize his position and make clear the division between right and wrong, Calvin asserts that what he is arguing is not a matter for dispute: 'Il n'est pas icy question de leur opinion ou de la miene. Je monstre ce que j'en trouve en l'escriture' (It is not a question of their opinion or mine. I am showing what I have found in scripture).[153] The apostles, sneers Calvin, would not be impressed with the Nicodemites' desire to avoid persecution because, in abjuring their faith, they become complicit with the idolatry of the world.[154] However, Calvin must

[145] On the Family of Love see Alastair Hamilton, *The Family of Love* (Cambridge: James Clark, 1981); Christopher W. Marsh, *The Family of Love in English Society, 1550–1630* (Cambridge: Cambridge University Press, 1994); David Wootton, 'John Donne's Religion of Love,' in Brooke and Maclean, eds, *Heterodoxy in Early Modern Science and Religion*, pp. 31–80; Zagorin, *Ways of Lying*, pp. 116–30.
[146] See, for example, McDiarmid, 'To Content God Quietlie', p. 186.
[147] Jean Calvin, *Three French Treatises*, ed. Francis M. Higman (London: Athlone, 1970), introduction, pp. 22–4; Richard Stauffer, 'Calvin', in Prestwich, ed., *International Calvinism*, pp. 15–38, at p. 24; François Higman, *Calvin*, trans. Philip Maret (London: Collins, 1963), pp. 24, 47.
[148] On Christians and Islam see Eliav-Feldon, *Renaissance Impostors*, pp. 59–60.
[149] Stauffer, 'Calvin', p. 24; Jean Calvin, *What a Faithfull Man, Whiche is Instructe in the Worde of God, Ought to do, Dwellinge Amongest the Papistes* (London, 1548), sigs C2v, C6r.
[150] Jean Calvin, *Excuse A Messieurs Les Nicodemites*, in Calvin, *Three French Treatises*, pp. 131–53, at p. 133.
[151] Calvin, *Excuse*, p. 135.   [152] Calvin, *Excuse*, p. 142.
[153] Calvin, *Excuse*, p. 141.   [154] Calvin, *Excuse*, pp. 144, 148.

surely have been disappointed by later events, especially in England. As Diarmaid MacCulloch has pointed out, the Church of England was actually designed and planned by Nicodemites, Protestants who had survived the reign of the Catholic Queen, Mary, such as William Cecil, Lord Burghley.[155]

Calvin's short tract was not among the many works of his which were translated into English in the late sixteenth century—unlike the slightly longer *Traité des Reliques* (1543), which outlines Calvin's conception of idolatry, and showed how 'telz mensonges sont couvers soubz ombre de devotion' (many lies are hidden by the shadow of devotion).[156] Even so it clearly had a significant influence, and a number of similar works influenced by Calvin's views appeared in English for those unable to read or obtain his French texts. Calvin and his followers were especially eager to stamp out heresy.[157] *Two epystles, one of Heinrich Bullinger, another of Jhon Calvin whether it be lawfull for a Chrysten man to communycate or be pertaker of the masse of the papysts, wythout offendyng God and hys neyghboure*, published in English in the same year as *Excuse A Messieurs Les Nicodemites* (1544), posed the rhetorical question (erotema) what light has to do with darkness or Christ to do with Belial.[158] Citing the example of Shadrach, Meshach, and Abednego, Daniel's three friends who survived in a furnace through their trust in God after they refused to worship Nebuchadnezzar (Daniel 3:1–30), Bullinger argues that 'outwarde Symulacion of wyckdnesse doth displease God'.[159] For Bullinger, 'the scripture requireth of us no closed, but an open confessyon', as Christians declared the truth to anyone not to a priest who then had the power to absolve them of their sins or punish them further.[160] Calvin's letters make similar points, warning Christians against complacency in tolerating the evil practices of the Catholics because 'the Godly ought not to flatter them selues in euell thynges lest they be careles in remaining therin'.[161] Equally forceful was John Hooper's *Whether Christian Faith Maye Be Kepte Secret in the Heart, Without Confession Therof Openly to the Worlde as Occasion Shal Serve* (1553), published just before the death of Edward VI and the accession of Mary. Hooper chose to practise what he preached and, although supporting Mary as the lawful Queen against the Protestant claims of the Northumberland faction, he refused to escape (although given a number of chances), remained steadfast to his radical views (despite

---

[155] Cited in Lady Anne Bacon, *An Apology or Answer in Defence of the Church of England*, ed. Patricia Demers (London: MHRA, 2015), introduction, p. 9; Jones, *Governing by Virtue*, p. 46.

[156] Jean Calvin, *Traité des Reliques*, in Calvin, *Three French Treatises*, pp. 47–97, at p. 78; *A Very Profitable Treatise made by M. Ihon Caluyne, declarynge what great profit might come to al christendome, yf there were a regester made of all sainctes bodies and other reliques*, trans. Stephen Wythers (London, 1561).

[157] Patrick Collinson, 'England and International Calvinism, 1558–1640', in Prestwich, ed., *International Calvinism*, pp. 197–223. I am very grateful to Andrew Pettegree for advice on Calvinist influence in England. On the increase in heresy trials after the Reformation see William Monter, 'Heresy Executions in Reformation Europe, 1520–1565', in Grell and Sribner, eds, *Tolerance and Intolerance*, pp. 48–64.

[158] Heinrich Bullinger, *Two Epystles, one of Heinrich Bullinger, another of Jhon Calvin whether it be lawfull for a Chrysten man to communycate or be pertaker of the masse of the papysts, wythout offendyng God and hys neyghboure* (London, 1544), sig. A3v.

[159] Bullinger, *Two Epystles*, sig. A5r.   [160] Bullinger, *Two Epystles*, sig. A7r.

[161] Bullinger, *Two Epystles*, sig. B1r.

rumours that he had recanted), and was burnt at the stake on 9 February 1555.[162] His treatise, like the letters of Bullinger and Calvin, contrasts the open nature of Protestant confession to the dark, private, and unchristian practices of Catholicism. Hooper, probably echoing Calvin, insists that heart and mouth be in accord: 'so is the confession outwardly of the same faith by mouth'.[163] He admits that the path of virtue is a narrow one: 'But how hard a thing it is to confesse Christ in the daies of trouble, not onely the Scripture but also daily experience in good men & women declare', but that it was a Christian's duty to avoid the all-encompassing sin of idolatry.[164] What God cannot tolerate is 'clooked hypocrisie', when 'people honoure me with the mouth, but their hartes be far from me', a distinction that surely is derived from Calvin's strictures against the pusillanimous lying of the Nicodemites.[165] The Christian's duty is to be a witness to the faith, whatever the consequences. Like Bullinger, Hooper employs a strategic rhetorical question to hammer home his point: 'Doth a Christian manne know the truth to bring his brother to a lye?'[166] Lying, as in the More–Tyndale debate a few years earlier, is not defined in a technically precise manner, but used as a public rebuke.

VI

Probably the most fascinating case of Nicodemism was that of Francesco Spiera (1502–48), an Italian Protestant lawyer.[167] Spiera enjoyed a comfortable living and was a well-respected citizen of Citadella in the Veneto, when he became a convinced Protestant. Hauled before the Inquisition in July 1548, he renounced his faith, but repented immediately, and believing himself to be already damned he sank into a terrible despair, from which he died in October.[168] Spiera's sad story came to the attention of Calvin—the Italian Reformation was notably Calvinistic in belief—and he wrote a preface to an account by Matteo Gribaldi (c.1505–64), translated into English in 1550, which was popular enough to be reprinted in 1570.[169] Calvin saw the story as yet another example of the Pope's tyranny and his desire to silence 'The voices of the Martires', as well as a cautionary tale of the perils

---

[162] On Hooper, see the *ODNB* entry; Brigden, *London and the Reformation*, pp. 460–7.

[163] John Hooper, *Whether Christian Faith Maye Be Kepte Secret in the Heart, Without Confession Therof Openly to the Worlde as Occasion Shal Serve* (London, 1553), sig. A2r. See also Zagorin, *Ways of Lying*, pp. 138–9.

[164] Hooper, *Christian Faith*, sigs A3v–A4r.   [165] Hooper, *Christian Faith*, sigs A4v–A5r.

[166] Hooper, *Christian Faith*, sig. A6r.

[167] See M. A. Overall, 'The Exploitation of Francesco Spiera', *C16J* 26 (1995), 619–37; Zagorin, *Ways of Lying*, pp. 88–9.

[168] Spiera's belief that he was already damned appears in Protestant accounts of his life: the truth is that Spiera probably recanted his faith in order to save his family: Overall, 'Spiera', p. 626.

[169] Gribaldi later became a follower of Michael Severtus, who was burnt at the stake for heresy in Geneva in 1553: see François Wendel, *Calvin: The Origins and Development of his Religious Thought*, trans. Philip Mairet (New York: Harper and Row, 1963), pp. 93–9. On Calvin's influence in Italy see Simone Maghenzani, 'The Protestant Reformation in Counter-Reformation Italy, c.1550–1660: An Overview of New Evidence', *CH* 83 (2014), 571–89.

of lapsing into the worst sin of all, despair and then suicide.[170] Gribaldi's text is notably sympathetic to a man who had committed a deadly sin, which is a sign, perhaps, of the change in emphasis of Christian teaching as the Ten Commandments eclipsed the Seven Deadly Sins.[171] Gribaldi describes Spiera as a Christian who had obtained an 'abundant knowledge of the trueth', and his betrayal of the faith is represented in terms that recall Jesus's demand that his disciples should be prepared to abandon their ordinary lives to serve him: ('If a man come to me, and hate not his father and mother, and wife and children, and brethern and sisters, moreover and his own life, he cannot be my disciple' (Luke 14:26 [Tyndale translation]):

> This wretched man . . . began diversely to reason with hymselfe, whether he should returne to Citadell, to confirme his recantation: either shoulde forsake all his goodes, and goe to some other place to repent. As he went in his journey, the spirite of God continually came into his mynde, and the pricke of Conscience prouoking him to repentance, and councellyng hym al waies not to goe to abiure: but rather to forsake Wife, Children, and the whole world: yea, and to suffer present death, rather than to abandon and recante the truthe whiche he knewe.[172]

Spiera is caught between his knowledge of the truth and desire to remain with his family in the world, a sign that he is not ready to become a true disciple, which is why he is so troubled in conscience and why his inability to resolve his dilemma leads to despair. It is easy to see why his story was so important for the Edwardian regime, demonstrating the evils of the papacy, as well as the need to be resolute, truthful, and honest in bearing witness to the true faith, much as Catholic images of Protestants butchering the faithful were designed to 'terrify a bourgeois lay audience'.[173] Spiera is compared to Peter denying Christ three times after his arrest (Matthew 26:69–75; Luke 22:54–62), lying to protect himself, exactly how Reformers saw Nicodemites.[174] In fact, as Simone Maghenzani has argued, the Reformation in the Venice area proceeded 'step by step'. The Reformers were eager 'not to create trouble', because Nicodemism was especially widespread despite the publication of Calvin's strictures against the practice in Florence in 1551, and, as a result, the Reformation was 'weak'.[175]

[170] Matteo Gribaldi, *A Notable and Marueilous Epistle Concerning the Terrible Judgemente of God, upon hym that forsweare of men, denieth Christ* (London, 1550), 'John Calvin to the Christian Reader', sigs A3r–A4r. On despair see Baseotto, *Despair*, ch. 1; on attitudes to suicide see Ariès, *Hour of Our Death*, pp. 123, 130, *passim*; Keith Thomas, *The Ends of Life: Roads to Fulfilment in Early Modern England* (Oxford: Oxford University Press, 2009), pp. 175–6; Eric Langley, *Narcissism and Suicide in Shakespeare and his Contemporaries* (Oxford: Oxford University Press, 2009), ch. 6.
[171] See above, pp. 17–18.
[172] Gribaldi, *Notable and Marueilous Epistle*, sigs A5v–A6r.
[173] On the success of the story in terrifying Protestants afraid of being damned see Overall, 'Spiera', p. 637; Margaret Spufford, *Small Books and Pleasant Histories: Popular Fiction and its Readership in Seventeenth-Century England* (Cambridge: Cambridge University Press, 1981), p. 38; Dillon, *Construction of Martyrdom*, p. 255.
[174] Gribaldi, *Notable and Marueilous Epistle*, sig. B1r.
[175] Maghenzani, 'Protestant Reformation in Counter-Reformation Italy', pp. 574, 576, 582; Overall, 'Spiera', p. 627.

The second, longer part of Gribaldi's treatise is a 'godly prayer against desperation', reminding the faithful that God will protect them so that no one should have to suffer Spiera's terrible fate. Spiera's story was retold in one of the strangest plays to emerge from England in the sixteenth century. Nathaniel Woodes's *The Conflict of Conscience*, published 1580, written *c.*1570, dramatized Spiera's story in the form of a Protestant morality play.[176] Little is known of Woodes except that he was ordained in Norwich, and then became rector of South Walsham, nine miles north-east of the East Anglian capital.[177] *The Conflict of Conscience*, based on his reading of the story in English, was his only play, and it was almost certainly never performed in public.[178] Erin Kelly speculates that Woodes's experience in Norwich with its 'tradition of performing cycle plays' probably provided a reason for the work, and the play can be read, like John Bale's, as a Protestant attempt to adapt a late medieval, now Catholic, tradition, perhaps written in response to the Protestant fear of Catholic plots in the 1570s.[179] Spiera is represented as Philologus, a scholar, who is uncertain how to act, caught between his realization of the truth and fear of the consequences, exactly as he is portrayed in Gribaldi's work, closely resembling the protagonists of the morality plays of the late fifteenth century, *Mankind* and *Everyman*.[180] In the prologue Satan boasts that he has sent Hypocrisy to advise the hapless Philologus, 'Who can full well in time and place, dissemble eithers parte', which indicates that hypocrisy is the natural ally of an education system, one that Woodes would have experienced at school and university, which required students to argue *in utramque partem*, on either side.[181] Furthermore, Woodes is showing that scholars like Spiera can find ways of avoiding the voices of

[176] On *The Conflict of Conscience* see Celesta Wine, 'Nathaniel Wood's *Conflict of Conscience*', *PMLA* 50 (1935), 661–78; Erin E. Kelly, '*Conflict of Conscience* and Sixteenth-Century Religious Drama', *ELR* 44 (2014), 388–419; Anna Riehl Bertolet, 'The "blindnesse of the flesh" in Nathaniel Woodes' *The Conflict of Conscience*', in Thomas Betteridge and Greg Walker, eds, *The Oxford Handbook of Tudor Drama* (Oxford: Oxford University Press, 2012), pp. 144–60; David Bevington, 'Christopher Marlowe's *Doctor Faustus* and Nathaniel Woode's *The Conflict of Conscience*', in Pincombe and Shrank, eds, *Oxford Handbook of Tudor Literature*, pp. 704–17. On Protestant drama see Andrew Pettegree, *Reformation and the Culture of Persuasion* (Cambridge: Cambridge University Press, 2005), ch. 4.

[177] Celesta Wine, 'Nathaniel Woodes: Author of the Morality Play *The Conflict of Conscience*', *RES* 15 (1939), 458–63; Venn, IV, p. 453.

[178] Nathaniel Woodes, *The Conflict of Conscience*, ed. Herbert Davies (Oxford: Malone Society, 1952), v–vi.

[179] Kelly, '*Conflict of Conscience*', p. 392. On Bale, see Thora Balslev Blatt, *The Plays of John Bale: A Study of Ideas, Technique and Style* (Copenhagen: G. E. C. Gad, 1968); Overall, 'Spiera', p. 634. East Anglia had a high percentage of Catholics and was where Mary built up her power base before assuming the throne in 1553: Haigh, 'Continuity of Catholicism', p. 191.

[180] See Andrew Hadfield, '*The Summoning of Everyman*', in Betteridge and Walker, eds, *Oxford Handbook of Tudor Drama*, pp. 93–108; David Bevington, *From Mankind to Marlowe: Growth of Structure in the Popular Drama of Tudor England* (Cambridge, MA: Harvard University Press, 1962), pp. 8–9, 15–18; Overall points out that Spiera was represented as Everyman in some accounts: 'Spiera', p. 629.

[181] Nathaniel Woodes, *The Conflict of Conscience* (London, 1581), sig. A4r. On the principle of *in utramque partem* and its significance for drama, see Ronald Knowles, *Shakespeare's Arguments with History* (Basingstoke: Palgrave, 2001).

their conscience and lapsing into a state of hypocrisy, lying to the world, if not themselves. But, as the play demonstrates, this lie harms them more than others.

Philologus recognizes the significance of Job, whom God tested to prove his faith, his argument summarized by his friend, Mathetes, serving as his conscience:

> This is the summe of all your talke, if that I gesse right,
> That God doth punnish his elect to keepe their faith in ure,
> Or least that if continuall ease, and rest enjoy they might:
> God to forget through haughtinesse, fraile nature should procure[.][182]

Mathetes has accurately predicted what will happen to Philologus, as Hypocrisy, aided by Avarice and Tyranny, start to dominate the world in the name of the Church and force the godly to choose whether to oppose the forces of darkness or to go underground. Indeed, Avarice celebrates the return of Hypocrisy, 'our Belsire', who saves him from having to hide from the godly who shun him:

> I meane the evil lucke which *Hipocrisy* had,
> When he was expelled out of this land
> For then with me the matter evill did stand.
> For I by him so shadowed was from light,
> That almost no man could me out espye,
> But he being gon to every mans flight,
> I was apparent ech man did descrye,
> My pilling and poling so that glad was I,
> From my nature to cease a thing most merveilous,
> And live in secret the tyme was so daungerous.[183]

The experience of Avarice when not protected by Hypocrisy mirrors and prefigures the experience of Philologus, the Nicodemite, when the forces of darkness replace the forces of light. Woodes is surely commenting on the dangerous and confusing nature of religious change after the Reformation in England, which, like the older William Baldwin, he would have directly experienced (he was probably born in *c.*1550).[184] Avarice is upbraided by the rather more courageous Tyranny—'Tush *Avarice* thou fearest a thing that is vayne, / For by me alone both you shalbe stayed'—a sly joke that in such terrible times even tyranny can seem impressive.[185] In good times people will disguise their vices; in bad times they will hide their virtues. Either way, the best solution is to be resolutely honest, recognizing virtue and eradicating vice.

Philologus defeats the forces of the papacy in argument, remaining steadfast in his belief that the gospel must be the final arbiter in matters of doctrine (*sola scriptura*). However, unlike the apostles who were prepared to abandon their families to follow Christ, he wilts when Suggestion conjures up an image of his suffering wife and children 'Sobbing and sighing . . . / Knocking their brestes, and wringing their hand: / Saying, they are brought to utter desolation, / By the meanes

---

[182] Woodes, *Conflict*, sig. B2r.   [183] Woodes, *Conflict*, sig. B4r.
[184] Wine, 'Nathaniel Woodes', p. 458.   [185] Woodes, *Conflict*, sig. B4r.

of their fathers willfull protestation'.[186] Philologus's resistance crumbles and he perceives himself caught in an impossible dilemma: 'Either my Lord God in hart to reject, / Or els to be oppressed by the Legates authoritie: / And in this world to be counted an abject: / My Landes, wife and children to neglect.'[187] On the one hand Philologus simply has to swear an oath to an authority he does not fully accept, as Englishmen and women did when ordered to swear the Oath of Supremacy and the Oath of Allegiance. On the other, he is being tested by God in the most extreme manner and has to testify to his faith in exceptionally trying circumstances. Philologus fails the test, gives in, and, in the most lukewarm manner possible, declares his loyalty to the Church, renounces his true faith, and becomes a Nicodemite:

> If it please your Lordship, I say even what you say
> And confesse your religion, to be most allowable,
> Neither will I gainsay your customes lawdable:
> My former follyes I utterly renownce,
> That my selfe was an Heretick I do here pronownce.[188]

Philologus's mealy mouthed words signal his insincere adherence to the Catholic Church, but they do not alleviate, so much as advertise, the nature of his sin and lapse into hypocrisy.

Returning home from the Inquisition, Philologus resists the assault of Conscience to repent, concentrating on worldly joys at the expense of the salvation of his soul. He understands what is happening to his soul—'So long as this prosperitie, and wealth by mee abide', we witness just how far he has fallen and understand Calvin's demand that the true Christian cannot remain among idolaters without professing the truth and risking the consequences. But he is then confronted by Horror who warns him of his impending fate now that he is in Satan's grip, and has abandoned his conscience. The mirror which he uses to blot out all thoughts of the afterlife will be transformed into 'the Glasse of deadly desperation', reflecting the truth rather than lies.[189] Philologus lapses into despair as a result of his sin in refusing to bear witness to his faith and, despite the arguments of Theologus and Eusebius, that Christ died for his sins and so has secured his salvation and that if he only repents like Peter after he denied Christ, then all will be forgiven.[190] Philologus can only reproduce an inverted parody of Calvin's insistence that the heart and the mouth must be in unison: 'I have no faith, the wordes you speake my hart doth not believe, / I must confesse that I for sinne, am justly throwne to hell'.[191] And, again, 'To pray with lips, unto your God, you shall mee soone intreate, / My spirit, to Sathan is inthrall, I can it not thence get'.[192]

Philologus assumes that he is damned—'Alas, what comfort can betide, unto a damned wretch? / what so I heare, see, feele, tast, speake, is turned all to woe'—which

---

[186] Woodes, *Conflict*, sig. F3r.
[187] Woodes, *Conflict*, sig. F3v.   [188] Woodes, *Conflict*, sig. G1r.
[189] Woodes, *Conflict*, sig. H2v. On Mirrors, truth, and conscience, see Herbert Grabes, 'Mirrors', *Sp. Enc.*, pp. 477–8; Herbert Grabes, *The Mutable Glass: Mirror-Imagery in Titles and Texts of the Middle Ages and English Renaissance* (Cambridge: Cambridge University Press, 1982), pp. 53–6.
[190] Woodes, *Conflict*, sig. H3r.   [191] Woodes, *Conflict*, sig. H3v.
[192] Woodes, *Conflict*, sig. H4r.

means that he surely is if he does not alter his course, one reason why the ending of the play was changed in the second edition so that the protagonist listens to reason and does not hang himself.[193] Woodes's morality play is a plea for honesty and a warning that Protestants must not hide beneath the cosy lie that they are preserving the faith through their caution. The truth is that such actions weaken the power of Christians to stand up to tyranny, as the faith is maintained through its witnesses who testify to the power of the scriptures. It is better to produce a long list of martyrs than to have hypocrites and cowards who survive through evil times, tainted by the company they were forced to keep, their faith distorted beyond recognition.

VII

Of course, not everyone saw matters this way. In the September eclogue of Edmund Spenser's *The Shepheardes Calender* (1579), we have a graphic and confusing image, which suggests that separating truth from lies is a fraught, dangerous, and confusing process, perhaps worse than leaving them intermingled.[194] Speaking of the good shepherd, Roffy, to his fellow shepherd, Hobbinol, the beleaguered Diggon Davie describes with admiration the vigilant ways in which the old man and his trusty dog, Lowder, protect the shepherds from the predatory wolf who disguises himself in sheep's clothing:

> Tho at midnight he would barke and ball,
> (For he had eft learned a curres call)
> As if a Woolfe were emong the sheepe.
> With that the shepheard would breake his sleepe.
> And send out Lowder (for so his dog hote)
> To raunge the fields with open throte.
> Tho when as Lowder was far awaye,
> This Woluish sheepe would catchen his pray,
> A Lambe, or a Kidde, or a weanell wast:
> With that to the wood would he speede him fast.
> Long time he vsed this slippery pranck,
> Ere Roffy could for his laboure him thanck.
> At end the shepheard his practise spyed,
> (For Roffy is wise, and as Argus eyed)
> And when at euen he came to the flocke,
> Fast in theyr folds he did them locke,
> And tooke out the Woolfe in his counterfect cote,
> And let out the sheepes bloud at his throte.[195]

---

[193] Woodes, *Conflict*, sigs I2v, I4r; Bevington, '*Doctor Faustus* and *The Conflict of Conscience*', p. 705. The pre-eminent English Calvinist William Perkins (1558–1602) argued that some sins of the apostates were unpardonable, such as blaspheming the Holy Ghost: Kendall, *Calvin*, p. 73.
[194] This section draws on my *Edmund Spenser: A Life* (Oxford: Oxford University Press, 2012), pp. 115–18.
[195] Edmund Spenser, *The Shepheardes Calender*, in *The Shorter Poems*, ed. Richard A. McCabe (Harmondsworth: Penguin, 1999), pp. 23–156, at pp. 122–3 (lines 190–207).

These are exceptionally confusing lines, the sense of which seems straightforward enough on a first reading, but which becomes less clear on a second reading, a disjunction that highlights their profound complexity. It is easy to understand that the good shepherd and his dog find and kill a wolf in sheep's clothing. However, a series of questions remain, not least whether such action is endorsed by the author.[196] The first line cited must refer to the disguised wolf, but why does he imitate the cry of a dog who has discovered a wolf? Does he think that he will fool the shepherd by imitating a dog as well as a sheep? Or is he boasting to the shepherd? Eager to give himself away? Or is the truth that he is not a master of disguise at all and it is actually quite simple to expose him because his moves are so obvious? Roffy does not pursue the wolf himself but sends out his dog who is described as having an 'open throte'. The dog is surely called Lowder because he can bark—or sing—at greater volume than anyone else, enabling the authorities to track his discoveries with ease. When put with Roffy's Argus eyes, it is clear that this pair are very hard to elude. There is also surely something disturbing about the description of Lowder's 'open throte', which suggests a greedy predator or wild animal in attack mode rushing at its prey, making the reader wonder if the cure is almost if not as bad as the disease. The disguised wolf is clearly adept at catching its prey, for all the efforts of Roffy and Lowder, and avoids Lowder easily enough, and it is only when he hides in the sheep pen that he can be caught. The last two lines of Diggon Davie's speech are the most disturbing and ambiguous. When the sheep's blood is let out of the disguised wolf's throat is this what he is in the process of digesting from his prey? Or are we to imagine his throat being cut to let out the blood? If so then is the blood actually his, making him part wolf and part sheep? And who actually sheds the blood, Lowder or Roffy? Have they become merged in their efforts to police the religion of the countryside?

The common Reformation image of the Catholic wolf letting out the blood of the Protestant sheep derives from Matthew 7:15: 'Beware of false prophets, which come to you in sheep's clothing, but inwardly they are ravening wolves' (Tyndale translation). Priests were depicted as wolves, casting aside their surplices, and slaughtering the sacrificial lamb (Christ, the Eucharist) with their teeth, spraying blood over the supine congregation.[197] In *The Shepheardes Calender* the image is reversed and it is the Protestant dog which slaughters the Catholic sheep-wolf. Perhaps, given the deliberately ambiguous use of pronouns here—a characteristic device of Spenser's—Roffy and Lowder have actually merged as one, creating a new hybrid creature with a thousand eyes and an open throat.[198] There can be no doubt

---

[196] The prevailing critical consensus that Spenser was a Protestant poet has often predetermined how his poetry has been read: see Anthea Hume, *Edmund Spenser: Protestant Poet* (Cambridge: Cambridge University Press, 1984), pp. 1–4; John N. King, *Spenser's Poetry and the Reformation Tradition* (Princeton: Princeton University Press, 1990), pp. 44–5.

[197] Andrew Cunningham and Ole Peter Grell, *The Four Horsemen of the Apocalypse: Religion, War, Famine and Death in Reformation Europe* (Cambridge: Cambridge University Press, 2000), pp. 54–6. See also Sutcliffe, *Challenge*, p. 220.

[198] Hadfield, *Spenser: A Life*, p. 179; Graham Atkin, 'Raleigh, Spenser, and Elizabeth: Acts of Friendship in *The Faerie Queene*, Book IV', in Julian Lethbridge, ed., *Edmund Spenser: New and Renewed Directions* (Madison: Fairleigh Dickinson University Press, 2006), pp. 195–213, at p. 204.

that the wolf is up to no good and this passage cannot be read as a defence of the Jesuits supporting Edmund Campion's argument that the order sought spiritual not political influence in England. Rather, it points out that rooting out Catholic influence is likely to end up being counterproductive, making Protestants uncomfortably similar to their opponents—another familiar argument in Spenser, most notably in his descriptions of the savage terror that would be needed to prevent rebellion in Ireland.[199] More worrying still, Diggon Davie's description suggests that it is very hard to tell Catholics and Protestants apart. It is surely no accident that we know very little about Spenser's religious beliefs outside his published writings. These are full of passages expressing strong opposition to aggressive international Catholicism, but provide little of substance that can really be thought of as Protestant.[200] Spenser's account is based, presumably, on personal experience, as Roffy was John Young, Bishop of Rochester, for whom Spenser had worked as a secretary, and sometime Master of Pembroke College, Cambridge, where he had studied.[201] It is hard to square Spenser's account of the problems of discovering the belief of an individual and the connections and transformations that inevitably take place in times of religious confusion with a Calvinist belief that declaring one's faith is what God demands. Even so, Spenser has all too often been seen as a moderate Calvinist, part of the Church of England's mainstream.[202] But the evidence of his writing would appear to suggest a sympathy for those who were rather less eager to declare their own faith, police that of others, and root out heresy.

The logic of Spenser's eclogue is a world away from the strident message of *The Conflict of Conscience*, published two years later. Spenser's poetic sequence provides no easy answers to questions of religious doctrine and allegiance, and, in places such as the passage cited from the September eclogue, suggests that a policy of forcing everyone to declare their hand may cause more problems than it solves. *The Shepheardes Calender* articulates the concerns and anxieties of the 1570s rather than providing obvious solutions.[203] Spenser's religious position was probably much closer to the Nicodemites than the Calvinists, and his early connections to the Family of Love through contact with exiles from the Low Countries fleeing the vicious wars of religion would appear to have left a lasting impact on his writing (he returned to his early translations written for one prominent exile, Jan Van Der Noot, in the early 1590s near the start of his major publishing success which

[199] Andrew Hadfield, *Spenser's Irish Experience: Wilde Fruyt and Salvage Soyl* (Oxford: Clarendon Press, 1997), pp. 137–8.
[200] Hadfield, 'Spenser and Religion'.
[201] Hadfield, *Spenser: A Life*, pp. 67–8; Paul E. McLane, *Spenser's* Shepheardes Calender: *A Study in Elizabethan Allegory* (Notre Dame: University of Notre Dame Press, 1961), pp. 158–74.
[202] The traditional views are Frederick M. Padelford, 'Spenser and the Theology of Calvin', *MP* 12 (1914), 1–18; Virgil K. Whitaker, *The Religious Basis of Spenser's Thought* (Stanford: Stanford University Press, 1950). More recent and nuanced arguments can be found in King, *Spenser's Poetry*, pp. 11, 62–4; Richard Mallette, *Spenser and the Discourses of Reformation England* (Lincoln: University of Nebraska Press, 1997), pp. 1–13 (which stresses the significance of the Calvinist William Perkins). There is a balanced overview by Peter Auksi, 'Calvin, Calvinism', *Sp. Enc.*, pp. 128–9.
[203] Lynn Staley Johnson, The Shepheardes Calender: *An Introduction* (University Park: Penn State University Press, 1990), p. 86.

established him as the most significant Elizabethan poet).[204] Spenser's writings run a close and mysterious line between revelation and disguise, often appearing as if they are about to reveal something that they then withhold, as might be expected in an age when duplicity was often necessary for survival.[205]

VIII

This stark dichotomy between a demand that the truth be declared, all lying condemned and expunged, and a cautious desire to keep revelation at arm's length characterized religious experience throughout Elizabeth's and James's reigns. Few writers can have understood this better than John Donne, born nearly twenty years after Spenser. Donne was from a well-established Catholic family, his brother dying in prison for harbouring a priest, but he later forged a successful career as Dean of St Paul's Cathedral and had considerable influence on the nature and character of the Church of England. It is hard to establish where Donne's religious sympathies really lay, whether he was always a Catholic at heart, or whether he was a sincere and committed convert.[206] It is no surprise that Donne, like Spenser, has been connected to the Family of Love, their evasive antinomian beliefs enabling him to avoid unwelcome attention to his beliefs, answer difficult questions in evasive ways and even lie.[207]

Donne's most significant work on the rights of authorities to force subjects to declare their religious belief is *Pseudo-Martyr*, published in 1610.[208] The work may well have had some form of official sanction as it seems very close to James's writings and it is possible that, as Anthony Raspa claims, *Triplici Nodo* (1607), James's defence of the Oath of Allegiance, 'inspired Donne to write *Pseudo-Martyr*'.[209] Donne praises this far-sighted policy as an obvious, practical solution

---

[204] Hadfield, *Spenser: A Life*, pp. 38–40, 278, 283.

[205] For one reading of this facet of Spenser's writing, see Richard Rambuss, *Spenser's Secret Career* (Cambridge: Cambridge University Press, 1993).

[206] See the essays in Mary Arshagouni Papazian, *John Donne and the Protestant Reformation: New Perspectives* (Detroit: Wayne State University Press, 2003); Murray, *Poetics of Conversion*, p. 74; and Dennis Flynn, *John Donne and the Ancient Catholic Nobility* (Bloomington: Indiana University Press, 1995), who makes a case that Donne never abandoned his Catholic faith. Kimberly Anne Coles argues that Donne imagines belief in somatic terms because of his perilous and conflicted position: 'The Matter of Belief in John Donne's *Holy Sonnets*', *RQ* 68 (2015), 899–931.

[207] Wootton, 'John Donne's Religion of Love'.

[208] For an excellent analysis, to which my comments here are significantly indebted, see Shanyn Altman, '"An Anxious Entangling and Perplexing of Consciences": John Donne and Catholic Recusant Mendacity', in *EJES: Mendacity in Early Modern Literature and Culture*, ed. Ingo Berensmeyer and Andrew Hadfield, 19 (2015), 176–88. See also Victor Houliston, 'An Apology for Donne's *Pseudo-Martyr*', *RES*, ns, 57 (2006), 474–86.

[209] Donne, *Pseudo-Martyr*, introduction, p. xxxv. Donne claims that James's writings inspired him in his dedicatory epistle to the King prefacing *Pseudo-Martyr* (pp. 3–4). It is most likely that he wrote *Pseudo-Martyr* to correct the errors in William Barlow's *An answer to a Catholike English-man* (1609), the officially commissioned defence of the oath, which disgusted him (Jeremy Maule, 'Donne and the Words of the Law', in David Colclough, ed., *John Donne's Professional Lives* (Woodbridge: Brewer, 2003), pp. 19–36, at p. 28). Donne may have been officially sanctioned to do this: see R. C. Bald, *John Donne: A Life* (Oxford: Clarendon Press, 1970), pp. 218–21 (I am grateful to Shanyn Altman for

for all James's subjects: 'If therefore the matter of this oath be so evident, as being Morall, & therefore constant and ever the same, that it can never neede his judgement, because it can in no case be sinne, the scruple which some have had, that by denying this power absolving, his spiritual power is endamaged, is vaine and frivolous.'[210] The oath, according to Donne, is a sensible measure because it is temporal not spiritual and so cannot envelop the swearer in sin. Therefore, it liberates men and women to act as they please and as their consciences see fit. Donne acknowledges the need for oaths and makes a telling contrast between the false oaths imposed by the Catholic Church and the necessary oath undertaken by the loyal subject of the British King:

> And at no time, and to no persons, can such *Oathes* be more necessary, then to us now, who have been awakened with such drummes as these, *There is no warre in the world so just and honourable, be it civill or forraigne, as that which is waged for the Romane Religion.* And especially in this consideration are *Oathes* a fit and proper wall and Rampart, to oppose against these men, because they say, *That to the obedience of this Romane Religion, all Princes and people have yielded themselves, either by Oath, vow, or Sacraments, or every one of them.* For against this their imaginary oath, it is best, that a true, reall, and lawfull oath be administered by us.[211]

Donne draws a pointed contrast between the true and proper Oath of Allegiance, and the false and deluded oath of absolute loyalty demanded by the Catholic Church. In fact, the oath demanded by the legitimate secular authority is a reaction to the wicked and destructive promise extorted by the Pope to fulfil his deluded claims to hegemony over kings and their subjects. James's oath is a vital form of protection against claims that will encourage religious persecution and so undermine the fabric of religious and secular life. The worst confusion that can be wrought, according to Donne, is to mis-recognize and conflate these two forms of authority: 'Nor is there any thing more monstrous, and unnaturall and disproportioned, then that *spirituall* power should conceive or beget *temporall*: or to rise downwards, as the more degrees of height, and Supremacie, and perfection it hath, the more it should decline and stoope to the consideration of secular and temporall matters.'[212] Donne shows his delight in paradox: the more religion concerns itself with secular matters and claims supremacy over political powers the less spiritual it becomes, sullying and diluting the sacred and undermining the legitimate authority of the prince.[213] For Donne the crucial point is that individuals should all be responsible for their own souls and salvation. Earthly authorities and institutions

---

advice on the composition of *Pseudo-Martyr*). For the wider context of the debate see Dillon, *Construction of Martyrdom*, ch. 1.

[210] Donne, *Pseudo-Martyr*, p. 254.
[211] Donne, *Pseudo-Martyr*, p. 242. See also Pricket, *Iesuits Miracles*, sig. E1r.
[212] Donne, *Pseudo-Martyr*, p. 200.
[213] Michael Mccanles, 'Paradox in Donne', *SR* 13 (1966), 266–87; Gillian R. Evans, 'John Donne and the Augustinian Paradox of Sin', *RES* 33 (1982), 1–22.

should leave them to act alone, not mislead them, or force people to act against God's will:

> when all things are in such sort wel composed and established, and every subordinate Wheele set in good order, we are guilty of our owne damnation, if wee obey not the Minister, and the Minister is guilty of it, if hee neglect to instruct us, so is the Prince guilty of our spiritual ruine, and eternall perishing, if hee doe not both provide able men to give us spirituall foode, and punish both their negligence and our transgressions.[214]

The penalties for confusing the spiritual and the secular are catastrophic. Not only is proper rule compromised and realms placed in unnecessary danger but everyone concerned is in grave danger of eternal damnation.

Such passages remind us of the central point of *Pseudo-Martyr*, that death in the service of illegitimate authority is not merely futile, but diabolical, likely to imperil the soul of the victim rather than elevate him or her to heavenly bliss. It is the duty of authorities to facilitate the salvation of the subjects entrusted to their care, something best achieved by leaving them alone to make their own decisions rather than coercing them and so removing the power of choice. Worst of all are the Jesuits who press the men who have taken their oath to sacrifice themselves for the glory of the Church.[215] Chapter four details the failings of their doctrine, concluding 'That the desire of Martyrdome might be vicious, & that, as the Roman authors observe in the first times, it had been so; and, That by the Romane doctrine it must of necessity be so, we have added now, that the *Jesuites* more then any, inflame thereunto'.[216]

Donne is invariably concerned to limit pointless and wasteful sacrifice, blaming deluded and aggressive spiritual authorities for sending men and women to their deaths under the guise of martyrdom. *Pseudo-Martyr* is central to our understanding of Donne's intellectual and religious beliefs during James's reign, so that it explains his loyal adherence to the monarch and—in part—his decision to pursue a career in the Church of England.[217] Donne had lived under the threat of imprisonment and possible execution throughout his life, but the Oath of Allegiance provided a means of security and the squaring of conscience.[218]

Accordingly, Donne argues for a balance between extremes: 'we must neither pursue persecution so forwardly, that our natural preservation be neglected, nor runne away from it so farre, that Gods cause be scandaliz'd, and his Honour diminished'.[219] Donne argues that it is the Jesuits/Roman Catholics who have abandoned the Church after the Reformation and left 'her diseases to putrifie and fester within her bowels', assuming an illegitimate authority that undermines its

---

[214] Donne, *Pseudo-Martyr*, p. 144.

[215] Lander, *Inventing Polemic*, p. 152; Pricket, *Iesuits Miracles*, sig. B3r.

[216] Donne, *Pseudo-Martyr*, p. 120.

[217] David Nicholls, 'The Political Theology of John Donne', *TS* 49 (1988), 45–66, p. 65.

[218] On Donne's complicated relationship to casuistry and conscience see A. E. Malloch, 'John Donne and the Casuists', *SEL* 2 (1962), 57–76.

[219] Donne, *Pseudo-Martyr*, p. 28.

true status.[220] Therefore, to die for such a cause is suicide not martyrdom, and Donne urges his opponents not to expose themselves to '*certaine* ruine, upon *uncertaine* foundations'.[221] Donne ridicules the ambiguous practices of the papacy towards lying, and its ludicrous understanding of the authority it possesses through its decretals and canon law:

> And when they list urge a *Canon*, any litle rag torn or fallen off from thence, must bind the Church *de fide*, as a cathedrall, and Decretall resolution: for so says he, that made the Notes uppon *Cassianus*, excusing *Origen*, *Chrysostome*, & some other Fathers, for inclining to *Platoes* opinion of *allowing some use of lies, in wise men, That it was lawfull till the Church had defined the contrary: But now*, sayes he, *the* question of *Usurie*, the Pope says, *Since the Scriptures forbid lies, even for defense of any man life, much lesse may usury be permitted*. But, if in this question of lying, the band did not arise out of the evidence and truth of the matter it selfe, but relied upon the authority of the Popes *declaration*, and *decision*, can such a ragge casually and incidentally fallen into a letter of another purpose, by way of comparison, binde the whole Church, *De fide*?[222]

Donne is showing just how flimsy and misleading the Pope's authority is. Declarations of great significance are made in a whimsical fashion and scraps of paper that really deal with one issue are made to stand as authoritative pronouncements on related matters that happen to be contained within the same document. This explains the dramatic shift in the Church's position from a defence of the Church Fathers who, following Plato, argued for lying in certain extreme situations, to an Augustinian prohibition on lying under any circumstances.[223] The stated reasoning of the papacy is that certain acts, gestures, and positions were possible before the Church decreed that they were sinful, but now they are prohibited. The reality is, according to Donne, a chaotic policy which only serves to expose the lack of serious authority that the leader of the Church possesses. In *Pseudo-Martyr* Donne is careful neither to defend nor to condemn lying as such: his target is the illegitimate authority of the Catholic Church, a contrast to the legitimacy of the monarchy.[224] The door is open for Catholics to serve both masters if they wish, a sensible course of action that he recommends. The Church, the institution that mankind has allowed to putrefy and fester, can be served in many ways and, for Donne, the great shame is that the Catholics have left it to serve the Pope. Now they have a chance to return and so help the wider cause of Christendom if only they take the Oath of Allegiance. Swearing to adhere to it may be difficult but it is not, in itself, a lie that imperils the soul, unlike those taken by the pseudo-martyrs. Once this basic act has been undertaken, the rest, including the decision about if

---

[220] Donne, *Pseudo-Martyr*, p. 111; see also Tutino, *Law and Conscience*, p. 135.
[221] Donne, *Pseudo-Martyr*, p. 157.   [222] Donne, *Pseudo-Martyr*, pp. 198–9.
[223] See John Cassian, *The Conferences*, trans. Boniface Ramsey (Mahwah, NJ: Newman Press, 1997), pp. 583–4; Ehrman, *Forgery and Counter-forgery*, p. 135. On Chrysostom, see above, pp. 130–1.
[224] Although in the unpublished *Biathanatos*, Donne argues that suicide 'is not so intrinsically ill as to Ly' (John Donne, *Selected Prose*, ed. Neil Rhodes (Harmondsworth: Penguin, 1987), p. 64) (I am grateful to Shanyn Altman for this point).

and when to lie, is left to the individual. Like Spenser, Donne would seem to be a Nicodemite at heart.

If the range of the apparently casually cited authorities demonstrates his scholarly interest in definitions of lying, elsewhere Donne is more amusing and polemical on the subject. *Ignatius His Conclave* (1611), the last of Donne's controversial prose works to be written, is probably the most enjoyable to read, a robust, polemical satire of the Jesuits.[225] Donne has an 'extasie' and his soul is transported to Hell where he meets the forces of evil who surround Lucifer. These include Pope Boniface III, who established papal power in the seventh century, Muhammad, and St Ignatius Loyola (1491–1556), the founder of the Jesuits, who is shown to be able to outwit the Devil himself. Accordingly, he establishes himself at the end of the work as the chief innovator who has distorted and inverted true religion.[226] So much does the Devil fear Ignatius that he sends him off to colonize the moon where he will be less threatening to the master of evil. Probably the most interesting passage in the satire is the exchange between Machiavelli, the arch-exponent of political ruthlessness, and Ignatius, who adopts even more aggressive principles in furthering his religious empire.[227] Machiavelli states that he delights in killing; that he enjoys the different types of death that his authority can generate; and that he has a connoisseur's appreciation of the distinction between forms of slaughter: 'For I my selfe went always that way of bloud, and therefore I did euer preferred the sacrifices of the *Gentiles*, and of the *Iewes*, which were performed with effusion of bloud (whereby not only the people, but the Priests also were animated to bold enterprises) before the soft and wanton sacrifices of *Christians*'.[228]

Machiavelli is a devil and well worth the high esteem he receives in Hell. However, his labours to confuse political and religious authority and so damn the souls of those foolish enough to listen to him are negligible compared to those of the greater master, Ignatius, who points out his superiority in a disdainful speech. Arguing—as Donne did in *Pseudo-Martyr*—that the Pope is able to define his own authority as supreme pontiff, Ignatius claims that they have nothing to learn from his newfangled doctrines:

> This then is the point of which wee accuse *Machieull*, that he carried not his Mine so safely, but that the enemy perceiued it still . . . yet I doe not obstinately say, that there is nothing in *Machieuls commentary*, which may bee of vse to this Church. Certainely there is very much; but we are not men of that pouerty, that wee neede begge from others, nor dignify those things with our prayers, which proceede not from our selues.[229]

[225] See Anne Lake Prescott, 'Menippean Donne', in Shami, Flynn, and Hester, eds, *Handbook of Donne*, pp. 158–79, at pp. 168–72.
[226] Stefania Tutino, 'Notes on Machiavelli and Ignatius Loyola in John Donne's *Ignatius his Conclave* and *Pseudo-Martyr*', *EHR* 99 (2004), 1308–21.
[227] Anglo, *Machiavelli*, pp. 374–414.
[228] John Donne, *Ignatius His Conclaue* (London, 1611), p. 35.
[229] Donne, *Ignatius*, pp. 74–5.

As Ignatius points out, the Church has a long history of duplicity and deception that renders Machiavelli's ideas virtually redundant, which is why he is damned with such faint praise. In particular Ignatius pours scorn on Machiavelli's discovery of lying as a strategy, showing that the Church has a distinguished tradition of far worse behaviour from Herod to the Jesuit doctrine of equivocation: 'The libertie of lying, is neither new nor safe as almost all *Machiauells* precepts are . . . stale and obsolete.'[230] The Catholic Church does not need such allies—even though they are reprehensible enough—because it can do much better if left to its own devices. The Jesuits have found more than enough ways already to lure the unwary to their doom.[231] In doing so they are simply revealing themselves to be the natural culmination of all that is Satanic in Catholicism, creating a series of plausible but false doctrines designed to cause death and damnation, the most pernicious of which is the need for the pseudo-martyr, a victim of cruel papal duplicity.

---

[230] Donne, *Ignatius*, pp. 77–8. [231] Anglo, *Machiavelli*, pp. 408–9.

4

Rhetoric, Commonplacing, and Poetics

I

Anxieties about lying subsuming the articulation of the truth are ever present in the theory and practice of rhetoric.[1] Misused, the tools of the orator support the proliferation of falsehood rather than spread of truth. The study of rhetoric, as every historian of education has argued, was the focus of the educational reforms of the sixteenth century and characterized educational systems in Europe until the eighteenth century.[2] Placing more emphasis on the study of rhetoric was the central aspect of the transformation in school and university teaching that witnessed traditional medieval practices designed to prepare the educated for clerical life mutate into teaching methods that prepared students for a wider range of professions and careers, teaching them how to write and argue and so be employable as secretaries, bureaucrats, teachers, and also writers.[3] Cultures of education, religion, work, and writing were in step.[4] Rhetoric brought with it great benefits: an ability to write, argue, and speak in a variety of sophisticated ways for any number of causes, learned through the practice of studying topics *in utramque partem*.[5] But it also created attendant anxieties that the certainty of truth generated by the study of logic was giving way to an art that could benefit the devious as much as, if not more than, the honest. The humanist logic of 'places'—related to the commonplace tradition—designed by Rudolf Agricola and popularized by Petrus Ramus (Peter Ramus) made available a logic that could be applied to specific situations and so was easy to teach and understand, which rivalled and largely obscured the scholastic tradition of Aristotelian formal logic. Agricola's logic, in Lisa Jardine's words, 'marks a conscious move towards and account of systematic reasoning which includes reasoning which falls short of the

---

[1] For one example see Nashe, *Works*, III, p. 120.

[2] See, for example, Kenneth Charlton, *Education in Renaissance England* (London: Routledge, 1975); David Cressy, *Education in Tudor and Stuart England* (London: Arnold, 1975); Helen M. Jewell, *Education in Early Modern England* (Basingstoke: Palgrave, 1998).

[3] Lisa Jardine, 'The Place of Dialectic Teaching in Sixteenth-Century Cambridge', *SR* 21 (1974), 31–62; Mack, *History of Renaissance Rhetoric*, pp. 13–33.

[4] Lynne Enterline, *Shakespeare's Schoolroom: Rhetoric, Discipline, Emotion* (Philadelphia: University of Pennsylvania Press, 2102), ch. 1.

[5] Joel B. Altman, *The Tudor Play of Mind: Rhetorical Inquiry and the Development of Elizabethan Drama* (Berkeley: University of California Press, 1978); Knowles, *Shakespeare's Arguments with History*.

deductively rigorous, and towards the development of language use', so making logic an ally of rhetoric.[6]

In England, as Peter Mack has pointed out in his authoritative history of Elizabethan rhetoric, the standard university set text was Quintilian, along with Cicero's speeches, which were the principal examples used in *Institutio Oratoria* (*The Orator's Education*).[7] Quintilian, who was widely read in England and had a major influence on conceptions of rhetoric, is repeatedly anxious about the abuse of rhetoric to produce falsehood.[8] His defence of the art is based on the assumption that the knowledgeable rhetorician will know when he is lying. In Book Two, Quintilian responds to objections that rhetoric is not really an art with a robust defence of its truthfulness:

> Their second slander is that no art assents to false propositions, because it cannot exist without a cognitive presentation which is invariably true, whereas rhetoric does assent to falsehoods, and therefore is not an art. I am prepared to admit that rhetoric does sometimes say untrue things as if true, but I would not concede that it is therefore in a state of false opinion; there is a great difference between holding an opinion oneself and making someone else adopt it. Generals often use falsehoods: Hannibal, when hemmed in by Fabius, gave the enemy the illusion that his army was in retreat by tying brushwood to the horns of oxen, setting fire to them, and driving the herd at night up the mountains ... Similarly an orator, when he substitutes a falsehood for the truth, knows it is false and that he is substituting a falsehood for the truth; he does not therefore have a false opinion himself, but he deceives the other person. When Cicero boasted that he had cast a cloud of darkness over the eyes of the jury, in the case of Cluentius, he saw clearly enough himself.[9]

The passage is characteristic of Quintilian's style and method: a definition followed by an illustrative example, a mode of argument followed by most Renaissance rhetoricians.[10] But here, one suspects, the educator is less than comfortable with what he is forced to admit. Quintilian argues that rhetoric does not deceive those educated in its arts who know how to use and read rhetorically crafted arguments correctly. But it can and does mislead the less prepared and protected who are taken in by its wiles. Therefore, Quintilian has to admit that rhetoric can be an art of lying. The example of Hannibal's skilful military manoeuvre does not really remove such concerns as this is an extreme case in which the general is placed in a position in which deception is the best pragmatic course. It does not answer the question of whether a rhetorician can deceive an audience when he wants to or whether rhetoric can be used to defend something that he knows is not in the interests of the audience, such as tyranny. The second example of Cicero bamboozling a jury and

---

[6] Lisa Jardine, 'Humanist Logic', in Schmitt and Skinner, eds, *Cambridge History of Renaissance Philosophy*, pp. 173–98, at p. 182.

[7] Mack, *Elizabethan Rhetoric*, pp. 51–4.

[8] See, for example, William Scott, *The Model of Poesie*, ed. Gavin Alexander (Cambridge: Cambridge University Press, 2013), pp. 24, 66, *passim*; George Puttenham, *The Arte of English Poesie*, ed. Gladys Doidge Willcock and Alice Walker (Cambridge: Cambridge University Press, 1970, rpt of 1936), pp. 203, 217, *passim*.

[9] Quintilian, *Institutes*, 2.17.18–21.

[10] Jorge Fernández López, 'Quintilian as Rhetorician and Teacher', in Dominik and Hall, eds, *Companion to Roman Rhetoric*, pp. 307–22.

openly boasting of his triumph, refers to one of Cicero's most celebrated and audacious oratorical performances, his defence of Aulus Cluentius Habitus. Cluentius had been accused of murdering his stepfather, Oppianicus, but had been acquitted after Cicero had defended him with considerable brio, launching a series of surprise attacks against the unjust verdicts delivered by judges and juries in earlier trials, and only reaching the case of Cluentius in the final section of his speech. It is not clear whether Cluentius was innocent or whether Cicero believed him to be, which overshadows the orator's concluding lines, 'whereas the place for prejudice is a public meeting, a court of law is the abode of truth'.[11]

In the concluding book of *The Orator's Education* Quintilian tries to resolve this dilemma through his contention that Cato the Elder's definition of the orator as 'a good man, skilled in speaking' should define the process of creating the *homo rhetoricus*.[12] But the door is open to the familiar charge that the art of rhetoric is the art of lying, the accusation that Socrates had made against the Sophists, notably in the *Gorgias* and *Protagoras*.[13] And, indeed, this was precisely the worry that would not go away, and which characterized the anxieties expressed throughout the one substantial treatise on lying that was printed in sixteenth-century England, Mathieu Coignet's *A Politique Discourse upon Trueth and Lying*.

Other classical treatises on rhetoric expressed similar anxieties, often in oblique and subtle ways that helped to make the point that rhetoric may be much more of a potent force than logic. Aristotle's *The Art of Rhetoric* argues that orations should be based on the building-block of the enthymeme (a syllogism in which one premise or the conclusion is not stated). The first enthymeme that Aristotle produces is surprising, being perfectly balanced between truth-telling and lying:

> One line of positive proof is based upon consideration of the opposite of the thing in question. Observe whether that opposite has the opposite quality. If it has not, you refute the original proposition; if it has, you establish it. E.g., 'Temperance is beneficial; for licentiousness is hurtful'.
>
> Or, as in the Messenian speech, 'If war is the cause of our present troubles, peace is what we need to put things right again.' Or—
>
> > For if not even evil-doers should
> > Anger us if they meant not what they did,
> > Then can we owe no gratitude to such
> > As were constrained to do the good they did us.
>
> Or—
>
> > Since in this world liars may win belief,
> > Be sure of the opposite likewise—that this world
> > Hears many a true word and believes it not.[14]

---

[11] Cicero, *Murder Trials*, trans. Michael Grant (New York: Dorset Press, 1975), pp. 111–253, at p. 253.

[12] Quintilian, *Institutes*, 12.1.1. Cicero makes the same equation: see Denery, *The Devil Wins*, pp. 169–70.

[13] John Dugan, 'Modern Critical Approaches to Roman Rhetoric', in Dominik and Hall, eds, *Companion to Roman Rhetoric*, pp. 9–22, at p. 13.

[14] Aristotle, *The Art of Rhetoric*, trans. Anon. (London: Collins, 2012), pp. 133–4. The Messenians fought a series of wars with the Spartans in the eighth century; the quotation about lying comes from Euripides's *Thyestes*, which only survives as a fragment: see Aristotle, *The Art of Rhetoric*, trans.

The final enthymeme leaves ideas of truth/lies suspended, suggesting that there is not really any hope of progress.[15] Some lies will be believed and some will fail to persuade those who encounter them, and the notion that habitual liars would not be believed when they told the truth was proverbial in sixteenth-century England.[16] This enthymeme suggests that there is no logic to which lies will be believed and that either the process of their dissemination is random, or that it is rhetoric that really counts. Aristotle, like Plato, is opposed to what he sees as the misleading wiles of the Sophists, but here he admits that they might hold the upper hand.

A similar sense of unease is frequently reproduced in rhetorical and poetry manuals produced in early modern England, published as a response to the growth and development of the interest in rhetoric as an educational tool and a prized ability that would lead to gainful employment. A troubled passage concludes Leonard Cox's learned discussion of how a speaker might begin an oration in *The Arte or Crafte of Rhetoryke* (1530). Cox turns to the mode of insinuation, which he suggests is a risky but sometimes powerful way of speaking. Cox writes about the difficulties of praising a figure such as Thersites in Homer's *Iliad*, because he is somewhat less than heroic being the 'moost foule and euyll fauored of all the Grekes that came to the batayle of Troye', being 'gogle eyed and lame on the one legge with croked and pynched shulders and a longe pyked hede balde in very many places'.[17] Cox points out that poets have not been able to tell the truth in such circumstances:

> Nowe if one wolde take vpon hym to make an oracioon to the prayse of this losel whiche mater is of litle honesty in it selfe he must vse in stede of a preface an insinuacion. That what thynge poetes or commune fame doth eyther prayse or dispraise ought nat to be gyuen credence to but rather to be suspecte. For ones it is the nature of poetes to sayne and lye as bothe Homere and Virgile which are the princes and heddes of al poetes do witnesse them selfe. Of whome Homere sayth that poetes make many lies and Virgile he saith: The moost part of the sene is but deceyte.
>
> Poetes haue sene blake soules vnder the erthe poetes haue fayned and made many lyes of the pale kyngdome of Plato and of the water of Stigie and of dogges in hell.[18]

There is surely an unease that surrounds this passage, a fear that poets will tell lies in order to avoid telling unpalatable truths to power. Even the greatest classical poets admit that this is the case and is something that has to be accepted. Accordingly, reading poetry is a complicated and demanding exercise as it is never really clear whether they are actually telling the truth at any point or using their powers of insinuation to produce oblique and ironic praise of something that is really disturbing or threatening or not worthy of their words. The truth is that poets

John Henry Freese (London: Heinemann, 1926), p. 297; T. B. L. Webster, *The Tragedies of Euripides* (London: Methuen, 1967), pp. 113–15.

[15] For discussion see Irene E. Harvey, *Labyrinths of Exemplarity: At the Limits of Deconstruction* (Albany, NY: SUNY Press, 2012), pp. 249–50.

[16] Tilley, *Proverbs*, L217 (p. 377).

[17] Leonard Cox, *The Arte or Crafte of Rhetoryke* (London, 1530), sig. B4v.

[18] Cox, *Arte or Crafte of Rhetoryke*, sig. B3r.

rarely have to praise deformed and unsavoury creatures like Thersites, but are called on to praise tyrants and other powerful criminals who may be alluded to in the final sentence describing the 'blake soules' in hell. Cox, of course, may have been wary of pointing this out in his treatise, given his proximity to Henry VIII—he later praised the marriage of Henry and Anne in his translation of Erasmus's paraphrase of Paul's letter to Titus—performing the act of insinuation in recounting how poets were forced to insinuate their real messages if they wanted them to have any impact on those in power.[19]

In Richard Sherry's similarly pioneering *A Treatise of Schemes and Tropes* (1550), the author provides a definition of 'Antithesis (*Contrarium*)' as 'when the reason standeth by contrary wordes or contraries be rehearsed by comparison'.[20] The figure lends itself to discussions of duplicity and lying which Sherry duly provides: 'He that in familiare communicacion and company of hys friendes wyl neuer say truth, thinkest then y[f] he wil absteine from a lye in a common audience.'[21] It has the capacity to perform what it might be thought to mean, that the orator produces words at odds with what he speaks, just as the liar in familiar company may or may not tell the truth when addressing a public audience.

II

Anxiety about lying also dominated literature about commonplacing which was intimately connected to the theory and practice of rhetoric in sixteenth-century Europe, as rhetorical practice based on the significance of 'places'—specific instances of arguments designed for particular situations—began to dominate the formal teaching of rhetoric.[22] Commonplaces were, of course, good when they could be shown to inspire useful thought about everyday matters, bad when they served to support thoughtless and self-serving behaviour, a problem inherent in proverbs, maxims, and any portmanteau statement, as early modern writers acknowledged. Erasmus's *Colloquies* contain a number of dialogues about lying, sharp practice, and double-dealing, most notably 'The Liar and the Man of Honour: Pseudochei et Philetymi'.[23] Pseudocheus, whose name can be translated as 'liar', explains that there is no particular reason why he lies, although practising in various ways over the years has made him more skilful and adept at his calling:

---

[19] *ODNB* entry; Leonard Cox, *The Paraphrase of Erasmus Roterdame vpon the epistle of saint Paule vnto his discyple Titus* (London, 1534).

[20] Richard Sherry, *A Treatise of Schemes and Tropes very profytable for the better vnderstanding of good authors, gathered out of the best grammarians [and] oratours* (London, 1550), sig. D5r. See also Sonnino, *Handbook*, pp. 62–3. On Sherry (b.*c*.1505) little is known outside his published works: see the *ODNB* entry.

[21] Sherry, *Treatise of Schemes and Tropes*, sig. D5r.

[22] See, for example, Heinrich F. Plett, *Rhetoric and Renaissance Culture* (Berlin: Walter de Gruyter, 2004), pp. 134–5.

[23] Erasmus, *Collected Works*, 39, pp. 344–50.

PHILETYMUS: What's the source of your constant flow of lies?

PSEUDOCHEUS: What's the source of spider's webs?

PHILETYMUS: Then it's not a work of art but of nature?

PSEUDOCHEUS: Nature gave the seed. Art and practice developed the skill.

PHILETYMUS: Aren't you ashamed of yourself?

PSEUDOCHEUS: No more than the cuckoo of her song.

PHILETYMUS: But *you* can change your tune, and man was endowed with speech in order to proclaim truth.

PSEUDOCHEUS: Oh, yes—when it's profitable. But it's not always convenient to tell the truth.[24]

Pseudocheus is, of course, practising his art in this opening exchange. One did not have to be an expert on insects or particularly well versed in beast fables to know that spiders spun webs to catch flies, knowledge that later informs John Heywood's allegorical *The Spider and the Fly* (1556).[25] Pseudocheus is pretending that there is no reason why he lies other than a natural propensity that he possesses, but this is not a belief that he sincerely holds and his answering a question with a question is a means of diverting attention from his obvious moral failing. His analogy undermines itself as there is a definite and easily obtainable answer to his question just as there is undoubtedly a similarly obvious answer to Philetymus's, that is, that Pseudocheus lies for personal advantage and because he does not care about anyone other than himself. The analogy fails because a spider has to consume insects whereas he is not designed by nature to lie. Truth is not something that can or should be adhered to merely when it is convenient.

The colloquy asks difficult questions because it deliberately avoids the normal starting point of discussions in moral philosophy and theology—were there any circumstances in which one might be permitted to tell lies?—and in doing so forcing the reader to think hard about what he or she actually knows. Elsewhere Erasmus refers to this problem as 'that notorious and confusing question'.[26] Here we are confronted with the nature/nurture distinction and asked whether lying is something that is inherent in human nature, a debate that chimes with modern, scientifically based concerns about lying.[27] Pseudocheus has been created by Erasmus to test commonplaces—which are here represented in sceptical terms as philosophical clichés—about the inherent goodness of human nature and the capacity of man to imitate God, most famously expressed in Pico della Mirandola's *Oration on the Dignity of Man* (1486).[28] If Pseudocheus is as bad as he claims to be

---

[24] Erasmus, *Collected Works*, 39, p. 344.

[25] T. H. White, *The Bestiary: A Book of Beasts* (New York: Putnam, 1954), p. 187; Alice Hunt, 'Marian Political Allegory: John Heywood's *The Spider and the Fly*', in Pincombe and Shrank, eds, *Oxford Handbook of Tudor Literature*, pp. 337–55.

[26] Erasmus, *Collected Works*, *Lingua*, 29, pp. 249–412, at p. 330.

[27] Robert W. Mitchell, 'Animals as Liars: The Human Face of Nonhuman Duplicity', in Lewis and Saarni, eds, *Lying and Deception*, pp. 59–89; Metcalf, *They Lie, We Lie*, introduction; Leslie, *Born Liars*, pp. 1–22.

[28] Pico della Mirandola, *Oration on the Dignity of Man*, in Ernst Cassirer, Paul Oskar Kristeller, and John Herman Randall, Jr, eds, *The Renaissance Philosophy of Man* (Chicago: University of Chicago Press, 1948), pp. 215–54.

then he calls into question God's purpose in creating mankind, a version of the Cretan liar paradox, which, in demonstrating that not everything can be a lie, suggests that nothing can be entirely negative. Perhaps it is best to read this particular colloquy in terms of Erasmus's intellectual feud with Luther over the freedom or bondage of the will, and an attack on the assumption that mankind's essential feature was depravity, something Erasmus argues God could not have planned.[29]

Erasmus explores such paradoxes throughout the colloquy. Philetymus's earnest explorations attempt to get to the heart of Pseudocheus's commitment to avoiding telling the truth:

> PHILETYMUS: So it helps sometimes to have sticky fingers. And that this failing is closely related to yours is attested by a popular proverb.
>
> PSEUDOCHEUS: Each failing rests on good authority: one on Ulysses, so highly praised by Homer, and the other on Mercury, even though a god, if we trust the poets.
>
> PHILETYMUS: Then why are liars commonly cursed, thieves even crucified?
>
> PSEUDOCHEUS: Not because they lie or thieve but because they bungle the job, either acting contrary to their own nature, or lacking sufficient experience in the art.[30]

Pseudocheus is using commonplaces in exactly the wrong way, transforming maxims into proverbs, to support opinions he already holds and so justify his reprehensible behaviour. In doing so he is acting against the spirit of the *Colloquies*, assuming a fixed position rather than using statements and apparent truisms to explore problems which require sustained and nimble thought not dogmatic assertion and repetition. Pseudocheus suggests that he has two failings, a tendency to lie related to a desire to steal, the two closely linked in the popular imagination by the proverb, 'show me a liar and I'll show you a thief'.[31] In order to justify his behaviour Pseudocheus uses the support of classical examples, Ulysses, the wily, crafty liar whose cunning enables him to escape from the ruins of Troy and so be reunited with his equally resourceful wife, Penelope; and Mercury, 'the patron and inventor of thieving', a skill closely associated with Mercury's other talent, that of rhetoric, as Erasmus outlines in *Adage* II I 85, 'Communis Mercurius' (Share Mercury).[32]

Pseudocheus is a leaden and unimaginative reader of literature, resembling Martin Amis's character John Self in *Money* (1984) who is confused by *Animal Farm* because it is obvious that animals cannot talk.[33] Pseudocheus has simply looted works of high cultural status and used choice phrases to support his untenable position. It is evident to readers that Homer's representation of Ulysses's

---

[29] *Luther and Erasmus: Free Will and Salvation*, ed. Ernest Gordon Rupp and Philip Saville Watson (Westminster: John Knox Press, 1969).

[30] Erasmus, *Collected Works*, 39, p. 345.   [31] Erasmus, *Collected Works*, 39, p. 348.

[32] Erasmus, *Collected Works*, 33, pp. 65–7.

[33] Martin Amis, *Money: A Suicide Note* (London: Vintage, 2011, first published 1984), pp. 203–12.

voyage home in *The Odyssey* is not just an endorsement of human failings, as Pseudocheus claims: the cunning, deviousness, and bloody-mindedness of Ulysses are, after all, precisely the sort of human vices and virtues that led to the Trojan War in the first place, as readers of *The Iliad* would have been all too aware. Erasmus is referring to another central debate that absorbed sixteenth-century European intellectuals, the relationship between literary representation and the truth.[34] Pseudocheus takes literature seriously as a store of useful truths in order to justify his own, natural desire to lie, an untenable position that is seemingly unaware of the debate (unless he is lying). More significantly, Pseudocheus is spiritually blind, missing the reference that Philetymus provides to Christ's crucifixion, and the thieves who died beside him, one of whom repented and was rewarded with a place in Paradise later that day (Luke 23: 33–43). Crucifixion was abolished as a punishment by Constantine I in the fourth century so Erasmus is not expecting his readers to relate this aspect of the colloquy to contemporary life.[35] For Pseudocheus the crime is irrelevant as malefactors are only punished because they fail to do their jobs properly.

Erasmus's point is that Pseudocheus is able to defend his untenable position because he is a wilfully blind reader, one who simply refuses to see the truth and who cannot understand that commonplaces are starting points for a discussion not finishing points or universal truths that will trump everything else. On their own, commonplaces and parables can mislead as well as instruct: it is their place within the narrative concerned that really matters: 'A parable coming out of a fool's mouth shall be rejected; for he doth not speak of it in due season.'[36] Whether he is lying in adopting the stance he does or genuinely deluded probably matters less than his refusal to accept or understand that his arguments and actions are pernicious. The colloquy ends with the two interlocutors as far apart as they were at the start of their dialogue:

PSEUDOCHEUS: Just mark off the skill of professionals. By these methods there's the greater profit, or certainly just as much; and there's less risk.

PHILETYMUS: Bad luck to you with your tricks and lies! I don't care to bid you farewell.

PSEUDOCHEUS: Snarl away in your filthy rags of righteousness. Meanwhile I'll live enjoyably with my thefts and lies under the patronage of Ulysses and Mercury.[37]

For Pseudocheus the world is a place where every man is for himself and the winner takes all, his stories of prodigious feats of lying demonstrating that he is indifferent to any suffering caused by his actions and does not hesitate to blame someone else for his crimes when he can get away with it. The dialogue ends with nothing resolved and the two men, the liar and the man of honour, returning to their separate moral worlds. What the colloquy shows the reader is the bleak nature of

---

[34] Herman, *Squitter-wits*, pp. 13–59.   [35] *Christian Church*, p. 438.
[36] Erasmus, *Collected Works*, 29, p. 324 (quoting Ecclesiasticus 20:22 (Vulgate)).
[37] Erasmus, *Collected Works*, 39, p. 348.

the world if lying is permitted or even celebrated as a central facet of human behaviour: Erasmus habitually espoused a mean, one that is not achieved here.[38] Combatting the brutal logic of Pseudocheus involves sophisticated reading strategies, an understanding that texts do not tell us obvious truths but that the significance of a difficult work has to be painstakingly extracted by a sympathetic expert, like Erasmus himself. Pseudocheus is not good enough to be allowed to read literature without guidance and Philetymus, decent as he is, is unable to counter Pseudocheus's reductive readings of complicated literary works. In many ways the colloquy is an anti-Reformation text, a counterpart to Thomas More's arguments about scripture with William Tyndale, a warning about what misreadings, heretical, stupid, and pernicious, and only occasionally true and illuminating, will result if no one controls interpretation and teaches people how to read properly. *The Odyssey* will be reduced to a manual about how to lie most effectively, which, as Erasmus's analysis of the eloquence of its principal characters and praise of Ulysses's self-restraint in other writings demonstrates, is not a reading he ever endorses.[39]

Erasmus's writings condemn lying in sustained as well as relatively casual ways, as a vice that, if tolerated, undermines the basic contract between speakers that makes engagement possible. Folly starts her oration in *The Praise of Folly* (1509) arguing that she will tell her own story, a practice that is rather more honest and less immodest than that of princes who 'hire some flattering orator or lying poet from whose mouth they may hear their praises, that is to say, mere lies'.[40] More significant is the discussion in *Lingua*, as lying 'often appears as the chief vice of the tongue' in literature on speech.[41] Erasmus articulates the familiar model of language as a perfect form of communication given to man by God, 'a natural language, reflecting the nature of things': 'Only God perceives what lurks in the heart of man. But the tongue was given to men so that by its agency as messenger one man might know the mind and intention of another.'[42] Erasmus, following most ancient authorities, admits the exception of jokes, 'lying tales . . . used only to raise laughter'.[43] But, as a rule and following the example of Christ, 'it is most shameful for the tongue to be at variance with the heart'.[44]

Erasmus then launches a sustained attack on the failure of mankind to live up to God's linguistic bargain:

[38] Erasmus, *Collected Works*, 29, p. 286.   [39] Erasmus, *Collected Works*, 29, pp. 270, 304–5.

[40] Erasmus, *Praise of Folly*, trans. John Wilson (New York: Dover, 2003), p. 6.

[41] Mark D. Johnston, 'The Treatment of Speech in Medieval Ethical and Courtesy Literature', *Rhetorica* 4 (1986), 21–46, p. 29. On the significance of Erasmus's treatise see Nathalie Vienne-Guerrin, ed., *The Unruly Tongue in Early Modern England: Three Treatises* (Madison: Farleigh Dickinson University Press, 2012), introduction, xxi.

[42] Ashworth, 'Traditional Logic', p. 156; Erasmus, *Collected Works*, 29, p. 314.

[43] Erasmus, *Collected Works*, 29, p. 314. Thomas Wilson has a long section on 'Pleasaunt dissembling', which shows readers how to make jokes about lying in order to disarm liars: Thomas Wilson, *The Arte of Rhetorique* (London, 1560), pp. 149, 150.

[44] Erasmus, *Collected Works*, 29, p. 315.

But now even among Christians, O everlasting God, how rare is honesty of speech? How many men are there who have become so accustomed to lying that they do not even know they lie? In comedies this is treated as a feature of the slave character, but in our way of life it is scarcely thought improper in priests and monks, and when it occurs in our leaders is even given the name of policy. I need not mention at this point those whose whole life is nothing but a lie. For they do not only lie in their speech, always keeping on their lips religion, the church, and Christ, the faith and the gospel, but even in their feigned countenance, their portentous apparel, their diets, titles, and ceremonies, they lie before the whole world, bringing great damage to the religion which they dishonestly profess.[45]

In 1525 Erasmus's hope was to shame the Church into reforming and so make it better able to combat Luther's principled assault, but it is easy to see why such passages helped provide ammunition for the Protestant cause and made Erasmus seem like a weak Nicodemite, aware of the truth but too self-interested to act.[46] Erasmus is using the term 'lie' in its popular, polemical sense, insulting his opponents within the Church in the hope of shaming them into a reformation of their ways and effective action against the gathering pace of the Reformation. As such, the passage is relatively unremarkable and belongs to the style of ferocious religious debate over the nature of truth in the first half of the sixteenth century.[47] More significant is the claim that lying has become such a habit that people do not even know they are lying. For virtually all authorities on lying, including Augustine, this is impossible, as lying involves pretending to believe something one does not. However, Erasmus is making a much more forceful and aggressive point: the common culture of lying has reduced people from being thinking active citizens who have the free will to choose into slaves who are unable to make decisions for themselves. In making this insulting intellectual manoeuvre Erasmus is linking a number of contemporary issues. Comparing people who fail to exercise their free will to slaves follows Aristotle who claimed in *The Politics* that the lower sections of humanity were 'natural slaves' and, as the medieval logician Giles of Rome argued, 'it is appropriate for such people to be placed in subjection to others'.[48] For Aristotle 'all men who differ from others as much as the body differs from the soul, or an animal from a man . . . are by nature slaves, and it is better for them . . . to be ruled by a master'.[49] Slaves need constant guidance as they lack rational capacity and require proper government and guidance just as the body needs to be controlled by the soul and not vice versa. Christians have transformed themselves into slaves through a failure to govern the tongue, tell the truth, and avoid lies.

Erasmus cleverly combines a series of factors in making his claim, challenging his readers to understand the nature and significance of his criticism of the Church. In

---

[45] Erasmus, *Collected Works*, 29, p. 315.
[46] Alastair Duke, *The Reformation and Revolt in the Low Countries* (London: Black, 2003), p. 83.
[47] Evans, *Problems of Authority*, pp. 241, 261, *passim*.
[48] Cited in Quentin Skinner, 'Political Philosophy', in Schmitt and Skinner, eds, *Cambridge History of Renaissance Philosophy*, pp. 389–452, at p. 407.
[49] Aristotle, *The Politics*, ed. and trans. Ernest Baker (Oxford: Oxford University Press, 1946), p. 13.

suggesting that the Church has lapsed into slavery he is surely alluding to the debates taking place in Spain about the nature of the natives in the New World discovered by Columbus in 1492.[50] Why had such people never received the word of God? Were they natural slaves placed by God in remote lands who should now be ruled by Christians? Erasmus is suggesting that in becoming slaves through living a lie the Church had forfeited all right to rule over the New World unless they mended their ways. The reference to slaves in comedy is another allusion to Aristotle, this time the *Poetics*, which argues that comedy represents 'inferior people' who provoke laughter because 'the laughable is a species of what is disgraceful'.[51] It is implicit in Aristotle's argument that slaves feature significantly in comedy: 'there is such a thing as a good woman and a good slave, even though one of these is perhaps deficient and the other generally speaking inferior'.[52] The Church is making itself ridiculous, the subject of a human comedy of self-interest, greed, mendaciousness, and, above all, lying hypocrisy. Perhaps most dangerously—and presciently—Erasmus is suggesting that the clergy have transformed themselves into creatures enslaved to their bodies and appetites, a bondage of the will that obliterates the capacity for reason and justifies the dark view of human nature of the Reformers.

Erasmus's strictures about lying are far-reaching and serious. *Lingua* explains what is at stake in a colloquy such as 'The Liar and the Man of Honour'. Furthermore it shows that the significance of debates about lying is often less in the formal properties and distinctions involved and more in an articulation of the effects of individual acts of lying and the creation of a culture of lying. Like More, Erasmus is especially concerned about the erosion of a culture of oaths, and the ability of an individual to override solemn promises with an apparently casual disregard, stemming from not understanding the nature of a contract between man and God stretching into the future. Oaths have become more esteemed as public acts and so more easily violated leading to a culture of insincerity that is far more pernicious than one which did not require excessive swearing. Princes swear, as do churchmen and university teachers: 'The men who enter on public office are sworn in, and then exercise that office as if they had sworn to forswear themselves.'[53] Peter's failings when he denied Christ three times are routinely condemned 'yet it seems a sport for us to perjure ourselves, as if perjury in God's name were anything less than denying him'.[54] The terrible failures of a common culture of lying will lead to serious issues for the Church as promises to God are broken. Erasmus outlines the slippery slope: 'It is a dangerous sickness when anyone is provoked to silly talk by a restless tongue, but far more dangerous when someone is led to talk silly nonsense by a shameless delight in lying itself.'[55] What starts as an annoying, localized series of failings eventually becomes diabolic with nothing to stop it:

---

[50] Anthony Pagden, *The Fall of Natural Man: The American Indian and the Origins of Comparative Ethnology* (Cambridge: Cambridge University Press, 1986), ch. 3.

[51] Aristotle, *Poetics*, ed. and trans. Malcolm Heath (Harmondsworth: Penguin, 1996), p. 9.

[52] Aristotle, *Poetics*, p. 24.   [53] Erasmus, *Collected Works*, 29, p. 317.

[54] Erasmus, *Collected Works*, 29, p. 317.   [55] Erasmus, *Collected Works*, 29, pp. 326–7.

For if those who benefit men by lying are offensive to him [God], surely those men are far more offensive to him who by their lying cause ruin to body and soul, and by falsehood bring into the power of Satan whom Jesus Christ, the eternal Truth, has set free from Satan's falsehood? For he did not stand firm in the truth, but from the beginning was a liar and the father of lies.[56]

Lying reverses Christ's sacrifice for mankind and reintroduces the prospect of widespread damnation (again, it is likely that there is a reference here to Luther's understanding of human depravity). Slips of the tongue, a failure to control it properly, will have untold consequences: 'Whoever lies, forswears, cheats, or teaches impiety, or urges unjust behaviour, or sows discord among his brethren, whoever competes, quarrels, or accuses, speaks with the tongue of the devil.'[57]

III

William Baldwin's *A Treatise of Moral Philosophy* was undoubtedly the most popular work of philosophy produced in sixteenth-century England. Baldwin's work appeared in the first year of Edward VI's reign and was reprinted six times before Elizabeth acceded to the throne; a further ten times during her reign in various enlarged versions; and a further seven times before the Interregnum.[58] In this achievement it was second only to the Bible.[59] Baldwin's work is not, strictly speaking, a treatise at all, and it is certainly not 'a formal or methodical discussion or exposition of the principles of the subject'.[60] Rather, *A Treatise of Moral Philosophy* is a work inspired by Erasmus's encyclopedic collections which seeks to reconcile Christian and classical philosophy.[61] Most of the work consists of a collection of commonplaces, which provide the reader with a series of maxims by philosophers, perspectives and proverbs that can be applied in a variety of situations: in later editions this element became even more pronounced as Baldwin's critical apparatus faded into the background.[62] Influenced by the spectacular success and spread of Ramism in the second half of the sixteenth century, the means of preserving useful phrases and sayings, the commonplace method, was starting to dominate European scholarship and approaches to learning by the middle of the sixteenth century, leaving its mark on a variety of forms of writing.[63] In Ann Moss's words, 'printed vernacular commonplace books may be signs of a socially cohesive effect exerted

---

[56] Erasmus, *Collected Works*, 29, p. 327.   [57] Erasmus, *Collected Works*, 29, p. 405.

[58] Gaudet, 'Baldwin's *Treatise of Moral Philosophy*', pp. ii, 36–7.

[59] R. W. Maslen, 'William Baldwin and the Politics of Pseudo-Philosophy in Tudor Prose Fiction', *SP* 97 (2000), 29–60, p. 31.

[60] *OED* 1a.

[61] Gaudet, 'Baldwin's *Treatise of Moral Philosophy*', pp. 48–56. On Erasmus see Brian Cummings, 'Encyclopedic Erasmus', *RS* 28 (2014), 183–204.

[62] Gaudet, 'Baldwin's *Treatise of Moral Philosophy*', pp. 78–87.

[63] Howard Hotson, *Commonplace Learning: Ramism and its German Ramifications, 1543–1630* (Oxford: Oxford University Press, 2007); Neil Rhodes, *Shakespeare and the Origins of English* (Oxford: Oxford University Press, 2004), pp. 149–88; Jennifer Richards, *Rhetoric* (Abingdon: Routledge, 2008), pp. 85, 87.

beyond the limits of the classroom by the commonplace-book habits of thought'.[64] And, as Sydney Anglo points out, that the expression of political views invariably took the form of maxims, aphorisms, and other commonplaces was considered 'both desirable and normal': Machiavelli and his nemesis Gentillet relied on aphorisms to underpin their work, as did works that they both influenced such as *Vindiciae Contra Tyrannos*.[65] Following Quintilian, orators and writers assumed that it was important to appeal to what was familiar to 'persuade the audience by rousing the emotions'.[66] Baldwin's book is a useful guide to what was available to ordinary literate readers as well as a barometer of the state of knowledge about lying. Baldwin mixes sayings from major philosophers and English authorities to produce a practical guide for 'would-be governors and gentlemen' eager to master the basics of moral philosophy, understand debates, and, therefore, ready to put principles into action.[67]

Baldwin provides a list of commonplaces, 'Of lieng and diseit':

> *Socrates*, Llinge is a sicknes of the sowle, which cannot bee cured, but by shame or reason.
> *Seneca*, There is no difference, between a greate teller of tidings and a lyar.
> *Hermes*, Beware of lyers and flatterers: and if thou be in aucthoritie punishe them.
> Flye the companye of a Lyar, but if thou must needs keepe companye wyth him, beware that in any case thou beliue him not.
> *Plato*. There is no goodness in a lyar.
> Beliue not him whiche telleth thee a lye by another bodye, for hee will in like manner make a lie of thee to an other man.
> He ought not to lie that taketh upon him to instruct other.
> It is laweful for a gouernour for the maintenaunce of his estate, and sauegard of his people: but not for a subiect to lye in any cause.
> *Solon*. The rewarde of a lier is, that hee bee not beleued of that he speaketh.
> *Pithagoras:* A common lyar, not to be double in his tale, needeth a good memory.
> A boster is more to be despised then a liar.
> A wicked soule is knowen by that it deliteth in lies.[68]

Apart from the description of Plato's 'noble lie'—which would not necessarily have been known to English Renaissance readers—there is little here that characterizes any specific philosopher and, in the absence of sources, it is hard to attribute these maxims to any particular thinker.[69] In fact, Baldwin borrows heavily from *The*

---

[64] Ann Moss, *Printed Commonplace-Books and the Structuring of Renaissance Thought* (Oxford: Clarendon Press, 1996), p. 208.

[65] Anglo, *Machiavelli*, pp. 298–9, 344. See below, pp. 234–9.

[66] Fitzmaurice, *Humanism and America*, p. 113.   [67] Maslen, 'Baldwin', p. 31.

[68] William Baldwin, *A Treatise of Morall Phylosophie, contaynyng the sayinges of the wyse. Gathered and Englyshed* (London, 1547), fos 184–5.

[69] On the 'noble lie', see Plato, *The Republic*, trans. Desmond Lee (rev. edn, Harmondsworth: Penguin, 1974), pp. 177–82 (412b–415d); Jane S. Zembaty, 'Plato's *Republic* and Greek Morality on

Dicts and Sayings of the Philosophers, a translation of a popular thirteenth-century compilation, *Liber Philosophorum Moralium Antiquorum*, by Lord Anthony Woodville, Earl Rivers (*c.*1440–83), whose tragedy Baldwin narrated in additions made to *The Mirror for Magistrates* (1563), as well as Ficino's works on Hermes Trismegistus.[70] The *Dicts* is an especially significant work which had a profound effect on later writing, because it was the first book printed in England, and also circulated widely in manuscript form.[71]

The *Dicts* provides readers with a handy collection of proverbs and maxims on lying culled from the writings of philosophers. Readers are told, following Christ's injunction in Matthew 5:37, to 'let trouth be alwey in your mouthe, and swere not but ye and nay, enforce you not to cause them swere that ye knowe wille lye'.[72] Hermes Trismegistus warns his readers that a 'reportour or contreuer of wordes' is inevitably a liar because he distorts the words either at source, or when he delivers the message, and urges rulers to punish criminals fairly and openly and so keep them from the attention of liars.[73] Pythagoras states that the tongue of an evil man is sharper than a spear and advises good men to be careful of their speech but to be patient when exposed to liars.[74] And Plato counsels men to adhere to the truth because goodness and truth connect men and women but lies and evil behaviour divide them. Accordingly, evil men, suspicious by nature, are more likely to believe lies.[75]

Baldwin's collection of examples provides the reader with an understanding that lying is reprehensible and should be avoided, especially with Socrates—here separated from Plato—describing it as 'a sicknes of the sowle' which is extremely difficult to cure, and Pythagoras asserting that the wicked enjoy lying. Taken together, the sayings collected in both books can be read to support the two generally accepted but opposed perceptions of lying deriving from Augustine and Jerome, that is, that lying was utterly forbidden as antithetical to God's designs, and that lying was possible in certain, limited circumstances. Even Socrates's condemnation is tempered by the suggestion that lying can be cured by shame or reason, an understanding that there are many ways to control and prevent the spread of deliberate falsehood. Seneca

Lying', *JHP* 26 (1988), 517–45; Ehrman, *Forgery and Counter-forgery*, p. 540. Plato was known through the 'distorting window' of Ficino's Latin edition: Anthony Grafton, 'The Availability of Ancient Works', in Schmitt and Skinner, eds, *Cambridge History of Renaissance Philosophy*, pp. 767–91, at p. 769.

[70] Curt F. Bühler, 'A Survival from the Middle Ages: William Baldwin's *Use of the Dictes and Sayings*', *Speculum* 23 (1948), 76–80; N. F. Blake, *Caxton and his World* (London: Andre Deutsch, 1969), pp. 85–6; J. S. Gill, 'How Hermes Trismegistus Was Introduced to Renaissance England: The Influences of Caxton and Ficino's "Argumentum" on Baldwin and Palfreyman', *JWCI* 47 (1984), 222–5. On The tragedy of Lord Rivers, see Lily B. Campbell, ed., *The Mirror for Magistrates* (Cambridge: Cambridge University Press, 1938), pp. 245–66. On Rivers, see *ODNB* entry.

[71] *The Dicts and Sayings of the Philosophers: The Translations Made by Stephen Scrope, William Worcester and an Anonymous Translator*, ed. Curt F. Bühler (London: EETS, 1941), introduction, p. ix; Samuel Willard Crompton, *The Printing Press: Transforming Power of Technology* (New York: Infobase, 2004), p. 25; A. E. B. Coldiron, *Printers without Borders: Translation and Textuality in the Renaissance* (Cambridge: Cambridge University Press, 2015), pp. 65–91.

[72] Anthony Wydeville [Woodville], *The Dictes or Sayengis of the Philosophers* (London, 1477), p. 12.
[73] *Dicts*, pp. 20, 30.   [74] *Dicts*, pp. 40, 52.   [75] Wydeville, *Dictes*, p. 116; *Dicts*, p. 140.

suggests that a liar is indeed culpable, but so is 'a greate teller of tidings', which probably means someone who tells tall tales, or, less likely, a writer of fiction.[76] However we read the comparison, the maxim would not have pleased Augustine, who would have seen it as the start of a slippery slope towards moral relativism. Hermes does advise rulers to punish liars and flatterers, conventional wisdom that sought to ensure that rulers received the best advice, and he tells readers to avoid liars.[77] But if that is not possible, which was surely the case for most people who did not mix exclusively with the saintly, then one simply had to be on one's guard. Solon provides the concomitant advice that liars risk not being believed, as does Plato whose second saying observes that lying often becomes a habit. Most unusual is the advice of Pythagoras that boasters are worse than liars, a judgement that would have astonished Aquinas and, again, risks the sort of moral relativism that many in the sixteenth century found so dangerous.[78] The observation of Pythagoras that liars need a good memory, developed later by Montaigne, cuts both ways. It can be read as a moral injunction to avoid lying by pointing out its pitfalls; or cynical, politique advice to those who may be forced to lie, alluding to an especially difficult and highly valued skill that would be required to succeed.[79]

Baldwin's *Treatise* develops out of an educational tradition that valued arguing *in utramque partem*, in itself an acknowledgement that many dilemmas were difficult to solve and answers to complex problems worth debating were unlikely to be straightforward. It stands as a pointed contrast to later works such as Robert Cawdrey's *A Treasurie or Storehouse of Similies* (1600), which were written to counter what he clearly regarded as the dangerous relativism of the rhetorical tradition.[80] Cawdrey, who had noted puritan sympathies, was eager to provide useful manuals that would help keep the minds of his fellow countrymen of 'all estates', as the title advertised, focused on the Bible by making its wisdom more easily digestible. While Baldwin was encouraging his readers by providing them with the tools to think and write about important issues, Cawdrey's entry for lying shows him trying to direct their thoughts one way:

1 As hee sinneth most greeuously that deceiueth blinde men, or trauelling men, by shewing them a contrary way: Euen so much more heinously often deth hee, that in matters of religion, doctrine, and godlinesse, do bring men into

---

[76] On the complicated debates about literature, fiction, and lies in fifteenth- and sixteenth-century Europe see José Maria Pérez Fernández, *Communication, Commerce and Community: Translation and the International Republic of Letters*, work in progress, ch. 4. I am grateful to Prof. Pérez Fernández for showing me this work in typescript.

[77] Greg Walker, *The Politics of Performance in Early Renaissance Drama* (Cambridge: Cambridge University Press, 1998), p. 212.

[78] *Summa Theologica*, II.ii.112 (pp. 1666–8).

[79] On interest in memory in Renaissance Europe see Frances A. Yates, *The Art of Memory* (Harmondsworth: Penguin, 1966). It was often argued that memory was one of the highest forms of intelligence: see Philippa Berry, 'Disjointed Times, and Half-Remembered Truths in Shakespearean Tragedy', in Richard Dutton and Jean E. Howard, eds, *A Companion to Shakespeare's Works*, 4 vols (Oxford: Blackwell, 2003), pp. 95–107, at p. 98. On Montaigne, see below, pp. 179–87.

[80] Brian Vickers, 'Some Reflections on the Rhetoric Textbook', in Peter Mack, ed., *Renaissance Rhetoric* (Basingstoke: Macmillan, 1994), pp. 81–103, at p. 97.

errours through Lying, because he doth therby as it were, thrust them out of the kingdom of heauen. *Ex. X, 3.6, 8, 10. Iere. 23.25, 26. I Tim. 4.2, 3. Esa: 9.15, 16.*

2 As the diuel is the Father of lyes: So Lying is an euident token of his children. *Ioh. 8.44.*

3 As vncomely as magnificall talke is for a poore foole: So vnmeete is Lying and vntrue talke for a Prince. *Prov. 17.7.*[81]

The use of the language of sight in the first simile makes it clear that correct vision will lead men and women to heaven and that lying is a pernicious way of hindering the true path established by God. The second simile states the familiar link between lying and the Devil, its absolute nature refusing the possibility that there can be any exceptions as various Church Fathers argued. Cawdrey's third and final simile might even be read as a counter to the Platonic tradition which accepted that rulers were permitted to tell 'noble lies' for the sake of those they governed, producing fictions that would help bond together the commonwealth, such as the story of the children made of gold, silver, bronze, and iron, who had to change classes if they appeared at the wrong social level through a random genetic combination.[82] Instead people should know their place on earth in order to be treated equally in the eyes of God. Lying, according to Cawdrey's figure of speech, is a more serious crime for those in positions of power, a sentiment that connects his commonplace to that of Hermes in Baldwin's *Treatise* when he demands that those in authority have a duty to punish liars.

But if Cawdrey's similes guide the reader to an Augustinian position on lying, whether consciously or not, they are still intended, like Baldwin's, to provide material that the reader can use. They only really make sense if actually tested in particular situations. Baldwin employs the maxims he has collected on lying in his tragedy of Sir Anthony Woodville, Lord Rivers, in the 1563 edition of *The Mirror for Magistrates*, a deft and cunning manoeuvre, given the influence of Rivers's work on the *Treatise*. Rivers's ghost appears to Baldwin and laments his life as a counsellor to mighty kings, a role that has forced him to keep silent in the presence of immorality. The ghost reflects on the sad fate of the compromised courtier, his major contribution to wisdom from beyond the grave:

> For hytherto slye wryters wyly wittes
> Which have engrossed princes cheefe affayres,
> Have been lyke horses snaffled with the byttes
> Of fansye, feare, or doubts full diepe dispayres,
> Whose raynes enchained to the chefest chayres,
> Have so ben strayned of those that bare the stroke
> That truth was forst to chow or els to choke.
>
> Thys caused such as lothed lowd to lye,

[81] Robert Cawdrey, *A Treasurie or Storehouse of Similies: Both Pleasaunt, delightfull, and Profitable, for all estates of men in generall* (London, 1600), pp. 454–5. I owe this reference to Abigail Shinn.
[82] Plato, *Republic*, p. 182.

To passe with silence sundry prynces lyues.
Lesse faut it is to leave, then to leade awry:
And better dround, that ever bound in gyves.
For fatall fraude this world so fondly dryves,
That whatsoeuer writers braines may brue
Be it neuer so false, at length is tane for true.

What harme may hap by help of lying pennes
How wrytten lyes may lewdly be maynteyned.
The lothly rytes, the divilysh ydoll dennes
With gyltles blud of virtuous men bestayned,
Is such a proofe as all good hartes haue playned.
The taly groundes of storyes thoroughly tryes,
The deth of martyrs vengeauns on it cryes.[83]

Rivers's dilemma recalls that of Raphael Hythloday in *Utopia*, his fear that advising the great would compromise his ideals, force him to become a flatterer rather than a free man able to speak frankly, and start lying. As he complains to More, 'If I'm to speak the truth, I will have to talk in the way I've described [i.e. obliquely]. Whether it's the business of a philosopher to tell lies, I don't know, but it isn't mine. Perhaps my advice may be repugnant to the king's councillors, but I don't see why they should consider it eccentric to the point of folly.'[84] Hythloday will never become a counsellor to a monarch—unless his conception of Plato's ideal ruler summons him—because he does not wish to sacrifice his right to tell the truth and be forced to compromise and to tell lies. Baldwin's ghost of Lord Rivers represents him in the same way, but as a man who made the wrong decision and took the wrong path. He serves as a warning to ambitious magnates and magistrates not to reach too far, reminding them of the double penalty they may well pay for such service: a loss of personal integrity and eventually disgrace, betrayal, and death.

The reader does not have to take Lord Rivers's judgement of his fate entirely at face value. Of all the ghosts who speak to the assembled group of contemporary writers, Lord Rivers is probably the most eloquent, undoubtedly represented in this way by Baldwin because of the influence that his writing had on Baldwin's *Treatise*, published before the *Mirror*.[85] Rivers concentrates on the fate of writers, and he is portrayed as much as an intellectual as a politician in his tragedy. Rivers complains that truth is not something that princes can endure, and those who have been most vociferous in trumpeting its virtue fall silent when exposed to the lies of princes, perhaps a recollection of Raphael Hythloday's complaints in *Utopia*, which had been published in Ralph Robinson's English translation in 1551.[86] Rivers was

---

[83] Campbell, ed., *Mirror*, pp. 246–7 (lines 29–49).

[84] Thomas More, *Utopia*, ed. George M. Logan and Robert M. Adams (Cambridge: Cambridge University Press, 1989), p. 36.

[85] The *Treatise* appeared in 1547; the first edition of the *Mirror* in 1559, and *The Tragedy of Lord Rivers* opened the 1563 edition.

[86] Although it needs to be acknowledged that Robinson does not use the word 'lies' in his rendition of Raphael Hythloday's words cited above: 'For if I wolde speake thynges that be trewe, I muste eades speake suche thinges: but as for to speake false thinges, whether that be a philosophers part or no I can not tell, truely it is not my part. Howebeit thys communicatyon of myne, thoughe peraduenture it

represented as a noble and honourable man in the chronicles, behaving with decency and fortitude in the impossibly trying times in the last years of the civil wars. It is clear that he does not deserve his fate at the treacherous hands of Richard III, whose cause he had loyally supported. Furthermore, he was known to be pious and had gone on various pilgrimages and a crusade when he could have had more influence on political events, something his ghost highlights in his writing. Rivers's success owed much to fortunate dynastic alliances, his sister becoming wife of Edward IV in 1564 much to the fury of the Earl of Warwick who was negotiating a French match, a union that made the Woodvilles powerful but also vulnerable.[87] But it is surely his role as a writer that makes him such an interesting figure for Baldwin.

The first stanza cited above is a conspicuously poetic passage with its extravagant metaphors representing writers as wild horses who have been bridled with bits that censor their ability to write freely through fear, doubt, despair, and the false use of the imagination in times of acute anxiety. The lines articulate a common fear in the period, as censors sought to determine whether writers meant what they wrote and writers sought to evade attention through the cunning use of ambiguity.[88] The horse metaphor enables Baldwin to make a pun on reins/reigns, as these writers are tied to chairs, that is, chariots/thrones, so that as they are whipped by their riders, the horses/writers eat or choke on their truth. The stanza is a conspicuous *tour de force* that defends Lord Rivers's position: at least, in his own eyes. The truth may be that this is an example of the fanciful use of the imagination that he imagines he is combatting, and that he is represented as not being as honest about his behaviour as he imagines he is, but self-serving in excusing himself for the sins of his times. The reader has to decide, as well as judge how culpable Lord Rivers was, whether he is being more or less honest, deluding himself, or lying.

Certainly the last stanza cited qualifies our understanding of his life. Lord Rivers has represented himself as a foolish victim of a tyrannical ruler, who forced writers to pull his chariots like a Roman emperor or an Oriental despot.[89] As the passage continues, the issue of lying looms ever larger. Lord Rivers realizes the harm caused by 'lying pennes', which enable awful lies to be maintained, as they continue to oppress the tyrant's subjects. He connects these lies to Satanic rites and devilish liars stained with the blood of the virtuous, not only confirming that wicked souls delight in lying and that the Devil is the father of lies, but, in making this connection, pointing out just how much damage a hired pen can do. The last line—'the deth of martyrs vengeauns on it cryes'—has a particular resonance in England after the creation of so many martyrs in the middle years of the century.[90]

maye seme vnplesaunte to them, yett can I not see whie it should seme strauge, or foolisshelye new fangled' (Thomas More, *A Fruteful, and Pleasaunt Worke of the Beste State of a Publyque weale, and of the Newe Yle called Utopia*, trans. Ralph Robinson (London, 1551), sig. F7r).

[87] *ODNB* entry; Thomas More, *The History of King Richard III and Selections for the English and Latin Poems*, ed. Richard S. Sylvester (New Haven: Yale University Press, 1976), pp. 18–21.

[88] Dominique Brancher, '"When the Tongue Slips it Tells the Truth": Tricks and Truths of the Renaissance Lapsus', *RS* 30 (2016), 39–56, pp. 50–3.

[89] René Graziani, 'Philip II's Impressa and Spenser's Souldan', *JWCI* 27 (1964), 322–4.

[90] Lucas, Mirror *and the Politics*, p. 205.

Writers for the wrong cause—and perhaps the right cause too—have much to answer for and their failings have led to significant bloodshed.

The passage leaves the reader with a series of dilemmas. On the one hand Lord Rivers is clearly more culpable than many of the other ghosts who speak in the *Mirror*, as he has the wit and eloquence to know that lying is never a good option. He later shows that he has understood how to read history by citing the example of Richard II, a king whose tragedy was told in the first edition of the *Mirror*. There, Richard confesses that he was 'a Kyng that ruled all by lust, / That forced not out of virtue, ryght, or lawe, / But always put false Flatterers most in trust'. Accordingly, Lord Rivers represents Richard as a ruler cut off from his people who 'carelesly despyse[d] / To hear the oppressed peoples heavy cryes' and so was deposed by 'crafty Lawyers'.[91] Baldwin's joke is that intelligent ghosts like Lord Rivers are learning from work published long after their deaths. When betrayed by Gloucester, Lord Rivers laments the ways in which he has been deluded by suspiciously enthusiastic shows of friendship in pointed lines that count as much against as for him: 'For commonly in all dissimulations / The excess of glavering [flattery] doth the guile detect'.[92] But, this only demonstrates that he has been hoist by his own petard: a sophisticated writer who has kept silent at crucial times and supported dishonesty now fails to spot it when he is the victim, his critical faculties presumably dimmed by his shameful service to the powerful and the consequent rewards. Lord Rivers laments his fate in bathetic lines that are clearly humorous: 'Why such dissemblers as would seme to laugh / Breth not Tihhy, but brave out, hah hah hah [i.e. bray out rather than titter]'.[93] At this point he is clearly the butt of the joke and the fates are laughing at him for his failure to read more astutely, as he faces a barrage of public contempt.

On the other hand, we might feel some sympathy for Lord Rivers. As I have already pointed out, Baldwin is invariably described as a Protestant by commentators.[94] If so, then how did Baldwin make it through the bewildering regime changes of the mid-Tudor period? Was Rivers a clever and principled writer who was simply unlucky and who made the sort of compromises that most people had been forced to make in recent memory, including Baldwin himself? Were not most people forced to lie in times of crisis, even if they were principled enough to avoid dissembling at other times? Furthermore, what was the truth? Lord Rivers refers to martyrs, and it may well be that Baldwin's reader would have understood this to mean the victims of Mary's persecutions. But we would do well to remember that at the start of *Beware the Cat* we are confronted with the body parts of the victims of Edward's regime, Catholics who were executed in defence of their faith in 1549, graphically demonstrating that persecution was a two-way street.[95] Furthermore, in

[91] Campbell, ed., *Mirror*, p. 113 (lines 31–3); p. 253 (lines 214–15, 219).
[92] Campbell, ed., *Mirror*, p. 260 (lines 409–10).
[93] Campbell, ed., *Mirror*, p. 260 (lines 418–19).
[94] See, for a recent example, John A. Wagner, 'Baldwin, William', in John A. Wagner and Susan Walters Schmid, eds, *Encyclopedia of Tudor England*, 3 vols (Santa Barbara: ABC-Clio, 2012), pp. 86–8.
[95] See above, p. 133.

their writings both Baldwin and Lord Rivers had compiled lists of maxims that included entries on lying and dissimulation, collections of sayings which did not—and could not—resolve the issue by telling readers what truth was, and instead left the onus on readers to choose the right path. Lord Rivers has lived through a time when writers—including, by implication, himself—told lots of lies, although we never actually learn what these are. He concludes:

> Far better therefore not to wryte at all
> Than stayne the truth for any maner cause,
> For this they meane to let my story fall
> (Thought I) and ear my tyme theyr volume clause.
> But after I knew it only was a pause,
> Made purposely, most for the readers ease,
> Assure thee Baldwyn, highly it dyd me please.[96]

This is an odd, contorted, and slyly self-referential stanza that is both humorous and poses a searching question.[97] In the opening two lines Lord Rivers appears to be arguing that keeping silent is the better option if truth cannot be guaranteed, coming as it does after a series of reflections on the problems of being forced to tell lies if one serves a prince. However, in the third line the reader realizes that things are not quite as they seem when Lord Rivers explains that this is what he thought 'they' (the authors of the *Mirror*) meant by excluding his story from the first edition. He then realizes that his tragedy was missed out simply to aid the reader's enjoyment and he is now able to set the record straight.

Of course, this is not true, because Lord Rivers as he appears in the *Mirror* exists as he is imagined by Baldwin, so to have him address his author and thank him for allowing him to tell his story can only be ironic. We do not know why the tragedy was not included in the first edition: Lord Rivers's argument can be read to suggest that it was because of fear of censorship.[98] We can be sure that it was not simply because of a desire to please the audience, something that Lord Rivers has just realized. The joke draws attention to the question of the relationship between writing, truth, and lies. In telling a joke about lying, Baldwin is following one of Augustine's exceptions to possible accusations of lying, one that moral philosophers have invariably followed. In chapter 2 of *De Mendacio* Augustine sets aside 'jocose lies, which have never been considered as real lies, since both in the verbal expression and in the attitude of the one joking such lies are accompanied by a very evident lack of intention to deceive, even though the person be not speaking the truth'.[99] Baldwin's Lord Rivers is joking, but is he intending to deceive the reader? It is hard to tell. The serious point may well be that it is difficult to write without risking either telling lies or being accused of telling lies, a problem that is here deflected in a joke. The anxiety expressed is that the only way to ensure that

---

[96] Campbell, ed., *Mirror*, p. 247 (lines 50–6).

[97] On the humour in the *Mirror* see Mike Pincombe, 'Tragic and Untragic Bodies in *The Mirror for Magistrates*', in Archer and Hadfield, eds, Mirror for Magistrates *in Context*.

[98] Lucas, Mirror *and the Politics*, p. 206.

[99] Augustine, *Treaties on Various Subjects*, p. 54; Griffiths, *Lying*, pp. 34–5.

one does not lie is to, first, withdraw from the world of politics and so have no influence on the world; and, going further still, perhaps even refusing to write at all. Just as it is all too easy to stray into heresy without wanting to or meaning to, so, Baldwin/Lord Rivers seems to be arguing, can one sleepwalk into telling lies.[100]

As he is waiting to die in Pontefract Castle, Shakespeare's Lord Rivers faces his gaoler, Sir Richard Ratcliffe, one of Richard III's henchmen, and proclaims that he is a subject who will die 'For truth, for duty and for loyalty'. Furthermore, remembering that this was where Richard II was 'hacked to death', the killing that sparked the cycle of vicious civil wars, Lord Rivers gives to the castle 'our guiltless blood to drink'.[101] Shakespeare's truth-telling figure surely owes much to Baldwin's portrayal of Lord Rivers, even though the subtle debate on lying has been removed.[102]

IV

Erasmus condemns lying in straightforward terms, but he is acutely aware of the problem of maintaining such clear distinctions between truth and lies, good and evil behaviour, when representing the world. In his writings it is the effects of lying that are most terrifying not the act itself. In the colloquy 'Things and Names' Beatus and Boniface argue about the relationship between truth and reality, and show how far language in sixteenth-century Europe had moved away from the correspondence model God had first given to mankind.[103] Their anger at the delaying tactics of bad debtors leads to a discussion of liars:

> BEATUS: Have you never had the experience of finding that someone who had promised to repay a loan by a certain day failed to keep his bargain?
> BONIFACE: Often, even when he'd sworn he'd pay—not once but over and over.
> BEATUS: Unable to pay, perhaps.
> BONIFACE: Oh, they were able, all right, but they thought it more to their advantage not to repay the debt.
> BEATUS: Isn't that lying?
> BONIFACE: Quite obviously.
> BEATUS: Would you dare reproach a 'creditor' of that sort with 'Why do you lie to me so often?'
> BONIFACE: Not unless I were ready for a fight.
> BEATUS: Don't stonecutters, carpenters, goldsmiths, and clothiers make daily commitments of the same sort, promising something by a certain day but not keeping their word even if the matter's important to you?

---

[100] On the problem of heresy see Cummings, *Literary Culture*, ch. 6.
[101] William Shakespeare, *King Richard III*, ed. James R. Siemon (London: Black, 2009), 3.3.3, 13.
[102] For possible influences see *Narrative and Dramatic Sources*, III, pp. 230, 233, 243.
[103] See Richard Waswo, *Language and Meaning in the Renaissance* (Princeton: Princeton University Press, 1987), pp. 95, 119.

BONIFACE: They have an astonishing cheek. Add to these the lawyers with their promises of getting something done.

BEATUS: You can add six hundred names, yet none of these persons will stand for 'liar.'

BONIFACE: The world abounds with liars of this kind.[104]

On the one hand lying is to be condemned, as Beatus and Boniface, resembling Erasmus in *Lingua*, recognize. On the other, lying is necessary if one is to exist in the world given the complications of ordinary life, and the high-minded and self-righteous words of both speakers will do nothing to stop it taking place: the complicated nature of honesty in the early modern period, as Jennifer Richards has pointed out, 'only emerges *in* conversation'.[105] It is implausible that all these tradesmen and lawyers are wicked people; equally, what they do in order to keep their heads above water is reprehensible. Lying, as William Baldwin also realized, is as hard to prevent as it is easy to condemn, which is why an analysis of lying is most meaningful through a series of examples rather than precepts.

Such logic informs the essays of Montaigne, translated into English in 1603, but clearly known and exerting influence before that date, not least through the offices of his well-connected translator, John Florio.[106] Like Baldwin and Erasmus, Montaigne starts with commonplaces and definite statements in his essays, his titles invariably being commonplaces.[107] 'Of Lyers' explores the veracity of a series of pieces of received wisdom through a number of examples, and concludes by leaving the reader to puzzle what has been learned at the end: the *Essays* were often read as 'a communally-constructed document'.[108] The essay starts with a discussion of memory, specifically his own failure to remember anything: 'There is no man living, whom it may lesse beseeme to speake of memorie, than my selfe, for to say truth, I have none at all.'[109] The joke is that this is the opening sentence of an essay on liars, forcing the reader to wonder whether Montaigne is actually telling the truth and always planned to write about liars or whether this really started life as an essay on memory and turned into a piece on lying. Montaigne's lack of memory has saved him from a 'worse mischief, that would easily have growen upon me, that is to say, ambition', a judgement that the author may, of course, know not to be true.[110] He is able to approach his subject via an oblique route, as he lists the vices that his failing enables him to eschew. He cannot give long and dull speeches,

---

[104] Erasmus, *Collected Works*, 40, p. 812.

[105] Jennifer Richards, *Rhetoric and Courtliness in Early Modern Literature* (Cambridge: Cambridge University Press, 2003), p. 28.

[106] Stuart Gillespie, *Shakespeare's Books: A Dictionary of Shakespeare's Sources* (London: Athlone, 2000), pp. 342–9; William M. Hamlin, *Montaigne's English Journey: Reading the Essays in Shakespeare's Day* (Oxford: Oxford University Press, 2013), pp. 1–36; Stephen Greenblatt and Peter G. Platt, eds, *Shakespeare's Montaigne: The Florio Translation of the* Essays: *A Selection* (New York: New York Review of Books, 2014).

[107] Hamlin, *Montaigne's English Journey*, p. 130.

[108] Hamlin, *Montaigne's English Journey*, p. 34.

[109] Michel de Montaigne, 'Of Lyers', in *Essayes*, I, pp. 44–9, at p. 44.

[110] Montaigne, 'Of Lyers', p. 45.

unlike some friends, 'their memory hath ministred them a whole and perfect matter, who reconcile their narration so farre-backe, and stuff-it with so many vaine circumstances, that if the story bee good, they smother the goodnesse of it: if bad, you must needs either curse the good fortune of their memorie, or blame the misfortune of their judgement'.[111] Montaigne is showing the reader that he is firmly in control of his material and this short essay will possess real substance, as the comparison of skilful narration to skilful horse riding indicates. Unlike the old men who forget their stories, repeat themselves and lapse into tedium, Montaigne knows how to fashion his material because he understands his limits and has the virtue of self-control. And he can afford to be more benign than most people because he does not remember injuries done to him by others.

The commonplace that Montaigne elects to explore, reached a third of the way into the essay, is that attributed to Pythagoras and included in William Baldwin's collection of philosophical commonplaces, that a liar requires a good memory.[112] Montaigne, through his professed inability, is saved this heinous human vice. He distinguishes between the lesser—but still significant—crime of telling a lie, 'to speake that which is false, but was reputed true', and to lie, which 'implieth and meaneth to goe against ones conscience: and by consequence it concerneth onely those, who speake contrary to that which they know'.[113] The distinction that he provides is a technical one between a noun and a verb, but it resembles the discussion of lying in Erasmus and the problem of establishing a culture which supports lying. Montaigne discusses the corrosive effects of sustaining an elaborate and difficult lie, emphasizing how it is invariably painful to preserve untruth consistently:

> When they disguise or change, if they be often put to the repetition of one thing, it is hard for them to keepe still in one path, and very strange if they lose not themselves: because the thing, as it is, having first taken up her stand in the memory, and there by the way of knowledge and writing, imprinted it-selfe, it were hard it should not represent it selfe to the imagination, displacing and supplanting falsehood, which therein can have no such footing, or settled fastnesse: and that the circumstances of the first learning, still diving into the minde, should not cause it to disperse the remembrance of all false or bastardizing parts gotten together.[114]

The lie takes on a life of its own, becoming part of the liar's memory, which confuses the gap between reality and falsehood. A powerful memory is required to carry off such a difficult feat and the act of lying succeeds only in relation to the talents and abilities of the liar. Put another way, lying transforms good qualities into bad, corrupting what should be admirable human qualities. The essay, therefore, is more about liars than lying, and, in this first half, Montaigne shows what happens to those who choose this path.

[111] Montaigne, 'Of Lyers', p. 45.
[112] A widespread commonplace: see Tilley, *Proverbs*, L219 (p. 377).
[113] Montaigne, 'Of Lyers', p. 46.   [114] Montaigne, 'Of Lyers', p. 46.

Lying undermines our humanity, because 'Nothing makes us men', and binds us together, 'but our word'.[115] Montaigne argues that children receive harsh punishment for many apparent crimes which are really innocent, but the 'ill and detestable vice' ought to be harshly confronted to prevent it taking hold:

> Onely lying, and stubbornesse somewhat more, are the faults whose birth and progresse I would have severely punished and cut off; for they grow and increase with them: and if the tongue have once gotten this ill habit, good Lord, how hard, nay how impossible it is to make her leave it? Whereby it ensueth, that we see many very honest men in other matters, to bee subject and enthralled to that fault.[116]

Montaigne's point is the same as that of Erasmus: that if lying secures a place in the human psyche then the long-term effects will be devastating. He professes to hate lying so much that he could not ward off 'extreme and evident danger, by a shamelesse and solemne lie', a sentiment that derives from Augustine who is immediately cited: 'We are better in the companie of a knowne dogge, than in a mans societie, whose speech is unknown to us.'[117] Thomas Lupton, appearing in print in the same year (1580) that Montaigne's *Essays* were published in France, has his character Omen produce an equally strong reaction to lying, and describe a detailed sliding scale of punishments that his fictional country adopts, envisaging laws that will require energetic and expensive policing:

> Lying is so much detested with us, that if one lye in sporte, he shall be punished in earnest: for, if one make a pleasant lye, thoughe he hurte no body therewith, for the first suche lye he shal be reproued, for the second such Lye he shall be fiue dayes imprisoned: and for the thyrde suche Lye, and euerye other such Lye after, he shal be banished from the place he dwelleth in for the space of three monthes: but if one with us shold make a Lye to the deceyuing or hurting of any, or speake a Lye before a magistrate or a Iudge, then the partie for euery suche Lye, shal be constrained to holde his peace, and to speake neuer a worde to anye person the space of three months after, unlesse hee shall bee required of some Ruler for some urgent matter: and he shal ware on his Sleeve all that while, an H. and an L. for a Hurtful Lyar.[118]

Clearly Lupton, unlike Sir Henry Wotton, did not imagine a liar serving his country as an ambassador.[119] Liars who actually hurt people through their false words 'immediatelye shall be hurte, wounded or maimed on the same part of hys bodye, and in suche order, as the partie was hurte by meanes of the saide Lye'.[120] Omen, when challenged, provides the example of a man who lied to his neighbour, telling him that someone else had called him a drunkard and a liar whose word was

---

[115] Montaigne, 'Of Lyers', p. 47.   [116] Montaigne, 'Of Lyers', p. 47.

[117] Montaigne, 'Of Lyers', pp. 47–8; Michel de Montaigne, *The Complete Works*, trans. Donald M. Frame (New York: Knopf, 2003), p. 28.

[118] Lupton, *Siuqila*, sig. L3v. We later witness this mode of justice in action (sig. P4v).

[119] Wotton (1568–1639) famously quibbled on lying in the manner of Garnet's manual, when he remarked that 'An ambassador is an honest man sent to lie abroad for the good of his country': *ODNB* entry; *The Life and Letters of Sir Henry Wotton*, ed. Logan Pearsall Smith, 2 vols (Oxford: Clarendon Press, 1907), I, p. 126.

[120] Lupton, *Siuqila*, sig. L4r.

never to be trusted. The neighbour attacked the innocent party and in the ensuing melee lost an eye. The ruler demanded that 'the lyke eye' of the real liar be put out, a literal manifestation of Exodus 21:24.[121] His interlocutor, Siuqila, is impressed: 'Oh suche a law with us, and so well executed, would teach many a one to tel trueth, that do now almost nothing but lye.'[122] But, sadly, the contrary state exists as society values liars over truth-tellers, rewarding them with a silver whetstone to sharpen their knives.[123]

Montaigne has already provided the reader with a warning that 'the opposite of truth hath many-many shapes, and an undefinite field'. What seemed definite and clear cut a couple of sentences earlier, that lying is evil and should be avoided at all costs, now starts to seem rather less certain. If falsehood has so many forms and shapes how can we ever be sure that we have correctly identified it? Can we trust Montaigne when he states that he would never tell a lie, not even to save his life? After all, like the unknown man in Augustine's commonplace, we, the readers, do not know him. This may not be because Montaigne is a particularly untrustworthy man who wishes to tell lies, but because as soon as we start believing that things can be fixed and certain, the confusing and insecure nature of reality with its numerous forms of falsehood challenges what we imagine is truth.[124] And what of Augustine's statement? Does this mean we should stick with what we know and not try to find anything out? Surely that is against the spirit of the *Essays*. We should never trust commonplaces or let them have the final word. Indeed, the essay can be seen to unravel in other ways: if memory binds us together, then lying, the vice that only those with an exceptional memory can practice successfully, then serves to set us apart.[125] And, as Montaigne would have been well aware, another commonplace was that what connects us is lying because 'All men are liars.'

This essay concludes with two significant anecdotes about lying, again demonstrating the importance of trying to understand lying through examples and particular cases rather than abstract statements and definitions, especially as the essayist has declared that falsehood takes manifold shapes. The first anecdote concerns a diplomatic incident based on a story told by Francis I (1494–1547), King of France from 1515 until his death. Francis boasts that he outwitted his formidable foe, Francesco Sforza (1495–1535), Duke of Milan.[126] The Duke is unable to deal openly with the French because he is a client of the Holy Roman Emperor, Charles V (1500–58). In order to discover what is going on at the Italian court ('to keepe ever some intelligence in *Italy*'), the King dispatches 'a Gentleman of *Millane*', Merveille, one of his equerries, with 'secret letters of credence' and 'other letters of commendation to the Duke in favour of his particular affaires, as a maske and pretence of his proceedings'. The plot is discovered by the Emperor and Merveille is executed one night after a speedy two-day trial that found him guilty of

---

[121] Lupton, *Siuqila*, sig. L4v.   [122] Lupton, *Siuqila*, sig. L4v.
[123] Lupton, *Siuqila*, sig. L4v.
[124] Shormishtha Panja, 'Introduction', in Panja, ed., *Shakespeare and the Art of Lying*, pp. 1–13, at p. 8.
[125] Andrea Frisch, 'Montaigne and the Ethics of Memory', *L'Esprit Créateur* 46 (2006), 23–31.
[126] On the role of Francis I in European diplomacy see Mattingly, *Renaissance Diplomacy*, pp. 163–71.

murder. An ambassador, Francesco Taverna, 'a man very famous for his rare eloquence, and facilitie in speech', is sent to France to excuse the conduct of his master after the King makes it clear that he wants justice 'for such an outrage committed upon his servant'. He provides the King with a 'long counterfeit deduction of this storie', establishing a plausible series of lies as well as claiming that the Duke had no idea that Merveille was the King's servant and, in effect, a spy. The King counters with a series of searching questions and eventually traps the Italian ambassador,

> Prest him so farre with the execution done at night, and as it were by stealth, that the seely man, being much entangled and suddenly surprised, as if he would set an innocent face on the matter, answered, that for the love and respect of his Majestie, the Duke his Master would have beene very loth that such an execution should have beene done by day. Heere every man may guesse whether he were taken short or no, having tripped before so goodly a nose, as was that of our King *Francis* the first.[127]

The second anecdote also concerns Francis I, here as the possible victim of a sly diplomatic operator, well known for his devious manoeuvres. Pope Julius II, Giuliano della Rovere (1443–1513), 'the Warrior Pope', sent an ambassador to England to forge an alliance against France.[128] After the ambassador has spoken, the King, Henry VIII, explains how complicated a campaign against France will be. The ambassador 'fondly and unfitly replied' that he has already considered the difficulties and 'had told the Pope of them'. Therefore, the King started to realize that the ambassador, whose mission was 'with all speed, and without more circum-stances to undertake and undergoe a dangerous warre', really favoured France rather than the papacy: 'whereof advertising [telling] his Master, his goods were all confiscate, himselfe discgraced, and he very hardly escaped with life'.[129]

However we read these two stories they do not support the apparent trajectory of the essay up to the start of the first one, that truth and falsehood can be kept separate. The reader is suddenly thrust into the world of diplomacy and inter-national conflict in which virtually everybody is lying: the King of France and his secret ambassador; the Duke of Milan and his ambassador; and the Pope and his ambassador. The only relatively innocent figure here is Henry VIII, which is probably a sly joke given his international reputation for duplicity, broken prom-ises, and aggressive diplomacy.[130] And we conclude Montaigne's essay with Henry confiscating the diplomat's goods and threatening his life. Montaigne's point is that separating truth and lies is easy enough in theory but virtually impossible in practice, a similar conclusion to that of thinkers such as William Baldwin. Francis

[127] Montaigne, 'Of Lyers', pp. 48–9. See Chaudhuri, 'Being True to Yourself', p. 67.
[128] On Julius II see *Popes*, pp. 255–6.   [129] Montaigne, 'Of Lyers', p. 49.
[130] Catherine Fletcher, 'Performing Henry VIII at the Court of Rome', and Susan Brigden, 'Henry VIII and the Crusade Against England', in Thomas Betteridge and Susannah Lipscombe, eds, *Henry VIII and the Court: Art, Politics and Performance* (Farnham: Ashgate, 2013), pp. 179–94, 215–34. A more positive account of Henry's reign is provided in William Thomas's defence of Henry to an audience in Italy: Thomas, *Works*, pp. 1–127.

I is a successful king because he is able to expose the lies of his opponent. But he exists in a world in which lying is endemic and 'lie-catchers' are good at their jobs principally because they are also skilful practising liars.[131] Lying may well be an 'ill and detestable vice' but the stories told by Montaigne indicate how far away Europe is from being able to manage without lying, the necessary tool of the experienced diplomat. Francis I acts as the protector of France, understanding the ruthless world of diplomacy, which enables him to protect his nation.

The other story, involving Julius II's conspiracy to set England and France at odds is an even more twisted tale of intrigue. France is spared being caught in a pincer movement through the actions of an ambassador who 'was more affected to the French side'. We do not learn whether the ambassador was simply acting out an enthusiasm for France; a patriotic sense of duty which is not revealed here; or, as is most likely, he was in the pay of the French. The story has no obvious moral compass: the Pope is shown to be acting in exactly the same underhand way as secular monarchs, and it is the ambassador who intervenes on behalf of the French who is severely punished. Rather, the point is that in a world of duplicity and self-interest, understanding that everyone is ruthlessly wedded to securing their own advantage and being able to act accordingly counts more than moral behaviour. The first story shows France acting with appropriate cunning and understanding what can be achieved in private and public in order to further its interests; the second would appear to go a stage further in suggesting that the French have acted to thwart the machinations of their rivals and, in the process, have hung out their client to dry.

The larger point of this complicated, divided essay is left open. It is easy enough to understand that the practices of the world are at odds with the precepts of Christian morality, and that lying will have to continue for the foreseeable future, whatever people might really want. As is routinely pointed out, Montaigne was writing against the background of ever-expanding state power and the indiscriminate slaughter of civil war, hardly conditions under which it was easy or even possible to assert the value of altruistic behaviour.[132] But the reader is then left to decide whether the problem rests with the moralists or the pragmatists: could the world be any better than it is, and more in line with Christian thinking? Or would acting in line with such principles merely expose the protagonists to terrible danger? Montaigne provides no obvious answer, apart from demonstrating that easy answers based on commonplaces will not suffice. Commonplaces aid thought when they begin discussions, not when they conclude them.

Montaigne provides an equally balanced discussion of the problem of lying in his other essay directly dealing with the subject, 'Of Giving the Lie' (II.18). As in the

---

[131] Ekman, *Telling Lies*, pp. 50, 53.

[132] James Coleman, 'Montaigne and the Wars of Religion', in Keith Cameron, ed., *Montaigne and His Age* (Exeter: University of Exeter Press, 1981), pp. 107–20; David Quint, *Montaigne and the Quality of Mercy: Ethical and Political Themes in the 'Essais'* (Princeton: Princeton University Press, 1998).

earlier essay, Montaigne condemns lying in the strongest possible terms, as a means of dishonouring man's contract with God:

> It is impossible more richly to represent the horror, the vilenesse and the disorder of it . . . Our intelligence being onely conducted by way of the Word: Who so falsifieth the same, betraieth public society. It is the onely instrument, by meanes wherof our wils and thoughts are communicated: it is the interpretour of our soules: If that faile us we hold our selves no more, we enter-know one another no longer. If it deceive us, it breaketh al our commerce, and dissolveth al bonds of our policie.[133]

This list of the malign consequences of lying would seem clear enough, but, as in 'On Lying', the essay provides an unsettling twist, as Montaigne moves from discussing lying to giving the lie. Montaigne recognizes the power of lying as an insult: 'Thus have I often considered, whence this custome might arise, which we observe so religiously, that we are more sharply offended with the reproach of this vice, so ordinary in us, than with any other; and that bit is the extremest injury, may be done us in words, to upbraid and reproch us with a lie.'[134] Perhaps the most significant phrase here is 'so ordinary in us'. Is lying ordinary because there is little we can do to expunge it? Or a sign of how inured we are to its significance and serious consequences? The statement cuts both ways and the reader is unsure whether lying is correctly considered a terrible vice that should be eliminated, or whether it has become a meaningless insult designed to rile the injured party.

The essay concludes with a reflection on the social practices of the Greeks and Romans and their ability to hurl the most extreme insults at each other:

> And I have often thought it strange, to see them wrong and give one another the lie, and yet never enter into quarrell. The lawes of their duty, tooke some other course than ours. *Caesar* is often called a thiefe, and sometimes a drunkard to his face. We see the liberty of their invectives, which they write one against another: I meane the greatest Chieftaines and Generals in war, of one and other Nation, where words are onely retorted and revenged with words, and never wrested to further consequence.[135]

The essay accepts, therefore, the grave nature of an accusation of lying, but arguing that the effects of doing so are to offset and absorb conflict rather than to foster it. Montaigne undoubtedly has the forensic oratory of Cicero, the subject of a critical essay in the first book, and others in mind here, and one of the points of this essay is that the study of the past may prove useful in providing us with material to think about vital issues that we think we understand, and enabling us to challenge the misleading statements of the commonplace tradition.[136] Do certain forms of apparently reprehensible behaviour cancel out others rather than reinforcing them? In asking this question the essay complements 'Of Lying', demonstrating

---

[133] Montaigne, 'Of Giving the Lie', in *Essayes*, II, pp. 390–4, at pp. 393–4. For comment see Craig Muldrew, *The Economy of Obligation: The Culture of Credit and Social Relations in Early Modern England* (Basingstoke: Palgrave, 1998), p. 184.
[134] Montaigne, 'Of Giving the Lie', p. 393.   [135] Montaigne, 'Of Giving the Lie', p. 394.
[136] Jeffrey Martin Green, 'Montaigne's Critique of Cicero', *JHI* 36 (1975), 595–612; Peter Mack, *Reading and Rhetoric in Montaigne and Shakespeare* (London: Black, 2010), p. 34.

that in a complicated world riven by conflict obvious answers to central questions of human existence will not suffice.

As a counterpoint to the case of the ancients, Montaigne cites the apparent beliefs of

> Certaine Nations of the new *Indiaes* (whose names we need not declare, because they are no more; for the desolation of this conquest hath extended it selfe to the absolute abolishing of names and ancient knowledge of Places, with a marvellous and never the like heard example) offered humane bloud unto their Gods, but no other than that which was drawne from their tongues and eares, for an expiation of the sinne of lying as well heard as pronounced.[137]

Here we witness extreme honesty and the effects of a severe policy against lying, one that contrasts unfavourably with that of the ancients who avoided conflict—at least amongst themselves—by tolerating ferocious public accusations which were clearly often lies. Between the two extremes we have Europeans, ostensibly Christian but actually ferocious in their desire for conquest, their bloodthirstiness making a mockery of any moral stance here. Any reader who wishes to protest at the savagery of native customs has to balance this against the 'desolation' wrought by the European conquest of the Americas, a pointed contrast that has to be read against the more celebrated description of the cannibals who have no words for 'lying, falsehood, treason, dissimulations, covetousness, envie, detraction, and pardon', and whose practice of eating their slain enemies pales into insignificance beside the barbarous practices of European warfare.[138] In pointing out the chasm between the ideal of benign conquest and the reality of brutal destruction, Montaigne, following Las Casas, is giving the lie to his opponents.[139]

Montaigne's *Essays* frequently suggest a detached bemusement and sadness at the state of the world, less a philosophical position than a judgement based on the overwhelming evidence of the times. Montaigne was eager to cultivate the self-image in his writing of an honest, slightly rude rustic aristocrat at odds with the superficial values of the increasingly 'civilized' French court.[140] Accordingly, lying is simultaneously regarded as a terrible crime and something of almost no consequence: indeed, it is hard to know where a moralist might start trying to rid the world of lying other than pointing out that it should be avoided if possible. Montaigne's English follower, William Cornwallis the younger (c.1579–1614), distinguishes between the relatively innocent practice of dissimulation which might be necessary 'if a man be fallen vpon a wife that he cannot love, yet he must vse her well, and if he cannot performe the expresse commandement, yet at least to come as near as he can', and the malign practice of lying which makes habitual liars 'beate away repentance, and remorce, with palpable vntruthes'.[141] But this distinction, in

---

[137] Montaigne, 'Of Giving the Lie', p. 394.
[138] Montaigne, 'Of the Cannibals', in *Essayes*, I, pp. 215–29, at p. 220.
[139] Bartolomé de las Casas, *A Short Account of the Destruction of the Indies*, trans. Nigel Griffin (Harmondsworth: Penguin, 1992).
[140] Carroll, *Blood and Violence*, pp. 310–11.
[141] William Cornwallis, *Essayes* (London, 1600), p. 592. Cornwallis's coy language imitates that of Montaigne, whose work he had seen in manuscript: R. E. Bennett, 'Sir William Cornwallis's Use of Montaigne', *PMLA* 48 (1933), 1080–9. On Montaigne's sexual language see Hamlin, *Montaigne's English Journey*, ch. 2. On Cornwallis see the *ODNB* entry.

an essay largely about avoiding flattery, does little more than repeat injunctions against lying while excusing similar practices that are milder forms of the same, a means of arguing that would not have satisfied Montaigne.

Commonplaces are always useful: Montaigne was well known for placing statements from philosophers and the Bible on the beams of his library.[142] As Ann Moss has argued, Montaigne makes extensive use of the language of the commonplace-book throughout his writings. His constant 'quotation of excerpts mainly from Latin authors ... points indubitably to the commonplace-book', but, as any reader of the *Essays* will realize, he 'deliberately disassociates' his writing and thinking from the confines of the form.[143] Like Erasmus and William Baldwin, such knowledge is only ever a starting point and, if taken at face value, what is useful becomes misleading, false, and even a lie.

V

When rhetorical handbooks and guides to commonplacing are refigured in works on poetics towards the end of the sixteenth century fears about truth and lying are not diminished.[144] One of the most interesting sections of George Puttenham's *Arte of English Poesie* (1589) is chapter 18 of the long third book, 'Of Ornament', 'Of sensable figures altering and affecting the mynde by alteration of sence or intendements in whole clauses or speeches'.[145] The rather forbidding and technical-sounding title actually contains a discussion of figures and modes of writing that dissemble and mislead readers.[146] The previous chapter had discussed how through the use of certain figures 'the sence of single wordes is altered' and Puttenham now states that he plans to demonstrate how other literary devices, such as 'the Courtly figure *Allegoria*', alter 'whole and entire speech ... that our wordes and our meanings meete not'.[147] No one can hope to succeed who does not have a grounding in allegory, which means that it is central to Puttenham's conception of the purpose of learning rhetoric and poetry:

> The vse of this figure is so large, and his virtue of so great efficacie as it is supposed no
> man can pleasantly vtter and perswade without it, but in effect is sure neuer or very
> seldome to thriue and prosper in the world, that cannot skilfully put in vre, in somuch
> as not onely euery common Courtier, but also the grauest Counsellour, yea and the
> most noble and wisest Prince of them all are many times enforced to vse it ... Of this

---

[142] Mack, *Montaigne and Shakespeare*, p. 174.

[143] Moss, *Printed Commonplace-Books*, pp. 212–13.

[144] On the relationship between rhetoric and poetics, which was frequently imagined as a branch of rhetoric, see Brian Vickers, ed., *English Renaissance Literary Criticism* (Oxford: Oxford University Press, 1999), introduction, pp. 10–22; Glyn P. Norton, ed., *The Cambridge History of Literary Criticism, Vol. III: The Renaissance* (Cambridge: Cambridge University Press, 1999), introduction, pp. 7–8; William Webbe, *A Discourse of English Poetry*, ed. Sonia Hernández-Santano (Cambridge: MHRA, 2016), introduction, pp. 11–12.

[145] See John Hollander, *Melodious Guile: Fictive Pattern in Poetic Language* (New Haven: Yale University Press, 1990), pp. 3–4.

[146] Puttenham, *Arte of English Poesie*, pp. 186–96.

[147] Puttenham, *Arte of English Poesie*, p. 186.

figure therefore which for his duplicitie we call the figure of [*false semblant or dissimulation*] we will speake first as of the chief ringleader and captaine of all other figures, either in the Poeticall or oratorie science.[148]

Puttenham places more emphasis on the significance of allegory than rhetoricians such as Quintilian, who does not represent it as such a leading mode, nor makes a particular link between allegory, advancement, and modes of behaviour.[149] Puttenham has enshrined the anxiety that classical orators had about the value and purpose of rhetoric in the rhetorical figures themselves so that, at this point in his treatise, rhetorical skill and duplicity exist in a symbiotic relationship: insecurity is the counterpart to ambition.[150] Everyone at court has to be versed in the art of rhetoric, which makes them adept at dissimulation, able to separate speech and its meaning.

Puttenham acknowledges that, according to the logic of his argument, lying has to be tolerated, even encouraged: 'And ye shall know that we may dissemble, I meane speake otherwise then we thinke, in earnest as well as in sport, vnder couert and darke termes, and in learned and apparent speaches, in short sentences, and by long ambage and circumstances of wordes, and finally aswell when we lye as when we tell truth.'[151] This is a carefully constructed sentence in which each clause builds on and qualifies the previous one, the whole enveloped between the two terms for deliberate falsehood, as 'dissemble' is transformed into the more pejorative 'lye'. The study of rhetoric will enable its practitioners to separate what they say and what they mean, the fundamental prerequisite for telling lies when the speaker pretends to believe something they do not in order to mislead those to whom he or she is talking. The qualification 'in earnest as well as in sport' makes it clear that Putttenham is not simply thinking about joking and irony, exceptions to accusations of lying from Augustine onwards. The reference to 'couert and darke termes', a description that may have inspired Spenser's reference to his allegory as a 'darke conceit', provides a further suggestion of the close relationship between rhetoric and subterfuge.[152] The penultimate section (three clauses) covers every aspect of rhetorical performance so that dissembling cannot be confined to certain features that an orator can employ: speeches, both prepared (learned) and occasional (apparent); short sentences; and long and circumlocutory sentences (ambage) as well as word order, accidental or carefully chosen. Therefore we are prepared for the balance of the last clause which makes rhetoric into a neutral and equivocal art in which lying and truth-telling cannot be distinguished. For Puttenham, as this careful and persuasive sentence demonstrates, to adopt the art of rhetoric is to accept that one will have to lie.

The final third of *The Arte of English Poesie* centres nervously around this issue of the relationship between lying and rhetoric. Puttenham sees riddles as forms of allegory because in telling them we 'dissemble againe vnder couert and darke

---

[148] Puttenham, *Arte of English Poesie*, p. 186.   [149] Quintilian, *Institutes*, 8.6.44–59.

[150] Catherine Nicholson, *Uncommon Tongues: Eloquence and Eccentricity in the English Renaissance* (Philadelphia: University of Pennsylvania Press, 2014), p. 137.

[151] Puttenham, *Arte of English Poesie*, p. 186.

[152] Edmund Spenser, *The Faerie Queene*, ed. A. C. Hamilton (Harlow: Longman, 2001), p. 714.

speaches... of which the sence can hardly be picked out'.[153] Riddles, of course, cannot be equated with lies, but in equivocating and misleading the hearer they have to run the risk of lying, much as prophecy does in hedging its bets and attempting to provide a clear sense of allegorical truth which can then be denied.[154] More significantly, Puttenham argues that 'We dissemble after a sort, when we speake by common prouerbs', a further sign that the commonplace tradition that dominated education systems and processes in the period was regarded with suspicion not as an automatic fount of wisdom.[155] Proverbs and commonplaces could be manipulated to mean virtually anything, as Baldwin, Erasmus, and Montaigne demonstrate, either providing a starting point that will undoubtedly be overturned during the discussion in question, or even, as in Montaigne's writings, stating the opposite of what the speaker/writer appears to mean. Puttenham cites two proverbs which, while they do not contradict each other, provide contrasting pieces of wisdom:

> *As the olde cocke crowes so doeth the chick:*
> *A bad Cooke that cannot his owne fingers lick.*[156]

Both are common in contemporary literature.[157] It is only Puttenham who seems to have linked the two and so provided the rhyme. The first proverb means that 'the young learne by the olde, either to be good or euill in their behauiors'; the second is rather perversely interpreted to mean 'that he is not to be counted a wise man, who being in authority, and hauing the administration of many good and great things, will not serue his owne turne and his friends whilest he may'.[158] Is Puttenham being serious here? Or proving his point by bending the truth? The second proverb has a more obvious meaning, that the cook has to be trusted to produce food that s/he is prepared to eat, with the secondary meaning that cooks have their fingers in the soup (i.e. are corrupt). In foregrounding the secondary meaning Puttenham is showing how commonplaces can be manipulated by their user and so do not provide obvious wisdom, but are often examples of dissimulation. The second proverb has this ambiguity when it appears in *Romeo and Juliet* as the Capulets plan a hasty wedding feast to unite Juliet and Paris:

Capulet So many guests invite as here are writ.
> [*Exit Servingman.*]
Sirrah, go hire me twenty cunning cooks.
Servingman You shall have none ill, sir, for I'll try if they can lick their fingers.
Cap. How! Canst thou try them so?
Ser. Marry sir, 'tis an ill cook that cannot lick his own fingers; therefore he that
   cannot lick his fingers goes not with me.[159]

---

[153] Puttenham, *Arte of English Poesie*, p. 188.
[154] Howard Dobin, *Merlin's Disciples: Prophecy, Poetry, and Power in Renaissance England* (Stanford: Stanford University Press, 1990), pp. 124, 158.
[155] Puttenham, *Arte of English Poesie*, p. 189.   [156] Puttenham, *Arte of English Poesie*, p. 189.
[157] Tilley, *Proverbs*, C491 (p. 108), C636 (p. 118); Lupton, *Siuqila*, sig. Z2v.
[158] Puttenham, *Arte of English Poesie*, p. 189.
[159] William Shakespeare, *Romeo and Juliet*, ed. Brian Gibbons (London: Methuen, 1980), 4.2.1–7 (pp. 201–2).

The proverb works here because both meanings are employed: only good cooks can bear to lick their fingers, and cooks who 'lick their fingers' may be crooks. Puttenham writes as if the proverb has only one obvious meaning—the secondary one that depends on a quibble—in order to couple it with the first one. His explanation suggests that a person in authority (metonymically, a cook) is expected to dole out favours to all and sundry while he occupies the office in question, which will probably not be for ever, such are the wiles of fortune and the risks of this mode of behaviour. Hence, the young chicks will learn to act like this, distributing favours to cement their position, from the old cock, which resembles life at court where courtiers need to have the ability to dissemble and to lie. Puttenham may, of course, not really believe this interpretation of the two proverbs he has yoked together and he may not think that this is proper courtly behaviour. But in producing this striking reading that links commonplaces to lying he is writing in an established tradition of thinking about commonplaces and rhetorical theory. Successful courtiers who have mastered the art of rhetoric are both old cocks and skilful cooks.

Puttenham lists numerous other forms of dissembling: mockery, sarcasm, and the 'mery skoffe', a form of civil pleasantry which alleviates social embarrassment, and so on.[160] He also discusses hyperbole, another figure of 'false semblant'.[161] Here the logic of dissembling is pushed to its limit and, following the Romans, Puttenham refers to hyperbole as '*Dementiens* or the lying figure'.[162] Puttenham uses the familiar device of prosopopoeia, transforming Hyperbole into a person he can address:

> I for his immoderate excesse cal him the ouer reacher, right with his original or [*lowd lyar*] & me thinks not amisse: now when I speake that/which neither I my selfe thinke to be true, nor would haue any other body beleeue, it must needs be a great dissimulation, because I meane nothing lesse then that I speake, and this maner of speech is vsed, when either we would greatly aduance or greatly abase the reputation of any thing or any person, and must be vsed very discreetly, or els it will seeme odious, for although a prayse or other report may be allowed beyond credit, it may not be beyond all measure[.][163]

Hyperbole is the closest that a speaker/writer can get to lying, part of a game that will always threaten to spiral out of control. It should not surprise us that the first example cited is a genuine political case, from a parliament in Henry VIII's reign when a 'graue and wise Counsellour' transformed himself into 'a grosse flattering

---

[160] Puttenham, *Arte of English Poesie*, pp. 189–91.

[161] See Daniel Javitch, *Poetry and Courtliness in Renaissance England* (Princeton: Princeton University Press, 1978), pp. 89–90; Katrin Ettenhuber, 'Hyperbole: Exceeding Similitude', in Sylvia Adamson, Gavin Alexander, and Katrin Ettenhuber, eds, *Renaissance Figures of Speech* (Cambridge: Cambridge University Press, 2007), pp. 197–216, at pp. 199–202. See also Sherry, *Treatise of Schemes and Tropes*, sig. E3v; Sonnino, *Handbook*, pp. 68–9; Kerr, ed., *Penguin Book of Lies*, p. 110.

[162] Puttenham, *Arte of English Poesie*, p. 191.

[163] Puttenham, *Arte of English Poesie*, pp. 191–2. Wilson also employs the idea of a 'loude lye' (*Arte of Rhetorique*, p. 149). Henry Peacham argues that a prosopopoeia of truth can be used 'against false testimonies, lies and perjurie, against wicked hipocrisie and cursed heresie, against feare, favour and avarice which are her enemies in the seats of judgement': *The Garden of Eloquence* (London, 1593), p. 136.

foole' through his hyperbolic praise of the King. The speaker claims that to list Henry's virtues would be as great a task as if he were asked to 'number the stares of the skie, or to tell the sands of the sea'. Puttenham roundly condemns him for straying from a pardonable lie into an absurd one, always the danger of using hyperbole overenthusiastically. Accordingly, Puttenham provides an acceptable alternative which, 'if he had vsed it thus, it had bene better and neuerthelesse a lye too, but a more moderate lye and no lesse to the purpose of the kings commendation'. Praising the King as having virtues that words cannot express, numerous 'kingly merites', and deserving everlasting honour and renown, is still an 'vntruth' if 'we shall measure it by the rule of exact veritie', but more obviously within the bounds of acceptable hyperbole.[164]

Once lying has been admitted as acceptable practice it has to be carefully regulated to prevent falsehood from getting out of hand. The courtier and the poet need 'in plaine termes, cunningly to be able to dissemble' the honesty of the admission, a striking contrast to its substance.[165] The courtier poet has to learn to regulate his dissembling and lying. Whereas foreign courtiers might dissemble to excess, regularly attending church but never actually praying, and giving a penny to a beggar while spending a pound on a harlot, their English counterparts need to be honest men rather than hypocrites:

> Therefore leauing these manner of dissimulations to all base-minded men, & of vile nature or misterie, we doe allow our Courtly Poet to be a dissembler only in the subtilties of his arte: that is, when he is most artificiall, so to disguise and cloake it as it may not appeare, nor seeme to proceede from him by any studie or trade of rules, but to be his natural: nor so euidently to be descried, as euery ladde that reads him shall say he is a good scholler, but will rather haue him to know his arte well, and little to vse it.[166]

Puttenham's words can be read as a counterpart to those of Quintilian claiming that rhetoric cannot be a dangerous art because only a good man can be a good orator and know the limits of rhetoric. Puttenham performs the same manoeuvre in terms of his nation and its identity, claiming that the English poet will know how to use the skills he has acquired properly and moderately, only dissimulating 'when he is most artificiall', and providing clear markers so that any potential excess can be contained.[167] English writers will adopt and adapt Italian practices of *sprezzatura* in order to express modesty and confine behaviour within agreed boundaries, rather than, as Puttenham suggests, in the Italian mode, which enables courtiers there to hide their immoral behaviour. The English court, in increasing its artificiality sensibly and dissembling in controlled and reasonable ways, seals itself off from the vices of the wider world and so enables its courtiers to become more adept at distinguishing between proper behaviour at court and improper behaviour in the world outside.

---

[164] Puttenham, *Arte of English Poesie*, p. 192.   [165] Puttenham, *Arte of English Poesie*, p. 299.
[166] Puttenham, *Arte of English Poesie*, p. 302.
[167] On Puttenham and national identity, see Hadfield, *Literature, Politics and National Identity*, pp. 122–31.

VI

While Puttenham pushes ideas about lying one way in his pioneering analysis of poetics—before he draws back—Sir Philip Sidney travels in the opposite direction in his *Apology for Poetry*, written earlier (*c.*1579), but not published until after Puttenham's *Arte* (1595). Sidney's work does not simply rely on passages heavily indebted to rhetoric but is a rhetorical performance in itself.[168] Like Puttenham's, Sidney's treatise is shot through with anxiety about the relationship between literature, society, and class, an indication of how carefully both were thinking about the place of literature in the world, which is why they were both so concerned with issues of truth and lies.[169] In a famous passage Sidney clearly gestures towards larger issues than the ones he is ostensibly addressing. He refers to the 'imputations' that are directed against poetry, the second being that poetry is 'the mother of all lies':

> To the second [imputation] therefore, that they should be the principal liars, I answer paradoxically, but truly, I think truly, that of all writers under the sun the poet is the least liar, and, though he would, as a poet can scarcely be a liar. The astronomer, with his cousin the geometrician, can hardly escape, when they take upon them to measure the height of the stars. How often, think you, do the physicians lie, when they aver things good for sicknesses, which afterwards send Charon a great number of souls drowned in a potion before they come to his ferry? And no less of the rest, which take upon them to affirm. Now for the poet, he nothing affirms, and therefore never lieth. For, as I take it, to lie is to affirm that to be true which is false; so as the other artists, and especially the historian, affirming many things, can, in the cloudy knowledge of mankind, hardly escape from many lies. But the poet (as I said before) never affirmeth.[170]

This is an extraordinary passage—although not unique, as a serious literature developed throughout Europe which justified and encouraged the practice of dissimulation in the visual arts—that concentrates on the issue of truth and falsehood, making its point through a series of powerful rhetorical devices.[171]

The charge that poets were liars was familiar enough, as editors and critics have frequently pointed out.[172] Sidney is, of course, answering Plato's attack on poets as

---

[168] See, for example, O. B. Hardison, Jr, 'The Two Voices of Sidney's *Apology for Poetry*', *ELR* 2 (1972), 83–99; Wesley Trimpi, 'Sir Philip Sidney's *An Apology for Poetry*', in Norton, ed., *Cambridge History of Literary Criticism*, pp. 187–98.

[169] For recent discussions see Kevin Pask, *The Emergence of the English Author: Scripting the Life of the Poet in Early Modern England* (Cambridge: Cambridge University Press, 1996), ch. 2; Robert Matz, *Defending Literature in Early Modern England: Renaissance Literary Theory in Social Context* (Cambridge: Cambridge University Press, 2000), pp. 63–6; Robert E. Stillman, *Philip Sidney and the Poetics of Renaissance Cosmopolitanism* (Farnham: Ashgate, 2013), p. ix.

[170] Sidney, *Apology*, pp. 102–3.

[171] See also Sir John Harington, *A Brief Apology of Poetry* (1591), in Gavin Alexander, ed., *Sidney's 'The Defence of Poetry' and Selected Renaissance Literary Criticism* (Harmondsworth: Penguin, 2004), pp. 260–73, at p. 265. Harington's work borrows heavily from Sidney's and is a sign of its influence: see also Scott, *Model of Poesie*, introduction, pp. li–lv. On dissimulation in the visual arts see Sara Galletti, 'Rubens's *Life of Maria de' Medici*: Dissimulation and the Politics of Art in Early Seventeenth-Century France', *RQ* 67 (2014), 878–916.

[172] Sidney, *Apology*, p. 203; E. R. Curtius, *European Literature and the Latin Middle Ages*, trans. Willard R. Trask (Princeton: Princeton University Press, 1983, rpt of 1953), p. 206.

liars in the *Republic*, but the passage surely does not stop there and has a much wider relevance. Sidney may well have a range of works in mind, in particular Henry Cornelius Agrippa's *Of the Vanitie and Uncertaintie of Artes and Sciences*, translated into English in 1569, where Agrippa accuses poets of telling fables 'with fardels [bundles] of lies'.[173] He could also have been thinking of other familiar and popular works such as Richard Reynoldes's treatise on rhetoric (1563), which also castigated poets for telling such outrageous and damaging lies:

> the vanities of Poetes are to bee reproued, and their forged inuencions to bee reiected: in whose writynges, so manifestlie are set forthe as a truthe, and Chronicled to the pesteritie of ages and times, soche forged matters of their Poeticall and vain wittes. Who hath not heard of their monsterous lies against God ... The vain inuention of Poetes ... [whose] lies exceade all nomber, because thei hee infinite, so also thei passe all truthe, reason, and iudgemente.[174]

Reynoldes's target is classical literature because it represented a plurality of gods, and because of its wild exaggerations: 'Accordyng to the folie and supersticiousnes of those tymes, thei inuented and forged folie vppon folie, lye, vpon lye, as in the battaill of Troie, thei aggrauate the dolour of the battaill, by pitifull and lamentable inuencion.'[175] Plato, therefore, was right to banish poets from the ideal Republic.[176]

In Sidney's account the personal belief of the speaker is heavily emphasized: 'truly, I think truly', foregrounding the speaker's belief in what he is saying about truth/lies. 'Truly', as Robert Maslen has pointed out, is Sidney's favourite word in the *Apology*, used thirty-four times, 'invariably ... at moments when he is at his most controversial'.[177] In doing so Sidney is undoubtedly comparing himself to Cicero, whose powerful voice throughout his writing and use of the first person in his multifarious roles as orator, accuser, theorist, and friend established the voice of Roman literature for subsequent generations of readers. Sidney acknowledges the significance of Cicero in the *Apology*, and the relationship between the establishment of rhetoric as a science, legal testimony, and, by implication, English literature.[178] Sidney did not adopt a Ciceronian style, and he satirized those writers who slavishly followed Renaissance ideas of Ciceronianism, but used Cicero's strong voice to create his own, placing emphasis on the significance of his personal voice and his testimony in order to validate his version of the truth.[179] Sidney refers to

---

[173] Henricus Cornelius Agrippa, *Of the Vanitie and Uncertaintie of Artes and Sciences*, trans. Jan Sanford (London, 1569), sig. D3r. Agrippa's target is classical myth rather than modern poetry.

[174] Richard Reynoldes, *A Booke Called the Foundacion of Rhetoricke* (London, 1563), sig. G1r.

[175] Reynoldes, *Foundacion of Rhetoricke*, sig. G1r.

[176] Russell and Winterbottom, eds, *Classical Literary Criticism*, pp. 14–50. Reynoldes does admit that fables might have some value, as a fable is 'a forged tale, containing in it by the colour of a lie, a matter of truthe' (Reynoldes, *Foundacion of Rhetoricke*, sig. A3v).

[177] Sidney, *Apology*, introduction, pp. 4, 60.

[178] Gavin Alexander, *Writing after Sidney: The Literary Response to Sir Philip Sidney, 1586–1640* (Oxford: Oxford University Press, 2006), p. 31.

[179] On Sidney's relationship to Ciceronian style see Hardison, Jr, 'Two Voices', pp. 83–4. See also Sidney, *Correspondence*, ed. Kuin, I, p. 111. On Ciceronianism see Javitch, *Poetry and Courtliness*, pp. 21–2; Ann Moss, 'Literary Imitation in the Sixteenth Century: Writers and Readers, Latin and French', in Norton, ed., *Cambridge History of Literary Criticism, Vol. III*, pp. 107–18.

Cicero's great speech against the conspirator Catiline, whose plot to overthrow the Roman Republic was exposed by Cicero in 63 BCE, a favourite source for rhetorical handbooks.[180] He professes admiration for Cicero's performance of truthfulness which exposes the lies and deceptions of his enemies even as he feigns emotions to do so:

> Tully, when he was to drive out Catiline, as it were with a thunderbolt of eloquence, often used that figure of repetition, *Vivit. Vivit? Imo vero etiam in senatum venit, &c.* [he lives. Lives? Why, he even comes into the Senate!] Indeed, inflamed with a well-grounded rage, he would have his words (as it were) double out of his mouth, and so do that artificially which we see men do in choler naturally.[181]

Cicero is able to perform honesty and truthfulness, and his effectiveness, according to Sidney, is because he genuinely feels and understands the horror of Catiline's crime. In placing such emphasis on public performance to lead witnesses to the truth, Sidney is working within the paradigms established by Quintilian, whose work was based to a large extent on the example of Cicero, and who made the empathy established by the orator between himself and the audience such a vital part of the armoury of the rhetorically trained speaker and writer.[182] However, this argument is also vulnerable to the same charges that might be levelled against Quintilian, that rhetoric works well when in the service of the good, but that it provides useful tools for the unscrupulous to work with as well, a problem that can only really be solved through the assertion that a good rhetorician must be a good man.

Sidney claims that literature has a particular relationship to the establishment of the truth, a mimetic witness, which marks it out as a privileged form of writing.[183] Even the most scrupulous scientists lie more than poets do, and practical men, physicians, have to lie in the course of their work, a reference to Augustine's strictures against doctors misleading their patients when they are gravely ill in the hope of doing some good.[184] The classical reference to Charon's ferry perhaps occludes a deeper anxiety that in trying to save the life of a patient some individuals

[180] Sherry, *Treatise of Schemes and Tropes*, sig. D5r.

[181] Sidney, *Apology*, p. 114. Translation from Sir Philip Sidney, *A Defence of Poetry*, ed. J. A. Van Dorsten (Oxford: Oxford University Press, 1973), p. 104. The words are from the opening of Cicero's first *Oratio in Catilinam*. For analysis see B. A. Krostenko, 'Text and Context in the Roman Forum: The Case of Cicero's *First Catilinarian*', in Walter Jost and Wendy Olmsted, eds, *A Companion to Rhetoric and Rhetorical Criticism* (Oxford: Blackwell, 2004), pp. 38–57.

[182] On Cicero and Quintilian see Arthur F. Kinney, 'Continental Poetics', in Jost and Olmsted, eds, *Companion to Rhetoric and Rhetorical Criticism*, pp. 80–95, at p. 85; John O. Ward, 'Cicero and Quintilian', in Norton, ed., *Cambridge History of Literary Criticism, Vol. III*, pp. 77–87.

[183] Leonard Barkan, 'Making Pictures Speak: Renaissance Art, Elizabethan Literature, Modern Scholarship', *RQ* 48 (1995), 326–51.

[184] The Hippocratic oath does not forbid lying to help a patient. The ethics of lying to patients and detecting their lies is still a debated issue for health care professionals: see John J. Palmieri and Theodore A. Stern, 'Lies in the Doctor–Patient Relationship', *The Primary Care Companion to the Journal of Clinical Psychiatry* 11 (2009), 163–8. Galen was much clearer that the relationship between doctor and patient was based on trust whereas Hippocrates was more worried about patients lying to doctors and believed that the real issue was to remove error and establish the nature of the patient's condition: Jacques Jouanna, *Greek Medicine from Hippocrates to Galen: Selected Papers* (Leiden: Brill, 2012), pp. 273–5.

may die without a proper acknowledgement of their sins, and, even if Protestants no longer believed in the rite of extreme unction, the deathbed scene and the ideal of the good death were central aspects of Christian belief and ritual.[185] Lies are an unavoidable feature of everyday life. The only exception made is for poets who are defined by their medium and chosen profession as non-liars. Literature, for Sidney, becomes a means of avoiding the need to affirm one's faith in anything and is defined against the possibility of deception and error, a position that, as R. S. White has argued, owed much to the concept of the 'legal fiction', something invented— and, therefore, a lie—in order to secure the truth.[186] Sidney appears to be using what we might term a maximalist definition of lying, including everything from deliberate falsehood to errors, which is why he is able to define, somewhat tongue-in-cheek of course, historians as liars.[187]

The brutal reality of sixteenth-century history placed murderous religious differences at the centre of everyone's consciousness, specifically the need to declare or hide one's faith in a time of bewildering and invariably destructive change.[188] Sidney, more than most, had direct experience of the brutal realities of sectarian conflict so it is hard to believe that, writing in the 1570s, Sidney did not have his knowledge of the late-sixteenth-century Wars of Religion on his mind, especially as he places such significance on the value of testimony in the *Apology*. Sidney had important Catholic and Protestant connections, many very personal, which illustrate the complicated web of alliances that routinely affected the governing class, especially in mid-Tudor England.[189] On the one hand he was the godson of Philip II, King of Spain and had been friendly with the Jesuit Edmund Campion, and had met him in Prague in 1577, four years before Campion's execution which must surely have been fresh in his mind when he was writing the *Apology*, which he probably started around 1580.[190] On the other, he was the future son-in-law of Sir Francis Walsingham, and had witnessed the St Bartholomew's Day Massacre (1572) at first hand with his father-in-law in his house in Paris, and was closely associated with the more forward Protestants who wanted to intervene in Europe to help the Dutch against his godfather's country.[191] Sidney was hardly a stranger to religious controversy and its impact, and the unpleasant reality that it was almost

---

[185] Ariès, *Hour of Our Death*, pp. 14–18, 23–4. On the persistence of traditional beliefs and rituals see David Cressy, *Birth, Marriage, and Death: Ritual, Religion, and the Life-Cycle in Tudor and Stuart England* (Oxford: Oxford University Press, 1997), ch. 18.

[186] White, *Natural Law*, p. 102.

[187] On Sidney and history see Elizabeth Story Donno, 'Old Mouse-Eaten Records: History in Sidney's *Apology*', *SP* 72 (1975), 275–98; Rebecca W. Bushnell, *A Culture of Teaching: Early Modern Humanism in Theory and Practice* (Ithaca, NY: Cornell University Press, 1996), p. 156.

[188] Zagorin, *Ways of Lying*, introduction; Snyder, *Dissimulation*, ch. 1.

[189] Alan Stewart, *Philip Sidney: A Double Life* (London: Chatto & Windus, 2000), pp. 102–14, 175–7, *passim*; Stillman, *Philip Sidney*, pp. 35–62, *passim*.

[190] Katherine Duncan-Jones, *Sir Philip Sidney, Courtier Poet* (London: Hamish Hamilton, 1991), pp. 3, 124–7; Sidney, *Apology*, ed. Maslen, introduction, pp. 2–3.

[191] Duncan-Jones, *Sidney*, p. 60; Roger Howell, *Sir Philip Sidney: The Shepherd Knight* (London: Hutchinson, 1968), pp. 46–7, *passim*; Andrew D. Weiner, *Sir Philip Sidney and the Poetics of Protestantism: A Study of Contexts* (Minneapolis: University of Minnesota Press, 1978).

impossible not to tell lies in the course of everyday life. His comments in the *Apology* are a robust defence of his own literary efforts and his right to say what he thought fit in them, an acknowledgement of the need to write well and to prevent literature sliding into banal untruthfulness.[192] More significantly, they are a desire to defend poetry as a place which is beyond the terrifying reality of quotidian existence, where the big and small lies of everyday life cannot intrude.

[192] I owe this point to Keston Sutherland.

5

Courtesy, Lying, and Politics

I

Did small lies lead to big lies, or was it only the big ones that really mattered? Was it possible to contain lying within circumscribed boundaries, or did the capacity to lie just get more overwhelming the more a liar lied? The relationship between issues of truth and falsehood/lying is a major concern of many sixteenth-century works of literature, in particular Edmund Spenser's complicated and diverse romance-epic, *The Faerie Queene* (1590, 1596), a poem always caught between the forward movement of epic and the sideways dilation of romance.[1] While the one literary genre moves the reader forward to the truth, the other finds the real core of the matter in the ways in which the knights are interrupted from their quest: the ostensible purpose of the quest retards rather than advances the serious action.[2] Lying is clearly a central concern for all the virtues Spenser outlines, most especially Book I, the Book of Holiness, and Book VI, the Book of Courtesy, providing a neat link between apparently deep and ostensibly superficial values. A central lesson that the poem teaches the reader is to beware of hasty judgements as moral and religious instruction will be found in the most unlikely places.[3] It is noticeable how infrequently Spenser actually uses the words 'lie', 'lying', or 'liar', even though the quests of the knights are directly involved with questions of truth and falsehood. This apparent omission actually serves to draw our attention to the central importance of lying in the poem's wandering and divergent plots.

In the opening canto, having dispatched the monster, Error, the Red-Cross Knight encounters a suspicious old man, dressed as a monk, whom we soon learn is called Archimago, the arch magician, maker of images:

> For that old man of pleasing wordes had store,
> And well could file his tongue as smooth as glas;
> He told of Saintes and Popes, and euermore
> He strowd an *Aue-Mary* after and before.[4]

---

[1] There is relatively little comment on lying in *The Faerie Queene*, apart from some relevant remarks in James Nohrnberg, *The Analogy of* The Faerie Queene (Princeton: Princeton University Press, 1976), pp. 121, 124, 128–9, *passim*.

[2] Patricia Parker, *Inescapable Romance: Studies in the Poetics of a Mode* (Princeton: Princeton University Press, 1979); Colin Burrow, *Epic Romance: Homer to Milton* (Oxford: Clarendon Press, 1993), p. 2.

[3] A. Bartlett Giamatti, *Play of Double Senses: Spenser's* Faerie Queene (New York: Norton, 1975), pp. 94–105.

[4] Spenser, *Faerie Queene*, 1.1.35, lines 6–9.

Archimago clearly represents either the late medieval Church, or more recent forms of Catholicism, with his stories of popes and saints, and frequent recourse to Ave Marias, the most basic and widespread of Catholic prayers—as well as suggesting an uncomfortably close link between poets ('makers') and traditional forms of worship.[5] In doing so is he actually lying to the Red-Cross Knight and Una? Or is Archimago sincere in his delusion? The narrator's words suggest that s/he thinks that the magician is deceiving them, but nothing is made explicit, and it is not clear whether the duplicity is conscious or misconceived. Can we really trust the narrator at this point in the story? The description that Archimago could 'file his tongue as smooth as glas' would seem to suggest that there is an intention to deceive and articulate a series of lies, disguising the truth like a cunning rhetorician. Is that Archimago's plan or is he simply obeying orders? Does it matter if he is lying anyway? Heresy, like treason, regardless of the sincerity involved, is a crime even if it cannot be defined as lying, because if we accept the truth of the Reformation then everything that Archimago says and does is a Romish lie as Protestant polemicists such as John Bale—and many others—argued.[6] Or is Spenser deliberately avoiding using the terms 'lie' and 'lying' because, in fact, the difference between Protestants and Catholics was not as clear as many liked to think?[7]

What Spenser does not write is as important as what he does: the description of Archimago's behaviour indicates that he cannot be trusted and wants to mislead the Knight and his lady, but he is not explicitly represented as a liar. Protestant accounts of the Catholic cults of Mary and of saints were not usually so reticent.[8] Other incidents in the poem also skirt around the issue of lying while signalling its obvious importance. In Book V, canto 9, Artegall and Talus enter the court of Mercilla where they see the terrible fate of the poet Bon Font:

> There as they entred at the Scriene, they saw
> Some one, whose tongue was for his trespasse vyle
> Nayld to a post, adiudged so by law:
> For that therewith he falsely did reuyle,
> And foule blaspheme that Queene for forged guyle,
> Both with bold speaches, which he blazed had,

---

[5] Cunningham, *Introduction to Catholicism*, pp. 163–8; MacCulloch, *Reformation*, p. 100. On Archimago and poets as 'makers' see David Quint, 'Archimago and Amoret: The Poem and its Doubles', in Patrick Cheney and Lauren Silberman, eds, *Worldmaking Spenser: Explorations in the Early Modern Age* (Lexington: University Press of Kentucky, 2000), pp. 32–42; Sidney, *Apology*, p. 84.

[6] Leslie P. Fairfield, *John Bale: Mythmaker of the English Reformation* (Indiana: Purdue University Press, 1976), chs 3–4. On the relationship between Bale and Spenser's Book 1, see Florence Sandler, 'The *Faerie Queene*: An Elizabethan Apocalypse', in C. A. Patrides and Joseph Wittreich, eds, *The Apocalypse in English Renaissance Thought and Literature* (Manchester: Manchester University Press, 1984), pp. 148–74; King, *Spenser's Poetry*, pp. 71–2.

[7] Hadfield, 'Spenser and Religion'. For an alternative view, see, for example, Hume, *Spenser: Protestant Poet*.

[8] Helen Parish, '"Monks, Miracles and Magic": The Medieval Church in English Reformation Polemic', *Reformation* 8 (2003), 117–42; Eric Ives, *The Reformation Experience: Living Through the Turbulent Sixteenth Century* (Oxford: Lion, 2012), pp. 163–4, 170, *passim*; Sarah Tarlow, *Ritual, Belief and the Dead in Early Modern Britain and Ireland* (Cambridge: Cambridge University Press, 2011), pp. 39, 166.

And with lewd poems, which he did compyle;
For the bold title of a Poet bad
He on himselfe had ta'en, and rayling rymes had sprad.

Thus there he stood, whylest high ouer his head,
There written was the purport of his sin,
In cyphers strange, that few could rightly read,
BON FONT: but *bon* that once had written bin,
Was raced out, and *Mal* was now put in.
So now *Malfont* was plainely to be red;
Eyther for th'euill, which he did therein,
Or that he likened was to a welhed
Of euill words, and wicked sclaunders by him shed.[9]

Spenser uses a whole series of words defining and explicating deception and deceitfulness, 'blaspheme', 'forged guyle', 'bold', 'blazed', 'lewd', 'rayling', 'cyphers', 'euill words', and 'wicked sclaunders'. However, as before, he never once actually states that the poet lies or is labelled as a liar. The reader is told that s/he can read this incident clearly now that the poet's name is given in block capitals, but it is not actually stated that he does not tell the truth, that he lies about anything. What Bon/Malfont says may offend people and seem misleading as well as offensive, and he may be defaming or slandering the monarch or someone high up at court. But what he has written or spoken could equally well be true: the fact that his words have fallen foul of those in authority perhaps indicates that the poet is at fault, perhaps signals their guilt/error.[10] He exists as a doppelgänger of Archimago, a maker of images, which may be true or false, and are certainly hard to read.

These distinctions are clearly important. What we witness in *The Faerie Queene* is a language about deception, about truth and lying, that very rarely mentions the word 'lie', even when readers probably think it should do, or might even imagine that it does. The term is rarely used and these few examples are scattered throughout the long poem. The false visions and prophecies that Guyon encounters in the Chamber of Memory in the House of Temperance are described as 'lies' at the end of a long list of their negative qualities:

Like many swarmes of Bees assembled round,
After their hiues with honny do abound:
All those were idle thoughts and fantasies,
Deuices, dreames, opinions vnsound,
Shewes, visions, sooth-sayes, and prophesies;
And all that fained is, as leasings, tales, and lies. (2.9.51, lines 4–9)

As Jennifer Summit argues, this description shows how anxious Protestants were when they had to rely on Catholic records to reconstruct the past.[11] Spenser's

---

[9] Spenser, *Faerie Queene*, 5.9.25–6.

[10] M. Lindsay Kaplan, *The Culture of Slander in Early Modern England* (Cambridge: Cambridge University Press, 1997), pp. 34–63.

[11] See Jennifer Summit, 'Monuments and Ruins: Spenser and the Problem of the English Library', *ELH* 70 (2003), 1–34.

representation of the dysfunctional Chamber of Memory, a sign of a faulty and limited intelligence at work, can be related to the question of whether Archimago is actually lying or is sincere in his delusion when he talks about saints and popes and utters the Ave Maria, and whether a vestige of truth can be recovered from his actions and statements. The question is left tantalizingly open and the reader has to decide whether any elements from England's religious past can be rescued and integrated into the present conception of Christianity; whether they should be dismissed as lies; or whether separating the two is an impossible task.

Later, the narrator labels Duessa, Una's rival and an ally of Archimago, a liar when she reappears at the start of Book IV, having transformed herself into Ate.[12] Ate is represented as the 'mother of debate', a sobriquet that links her to Elizabeth's well-known description of Mary Stuart as the 'daughter of debate' in a poem that circulated widely in manuscript verse anthologies which was then published in George Puttenham's *Arte of English Poesie*, which made the link explicit.[13] The connection is especially significant in Spenser's poem because Duessa's final guise is as Mary who is executed for her 'vyld treasons, and outrageous shame' against Mercilla (Elizabeth) in the same canto in which we witness the punishment of Bon/ Malfont, linking the fate of Duessa to that of the unfortunate poet.[14] Here the narrator states that 'Her lying tongue was in two parts divided, / And both the parts did speake, and both contended', showing how a forked tongue cannot produce unity and truth, but will always be sending out contradictory messages, being the opposite of 'integrity (the moral version of one-ness)'.[15]

These words are clearly recalled and refigured in the final stanzas of Book VI, the last section of the poem published in Spenser's lifetime. Calidore, the Knight of Courtesy, approaches his nemesis, the Blatant Beast:

> Tho when the Beast saw, he mote nought auaile,
> By force, he gan his hundred tongues apply,
> And sharpely at him to reuile and raile,
> With bitter termes of shamefull infamy;
> Oft interlacing many a forged lie,
> Whose like he neuer once did speake, nor heare,
> Nor euer thought thing so vnworthily[.]   (6.12.33, lines 1–7)

At last, we have the truth about lying, because we have known all along that Book 6 is really about this issue which is inextricably related to courtesy and courteous behaviour. Courtesy is the root of 'civil conversation' but the Knight of Courtesy loves 'simple truth and stedfast honesty', two definitions that are not necessarily at

[12] Humphrey Tonkin, *The Faerie Queene* (New York: Unwin, 1989), p. 137; Harry Berger, Jr, *Revisionary Play: Studies in the Spenserian Dynamic* (Berkeley: University of California Press, 1988), p. 64.

[13] Spenser, *Faerie Queene*, 4.1.19, line 1; Elizabeth I, *Collected Works*, ed. Leah S. Marcus, Janel Mueller, and Mary Beth Rose (Chicago: University of Chicago Press, 2000), pp. 133–4; Puttenham, *Arte of English Poesie*, p. 248.

[14] Spenser, *Faerie Queene*, 5.9.40, line 8. For analysis see Richard A. McCabe, 'The Masks of Duessa: Spenser, Mary Queen of Scots, and James VI', *ELR* 17 (1987), 224–42.

[15] Spenser, *Faerie Queene*, 4.1.27, lines 6–7. OED, 'integrity', n., 1a.

odds but which might well be and which also raise the spectre of the binary divisions established by Augustine between the heavenly and earthly cities.[16] Rhetoric is the basis of the art of civil conversation so it is surely important to note that Spenser locates the problem of truth/falsehood here rather than in debates about religion.[17] For so many writers lying is conceived in directly religious terms, as an offence against God as well as one's neighbours, but Spenser seems to turn these common assumptions around and show that the abuse of truth actually precedes religious concerns. It is only when the beast attacks and despoils a monastery that s/he is defined as a liar.[18] It is not clear that the text supports an easy and satisfying discourse of religious truth and diabolic lies even when it seems to do so; Spenser suggests that there is no straightforward relationship between truth, lies, and religion. Ben Jonson claimed that Spenser was attacking the Puritans when he represented the Blatant Beast rampaging through the established Church, a judgement which, if correct, complicates our understanding of Spenser's relationship to Protestantism.[19] Possibly, the text is even more sophisticated than Jonson assumes, with Spenser showing how practices of lying lead eventually to sacrilege and idolatry, and so indicating that the problem may be intractable, a common feature of all religions, however stringently belief is policed.

What we witness in Book 6 is the initially comic and eventually terrifying realization that there is no central concept of truth, nothing that holds everything together. Calidore is forced to 'tread an endlesse trace withouten guyde' because he is supposed to be courteous and follow the truth without any means of connecting the two in a coherent model established by a strong central authority.[20] As a result, whatever his best intentions, he often ends up telling lies. Calidore's quest is compromised before it begins, the Knight of Courtesy knowing that he has to discover a virtue which has a close relationship to truth and truthful speech but which he does not—and cannot—understand, because its truth is hidden from him. Accordingly, situations drift, as readers expect in a romance rather than an epic, and we can never be sure what the truth actually is, nor whether we will ever discover it. In such a world lying, both petty and serious, flourishes.

Early on in Calidore's quest he discovers Calepine and Serena *in flagrante delicto*, which leads to a comic series of misunderstandings, refracted through the knowing comments of the narrator. Calidore seems to have no idea that his presence may not be entirely welcome and he inaugurates a long debate about courtesy with Calepine which has a number of comic and serious consequences:

> With which his gentle words and goodly wit
> He soone allayd that Knights conceiu'd displeasure,

---

[16] Spenser, *Faerie Queene*, 6.1.1, line 6; 6.1.3, line 9; Augustine, *City of God*, pp. 5–6.

[17] Richards, *Rhetoric and Courtliness*, pp. 29–33.   [18] Spenser, *Faerie Queene*, 6.12.23–5.

[19] Robert Cummings, ed., *Edmund Spenser: The Critical Heritage* (London: Routledge, 1971), p. 136.

[20] Spenser, *Faerie Queene*, 6.1.6, lines 2–3. For analysis see Humphrey Tonkin, *Spenser's Courteous Pastoral: Book VI of* The Faerie Queene (Oxford: Oxford University Press, 1972), pp. 16–18; A. Leigh Deneef, *Spenser and the Motives of Metaphor* (Durham, NC: Duke University Press, 1982), pp. 134–41; Jonathan Goldberg, *Endlesse Worke: Spenser and the Structures of Discourse* (Baltimore: Johns Hopkins University Press, 1981).

That he besought him downe by him to sit,
That they mote treat of things abrode at leasure;
And of aduentures, which had in his measure
Of so long waies to him befallen late.
So downe he sate, and with delightfull pleasure
His long aduentures gan to him relate,
Which he endured had through daungerous debate.

Of which whilest they discoursed both together,
The faire *Serena* (so his Lady hight)
Allur'd with myldnesse of the gentle wether,
And pleasaunce of the place, the which was dight
With diuers flowres distinct with rare delight,
Wandred about the fields, as liking led
Her wauering lust after her wandring sight,
To make a garland to adorne her hed,
Without suspect of ill or daungers hidden dred.[21]

Calidore exercises his skills in 'civil conversation', which, as Jennifer Richards has pointed out, Cicero linked to the virtue of 'honestas', and appears to extract himself from an embarrassing situation, but at the cost of telling the truth.[22] However, things cannot be quite as they seem: the opening lines are arch in the extreme, as is the description of Serena wandering off because it is a lovely day and she fancies a walk.[23] The humour of this episode relies on our knowledge that such encounters are surely rather awkward, and that the two lovers are not quite as sanguine about the interruption as they appear to Calidore, as the Knight of Courtesy has caused their separation.[24] Although he thinks he is behaving courteously in discussing the virtue, perhaps it is they who are truly courteous in preventing him from feeling uncomfortable, and in covering up their true feelings. The description of this scene necessarily contains a lie: either the narrator is lying to us or Calepine is lying to Calidore, having to act courteously and hide the truth of his feelings. A mild enough example, of course, but Spenser is showing just how out of joint the times are for equating truth and courtesy against lying and falsehood, or, pointing out that a simple faith in truth is never really possible. In the following stanzas the Blatant Beast, later the figure of lying itself, appears to whisk Serena away, an early sign of connections that become more obvious later in the book and that we are witnessing the slippery slope from white social lies to ones of cosmic significance.[25]

Spenser's representation of truth and lies is not obviously based on religion: or, rather, the connection between the two is not immediately apparent. We do not move towards holiness and religion in *The Faerie Queene*: instead, we start with a book of holiness, move on to temperance and chastity, virtues relating to the body, through friendship and justice to courtesy, which is where Spenser provides us with

---

[21] Spenser, *Faerie Queene*, 6.3.20–1.
[22] Richards, *Rhetoric and Courtliness*, pp. 26–8, 48–51.
[23] See Arnold Williams, *Flower on a Lowly Stalk: The Sixth Book of* The Faerie Queene (East Lansing: Michigan State University Press, 1967), p. 46.
[24] Tonkin, *Spenser's Courteous Pastoral*, p. 50.　　　[25] Spenser, *Faerie Queene*, 6.3.24–6.

a discussion of lying, signalling the debate in careful and pointed ways. *The Faerie Queene* turns away from religion until we return at the very end of the published poem as the Blatant Beast despoils the monasteries. Calidore pursues the Beast until he eventually finds him:

> Through all estates he found that he had past,
> In which he many massacres had left,
> And to the Clergy now was come at last;
> In which such spoile, such hauocke, and such theft
> He wrought, that thence all goodnesse he bereft,
> That endlesse were to tell. The Elfin Knight,
> Who now no place besides vnsought had left,
> At length into a Monastere did light,
> Where he him fou[n]d despoyling all with maine & might.[26]

We start the book looking for truth and end it overwhelmed by lies, but how this terrible reversal takes place is—deliberately—never made entirely clear.

Spenser's narrative suggests that we should not think of religion in isolation from other forms of writing, discourses, institutions, or authorities: we are reminded that religion was understood as part of the world, not a category that could be separated from it and used to explain everything.[27] On the one hand we need to be alert to the possibility of lying, as lies can occur in a wide variety of places, and, therefore, we might not even recognize a significant lie or realize that one has just been articulated, even though it could have the most devastating consequences, as the episode of Serena, Calepine, and Calidore indicates. On the other, Spenser's allegory makes Puttenham's definition of 'false semblant' a literal reality, showing that lying and dissimulation can never be entirely avoided. The realization that this is true may well, of course, be a strange blessing rather than a curse: or, rather, it could be a relief to admit that lying will never actually disappear, and that we will never be able to obtain impossible standards of purity.

Spenser does not provide a solution to this conundrum, ending his unfinished poem with the prospect of his own writing being subsumed by the lies and falsehoods uttered by the Blatant Beast:

> He growen is so great and strong of late,
> Barking and biting all that him doe bate,
> Albe they worthy blame, or cleare of crime:
> Ne spareth he most learned wits to rate,
> Ne spareth he the gentle Poets rime,
> But rends without regard of person or of time.
>
> Ne may this homely verse, of many meanest,
> Hope to escape his venemous despite,
> More then my former writs, all were they clearest
> From blamefull blot, and free from all that wite,
> With which some wicked tongues did it backebite,

---

[26] Spenser, *Faerie Queene*, 6.12.23.   [27] Cummings, *Mortal Thoughts*, pp. 1–18.

> And bring into a mighty Peres displeasure,
> That neuer so deserued to endite.
> Therfore do you my rimes keep better measure,
> And seeke to please, that now is counted wisemens threasure.[28]

Spenser describes a world in which the distinctions between telling the truth and lying have collapsed, leaving a vacuum which prevents any form of reasoned argument or sensible interaction, let alone critique. The principal cause of this dangerous problem is a failure to control language so that no one can determine whether anyone is actually speaking the truth, an obvious development of the image of Bon/Malfont, the poet with his tongue nailed to a post in Book 5. The poem is not immune from such attacks, and Spenser is both predicting the fate of his *magnum opus*, and following through the logical consequences of the confusing and contradictory definitions of courtesy at the start of Book 6.

Even so, despite these general caveats, there is an implicit assertion that the poet himself is one of the few people who is capable of telling the truth and that he is the victim of malicious lies, through the falsehoods uttered by the 'mighty Pere' who has found the poet and his work displeasing. The pointed use of the word 'displeasure' implies a courteous reaction to a transgression, but really indicates a vindictive campaign. The peer is usually assumed to be William Cecil, Lord Burghley, whom Spenser had attacked in *Mother Hubberds Tale*, as Spenser later acknowledges that he had offended the Queen's most important politician in *The Ruins of Time*.[29] Spenser's attack on the chaos of the late 1590s implies that there is a widespread problem which may have a particular cause. Book VI of *The Faerie Queene* started with the fear that the inevitable lies that courtesy demands might lead to much more obvious transgressions: at the end we understand that it is almost impossible to know whether widespread chaos and the breakdown of the intellectual and social order is the result of a particular action or a general cultural shift, or whether, indeed, the distinction matters and can be identified. Once we live in such times, Spenser seems to be suggesting, when truth and lies are not clear and distinct, the damage is already done and there is no obvious way back because we cannot know what we have lost or what we can restore.

II

Spenser's anxiety emerged from a culture that placed significant emphasis on courteous speech and behaviour, but was also afraid of them, just as it both valued and feared the practice of rhetoric. Near the start of the fourth book of Castiglione's *Book of the Courtier* Fregoso Ottaviano makes a long speech extolling the merits of the true courtier and his ability to correct the vices of a modern prince who is

---

[28] Spenser, *Faerie Queene*, 6.12.40, lines 4–9, and 41.
[29] For a recent account of Spenser's representation of his quarrels see Bruce Danner, *Edmund Spenser's War on Lord Burghley* (Basingstoke: Palgrave Macmillan, 2011).

otherwise ill-served by his friends and enemies. In a passage signalled by a marginal note, 'Lies engender ignorance and self seeking', Ottaviano asserts that princes need courtiers to save them from the worst vices, 'ignoraunce and selfe seeking... the roote of these two mischeeues is nothing elles but lyinge, which vice is worthelie abhorred of God and man, and more hurtful to Princis then any other'.[30] Courtiers are needed to save princes from their friends who are more dangerous than their enemies. Beside the marginal notes to help the reader marked 'Friendes' and 'Flattery', Ottaviano claims that few close to a prince

> haue a respect to reprehende their vices so freelye as they do priuate mens: And many times to coorie fauour and to purchase good will, they giue themselues to nothinge elles but to feede them with matters that may delite, and content their minde, thoughe they be foule and dishonest. So that of friendes they beecome flatterers, & to make a hande by that streict familiaritie, they speake and woorke alwaies to please, and for the most part open the way with lyes, which in the Princis minde engender ignorance, not of outwarde matters onlie, but also of his owne selfe. And this may be said to be the greatest & fowlest lye of all other, bicause the ignorant minde deceiueth himself and inwardlie maketh lyes of himself.[31]

The courtier needs to save the prince from himself. The prince has to listen to lies which have the power to deceive him uttered by his close advisors, because they do not have enough independence to advise him properly and articulate the criticism that even the most virtuous ruler will invariably need at times. The effect of being exposed to so much deception and lying has a corrosive effect on the prince whose mind becomes divided from itself and starts to tell lies. Augustine had argued that lying to oneself was impossible, but a divided mind, if such a thing is possible, could lie to its other part.[32] Castiglione has Ottaviano represent a prince whose mind is in fragments as a result of being overwhelmed by lies, undermining the ideal that the court should represent. The prince's ignorance of how to govern properly creates a breeding ground for lies which proliferate and characterize the nature of the court, transforming it into a place of falsehood and corruption.

The problem is resolved in Pietro Bembo's long oration which concludes the *Courtier*. Bembo shows how the courtier is able to unite erotic and heavenly love through his thought and behaviour, making the Platonic republic an earthly reality. The courtier can guide the prince and so help establish the ideal state through his conduct, saving his ruler from both friends and enemies. The courtly ideal works to reform and save the court from within, as Ottaviano makes clear:

> I saye therfore that sins nowadayes Princis are so corrupt through yl vsages, ignorance & false self seekinge, and that yt is so harde a matter to geue them the knowelage of the truth and to bende them to vertue, and men with lyes and flatterie and such naughtye meanes seeke to coorie fauour wyth them, the Courtier by the meane of those honeste qualities... may soone, and ought to go about so to purchase him the good will and

---

[30] Baldesar Castiglione, *The Courtyer of Count Baldessar Castilio*, trans. Thomas Hoby (London, 1561), sig. Nn1r.
[31] Castiglione, *Courtyer*, sig. Nn1v.   [32] See above, p. 26.

allure vnto him the minde of his Prince, that he maye make him a free and safe passage
to commune with him in euery matter with out troublinge him.[33]

Only through the honesty of the courtier's arts can the prince and his court be
reformed and the truth be spoken openly. What might seem like dissimulation, the
sprezzatura of the courtier, is in fact truthfulness. Hoby's translation of this complex
word as 'recklessness' might seem particularly appropriate, an indication of the
courtier's disregard for the consequences of his actions in speaking truth to
power.[34] The verb 'reck', from Old English, means 'take care or thought for',
and Hoby's courtier, following the prescribed ideal of aristocratic carelessness,
ignores his own safety through his behaviour because he has his mind on higher
matters, the Platonic ideal of the court.[35]

A number of courtesy books appeared in English in the second half of the
sixteenth century, a sign of the widespread social desire to transform the upper
classes from the old warrior caste of the Middle Ages into sophisticated and adept
courtiers, as well as the increasing value of education and manners throughout
Europe.[36] It is an indication of the ubiquity of the language of courtesy during
Elizabeth's reign that John Awdely's *The Fraternity of Vacabondes* (1561, 1575), a
work about urban crime not courts, could contain a description of a 'courtesy man'.
A courtesy man was a child who 'can behave himself mannerly' and 'make humble
salutations and low curtsey' in order to befriend newcomers to London before
demanding money on behalf of demobbed soldiers, or to gain entry to 'hostelries or
other places' in order to steal sheets and coverlets.[37] Ideas of courtesy had passed
into popular culture, along with the anxiety that courtesy encouraged insincerity,
lying, and crime. Sir Thomas Overbury in his *Characters* placed the courtier after
the dissembler and before the golden ass and the flatterer, representing him as
someone who 'puts more confidence in his words than meaning . . . and follows
nothing but inconstancy . . . honours nothing but fortune. Loves nothings.'[38]

Courtesy books described how courtiers should speak and dress; how they
should appear in public; and how to sustain the good impression they would
make if they followed proper advice: in short, a semiotic guide to gesture, utterance,
and behaviour.[39] They also gave much more practical advice about using forks,

[33] Castiglione, *Courtyer*, sig. Nn2v–Nn3r.

[34] Peter Burke, *The Fortunes of the Courtier* (Cambridge: Polity, 1995), p. 70; Jennifer Richards,
'Assumed Simplicity and the Critique of Nobility: Or, How Castiglione Read Cicero', *RQ* 54 (2001),
460–86, pp. 461–2.

[35] *OED*, 'reck', v., 1b.

[36] Norbert Elias, *The Civilizing Process: Sociogenetic and Psychogenetic Investigations*, trans. Edmund
Jephcott (rev. edn, Oxford: Blackwell, 1994), pp. 68–70; Burke, *Fortunes of the Courtier*, pp. 139–57;
Fitzmaurice, *Humanism and America*, p. 105.

[37] John Awdely, *The Fraternity of Vacabondes* (London, 1575), sigs A3v–A4v (the first edition
survives only as a title page); Arthur F. Kinney, ed., *Rogues, Vagabonds, and Sturdy Beggars: A New
Gallery of Tudor and Early Stuart Rogue Literature Exposing the Lives, Times, and Cozening Tricks of the
Elizabethan Underworld* (Amherst: University of Massachusetts Press, 1973), pp. 94–5.

[38] Thomas Overbury, *Sir Thomas Overbury his Wife. With additions of New Characters, and many
other wittie conceits never before printed* (London, 1614), sig. E5r.

[39] Catherine Bates, *The Rhetoric of Courtship in Elizabethan Language and Literature* (Cambridge:
Cambridge University Press, 1992), p. 44; Kerrigan, *Shakespeare's Binding Language*, pp. 38–9.

blowing one's nose, using perfumes, spitting, and so on.[40] Courtiers had to be able to speak and write with eloquence and insouciance, disguising what they might really feel, be artful, entertaining and witty in conversation.[41] However, while such speech and writing required dissimulation, courtiers should never cross the line and start to tell lies. Spenser, who, as has often been noted, was no friend to the court, provided a critique of this particular fault line.[42] But his analysis only exploited what was already in the public domain.

Giovanni Della Casa's *Galateo: A Treatise of Manners and Behaviours*, was published in translation in 1576, 'a collection of precepts on how we should behave in public places', and had a major influence on later Elizabethan literature, as was acknowledged soon after its publication.[43] Gabriel Harvey, Spenser's friend and tutor, argued that both Guazzo and Galateo were 'neuer so happy' as when they were names bandied around by so many Cambridge students, and referred to Edward de Vere, seventeenth Earl of Oxford, satirically, as Galateo, in 1579, a sign of that work's currency in Spenser's circle.[44] John Lyly's *Gallathea*, one of the comedies that had such an impact on the development of Elizabethan drama, was first performed before the Queen in the early 1580s.[45] The play is surely a response to the influence of Della Casa's work in court circles, as Gallathea was the perfect woman created by the sculptor Pygmalion, a counterpart to the perfect courtier.[46]

Robert Peterson's translation was always designed to have a wide influence. It was dedicated to Robert Dudley, Earl of Leicester, the most important patron of the arts from Elizabeth's accession to his death in 1588.[47] The treatise is published in black letter, often called 'Old English', in this period the easiest font for English readers to use, which signalled the desire for wide readership rather than the elite status of roman script, a physical sign that this work on courtesy was not just for the elite, like Leicester, but more ordinary readers too.[48] The epistle to Leicester is followed by six dedicatory poems in Latin and English, clearly designed to demonstrate the interest the work had already generated.[49]

---

[40] Elias, *Civilizing Process*, pp. 109–82.

[41] Peter Burke, 'Civility', in *Tudor England: An Encyclopedia*, pp. 139–40.

[42] Andrew Zurcher, *Edmund Spenser's 'The Faerie Queene': A Reading Guide* (Edinburgh: Edinburgh University Press, 2011), p. 169; Javitch, *Poetry and Courtliness*, p. 133; Alan Sinfield, *Literature in Protestant England, 1560–1660* (New York: Barnes and Noble, 1983), pp. 39–42.

[43] Giovanni della Casa, *Galateo, or, The Rules of Polite Behaviour*, trans. M. F. Rusnak (Chicago: University of Chicago Press, 2013), introduction, p. x.

[44] Spenser, *Variorum*, X, pp. 460, 467; Nelson, *Monstrous Adversary*, pp. 225–6; Joan Simon, *Education and Society in Tudor England* (Cambridge: Cambridge University Press, 1979), p. 361.

[45] On the influence of Lyly's drama on Elizabethan culture see Bates, *Rhetoric of Courtship*, pp. 83–8; Andy Kesson, *John Lyly and Early Modern Authorship* (Manchester: Manchester University Press, 2014), pt 2.

[46] Philippa Berry, *Of Chastity and Power: Elizabethan Literature and the Unmarried Queen* (London: Routledge, 1989), p. 125.

[47] Eleanor Rosenberg, *Leicester, Patron of Letters* (New York: Columbia University Press, 1955).

[48] On the font see Stephen Galbraith, ' "English" Black-Letter Type and Spenser's *Shepheardes Calender*', *Sp. St.*, 23 (2008), 13–40.

[49] Giovanni della Casa, *Galateo of Maister John Della Casa. Or rather, a treatise of manners*, trans. Robert Peterson (London, 1576), sigs A1r–A4r.

Della Casa counsels measure and proportion in all things throughout, warning of the dangers of an imbalance of humours: 'for who so applieth himself to much, to feede other mens humors, in his familiar conuersation, and behauiour with men, is rather to be thought a Jester, a Jugler or flatterer, then a gentleman wel taught and nourtured'.[50] Rational control of the passions is paramount, and abuse of speech a serious problem that undermines social conventions and order.[51] While counselling gentlemen and courtiers in the arts of gracious behaviour, Della Casa is concerned to warn them of the perils of dissimulation and deception. Accordingly, he advises against playing games which cannot be supported by genuine substance in order to increase one's standing: 'doe they very yll, yf now & then pull out a letter out of theyr pocket, to reade it: as if they had greate matters of charge, and affaires of the common weale committed unto them'.[52]

Therefore, it is not surprising that Della Casa has a particularly fierce aversion to dreams as they invariably delude the dreamer, unsettling and disturbing the rational minds of those foolish enough to take them seriously.[53] However, he recounts one particularly instructive and morally improving dream. Della Casa tells the story of Flaminio Tomarozzo, a Roman gentleman, 'not unlearned and grosse: but full of knowledge and singular witte', who, nevertheless, is afflicted by a powerful dream. Tomarozzo imagines that he is sitting in an apothecary's shop which, for some unexplained reason, is overrun by people who either consume the drugs in the shop or destroy the containers. One small glass of water is left untouched until a tall 'aged and very graue man' surveys the wreckage until his eyes light upon the glass. He duly drinks the contents and leaves. The dreamer asks the apothecary who the man is and receives the answer, 'My sonne, this is the Lord God. And the water, that hee dranke, and all the reast refused & would not taste as you saw: was discretion: which you know wel ynough men will not taste of, by any meanes.'[54]

This is the exception that proves the rule: a dream that provides direct access to the truth and instructs the dreamer how to behave, charting a course that is constantly wary of excess, relying on discretion/reason and never surrendering to the delusive effects of the passions. The water of God is far more spiritually uplifting that all the drugs in the shop, as the wise apothecary recognizes (presumably the analogy starts to break down here as the apothecary needs to sell some drugs in order to prosper).[55] Flaminio Tomarozzo's dream is valuable precisely because it is

---

[50] Della Casa, *Galateo*, sig. B2v.   [51] Tilmouth, *Passion's Triumph*, pp. 15–36.
[52] Della Casa, *Galateo*, sigs C4v–D1r.
[53] Compare Spenser, *Faerie Queene*, 2.9.51, where the dreams of the disordered mind are represented as 'leasings, tales, and lies' (line 9). Not all Renaissance thinkers were quite so hostile to dreams: see Peter Holland, '"The Interpretation of Dreams" in the Renaissance', in Peter Brown, ed., *Reading Dreams: The Interpretation of Dreams from Chaucer to Shakespeare* (Oxford: Oxford University Press, 1999), pp. 125–46; Rona Goffen, 'Renaissance Dreams', *RQ* 40 (1987), 682–706.
[54] Della Casa, *Galateo*, sigs F1r–v.
[55] On the anxieties generated by the rise of apothecaries' shops see Patrick Wallis, 'Consumption, Retailing, and Medicine in Early-Modern London', *Ec.HR* 61 (2008), 26–53. An apothecary's shop is represented in this manner in Middleton and Dekker's *The Roaring Girl* (*c*.1611), scene 3 (James Knowles, ed., *The Roaring Girl and Other City Comedies* (Oxford: Oxford University Press, 2001), pp. 239–49). Apothecaries' shops were well established in Florence, which had a strong economy based

not really a dream, as it resembles 'the Cogitations & thoughts of an awakened minde... the virtue sensitive: then the visions and syghts of a drowsie head' and Della Casa does not deny that 'the dreames of good men and learned, be better then theirs of the wicked and more unlearned sorte'.[56]

More often, however, dreams should not be trusted because they are like lies:

> There can bee nothing in the worlde more vaine then Dreames: ye there is one thing more light then they, and that are *Lyes. For there is yet some shadowe, and, as it were, a certaine feeling of that which a man hath seene in his dreame. But there is neyther shoadowe nor bodye of a trueth in a lye.* And therefore we should lesse busie mens eares, and their minds to harken to lyes, then to dreames, because they bee otherwhile receiued for truethes. (Emphasis in original)[57]

In the end lies are always uncovered and no one listens to liars. So why do people indulge in this high-risk and ultimately futile practice?

> You shal understand, ther be many that use to lye, not minding any yll purpose in it, or to make their owne peculiar profit by it, to hurt other men or shame their neighbour: onely they doe it, for a pleasure they take to tell a lye: as men that drinke not, all for thirst: but for a pleasure they take, to taste of the wine. Other some doe tell lyes, to make a vaine glorious boasting of them selues: vaunting and telling in a brauery, what wonderfull exploits they haue done, or bearing men in hand, they be great doctors and learned men.[58]

Della Casa moves swiftly from dreams to lies, delusive elements of human existence that have to be shunned. It soon becomes clear that Flaminio Tomarozzo's dream in the apothecary's shop assumes a central importance in Della Casa's thinking. The dream is a fantasy of an unconscious experience that can be rendered perfectly visible and transparent, preventing the need for the sort of hard work that is required in becoming a successful courtier, able to disguise the extensive labours that enable the appearance of insouciant ease. Della Casa's analysis of lying follows naturally from Tomarozzo's dream. He is eager to assert that lying is easy to detect, uncover, and decode because not only are lies generally obvious enough but the motives for them are equally facile, unsophisticated, and unworthy of the serious courtier. According to Della Casa, men lie because they enjoy it—a category that Augustine recognized—and so continue to lie even though they know that there is no hope of their escaping the consequences.[59] Or they lie because they cannot resist boasting in order to provide themselves with short-term advantages; again, either because they are too foolish to realize the consequences or simply because they cannot control their baser passions.

on guilds, when Della Casa (1503–6) was writing: John M. Najemy, *A History of Florence, 1200–1575* (Oxford: Blackwell, 2006), pp. 39–44.

[56] Della Casa, *Galateo*, sigs F1v–F2r.
[57] Della Casa, *Galateo*, sig. F2r; Monseignor Della Casa, *Galateo* (Milan: Rizzoli, 1950), p. 35.
[58] Della Casa, *Galateo*, sigs F2r–v; Monseignor Della Casa, *Galateo*, p. 35.
[59] On Augustine, see above, p. 29. See also Snyder, *Dissimulation*, p. 34.

Della Casa has provided a satisfyingly straightforward and logical analysis of lying. Lying is doomed to failure because truth always triumphs—eventually. Therefore liars are like the deranged people in the dream of the apothecary shop, their wills overcome by passion, unable to help themselves, the goal of short-term pleasure obliterating any sensible calculation about the longer term. Della Casa draws an implicit contrast between their ugliness and the grace and beauty of the accomplished courtier. This analysis has many obvious advantages, not least that it enables Della Casa to make an absolute distinction between the civilized and admirable behaviour of the courtier and the irrational and base behaviour of the liar, a pointed contrast to the confusing world of *The Faerie Queene*, Book VI. Instead of a rather messy and anxious division between one form of dissimulation that is valuable and another that has to be condemned, we have an absolute distinction between good and evil that makes choices easy, and difficult moral and intellectual judgements far less daunting than they really are. As Jon Snyder has pointed out, *Galateo*'s arguments are based on an 'often problematic . . . relationship between etiquette and ethics', and the reluctant understanding that 'self-improvement was not necessarily ethical improvement'.[60] Accordingly, strategies of argument are adopted—analogical, metaphorical, rhetorical—which suggest that telling the truth and practices of lying can be distinguished without immense difficulty. Della Casa works hard to achieve this illusion, but his text cannot disguise the problematic nature of this division, and the anxiety that courtiers and liars may not be as far apart as he would like them to be is everywhere apparent.

Galateo clearly does not function as an advice book for aspiring courtiers, or those wishing to understand the modes of behaviour that operate in European courts, by providing strict and careful definitions that can easily be recognized and imitated or avoided. Rather, it establishes a series of dichotomies—between gracious and ungracious behaviour, between the control of the will and the licence of appetite, and between truth and lying—making it clear which is the correct choice and mode of living. Della Casa's treatise outlines a semiotics of courtly and anti-courtly behaviour, which means that the author does not limit his understanding of lying to the verbal: 'In Silence too, after a sorte, without speache, a man may tell a lesynge: I meane with his gestures and grace[.]'[61] Hence walking and deportment can function as types of lies. Men 'being of meane, or rather base condition and calling, use suche a solemnitie in all their doings, and marche so stately, and speake with suche a prerogatiue . . . proudly prying about them like Peacockes: that it is a very death to behold them'.[62] Again, Della Casa is making the distinction between right and wrong rather too straightforward: the gestures represented here are ridiculous, easy to laugh at, and self-evidently false, in pointed contrast to the carefully disguised and controlled gestures of the courtier.

Such taxonomies of lying were always open to parody. In *As You Like It* Shakespeare has Touchstone recount how he chose to fight for Audrey's honour on the 'seventh cause', 'a lie seven times removed'. Shakespeare's satire of well-known

---

[60] Snyder, *Dissimulation*, p. 33; Carroll, *Blood and Violence*, p. 309.
[61] Della Casa, *Galateo*, sig. F2v.   [62] Della Casa, *Galateo*, sig. F2v.

taxonomies of lying in duelling manuals involves the fool arguing that a quarrel over the cut of a courtier's beard involved the 'Countercheck Quarrelsome', a basic public insult accusing the speaker of lying.[63] Touchstone further explains that the disputants get no further than the 'Lie Circumstantial' and do not reach the 'Lie Direct' as they 'measured swords and parted', indulging in elaborate and aggressive behaviour that leads to no resolution.[64] Readers of Jones's *Booke of Honor* or *Sauiolo His Practise* would have understood that Touchstone and his opponent do not get anywhere near meeting the precise level of insult required to justify a duel, as no specific allegation is made.[65] Touchstone is surely misrepresenting his behaviour in a manner that undermines his indignant assertion of his right to be treated as a gentleman.

This fault line, a belief that distinguishing right and wrong is a relatively straightforward issue, is exposed in Della Casa's extensive discussion of ceremonies. Della Casa acknowledges that it is the duty of a courtier to experience and participate in a number of ceremonies, which will structure life at the court in most countries. By ceremonies, Della Casa specifically means rules of polite speech which inevitably require circumlocution and he is consciously and conspicuously blunt about their function:

> [I]t is a deadly paine to here them, & specialy if they be men, in the Judgement of the world, of good understanding and wisdom. What a fetching about is this, ere they come to the matter? *Sir I beseche you pardon mee, if I doe not say well. I will speake like a gros man as I am: & grosly according to my pore skil. And Sir, I am sure you will but mocke me for it. But yet, to obey you.* (Emphasis in original)[66]

This might seem to be a relatively trivial point that can be adjusted through an application of the sensible control of the will, but the implications of excessive speech are related in Della Casa's mind to more substantial issues: '*Ceremonies*, I saye (in my Judgement,) differ not much from lyes & dreames, for their own very vainesse it selfe.'[67] As in *The Faerie Queene*, what might seem insignificant is carefully related to matters of great importance as abuses of speech are shown to have serious consequences. Della Casa provides a brief history of such court ceremonies, which he argues were imported into secular life from the Church where proper religious ceremonies took place, 'after, men did begyn, to reuerence eche other with curious entertaynements, more then were conuenient, and would be called masters and Lords, amongst them selues, yealding bending and bowing their bodyes, in token of reuerence one to another, uncouering their heads, using high titles and Styles of honour, and kissing their hands as if they were holye

[63] Jones, *Booke of Honor*, pp. 5–12. Jones's book is a compilation of other works on duelling.
[64] William Shakespeare, *As You Like It*, ed. Agnes Latham (London: Methuen, 1975), V.iv.67–86; Kerrigan, *Shakespeare's Binding Language*, pp. 219–20. I owe this Shakespeare reference to Bill McEvoy.
[65] Jones, *Booke of Honor*, pp. 8–9; Vincento Saviolo, *Vincentio Sauiolo His Practise In Two Bookes* (London, 1595), sigs R3r–X1r.
[66] Della Casa, *Galateo*, sig. F4r; Monseignor Della Casa, *Galateo*, p. 43.
[67] Della Casa, *Galateo*, sigs F4v–G1r.

things'.[68] Excessive courtly behaviour does more than risk insincerity and mark the overenthusiastic courtier as a buffoon who is trying too hard to display *sprezzatura*, like the ridiculous Osric in *Hamlet*, who is still a 'boor' however hard he 'plays the courtier'.[69] It risks the sin of idolatry, possibly even blasphemy, contempt for God, which Aquinas argued was worse than murder.[70] For readers of *Galateo* in Protestant England the connection between a court culture that appropriated religious language and the perversion of the true faith would have been obvious enough. Adopting religious forms, gestures, and language for everyday behaviour undermined both the secular and the sacred. For Reformers the relationship between inappropriate images and behaviour was clear, as the traditional belief that an appeal to the senses, in particular sight and hearing, dangerously obscured proper devotion.[71]

The adoption of ceremonies at court, therefore, introduced the serious possibility of undermining appropriate religious belief, obscuring the truth and making the courtier a liar. The true courtier, according to Della Casa, must not be afraid to speak truth to power and must not indulge in the tempting vice of flattery in order to secure self-advancement. Insincere courtiers who fail to control their speech and actions will commit grave political as well as religious crimes. Della Casa explicitly links lying, the adoption of ceremonies in court life, and treason: 'Then not *Lesinges* alone, but also *Treacheries* and *Treasons*, shalbe called *Ceremonies*.'[72] He acknowledges that most treason was usually a crime of words rather than actual deeds, whether real or imagined, an insight that links him, once again, to Spenser. Lying is the transgression that connects these serious crimes, the failure of the individual to tell the truth having more serious effects than the petty liar who adopts ceremonies realizes: 'So that wee are to noate, that *Ceremonies* are used, eyther for a *Profit*, or for a *Vanitie*, or for a *Duetie*. And euery lye that is told for a mans priuate profit: is a deceite, a sinne, and a dishonest parte: for, in what so euer it bee, *A man can neuer honestly lye*.'[73] The warning to the courtier is stark but, in the end, only he or she can really know if they are telling lies. Ceremonies encourage dishonesty and are inherently duplicitous but a foolish courtier oblivious to the implications of the habits and practices of the court may not actually be lying. In reality, this is an unlikely scenario, and the converse is the usual case: ambitious courtiers will inevitably tell lies. Men on the make are generally self-interested but pretend not to be, so that, accordingly, they must lie all the time. There is a serious warning in the statement '*A man can neuer honestly lie*', which implies that men who put themselves in situations where lying is endemic, such as the court, will become liars if they are not already practised in the dark art. From this base their sins will grow

---

[68] Della Casa, *Galateo*, sig. G1r.
[69] William Shakespeare, *Hamlet*, ed. Harold Jenkins (London: Routledge, 1982), V.ii.81–180; Margreta de Grazia, Hamlet *Without Hamlet* (Cambridge: Cambridge University Press, 2007), p. 34.
[70] *Christian Church*, pp. 215–16; *Summa Theologica*, Qu. 13, Art. 4, Reply Obj. 1 (III, p. 1226).
[71] Matthew Milner, *The Senses and the English Reformation* (Farnham: Ashgate, 2013), p. 4; Hunt, *Art of Hearing*, pp. 21, 24; Stuart Clark, *Vanities of the Eye: Vision in Early Modern European Culture* (Oxford: Oxford University Press, 2007), pp. 161–203. See also Heal, *Reformation*, pp. 262–70; Eire, *War Against the Idols*, pp. 280–1.
[72] Della Casa, *Galateo*, sig. G1v.   [73] Della Casa, *Galateo*, sig. G2v.

and become ever more serious, their flatteries and self-interest leading to idolatry and treason.

Galateo is not what it seems to be. It is less a manual advising the courtier how to behave, like *The Book of the Courtier*, than a series of stern warnings of what to avoid, a work of court literature that is sceptical about the value of court life as it stands and is eager to inspire root-and-branch reform. The problem with the court is that it is a place where lies are not merely encouraged but are enshrined in the very practices that make the court the centre of political and cultural life. Della Casa writes as an insider and asserts that 'our speache must be plaine'.[74] *Galateo* contains a long disquisition on the nature and practice of language which is as austere and demanding as that of many Reformers who demanded that the Bible be translated into the language of the common man:

> [T]he words you shall vse, must haue no double vnderstanding, but simple. For by coupling suche words together: wee frame that speache that is called *Aenigma*...
>
> Againe, our words would be, (as nere as they might be) aptly and properly applied to that thing we go about to deliuer, & as little as may be, common to other matters: for, in so doing, a man shall weene, the matter it selfe is openly laide before hym: & that it is not expressed with words, but pointed foorthe with the finger.[75]

Della Casa stands in contrast to Giovanni Battista Nenna, author of an influential treatise on nobility which emerged out of the same intellectual milieu as *Galateo*, who argues that the upper classes must not 'follow the lying opinion of the rude vulgar sorte, which for the most part, doe fall into great errors'.[76] Instead, Della Casa suggests that words and things should coincide as closely as possible, qualifying his principle with 'as nere as they might be', a desire to return to a purer form of speech that is cleansed of duplicity. Language should be able to express what is meant without fear of ambiguity, the counterpart to the perceived need to cleanse the court of its pernicious habitual lying. Accordingly, misleading figures of speech, which come under the umbrella term '*Aenigma*', or 'Gergo', 'a very doubtfull manner of speache, as it were in Riddles: and very ambiguous' defined in a marginal note, need to be avoided.[77] '*Aenigma*' is for Della Casa what 'Hyperbole' is for Puttenham.[78] The reference to pointing forth with the finger further expresses a desire to remove misleading and ambiguous gestures from communication, reducing shades of meaning to a single direction. The pointing finger is the manicule, the most common symbol inserted into the margins of printed books.[79] Here it

[74] Della Casa, *Galateo*, sig. L2v.
[75] Della Casa, *Galateo*, sigs L2v–L3r; Monseignor Della Casa, *Galateo*, pp. 66–7. David Norton, *A History of the Bible as Literature, Volume 1: From Antiquity to 1700* (Cambridge: Cambridge University Press, 1993), p. 94.
[76] Giovanni Battista Nenna, *Nennio, or A Treatise of Nobility Wherein is Discoursed What True Nobilitie is, with such qualities as are required in a perfect gentleman*, trans. William Jones (London, 1595), p. 34. On the context see Rudolph M. Bell, *How to Do It: Guides to Good Living for Renaissance Italians* (Chicago: University of Chicago Press, 2000), p. 282.
[77] Della Casa, *Galateo*, sig. L2v. [78] See above, pp. 190–1.
[79] William H. Sherman, 'Toward a History of the Manicule', in *Used Books: Marking Readers in Renaissance England* (Philadelphia: University of Pennsylvania Press, 2010), pp. 25–52.

signifies the stability of truthfulness in courtly language, a desire that words should refer to things with no fear of ambiguity.

III

In 1566 writing to his twelve-year-old son, Philip, a pupil at Shrewsbury School, Sir Henry Sidney gave him a considered piece of fatherly advice. Along with many other things, Sir Henry suggested that his son read carefully and learn from what he was reading, so he could 'enrich [his] tongue with words, and [his] wit with matter', enabling his judgement to grow as he matured.[80] Philip should learn how to obey others in order to understand how to make people obey him when he grew up. Sir Henry exhorted his son to 'Be courteous of gesture, and affable to all men, with diversity of reverence, according to the dignity of person', advice that could have come from *Galateo* or another courtesy manual.[81] Sir Henry returned to the subject of language towards the end of the letter:

> Think upon every word that you will speak, before you utter it, and remember how nature hath rampired up (as it were) the tongue with teeth, lips, yea and hair without lips, and all betokening reins, or bridles, for the loose use of that member. Above all things tell no untruth, no not in trifles. The custom of it is naughty, and let it not satisfy you, that, for a time, the hearers take it for a truth; for after it will be known as it is, to your shame; for there cannot be a greater reproach to a gentleman, than to be accounted a liar.[82]

Philip is advised to understand and control his language, balancing his mental and physical attributes in order to regulate both his speech and gestures. Sir Henry roots his analysis in his son's body reminding him that he has to consider the organs that produce speech—tongue, teeth, and lips, as well as his facial hair (although this is probably an affectionate joke, given Philip's age and the rather overbearing nature of the letter, and may also be a family joke as Philip remained beardless for a relatively long time)—along with his mental faculties.[83] Throughout his letter Sir Henry stresses the need for regulation and moderation, steering between two extremes through the exercise of considered judgement and reason. Philip is urged to excise unruly elements within his character and body so that everything that makes him what he is can be understood and utilized to his greatest advantage, establishing him as an exemplary citizen ready to take his place in the natural and

---

[80] Sir Henry Sidney to Sir Philip Sidney, 1566, reprinted in Vicesimus Knox, ed., *Elegant Epistles: Being a Copious Collection of Familiar and Amusing Letters* (Dublin, 1790), pp. 204–5, at p. 204. See also G. W. Fisher, *Annals of Shrewsbury School* (London: Methuen, 1899), p. 10. I am grateful to Dr Angela Andreani for this reference.

[81] Knox, ed., *Elegant Epistles*, p. 204.   [82] Knox, ed., *Elegant Epistles*, p. 205.

[83] Sir Henry's joke is aided by the fact that puberty was much longer in the Elizabethan period and facial hair grew later than it does now: Paul Griffiths, *Youth and Authority: Formative Experiences in England, 1560–1640* (Oxford: Clarendon Press, 1996), p. 121; Herbert Moller, 'The Accelerated Development of Youth: Beard Growth as a Biological Marker', *CSSH* 29 (1987), 748–62; Stewart, *Sidney*, p. 262.

social order and so serve the state as best as he can.[84] Sir Henry sees lying as the most serious transgression of these values because it will diminish his son's reputation and honour, limiting his ability to carry out his duties as a gentleman and a courtier. Liars may be able to succeed in the short term, hence the superficial appeal of lying as a strategy. In the longer term, however, lying will always be exposed and will do the liar far more damage than credit. Accordingly, Sir Henry, dispensing advice that corresponds nicely with the conclusions of Della Casa and Spenser, warns his son never to tell lies, not even tiny ones, for fear that these will return to haunt him and that he will start to imagine that telling lies may be acceptable. Sir Henry is making a strong link between courtesy and lying, articulating the fear that social conventions of politeness and good manners will dictate that apparently trivial lies can be tolerated, which will prevent the liar from changing his habits and so he will develop into a fully fledged liar. Philip is to 'Study and endeavour . . . to be virtuously occupied' so that he shall 'make such a habit of well doing' that he 'shall not know how to do evil, though [he] would'.[85] The key word is 'habit', which refers to 'custome' a few sentences earlier, the fear that in the battle between good and evil, it is the everyday practices that will do most harm as they will not be stopped because they fall beneath everyone's radar, and eventually, like little lies, develop into serious problems. Courtesy is both a blessing and a curse, on the one hand helping to provide the means of control, but on the other providing the means of insincerity which can unbalance and destroy the whole edifice, which is why lying is the central fear of the father, and why he has to urge his son to police himself so carefully.

George Pettie's translation of Stefano Guazzo's *Ciuile Conuersation* (1581) articulates similar fears about the relationship between courtesy and lies. When the subject turns to lying, William Guazzo, the author's brother who is using conversation with friends to cure him of his melancholy, states: 'I cannot for my part away with the company of those other lyars, which at no time tell trueth, though it turne not to the hurt of any.'[86] Even apparently harmless lying cannot be countenanced because, at best, it wastes precious time. One of the great strengths of Pettie's translation is the reproduction of Guazzo's language in 'the robust vigour and earthy flavor of the common speech', so making ideas about courtesy relevant to the everyday (as the example of the 'courtesy man' demonstrates).[87] Guazzo's

---

[84] Arthur B. Ferguson, *The Articulate Citizen and the English Renaissance* (Durham, NC: Duke University Press, 1965), pp. 133–61.

[85] Knox, ed., *Elegant Epistles*, p. 205.

[86] Stefano Guazzo, *The Ciuile Conuersation*, trans. George Pettie (London, 1581), sig. F2r. On William Guazzo see Jennifer Richards, 'Health, Intoxication, and Civil Conversation in Renaissance England', in Phil Withington and Angela McShane, eds, *Cultures of Intoxication: P. & P. Supplement* 9 (2014), 168–86, p. 181.

[87] John Leon Lievsay, *Stefano Guazzo and the English Renaissance, 1575–1675* (Chapel Hill: University of North Carolina Press, 1961), p. 71. On Pettie as translator see also Jason Lawrence, *'Who the devil taught thee so much Italian?': Italian Language Learning and Literary Imitation in Early Modern England* (Manchester: Manchester University Press, 2005), p. 44.

interlocutor in the dialogue, Annibale Magnocavelli, his friend and neighbour, provides a list of the types of liars that are commonly encountered:

> We haue now to speake of lyers, who swarue from the trueth, ... And first and formost, lyars are flatterers, dissemblers, boasters, & vaine glorious, neuer ceassing to set foorth their owne praises, enterlacing lyes amongest them: a fault though not great, yet which greatly misliketh vs. For there is nothing spites vs more, then to heare a man commend himselfe.[88]

Guazzo provides a demotic overview of the modes of lying in early modern England, again suggesting that lying starts in humble ways and then becomes more serious and dangerous. Boasting is a clear affront to courteous forms of behaviour and is a type of lying because, like hyperbole, it exaggerates and so distorts—or swerves from—the truth. Looked at another way, however, and it might be described as the opposite of *sprezzatura*, the disguise of what one really means or does, which Hoby astutely rendered as recklessness.[89] Whichever way the courtier turns, lying is sure to follow, making a mockery of attempts to condemn liars as those who undermine the values of courtesy, an insight common to Spenser and the 'courtesy man'.

In order to escape from this impasse Annibale resorts to a commonplace, which is highlighted in the text: '* And therfore wise men ought to print in their heart the saying of *Pithagoras*, who being demaunded when men did any thing which might make them like to God: answered, when they tell the trueth. *'[90] Truthfulness is next to Godliness, as in the opening book of *The Faerie Queene*, whereas Satan is the father of lies.[91] Guazzo is, yet again, making the connection between small transgressions and large ones, the former inevitably leading to the latter. He also links justice and truth through a familiar image: 'iustice resembled a pure virgin, for that the puritie therof is spotted by leasings', which not only makes the connection between courtly vices, lying, and crimes of language—slander, defamation, perjury—but also prefigures the narrative trajectory in *The Faerie Queene* where the failure of justice leads to the confusion of courtesy and, eventually, the inability to tell truth and lies apart.[92] Guazzo points the finger at the courtier whose lies are more culpable than those of poor people needing to survive: 'though lying bee unseemely for euery man, yet is it more tolerable in one of base calling, and who is driven thereto of necessitie : And therefore in holy Scripture, a ryche man being a lyar is greatly reproued.'[93] The courtesy man shadows the courtier. Lying is a perennial problem when people do not have enough to survive easily, which is why telling the truth in the upper circles of society is so vital. Not only must courtiers

---

[88] Guazzo, *Ciuile Conuersation*, sig. F1v. On lying and flattery see also Bullein, *Pestilence*, p. 1.

[89] Skinner, *Visions of Politics*, I, p. 181.

[90] Guazzo, *Ciuile Conuersation*, sigs F2r–v. On Pythagoras's words see Giovanni Santinello, *Models of the History of Philosophy: From its Origins in the Renaissance to the 'Historia Philosophica'* (Dordrecht: Kluwer, 1993), p. 151.

[91] Douglas Brooks-Davies, *Spenser's Faerie Queene: A Critical Commentary on Books I and II* (Manchester: Manchester University Press, 1977), pp. 9–10.

[92] Hadfield, *Spenser's Irish Experience*, ch. 5.

[93] Guazzo, *Ciuile Conuersation*, sig. F2v.

establish themselves as paragons of virtue to inspire everyone else beneath them on the social ladder but they must ensure that the virgin of Justice remains spotless.

Annibale reproduces another commonplace, this time in rhyme, to repeat a version of the familiar message that lying will always hurt the known liar most:

> *The Liar neuer is beleeued, although an oth he take,*
> *The honest euer is beleeued, although a lye he make.*[94]

It is a commonplace that Angelo ruthlessly exploits in *Measure for Measure* when he threatens Isabella.[95] Guazzo's source is Dante's discussion of truths that look like lies in the *Inferno* and the need to avoid being contaminated by such compromised speech and writing in order to be able to make a clear distinction between the two:

> Sempre a quell ver c'ha faccia di menzonga
> de l'uom chiuder le labra fin ch'el puote,
> però che sanza colpa fa vergogna[.]
>
> A man should always close his lips, as far as he can, to the truth that has the face of a lie, since without fault it brings him shame[.][96]

Having used this reference to make the connection between lying and injustice, Guazzo introduces the binding nature of the oath. Liars cannot make these public promises because their protestations of innocence will never be believed and they have fatally undermined the fundamental element that binds society together, which was the point that Sir Henry Sidney made to young Philip. But, conversely, the man with a long-standing reputation for honesty can get away with a lie.[97] The couplet is delicately balanced between a plea for honesty and truthfulness and a Machiavellian understanding of realpolitik, knowing when it is possible to deceive the people like a fox and tell lies because your reputation will disguise the transgression.[98]

Annibale agrees that at times it is commendable to tell lies if they are 'to some honest ende'.[99] William Guazzo then tells a story to support Annibale's point:

> There commeth to my mind, touching these kindes of lyes, a pleasant example, happened in the Court, where I knewe a Princes sonne, being about twelue yeeres old, who in behauiour and good conditions surpassed al other his equals in the Court, but hee had one childishe fault, which neither by admonishing, neither by reprehending, neither by threatning, hee coulde bee made to leaue. Which was this, Hee woulde through negligence suffer his nose alwaies to be sneueled, & tooke no care to wype it: while his gouerner tooke paines to amend this fault, there commeth on a time to this

[94] Guazzo, *Ciuile Conuersation*, sig. F3r.

[95] On the use of commonplaces in the play see Darryl J. Gless, *Measure for Measure, the Law and the Convent* (Princeton: Princeton University Press, 1979), pp. 212, 227.

[96] Dante, *Inferno*, trans., John D. Sinclair (Oxford: Oxford University Press, 1961), Cano 16, 124–6 (pp. 210–11); Jackson Campbell Boswell, *Dante's Fame in England: References in Printed British Books, 1477–1640* (Newark: University of Delaware Press, 1999), p. 62.

[97] Anglo, *Machiavelli*, p. 604.

[98] Niccolò Machiavelli, *The Prince*, ed. Quentin Skinner and Russell Price (Cambridge: Cambridge University Press, 1988), pp. 61–3.

[99] Guazzo, *Ciuile Conuersation*, sig. F3r.

child, to craue his deuotion, a poore old man, whose nose by some infirmitie was become meruellous great, deformed, ful of pimples, precious, & monstrous: the childe with a certain feare mixed with compassion, was much mooued at it, whervpon his discrete gouernour began to say vnto him, that hee had knowne that poore man a long time, and remembred hee had seene him in his youth with a little nose, well fashioned and sound, but that afterwarde the sneuil and filth for want of wyping and making it cleane had brought it into that case. The childe was put into such a feare by these words, that hee began foorthwith to spit, and to blowe and wype his nose in such sort, that hee neuer after needed to bee put in minde of it. And therefore this lye was profitable to the Prince, and commendable for the gouernour.[100]

The story creates a significant narrative crux in *The Ciuile Conuersation*, leading the conversation away from a subject of intense seriousness which threatens to undermine the assumptions behind a work on the benefits of civility and courtiership, certainly one that would not have helped relieve William Guazzo's melancholy. Annibale therefore provides his companion with an opportunity which he immediately seizes, suggesting that he is well on the way to recovery. Discussions of lying are central to works on courtesy but they always run the risk of undermining the subject, prising apart the delicate balancing act that courtesy requires and introducing a moral discourse of extremes at odds with the studied ambiguity that the courtier needs to understand. The story is an act of courtesy, demonstrating what is being argued, and leading the subject back to a productive area. William Guazzo makes a clear distinction between lies that help people and lies that cause harm, taking the side of Jerome rather than Augustine. The governor is able to correct a small fault in the prince and so restore him as an accomplished young man of great potential, correcting his tiny flaw, a pointed contrast to the corrosive nature of telling small untruths which will eventually lead to large, disfiguring lies. In eliminating a small but significant fault the governor justifies his position at court. As Norbert Elias has pointed out, blowing one's nose in a discrete fashion was one of the main indicators of the civilizing process, the type of detail that a prince would have to learn if he wished to command respect when in a position of authority.[101] The story shows a court in proper order, able to sort out minor problems in a sensible way and understanding the difference between different types and levels of lying.

But this is a reading that takes the text at face value. Looked at another way, the story helps to paper over the cracks and disguise the very real dangers that lying poses. We see a court in which results are achieved through telling lies and which, therefore, may be based on dissimulation and lying. It has been argued that the Italian Wars (1494–1559) 'shattered the system of city-states that had long maintained a balance of power on the peninsula, replacing it by and large with the Old Regime patchwork of absolutist states', suggesting that the art of the courtier developed as part of a wider political transformation of the Italian peninsula.[102] The story of the prince's nose recounts a lie told for 'some honest ende' that works

---

[100] Guazzo, *Ciuile Conuersation*, sig. F3r.   [101] Elias, *Civilizing Process*, pp. 121–9.
[102] Snyder, *Dissimulation*, p. 68.

as its author intended, causes no harm, and leads to future benefits for the whole court. This is, of course, true of some lies and every reader can think of examples. However, such well-intentioned lies do not always work out as well as this story, and Annibale's response returns us to a more ambiguous understanding of the nature of lying:

> It is very true: and as suche lyars are to bee praised, so the other are to bee blamed, and to bee registred amongst those which are neither to bee desired nor auoided. Besides, there are certain curious felowes to be discommended, which trouble euerie one in vsing alwaies this worde *Wherfore*, being desirous to enter too farre into other mens matters, which is perchaunce a fault greater then it is taken for: for there is neuer any curious person, but hee is likewise malicious, and besides, ouer talkatiue, playing the tale bearer from one to another, and therefore the Poet blameth him which is inquisitiue of that hee hath nothing to doe withall.[103]

Annibale's words show how the conversation has moved on but also registers the unease that the subject of lying generates. Lying, as they both accept, can be beneficial, but the practice has also to be blamed in other circumstances, especially when produced by liars with rather less wholesome intentions. In the next sentence he changes the subject and moves sideways, through the use of 'Besides', onto the problem of excessive inquisitiveness and the telling of tales, a related fault of the tongue. The second sentence reproduced here makes a significant connection between those who habitually use the word '*Wherfore*', seeking explanations for things which may not be appropriate, and liars, both sins of the tongue.[104] While the latter are now represented as not as bad as they were a few paragraphs ago, liars being 'neither to bee desired nor auoided', the former are connected to the most serious crimes. In stating that 'there is neuer any curious person, but hee is likewise malicious', those who seek to know what they cannot in order to tell tales speak with malign intentions that constitute treason and other grave actions against the security of the state.[105]

Although it seems to have been sidestepped here, it is inevitable that the fear of lying will return to haunt the discussion, and later Annibale has to admit that courts are full of liars who threaten their integrity: 'Courtiers remained a byword for corruption.'[106] Annibale resorts to yet another commonplace to ground his analysis:

> [W]herevppon it is sayd,
> *Of surly seruantes, euery court is full.*

> That vyce is accompanyed wyth lying (a thynge of all others moste seruile) framing themselues neuer to tell the trueth to their maysters, nor perchaunce to theyr ghostly fathers[.][107]

The pun on servile/surly, a more pointed contrast in early modern English than now, is exploited to encapsulate the contemptible nature of the self-interested

---

[103] Guazzo, *Ciuile Conuersation*, sigs F3r–F3v.   [104] See Cressy, *Dangerous Talk*, ch. 1.
[105] Baldwin Smith, 'English Treason Trials', p. 474; Bellamy, *Treason*, pp. 33–4.
[106] Anglo, *Machiavelli*, pp. 588–9.   [107] Guazzo, *Ciuile Conuersation*, sig. Gg2r–Gg2v.

courtier, who is simultaneously haughty and arrogant and constantly flattering his masters.[108] The courtier lies by disguising his true feelings and motivations, his desire for self-advancement, sense of self-worth and entitlement, and in exaggerating the merits of his prince in order to achieve his goals. The court is designed to bring out the worst in ambitious people, as there are no checks and balances to control the desires of the individual who is therefore encouraged to lie in order to get as far up the greasy pole as possible.

Guazzo's analysis, which warns the courtier of the dangers of courtly behaviour as well as showing the would-be courtier how to behave at court, is taken further still by Lodowick Bryskett. Bryskett (c.1546–1609/12) was the son of a merchant from Genoa who had settled in England. He acted as Philip Sidney's tutor and accompanied him on his grand tour (1572–4), and had a career in the Irish civil service, acquiring land in Ireland, like his friend Edmund Spenser.[109] Bryskett's most significant literary work, *A Discourse of Civil Life*, an adapted translation of Giambattista Giraldi Cinthio's *Tre dialoghi della vita civile* (1565), was not published until late in his life (1605). However, the discussion between the assembled company of soldiers, courtiers, and Dublin citizens in a Dublin suburb shows that the work had its origins in the early 1580s, and it contains one of the earliest references to *The Faerie Queene*, then circulating in manuscript. Bryskett, therefore, provides a neat link between Sidney and Spenser, which suggests that the comments on the relationship between courtesy and lying in the *Discourse* emerge from the same intellectual milieu as those in Sir Henry Sidney's letter to his son and those in *The Faerie Queene*.

Like other writers on courtesy Bryskett is especially eager to counter the dangers of flattery. Aristotle provides the philosophical underpinning of the argument, his words expanded into an elaborate metaphor:

> These, who (as Aristotle saith) bend all their wits to euill, with continuall lying and soothing, make yong men beleeue that they are excellent in all things aboue course of nature; whereunto they (simple) giuing a readier eare then they should, become so blind and foolish, that they discerne not their owne good: but pricked forward with those false praises, apply themselues to that onely which is pleasant and delightfull, and become a prey vnto their flatterers, who like Parasites affirme all that they heare their master say, and denie whatsoeuer he denieth.[110]

Flattery is the vice which derails the court's claim to ethical substance and superiority to the rest of society, and Bryskett provides stern warnings of princes who have been deceived by 'lying companions' and urges them to beware of the 'deceit

[108] *OED*, surly, *adj.*, 2a.
[109] On Bryskett's life see the *ODNB* entry; Henry R. Plomer and Tom Peete Cross, *The Life and Correspondence of Lodowick Bryskett* (Illinois: University of Illinois Press, 1927); Hadfield, *Spenser: A Life*, pp. 186–9, *passim*.
[110] Lodowick Bryskett, *A Discourse of Ciuill Life containing the ethike part of morall philosophie. Fit for the instructing of a gentleman in the course of a vertuous life* (London, 1606), sig. O4v; Jane S. Zembaty, 'Aristotle on Lying', *JHP* 31 (1993), 7–29, pp. 10–11.

of flatterers'.[111] Encouraging young men to believe that they are better than they really are has the disastrous effect of eliminating the possibility of self-criticism and so fostering uncontrollable pride which impedes the possibility of good government: false civility destroys the civil order. Bryskett is referring to Aristotle's strictures on boasting and its pernicious consequences in *The Nicomachean Ethics*, a vice he carefully links to lying, as George Pettie does, in order to distinguish the relatively benign boaster who sings his own praises and the much more dangerous figure who boasts to gain advantage, 'as one man is a liar because he enjoys the lie itself, and other because he desires reputation or gain'.[112] A courtly culture of boasting and flattery ('lying and soothing') will have a terrible impact on the society that the court is supposed to govern, because there will be no possibility of fair and sensible criticism.[113] The courtiers are (almost) as much victims as everyone else because they are unable to 'discern their own good', as lies 'are ordinarily harmful to other individuals and the *polis*'.[114] In Aristotelian terms Bryskett represents a society that has lost control of the mean, the vital position for both ethical and political philosophy, and so will veer towards undesirable and unstable extremes.[115]

Bryskett's *Discourse*, like Spenser's *Faerie Queene*, is structured around a contrast between the court and military life, a dichotomy that shows the latter to be more obviously related to cardinal virtues than the former. Bryskett delivers a long speech to the assembled company which ends by concluding that lying is the worse vice as it undermines the principles of government, because 'he which respected not truth in matters of moment, destroyed as much, as in him lay, the societie and ciuill conuersation of men, since no man can trust or beware of a lyer'.[116] It is important to instil a respect for the value of truth in young children: 'as Plutarch reporteth ... all iniuries and wickednes proceeded from a lyer'.[117] Bryskett is referring to Plutarch's *Moralia*, a translation of which was published by Philemon Holland (1603), already well known for his translation of Livy: 'children ought to be inured from their very infancie in one thing which is most holy and beseeming religious education, and that is, to speake the truth: For surely, lying is a base and servile vice, detestable and hatefull among all men, and not pardonable so much as to meane slaves, such as haue little or no good in them'.[118] Lying is so serious a vice that while truth-telling enables men to resemble God, 'by lying a man was worthy to loose the title of a man'.[119] Accordingly, Pan, son of Mercury, and the inventor of speech,

---

[111] Bryskett, *Discourse*, sig. P2v. On the danger of flattery see David Colclough, 'Talking to the Animals: Persuasion, Counsel, and their Discontents in *Julius Caesar*', in David Armitage, Conal Condren, and Andrew Fitzmaurice, eds, *Shakespeare and Early Modern Political Thought* (Cambridge: Cambridge University Press, 2009), pp. 217–33, at pp. 217–21.

[112] Aristotle, *The Nicomachean Ethics*, trans. David Ross (Oxford: Oxford University Press, 1980), p. 102.

[113] *OED*, soothing, 1, 'Flattering, blandishing; specious, plausible'.

[114] Zembaty, 'Aristotle on Lying', p. 29.

[115] Aristotle, *Nicomachean Ethics*, pp. 37–43; Aristotle, *The Politics*, p. 178.

[116] Bryskett, *Discourse*, sig. J4v.   [117] Bryskett, *Discourse*, sig. J4v.

[118] Plutarch, *The Philosophie, commonlie called, The Morals*, trans. Philemon Holland (London, 1603), p. 13. On Holland, see *ODNB* entry.

[119] Bryskett, *Discourse*, sig. J4v. Compare Sidney, *Apology*, p. 86.

assumes human form in the upper part of his body, which 'betokeneth truth'; but the lower half, 'being crooked, and of shape of a goate, fals and yntrue speaking was signified', signifying that when men fail to speak the truth they become monsters.[120]

Bryskett's next manoeuvre is especially interesting, cementing the link between his analysis and that of Spenser as he connects poets to military men, effectively circumventing the court as a place where the truth can be told and lying opposed. Bryskett refers to the Persians, among whom 'a lie was reputed a most heinous offence', a detail taken from Xenophon's *Cyropedia*, the biography of Cyrus the Great (*c.*576–529 BCE), the Athenian soldier who had been a student of Socrates and who sought to inform his military practice with his teacher's philosophical ideals.[121] Bryskett connects the virtuous military-minded Persians to the present day, reminding his readers of the importance of honour:

> [W]e see that euen now among vs, it is reputed so great a shame to be accounted a lyer, that any other iniury is cancelled by giuing the lie; and he that receiueth it, standeth so charged in his honor and reputation, that he cannot disburden himselfe of that imputation, but by striking of him that hath so giuen it, or by chalenging him the combat.[122]

Bryskett, writing from a colonial city remote from the courtly centre, has manipulated the discussion of lying so that it has become entwined with a military culture of honour, as the challenge of 'giving the lie' was directly associated with duelling.[123] The assembled company are obviously more in tune with such values as none of them are courtiers: there is one cleric, one doctor, two lawyers, one poet/secretary, and five military men.[124] One of the soldiers, John Norris (1547/50–97), interrupts Bryskett, inspired by the words 'spoken of truth, and of the lie'.[125] Norris asks whether the speaker might continue his theme and tell him if the current military culture of giving the lie is acceptable, as the matter has grown 'confused and dangerous, so as a man can hardly tell, how to carry himselfe in so many occasions'.[126]

Bryskett explains that challenging an opponent to a duel has never been acceptable practice and that an exploration of histories will reveal that 'for reuenge of iniury, for want of proofes, for points of honour, or for any such like causes, this

---

[120] Bryskett, *Discourse*, sig. J4v.

[121] Bryskett, *Discourse*, sig. J4v. For the connection see Andrew Hadfield, 'War Poetry and Counsel in Early Modern Ireland', in Valerie McGowan-Doyle and Brendan Kane, eds, *Elizabeth I and Ireland* (Cambridge: Cambridge University Press, 2014), pp. 239–60, at pp. 258–9. For analysis of the importance of the *Cyropedia* in early modern England see Jane Grogan, *The Persian Empire in English Renaissance Writing, 1549–1622* (Basingstoke: Palgrave Macmillan, 2014), pp. 33–68.

[122] Bryskett, *Discourse*, sigs J4v–K1r.

[123] Markku Peltonen, *The Duel in Early Modern England: Civility, Politeness and Honour* (Cambridge: Cambridge University Press, 2003), p. 3.

[124] Hadfield, *Spenser: A Life*, p. 180.

[125] On Norris see John S. Nolan, *Sir John Norreys and the Elizabethan Military World* (Exeter: University of Exeter Press, 1997); David Edwards, ed., *Campaign Journals of the Elizabethan Irish Wars* (Dublin: IMC, 2014), pp. 216–19, 284–6

[126] Bryskett, *Discourse*, sig. K1r.

wicked and vnlawfull kinde of fight, was euer graunted or allowed in auncient time'.[127] Bryskett's answer is not to turn to the values and practices of the court to correct military culture but to reform it from its own history, referring Norris to classical learning for his answer:

> For when any difference or controuersie fell out among men of honor, which might concerne their credit and reputation for matter of valor, they neuer tried the quarrell by combat betweene themselues, but stroue to shew which of them was most worthy honor, by making their valour well knowne in fight against their common enemies, as in *Caesars* Commentaries we haue a notable example. And the singular fights or combats, that are mentioned in the Greeke or Latine histories, or fained by the Poets, happened euermore betweene enemies of contrary nations, or otherwise in time of publike warre, though perhaps the quarrell might be priuat betweene some of the chiefe men of both camps, as betweene *Turnus* and *Aeneas, Paris* and *Menelaus. Turnus* labouring that *Aeneas* might not haue *Lauinia* to his wife: and *Menelaus* seeking to recouer his wife whom *Paris* had taken from him... The name of Duellum was giuen by the Latins, not to singular fight betweene man and man, but to the generall warre betweene two nations or States, as may be seene by Plautus, Horace, Liuie, and other authors.[128]

For Bryskett as for Spenser, soldiers and poets share the same culture making them natural allies, united most obviously against the court, which, by implication, does not understand their world and which demands a literature and culture which is not committed to telling the truth.[129] Indeed, the force of the analysis here, although it is not explicitly stated, is that the culture of duelling, giving the lie, and false honour is something that has been imported from the court and infected military discipline. Bryskett is careful to reference all genres in his description of the value of a humanist education in order to make the point that writers and soldiers belong to the same world. The army needs to remember its classical roots and sense of true honour by attending properly to the classical education provided in schools. Soldiers should not simply read the most obvious military work, Caesar's commentaries on his campaigns in Gaul and Britain, one of the first works studied in school, but also work hard to understand: the classical epics of Homer and Virgil, the plays of Plautus, the poems of Horace, and the history of Livy.[130]

Bryskett probably wishes to direct Elizabethan soldiers to specific episodes in Caesar's account of his campaigns, such as the description of the surrender of the leader of the revolt in Gaul, Vercingetorix, after Caesar's victory. Vercingetorix

---

[127] Bryskett, *Discourse*, sig. K1v. See also Malcolm Gaskill, *Crime and Mentalities in Early Modern England* (Cambridge: Cambridge University Press, 2003), pp. 209–10; Maria Mendes, 'Hamlet's Ordeals', *Law and Hum.* 8 (2014), 269–89, p. 286.

[128] Bryskett, *Discourse*, sig. K1v.

[129] On the wealth of military poetry and the significance of its neglect in modern scholarship see D. J. B. Trim, 'The Art of War: Martial Poetics from Henry Howard to Philip Sidney', in Pincombe and Shrank, eds, *Oxford Handbook of Tudor Literature*, pp. 587–605.

[130] On the place of Caesar's commentaries in the curriculum see T. W. Baldwin, *William Shakespere's Small Latine and Lesse Greeke* (Illinois: University of Illinois Press, 1944), p. 80.

accepts the blame for the disaster that has befallen his people, making it clear that his intention was never to glorify himself. Calling an assembly, he

> declared vnto them how he had taken that war in hand, not for anye necessitye that he was driuen to himselfe, but for the liberty of the whole Realme: and for asmuche as there was no shift but to geue place vnto fortune, he offered himselfe vnto them both waies, choose whether they would satisfy the Romanes with hys death, or yeld him into their handes aliue.[131]

This culture of truthful honour is diametrically opposed to a court culture of lying and flattery. Bryskett tells us that just as military men tell the truth and take the consequences so do ancient philosophers like Diogenes the cynic, who 'was so great an enemy to flattery, that he chose rather to liue in his tub, then in the courts of mightie Princes, who offered him fauour and entertainment, disdaining to haue abundance of things gotten by so vile a vice'.[132] In contrast is Aristippus, a former disciple of Socrates who, despite his good education, is best known via an anecdote in Vitruvius's *On Architecture*, which suggested that he was a philosopher easily bought, who 'did so degenerate from the doctrine and behauior of his master, that he became a parasite to *Dionysius* tyrant of Sicile, esteeming more the profit he got that way, then the reputation he might haue won by the profession of Philosophie'.[133] The honest philosopher works in harsh conditions that resemble those of the soldier on campaign, preserving his integrity; the dishonest one accepts the terms and conditions of the court and so becomes a lying parasite for the sake of worldly gain.[134]

The same conflict between truth and lying structures Sir Thomas Hoby's translation of Castiglione completed at the start of Elizabeth's reign. Like Bryskett, Castiglione saw the danger that lying posed and he realized that it would undermine the Neoplatonic values which he argued the court should represent and exemplify.[135] But he provided a radically different solution to the problem. Castiglione claimed that courtly values should be corrected rather than rejected. If courtiers applied ever more intelligent, refined, and rigorous courtly values they would be able to express the highest possible earthly values and so glance at the

[131] Julius Caesar, *The Eyght Bookes of Caius Iulius Cæsar Conteyning his Martiall Exploytes in the Realme of Gallia and the countries bordering vppon the same*, trans. Arthur Golding (London, 1565), fo. 237.

[132] Bryskett, *Discourse*, sig. P3v. John Marston made the link between cynicism and satire in *The Scourge of Villainy* (1598): see David Mazella, *The Making of Modern Cynicism* (Charlottesville: University of Virginia Press, 2007), p. 68. I owe this point to Neil Rhodes.

[133] Bryskett, *Discourse*, sig. P3v; Vitruvius, *On Architecture*, trans. Robert Schofield (Harmondsworth: Penguin, 2009), p. 163.

[134] See also Nicholas Breton's *The Scholler and the Souldier, A Discipline Pithily Passed Betweene Them, The One Defending Learning, The Other Martiall Discipline*, in *The Wil of Wit, Wits Will, or Wils Wit, Chuse you whether Containing Fiue Discourses, The Effects Whereof Follow* (London, 1597). The soldier and the scholar find a common hero in Marcus Aurelius, and the scholar asks the soldier not to 'condemne schollers for serving Ladies' (sig. IVr), an implicit criticism of courtiers.

[135] Burke, *Fortunes of the Courtier*, p. 30; John Hale, *The Civilization of Europe in the Renaissance* (London: HarperCollins, 1993), p. 207; Jill Kraye, 'Moral Philosophy', in Schmitt and Skinner, eds, *Cambridge History of Renaissance Philosophy*, pp. 303–86, at pp. 355–6.

heavenly reality of the spiritual world, seeing, as Plato had argued, the shadows in the cave that reflected ideal truth.[136] *The Book of the Courtier* was written in reaction to the old-fashioned military values that had dominated the behavioural codes of the European nobility, pitting the sophisticated values of the court against—what were seen as—the dangerous and often boorish values of the late medieval aristocracy.[137] Furthermore, Castiglione's conception of the ideal court can be seen as part of an intellectual shift against military culture, represented most famously in Erasmus's adage, 'dulce bellum inexpertis'.[138] Castiglione is clear that the courtly ideal has replaced military values for the aristocracy, and the way forward is to reject a culture of bellicosity. Princes will require military expertise but they should 'make their people warlyke, not for a greedie desire to rule, but to defende themselues the better and their owne people, from whoso woulde attempt to bringe them in bondage'.[139]

The Book of the Courtier was a bestseller in England, reprinted eight times before the accession of James I, and became so well known that it inspired a series of parodies of the courtier's behaviour that it defined and recommended.[140] In 1570 Roger Ascham argued that on its own the *Courtier* removed the need for overseas travel, given that it was available in an easily obtained English translation: 'The Cortegian, an excellent booke for a ientleman aduisedlie read, and diligentlie folowed, but one yeare at home in England, would do a yong ientleman more good, I wisse, then three yeares trauell abrode spent in *Italie*.'[141] And, even before Hoby's translation was published, an anti-court discourse had developed criticizing the life of the courtier as one of unfulfilled ambition, hypocrisy, and lying. Antonio de Guevara's *A Dispraise of the Life of a Courtier, and a Commendacion of the Life of the Labouryng Man* (1548), translated by Francis Bryan, was based on a pointed contrast, one that Spenser reproduces to a large extent in *The Faerie Queene*, Book VI, between the honest and decent life of the labourer in the fields and the 'dissemblyng folly' of the life of a courtier who 'for the obteinyng of a litle fauour, do against nature, flatter, & begge'.[142] Bryan's translation of Guevara contributed to a Protestant tradition of pastoral satire and anti-court rhetoric that came to the

---

[136] Plato, *Republic*, pp. 316–25 (514a–521b); Robin Kirkpatrick, *The European Renaissance 1400–1600* (London: Routledge, 2014), p. 170.

[137] Jonathan Dewald, *The European Nobility, 1400–1800* (Cambridge: Cambridge University Press, 1996), p. 35.

[138] Elias, *Civilizing Process*, pp. 47–52; Philippe Contamine, *War in the Middle Ages*, trans. Michael Jones (Oxford: Blackwell, 1984), p. 292.

[139] Castiglione, *Courtyer*, sig. Pp4v. See also Paul Chilton, 'Humanism and War in the Work of Rabelais and Montaigne', in J. R. Mulryne and Margaret Shewring, eds, *War, Literaure and the Arts in Sixteenth-Century Europe* (Basingstoke: Macmillan, 1989), pp. 119–43, at pp. 132–3.

[140] Duncan Salkeld, *Shakespeare Among the Courtesans: Prostitution, Literature and Drama 1500–1650* (Farnham: Ashgate, 2012), pp. 72–3.

[141] Roger Ascham, *The Scholemaster* (London, 1570), sig. G4v; Salkeld, *Shakespeare Among the Courtesans*, p. 51; A. E. B. Coldiron, 'Form[e]s of Transnationhood: The Case of John Wolfe's Trilingual *Courtier*', RS 29 (2015), 103–24, pp. 109–11.

[142] Antonio de Guevara, *A Dispraise of the Life of a Courtier, and a Commendacion of the Life of the Labouryng Man*, trans. Francis Bryan (London, 1548), sig. D1r. On Spenser see Tonkin, *Spenser's Courteous Pastoral*, ch. 6.

fore during Edward VI's reign.[143] The court was a place where lying was not just tolerated as an excusable vice, but actively encouraged:

> If he [the courtier] be disposed to banquetyng, euery where he shall fynde gluttons, If he will manifestly & shamefully lye, he shall fynde companions ready that will approue his lies: If he wil steale, he shal fynde theim that will instructe him many wayes therto: If he will play, there is so many cardes and so many dise, that it is shame to see it: If one will be falsely forsworne, he shal fynde theim that will geue money for forswearyng: Fynally, if he wil vtterly geue himself to do euil, in the court he shall see perfecte examples.[144]

It is clear that other courtesy books, while they accepted Castiglione's diagnosis of the failings of court culture, told a different story. Most had rather less confidence in the ability of the court to correct its vices and establish itself as an ideal centre of government that could act as a beacon to the rest of society. Nicholas Breton's dialogue *The Court and Country* (1618) suggests that the countryman has the better of the argument. He associates the court with lying, pointedly reminding the courtier that 'a Lyer is held little better then a theefe, and it is a lesson we learne our little Children, speake truth, tell truth . . . let your tongues and your hearts goe together', and in his last speech he provides a backhanded compliment to the courtier in acknowledging that 'truth is no lyer; all in the Court are not Court-iers'.[145] While Castiglione saw the courtier as someone who could understand the truth, Della Casa, Bryskett, and Spenser seem to have regarded the court as too corrupt, too wedded to flattery, corruption, boasting, and lying to be anything other than a false beacon. Instead true courtesy required a return to the austere values of military culture, placing learning and soldiery side by side as twin repositories of proper values, what we might think of as a 'Tacitean moment', which sought to restore the hard truthfulness of military values instead of the false values of the lying court that wanted to banish them.[146]

IV

If courtiers attracted the danger of being labelled liars, it was a low-grade risk compared to that of politicians, especially after the advent of Machiavellianism. *The Prince*, although circulating in manuscript as early as 1513, was first published in 1532, four years after the *Courtier*, and the two were inextricably linked in the

---

[143] King, *English Reformation Literature*, p. 241. Bryan, noted for his plain speaking, was a friend of Sir Thomas Wyatt: Brigden, *Wyatt*, pp. 238–9, 329–30, *passim*.

[144] Guevara, *Dispraise*, sig. F3v.

[145] Nicholas Breton, *The Court and Country, or A Briefe Discourse Dialogue-wise Set Downe Betweene a Courtier and a Country-man Contayning the Manner and Condition of their Liues, with many delectable and pithy sayings worthy obseruation* (London, 1618), sigs C4r, IVr. See Bellany, *Court Scandal*, pp. 4–5.

[146] James B. Rives, '*Germania*', in Victoria Emma Pagán, ed., *A Companion to Tacitus* (Oxford: Blackwell, 2012), pp. 45–61, at p. 51; Alan T. Bradford, 'Stuart Absolutism and the "Utility" of Tacitus', *HLQ* 45 (1983), 127–55; Malcolm Smuts, 'Court-Centred Politics and the Uses of Roman Histories, *c*.1590–1630', in Kevin Sharpe and Peter Lake, eds, *Culture and Politics in Early Stuart England* (Basingstoke: Macmillan, 1994), pp. 21–44.

European intellectual imagination.[147] Both were advice books and so were seen to have created a culture in which sophistication and dishonesty had become intermingled.[148] Francesco Guicciardini's discussion of the relationship between the courtier and the citizen, as John Pocock points out, could not have been written without a knowledge of both Castiglione and Machiavelli.[149] In England the two authors were linked in the mind of Gabriel Harvey—often a useful guide to reading habits at Cambridge—who complained of students' preference for modern over ancient letters, and their general taste for the range of fashionable modern Italian poetry and courtesy books: '*Machiavelli* a great man: *Castillo* of no small reputation: *Petrarch*, and *Boccace* in euery mans mouth: *Galateo*, and *Guazzo* neuer so happy: ouer many acquainted with *Vnico Aretino*: The *French* and *Italian* when so highlye regarded of Schollers? The *Latine* and *Greek*, when so lightly?'[150] In Scotland, where Machiavelli was translated by William Fowler, the two authors existed together in the private library of King James VI, probably influenced by the political and literary taste of his tutor, George Buchanan.[151] There were surely many readers throughout the British Isles who made connections between the two writers, seeing them as representatives of related strands of the culture of lies and deceit that dominated Italian life.[152]

One did not have to read Machiavelli to know that he was a liar who encouraged lying, as Christopher Marlowe's prologue to *The Jew of Malta* (1589–90) makes clear:

> MACHIAVEL. Albeit the world think Machiavel is dead,
> Yet was his soul but flown beyond the Alps;
> And, now the Guise is dead is come from France,
> To view this land, and frolic with his friends.
> To some perhaps my name is odious,
> But such as love me guard me from their tongues;
> And let them know that I am Machevil,
> And weigh not men, and therefore not men's words.
> Admired I am of those that hate me most:
> Though some speak openly against my books,
> Yet will they read me, and thereby attain
> To Peter's chair; and, when they cast me off
> Are poisoned by my climbing followers.
> I count religion but a childish toy,
> And hold there is no sin but ignorance.[153]

[147] Roberto Ridolfi, *The Life of Niccolò Machiavelli*, trans. Cecil Grayson (London: Routledge, 1963), pp. 149–54.

[148] Quentin Skinner, *Machiavelli* (Oxford: Oxford University Press, 1981), pp. 21–47; Skinner, *Foundations*, I, pp. 214–15.

[149] J. G. A. Pocock, *The Machiavellian Moment: Florentine Political Thought and the Atlantic Republican Tradition* (Princeton: Princeton University Press, 1975), pp. 153–4.

[150] Spenser, *Variorum*, IX, p. 460.

[151] Alessandra Petrina, *Machiavelli in the British Isles: Two Early Modern Translations of* The Prince (Farnham: Ashgate, 2009), p. 41.

[152] John Stoye, *English Travellers Abroad, 1604–1667* (rev. edn, New Haven: Yale University Press, 1989), p. 71.

[153] Christopher Marlowe, *The Jew of Malta*, ed. N. W. Bawcutt (Manchester: Manchester University Press, 1978), Prologue, 1–15.

Just as lies spread throughout courts where the vice of flattery is not checked, then down through the prince's territories, so do they travel over the Alps and infect European political culture via the hidden works of the Machevil. The same connection was made a few years later by the diarist John Manningham, discussing Cain's murder of Abel: 'he used dissembling flattering speeches to draw him to such a place where he might with advantage execute his purpose . . . A common practice in this world . . . a Machivilian tricke; they will match the Divel in this age.'[154] Marlowe's cunning lines are impossible to challenge or refute: no one admits to reading Machiavelli, even though many do, often those who are most eager to deny the knowledge. Marlowe parodies religious language in the line 'But such as love me guard me from their tongues', asserting that Machiavelli's followers make a distinct separation between the tongue and the heart in pointed contrast to the proper behaviour of the good Christian.[155] Only careful adherence to the Machiavellian code of paranoid suspicion and constant deviousness saves popes from poisoning at the hands of their ambitious rivals. This culture has now reached France, as the Massacre of St Bartholomew's Day demonstrates, but the Machevil's prologue is designed to make the London audience anxious that anyone or everyone they know are likely to be secret Machevils, especially those who speak out openly against the Florentine's doctrines.[156] It is hard not to read the play as a reflection on the culture of lying and equivocation established in the wake of the Jesuit mission. However, equating lying with Catholicism will not circumscribe or fully explain the ubiquity of falsehood: the Machevil's machinations go deeper still and it is clear that lying has the potential to afflict all religions or even, more radically still, question their truthfulness and purpose, 'the triumph of the more consummate evil over the less consummate.'[157]

In asserting that there is no sin but ignorance, the Machevil may be recalling Fregoso Ottaviano's link between ignorance and lying in the *Courtier*, further demonstrating the close relationship between the two works in the English mind. The prologue is directly concerned with hypocrisy and disguise, and so forces the audience to think whether this culture has already taken root and they need to conform and survive, or whether they can successfully weed it out and re-establish honest values. The use of theological language works as an obvious parody of the papacy which pretends to be religious but is really in thrall to the devilish wiles of the spirit of Machiavelli. The plot of the play itself outlines a general cynical understanding of religion among the communities who interact in Malta. Neither the Christians and Jews who live there with some Turkish slaves nor the Ottomans who besiege the city to claim their unpaid tribute exhibit genuine faith, but exploit

---

[154] *Diary of John Manningham*, p. 169.

[155] Patrick Cheney, *Marlowe's Counterfeit Profession: Ovid, Spenser, Counter-Nationhood* (Toronto: University of Toronto Press, 1997), p. 139.

[156] John Roe, *Shakespeare and Machiavelli* (Woodbridge: Brewer, 2002), p. 7; Coburn Freer, 'Lies and Lying in *The Jew of Malta*', in Kenneth Friedenreich and Roma Gill, eds, '*A Poet and a Filthy Play-maker*': *New Essays on Christopher Marlowe* (New York: AMS Press, 1988), pp. 143–67.

[157] Anglo, *Machiavelli*, p. 363.

religion for their own purposes when it suits them.[158] The action alludes to the
Siege of Malta (1565), an event that can be read alongside the Massacre at Paris as a
crisis point in recent European history which Marlowe was able to exploit to show
how insignificant cultural differences were between groups that imagined themselves to have a distinct and superior identity.[159] Religion is regarded as a 'childish
toy', one that enables people to swindle others out of their property through
arbitrary laws or to enclose groups of young women in the hope of sexual
gratification. The vices depicted in the play and its representation of a culture of
lying and hypocrisy are initially imagined to have an origin in religion. However,
religion is shown to be emptied of significance through the ubiquitous practice of
lying, which makes its values irrelevant to the protagonists. The central character,
Barabas, tells his daughter that 'It's no sin to deceive a Christian, / For they themselves
hold it a principle', and when she is the last nun to die after her conversion, friar
Bernardine cynically undercuts her testimony of faith: '*Abigail*: And witness that I die
a Christian. [Dies] / Ay, and a virgin too, that grieves me most'.[160] Lying appears to
have its origins in the significant issues posed by religion and politics, but, yet again,
the play forces the audience to wonder whether it is the small apparently minor or
even insignificant lies of everyday life that really matter as they corrode the values by
which life should be lived. The Machevil becomes irrelevant to the play, a neat irony
given that he has become the most famous literary representation of Machiavelli. As
Barabas is boiled alive on stage—a punishment for poisoners after the 1531 Act which
made it a treasonable crime (although the Act was repealed in 1542)—the Machevil
does not return to gloat or point a moral.[161] And it is worth noting that Barabas is a

---

[158] See Matthew Dimmock, *New Turkes: Dramatizing Islam and the Ottomans in Early Modern England* (Farnham: Ashgate, 2005), pp. 168–9.

[159] Emily C. Bartels, *Spectacles of Strangeness: Imperialism, Alienation, and Marlowe* (Philadelphia: University of Pennsylvania Press, 1993), p. 88; Julia Reinhard Lupton, '*The Jew of Malta*', in Cheney, ed., *Cambridge Companion to Marlowe*, pp. 144–57, at pp. 145–6. On the siege see Ernle Bradford, *The Great Siege: Malta 1565* (Harmondsworth: Penguin, 1964). On the impact of the Massacre of Paris on print see Kingdon, *Myths about the St. Bartholomew's Day Massacres*; Anglo, *Machiavelli*, pp. 229–70.

[160] Marlowe, *Jew of Malta*, II.iii.311–12; III.vi.40–1. Barabas's name derives from the murderer and thief who was released by Pilate instead of Christ, often linked to the Antichrist: G. K. Hunter, 'The Theology of Marlowe's The Jew of Malta', *JWCI* 27 (1964), 211–40, pp. 213–14; Aaron Kitch, *Political Economy and the States of Literature in Early Modern England* (Farnham: Ashgate, 2009), p. 118.

[161] Barabas's fate might have reminded the audience of the fate of Richard Rouse (Roose), the cook who tried to poison Archbishop John Fisher in 1531, claiming that he thought he had put a laxative in the gruel he served (no one believed him). A special Treason Act was passed (it was repealed in 1547 in Edward VI's first parliament) so that Roose could be singled out for a particularly gruesome punishment which reflected the nature of his crime, and he was boiled to death in a cauldron (Henry Clifford, *The Life of Jane Dormer, Duchess of Ferrara*, ed. E. E. Estcourt and Joseph Stevenson (London: Burns & Oates, 1887), pp. 78–9; J. R. Tanner, ed., *Tudor Constitutional Documents, A. D. 1485–1603, with an Historical Commentary* (Cambridge: Cambridge University Press, 1930), p. 381). On the significance of Roose's crime which led to the first use of parliamentary attainder in Henry VIII's reign, paving the way for the treatment of Ann Barton, the Maid of Kent, Thomas More, Anne Boleyn, and others, see William R. Stacy, 'Richard Roose and the Use of Parliamentary Attainder in the Reign of Henry VIII', *HJ* 29 (1986), 1–15; K. J. Kesselring, 'A Draft of the 1531 "Acte for Poysoning"', *EHR* 116 (2001), 894–9.

poisoner, poisoning his daughter with rice-porridge (III.vi.64–5), which provides a neat link between lying and poisoning.[162] We witness a litany of petty, greedy humans behaving badly, none able to comprehend the significance of any larger ideas or realize that their behaviour should be condemned and curtailed, a world that bears more than a passing resemblance to the one represented in *Beware the Cat*. Is Marlowe pointing out a moral or recognizing that audiences will flock to plays which confront them and challenge received ideas?[163] If there is a moral it is surely that lying and hypocrisy do not depend on the Machevil and that any changes that could be made had to take place in more basic and obvious ways.[164] Human beings are adept at finding ways of behaving badly in most circumstances anyway and do not require an outside figure to encourage them: in fact, and this may be the most scandalous moral of the play, the existence of such figures may help to spread vice by providing an enemy and so convincing people that they are in the right. Such ignorance leads to lying and hypocrisy and is clearly a sin.

The Machevil's comments would seem to follow from Marlowe's earlier reflections on lying in *Tamburlaine, Part Two* (1587–8), a play which also shows different groups cynically immune to religious language and ideas and so able to lie at will. The Christian forces led by Sigismund of Hungary decide to break their oaths to the Turks because making a promise to an infidel is not binding:

> *Frederick.* Now, then, my lord, advantage take hereof,
> And issue suddenly upon the rest:
> That in the fortune of their overthrow,
> We may discourage all the pagan troop,
> That dare attempt to war with Christians.
> *Sigismund.* But calls not then your grace to memory
> The league we lately made with king Orcanes,
> Confirmed by oaths and articles of peace,
> And calling Christ for record of our truths?
> This should be treachery and violence
> Against the grace of our profession.
> *Baldwin.* No whit, my lord: for with such infidels,
> In whom no faith nor true religion rests,
> We are not bound to those accomplishments,
> The holy laws of Christendom enjoin:
> But as the faith which they profanely plight
> Is not by necessary policy,
> To be esteemed assurance for ourselves,
> So what we vow to them should not infringe
> Our liberty of arms and victory.
> *Sigismund.* Though I confess the oaths they undertake,

---

[162] I owe the point about poisoning and lying to Neil Rhodes.

[163] Ruth Lunney, *Marlowe and the Popular Tradition: Innovation in the English Drama before 1595* (Manchester: Manchester University Press, 2002), p. 123.

[164] Paul Whitfield White, 'Marlowe and the Politics of Religion', in Cheney, ed., *Cambridge Companion to Marlowe*, pp. 70–89, at p. 86.

Breed little strength to our security,
Yet those infirmities that thus defame
Their faiths, their honours, and religion,
Should not give us presumption to the like.
Our faiths are sound, and must be consummate,
Religious, righteous, and inviolate.
Frederick. Assure your grace, 'tis superstition
To stand so strictly on dispensive faith[.][165]

For these Christians, faith overrides any public duty to tell the truth, and enables them to break oaths sworn in public with pagans, the central dilemma which confronted Christians at odds with the state throughout Europe. The episode derives from an episode recounted in John Foxe's *Acts and Monuments of the Christian Church* (1570).[166] Marlowe has altered the details so that we can be clear that the breaking of a promise is the principal issue at stake here, as Foxe's account supports the actions of the Christian alliance against 'that barbarous nation and cruel enemies to the name and religion of Christ' and makes no mention of Sigismund's oath-breaking.[167] Needless to say, the Christian perfidy misfires and their armies are overwhelmingly defeated by the Turks in battle in the next Act, perhaps a sign that God was really on the side of the Turks; that he was eager to punish the Christians for breaking oaths; or that he is indifferent to human actions.

Both parts of *Tamburlaine* were performed in the wake of Elizabeth's Act Against Jesuits and Seminarists (1585), the execution of Mary Stuart (1587), and, perhaps, the defeat of the Spanish Armada.[168] *Tamburlaine* could therefore be read as an anti-Catholic play, reflecting on the devious practices of those who would undermine the realm with their lies, especially as Marlowe is following John Foxe and Martin Luther's narration of the episode, both of whom represent the events as the consequence of Catholic treachery.[169] There is indeed a long critical history which reads Marlowe as a fanatically anti-Catholic author.[170] However, the grand sweeping geographical spectacle of *Tamburlaine* does not make it seem like a play directed at an enemy within or one that champions Christendom against its external enemies.[171] Furthermore, the Turks are given the chance to reflect on the defeat of the Christians and express their shock at

[165] Christopher Marlowe, *Tamburlaine*, ed. J. W. Harper (London: Black, 1971), *Part Two*, II. i.22–50.
[166] Cited and analysed in Vivien Thomas and William Tydeman, eds, *Christopher Marlowe: The Plays and Their Sources* (London: Routledge, 1994), pp. 135–8.
[167] Thomas and Tydeman, eds, *Marlowe*, p. 138.
[168] Both parts of *Tamburlaine* are usually dated to 1587: evidence that they may have appeared in 1588 is provided in G. R. Hubbard, 'Possible Evidence for the Date of Tamburlaine', *PMLA* 3 (1918), 436–43.
[169] Thomas and Tydeman, eds, *Christopher Marlowe*, p. 78.
[170] Paul H. Kocher, 'François Hotman and Marlowe's *The Massacre at Paris*', *PMLA* 56 (1941), 349–68; Julia Briggs, 'Marlowe's *Massacre at Paris*: A Reconsideration', *RES*, ns, 34 (1983), 257–78.
[171] On the play's engagement with geography, see Bernhard Klein, *Maps and the Writing of Space in Early Modern England and Ireland* (Basingstoke: Palgrave, 2001), pp. 15–19.

their duplicity. The words of Orcanes, King of Natolia, further draw attention to the nature of their crime:

> Can there be such deceit in Christians,
> Or treason in the fleshly heart of man,
> Whose shape is figure of the highest God?
> Then if there be a Christ, as Christians say,
> But in their deeds deny him for their Christ:
> If he be son to everlasting Jove,
> And hath the power of his outstretched arm,
> If he be jealous of his name and honour,
> As is our holy prophet Mahomet,
> Take here these papers as our sacrifice
> And witness of thy servant's perjury.[172]

It is hard to avoid the conclusion that *Tamburlaine* was designed to be read as a critique of bad faith, of self-interest disguised as a holy principle that needs to be exposed and ridiculed, rather than a specifically sectarian attack on Catholicism as we find when Luther and Foxe narrate episodes involving the Ottoman Empire.[173]

It is also difficult to decide whether Marlowe actually read Machiavelli and, if he did, whether he did so between writing *Tamburlaine* and *The Jew of Malta*.[174] Or whether he accessed Machiavelli through the work of Innocent Gentillet, who cites substantial passages from his writings.[175] The most significant point is that Marlowe represents lying as an all-consuming evil which has the power to subsume everything: his plays are designed to instil paranoia in an audience unsure what they can trust, very like the experience of reading *Beware the Cat*. Machiavelli merely adds an extra gloss to what is already present in both parts of *Tamburlaine* and *The Massacre at Paris*. The plays do not provide any answers to the questions they pose. Neither at the conclusion of *Tamburlaine*, when the protagonist dies after burning the Koran, nor at the end of *The Jew of Malta*, does the audience know whether lying actually works or whether honesty would have been a better policy.[176] Nor do we really know whether small lies lead to big ones, or whether it is the large ones that really matter.

---

[172] Marlowe, *Tamburlaine, Part Two*, II.i.36–46.

[173] See Richard Hillman, *Shakespeare, Marlowe and the Politics of France* (Basingstoke: Palgrave, 2002), ch. 4; Maus, *Inwardness*, ch. 3.

[174] John Roe refuses to state whether Shakespeare read Machiavelli (Roe, *Shakespeare and Machiavelli*, p. 1); John Wilders was convinced that he had (John Wilders, *The Lost Garden: A View of Shakespeare's English and Roman History Plays* (London: Macmillan, 1978), p. 48).

[175] Irving Ribner argues that Gentillet had significant influence in the anglophone world: 'Marlowe and Machiavelli', *CL* 6 (1954), 348–56. Sydney Anglo is more sceptical, *Machiavelli*, pp. 417–33; as is Felix Raab, *The English Face of Machiavelli: A Changing Interpretation, 1500–1700* (London: Routledge, 1965), pp. 56–7.

[176] On the significance of Tamburlaine burning the Koran see Matthew Dimmock, *Mythologies of the Prophet Muhammad in Early Modern English Culture* (Cambridge: Cambridge University Press, 2013), pp. 118–21.

Marlowe's representation of Machiavelli had a significant influence on perceptions of lying and politics. Thomas Churchyard echoes Marlowe's prologue when he states, with obvious irony, that

> Fine Macheuill, is now from Florence flown
> To England where, his welcome is too great,
> His busie books, are here so red and known
> That charitie, thereby hath lost her heat
> Poore printers doe, in Ludgate die for meat
> Who doth for det, in danger long remaine
> Must fall down flat, and seldom rise againe.[177]

A marginal note states, with undisguised bitterness, 'Marcheuill is now made an English man'. Churchyard's complaint that he had been forced into poverty by hostile forces and the deluded fashions of the reading public, was one he frequently made.[178] Churchyard presumably has in mind the conspicuous success of the publisher John Wolfe (1548?–1601) in selling Italian books, notably those by Machiavelli—*Il Principe* and *I Discorsi* were printed together in 1584 with the false imprint 'Palermo' so that Wolfe could pretend that they had been imported (which may have further informed Marlowe's understanding of the cynical duplicity associated with Machiavelli and his works).[179] In contrast to the success of booksellers who make a killing out of immoral foreign publishing, poor English publishers languish in the debtor's prison at Ludgate.[180] Their fate was further thrown into relief by the richly decorated gate which sported the genealogical line of English kings from the mythical Lud, founder of London according to Geoffrey of Monmouth, to Elizabeth I, signalling the nation's independence from and rivalry to Rome.[181] Churchyard is lamenting that the honest values of the traditional English writer now fallen on hard times (i.e. Churchyard himself) are no longer valued because everyone is a Machiavellian or is reading Machiavelli in order to uncover the lies that now dominate English society, an accurate, albeit literal, reading of Marlowe's prologue.

[177] Thomas Churchyard, *A Musicall Consort of Heauenly Harmonie (compounded out of manie parts of musicke) called Churchyards Charitie* (London, 1595), sig. C3r. I owe this reference to Matthew Dimmock.
[178] Matthew Woodcock, *Thomas Churchyard: Pen, Sword, and Ego* (Oxford: Oxford University Press, 2016), ch. 17.
[179] See Peter S. Donaldson, *Machiavelli and Mystery of State* (Cambridge: Cambridge University Press, 1992), ch. 3; Harry R. Hoppe, 'John Wolfe, Printer and Publisher', *The Library*, 4th series, 14 (1933), 241–89.
[180] Ahnert, *Rise of Prison Literature*, p. 15; Jean E. Howard, *Theater of a City: The Places of London Comedy, 1598–1642* (Philadelphia: University of Pennsylvania Press, 2011), p. 70.
[181] Tiffany Stern, *Making Shakespeare: From Stage to Page* (London: Routledge, 2004), pp. 9–11; Geoffrey of Monmouth, *The History of the Kings of Britain*, trans. Lewis Thorpe (Harmondsworth: Penguin, 1966), p. 106.

V

Machiavelli became a byword for lying, not just in terms of politics, but in every walk of life, as Marlowe and Churchyard demonstrate, even though his aims in writing were at odds with his popular image.[182] Was Machiavelli actually attempting to change the nature of an understanding of lying by removing God from his calculations, as many writers in the later sixteenth century alleged; or was he really, as C. S. Lewis argued many years ago, simply being immoral?[183] Machiavelli only discussed lying in one passage in *The Prince*, although the possibility of a ruler acting dishonestly is endorsed throughout the work. The fact that people lied for selfish and political ends was acknowledged in late medieval commonplace collections such as *The Dicts and Sayings of the Philosophers*, although these works always condemned liars and lying. Mainstream political discourse on lying often referred to Cicero, in particular *De Officiis* (*On Duties*), whose precepts on behaviour were often copied verbatim by moralists.[184] Machiavelli conceived *The Prince* as a modern version of Cicero's treatise, updating and refiguring some sections, rethinking, transforming, and inverting others.[185]

Cicero is unequivocal in his condemnation of lying. He makes his feelings clear not through a discussion of obvious villains, but by attacking prominent Romans he otherwise admires, who have sullied their reputations because of their lies. Cicero discusses the case of Gaius Marius (*c.*157–86 BCE), a relative by marriage to his grandmother, who had a distinguished war record in defence of Rome, but who had engaged in sharp practice in order to secure election as a consul. Cicero is clear that in such cases the good and the bad cannot be separated:

> Marius' usurping of the popular gratitude due to his colleagues and to the tribunes of the people seemed to be not so dishonourable, while to become consul because of it, which had been his aim, seemed extremely beneficial. But there is one rule for all cases; and I desire you to be thoroughly acquainted with it: either the thing that seems beneficial must not be dishonourable, or if it is dishonourable, it must not seem beneficial. Well then? Can we judge the one Marius or the other a good man? Unravel and sift your understanding in order to see the form and concept of a good man that is there. Does it become the good man to lie or slander for his own profit, or to usurp or to deceive? Unquestionably, no.[186]

Marius has to be judged as a single individual responsible for his actions good and bad; one cannot split him in half and argue that there are two different Mariuses who can be judged accordingly. Marius, so this description informs us, may have done good things but cannot be accounted a good man because he has lied to

---

John M. Najemy, 'Machiavelli and History', *RQ* 67 (2014), 1131–64, p. 1161.
Lewis, *English Literature*, p. 51. For Quentin Skinner, Machiavelli's real aim was to recover the lost liberty of the northern Italian city states: *Machiavelli*, pp. 48–77.
Machiavelli, *The Prince*, introduction, p. xv.
Machiavelli, *The Prince*, introduction, pp. xv–xxi.
Cicero, *On Duties*, ed. M. T. Griffin and E. M. Atkins (Cambridge: Cambridge University Press, 1991), p. 130.

achieve the positions of power which enabled him to undertake them. Cicero takes the reader through the stages of his argument carefully so that his conclusion is secure. Following Stoic principles he equates the honourable and the good and the dishonourable and the bad, then reminds his readers, following basic principles of the syllogism, that nothing that is dishonourable can be good in order to persuade them that Marius, despite all the benefits that he has brought Rome, cannot, therefore, be a good man.[187]

Machiavelli sought to challenge such logic in *The Prince* when he argued that a prince needed to be as cunning as a fox as well as strong as a lion, forcing his readers to take the logic of the beast fable seriously—a doctrine that impressed readers such as Justus Lipsius.[188] Machiavelli challenges Cicero's argument that the good man (Machiavelli assumes that rulers are generally men) must be wholly good in arguing that a separation between appearance and reality—tongue and heart—is not only possible but a desirable quality in the good ruler. The good ruler needs to appear to be 'merciful, trustworthy, humane, upright and devout', but 'having and always cultivating them is harmful, whereas seeming to have them is useful'.[189] He must have the ability to lie convincingly so that his subjects are confident that he is a competent and diligent ruler who will make their lives better if he stays in power: in particular by protecting their property. In contrast, the ruler must use every means possible to ensure that his subjects cannot deceive him: '[The prince] should contrive that his actions should display grandeur, courage, seriousness and strength, and his decisions about the private disputes of his subjects should be irrevocable. He should maintain this reputation, so that no one should think of lying to him or scheming to trick him.'[190] The ruler can—and should—lie to his subjects, but ensure that they cannot lie to him.

Although Machiavelli had the specific conditions of Italy at the end of the fifteenth and the start of the sixteenth century in mind, his message was taken as if it were a general dictum.[191] In Ben Jonson's *Every Man Out of His Humour* (1599), Cordatus complains that one should not assume that all emperors were like Nero nor all statesmen like the Machiavel, indicating that these equations were commonly made.[192] The majority of political thinkers and commentators sided with Cicero, and resistance to Machiavelli usually sought to reverse Machiavelli's critique of Cicero. Innocent Gentillet's attack on his recommendation of the deceptive arts of government was a Huguenot response to the horror of the Massacre

[187] On the Stoic principles see Cicero, *On Duties*, p. 112, n. 1.
[188] Annabel Patterson, *Fables of Power: Aesopian Writing and Political History* (Durham, NC: Duke University Press, 1991), p. 72. On Lipsius and Machiavelli see Zagorin, *Ways of Lying*, p. 124. Aesop was among the most translated and adapted Greek authorities in early modern Europe: see Robert Cummings, 'Classical Moralists and Philosophers', in Gordon Braden, Robert Cummings, and Stuart Gillespie, eds, *The Oxford History of Literary Translation in English, Vol. 2: 1550–1660* (Oxford: Oxford University Press, 2010), pp. 371–89, at pp. 379–80; Seth Lerer, 'Aesop, Authorship, and the Aesthetic Imagination', *JMEMS* 37 (2007), 579–94, p. 579.
[189] Machiavelli, *The Prince*, p. 62.   [190] Machiavelli, *The Prince*, p. 64.
[191] The importance of the context of Machiavelli's ideas has long been acknowledged: see J. R. Hale, *Machiavelli and Renaissance Italy* (Harmondsworth: Penguin, 1972).
[192] Ben Jonson, *Every Man Out of His Humour*, in *Jonson*, I, p. 326 (2.3.345–6).

of St Bartholomew's Day.[193] For Gentillet, Machiavelli 'was the greatest liar and imposter that had ever been'.[194] His recommendation of bad instead of good maxims replicated the overthrow of the good government of the Roman Republic and plunged France into the tyranny of the Julio-Claudians, a rhetorical analysis based on classical sources that would counter Machiavelli's.[195] Accordingly, Gentillet's text, complete with letters in the margins for ease of reference, is designed as a response to Machiavelli's dangerous commonplaces which, allied to the unscrupulous Catholic treachery they helped to inspire, threaten to destroy proper civilized values. Everyone knows, argues Gentillet, that the recent massacres 'were all coloured with false imputations, by these *Messers Machiavellists*'.[196] Princes should be just and magnanimous not devious and cunning. Gentillet argues that Machiavelli's recommendation that a prince needs to know how to behave like a lion or a fox reduces men to beasts, rather than serving as a beast fable. Princes should only use force if they have reason on their side so warfare should be a moral extension of normal government, not an exception: 'in warre a man may lawfully use subtilties against his enemies, if so be his faith and the rights of warre be not violated, and this is not called foxlike subtiltie, or unlawful deceiving, but it ought to be called militarie prudence'.[197] Gentillet is determined to bring political discourse back to the moral mainstream in order to combat Machiavellian policy. For Machiavelli 'a prince is not bound unto right, faith, or religious promise' and the School of Machiavelli cannot speak of such values 'unlesse it be to mocke at them'.[198] In taking this course of action they break the 'most holy bands of humane societie', just as they undermine Ciceronian ideals of friendship and other virtues which make civilized existence possible.[199] Gentillet is arguing—like Guazzo—that the promise or the oath should be central to public relationships and civil society, and he produces a series of examples from ancient Roman and recent French history to illustrate his point.

Gentillet tells the story of Hannibal and Marcellus from Livy's *History of Rome*, countering Machiavelli's use of Livy in his *Discourses*.[200] Hannibal, having killed the Roman general Marcellus, recovered his seal ring and wrote to the local Salapians in Marcellus's name saying that he (the Roman general) was about to arrive and to make the garrison ready for him. Marcellus's lieutenant, understanding Hannibal's nature, realized that this was a trick and warned the Salapians of the imminent danger that faced them. When Hannibal approached the garrison and sent on his Latin-speaking soldiers, the Salapians allowed six hundred in and 'then let they fall the port-cullis, and cut in pieces all of them which entred, which caused

[193] Victoria Kahn, 'Reading Machiavelli: Innocent Gentillet's *Discourse on Method*', *PT* 22 (1994), 539–60, p. 540.
[194] Anglo, *Machiavelli*, p. 281.
[195] Innocent Gentillet, *A Discourse Vpon the Meanes of Wel Governing and Maintaining in Good Peace, a Kingdome, or Other Principalitie*, trans. Simon Patericke (London, 1602), sigs B1r–D3v; Anglo, *Machiavelli*, pp. 298–300; Kahn, 'Reading Machiavelli', p. 543.
[196] Gentillet, *Discourse*, sig. V3r.   [197] Gentillet, *Discourse*, sig. V4v.
[198] Gentillet, *Discourse*, sig. V4v.   [199] Gentillet, *Discourse*, sigs V4v, V2r.
[200] Livy, *The Romane Historie*, trans. Philemon Holland (London, 1600), pp. 649–50; Kahn, 'Reading Machiavelli', p. 544.

Anniball thus to be taken in his own net'.[201] The story neatly reverses Machiavelli's recommendation of the subtle policy of Cesare Borgia (Duke Valentino), who used the brutal Remirro de Orco, 'a cruel and energetic man', to establish law in the newly conquered province of Romagna, then had him cut in 'two pieces in the square at Cesena', a 'terrible spectacle' which leaves 'the people both satisfied and amazed'.[202] The moral is straightforward: foxes are likely to be caught in their own traps and, according to Gentillet's reading of history, Machiavelli's maxim is revealed to be false and delusive, not cunning realpolitik. The real maxim that princes should follow is: 'Subtile and audacious counsels are at first very agreeable and pleasant, but to guide, they are difficult and hard, and full of sorrow in the end.'[203] Tyrannical and cruel behaviour based on lying and duplicity is not simply morally wrong but foolish and short-sighted, bad policy as well as bad ethics.

Gentillet also tells a rather convoluted story of Louis I, Duke of Anjou, and his attempts to conquer Naples and Sicily in 1383: again, the pointed attack on Machiavelli, reminding the world of good, honest French success in Italy, is clear. Needing to defeat his rival, Charles de la Paix, who is secure within the Egg-Castle (Castel dell'Ovo) of Naples, the Duke is approached by an Enchanter, who would help him conquer the castle as he helped Charles de la Paix before him. The Enchanter claims that he can produce a thick cloud from the sea which will form a bridge to the castle, terrifying the besieged who will immediately surrender. Unfortunately there is a drawback: if any of the Duke's soldiers make the sign of the cross, 'or do in any ways crosse their legs or their arms, or otherwise', while crossing the bridge 'all will fall to the ground, and goe to nothing'.[204] The Duke decides against using the Enchanter, even though—or perhaps because—he boasts that 'he [Charles de la Paix] feareth me more than all the forces that can come against him'.[205] The Duke decides that he will not only release Charles de la Paix from his fear but he will conquer the castle through legitimate military means, because he has the strength to do this, and he has the Enchanter beheaded. The moral of this odd story, which can also be read as a response to Machiavelli's praise of Cesare Borgia's actions, is that 'generous hearts doe always disdaine crafts, subtilties and deceits', preferring honest courses of action.[206] However, just as Cesare Borgia's cunning brilliance was cut short by his premature death, so was the honesty of Louis I, who died on campaign in 1384 attempting to press his claim to be King of Naples.[207] What Gentillet fails to mention is that the Duke's campaign was not successful, and was clearly faltering by the time of his death, and that he never actually reached Naples.[208] Gentillet wants to argue that lying and deceit never succeed but the historical record he employs is somewhat less helpful than he claims.

---

[201] Gentillet, *Discourse*, sig. V4v.
[202] Machiavelli, *The Prince*, p. 26; Gentillet, *Discourse*, sig. R4v; Kahn, 'Reading Machiavelli', p. 550. See also Walter Raleigh, *The History of the World* (London, 1617), Pt 1, Bk 5, p. 711.
[203] Gentillet, *Discourse*, sig. V4v.   [204] Gentillet, *Discourse*, sig. V5r–v.
[205] Gentillet, *Discourse*, sig. V5v.   [206] Gentillet, *Discourse*, sig. V45v.
[207] Machiavelli, *The Prince*, pp. 23–9.
[208] *Popes*, p. 229; Katherine Jansen, Joanna Drell, and Frances Andrews, eds, *Medieval Italy: Texts in Translation* (Philadelphia: University of Pennsylvania Press, 2010), p. 526.

Jean Bodin, whose major political treatise was published just after Gentillet's, has an equally traditional notion that politics and morality should reinforce each other: unsurprising, as the 'various accommodations Bodin made during his life leave little room for doubt that he practiced Nicodemism, assuming a posture of outward conformity in contradiction to his personal beliefs and thereby licensing dissimulation'.[209] Writing about deceptive merchants, Bodin makes a more general point following Cicero:

> Yet that is euery where which *Cicero* writeth, *Sordidos iudicari qui mercantur a mercatoribus quod eodem loco ac momento vendant*, Them to be deemed but base, which buy of marchants that which they hold euen in the same place, and selfe same moment againe sell: for why, they should gaine nothing, except they should lye loudly: whereas nothing is more foule than vanitie and lying.[210]

Politicians, like merchants, need to tell the truth and not indulge in misleading the people they should serve honestly. Lies not only diminish the nature of the person's achievements but they also devalue the goods they are trying to sell and generate a climate of fear and suspicion. The use of the word 'base' could be applied to a lowering of social rank, but, more significantly, the coinage, which could be debased. Duplicitous merchants, therefore, are guilty of interfering with the social order and the trust that money requires in order to function properly, the stamp of the crown guaranteeing the value of the coin.[211] Debasing the coinage was the prerogative of the monarch whose face appeared on the coin as a stamp of authority: interfering with the coinage in any country was treason, an assault on the monarch's integrity, like lying to compass his or her death.[212] Bodin's use of an intensifying adverb, 'lye loudly', suggests both the relatively unsophisticated nature of the behaviour of lying merchants, as they trumpet their wares in the bazaar in order to sell them as quickly as possible, and the serious and distorting nature of lying which destroys balanced conversation between equals.[213]

While writers claimed that Machiavelli dominated political discourse, the truth was that Cicero's belief in a virtuous public culture undoubtedly had more real influence on the ways in which lying, dissimulation, and hypocrisy were discussed.[214] Bodin is undoubtedly following Cicero in *De Officiis* when he castigates the profession of unscrupulous traders who 'buy from merchants then sell again

---

[209] Zagorin, *Ways of Lying*, p. 283.

[210] Jean Bodin, *The Six Bookes of a Common-weale*, trans. Richard Knolles (London, 1606), p. 400.

[211] *OED* base, v, 8. C. E. Challis, *The Tudor Coinage* (Manchester: Manchester University Press, 1978), pp. 81–112.

[212] John P. D. Cooper, *Propaganda and the Tudor State: Political Culture in the Westcountry* (Oxford: Clarendon Press, 2003), p. 88; Bellamy, *Treason*, p. 60; D. M. Loades, *The Reign of Mary Tudor: Politics, Government and Religion in England 1553–58* (2nd edn, Harlow: Longman, 1991), p. 250.

[213] Braggadocchio and Trompart are notably loud liars in *The Faerie Queene*, unsubtle and unsophisticated in their attempted deceptions: Peter Bayley, 'Braggadocchio', and Elizabeth J. Bellamy, 'Trompart', *Sp. Enc.*, pp. 109–10, 701.

[214] Howard Jones, *Master Tully: Cicero in Tudor England* (Nieuwkoop: De Graaf Publishers, 1998), pp. 21–46. William Cecil, Lord Burghley, was invariably cast as a disciple of Machiavelli in Catholic libels: Lake, *Bad Queen Bess?*, p. 349.

immediately', as 'they would make no profit unless they told sufficient lies, and nothing is more dishonourable than falsehood'.[215] Indeed, Cicero is eager to connect the sin of lying in politics to deception and falsehood in everyday life, making lying a central problem for the Republic that had to be fought using the weapons of ordinary legal practice. It is hardly surprising that Cicero was often represented primarily as a moralist in Tudor England.[216] Cicero tells the story of Gaius Canius, a wealthy Roman who wishes to buy a country estate in Syracuse. Gaius is lavishly entertained by the local banker, Pythius, who has a large number of local fishermen load their catch on the shore and Gaius is so impressed that, 'inflamed with greed', he buys the estate. But when he arrives there are no fishermen or fishing boats to be found and he realizes that he has been duped. Cicero is quite clear that Gaius is not an attractive character and we should not really feel sorry for him. But his case raises an obvious legal issue as he has been the victim of 'malicious fraud', a crime that is morally wrong and so must be stamped out:

> Both Pythius, therefore, and everyone else who does one thing and pretends another is treacherous, dishonest and ill-intentioned. No action of this sort can be beneficial, imbued as it is with so many vices . . . both pretence and dissembling must be removed from our whole lives: the good man, then, will neither pretend nor dissemble, whether in order to sell or to buy at a better price.[217]

And, of course, if this moral dictum is true of trade, it is also true of other aspects of life, especially those involving government of the self, others, and the state.[218] Lying in small or large ways, according to Cicero, was equally reprehensible, undermining the moral nature of the social fabric. Yet again discussions of lying can be divided between those, like Cicero, who argue that lying is fundamentally wrong, and those, like Machiavelli, who argue that, right or wrong, lying was simply part of life and the sooner we got used to that truth, the better. Authors of courtesy manuals and treatises on politics invariably argued that small lies led to big lies, as Spenser suggested would happen in the last book of *The Faerie Queene*. The more serious question was: did this process actually matter? Was lying actually a problem? Or did readers simply need to accept that lying was fundamental to the human condition? Put another way, did one trust Cicero or Machiavelli? Everyone asked these questions in the sixteenth century but, at a time of conflict, divided loyalties, ingenious duplicity, allied to faith that the truth will out, it is hardly surprising that no one answer held sway.

---

[215] Cicero, *On Duties*, p. 58. On the significance of mountebanks as dishonest traders see Neil Rhodes, 'Orality, Print and Popular Culture: Thomas Nashe and Marshall McLuhan', in Matthew Dimmock and Andrew Hadfield, eds, *Literature and Popular Culture in Early Modern England* (Aldershot: Ashgate, 2009), pp. 29–44, at p. 34.

[216] Cummings, 'Classical Moralists and Philosophers', pp. 380–2.

[217] Cicero, *On Duties*, p. 122.

[218] Cicero, *On the Commonwealth and On the Laws*, ed. James E. G. Zetzel (Cambridge: Cambridge University Press, 1999), pp. 41, 106.

6

Testimony

I

Early modern England depended on the authority of eyewitnesses who would provide truthful testimony, mediated knowledge that could be trusted.[1] Thomas Lupton, who singled out the bearing of false witness as a particular problem in Elizabethan England, was especially concerned to dismiss the Jesuits as 'lying witnesses', enemies of truth who undermined the values that should be upheld by proper Christians.[2] Lupton's fictional character Siuqila admits that he is a sinner made of flesh and blood 'or else I were a lyar' only to have his bluff called by his interlocutor, Omen, who points out that what he says cannot be trusted 'nor put . . . in proofe'.[3] Rather more impressive and thoughtful commitment to truth-telling is required of a reliable witness. A culture which assumed that witnesses were honourable and told the truth unless proved otherwise was always vulnerable if they turned out to be duplicitous. Medicus in William Bullein's *Dialogue Against the Fever Pestilence* succinctly expresses the dilemma through a tautology: 'That which we do see we do testifie, and that which we do testifie is true. Therefore no man ought in matters whiche appertaineth to the state of life to write fables or lyes, but that whiche is of great aucthoritie and of good experience.'[4] Bullein's immediate point is about medicine but the dialogue ranges far wider and he is also arguing that fictions have their place but only when they are produced by experienced and trustworthy writers who know exactly what they are doing. Bullein's concerns are repeated in a variety of other works, illustrating the ubiquity of the fear that authority depended on testimony which could well be false. There was particular anxiety about the authority of the historical evidence provided by the ancients, and whether their testimonies could and should be challenged.[5] Used badly, testimony

---

[1] Holger Schott Syme, *Theatre and Testimony in Shakespeare's England: A Culture of Mediation* (Cambridge: Cambridge University Press, 2012), p. 33; Shapiro, *Culture of Fact*, p. 13.

[2] Thomas Lupton, *The Christian against the Iesuite* (London, 1582), sigs B4v–C1r. On 'false witnesses' see Lupton, *Siuqila*, sigs N1v–N2r. For another case see Anon., *A Libell of Spanish Lies* (London, 1596). False witness statements, made for a variety of reasons, are the cause of most miscarriages of justice today: see A. Rattner, 'Convicted but Innocent: Wrongful Conviction and the Criminal Justice System', *LHB* 12 (1988), 283–93.

[3] Lupton, *Siuqila*, sig. B3r.   [4] Bullein, *Pestilence*, p. 36.

[5] Nicholas Popper, 'An Ocean of Lies: The Problem of Historical Evidence in the Sixteenth Century', *HLQ* 74 (2011), 375–400.

could undermine truth and 'generate slander rather than resolve it', so that access to the truth depended on the ability to read character.[6]

Testimony is often neglected as a subject in philosophical discussion but it is wrong to underestimate 'the epistemological significance of our reliance upon the word of others', as C. A. J. Coady defines the issue.[7] When the value of testimony is considered, the trustworthiness of the speaker is undoubtedly more significant than the nature of the evidence provided.[8] Shakespeare makes a related point in Sonnet 138: 'When my love swears that she is made of truth / I do believe her, though I know she lies', the speaker complicit with his mistress in accepting her deceit, and prepared to be drawn into her circle of lies, because of his affective bond with her (the joke being that he knows that she is not made (maid) of truth because he knows her (has had sex with her)).[9] Changes in the nature of evidence in the sixteenth century meant that 'From being an argument for confirmation, testimony was reconceptualized as providing facts for information and subsequent argument.'[10] With the dismantling of the power of the Church as an institution that provided the framework for the interpretation of doctrine and empirically observed phenomena and events, greater emphasis had to be placed on individual conscience and testimony as the guarantor of truth.[11] And, towards the end of the sixteenth century, the rising significance of contract law dictated that promises and intentions became ever more contested in legal disputes.[12] The testimony of eyewitnesses as evidence in trials, of unusual events, of strange phenomena, and of remote places, assumed greater significance in the sixteenth century and was particularly important for the development of modern science. William Harvey (1578–1657), in his study of the generation of animals, urged his readers 'to strive after personal experience, not to rely on the experience of others'.[13] According to Mary Poovey, Thomas Mun (1571–1641), director of the East India Company, 'simply *assumed* that his object of analysis was lawful. References to his own experience thus constituted a form of personal testimony . . . not allusions to experiments or observations from which he had derived his conclusions.'[14]

Harvey's dictum would seem to make sense and the exhortation to experience truth for oneself—with the corollary that the nearer we are to that experience the better—but it raises a number of problems. François Rabelais's satirical *Gargantua* (1534–5), well known to most of the writers discussed in this book, had already

[6] Kerrigan, *Shakespeare's Binding Language*, p. 302.
[7] C. A. J. Coady, *Testimony: A Philosophical Study* (Oxford: Clarendon Press, 1992), p. 120.
[8] Richard Moran, 'Getting Told and Being Believed', *PI* 5 (2005), 1–29, p. 5.
[9] *Shakespeare's Sonnets*, ed. Katherine Duncan-Jones (London: Thompson, 1997), 138, lines 1–2 (p. 391); Kerrigan, *Shakespeare's Binding Language*, p. 473.
[10] R. W. Serjeantson, 'Testimony and Proof in Early-Modern England', *SHPS* 30 (1999), 195–236, p. 226.
[11] Richard H. Popkin, *The History of Scepticism from Erasmus to Descartes* (rev. edn, Assen: Van Gorcum, 1960), p. 3; Jan-Melissa Schramm, *Testimony and Advocacy in Victorian Law, Literature, and Theology* (Cambridge: Cambridge University Press, 2000), p. 28.
[12] Raffield, 'Trials of Shakespeare', pp. 55–62.
[13] Cited in Shapin, *Social History of Truth*, p. 201.
[14] Mary Poovey, *A History of the Modern Fact: Problems of Knowledge in the Sciences of Wealth and Society* (Chicago: University of Chicago Press, 1998), p. 83.

satirized the gullibility of those who accepted the authority of testimony.[15] Describing the birth of the imaginary giant through his mother's left ear after her bowels are blocked by an astringent given to prevent the appalling diarrhoea which afflicts her after she has overeaten tripe sausages, the narrator addresses the audience directly: 'I doubt whether you will truly believe in this strange nativity. I don't care if you don't. But an honest man, a man of good sense, always believes what he is told and what he finds written down.'[16] As Richard Popkin has pointed out, the desire to base truth in individual experience and conscience meant that 'No effective standard of truth would be left.'[17] Testimony was often imagined as artless but had the clear function to 'prove a point' and carefully formulated rules in classical rhetoric.[18] Therefore, how can we know when eyewitnesses are telling the truth?[19] Were they always where they claimed to have been and seen what they stated they had? Was their testimony always truthful and devoid of lies? Are there signs that we can interpret to enable us to judge? Holger Schott Syme has pointed out that 'Where reports contradicted each other, a contest of authorities ensued', as had been the case throughout the Middle Ages.[20] The balance of authorities changed after the Reformation, but not the fundamental nature of the argument over truth. However, with more emphasis placed on individual testimony unfettered by institutional checks and balances there was an increased interest in lying as a subject and a practice.

Montaigne's description of the 'simple and rough-hewen fellow', who was 'a condition fit to yield a true testimonie' of the peoples of the New World, is a conscious fantasy of a perfect mediator, unavailable in the real world, as the subsequent representation of the unreliable witness acknowledges:

> For, subtile people may indeed marke more curiously, and observe things more exactly, but they amplifie and glosse them: and the better to perswade, and make their interpretations of more validitie, they cannot chuse but somewhat alter the storie. They never represent things truly but fashion and maske them according to the visage they saw them in; and to purchase credit to their judgement, and draw you on to believe them, they commonly adorne, enlarge, yea, and Hyperbolize the matter. Wherein is required either a most sincere Reporter, or a man so simple, that he may

---

[15] On the influence of Rabelais see Anne Lake Prescott, *Imagining Rabelais in Renaissance England* (New Haven: Yale University Press, 1998); Emily Butterworth and Hugh Roberts, 'Introduction: Gossip and Nonsense in Renaissance France and England', *RS* 30 (2016), 8–16, p. 8.

[16] François Rabelais, *Gargantua and Pantagruel*, trans. J. M. Cohen (Harmondsworth: Penguin, 1955), p. 52; Bernd Renner, 'From *Satura* to *Satyre*: François Rabelais and the Renaissance Appropriation of a Genre', *RQ* 67 (2014), 377–424, p. 403.

[17] Popkin, *History of Scepticism*, p. 4.

[18] R. W. Serjeantson, 'Testimony', in Adamson, Alexander, and Ettenhuber, eds, *Renaissance Figures of Speech*, pp. 180–94, at p. 185.

[19] For discussion see Coady, *Testimony*, pp. 262–76; Rob Iliffe, 'Lying Wonders and Juggling Tricks: Religion, Nature, and Imposture in Early Modern England', in James E. Force and David S. Katz, eds, *Everything Connects: In Conference with Richard Popkin, Essays in his Honour* (Leiden: Brill, 1999), pp. 183–209.

[20] Syme, *Theatre and Testimony*, p. 105. On medieval notions of authority see Curtius, *European Literature*, pp. 436–45, 515–18.

have no invention to build upon, and to give a true likelihood unto false devices, and be not wedded to his owne will.[21]

Montaigne is describing what people do when they provide testimony, so that the apparent direction of the passage needs to be reversed because it is the 'sincere Reporter' who is the exception not the 'subtile people'.[22] The desire to 'Hyperbolize the matter' reminds readers that Puttenham had defined hyperbole as the 'lying figure', showing that lying was an ordinary aspect of everyday life which could not be removed from testimony, but which would have to be decoded and counteracted.[23]

It is often repeated as fact that Robert Greene (1558–92) expired on 3 September after a 'fatall banquet' which involved 'a surfeit of pickle herringe and rennish wine', an unusual case of the cause of death apparently being recorded in late-sixteenth-century England.[24] The evidence comes from Greene's principal detractor, Gabriel Harvey (1552/3–1631), as well as his friend and ally, Thomas Nashe (1567–*c*.1600).[25] Greene's eventful life and death were represented in various works which have proved hard to attribute to any author with certainty.[26] However, even if their provenance is hard to determine, they all construct his life in terms of a particular narrative structure, that of the repentant prodigal, who is able to save his soul after an agonizing deathbed confession, atoning for his previous sins.[27] We cannot, of course, be sure that either Harvey or Nashe is actually telling the truth about Greene's death: significantly enough, no one knows who was at the fatal banquet, apart from one strange figure mentioned by Nashe.[28] Harvey is eager to expose the disgusting behaviour of an enemy who has been vigorously defended by his allies and so tells the story with considerable glee; Nashe has a different axe to grind, exploiting the detail as a means of showing that even if it were true—Nashe comments in parenthesis, '(if thou wilt needs haue it so)', which puts pressure on

---

[21] Montaigne, 'Of the Canniballes', *Essayes*, I, pp. 215–29, at p. 218.

[22] Andrew Hadfield, ed., *Amazons, Savages, and Machiavels: An Anthology of Travel and Colonial Writing, 1550–1650* (Oxford: Oxford University Press, 2001), p. 286.

[23] See above, pp. 190–1.

[24] As his *ODNB* biographer, Lori Humphrey Newcombe, notes, 'The multiple accounts of Greene's death are surprisingly consistent.' Lives were still largely based on funeral sermons at this time so reasons for death are rarely described in narrative accounts: see Alan Pritchard, *English Biography in the Seventeenth Century: A Critical Survey* (Toronto: University of Toronto Press, 2005), chs 1–2; Irena Backus, *Life Writing in Reformation Europe: Lives of Reformers by Friends, Disciples and Foes* (Farnham: Ashgate, 2008), introduction.

[25] For suggestions that Nashe had an equivocal attitude to Greene's work see Lorna Hutson, *Thomas Nashe in Context* (Oxford: Clarendon Press, 1989), p. 206; David Landreth, 'Wit Without Money in Nashe', in Stephen Guy-Bray, Joan Pong Linton, and Steve Mentz, eds, *The Age of Thomas Nashe: Text, Bodies and Trespasses of Authorship in Early Modern England* (Farnham: Ashgate, 2013), pp. 135–52, at pp. 142–6.

[26] See Lori Humphrey Newcomb, 'A Looking Glass for Readers: Cheap Print and the Senses of Repentance', in Kirk Melnikoff and Edward Gieskes, eds, *Writing Robert Greene: Essays on England's First Notorious Professional Writer* (Aldershot: Ashgate, 2008), pp. 133–56.

[27] Richard Helgerson, *The Elizabethan Prodigals* (Berkeley: University of California Press, 1976), pp. 79–94.

[28] Charles Nicholl, *A Cup of News: The Life of Thomas Nashe* (London: Routledge, 1984), pp. 123–4.

the reader to make a decision—Greene was still a better man and writer than Harvey could ever hope to be:

> My next businesse was to enquire after the famous Author: who was reported to lye dangerously sicke in a shoemakers house near Dow-gate: not of the plague, or the pockes, as a Gentleman saide, but of a surfett of pickle herring and rennish wine, or as some suppose, of an exceeding feare.[29]
>
> I and one of my fellows, Will. Monox (hast thou neuer heard of him and his great dagger?) were in company with him a month before he died, at that fatall banquet of Rhenish wine and pickled hearing (if thou wilt needs haue it so), and then the inuentorie of his apparel came to more than three shillings (though thou saiest the contrarie).[30]

Is either passage actually a testimony that borders on lying? Harvey seems to skirt around the issue of the incident's absolute truthfulness by claiming that all he is doing is repeating hearsay, and placing it in the context of a letter to a friend. We know that Harvey cared greatly about the letter form from the evidence of his letter book which shows that he habitually wrote letters designed for public consumption through print—the *Fovre Letters* being an example—as well as to private individuals, shaping and honing his epistles according to the addressee and a wider readership.[31] Harvey's letters cannot be taken at face value as private communications that we have intercepted, which is how his account of Greene's death seems to have been read. Even more doubts shadow the Nashe passage. McKerrow, Nashe's great editor, leaves the exasperated note about Will Monox, 'I can learn nothing of him.'[32] But is Monox a pseudonym: might the name mean 'one eye', from 'monoculus'?[33] McKerrow makes no mention of Monox's large dagger, but this detail sounds less testimony than taunt, a clue that all is not as it seems. Nashe even challenges the date of the supposedly fatal banquet, which he claims he attended, although it was a month before Greene's death. Accordingly, the weapon may not merely be an exaggeration, but a detail that draws attention to the fictional nature of the episode. The rhetorical question can always be used to signal its opposite (no one knows Will Monox because I have just made him up).

Other details instil further uncertainties in the reader. The details of the cost of Greene's suit are designed to counter Harvey's gibe that Greene died in poverty because he was such a neglected writer. And the timing of the banquet tells us that it was not the cause of his death. Nashe has systematically taken apart every detail that Harvey has given in his description of Greene's death, while not ever explicitly

---

[29] Gabriel Harvey, 'To my louing frend, Maister Christopher Bird of Walden', in *Fovre Letters and Certaine Sonnets* (1592), ed. G. B. Harrison (Edinburgh: Edinburgh University Press, 1966), p. 13.
[30] Thomas Nashe, *Strange News, Of the Intercepting Certaine Letters* (1592), in Nashe, *Works*, I, pp. 287–8.
[31] Gabriel Harvey, *Letter-Book of Gabriel Harvey, 1573–1580*, ed. Edward John Long Scott (London: Camden Society, 1884).
[32] Nashe, *Works*, IV, p. 173.
[33] Peter Farey, 'A Deception in Deptford: Christopher Marlowe's Alleged Death' (http://www.rey.prestel.co.uk/add1.htm) (accessed 23 October 2015).

denying anything ('if thou wilt needs haue it so').[34] If Nashe is writing in this manner, he is riddling or, in Augustine's terms, joking, rather than lying. Nashe's description may be a double bluff, the author adopting a pose of faux naivety so that he can bring in an event that Nashe pretends that he thinks Harvey has in mind knowing full well that the real cause lies elsewhere.

Whatever the truth, the success of Nashe's attack on Harvey depends on a readership who think—or, at least, ought to think—about the distinction between truth and lying, and have a sceptical attitude to the problematic nature of testimony as a means of establishing the truth, a theme that Nashe develops throughout his writing. Working out the intentions that lie behind this complicated exchange is not something that we are able to avoid, even if we cannot be certain of getting it right, and reaching a secure verdict. Accordingly, we are caught in a double bind, whereby we have to try and recover the intentions that produced texts in which the author has worked hard to disguise their purpose. If we read them too innocently we risk one form of faulty interpretation; if we read them as knowing statements anxious to veer away from the truth, we risk another.

II

It should not surprise us that the battle between truth and lies serves as a structural principle in Thomas Nashe's only explicit excursion into fiction, *The Unfortunate Traveller* (1594), a work which exploits the reader's anxiety about the testimony of travellers and the knowledge of the world that they provide. The novel narrates the picaresque adventures of the roguish Jack Wilton, a soldier in Henry VIII's invading army in France (1513). Jack returns from the campaign but after an outbreak of plague—one of the perennial themes in Nashe's works—he flees to Europe where he witnesses the Battle of Marignano (1515) at which the French forces under Francis I decisively defeated the Swiss confederation, then on to Münster where he observes the terrible effects of the civil wars in Germany after the Anabaptists under John of Leyden seize the city and are besieged by the Holy Roman Emperor, Charles V, and the Duke of Saxony, Magnus I (1535); attempting to return to England he meets Henry Howard, Earl of Surrey, his former master, at Middleborough, and travels with him through Europe to Italy, where they stop at Venice, Florence, and, finally, Rome; witnessing one too many executions, Jack marries his courtesan, flees Italy, and rejoins Henry VIII's army as he meets the French King, Francis I, at the Field of the Cloth of Gold (7–24 June 1520).[35] Nashe intermingles fact and fiction in his narrative, the absurd chronology and imaginary journey of Surrey to defend the honour of the 'fair

---

[34] Compare, 'if you will haue it' (*Have With You To Saffron-Walden* (1596), Nashe, *Works*, III, p. 53).

[35] For a summary see Donald J. McGinn, *Thomas Nashe* (Boston: Twayne, 1981), pp. 87–103. For the historical events see G. R. Elton, *Reformation Europe, 1517–1559* (London: Collins, 1963), pp. 38, 100–1; Scarisbrick, *Henry VIII*, pp. 74–80.

'Geraldine' are set against the background of real places and events.[36] Furthermore, Nashe clearly knew that Surrey never travelled to Italy; and Nashe only ever got as far as the Isle of Wight.

The detail in *The Unfortunate Traveller* is a blend of truth and lies, and the reader is never sure which parts of the story correspond to an external reality or, indeed, where the fictional stops and the factual starts, an unsettling experience given the text's close relationship to the violent history of sixteenth-century Europe.[37] Episodes based on classical legends exist side by side with observations of the brutal reality of contemporary warfare, many apparently accurate descriptions proving to be 'disingenuous mock-accuracy', in Lorna Hutson's words.[38] The description of the executions of the Jewish criminal Zadoch is surely based on the observation of a real execution (although not necessarily one witnessed by Nashe himself). As the account progresses, however, it becomes a fantastic set piece, a flight of fancy that is a testament to the author's ability to produce the disturbing effects of the truly grotesque:

> To the execution place was he brought, where first and formost he was stript, then on a sharpe yron stake fastened in the ground, had he his fundament pitcht, which stake ran vp along into his bodie like a spit, vnder his arme-hoales two of like sort, a great bonfire they made round about him, wherewith his flesh rosted not burnd: and euer as with the heate his skinne blistered, the fire was drawne aside, and they basted him with a mixture of Aqua fortis, allam water, and Mercury sublimatum, which smarted to the very soule of him, and searcht him to the marrowe. Then did they scourge hys backe parts so blistered and basted, with burning whips of red hot wire: his head they noynted ouer with pitch and tarre, and so enflamed it. To his priuie members they tied streaming fierworkes, the skinne from the crest of his shoulder, as also from his elbowes, his huckle bones, his knees, his ankles they pluckt and gnawd off with sparkling pincers: hys breast and his belly with seale skins they grated ouer, which as fast as they grated & rawed, one stoode ouer and lau'd with smithes cindry water and *aqua vito*: his nayles they halfe raised vp, and then vnderpropt them with Sharpe prickes like a taylers shop windowe halfe open on a holiday: euerie one of his fingers they rent vp to the wrist: his toes they brake off by the rootes, and let them still hang by a little skinne. In conclusion, they had a small oyle fire, such as men blow light bubbles of glasse with, and beginning at his feet, they let him lingringly burne vp limme by limme, till his hart was consumed, and then he died. Triumph women, this was the end of the whipping Jew, contriued by a woman, in reuenge of two women, her selfe and her maid.[39]

[36] See Andrew Hiscock, 'Blabbing Leaves of Betraying Paper: Configuring the Past in George Gascoigne's *The Adventures of Master F. J.*, Thomas Nashe's *The Unfortunate Traveller* and Thomas Deloney's *Jack of Newbury*', *English* 52 (2003), 1–20.
[37] See Raymond Stephanson, 'The Epistemological Challenge of Nashe's The Unfortunate Traveller', *SEL* 23 (1983), 21–36; Joshua Phillips, *English Fictions of Communal Identity, 1485–1603* (Farnham: Ashgate, 2010), pp. 195–203.
[38] Hutson, *Nashe in Context*, p. 232. See also Steve Mentz, *Romance for Sale in Early Modern England: The Rise of Prose Fiction* (Aldershot: Ashgate, 2006), where he describes *The Unfortunate Traveller* as 'dishonest romance' (p. 184).
[39] Nashe, *Works*, II, pp. 316–17.

Early modern executions throughout Europe were, as is well attested, brutal spectacles, staged to discourage crime, assert the power of the authorities, and shock would-be transgressors into obedience.[40] Readers of John Foxe and Richard Verstegan, the pre-eminent martyrologists of the Protestant and Catholic traditions whose works were circulating widely by the 1590s, would have had ample opportunity to observe the graphic images of tortured, burning, and mutilated bodies, even if they lived outside major population centres and so had not witnessed an execution at first hand. Tearing the flesh off the criminal's body with red-hot pincers was common in French executions.[41] Severed heads and body parts adorned most city walls at most times to remind citizens of the fate of traitors, as *Beware the Cat* demonstrates.[42] But there surely is a point at which this description changes from what most contemporary readers would have recognized as familiar, even normal practice, or the sort of judicial killing which they imagined took place in other European states, to a horrifying fantastic spectacle.[43] As Philip Thomson has pointed out, it is the '*unresolved* nature' of the grotesque that is particularly important, as the description of Zadoch's execution demonstrates.[44] The first sentence describing a stake entering Zadoch's anus is undoubtedly taken from the descriptions of Turkish executions, recounted by travellers such as Fynes Moryson.[45] The burning recalls the deliberate strategy of burning heretics who refused to renounce their faith throughout Mary's reign, abandoned by Elizabeth who classified opposition as traitors and chose hanging, drawing, and quartering as the primary method of execution.[46] The next sentence describing the basting with 'a mixture of Aqua fortis, allam water, and Mercury sublimatum' (nitric acid, alum, and mercury sulphate), all chemicals used by alchemists, should alert the reader's suspicions that the passage may be changing register as this is not an account of an execution that anyone has ever witnessed: perhaps the alchemical references are

---

[40] On the early modern execution as spectacle see Michel Foucault, *Discipline and Punish: The Birth of the Prison*, trans. Alan Sheridan (Harmondsworth: Penguin, 1977), ch. 2; on its representation in print see Julius R. Ruff, *Violence in Early Modern Europe, 1500–1800* (Cambridge: Cambridge University Press, 2001), p. 17. On Nashe and the spectacle of execution see Jonathan V. Crewe, *Unredeemed Rhetoric: Thomas Nashe and the Scandal of Authorship* (Baltimore: Johns Hopkins University Press, 1982), pp. 86–7.

[41] Anon., *A Spectacle for Vsurers and Succers of Poore Folkes Bloud, Whereby they may see, Gods iust dislike and reuenge, vpon their vncharitable and Vnciuill oppression, with a horrible murther committed by a young man, that hanged his owne Mother in August last* (London, 1606), p. 11.

[42] J. A. Sharpe, *Crime and the Law in English Satirical Prints, 1600–1832* (Cambridge: Chadwyck-Healey, 1986), pp. 56–7. For discussion see Patricia Palmer, *The Severed Head and the Grafted Tongue: Literature, Translation and Violence in Early Modern Ireland* (Cambridge: Cambridge University Press, 2014).

[43] Neil Rhodes, *Elizabethan Grotesque* (London: Routledge, 1980), p. 43. See also the illuminating discussion in John N. Vance, 'Gross Anatomies: Mapping Matter and Literary Form in Thomas Nashe and Andreas Vesalius', in Guy-Bray, Linton, and Mentz, eds, *Age of Thomas Nashe*, pp. 115–31.

[44] Philip Thomson, *The Grotesque* (London: Methuen, 1972), p. 21.

[45] Charles Hughes, ed., *Shakespeare's Europe: Unpublished Chapter of Fynes Moryson's Itinerary* (London: Sherratt & Hughes, 1903), p. 67.

[46] Duffy, *Fires of Faith*, pp. 76–8; Wagner and Schmid, eds, *Encyclopedia of Tudor England*, p. 1099.

designed to signal the transition.[47] But it is with the description of anointing the victim's head with tar which is then set alight and the attachment of fireworks to his penis that confirms any lingering suspicions that we have been transferred into the realm of grotesque fiction. From this sentence onwards the description becomes ever more far-fetched, so that when Zadoch's mutilated fingers look like the open shutters of a tailor's shop we know that this cannot be an eyewitness account of an actual event.[48] The bathos of the moral at the end brings the reader back to the reality of the criminal's death, but also forces the question of whether such punishment is appropriate, real, or just.

Zadoch is a stereotypical Jewish character represented in similar ways in a variety of discourses and literary works.[49] He takes his place alongside the vast array of such familiar figures who appear throughout Jack's travels: corrupt, devious, and passionate Italians; power-worshipping Germans; lovelorn aristocrats; brutal soldiers; trickster figures; hardened criminals; lascivious courtesans, and so on, all characters who would have been encountered in fiction rather than in life, *The Unfortunate Traveller* perhaps working as a satire not of society so much as the ways in which society is represented.[50] Just as material in the archives is shaped by literary modes, Nashe shows that so is our interaction with the world in the first place. We process material and think we know things because we have digested received images that we are then able to refigure as knowledge. Our understanding of the world is always mediated and we can never be sure whether we really know anything, whether the world deceives us or we deceive it. The only thing we can be sure about is if and when we lie, we know that we are at odds with reality, making lying, paradoxically, a guarantor of truth.

The problem is represented in spectacular terms when Jack is rescued from the gallows by a banished English earl. The earl knows that Jack did not murder Heraclide, 'a noble & chaste matrone', who committed suicide after she was raped by Bartol, 'a desperate Italian' working with Esdras of Granada, 'a notable Bandetto,

---

[47] Gary Edson, *Mysticism and Alchemy through the Ages: The Quest for Transformation* (Jefferson, NC: McFarland, 2012), p. 210. On Nashe's knowledge of alchemy see Stanton J. Linden, *Dark Hieroglipicks: Alchemy in English Literature from Chaucer to the Restoration* (Lexington: University Press of Kentucky, 1996), pp. 86–90, *passim*.

[48] McKerrow argues that 'The tortures inflicted on Zadoch are little worse than those suffered by Dr. Fian for witchcraft' (Nashe, *Works*, IV, p. 292). Dr Fian had his feet crushed by the 'boot' and his fingernails pulled out, but nothing resembling the treatment of Zadoch with chemicals or fireworks: Anon., *Newes from Scotland, declaring the damnable life and death of Doctor Fian a notable sorcerer, who was burned at Edenbrough in January last. 1591* (London, 1592?), sig. D2r–D2v. As McKerrow points out, Nashe could have read this tract.

[49] Constance C. Relihan, *Fashioning Authority: The Development of Elizabethan Novelistic Discourse* (Ohio: Kent State University Press, 1994), pp. 129–30; David S. Katz, *The Jews in the History of England, 1485–1850* (Oxford: Oxford University Press, 1994), pp. 102–3. More generally see James Shapiro, *Shakespeare and the Jews* (Columbia: Columbia University Press, 1996).

[50] On stereotypes see Andrew Hadfield, *Literature, Travel, and Colonial Writing in the English Renaissance, 1545–1625* (Oxford: Oxford University Press, 1998), p. 195. On Jack Wilton as a trickster see Joan Pong Linton, 'Counterfeiting Sovereignty, Mocking Mastery: Trickster Poetics and the Critique of Romance in Nashe's *Unfortunate Traveller*', in Naomi Conn Liebler, ed., *Early Modern Prose Fiction: The Cultural Politics of Reading* (London: Routledge, 2007), pp. 130–47. On the nature of the book's satire see Hutson, *Nashe in Context*, p. 220.

authorised by the pope because he had assisted him in some murthers'.[51] The
episode is a carefully constructed mixture of classical myth, the story of the rape of
Lucrece which led to the founding of the Roman Republic, and voguish tales of
Italian villainy, collected by William Painter, George Pettie, and others.[52] Rome,
which hardly any English writers saw first hand, was very much a city of the mind
for English readers, as Nashe makes clear.[53] Jack is about to fall victim to a fate that
many Englishmen and women imagined would probably be theirs if they were to
have the misfortune to find themselves in the eternal city, until the earl tells the
authorities that he had encountered Bartol, 'greeuuously wounded and bloodie' in a
barber's shop where he had confessed to the crime, having ended his partnership
with Esdras after a duel fought over Bartol's courtesan.[54] This testimony is enough
to save Jack.[55] Of course, we know that such strange coincidences and twists of
fortune rarely occur outside prose fiction and the public stage.

The earl then provides Jack with a long speech on the perils of overseas travel,
advising him that as he can return home, unlike the earl, he should do so as soon as
possible. The earl argues that nothing useful can be learned from travel that could
not have been acquired more easily and safely by other means:

> Alas, our Englishmen are the plainest dealing soules that euer God put life in: they are
> greedie of newes, and loue to be fed in their humors and heare themselues flattered the
> best that may be ... Rats and mice engender by licking one another, he must licke, he
> must croutch, he must cogge, lye and prate, that either in the Court or a forraine
> Countrey will engender and come to preferment ... Some alleadge, they trauell to
> learne wit, but I am of this opinion, that as it is not possible for anie man to learne the
> Arte of Memorie, whereof *Tully, Quintillian, Seneca, and Hermannus Buschius* haue
> written so manie bookes, except he haue a naturall memorie before: so is it not possible
> for anie man to attaine anie great wit by trauell, except he haue the grounds of it rooted
> in him before ... What is heere but wee maye read in bookes and a great deale more
> too, without stirring our feete out of a warme studie.[56]

The earl associates travel with the vices that result from lies and lying. The excessive
greed for news, here meaning novelty and newfangledness as much as the latest
information, makes the English gullible and easily deceived by unscrupulous flatterers eager to swindle them.[57] The desire to achieve success in foreign courts leads
to even more reprehensible behaviour, fawning, sycophancy, and, of course, lying.
Travel is associated not simply with unreliable testimony but, more significantly,

[51] Nashe, *Works*, II, p. 287.
[52] On Nashe's use of Lucrece see Linton, 'Trickster Poetics', p. 145; Katherine Duncan-Jones,
Ungentle Shakespeare: Scenes from his Life (London: Arden, 2001), pp. 71–2. On Italian tales see
Andrew Hadfield, 'Prose Fiction', in Michael Hattaway, ed., *A New Companion to English Renaissance
Literature and Culture* (Oxford: Wiley, 2010), II, pp. 423–36.
[53] On 'cities of the mind' see Andreas Huyssen, 'Introduction: World Cultures, World Cities', in
Andreas Huyssen, ed., *Other Cities, Other Worlds: Urban Imaginaries in a Globalizing Age* (Durham,
NC: Duke University Press, 2008), pp. 1–23, at pp. 2–5.
[54] Nashe, *Works*, II, p. 296.   [55] McGinn, *Nashe*, p. 95.
[56] Nashe, *Works*, II, pp. 298–9.
[57] On the fashion and appetite for news see Andrew Mousley, 'Self, State, and Seventeenth-Century
News', *The Seventeenth Century* 6 (1991), 149–68; Shapiro, *Culture of Fact*, p. 87.

with a corrosive influence on the personality of the traveller who becomes, as a result of travel, more dishonest and mendacious.

However, as this section of the speech continues, the nature and balance of the argument change and the alert reader may feel more at odds with the development of the earl's thinking. The earl argues that a belief that travel will lead to new knowledge or the development of new understanding is entirely without foundation. He claims that people are either predisposed to something or will be unable to master its complexities, like the art of memory. This is surely excessively pessimistic and deluded. The art of memory could be learned as so many manuals instructed readers, but perhaps the earl thinks that Jack is too ignorant to know about them.[58] If so, he is probably lying. And he surely cannot really believe that however pointless so much travel was—the grand tour often being a means of allowing young men to sow their wild oats by indulging in sex tourism under the guise of enculturation and preparation for adulthood—that travellers learned nothing at all except vice, unless he is simply thinking about his own experiences and universalizing them.[59]

The last sentence cited here would appear to undercut the argument of the earl and force the reader to worry about the nature of testimony. It would be true that one could learn everything through reading books and never be forced to venture into the wider world if one could trust them to tell the truth. But Montaigne's essay has already exposed the obvious epistemological problem with this assumption: books have their limitations as testimony, as do eyewitness accounts and personal observation.[60] Indeed, books had a far greater capacity to deceive people than travel as the case of Mandeville's *Travels* demonstrates. It would seem that the earl validates their use as a means of avoiding travel rather than because he particularly values them, especially if we remember that he claims that books on the art of memory are of little use because one cannot learn such skills. We should also remember that neither the earl nor Jack are entirely willing travellers. Sir Thomas Palmer, in his *An Essay of the Meanes How to Make our Trauailes, into Forraine Countries, the more Profitable and Honourable* (1606), divides travellers into three categories: voluntaries, non-voluntaries, and involuntaries.[61] While Jack is a non-voluntary traveller as a soldier and as part of the Earl of Surrey's entourage, the earl is an involuntary traveller, banished from his homeland for unstated reasons but surely as a result of behaviour that is unacceptable to the authorities. According to Palmer involuntaries are banished for two reasons: either 'for breach of Lawes in Court' or 'of such as the Prince vppon iust indignation banisheth the Land for a time certaine or not; wherby such are forced to trauell'.[62] Most likely we are to

---

[58] On the art of memory see above, pp. 179–80.

[59] On travel and sex see Ian Littlewood, *Sultry Climates: Travel and Sex Since the Grand Tour* (London: John Murray, 2001).

[60] Dolan, *True Relations*, pp. 9–10.

[61] Sir Thomas Palmer, *An Essay of the Meanes How to Make our Trauailes, into Forraine Countries, the more Profitable and Honourable* (London, 1606), pp. 1–3. See also Sebastian Sobecki, '"A Man of Curious Enquiry": John Peyton's Grand Tour to Central Europe and Robert Cecil's Intelligence Network, 1596–1601', *RS* 29 (2015), 394–410, pp. 406–7.

[62] Palmer, *Essay*, p. 8.

assume that the earl is a Catholic exile, as there were many such exiled communities in major European cities.[63] His refusal to learn and belief that he knows all the answers already may well suggest a stubbornness and wilful ignorance. Nashe's attacks on the Marprelate tracts when he was employed by Archbishop Whitgift (1589–90) criticize his puritan opponents for their want of wisdom. In *A Counter-cuffe Giuen to Martin Junior: by the Ventrous, Hardie, and Renowned Pasquill of England, Caualiero* (1589), Nashe, through the voice of Pasquill of England, a traveller who has returned to provide Martin Marprelate Junior with a rebuttal ('countercuff'), explains just how easy it is to procure ignorant clergy in England who will follow the Marprelate line: 'Downe with learning and Vniuersities; I can bring you a Free-mason out of *Kent*, that gaue ouer his occupation twentie yeeres agoe . . . These Bishops are somewhat too well grounded for greene-heades; so long as they keepe their place and power, it is impossible for thee to cast the Religion of this Land into a newe Molde euery newe Moone.'[64] *The Unfortunate Traveller*, with its rhetorical flourishes and subtle reversals which constantly unsettle a reader, is surely part of this same assault on wilful ignorance and refusal to think imaginatively.

As the earl's speech develops, the logic of his argument disintegrates, issuing a challenge to the reader. The earl argues that travel teaches the traveller nothing because the different countries and peoples of Europe exhibit particular character-istics which are already in the public domain and are easy to know and understand. Why would anyone need to travel to the countries in question, at great expense and with the possibility of the terrible consequences that Jack has experienced, in order to discover nothing new? The earl poses a series of rhetorical questions (interroga-tio, erotema): 'What is there in *Fraunce* to bee learned more than in *England*, but falsehood in fellowship, perfect slouenrie, to loue no man but for my pleasure, to sweare *Ah par la mort Dieu*, when a mans hammes are scabd.'[65] Spain is no better, and the earl complains that travellers simply bring back the latest fashions and a series of absurd, ill-informed opinions of no consequence denigrating England in comparison: 'if you vrge him [the traveller] more particularly wherein it exceeds, he can giue no instance but in *Spaine* they haue better bread than any we haue'.[66] Italy has even more pernicious effects on the English traveller. He brings back a ridiculous series of affected gestures, kissing his 'hand like an ape, cringe his necke like a starueling [someone who is starving], and play at hey passe repasse come aloft, when he salutes a man', apparently trivial problems which allude to the serious critique of ceremonies as blasphemous practices which have infected every-day life.[67] He also learns 'the art of athiesme, the art of epicurising, the art of

---

[63] Katy Gibbons, *English Catholic Exiles in Late Sixteenth-Century Paris* (Woodbridge: Boydell and Brewer, 2011).

[64] Nashe, *Works*, I, p. 62. 'Free mason' means stone-mason and Nashe would appear to have a particular person in mind. See also Powel Mills Dawley, *John Whitgift and the Reformation* (London: Black, 1955), p. 184; V. K. J. Brook, *Whitgift and the English Church* (London: English Universities Press, 1957), pp. 120–5.

[65] Nashe, *Works*, II, p. 300; Sonnino, *Handbook*, pp. 117–18.

[66] Nashe, *Works*, II, pp. 300–1.

[67] Nashe, *Works*, II, p. 301. On 'ceremonies', see above, pp. 211–2.

whoring, the art of poisoning, the art of Sodomitrie', all of which make him 'an excellent Courtier, a curious carpet knight...a fine close leacher, a glorious hypocrite'.[68] The Danes and the Dutch need little attention as they are both nations of drunks who 'doe nothing but fill bottomeles tubs, & will be drunke & snort in the midst of dinner'.[69]

This looks like knowledge but it is not. The earl is either lying or indulging in what moral philosophers call 'bullshit', when the speaker does not care whether what s/he claims is true and has no means of knowing whether any of it is.[70] The earl has provided a series of standard descriptions which the reader will recognize but, given that virtually no readers of *The Unfortunate Traveller* would have had a chance to visit the countries described—Nashe included—there is no means of disputing the earl's descriptions other than by reading other travellers' accounts. The work itself, especially the lurid and sensational sections recounting Jack's adventures in Italy, simply confirms what the earl claims.[71] His prejudiced observations are mainly what would have been available in contemporary travel accounts. The comments on Italy recall Roger Ascham's exhortation to his countrymen not to travel abroad and risk being infected by Italian vice, where an obsession with appearance produces fussy creatures who agonize over 'whether a man lust to weare Shoe or pantocle [slipper]'.[72] According to Ascham, 'three proper opinions' characterize all Italians: 'open contempte of Goddes worde: in a secret securitie of sinne: and in a bloodie desire to haue all taken away, by sword or burning, that be not of their faction'.[73] Therefore, the reader of *The Unfortunate Traveller* will not learn anything new from the earl's words, nor from the descriptions of the French, Dutch, or Danes.[74] The description of Spain may be more challenging given the necessarily limited contact with Spain in the later sixteenth century, as the Anglo-Spanish War dragged on through Elizabeth's reign.[75] The revelation that the main problem with travelling to Spain was the import of ridiculous fashions is certainly at odds with rather more serious accounts of the experience of mercenaries fighting in the Spanish armies in their European wars, or the fate of prisoners at the hands of the Inquisition.[76] The earl's

---

[68] Nashe, *Works*, II, p. 301. Nashe refers to Gabriel Harvey as an 'Italian Porredge seasoner' in *Have With You To Saffron Walden* (Nashe, *Works*, III, p. 93), which surely means a poisoner, locating the art of poisoning in Italy, and perhaps referring to the case of Richard Roose, which involved poisoned gruel, a variant of porridge (see above, p. 229, n. 161).

[69] Nashe, *Works*, II, p. 301.   [70] Carson, *Lying and Deception*, pp. 60–3.

[71] Michael J. Redmond, *Shakespeare, Politics, and Italy: Intertextuality on the Jacobean Stage* (Farnham: Ashgate, 2009), pp. 40–3.

[72] Ascham, *Scholemaster*, sig. K1r; Hadfield, *Literature, Travel, and Colonial Writing*, p. 196.

[73] Ascham, *Scholemaster*, sig. K1r.

[74] See Jean-Christoph Mayer, 'Representing France and the French in Early Modern English Drama', in Jean-Christoph Meyer, ed., *Representing France and the French in Early Modern English Drama* (Newark: University of Delaware Press, 2008), pp. 21–46; Ton Hoenselaars, *Images of Englishmen and Foreigners in the Drama of Shakespeare and His Contemporaries* (Cranbury, NJ: Associated University Presses, 1992), pp. 60–3, 79–81, 197–9, *passim*.

[75] R. B. Wernham, *After the Armada: Elizabethan England and the Struggle for Western Europe, 1588–1595* (Oxford: Oxford University Press, 1984).

[76] See above, pp. 11–13; Hadfield, ed., *Amazons, Savages and Machiavels*, pp. 106–15. On the horrors of life in the Spanish army see Geoffrey Parker, *The Army of Flanders and the Spanish Road, 1567–1659* (Cambridge: Cambridge University Press, 1972), ch. 7.

rapid tour through the nationalities of Europe is comic in its reliance on stereotypes which provides obvious humorous effects, in part, of course, at the earl's expense. But it is also comic in an Aristotelian sense, conspicuously representing people as worse than they really are, exaggerating for literary effect.[77]

The earl's account forces the reader to consider the value of testimony and whether it can ever provide useful knowledge without independent verification. We have no means of knowing whether the earl knows anything about any of the countries that he urges Jack not to visit and, therefore, whether he is lying about the extent of his knowledge, or whether he has formed an opinion based on his own limited experience which he feels the need to pass on to others. Furthermore, the reader may or may not know that the author has not visited any of the countries he represents in his fiction and that the representation of the places and people in the text are based on the testimonies of others and that the author may or may not know or care whether anything is actually true. Testimony could sometimes be valuable but was often unreliable, unverifiable, and sometimes dangerously misleading, and depended to a large extent on the character of the speaker, as Montaigne noted. Nashe exploits this epistemological problem in *The Unfortunate Traveller*, leaving the reader unsure whether he or she ought to travel to prove the earl's testimony and Jack's experiences wrong—or right.

III

Jack Wilton's experiences represent the reader with a world of fictions narrated by liars. *The Unfortunate Traveller* is, as its title indicates, written in the wake of the experience of the wider world for Europeans in the sixteenth century, as the Renaissance went global and individuals had to assimilate diverse knowledge, information, and testimony which challenged their understanding, but which probably contained as many lies and untruths as reliable information.[78] These tales reached a wide audience because they were printed, often in the form of tiny, cheap pamphlets, which spread strange and unusual stories of marvellous events, newly discovered phenomena, the malign actions of witches, grisly murders, and other signs of God's ability to demonstrate his control over human affairs within and beyond the borders of different countries as news networks developed throughout Europe.[79] Such works provide testimony of what was believed: but how should we understand the nature of this belief? Were they produced by sincere authors and publishers for an audience whose ideas they shared? Were they cynical productions

[77] Russell and Winterbottom, eds, *Classical Literary Criticism*, p. 53.
[78] For the context see Jerry Brotton, *The Renaissance Bazaar: From the Silk Road to Michelangelo* (Oxford: Oxford University Press, 2002), ch. 1; Jyotsna G. Singh, ed., *A Companion to the Global Renaissance: English Literature and Culture in the Era of Expansion* (Oxford: Blackwell, 2009).
[79] Pettegree, *Invention of News*, pp. 76–95; Joad Raymond, *Pamphlets and Pamphleteering in Early Modern Britian* (Cambridge: Cambridge University Press, 2003), ch. 4; Joad Raymond, ed., *The Oxford History of Popular Print Culture, Vol. 1: Cheap Print in Britain and Ireland to 1660* (Oxford: Oxford University Press, 2011), pt 4; Shapiro, *Culture of Fact*, p. 88.

fabricated by exploitative entrepreneurs eager to exploit the gullible for a quick profit, who knew that they were peddling lies? Was there a shared complicity, a guilty enjoyment of salacious gossip with no one really caring whether these stories were true or not? Or, perhaps most probably, did the producers and the audiences share a mixture of motives?

In 1597 John Wolfe published a pamphlet that was both unusual and familiar. *A Most Strange and Wonderfull Herring* provided a startling representation of a fish caught 'neere vnto Drenton sometime the old and chiefe Cittie of the kingdome of Norway' on 26 November 1597.[80] Short pamphlets and broadsheets recounting spectacular miracles and unusual phenomena were a staple of the late-sixteenth-century European print trade and it is easy to find similar works that represent strange portents and apparitions in the sky or in natural objects (Christ's face in a grain of wheat); unusual monsters, whether beached leviathans or dragons; and medical anomalies (Siamese twins are probably the most common).[81] Fish had a particular place in the Christian imagination as symbols of the faith, with the Bible comparing life to that of a fish struggling in a net, and, most significantly, the 'Greek word for fish being an acronym of Jesus Christ, Son of God'. Therefore, they were often heralded as divine symbols and portents.[82]

Wolfe's pamphlet has a striking image of the herring with its peculiar markings, showing each side of the strange fish (Figure 1). The accompanying text explains why these markings are significant and what they mean:

> on the one side whereof you may plainely behold the perfect shape of two armed men, the one hauing in his hand a launce, the other a sword, close buckled in their corslets, with burgancts on their heades, standing as it were in their defence, threatning and assayling one another. I know that many will giue as small credit hereunto, and as sleightly esteeme thereof as *Pharao* did of the flies, & the Iewes of Christs miracles . . . Moreouer there was toward the taile of this Herring the right portraiture of two rods, the one farre bigger then the other, seeming to bee bound together with two strong bandes apéece, which euery man must confesse to bee the vndoubted signe of dreadfull correction: according as the Psalmist speaketh, saying: *Thou shalt bruse them with a rod of Iron, and breake them in peeces like a Potters vessell* . . . But now behold on the other side of this Herring, were fiue Characters most perfectly ingrauen, some of them vsual, and wel knowne among vs at this day, others strange and not vnderstood: but what the God of all power and might will giue hereby to be known is left to better iudgement, notwithstanding let vs remember, that as it once pleased God by the finger of his power

---

[80] Anon., *A Most Strange and Wonderfull Herring taken on the 26. day of Nouember 1597, neere vnto Drenton sometime the old and chiefe cittie of the kingdome of Norway. Hauing on the one side the picture of two armed men fighting, and on the other most strange characters, as in the picture is here expressed. First printed in Dutch at Roterdam by Ian van Doetecam. And now translated into English* (London, 1597). Only one copy survives in Cambridge University Library, bound with a large collection of seventeenth-century pamphlets (shelfmark Dd*.3.26(E)).

[81] Walter L. Strauss, *The German Single-Leaf Woodcut, 1550–1600*, 3 vols (New York: Abaris, 1975); S. K. Barker, 'International News Pamphlets', in Andy Kesson and Emma Smith, eds, *The Elizabethan Top Ten: Defining Print Popularity in Early Modern England* (Farnham: Ashgate, 2013), pp. 145–56; Walsham, *Providence*, pp. 167–8; Andrew Hadfield, 'News of the Sussex Dragon', *Reformation* 17 (2012), 99–113.

[82] Cunningham and Grell, *Four Horsemen of the Apocalypse*, p. 86.

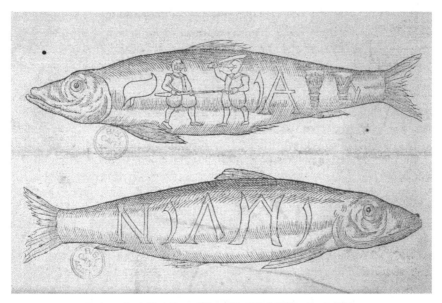

Figure 1. *A Most Strange and Wonderfull Herring* (1598).

to write on the wall a heauie sentence against *Balthasar,* so hath it pleased him at this present to write on this Herring vndoubtedly a heauie sentence against the sinnes of this age, thereby to call this drowsie worlde out of the damnable sléepe of sinne and wickednes, wherein it hath slugged so long a time.[83]

The author interprets the herring as a sign of God's wrath and his intention to punish mankind's wickedness unless people reform themselves and renounce their evil behaviour, a common theme in popular literature in the period, especially in the frequent times of plague.[84] The author is acutely aware that such prophecies are not always believed, an indication of a level of anxiety about duplicity and lying. However, he alleges that biblical examples will prompt readers foolish enough to discount the significance of the markings on the herring that Pharaoh ignored a host of warnings reminding him of his duty to free the Israelites (Exodus 8:21) and so made his people suffer. The markings nearer the tail of the herring are interpreted as rods bound together signifying the correction that God means to meet out to a world characterized by endless conflict, as stated in Psalm 2:9. The mysterious letters, which the author makes no attempt to decipher, are thought to recall those written by the mysterious hand on the wall at Balthasar's feast, which Daniel interpreted to mean that the fate of the kingdom lay in the balance because the King had hardened his heart against God (Daniel 5).

[83] Anon., *Most Strange and Wonderfull Herring*, sigs A2v–A3r.
[84] Carroll Camden, Jr, 'Elizabethan Almanacs and Prognostications', *The Library*, 4th series, 12 (1931), 83–108; Matthew Woodcock, '1603', in Raymond, ed., *Oxford History of Popular Print Culture*, pp. 578–89.

The herring pamphlet can therefore be read alongside a large body of material that saw signs in events that forecast the need for urgent reform, such as the sea monster washed up at Harwich, or the unfortunate woman with the horn in her forehead.[85] However, it is worth asking further questions of this text, as it may be a more significant work than has hitherto been recognized. Prognostications and prophecies should not always be taken at face value given the wealth of parodies and the frequent scepticism directed at the genre, something that the text draws attention to in acknowledging that there will be readers who do not take this pamphlet seriously.[86] Perhaps the pamphlet contains a series of signs that demonstrate that it contains more lies than truth.

The title page claims that the pamphlet is a translation of a work first published in Dutch by Jan Van Doetecam ('First printed in Dutch at Roterdam *by Ian van Doetecam, And now translated into English*'), a technically accomplished engraver from a family of artists, who were well known for producing high-quality maps.[87] This original text cannot be located—which does not mean that it does or did not exist given how many pamphlets have disappeared and how frequently only one copy of a popular work survives.[88] There clearly was a Dutch source as the same image exists in a copy of a broadsheet preserved in the National Library of Scotland: *Afbeeldinge Van Eenen Seer Wonderbaeren Harinck. Pourtraict d'un harenc, peche le 26. November, 159. a 3. Lieües de Dronten, la plus anienne ville capital du royaulme de Norvegue* (1598). This publication does not have an accompanying text, which suggests that the analysis of the significance of the herring is an original English work. When writing about the righteous wrath of God the author refers the reader to the behaviour of the bloody conqueror Tamburlaine: 'In scripture sword and pestilence is said to be the scourges of the Lord: and therefore that cruel and bloody tyrant *Tamberlaine* did iustly call himselfe the scourge of God, by whom he corrected the proud, rebellious and wicked world: bringing by bloody wars many kingdomes into his subiection.'[89] This must surely be a reference to Christopher Marlowe's play, which was printed in 1590, 1593, and 1597, describing the protagonist as the 'scourge of God' on the title page of the first two editions (Figure 2).[90]

---

[85] Anon., *A True Report and Exact Description of a Mighty Sea-Monster or Whale, cast vpon Langarshore ouer against Harwich in Essex, this present moneth of Februarie 1617* (London, 1617); Anon., *A Myraculous, and Monstrous, but yet most true, and certayne discourse, of a woman (now to be seene in London) of the age of threescore yeares, or there abouts, in the midst of whose fore-head (by the wonderfull worke of God) there groweth out a crooked horne, of foure ynches long* (London, 1588).

[86] For discussion see F. P. Wilson, 'Some English Mock-Prognostications', *The Library*, 4th series, 19 (1939), 6–43.

[87] See Anon., *The Van Doetecum Family: 1554–1606* (Rotterdam, Netherlands: Sound & Vision Interactive, 1998).

[88] Andrew Pettegree, 'Lost Books', paper given at The Biblioteca Hernandina and the Early Modern Book World: Towards a New Cartography (Corpus Christi College, University of Cambridge, 17 December 2013).

[89] Anon., *Most Strange and Wonderfull Herring*, sig. A3r.

[90] Or, perhaps, a reference to the 'Dutch Church libel', which was fixed on the French church wall in 1593, which attacked 'strangers' resident in England, and was signed 'Tamburlaine': see Arthur Freeman, 'Marlowe, Kyd, and the Dutch Church Libel', *ELR* 3 (1973), 44–52. If there is an allusion, the herring author would appear to be connecting the libel author's fear of chaos in London to the dangers posed by the conflict over a staple fish a few years later, suggesting that such imbalances and the aggression they generate are signs of celestial displeasure at man's actions.

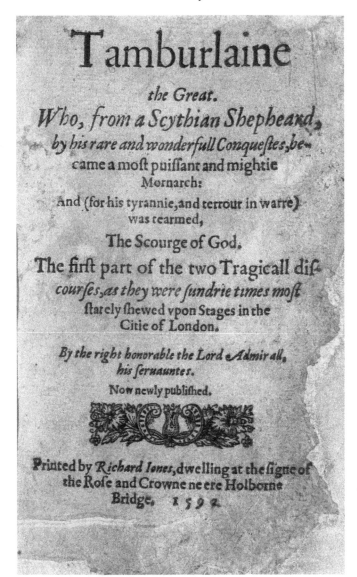

Figure 2. Christopher Marlowe, *Tamburlaine* (London, 1592), title page.

It is certainly hard to imagine a Dutch original that contained this comparison. Moreover, the reference suggests that the author was interested in literature and may have had a nuanced understanding of the genre he was employing, and the possibilities he had to exploit its nature.

There is something odd too about the story of the herring. The herring in the picture was caught in November 1597, but the representation of the letters on

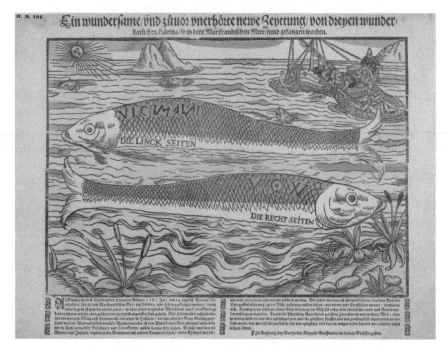

Figure 3. Wondrous Herring seen on 24 December 1587.

the side of the fish bear more than a passing resemblance to a herring caught on 24 December 1587, also off Norway, represented in German woodcuts.[91] The three herrings represented here (Figures 3–5) differ in some ways but it is clear that the more extensive writing on the one side of the herring is an attempt to reproduce the same markings and that the somewhat amorphous shape on the other has proved harder to represent.

Is it possible that the 1597 herring is, in fact, an updated and improved version of its 1587 counterpart? Has the shape in the middle mutated, whether through design or accident, into the figures of the two knights fighting?

Certainly the 1587 herring is the much better documented of the two and it is regularly referred to in histories of the fish.[92] This herring appeared at a particularly propitious time and seemed to be a sign of things to come. As Poul Holm has pointed out in his history of the brief flourishing of the Bohuslen herring industry (1556–89), the once mighty Danish fishing fleet declined sharply in the sixteenth century as the more efficient and powerful Dutch took over in the Baltic. However, the development of the war with the Spanish kept the Dutch occupied and the Danes enjoyed a bonanza period of profits, albeit with the constant prospect that the Dutch would return someday to reclaim the fish stocks. The discovery of the

---

[91] Strauss, *German Single-Leaf Woodcut*, I, p. 426; II, pp. 482, 500.

[92] Mike Smylie, *Herring: A History of the Silver Darlings* (Stroud: The History Press, 2004), pp. 67–8.

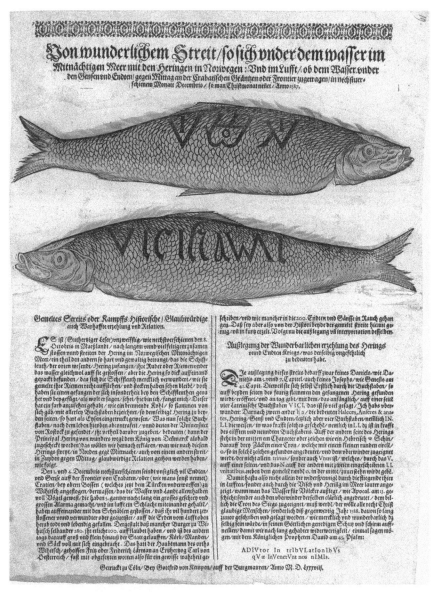

Figure 4. Wondrous Herrings in the Norwegian Sea, December 1587.

herring in 1587 excited the curiosity of the King, Frederick II (1534–88), father of Queen Anne of Denmark—soon to be the wife of James VI of Scotland and a firm believer in signs and prophecies—who asked the University of Berlin for advice.[93]

---

[93] Cunningham and Grell, *Four Horsemen of the Apocalypse*, p. 86. On James see Willson, *King James*, pp. 103–6.

Figure 5. Wondrous Herrings Found in Norway, 1587.

They interpreted the appearance of the fish as a warning that the Danes needed to mend their errant ways and turn their thoughts to God or the success of recent years would come to an abrupt end.[94] A broadside of 1588 deciphered the 'letters' on one side of the herring as *VICI MALUM*, 'I have conquered evil.' A more extensive reading by Ananias Jeraucurius claimed that the marks denoted an acrostic: '*Venit Iesus Christus iudicare, superbiam mundi peruersi*, or "Jesus Christ is coming to judge the arrogance of the corrupt world"'.[95] Frederick died in 1588; the Dutch–Spanish War declined in intensity and the Dutch were able to return to their old fishing grounds; as a result the Danish fishing industry was dramatically affected.[96]

---

[94] MacCulloch, *Reformation*, p. 556. MacCulloch assumes the two herring are different fish.

[95] Jonathan Green, Research Fragments (http://researchfragments.blogspot.co.uk/search?q=herring) (accessed 14 December 2015). See also Howard Hotson, *Paradise Postponed: Johann Heinrich Alsted and the Birth of Calvinist Millenarianism* (Dordrecht: Springer, 2000), pp. 100–4, who writes of two herring caught simultaneously on 21 November 1587, one of which was subjected to more extensive interpretation than the other.

[96] Poul Holm, 'The Bohuslen Herring: Interlude to Dutch Supremacy in the European Fish Market, 1556–1589', in L. M. Akveld, F. Broeze, F. S. Gaastra, G. Jackson, and W. M. F. Morzer Bruyns, eds, *In Het Kielzog Maritiem-Historische Studies aangeboden aan Jaap R. Bruijn, bij zijn vertrek als hoogleraar zeegeschiedenis aan de Universiteit Leiden* (Amsterdam: De Bataafsche Leeuw, 2003), pp. 182–8. See also Bo Paulson, *Dutch Herring: An Environmental History, C. 1600–1860* (Amsterdam: Aksant, 2008), pp. 95–6; James Travis Jenkins, *The Herring and the Herring Fisheries* (London: P. S. King and Son, 1927), chs 4–5.

As this history indicates, fishing was vitally important not just in producing food in a period of continual scarcity, but in determining the demography of Europe.[97] This was especially relevant in England, a country with a long coastline and access to substantial fish stocks. There were serious arguments put forward to increase fish consumption in order to protect the industry.[98] In 1580, the soldier-writer Robert Hitchcock (*fl.* 1573–91) had argued that developing herring fishing in particular would solve a host of England's economic and social problems, supplementing diet, boosting exports, and providing useful work for sturdy beggars and criminals.[99] In the early seventeenth century John Keymer, a client of Sir Walter Raleigh, who also worked for Sir Robert Cecil, made his celebrated claim 'that his Majesties Seas are far richer then the King of *Spains Indies*, and there is more made of Fish, taken by the *French, Biskers, Portugall, Spaniards, Hollanders, Hamburgers, Beemers, Embdeners, Scotish, Irish*, and *English* in one year, then the King of *Spain* hath in four years out of the *Indies*'.[100] As commentators have duly noted, 'No European government took as much interest in fishing as the English except the state of Holland,' which helps us understand why a Dutch pamphlet on herring might be translated into English.[101] Herrings, long a staple of the English and Scottish diet, especially on the east coast with ready access to the vast stocks of this prolific fish in the North Sea, were particularly important in the late 1590s and were much discussed. Most significantly, the principal English herring centre, Great Yarmouth, was locked in an unseemly quarrel with the neighbouring town of Lowestoft, whose citizens were disgruntled about the monopoly enjoyed by Yarmouth and the burdensome taxes imposed on the local area.[102]

In June 1595 Lowestoft took its quarrel to the Privy Council, lodging a petition that alleged that Yarmouth prevented the citizens of Lowestoft from buying white and red herring (i.e. fresh and smoked) from fishermen outside the town. According to the Lowestoft town council Yarmouth prevented this perfectly reasonable

---

[97] A. R. Mitchell, 'The European Fisheries in Early Modern Europe', in E. E. Rich and C. H. Wilson, eds, *The Cambridge Economic History of Europe, Volume 5: The Economic Organization of Early Modern Europe* (Cambridge: Cambridge University Press, 1977), pp. 133–84, at p. 135; Mark Kurlansky, *Cod: A Biography of the Fish that Changed the World* (London: Vintage, 1999).

[98] 'Arguments in Favour of Establishing Wednesday as an Additional Fish Day, February, 1563', in R. H. Tawney and Eileen Powers, eds, *Tudor Economic Documents*, 3 vols (London: Longman, 1924), II, pp. 104–10.

[99] Robert Hitchcock, *A Pollitique Platt for the Honour of the Prince, the greate profite of the publique state, relief of the poore, preseruation of the riche, reformation of roges and idle persones, and the wealthe of thousandes that knowes not howe to liue* (London, 1580). On Hitchcock, see the *ODNB* entry.

[100] John Keymer, *John Keymors Observation Made Upon the Dutch Fishing about the year 1601 demonstrating that there is more wealth raised out of herrings and other fish in His Majesties seas by the neighbouring nations in one year, then the King of Spain hath from the Indies* (London, 1664). On Keymor see the *ODNB* entry.

[101] Mitchell, 'European Fisheries', p. 178.

[102] My account is especially indebted to Robert Tittler, 'The English Fishing Industry in the Sixteenth Century: The Case of Great Yarmouth', *Albion* 9 (1977), 40–60; David M. Dean, 'Parliament, Privy Council, and Local Politics in Elizabethan England: The Yarmouth–Lowestoft Fishing Dispute', *Albion* 22 (1990), 39–64; R. C. L. Sgroi, 'Piscatorial Politics Revisited: The Language of Economic Debate and the Evolution of Fishing Policy in Elizabethan England', *Albion* 35 (2003), 1–24.

practice from happening through a variety of illegal methods: 'collecting tolls, frequently seizing ships, imprisoning fishermen, imposing hefty fines, and extracting "vehement promises never to sell herrings in Lowestofte Road againe"'.[103] In November the Council ruled in Lowestoft's favour, but the verdict was challenged by Yarmouth and by August 1596 the traditional rights of Yarmouth had been reinstated because of its successful appeals to the central authorities.[104] Lowestoft reappealed and a committee delivered another verdict upholding the status quo in April 1597. A bill was then presented to a parliamentary committee and 'committed after its second reading on 23 January 1598', but it did little to uphold the rights of Lowestoft.[105] Even so it was attacked by Yarmouth and its supporters as a threat to their ancient liberties and rights to fish herring, and the bill was eventually defeated in the House of Commons by eighteen votes.[106] The ill feeling between the towns lingered on into the early seventeenth century, but Yarmouth was always able to assert its superiority as a fishing port.[107]

The Yarmouth–Lowestoft dispute played a considerable role in defining the relationship between town councils and the Houses of Parliament and 'fishing remained a burning issue throughout the last two decades of Elizabeth's reign'.[108] Local interests were fought out on the national stage: Yarmouth had Robert Dudley, Earl of Leicester as its high steward until his death in 1588, then William Cecil, Lord Burghley until his death in 1598, before Robert Devereux, Earl of Essex (1598–1600); Lowestoft were undoubtedly aided by Sir John Fortesque and, probably, Thomas Sackville, Lord Buckhurst.[109] A sign of the significance of the quarrel is that 'The Elizabethan period saw the first comprehensive statutory regulation and protection of the English fishing industry.'[110] Even so, there was a widespread fear that the English would lose out to the Dutch in a herring war, just as the Danes had lost out in the Baltic. The Dutch were thought to be flooding the market even in the premier English herring stronghold of Yarmouth because the English had allowed their fleet to decline.[111]

Given the significance of the dispute it is hard not to assume that *A Most Strange and Wonderfull Herring* was consciously published to coincide with this crisis in the English fishing industry, as a warning to the two sides that God was unlikely to tolerate their fractiousness and wicked ways much longer. The pictures of the fighting men and the rods, unlikely to have been quite so clear on the fish itself, were clearly relevant to the situation in England in 1598, as two major ports on the East Anglian coast fought for mastery. The pamphlet poses a number of questions about its veracity that are difficult to answer, but which are directly relevant to

[103] Dean, 'Parliament', p. 46.

[104] Dean, 'Parliament', p. 50; Sgori, 'Piscatorial Politics', p. 12.

[105] See the account from Hayward Townshend's Journal in T. E. Hartley, ed., *Proceedings in the Parliaments of Elizabeth I, Vol. III: 1593–1601* (Leicester: Leicester University Press, 1995), pp. 239–40.

[106] Dean, 'Parliament', pp. 53–6.   [107] Dean, 'Parliament', p. 59.

[108] Sgroi, 'Piscatorial Politics', p. 18.   [109] Dean, 'Parliament', pp. 61–2.

[110] Sgroi, 'Piscatorial Politics', p. 1.

[111] Tittler, 'English Fishing Industry', pp. 58–9; Sgroi, 'Piscatorial Politics', p. 7.

issues of truth and lying in the period. If we assume that there is no Dutch original of the text, but that the images were copied, then is the story of the 1597 herring invented to delude readers? Or is it the case that the 1587 story was revisited and its provenance subtly rethought to make it relevant to the situation in England in 1598? And, if so, is this actually a lie, an attempt to make readers believe something that neither author nor publisher believes to be true?

It is hard to resist this last conclusion: even in a period when miraculous creatures appeared at regular intervals to warn people of the consequences of disobeying God, herrings with strange biblical markings did not appear very often, which is why the 1587 herring was so important and why there were so many woodcuts of it circulating in Europe. We then need to wonder why anyone would have produced such a pamphlet in 1598. Was it simply because such works would feed a market of readers eager to devour early newsbooks with tales of strange, uncanny stories that had to be explained? There were a number of publishers more than capable of bending the truth, as the case of the notorious John Trundle (1575–1629) indicates.[112] Or was it more likely that this was a work that took the moral decision to remind the warring citizens of Great Yarmouth and Lowestoft that they needed to end their quarrel for the sake of England and its immediate future? Perhaps a highly educated author knew what had happened ten years earlier in the Baltic and the fate of the once powerful Norwegian fishing industry, maybe through contacts in the international printing trade? There were few printers, publishers, or booksellers in England more connected to the international book trade than John Wolfe, known as the importer and publisher—often under a false imprint—of Italian books.[113]

Another explanation is that this could have been a strategic religious lie, rather like Jacob's deception of his father, or that of the virtuous Hebrew midwives. The author needed to tell the larger truth by manipulating the insignificant facts. The testimony of the eyewitness had to be altered in order to tell its story, and readers would realize the reason why God had decided to leave mankind a message on the side of a humble herring.

IV

The herring pamphlet must have been widely read. *Nashe's Lenten Stuffe* (1599), a work which, like the earlier *The Unfortunate Traveller*, explores the problem of truthful testimony, fiction, and lies, was surely influenced by such popular culture. In narrating the author's flight to Great Yarmouth after the suppression of *The Isle of Dogs* (1597), *Lenten Stuffe* provides an elaborate series of tales in praise of the red herring, outlining its contribution to world history and global culture in words that

[112] Gerald D. Johnson, 'John Trundle and the Book-Trade, 1603–1626', *SB* 39 (1986), 178–99; Walsham, *Providence*, pp. 45–7. Trundle's commercial instincts led him to publish the pamphlet on the Sussex dragon, the only sighting of a dragon in early modern England; pamphlets about the Overbury trial; and the pirated first quarto of *Hamlet*.
[113] On Wolfe see above, p. 233.

merge truth and fiction. In doing so Nashe reflects on issues of the real (in particular, economics) and the fantastic, mixing high and low culture, as well as highlighting the complicated relationship between the declaration of the truth and the production of lies.[114]

It is even possible—although there is no evidence—that the pamphlet was part of a more orchestrated plot given the interest of the Elizabethan authorities in promoting fish as a valuable food and commodity, and that a major figure was behind this particular pamphlet. William Cecil, Lord Burghley, was high steward of Great Yarmouth from 1588 until his death in 1598, and always took a keen interest in promoting the consumption of fish.[115] Wolfe's expertise in printing Italian books attracted Burghley's attention, who used Wolfe to print an Italian translation of a pamphlet defending the execution of Edmund Campion in 1584, and another four years later to spread the news of England's triumph over the Spanish Armada.[116] Perhaps the herring pamphlet was another ruse of Burghley's eager to make his case to a wider public in a cunning, underhand way.

Burghley was certainly adept at orchestrating opposition to policies and events which he thought threatened the security of the realm, realizing the power that the printing press could have in defining public opinion.[117] One of Burghley's most successful tactics was to place works in print that looked as if they were simply the expression of a popular outrage at the dangerous mechanics of mighty figures, which is why it should come as no surprise if the herring pamphlet proved to be yet another of his cunning schemes. So successful was his execution of his underhand policy that only now are some of Burghley's ruses coming to light. Burghley was behind the publication of a translation of George Buchanan's Latin text, *Detectio Mariae Reginae Scotorum* (1571), with the title *Ane Detectioun of the Duinges of Marie Quene of Scottes* (1571), appearing in the wake of the Northern Rebellion (1569–70), which planned to depose Elizabeth and place Mary on the throne. For Burghley the Rebellion was part of a dangerous international Catholic conspiracy, and he was keen to do all he could to prevent its spread and to raise public awareness of its obvious dangers, especially when the premier English Catholic peer, Thomas Howard, fourth Duke of Norfolk (1536–72) resumed his correspondence with Mary and revived earlier somewhat inchoate plans of marrying the

---

[114] On the relationship between the herring pamphlet and *Lenten Stuff* see Andrew Hadfield, 'A Red Herring?', *ELR* 45 (2015), 231–54. On economics see Henry S. Turner, 'Nashe's Red Herring: Epistemologies of the Commodity in *Lenten Stuffe* (1599)', *ELH* 68 (2001), 529–61; Kristen Abbott Bennett, 'Red Herrings and the "Stench of Fish": Subverting "Praise" in Thomas Nashe's Lenten Stuffe', *R. & R.* 37 (2014), 87–110.

[115] Dean, 'Parliament', pp. 61–2; Kitch, *Political Economy*, pp. 80–2; Tawney and Power, eds, *Tudor Economic Documents*, II, pp. 124–7.

[116] Fritz Levy, 'The Decorum of News', in Joad Raymond, ed., *News, Newspapers and Society in Early Modern Britain* (London: Frank Cass, 1999), pp. 12–38, at p. 23. The texts in question are Anon., *Atto della Giustitia d'Inghilterra* (London, 1584); Anon., *Essempio D'Vna Lettera Mandata D'Inghilterra A Don Bernadino Di Mendozza Ambasciatore in Francia per lo Re di Spagna* (London, 1588).

[117] Lake, *Bad Queen Bess?*, pp. 431, 448.

Scottish Queen.[118] Burghley was at the start of a long-drawn-out process that would eventually lead to the execution of Mary after her involvement in the Babington Plot—evidence for Mary's involvement may have been exaggerated or faked—nearly twenty years after she had first sought sanctuary in England.[119] Certainly the testimony of the Duke at his trial suggests that his plans amounted to little more than a half-baked and hare-brained scheme that was largely fantasy, and it is not clear that he really planned to marry Mary; that she knew much about his plans (he denied that she did); or, given the chaotic nature of his 'feckless behaviour' produced by the prosecution, that he was a dangerous traitor whose cunning plot threatened the security of the realm. Rather ungallantly the Duke argued that the fact that he had stated in a letter produced at the trial that he found Mary unattractive shows what service he was prepared to do his country in attempting to bring the two kingdoms closer together not, as the prosecution alleged, a result of his own ambition to rule.[120]

Buchanan's Latin text had been written as an explanatory letter to accompany the Casket letters, when they were used as evidence against Mary to justify incarcerating her in England in 1567.[121] These were letters and sonnets from Mary to her future husband, James Hepburn, fourth Earl of Bothwell, implicating Mary in the murder of her then husband, Henry Stuart, Lord Darnley, written between January and April 1567—and may also be unreliable as evidence.[122] Buchanan's *Detectio* appears to have remained in London, probably in Burghley's possession, until the arrest of Norfolk on charges of treason in 1571 made the work valuable once again.[123] Burghley helped arrange that a supposedly authentic 'Scottified' version of the Latin text should appear with the false imprint of St Andrews and be made widely available in England, disguising any connection to Elizabeth's government. Thomas Wilson (1523/4–81), the diplomat, politician and scholar, author of *The Art of Rhetoric* (1554) and *A Discourse Upon Usury* (1572), was probably the creative translator.[124] The printer, John Day, was already working on the major commission that was to dominate the rest of his working

[118] Kesselring, *Northern Rebellion*, pp. 150–62; Stephen Alford, *The Early Elizabethan Polity: William Cecil and the British Succession Crisis, 1558–1569* (Cambridge: Cambridge University Press, 1998), pp. 199–203; Stephen Alford, *Burghley: William Cecil at the Court of Elizabeth I* (New Haven: Yale University Press, 2008), pp. 158–9; Lake, *Bad Queen Bess?*, pp. 49–57. On Norfolk's trial see *State Trials*, I, pp. 957–1042.

[119] Guy, *'My Heart is My Own'*, pp. 181–4; Alford, *Watchers*, pp. 210–40; Wormald, *Mary Queen of Scots*, pp. 185–6.

[120] *State Trials*, I, p. 1001; Wallace MacCaffrey, *The Shaping of the Elizabethan Regime* (London: Cape, 1969), p. 279.

[121] James Emerson Phillips, *Images of a Queen: Mary Stuart in Sixteenth-Century Literature* (Berkeley: University of California Press, 1964), pp. 61–2.

[122] Guy, *'My Heart is My Own'*, pp. 396–417, concludes that the letters were doctored rather than faked. Rosalind Smith, *Sonnets and the English Woman Writer, 1560–1621: The Politics of Absence* (Basingstoke: Palgrave Macmillan, 2005), ch. 2, argues that the sonnets are genuine.

[123] Phillips, *Images of a Queen*, p. 62.

[124] Phillips, *Images of a Queen*, p. 62. On Wilson see *ODNB* entry. On the significance of *The Art of Rhetoric* see Hadfield, *Literature, Politics and National Identity*, pp. 108–17; see also Thomas Wilson, *A Discourse upon Usury*, ed. R. H. Tawney (London: Bell, 1925).

career and make him the pre-eminent Elizabethan publisher, John Foxe's *Acts and Monuments*.[125]

The long opening sentence of *Ane Detectioun* strikes a querulous note, warning subjects that they need to be resolute in defence of their liberty and not to allow their country to fall under the spell of foreign powers:

> Quhairas of thynges iudicially determinit within any dominioun, to haif accompte demandit by strangeris, is to sic as be not subiect to forane iurisdictioun, baith strange, and also for the strangenesse displeasant, to vs aboue all vther it ought to be most greuous, quha are driuen to this streight of necessitie, that quhase fautes we desire to couer, thair liues we are enforced to accuse, vnlesse we will our selues be accompted the most wicked persons that lyue.[126]

The sentence deliberately connotes authentic Scottishness in its opening word, making use of the familiar 'Qu' spelling as the equivalent of the English 'w' (repeated twice more in the sentence). The argument that the sovereignty of the nation has to be preserved at all costs and that strangers should not be permitted to rule has more force for being articulated by a speaker with an unfamiliar style/language to native English speakers, as it looks as if he is advising the English to learn from Scottish errors and follow their example in excluding Mary from the succession. The syntax resists straightforward interpretation but as the reader follows the sentence it becomes clear that the message urges readers to take what they might think of as regrettable actions in order to prevent greater evils, that is, support the execution of a queen. The paragraph opens with a direct statement, sounding as if the reader is overhearing a long, impassioned oration, that it might be thought grievous to suffer foreign rule. The clause appears as if it is heading towards a 'however', but then moves towards an intensification with the words 'to vs aboue all', making the sentence resemble a clever lawyer's argument that wrong-foots the reader into supporting the speaker all the more because s/he had not quite realized how much they were in agreement with the sentiments expressed. By the end the clauses build up towards an apparently reluctant climax: the logic of the paragraph is that we must perform these regrettable actions if we do not wish to become criminals ourselves.

The following sentence directly addresses Elizabeth as the lawful Queen: 'But a great part of this greef, is releued by your equitie (most excellent Quene) quha take it no lesse displeasantly to see your kinswoman, than we to see our Quene thus in speche of all men to be dishonorably reported, quha alswa are for your part no lesse desirous to vnderstand the truth, than we for ours to auoide sclaunder.'[127] This looks like support for Elizabeth but it is really a coercive attempt to force her hand to act against Mary, much like Foxe's representation of Elizabeth as the Emperor Constantine was designed to make her church government more religious and,

---

[125] Evenden, *John Day*, p. 132.
[126] George Buchanan, *Ane Detectioun of the Duinges of Marie Quene of Scottes* (London, 1571), sig. A2r.
[127] Buchanan, *Detectioun*, sig. A2r.

therefore, more Protestant.[128] Elizabeth, according to Wilson/Buchanan, has re-
lived a great part of the grief of her subjects eager not to suffer the misery of foreign
rule, but, the implication is, her justice (equity) needs to stretch a bit further in
order to cut off the threat of Mary. Buchanan's voice speaks with regret, as if in
sympathy with the dilemma that Elizabeth faces, claiming that Scots feel the pain
and shame of Mary's actions as they are reported, just as the English Queen is hurt
by the behaviour of her cousin. This fellow feeling will lead both loyal Scots and
English to conclude that the only honest and Christian way to act is to stop Mary's
threat by any means possible.

As Anne McLaren has argued, 'the uncharted political territory' of the 1570s
'threw into relief issues of regality, majesty and sovereignty', as Britain had to
grapple with the existence of two queens on one island.[129] *Ane Detectioun* played a
decisive role in blackening Mary's character and helped to fix an image of her in
English eyes as a treacherous murderess who had betrayed her people through her
own intemperate lusts and who, accordingly, should be executed.[130] Mary is
represented as evil, conniving, unscrupulous, and ruled by her lusts. When she is
told by the Protestant lords of Scotland that she cannot procure a divorce 'from that
day forwart sche neuer cessed to pursue hir intentioun of murdering the king'.[131]
This is because her unseemly desire for Bothwell rules her life, pursuing him in
ways that undermine her authority as monarch:

> Hir affectioun impatient of delay cauld not temper it self, but nedis she must bewray
> hir outragious lust, and in an vnconuenient time of the yere, despising all discommod-
> ities of the way & wether, & all dangers of theifis, she betooke hir self hedlong to hir
> iourney with sic a company as na man of any honest degree wald haif aduentured his
> life and his gudes amang tham.[132]

As Queen, her dignity and safety are paramount, as it is one of her primary duties
to secure the succession so that any action which places her in danger or which
links her to an unsuitable partner has a corresponding detrimental effect on the
people.[133] And, of course, the text establishes a pointed contrast to Elizabeth. Mary
is personally cruel, a word used frequently throughout *Ane Detectioun*, tormenting
her husband in unnecessary ways because he fails to satisfy her appetites. She tries,
but fails, to poison him, so finds other ways to vent her spleen:

> Quhen this practise framit nat fully to hir desire, sche goeth hir selfe to Glascow, that
> quhom being absent she could nat kill, sche might hir selfe in presence satisfie baith hir
> cruell hart and hir eyes with sight of hys present miseries. And as if hir selfe alone weir

---

[128] Frances A. Yates, *Astrea: The Imperial Theme in the Sixteenth Century* (London: Routledge, 1975), pp. 41–5.

[129] Anne C. McLaren, *Political Culture in the Reign of Elizabeth I: Queen and Commonwealth, 1558–1585* (Cambridge: Cambridge University Press, 1999), p. 184.

[130] John D. Staines, *The Tragic Histories of Mary Queen of Scots, 1560–1690* (Aldershot: Ashgate, 2009), ch. 1.

[131] Buchanan, *Detectioun*, sig. C2r.   [132] Buchanan, *Detectioun*, sig. B3v.

[133] Natalie Mears, *Queenship and Political Discourse in the Elizabethan Realms* (Cambridge: Cambridge University Press, 2005), chs 1–2.

nat sufficient to execute the cruell tormenting of hym, sche bringeth into his sight the ministers of hir haynous doinges, and hys auncient naturall enemies, and wyth these outragis trauailed to vexe hys saule at his last breath.[134]

Mary is a tyrant, unable to control herself, her marriage, or the nation that she rules.[135] When opposed, as she will be by all sensible godly people as they learn of her true nature, she is vicious and wreaks a terrible revenge on those who obstruct her desires. If her own people see her in this light then so must the English whose nation she plots to overthrow with the wicked tyranny of the papacy.[136]

In having this work published Burghley was acting against Elizabeth's wishes, as she was resolute in her opposition to the largely Protestant lobby that were eager to see Mary dead in order to protect her crown, fearing that the cure would be worse than the disease.[137] Elizabeth, although she had little time for Mary, was anxious not to execute another monarch, given the calls for her own assassination from Catholic quarters.[138] A literary equivalent of this case would be Cassius misleading the naive Brutus in *Julius Caesar*, placing false letters convincing him that the people want him to rise up and challenge Caesar, when the truth is that Cassius is conducting a 'deliberate propaganda campaign' in order to stage a *coup d'état*.[139] *Ane Detectioun* looks as if it is the expression of popular opinion, a keen desire to voice opposition to Mary which will force the English authorities to take note of the people's will. In reality it was, as John D. Staines has pointed out, part of a carefully orchestrated plot to ensure that Mary would never become Queen of England: 'The entire pamphlet amounts to one simple moral: Mary's character makes her an unfit ruler so don't be tempted to set her up in place of Elizabeth.'[140] Elizabeth did not know about Burghley's actions and neither, most probably, did Buchanan. The text as we have it is surrounded by falsehoods, even though part of it has a basis in truth. It is, in short, a lie: what looks like a truthful testimony of the wickedness of Mary's reign is not quite what it seems to be.

V

The same issues would seem to apply to popular pamphlet literature in general. Truthful testimony was invariably invoked but as an assertive and defensive measure which might have sought to guarantee the truthfulness of the evidence in question but which, in fact, drew attention to its unreliable nature. As Julius Ruff has argued,

---

[134] Buchanan, *Detectioun*, sigs H1v–H2r.
[135] Rebecca W. Bushnell, *Tragedies of Tyrants: Political Thought and Theater in the English Renaissance* (Ithaca, NY: Cornell University Press, 1990), pp. 15–19; Anon., *Vindiciae, Contra Tyrannos, or Concerning the Legitimate Power of a Prince over the People, and of the People over a Prince*, ed. George Garnett (Cambridge: Cambridge University Press, 1994), introduction, pp. I–liii.
[136] Buchanan, *Detectioun*, sig. F2r.
[137] Patrick Collinson, *Elizabethans* (London: Hambledon, 2003), pp. 46–55.
[138] Susan Doran, '"Revenge her most foul and unnatural murder": The Impact of Mary Stuart's Execution on Anglo-Scottish Relations', *History* 85 (2000), 589–612.
[139] Alan Stewart, *Shakespeare's Letters* (Oxford: Oxford University Press, 2008), p. 85.
[140] Staines, *Tragic Histories*, p. 49. See also Shrank, 'This fatall Medea'.

most of the pamphlet literature about violent crime printed in early modern England 'grossly misrepresented' the real nature of the offences described, reproducing what the audience wanted to read.[141] It would be easy to choose from a large variety of pamphlets, ballads, and other cheap print to prove Natalie Zemon Davis's point that representations of crime relied heavily on fictional models and existed in a shared culture that bound classes together, even though such works were commercially produced.[142] The case is particularly obvious when the violent crimes in question were committed by women, as the story of Frances Howard demonstrates, or if we consider the frequent cases of infanticide recorded in the period.[143] Criminal women were represented as unnatural, forms of the archetypal wicked woman, with either a popular or a more literary model, often derived from Ovid or Greek tragedy, in mind.[144]

One issue is that it is hard to attribute such manifestations of popular culture to a particular source in order to determine their veracity. Adam Fox's argument that 'It is difficult to know whether to describe a ballad as the product of oral, scribal, or print culture,' could almost as easily be applied to broadsides and pamphlets.[145] Murder pamphlets often assert that they represent the truth of an eyewitness's testimony, providing lists of names at the end of the text, but it is often clear that they cannot quite be what they claim to be and that their evidence is rather more problematic than the authors claim. Thomas Brewer's *The Bloudy Mother, or The Most Inhumane Murthers, committed by Iane Hattersley vpon diuers infants* (London, 1610) states that 'the names of those that at the bench gaue euidence against them, persons (for the most part) of good sufficiency, yet liuing, cannot but inforce a beleefe in any that haue sence to secure vpon such manifest markes of veritie'.[146] Susan Wiseman points out that the description of the number of infanticides apparently known to the local community suggests that all is not quite as it seems and that these witnesses were not telling the truth in representing the crime as a sudden revelation after an argument between Jane and her lover, Adam Adamson, is overheard.[147] Anne-Marie Kilday points out that the pamphlet represents the couple

---

[141] Ruff, *Violence*, p. 30.

[142] Alexandra Nicole Hill, '"Bloudy Tygrisses": Murderous Women in Early Modern English Drama and Popular Literature', PhD thesis, University of Central Florida Orlando, Florida, 2009, p. 27.

[143] See Cressy, *Agnes Bowker's Cat*, pp. 9–28.

[144] Sandra Clark, *Women and Crime in the Street Literature of Early Modern England* (Basingstoke: Palgrave Macmillan, 2003), pp. ix–xi; Hill, 'Bloudy Tygrisses', pp. 2–3; Pamela Joseph Benson, *Invention of the Renaissance Woman: The Challenge of Female Independence in the Literature and Thought of Italy and England* (University Park, PA: Penn State University Press, 1992), p. 9; Garthine Walker, *Crime, Gender and Social Order in Early Modern England* (Cambridge: Cambridge University Press, 2003), p. 75; Vanessa McMahon, *Murder in Shakespeare's England* (London: Black, 2006), p. 22.

[145] Adam Fox, *Oral and Literate Culture in England, 1500–1700* (Oxford: Oxford University Press, 2000), p. 5.

[146] Thomas Brewer, *The Bloudy Mother, or The Most Inhumane Murthers, committed by Iane Hattersley vpon diuers infants* (London, 1610), sig. A2r.

[147] Susan J. Wiseman, *Writing Metamorphosis in the English Renaissance: 1550–1700* (Cambridge: Cambridge University Press, 2014), p. 194.

burying the children in the picture on the title page, but then blames their deaths solely on Jane Hattersley, a significant discrepancy.[148]

Crime pamphlets proliferated in the first decades of the seventeenth century.[149] Many, not surprisingly, such as pamphlets about bizarre and weird phenomena, raise particular issues about testimony, truthfulness, and lying, given their sensational subject matter and nature, and the need for authors and publishers to make quick profits. In 1606 two pamphlets were published in the wake of a brutal crime and subsequent double execution in Hertfordshire on 4 August 1606. Both pamphlets were printed for the bookseller William Ferbrand (Firebrand), active from 1598 until 1609, which suggests that there is some connection between the pamphlets and their sources.[150]

The basic facts of the case would appear to be clear: Annis Dell, together with her son, George, murdered a child, Anthony James, at the inn they ran in Royston, Hertfordshire.[151] In order to disguise their actions they cut out the tongue of his sister, who then wanders off to become a beggar. Her brother's body is discovered and she then returns to the town some years later. Her speech miraculously recovers and she is able to tell the authorities what happened and the two villains are hanged.[152] Both pamphlets advertise the severing of the tongue as a key detail to attract readers on the title page.[153] But there are numerous discrepancies in the accounts given in the two pamphlets. *The Horrible Murther of A Young Boy* is sketchy and brief in its outline of events, and makes less effort to contextualize the crime; the other, *The Most Cruell and Bloudy Murther Committed by an Inkeepers Wife, called Annis Dell*, is over twice the length of *The Horrible Murther* and provides a more detailed account of the crime, as well as more literary and religious parallels to help explain the events.[154] It also ends rather abruptly and has a short

---

[148] Anne-Marie Kilday, *A History of Infanticide in Britain, c.1600 to the Present* (Basingstoke: Palgrave Macmillan, 2013), pp. 67–8.

[149] Raymond, *Pamphlets and Pamphleteering*, p. 118.

[150] On Ferbrand see *STC*, III, pp. 62–3. He had a series of shops, one of which was in 'Popes head Alley, right ouer against the Tauerne-doore': Samuel Rowland, *Letting of Humors Blood in the Head-Vaine* (London, 1607), title page. The longer of the two pamphlets was printed by Thomas Purfoot for Firebrand and John Wright; the shorter by Thomas Purfoot.

[151] The most sophisticated reading of the pamphlets is that of Lena Cowen Orlin, whose aim is to uncover the diverse and complicated nature of early modern women's history: 'A Case for Anecdotalism in Women's History: The Witness Who Spoke When the Cock Crowed', *ELR* 31 (2001), 52–77.

[152] The pamphlets are referred to in a number of works and read in various ways in John H. Langbein, *Prosecuting Crime in the Renaissance: England, Germany, France* (Cambridge, MA: Harvard University Press, 1974), pp. 48–9; Luc Borot, 'Early Journalism in Sixteenth- and Seventeenth-Century England: The Interface between Literature and "Popular Culture"', *YSPSR* 9 (1998), 41–58, pp. 47–9; Ruff, *Violence*, p. 34; Lake and Questier, *Antichrist's Lewd Hat*, pp. 16, 29, 176; Clark, *Women and Crime*, pp. 154–6.

[153] Anon., *The Horrible Murther of A Young Boy of three yeres of age* (London, 1606); Anon., *The Most Cruell and Bloudy Murther Committed by an Inkeepers Wife, called Annis Dell, and her Sonne George Dell, Foure yeeres since* (London, 1606).

[154] Sensational pamphlets occupied an uneasy place between sacred and secular language: see Peter Lake, 'Religion and Cheap Print', in Raymond, ed., *Oxford History of Popular Print Culture*, pp. 217–41, at pp. 226–8.

account of a witchcraft trial, that of Joanna Harrison, from the same court at the same time.[155]

The principal differences are significant and substantial. *The Most Cruell and Bloudy Murther* names the dead child as Anthony James; provides details of his parents, a yeoman and his wife, his happy childhood, and explains that the parents were murdered by a gang of nine villains and one especially ferocious and terrifying woman; that they abduct the children and proceed to the Dells' Inn where they hatch the plot to murder the boy and cut out his sister's tongue to hide their crime; and that while they are drinking they are observed by the Dells' servant, Nicholas Dracon, who asks whose the child is and is told by Annis Dell that he belongs to one of her guests. At the same time Anthony wanders into the street where he encounters a local tailor—like Nicholas Dracon we should probably assume that he gave evidence at the trial—who, admiring Anthony's green coat, measures the child in order to make a pattern. That evening the children are led away and Anthony is murdered, cow dung is pushed into his mouth to silence him and 'they slit his throat from one eare to another'.[156] George Dell then takes the lead in disposing of the body in a pond, having bound the corpse to a big stake. Annis leads the girl into the woods with the promise that she will be reunited with her parents and cuts out her tongue, throwing it into a pond with her dead brother's body. The villains depart leaving the Dells with money to rescue their ailing business, and, giving the girl a small sum, send her off as a beggar. The girl wanders to London where her wound is staunched by a kindly barber-surgeon, and she continues to beg throughout Essex for the next four years, only able to utter, 'Moka, Moka', and having to stretch the skin of her throat with her fingers in order to eat. Her brother's body is discovered in the pond and the Dells fall under suspicion. Annis is summoned by the local authorities as her husband is blind, but she swears under oath that she knows nothing of the crime. The girl comes back to Hatfield (the specific reason is not specified but she is an itinerant beggar), and starts to cry as she recognizes the place where her brother was murdered.[157] She is able to communicate by now and can answer questions using signs and gestures and we learn that her name is Elizabeth.[158] When she is shown her brother's distinctive green coat she knows the truth of his death.[159] While playing with another girl her speech miraculously returns after she hears the rhyme 'Cock a doodle doo', and she is able to answer all questions put to her (a detail common to both narratives). Elizabeth's answers are carefully examined by the local magistrates led by Ralph Conningsby and Sir Henry Butler, but they can find no fault with her testimony, no matter how hard they try

[155] For analysis see Anu Korhonen, 'The Witch in the Alehouse: Imaginary Encounters in Cultural History', in Jan Kusber, Mechthild Dreyer, Jörg Rogge, and Andreas Hütig, eds, *Historische Kulturwissenschaften: Positionen, Praktiken und Perspektiven* (Bielefeld: Transcript Verlag, 2010), pp. 181–205.
[156] Anon., *Most Cruell and Bloudy Murther*, sig. B1r.
[157] Beggars could be licensed if they had no other means of survival: Beier, *Masterless Men*, pp. 27–8.
[158] Anon., *Most Cruell and Bloudy Murther*, sig. B4r.
[159] On the coat see Elizabeth Hanson, 'Torture and Truth in Renaissance England', *Representations* 34 (1991), 53–84, p. 67.

(and they try very hard indeed).[160] The murderers admit their guilt and are duly executed.

The Horrible Murther provides few of these details and is generally a more limited version of the same story but with some important differences. The children are led to the Dells' Inn by a pedlar and 'his wife (or Puncke)', observed by the tailor.[161] The murdered boy is abandoned in a ditch 'with a great peece of wood tyed to his backe'.[162] The Dells fall under suspicion immediately, a warrant is issued for their arrest, and they are interviewed by Sir Henry Butler and another knight (presumably the author means Conningsby), the local Justices of the Peace. They admit that the children came into their house with the pedlars but, thinking they were thieves, they allow them to leave with a small amount of money, but have no idea where they went. The Dells are bound over to appear before the magistrates later but, as 'the time was not yet come wherein God had decreed to bring this cruell, barbarous, and bloody masacre to light', they are released.[163] The Dells spend a lot of money repairing and furnishing their house.

The story turns to the girl, who was abandoned and left to die in a large hollow tree. However, she is rescued by a stranger, 'not by chaunce, but surely by the providence and appointment of God', who then leaves her despite her pleas for help, afraid of the consequences of being found with a child.[164] The author, in contrast to the other, argues that no one knew what she did for the next four years but it can be assumed that she was probably able to make herself understood and begged throughout the local area. Returning to Hatfield, as in the first narrative, she starts to recognize where she is and remembers what happened there. She is led to the Dells' house by the tailor and others where she observes a key detail not recorded in the first narrative. The change to the interior design of the house is carefully narrated in this version: '[S]hee being within, stood staring wildelye round about her, at last shee spied a paire of stayres, to which shee went directlye, and comming to them, shee looked earnestlye on them, looking about the house againe, she first pointed to the stayres, and then to a Corner of the house, as who should say, these stayres did stand there.'[165] This convinces the neighbours that the child has been in the house before and the Dells are summoned again before the Justices. Under serious cross-examination, despite being examined separately, and despite the evidence of the tailor, they hold fast to their story that they have never seen the girl before. Butler is convinced of their guilt but does not have the evidence to convict them. The Dells' house is shut up and the girl is taken into town where she is well looked after, her newly found comfort enabling her to get out to play with

[160] On Sir Henry Butler (1538?–1608) see 'The Peerage' (http://www.thepeerage.com/p13766.htm) (accessed 15 January 2016); on Sir Ralph Conningsby (c.1555–1616) see 'The History of Parliament' (http://www.historyofparliamentonline.org/volume/1604-1629/member/coningsby-sir-ralph-1555-1616) (accessed 15 January 2016). The full list of JPs in Hertfordshire is given in J. S. Cockburn, ed., *Calendar of the Assize Records: Hertfordshire Indictments, James I* (London: HMSO, 1975), p. 29 (No. 155).

[161] Anon., *Horrible Murther*, sig. A2r.   [162] Anon., *Horrible Murther*, sig. A2v.
[163] Anon., *Horrible Murther*, sig. A4r.   [164] Anon., *Horrible Murther*, sig. A4v.
[165] Anon., *Horrible Murther*, sig. A4v.

other children. Hearing a cock crow, one of the children mocks the bird, and the tongueless girl, much to their amazement copies her. She is taken back to be interviewed by Butler and provides him with answers to the murder-mystery. She states that the man and the woman (the pedlar and his wife) who killed her parents took 'a great bagge of money from them', and then 'had giuen a great deale of that money to the olde woman: and that the olde woman did at that time lift vp her hands three times, and did sweare three times, that she would neuer tell any body who they were', which provides an interesting extra detail to give even more substance to the symbolic nature of this narrative.[166]

The Dells refuse to plead guilty and so 'put themselues to the ordinarie triall'. The child is brought before the bench, and 'stoode upon the Table betweene the Bench and the Jury'.[167] The court witnesses the miracle of the child's speech:

> Where after that the foresaid knight had opened some part of this foule offence, the childe was asked diuerse of the former questions: to which she answered as before. The taylor likewise was there, who tolde vnto the Iurie what he had seene. Then the Iurie was willed to goe togither: but before they went, they did looke into the childes mouth, but could not see so much as the stumpe of a tongue therein.[168]

The Dells are found guilty and hanged.[169] The pamphlet ends with an exhortation to trust in the providence of God, acknowledging that the pedlar and his wife have not been found and brought to justice, and the burial place of the parents is not yet known, 'But yet all in good time, if it be the will of the Amightie, both the one and the other shall come to light.'[170] No evidence survives to suggest they were ever apprehended or the bodies discovered.

The version of the story in *The Most Cruell and Bloudy Murther* is far more obviously literary, eloquent, and rhetorically crafted, suggesting that the author was highly educated and interested in diverse forms of writing, and had a keen sense of theatre. Both contain significant and carefully placed biblical references, but the second pamphlet is more providential in focus, and, as the penultimate quotation suggests, was written by someone with a working knowledge of local courts. The substance of the story is largely the same in both pamphlets but many important details differ. Nothwithstanding the publishing connections, the two accounts would appear to have been written independently of each other: they share numerous details but these seem to be generally agreed aspects of the story which were undoubtedly in general circulation not transmitted from one text to another and then refigured as part of a new narrative. The second version reads in places like an eyewitness account with the concentration on practical details that made up the case (the stairs, the organization of the courtroom). But we are left with the stubborn detail of the miracle of the child with no tongue speaking. Were both

[166] Anon., *Horrible Murther*, sig. B3r.   [167] Anon., *Horrible Murther*, sig. B3r.
[168] Anon., *Horrible Murther*, sig. B3r.
[169] As the assize record confirms: Cockburn, ed., *Assize Records: Hertfordshire*, p. 30 (No. 163).
[170] Anon., *Horrible Murther*, sig. B3v.

authors deluded? Were they lying? Or were they relying on false witnesses, perhaps aware that they were not reporting the truth, perhaps not aware, perhaps not caring?

The Most Cruell and Bloudy Murther is especially anxious about the nature and value of testimony, whether an account of events is truthful and how others might be able to judge its veracity. Annis Dell argues that 'shee had many guests, and many children lay at her house, of which number (for ought shee knewe) that might bee one, but who brougt them, from wheence they come, or whether they will, shee is not bound to take notice of', a defence that does not impress the narrator: 'This might haue been some instance of her innocency, but so to deny a question, the truth of which was not of sufficiency to heare her argues [sic], a suspition and mistrust of her selfe, and prooues her to be guilty.'[171] This is hardly conclusive proof, and seems like an odd point in the story to make such a claim as Annis Dell's answers are what might have been expected from both innocent and guilty parties in the circumstances. This statement suggests that the author is further away from the details of the case than the author of *The Horrible Murther* and is speculating about evidence and motives based on another account. The faulty answer of Annis Dell distinguishes her guilty testimony from the truthful testimony of Elizabeth:

> the Iustices were very carefull to sift her by seuerall examinations, to see if they could finde her alter or trippe in any part of her former discourse, as Sir *Raph Conesbye,* Sir *Henrie Butler,* Maister Auditor, and Master Auditor *Curle,* to the number of 14 Knights and graue Gentlemen of note Iustices of peace, tooke her seuerall examinations, when in the generall there could not be one found that differed in a sillable; nay though some of them threatned her with what vengeance God would stir vp for her in hell, and plagues here vpon earth, if she persisted to be a lyer, and a murtherer, both which would conclude in her (by the death of *Dels* wife and her sonne) if she perseuered in this testimony. Others in milder traine dealt with her, as by faire perswasions, golden promises, that froom ye state of a beggar, where till then she had liued, she should now be exalted and maintained by them in the same degree as their owne children, making them stand present obiects to alter her, neither of which could make her distant in any thing, but in briefe satisfied them with this answere. I must not lye, I haue that within me bids me tell truth.[172]

Elizabeth stands as a perfect witness incapable of uttering anything other than the truth, exactly like Montaigne's man 'not wedded to his owne will', possessing nothing beyond her innocence and need to explain what really happened. She endures the familiar combination of threats and cajolement, but her story does not alter, just as the Dells stand firm in guilty adversity in *The Horrible Murther*, until the evidence eventually overwhelms them and they admit their guilt. In *The Most Cruell and Bloudy Murther* it is the contrast between consciences that really matters as these determine the physical actions, a common motif in murder pamphlets

---

171 Anon., *Most Cruell and Bloudy Murther*, sig. B3r.
172 Anon., *Most Cruell and Bloudy Murther*, sigs B3r–v.

and a sign of the significance of the individual as both actor and provider of testimony.[173]

Even so, one of Butler's men decides to test Elizabeth further with a bizarre device that seems to be unique in English judicial procedure. He

> attired himselfe in a vizard with hornes, and (as we commonly say) like a Diuell, and out of a thicket stept before her, & threatned her, that in that place where shee first spake, hee would teare her in peeces for belying *George Dell* and his Mother; when the Girle though in common it doth appeare she should haue been frighted from her constancie) onely answered thus. Good Gaffer Diuell doe not hurt me, I speake nothing but truth, and what the thing within me instructeth me to speake[.][174]

Elizabeth remains unmoved and confirms that she speaks the truth as her inner conscience compels her (perhaps a confirmation that her tongue cannot intervene and distort the truth she carries within her?). Did this encounter really happen? Perhaps it did, as 'children as bystander witnesses were rarely called to testify', making this particular case unusual as conviction depended on the verbal evidence of a category of witness to whom juries rarely had to listen, which might have called for special measures.[175] Canon law, in theory at least, dictated that no child under fourteen could testify, and when minors did testify in court they had to have an 'adult bystander witness' with them.[176] Adults were often amazed that children could remember anything and provide coherent testimony as it was often assumed that they would simply ape what adults told them, which would explain why such drastic measures were taken here, especially when dealing with a child who had been through such a terrible trauma and mutilation, cured (at least temporarily) only by a miracle.[177] Children who claimed to be possessed by demons attracted widespread scepticism, with many thinking that 'children might be counterfeiting their ailments or accusations to gain attention or advance the aims of adults around them'.[178] A pamphlet which describes the brutal murder of an iron miner's wife extravagantly praises a small boy who has the courage to testify honestly to help convict his drunken father.[179]

Even so, the narration of the incident not only displays rather more delight in the event with what looks like a sly sense of irony (does the reader need to know that a figure with a horned mask might commonly be called a devil?), but a keen sense of spectacular theatre. Children were thought to be especially vulnerable to the wiles

---

[173] See also Anon., *Sundrye Strange and Inhumaine Murthers, lately committed the first of a father that hired a man to kill three of his children neere to Ashford in Kent, the second of Master Page of Plymouth, murthered by the consent of his owne wife* (London, 1591), sigs A2r–A2v.

[174] Anon., *Most Cruell and Bloudy Murther*, sig. B3v.

[175] Elizabeth A. Foyster, 'Silent Witnesses? Children and the Breakdown of Domestic and Social Order in Early Modern England', in Anthony Fletcher and Stephen Hussey, eds, *Childhood in Question: Children, Parents and the State* (Manchester: Manchester University Press, 1999), pp. 57–73, at p. 57; Shapiro, *Culture of Fact*, p. 16.

[176] Foyster, 'Silent Witnesses?', pp. 64–5.   [177] Foyster, 'Silent Witnesses?', p. 63.

[178] Michael Witmore, *Pretty Creatures: Children and Fiction in the English Renaissance* (Ithaca, NY: Cornell University Press, 2007), p. 173.

[179] Anon., *A Most Horrible & Detestable Murther committed by a bloudie minded man vpon his ovvne vvife and most strangely reuealed by his childe that was vnder fiue yeares of age* (London, 1595), sig. A3v.

of the Devil who could cunningly combine truth and lies.[180] Elizabeth is shown to be extraordinarily self-possessed, addressing the Devil in familiar, even insolent, terms, 'gaffer' meaning either 'my good fellow' or suggesting a simple, elderly rustic, a considerable achievement for a girl with no tongue.[181] In terms of an understanding of medieval/canon law it could be argued that she passes the ordeal (*judicium Dei*) to prove that she is a credible witness, and maintains her commitment to the truth, making it unimportant whether she believes that she is really speaking to the Devil or sees through the dramatic ruse.[182] On balance, it is hard to believe that the author accepts this version of events, given the wealth of literary allusions in the pamphlet and the ironic sophistication of the narration which is written with an understanding of what an audience might want and expect to hear; the employment of meta-narrative features; and an ironic detachment which resembles the style of the herring pamphlet rather than that of *The Horrible Murther*.

Elizabeth's words to the Devil recall the contemptuous ways in which Satan and other devils are addressed in the mystery plays and on the Jacobean stage, as they were often associated with the comedy of their inevitable defeat rather than their potential to terrify beleaguered mankind.[183] Indeed, throughout the pamphlet the author of *The Most Cruell and Bloudy Murther*, like the author of the herring pamphlet, shows a keen understanding of literature and drama, high and popular culture. The work opens with a reference to a description of the triumphant Egyptian King Sesostris, forcing four conquered kings to pull his chariot, which the author claims is from Herodotus. One looks back at the chariot wheels. When asked what he is doing he replies that he is looking at 'those things which were highest in the wheeles become lowest, and the lowest as soone become highest', a living manifestation of the arbitrary nature of the ubiquitous motif of the wheel of fortune.[184] The story is not actually from Herodotus, but part of a more common proverbial wisdom, and served as a prelude to George Gascoigne's translation of Euripides's *Jocasta*, the first Greek tragedy on the English stage.[185] Emrys Jones has pointed out that Gascoigne's dumbshow must have had an influence on Christopher Marlowe's representation of the two defeated kings, Trebizon and Soria, pulling Tamburlaine's chariot in *Tamburlaine, Part Two*, which, in turn, may be what this keen student of the stage has in mind in opening his account with such a striking image, which bears only a tangential relationship to the subsequent text.[186] This

---

[180] Witmore, *Pretty Creatures*, p. 180; Hanson, 'Torture and Truth', pp. 67–8.

[181] *OED*, gaffer, n., 1b, 2.

[182] Robert Bartlett, *Trial by Fire and Water: The Medieval Judicial Ordeal* (Oxford: Clarendon Press, 1986), p. 2. I owe this reference to Stuart Airlie.

[183] Christa Knellwolf King, *Faustus and the Promises of the New Science, C. 1580–1730: From the Chapbooks to Harlequin Faustus* (Farnham: Ashgate, 2008), p. 158; Frederik T. Wood, 'The Comic Elements in the English Mystery Plays', *Neophilologus* 25 (1940), 39–48.

[184] Anon., *Most Cruell and Bloudy Murther*, sig. A2r.

[185] Orlin, 'Case for Anecdotalism', pp. 52–3; Gillian Austen, *George Gascoigne* (Woodbridge: Brewer, 2008), pp. 55–6.

[186] Emrys Jones, *The Origins of Shakespeare* (Oxford: Clarendon Press, 1977), p. 123. It also provides a link to the herring pamphlet, both authors apparently having seen *Tamburlaine* and been impressed enough to refer to the play in their pamphlets.

scene with its striking opening line, 'Holla, ye pampered jades of Asia', was among the most frequent references made to Marlowe's plays in early modern England.[187]

The descriptions of Annis Dell as a 'bloody Tygris' and a 'She-wolfe' within a few lines of each other may well be proverbial, a common misogynist attack on powerful women.[188] But they were both descriptions applied to Queen Margaret, wife of Henry VI, in Shakespeare's first sequence of history plays, like the two parts of *Tamburlaine*, works that defined what was possible on the commercial stage in the 1590s. The dying York describes the triumphant Margaret as 'She-wolf of France', then as possessing a 'tiger's heart wrapt in a woman's hide'.[189] The second reference made its way into *Greene's Groatsworth of Wit* (1592), the first printed reference to Shakespeare, showing, as with the *Tamburlaine* allusion, how powerful this scene was and how the lines struck early readers.[190] The evidence is by no means conclusive but it does suggest that the author had an eye and an ear for striking dramatic moments that he put to good effect in his pamphlet. Queen Margaret would certainly be a suitable comparison to make to the powerful and ruthless Annis Dell.

The description of the miraculous restoration of Elizabeth's power of speech is more developed and elaborate in *The Most Cruell and Bloudy Murther* than in *The Horrible Murther*.[191] In the shorter pamphlet the girls imitate the sound of the cock crowing. God places a cock close to where the children play, 'his first messenger of this mightie miracle, like as a bird of the same name and nature, vsing the selfe same note, put Peter in minde that hee had denied his maister: from which his remembrance, sprung his true and heartie repentance'.[192] This might seem like a rather forced and creative comparison of events to Peter's betrayal of Christ in all four Gospels, but it further serves to remind readers of religious divisions as St Peter was the most contested of the apostles after the Reformation, and was the subject of

---

[187] Marlowe, *Tamburlaine, Part Two*, IV.iii.1. On the popularity of this scene see Nicholl, *Reckoning*, p. 5.

[188] Hill, 'Bloudy Tygrisses'; Helen Castor, *She-Wolves: The Women Who Ruled England Before Elizabeth* (London: Faber, 2011).

[189] William Shakespeare, *King Henry VI, Part 3*, ed. John D. Cox and Eric Rasmussen (London: Thomson, 2001), 1.4.111, 137.

[190] Henry Chettle and Robert Greene, *Greene's Groatsworth of Wit: Bought with a Million of Repentance* (1592), ed. D. Allen Carroll (Binghampton, NY: MRTS, 1994), p. 84; Stanley Wells, 'Allusions to Shakespeare to 1642', in Paul Edmondson and Stanley Wells, eds, *Shakespeare Beyond Doubt: Evidence, Argument, Controversy* (Cambridge: Cambridge University Press, 2013), pp. 73–87, at p. 73.

[191] The restoration of the power of speech of the abused woman surely also recalls the myth of Tereus and Philomel, familiar in so many Renaissance literary works: see Liz Oakley-Brown, *Ovid and the Cultural Politics of Translation in Early Modern England* (Aldershot: Ashgate, 2006), pp. 11, 26, *passim*. Beggars sometimes pretended to be mute: a trick explained in cony-catching pamphlets (Thomas Harman and Thomas Dekker call them 'Dummerers' (1566)): Orlin, 'Case for Anecdotalism', p. 75; A. V. Judges, ed., *The Elizabethan Underworld: A Collection of Tudor and Early Stuart Tracts and Ballads telling of the lives and misdoings of vagabonds, thieves, rogues, and cozeners, and giving some account of the operation of the criminal law* (London: Routledge, 1930), pp. 91–2, 375.

[192] Anon., *Horrible Murther*, sig. B2v.

vigorous attempts to Protestantize him as a repentant sinner returning to the fold after his denial of Jesus.[193] The children imitate the cock crowing:

> At last one of the children began (after their maner) to mocke the cockes, crying cocke-adoodle-doo: in the end this dumbe child, strayning her selfe, cried as the rest had done, cocke-adoodle doo, which made all the children amazde: and one of them that stoode next her, said: what, canst thou speake now? I that I can (said she) speaking it so plainly that they all vnderstoode her.[194]

The story is simple and straightforward, even if the relationship between events and the biblical precedent is somewhat less obvious. God sends the cockerel to remind mankind of the need for duty to him and repentance because he will use the natural world to expose crime and initiate the punishment of the guilty. *The Most Cruell and Bloudy Murther* contains yet another literary allusion embedded in a complicated representation of the event which reads like a bricolage of realist and symbolic details:

> one day, some month before Christmasse last, going to play with the Goodwifes daughter where shee soiourned in a Parke ioyning to Hatfield (commonly called the Kings Parke) as they were in sport together, a Cocke hard by them fell a crowing, when the other Girle mocking the Cocke with these words, Cocka doodle dooe, Peggy hath lost her shooe, and called to her Besse, canst not thou doe so? When presently the Girle in the like manner did so; which, drawing the other child into amazement, she presently left her, and ran home crying out as she went, the dumbe Girle Besse can speake, the dumbe Girle Besse can speake.[195]

Here we do not just witness an imitation of a cock crowing but we have the first recorded version of the familiar nursery rhyme, 'Cock a doodle Doo'.[196] The same allusion is made to Peter's betrayal of Christ and the importance of the cockerel as the harbinger of truth and repentance: 'that bird that put Peter in minde of his great sinne in denying our Sauiour and his Maister'.[197] But, in this account, we also learn that they were playing in what is commonly called the King's Park (does this detail have any significance?) and that Elizabeth is known to the other children as 'Besse'. Do such details confer authenticity on the account? Or are they details that appeal to the author's erudite sense of a literary culture that he wishes to demonstrate?

Elsewhere the author uses his understanding of human nature to add extra drama to the account, producing details that may well be true but which he cannot know for certain. We learn that showing Elizabeth/Besse the striking green coat of her

---

[193] See Karen Bruhn, 'Reforming Saint Peter: Protestant Constructions of Saint Peter the Apostle in Early Modern England', 33 *C16J* (2002), 33–49. Peter's denial of Christ was the subject of Robert Southwell's poem about his dilemma as a Jesuit who would undoubtedly have to face the prospect of martyrdom, which may provide a further layer to the story's significance: see above, pp. 84–7.

[194] Anon., *Horrible Murther*, sig. B2v.

[195] Anon., *Most Cruell and Bloudy Murther*, sig. C1r.

[196] Iona and Peter Opie, *The Oxford Dictionary of Nursery Rhymes* (rev. edn, Oxford: Oxford University Press, 1997), pp. 149–50; James Orchard Halliwell, *The Nursery Rhymes of England, Chiefly Collected from Oral Tradition* (London: Bodley Head, 1970, rpt of 1842), pp. 166, 213.

[197] Anon., *Most Cruell and Bloudy Murther*, sig. C1r.

murdered brother elicits a response in the girl 'as if in the sight thereof, she had seene another brother murthered', a wonder, 'the only table-talke in the Countrey, though often brought to the widdow Dels eare, she made slight of it, (perswading her sele belike)', that because she has power and status and the child no tongue, no harm can come to her. However, in doing so she was only deluding herself, because 'a guilty conscience Salamander-like liues alwayes in fire, that his dayes are dreadfull, his nights terrible, that he that admits sinne in himselfe, kils himselfe, that to vnhonest pleasure is begot a companion repenting'.[198] From Pliny onwards and in medieval bestiaries, salamanders were described as being able to live without being harmed in fire, to which they returned by instinct.[199] Accordingly, salamanders were associated with divine judgement, often the Apocalypse, indicating an ability to withstand trials that went beyond those that ordinary mortals could endure, and, like the medieval ordeal by fire, reminding humans of the torments they would experience in hell if they failed to repent their sins.[200] Henry Smith in his short pamphlet *The Trumpet of the Soule, Sounding to Judgement* (1591) makes this allusion: 'then shall the sinner be euer dying and neuer dead, like the Salamander that is euer in the fier and neuer consumed'.[201] William Perkins, author of *A Direction for the Government of the Tongue*, made the same connection between the salamander and the fate of the sinner in hell: 'But as the Salamander is alwaies in the fire, and neuer wasteth: so the wicked shall bee continually scorched in hell-fire, and yet shall neuer be consumed', as did Samuel Gardiner, in the same year that the two pamphlets about the Dell murder case were published.[202]

The most significant literary context for the representation of the murder of Anthony James may, in fact, be the least explicitly articulated, even though it applies to both versions of the story. Is this a story of a ritual murder?[203] Or, rather, a murder that looks like a ritual murder? In *The Most Cruell and Bloudy Murther* the child's throat is slit from ear to ear, his dead body tied to a stake before he is thrown into a 'botomelesse Pond', 'giuing him for his *requiem* farewell, no other funeral rites & Christian burial, but these words; sinke there in stead of a mother-graue.'[204] The account in *The Horrible Murther* is more forensic in telling the story of the recovery of the body, but also containing significant details:

[198] Anon., *Most Cruell and Bloudy Murther*, sig. B4v. A common motif in murder pamphlets: see Anon., *Sundrye Strange and Inhumaine Murthers*, sig. A2v; Anon., *Most Horrible & Detestable Murther*, sig. A2v–A3r.
[199] White, *Bestiary*, p. 184; Stephen Bateman, *Batman Uppon Bartholome* (London, 1582), p. 379; Edward Topsell, *Historie of Serpents, Or The second Booke of Liuing Creatures* (London, 1608), pp. 217–21.
[200] On salamanders and hell fire see Webster, *Works*, p. 631; on the ordeal and hell fires see Hunt Janin, *Medieval Justice: Cases and Laws in France, England, and Germany: 500–1500* (Jefferson, NC: McFarland, 2004), p. 14.
[201] Henry Smith, *The Trumpet of the Soule, Sounding to Judgement* (London, 1591), sig. B3v.
[202] William Perkins, *A Christian and Plaine Treatise of the Manner and Order of Predestination and of the Largenes of Gods Grace* (London, 1606), sig. E8v; Samuel Gardiner, *Doomes-Day Booke: or, An Alarum for Atheistes, A Watchword for Worldlinges, A Caueat for Christians* (London, 1606), p. 96.
[203] On the prevalance of ritual murder stories see Heiko A. Oberman, 'Containing Chaos in Early Modern Europe', in Grell and Scribner, eds, *Tolerance and Intolerance*, pp. 13–31, at pp. 22, 25.
[204] Anon., *Most Cruell and Bloudy Murther*, sigs B1r, B2r.

[T]he boy was found dead in a ditch or water not farre from the Towne, with a great peece of wood tyed to his backe. The Childe being taken out, it did plainely appeare that hee was murthered before he was throwne in, The poore harmelesse Infant being found thus cruelly murthered, and none that looked on him taking knowledge of him.[205]

Both accounts differ: the first has the boy thrown into a bottomless pond, the second a ditch; the first gives an eyewitness account of the funeral rites, such as they are. But they also have important details in common: the first has the boy's throat slit, the second states that he was clearly dead before being thrown into the water, and both describe the stake or large piece of wood tied to the body. Both accounts, therefore, contain striking elements of the myth of the Jewish ritual murder: specifically, the most notorious child murder in medieval England, that of Little Saint Hugh of Lincoln.[206] Hugh was a nine-year-old boy who disappeared in 1255, his body discovered in a well, and his murder blamed on the local community of Jews who were accused of having murdered him in a grotesque parody of Christian rituals, a re-enactment of their murder of Christ and a sign to the authorities that they were so implacably opposed to Christian values that they could never be tolerated. Accounts of the murder vary in detail. Matthew Paris's account in *Chronica Majora*, written in the aftermath of the case, has Hugh kidnapped, fattened, then scourged, tortured, and crucified in imitation of Christ in Lincoln in front of the assembled representatives of Jews from throughout England:

they at once appointed a Jew of Lincoln as judge to take the place of Pilate, by whose sentence, and with the concurrence of all, the boy was subjected to divers tortures They beat him till blood flowed and he was quite livid, they crowned him with thorns, derided him and spat upon him. Moreover, he was pierced by each of them with a wood knife, was made to drink gall, was overwhelmed with approaches and blasphemies, and was repeatedly called Jesus the false prophet by his tormentors, who surrounded him, grinding and gnashing their teeth. After tormenting him in divers ways, they crucified him, and pierced him to the heart with a lance. After the boy had expired, they took his body down from the cross and disembowelled it; for what reason we do not know, but it was asserted to be for the purpose of practising magical operations.[207]

The body is discovered when Hugh's understandably anxious mother enters the house of the mother of one of the children Hugh had been playing with and

[205] Anon., *Horrible Murther*, sig. A2v.
[206] *Saints*, p. 214. For analysis of Jewish ritual murder, to which my comments are indebted, see Karl Heinz Göller, 'Sir Hugh of Lincoln – From History to Nursery Rhyme', in Franz Link, ed., *Jewish Life and Suffering as Mirrored in English and American Literature* (Paderborn: F. Schöningh, 1987), pp. 17–32; Richard Utz, 'The Medieval Myth of Jewish Ritual Murder: Toward a History of Reception', *YWM* 14 (2000), 24–46. In her study of late medieval anti-Semitism Miri Rubin points out that 'the juxtaposition of Jew and children became more heavily weighted with episodic rumours of ritual murder': *Gentile Tales: The Narrative Assault on Late Medieval Jews* (New Haven: Yale University Press, 1999), p. 27.
[207] Matthew Paris, *English History*, trans. J. A. Giles, 3 vols (London: Bohn, 1852–4), III, pp. 138–9.

discovers his body thrown down a well. Thomas Fuller is briefer and has the boy snatched from his parents by 'impious Jews', and 'in derision of Christ and Christianity, to keep their cruel hands in use, by them crucified'.[208]

The most influential adaptation of the story, then as now, was that of Geoffrey Chaucer in *The Prioress's Tale*.[209] Even though the story told there is set in Asia, it is clear that the tale is designed to be read in terms of St Hugh, his murder connecting England to its recent past, as the final stanza makes clear:

> O Yonge Hugh of Lyncoln, slayn also
> With cursed Jewes, as it is notable,
> For it is but a litel while ago[.][210]

Chaucer combines two types of story in his tale, the Jewish ritual murder and the Marian miracle tale, another popular form, in which the mother of Christ leads people to understand the truth behind a crime or mystery.[211] In *The Prioress's Tale* the boy is murdered by a Jew, who, annoyed by his pious singing of the Gregorian chant in honour of Mary, *Alma Redemtoris*, cuts his throat and throws him into a deep pit used as a privy.[212] His mother, realizing where he might be, stands near the pit and her dead son continues singing *Alma Redemptoris*, 'So loude that al the place gan to rynge' (1803). He carries on, even when collected on a bier, then tells the Abbot who interviews him of the Jews' guilt. They are duly hanged and the boy is buried with proper Christian rites.

The Prioress's Tale describes the boy's mode of death three times within a hundred lines: 'This cursed Jew hym hente, and heeld hym faste, / And kitte his throte, and in a pit hym caste' (1760–1); the Abbot asks the dead boy, 'Tel me what is thy cause for to synge, / Sith that thy throte is kut to my semynge?' (1837–8); and he replies, 'My throte is kut unto my neckle boon' (1839). The Dell pamphlets tell a similar story which combines the murder and the miracle. In fact *The Most Cruell and Bloudy Murther*, the more literary of the two works, has the boy's throat cut and the girl's tongue cut out, which could be read as a dividing and doubling of the cruelty. Chaucer's Prioress insists 'Mordre wol out' (1766), which is the basic message of both *The Most Cruell and Bloudy Murther* and *The Horrible Murther* and

---

[208] Thomas Fuller, *The Worthies of England*, ed. John Freeman (New York: Barnes and Noble, 1952), p. 329.

[209] Lena Orlin observes the link between Chaucer's tale and the pamphlets but does not explore the connection in detail: 'Case for Anecdotalism', p. 59.

[210] Geoffrey Chaucer, *The Prioress's Tale*, in *Riverside Chaucer*, pp. 209–12, at p. 212 (lines 684–6). For comment see Jeffrey J. Cohen, 'Postcolonialism', in Steve Ellis, ed., *Chaucer: An Oxford Guide* (Oxford: Oxford University Press, 2005), pp. 448–62, at pp. 459–61.

[211] Göller, 'Hugh of Lincoln', pp. 22–3; Louise O. Fradenburg, 'Criticism, Anti-Semitism, and the Prioress's Tale', in Kathryn L. Lynch, ed., *Chaucer's Cultural Geography* (London: Routledge, 2002), pp. 174–92, at p. 172. More generally see Rubin, *Gentile Tales*, pp. 7–27; Marina Warner, *Alone of All Her Sex: The Myth and the Cult of the Virgin Mary* (Oxford: Oxford University Press, 2013), pp. xv, 245.

[212] On the significance of *Alma Redemptoris* in terms of the cult of Mary, see Warner, *Alone of All Her Sex*, pp. 119, 293.

suggests that these stories owe much to the tradition of Marian miracle tales.[213] Both make significant capital out of the contemptuous refusal to perform funeral rites, also present in Chaucer's tale and other versions of the ritual murder story.

Might the two pamphlets also be seen to retain traces of the crucifixion story which survives in Fuller's account of St Hugh? *The Horrible Murther* describes 'a great peece of wood tyed' to the boy's back; *The Most Cruell and Bloudy Murther* has a stake, which is described in some detail:

> *George Dell* presently stepping to the Woodstacke, and choosing out a good big stake, he with the helpe of the rest bound thereon the dead child with a hairen rope, and *George Dell* himselfe taking a long Pike staffe on his shoulder, lead them the way towards botomelesse Pond, being a mile from *Hatfield*, while the 2 theeues vpon the stake carried the boy[.][214]

Having the dead boy tied to a stake led between the two thieves is certainly suggestive of the crucifixion story in all four Gospels and it would be odd if this were a coincidence given the importance of that element of the Jewish ritual murder story.

For all the carefully placed factual elements in each of these versions, they cannot be accurate testimonies of what really happened, nor were they produced simply in order to tell the truth. *The Most Cruell and Bloudy Murther* in particular appears so anxious about truth-telling, so concentrated on drawing attention to the production of veracity, and so concerned with the dangers of the tongue and its sins, that it cannot be a guileless account. Furthermore, it is also worth noting that, major court scandals such as the Frances Howard/Sir Thomas Overbury trials aside, no other murder pamphlet published in the 1590s and early 1600s was narrated in more than one version. Five murder pamphlets were published in 1606: the two Dell pamphlets; *A Spectacle for Vsurers and Succers of Poore Folkes Bloud, Whereby they may see, Gods iust dislike and reuenge, vpon their vncharitable and Vnciuill oppression, with a horrible murther committed by a young man, that hanged his owne Mother in August last*, the story of a French usurer who was devoured by rats after he tried to swindle a woman out of a ring, and a tale of a youth executed after he strangled his mother; and two pamphlets written in the wake of the Gunpowder Plot, which provide the context needed to explain the nature of the Dell pamphlets.

The Divell of the Vault, or, The Vnmasking of Murther in a briefe declaration of the Cacolicke-complotted Treason, lately discouerd is a short narrative poem which details the crimes of the Jesuits and their threat to the state, culminating in their recent plot to commit murder by blowing up the Houses of Parliament. The poem surveys the crimes of subversive Catholics perpetrated throughout Europe in the Pope's name: the Massacre of St Bartholomew's Day, the Marian tortures and burnings, the Jesuit campaigns under Elizabeth, and the actions of Catesby and Percy, the two named conspirators. The poem contains the familiar descriptions of Catholics

---

[213] The motif of the severed tongue and the struggle to tell the truth may also owe something to Ovid's story of Tereus's rape and dismemberment of Philomel, and the adaptation in *Titus Andronicus*: see Ovid, *Metamorphoses*, trans. Mary M. Innes (Harmondsworth: Penguin, 1955), p. 149; William Shakespeare, *Titus Andronicus*, ed. Jonathan Bate (London: Routledge, 1995), introduction, pp. 88–92.

[214] Anon., *Most Cruell and Bloudy Murther*, sig. B1r.

as '*Romish* Wolues', and 'Crocadiles, / who weeping, wound and sting'.[215] It also juxtaposes Catholic practices of selling 'soules for Peter pence' with a warning of the influence of 'These Tygrish blood-sworne Iesuites'.[216] The Pope and the Jesuits were often referred to as tigers or described as tigerish.[217] Tigers were thought to be cunning beasts especially adept at disguising their true, vicious identity, exactly like the cunning Satanically inspired Jesuits, whose sole aim was to destroy the virtuous life of the true Christian.[218] As already noted, Annis Dell was described as a tiger, and a cockerel inspired the miracle of Elizabeth James's ability to speak without a tongue, a detail which the authors of both of the pamphlets compared to the cock crowing after Peter had betrayed Christ three times.[219] Put together these clues suggest a definite link between the account of the murder and the paranoia generated by the Gunpowder Plot.

It is surely no accident that the other murder pamphlet published in 1606 was George Closse's strikingly alliteratively titled *The Parricide Papist, or Cut-Throate Catholicke*, the story of an episode in Padstow when a son murdered a father who refused to convert back to Catholicism. Closse (*fl.* 1571–1621) was a Church of England clergyman who was often in trouble for financial mismanagement and sharp practice: this was his only venture into print.[220] Closse is clear that the crime is an abomination against nature and a sign of the evil that has overtaken the world in the last days dominated by the Whore of Babylon.[221] He employs the familiar image of the Catholics as wolves in sheep's clothing and attacks their use of equivocation.[222] Even though the father reproves his son, pointing out that the throne is occupied by a 'most religious King' and a worthy successor to Elizabeth, the son kills his father and then himself. Closse argues that the latter act follows from the former and is the logical conclusion of devotion to the Pope, whose doctrines will destroy the souls of those who are foolish enough to follow him.[223] Closse then exploits this link between murder and suicide to explain the Gunpowder Plot:

> But why (say they) is this rude phrase of *Cut-throate Catholicks* (so harshly sounding in vulgar eares) applyed to our pope-holy professors? Let *Northumberland*, aboue twentie yeres agoe murthering himselfe in ye Tower, *Arden* strangling himselfe in Newgate, and this our *Cornish Catholicke*, (so lately killing his father and himselfe) stand forth as

---

[215] Anon., *The Divell of the Vault, or, The Vnmasking of Murther in a briefe declaration of the Cacolicke-complotted Treason, lately discouerd* (London, 1606), sig. D2v–D3r. For discussion see Victoria Jane Buckley, 'Patterns of Mischief: The Impact of the Gunpowder Plot on the Jacobean Stage 1605–16', PhD thesis, University of Sussex, 2012, ch. 1.

[216] Anon., *Divell of the Vault*, sig. A4v.

[217] See, for example, James Aske, *Elizabetha Triumphans Conteyning the Dammed Practizes, that the diuelish popes of Rome haue vsed euer sithence her Highnesse first comming to the Crowne* (London, 1588), p. 9; John King, *Lectures Upon Ionas* (London, 1599), p. 506.

[218] See, for example, John More, *Three Godly and Fruitfull Sermons* (London, 1594), p. 6; Thomas Dekker, *The Ravens Almanacke* (London, 1609), sig. E1r.

[219] Orlin, 'Case for Anecdotalism', p. 62.   [220] On Closse see the *ODNB* entry.

[221] George Closse, *The Parricide Papist, or Cut-throate Catholicke A tragicall discourse of a murther lately committed at Padstow in the countie of Cornewall by a professed papist, killing his owne father, and afterwardes himselfe, in zeale of his popish religion* (London, 1606), p. 2.

[222] Closse, *Parricide Papist*, p. 16. See also Pricket, *Iesuits Miracles*, sig. D4r.

[223] Closse, *Parricide Papist*, pp. 6, 16.

freshbleeding examples to verifie it. Did not *Percy* and *Catesby*, which chose rather to die wilfully and desperately by the souldiers hand, then submit themselues, and liue to confesse their faults, satisfie the King and Commonwealth, and permit themselues a breathing time to repent them of their hideous attempts, beare witnes against them, & conuince them to be desperate Selfe-murtherers?[224]

Catholics, according to Closse, are not like Peter, who repented after denying Christ, but Judas, who hanged himself instead of returning to the fold:

> It is your religion that hath dubbed you *man-quellers, king quellers, selfe-quellers.* Are you not *Parricides?* alas, your maisters are not like *Peter,* that forsooke his Maister, & repenting did counteruaile his triple deniall, with a three-fold confession of him: but as your *Legend* noteth of *Iudas,* that had murthered his father, and committed incest with his mother, and became *Christes* disciple for a cullour to shadowe his horrible impieties, and betraying his maister lastly hanged himselfe: such succession rightly correspondeth with your Popedome, by bloodsheds they are hatched, grow great, and strengthen themselues.[225]

The Parricide Papist gives us a series of clues about how we might read the two which recount the murder of Anthony James. When read alongside Closse's work it is hard to see them as simply murder pamphlets, which is how they have invariably been read—not unreasonably—by historians and literary critics.[226] They also point to a moral panic and terror of insidious infiltration after the Gunpowder Plot, a fear that cunningly hostile Catholics were about to undermine the stability of Jacobean Britain. The pamphlets share a series of references with other works that explicitly deal with this perceived danger: in particular the reference to Peter and the cock crowing and the disguised tiger, exposing unnatural behaviour that threatens at a local level (the family, the relationship between adults and their duty to protect children), as well as on the national and international stage. The pamphlets are therefore directly concerned with the sins of the tongue, represented so graphically in Elizabeth James's severed organ of speech and the miraculous return of her ability to speak in order to reveal the truth as part of God's plan.[227]

They are both directly concerned with the truthfulness of testimony and the possibility of lying, anxious to establish the reliable account of Elizabeth, alongside that of the two different narrators who report her speech, and against the false, lying evidence of the Dells. The two narratives cannot simply be decoded as allegories of

---

[224] Closse, *Parricide Papist*, p. 15. Closse is referring to John Somerville (1560–83), John Arden's son-in-law, who strangled himself in the Tower of London after claiming that he wished to strangle Elizabeth: see the *ODNB* entry. Henry Percy, eighth Earl of Northumberland (1532–85), was shot through the heart while incarcerated in the Tower of London for the third time for conspiring to depose Elizabeth, an apparent suicide: see the *ODNB* entry.

[225] Closse, *Parricide Papist*, p. 12.

[226] Randall Martin, *Women, Murder, and Equity in Early Modern England* (Abingdon: Routledge, 2007), p. 26; Clark, *Women and Crime*, pp. 154–5; Greta Olson, *Criminals as Animals from Shakespeare to Lombroso* (Berlin: Walter de Gruyter, 2014), pp. 49–50.

[227] Then, as now, tales of murder concentrated on gory, violent details: see, for example, Anon., *The Manner of the Cruell Outragious Murther of William Storre* (London, 1603), sig. A3r; Anon., *The Most Horrible and Tragicall Murther of the Right Honorable, the Vertuous and Valerous Gentleman, Iohn Lord Bourgh* (London, 1591), sig. A4r.

a Catholic threat, as there is no obvious reason to assume that the Dells, or any other of the villains involved, are Catholics. Rather, they are stories that demand to be read analogously, terrifying tales of perfidy relevant for confusing and dangerous times.[228] The pamphlets are about lying, the deliberate intention of evil people in thrall to Satan to mislead the godly who must police the enemy within vigilantly. God's plans are uncovered when the symbolic cock restores Elizabeth's power of speech, enabling the girl to tell the truth and so provide the evidence to support what the reader has known all along, that the Dells, as Jews and Catholics have done so often in the past, committed an atrocity against Christians, murdering her little brother for no obvious reason other than spite and personal gain. Just as God miraculously thwarted the Gunpowder Plot, so did he reveal the crime that the Dells had committed, exposing their lies and establishing the truth. In the year of the Oath of Allegiance Catholics were being urged to behave like Peter and return to the ranks of the faithful, or be forced to continue in their popish lies.

But, of course, the pamphlets are underpinned by anxiety. They are designed to expose lies and the practice of lying, yet tell lies themselves, which is why they are so adamant in asserting throughout that they are establishing the truth and balance the truthful testimony of Elizabeth against the lies of Annis and George Dell. In doing so both, but in particular, *The Most Cruell and Bloudy Murther*, employ a rhetoric of veracity, embedding events, no matter how apparently far-fetched and unusual, within a narrative that uses a series of devices (assertions, factual details, providential and religious statements) of truth. Yet, surely, both authors know that they are not telling the whole truth. People do not speak once their tongues have been severed, and we never learn whether Elizabeth is able to continue speaking after the trial is over. The most obvious explanation is that she suffered a trauma rather than lost her tongue, but that would limit the impact of the narrative, its symbolism and its powerfully shocking nature.[229] *The Horrible Murther* even describes the jury inspecting her mouth to make sure that she is telling the truth about her mutilation.[230] *The Most Cruell and Bloudy Murther* painstakingly reconstructs the details of the case and reproduces conversations and dialogue which the author can only have known at second or third hand. These discrepancies could be innocent enough, and the authors may have believed the story they told. More likely they believed that such accounts provided a valuable service in times of peril, and in order to proclaim a higher truth they either did not care whether what they wrote was true or not, or were prepared to tell lies in the cause of truth, as Thomas More argued was reasonable and moral nearly a century earlier. The tide may well have been turning in favour of the testimony of the eyewitness as a guarantor of truth and away from the word of an acknowledged authority but this does not mean that we should believe all that we read.

---

[228] On reading analogously see Lorna Hutson, 'Fortunate Travelers: Reading for the Plot in Sixteenth-Century England', *Representations* 41 (1993), 83–103.

[229] Or that her inability to speak is either fabricated in the narrative, or an elaborate trick, as Orlin suggests: 'Case for Anecdotalism', p. 75.

[230] The names of the jury are given in Cockburn, ed., *Assize Records: Hertfordshire*, p. 30 (No. 160). See also Orlin, 'Case for Anecdotalism', p. 71.

7

Othello and the Culture of Lies between Conscience and Reputation

I

When Othello appears before the Venetian council to defend Brabantio's charge that he has bewitched his daughter into marrying him he dramatically recounts how the couple fell in love. It is not drugs or witchcraft that has won him Desdemona, but a story, his own traveller's tale:

> Her father loved me, oft invited me,
> Still questioned me the story of my life
> From year to year—the battles, sieges, fortunes
> That I have passed.
> I ran it through, even from my boyish days
> To th' very moment that he bade me tell it,
> Wherein I spake of most disastrous chances,
> Of moving accidents by flood and field,
> Of hair-breadth scapes i'th' imminent deadly breach,
> Of being taken by the insolent foe
> And sold to slavery; of my redemption thence
> And portance in my travailous history;
> Wherein of antres vast and deserts idle,
> Rough quarries, rocks and hills whose heads touch heaven
> It was my hint to speak—such was my process—
> And of the cannibals that each other eat,
> The Anthropophagi, and men whose heads
> Do grow beneath their shoulders. This to hear
> Would Desdemona seriously incline,
> But still the house affairs would draw her thence,
> Which ever as she could with haste dispatch
> She'd come again, and with a greedy ear
> Devour up my discourse[.][1]

---

[1] William Shakespeare, *Othello*, ed. E. A. J. Honigmann (London: Nelson, 1997), I.3.129–51. All subsequent references to this edition in parentheses in the text. On the significance of the accusation of witchcraft and early modern witch trials see B. J. Sokol and Mary Sokol, *Shakespeare's Legal Language: A Dictionary* (London: Athlone, 2000), p. 424.

Early modern travel accounts were invariably a combination of fact and fiction, as 'it was verisimilitude, not truthfulness, that counted for early modern audiences'.[2] A lying traveller, Mendax, appears in William Bullein's *Dialogue Against the Fever Pestilence*, who claims that he has witnessed many marvels in his extensive and incredible travels. On the island of Madagascar he encountered 'Kynges, Mahumitaines by religion, blacke as deuilles ... Some had no heddes, but eyen in their breastes.'[3] He also encountered many cannibals; on the island of Ruc, 'in the great Cans lande', he learned or witnessed that 'The people of the land do liue by eating the flesh of women', and in Cuba encountered the cannibals who live in caves, rocks, and woods where 'women will eate their owne children, and one man an other'.[4] The reference to the 'Great Khan', surely signals that the reader should understand that Mendax has been reading Mandeville, who claimed to have served in the court of the Great Khan for fifteen months. Mandeville had become the archetype of the lying traveller in the sixteenth century, joining the great fictional lying traveller of the ancient world, Ulysses.[5] In conclusion Mendax asserts, 'for this is true or els I doe lye', a commonplace that undermines his case and which is ripe for witty reversal, as Roger's riposte demonstrates: 'thy laste words are true, and all the reste are lies'.[6]

In this context, however, Othello, a North African general in the service of a major cosmopolitan European power, is, of course, lying in providing his audience with what they want to hear, constructing himself as a European traveller or an ancient historian, and an English audience would have understood him to be lying under oath.[7] He is not lying about Desdemona's reaction to his speech, and 'he represents himself as incapable of even innocent hypocrisy': in contrast to the self-aggrandizing Mendax, Othello, isolated in Venice as many critics have pointed out, is a sympathetic figure at this point in the play.[8] Desdemona confirms that she loves Othello and wishes to follow him wherever he is posted because she 'saw Othello's visage in his mind' (253), his words enabling her to see into his true character, and

---

[2] Elizabeth Horodowich, 'Venetians in America: Nicolò Zen and the Virtual Exploration of the New World', *RQ* 67 (2014), 841–77, p. 845; Shapiro, *Culture of Fact*, p. 72.

[3] Bullein, *Pestilence*, p. 98.   [4] Bullein, *Pestilence*, pp. 98, 100.

[5] On Mandeville see Malcolm Letts, *Sir John Mandeville: The Man and his Book* (London: Batchworth, 1949), pp. 64–75; on Ulysses see Chris Emlyn-Jones, 'True and Lying Tales in *The Odyssey*', *GR* 33 (1986), 1–10.

[6] Bullein, *Pestilence*, p. 111. See also the conclusion to T. N.'s *A Pleasant Dialogue* (London, 1579), which contains an aged pilgrim's fictitious account of the 'great province of Crangalor', an ideal state, yet concludes with the epigrammatic 'Pilgrime for thy telling troth, / Perhap thou shalt be shent: / In recompence of all thy toyle, / And time godly spent' (sig. D2v) (I owe this reference to Cathy Shrank).

[7] See Popper, 'Ocean of Lies', p. 394. For a related analysis of Othello and 'fraud' see Charles Ross, 'Avoiding the Issue of Fraud: 4, 5 Philip & Mary c.8 (the Heiress Protection Statute), Portia, and Desdemona', in Constance Jordan and Karen Cunningham, eds, *The Law in Shakespeare* (Basingstoke: Palgrave Macmillan, 2007), pp. 91–108, at pp. 100–6. Interestingly enough, Ira Aldridge (1807–67), the first black actor to play Othello with international success, refigured his own origins in terms of Othello's story, the parallel between his imagined early life and 'Othello's story was evidently too good to be missed by an actor with imagination': Herbert Marshall and Mildred Stock, *Ira Aldridge: The Negro Tragedian* (Carbondale: Southern Illinois University Press, 1968), p. 17.

[8] Maus, 'Proof', p. 42. See, for example, Graham Holderness, *Shakespeare and Venice* (Farnham: Ashgate, 2013), p. 116.

accept the violent path to marital bliss (250).[9] Lies may have been told but then, as Shakespeare wrote elsewhere, 'The course of true love never did run smooth.'[10]

Perhaps the situation is more complex still: according to his testimony, Othello makes his speech because he understood that Desdemona gave him a 'hint' to speak as he did, his understanding was that she wanted to hear his exciting traveller's tale and was encouraging him to woo her. Her evidence supports this reading and suggests that the couple had a mutual understanding, making Othello's original speech a shared fiction, which Desdemona may have understood was not really true and was delivered for her enjoyment. For Iago and, one suspects, Brabantio, Othello was simply lying, and Iago will later exploit the notion of a 'hint', a virtually undetectable sign which is open to equivocation, to destroy Othello.[11]

The minor lie that Othello tells in his speech is that his tale is not crafted, whereas what we witness, mirroring Desdemona's experience, is a polished and carefully designed tale within a tale, a representation of the effects of rhetoric on one audience (Brabantio's household) now designed to have a similar effect on another (the Venetian council). When the Duke responds, obviously spellbound, 'I think this tale would win my daughter too' (172), we know that Othello has delivered a masterpiece of rhetoric that would have impressed Cicero or Quintilian who were both always keen to stress the emotional effect of good rhetoric, which has gone way beyond its purpose in defending the speaker in court.[12] Quentin Skinner has argued that although Othello's speech is by no means brief, 'his *narratio* follows all the classical principles, and the duke feels able to salute its rhetorical power'.[13] As classical rhetoricians often pointed out, variation, repetition, and proliferation were usually astute tactics when providing persuasive testimony.[14]

The major lie is that his account of his travels simply cannot be true. Men's heads do not grow beneath their shoulders. They appeared frequently in maps and influential geographical surveys such as *The Nuremburg Chronicle* and Sebastian Münster's *Cosmography* which were reproduced and circulated long after their

[9] William Empson, *Seven Types of Ambiguity* (Harmondsworth: Penguin, 1961, rpt of 1930), p. 94; Maus, 'Proof', p. 45. Ayanna Thompson points out that Desdemona's reaction is in marked contrast to that of Portia when told a similar tale by the Prince of Morocco: *Othello*, ed. E. A. J. Honigmann, with a new introduction by Ayanna Thompson (London: Bloomsbury, 2016), p. 21. On the significance of the sexual nature of Desdemona's speech and the way in which it has unintended consequences see A. D. Nuttall, *A New Mimesis: Shakespeare and the Representation of Reality* (London: Methuen, 1983), pp. 138–9.

[10] William Shakespeare, *A Midsummer Night's Dream*, ed. Harold F. Brooks (London: Methuen, 1979), 1.1.134 (p. 13).

[11] 'Hint' is a complex word which warrants further investigation. The *OED* cites *Othello* (hint, n., Ia, 2a), but the first usage appears to have been in Thomas Nuce's translation of Seneca's *Octavia* (1566), when Nero desires an end to ambiguity: 'Swordes bloudy dynt / Shall cause them else at me to take their hynt' (sig. D4v). The word appears to have passed into more common usage, especially in biblical commentaries and theological works, in the early 1600s, describing classical and biblical notions of complicated signs that can be misread, and the obscure ways in which communication takes place (Nuce was a clergyman: see the *ODNB* entry). I am grateful to Duncan Fraser for drawing my attention to the significance of the word.

[12] Fitzmaurice, *Humanism and America*, pp. 113–14.

[13] Quentin Skinner, *Forensic Shakespeare* (Oxford: Oxford University Press, 2014), p. 186.

[14] Serjeantson, 'Testimony', p. 186.

contents were outdated, the material derived from Mandeville's *Travels*, or one of Erasmus's stranger texts about the state of the world.[15] But the first known account of such men, Herodotus's report of eastern Libya, with its list of marvellous beasts and humans, was clearly sceptical: 'It is here that the huge snakes are found—and lions, elephants, bears, asps, and horned asses, not to mention dog-headed men, headless men with eyes in their breasts (I don't vouch for this, but merely repeat what the Libyans say), wild men and wild women, and a great many other creatures by no means of a fabulous kind.'[16] Accounts of cannibals were notorious because invariably what travellers discovered were remains and signs, such as the abandoned cannibal meal; or they were told stories by the particular peoples whom they encountered that their hostile neighbours were the man-eaters that the Europeans feared so greatly.[17] There was increased scepticism about certain claims and testimony, and it is surely no coincidence that Shakespeare wrote *Othello* after Richard Hakluyt had removed the translation of Mandeville's *Travels*, the most notorious account then known by a 'lying traveller', from the revised and expanded edition of his *Principal Navigations, Voiages and Discoueries of the English Nation* (1599, 1600), replacing Mandeville with Odoric of Pordenone.[18] In Stephen Greenblatt's words, 'marvels were becoming more embarrassing than authenticating'.[19] Even after the major discoveries rendered its information outdated and misleading many readers continued to rely on Sebastian Münster's appealing and well-organized *Cosmographia* (1544).[20]

The most likely source for Othello's account of his travels is indeed Mandeville, his dubious status as an authority reinforced by Hakluyt's recent decision to remove the account. Mandeville describes the peoples who inhabit the Andaman Islands in

[15] Desiderius Erasmus, *Here Folowith a Scorneful Image or Monstrus Shape of a Maruelous Strange Fygure Called, Sileni Alcibiadis Presentyng Ye State [and] Condicio[n] of this Present World*, trans. Anon. (London, 1543); Ruth Samson Luborsky and Elizabeth Morley Ingram, *A Guide to English Illustrated Books, 1536–1603*, 2 vols (Tempe, AZ: MRTS, 1998), II, image 176; Crawford, *Marvelous Protestantism*, p. 5. On Mandeville's influence see Letts, *Mandeville*, p. 38.
[16] Herodotus, *The Histories*, trans. Aubrey de Sélincourt and A. R. Burn (Harmondsworth: Penguin, 1972), p. 334.
[17] Peter Hulme, *Colonial Encounters: Europe and the Native Caribbean, 1492–1797* (London: Methuen, 1986), pp. 80–3; Peter Hulme, 'Introduction: The Cannibal Scene', in Francis Barker, Peter Hulme, and Margaret Iversen, eds, *Cannibalism and the Colonial World* (Cambridge: Cambridge University Press, 1998), pp. 1–38.
[18] On 'lying travellers', see Malcolm Letts, 'Of Lying Travellers', *CR* 96 (1920), 95–100. On Hakluyt see Claire Jowitt, 'Hakluyt's Legacy: Armchair Travel in English Renaissance Drama', in Daniel Carey and Claire Jowitt, eds, *Richard Hakluyt and Travel Writing in Early Modern Europe* (Farnham: Ashgate, 2012), pp. 295–306, at p. 304. Charles Moseley suggests that Mandeville was probably removed because of the need for new material to be included not because of the fictitious nature of his account: ' "Whet-stone Leasings of Old *Maundeulie*: Reading the *Travels* in Early Modern England', in Ladan Niayesh, ed., *A Knight's Legacy: Mandeville and Mandevillian Lore in Early Modern England* (Manchester: Manchester University Press, 2011), pp. 28–50, at pp. 33–4.
[19] Stephen Greenblatt, *Marvelous Possessions: The Wonder of the New World* (Oxford: Oxford University Press, 1991), pp. 30–2. Many contemporary accounts noted this problem: see, for example, Tomasso Garzoni, *The Hospitall of Incurable Fooles*, trans. Edward Blount or Thomas Nashe (London, 1600), p. 4.
[20] Letts, 'Of Lying Travellers', p. 97.

the Bay of Bengal as a diverse collection of monsters.[21] Some are enthusiastic and indiscriminate cannibals, 'people of evil customs, for fathers eat their sons and sons their fathers, husbands their wives and wives their husbands', and others are 'ugly folk without heads, who have eyes in each shoulder'.[22] Othello is represented as a lying traveller at a moment when scepticism about the testimony of travellers, voiced most powerfully in Montaigne's essay on the cannibals, was rife. If Montaigne does not have Mandeville, Marco Polo, and others in mind, then surely many of his readers made the connection between historical accounts of man-eating and contemporary ones.[23] And if we are sceptical about Othello's account of the peoples he has encountered should we not also wonder whether he crossed huge deserts, saw enormous caves and colossal mountains, or whether he was actually sold into slavery when captured by his enemies (another commonly available narrative at the time).[24]

There is no way of verifying Othello's account of his life: no one witnessed his actions, because, as Ernst Honigmann points out, 'he refers to a time before he entered the service of Venice'.[25] The one character who appears to understand what has taken place is Iago, who complains to Roderigo, 'Mark me with what violence she first loved the Moor, but for bragging and telling her fantastical lies' (2.1.220–1), a recognition of the tempestuous nature of Othello's and Desdemona's passion, as well as a chilling prefiguration of her fate in Act 5. Othello's speech has no precedent in its source, Cinthio's *Gli Hecatommithi*, which indicates the significance of the council scene as well as Iago's response in the plot of *Othello*.[26] In spectacular and disturbing fashion, lying is introduced into Shakespeare's play.

Othello's testimony needs to be read against another purported eyewitness account.[27] Iago claims that he witnessed Cassio involuntarily confessing his love for Desdemona in the middle of the night in the barracks:

[21] See John Gillies, *Shakespeare and the Geography of Difference* (Cambridge: Cambridge University Press, 1994), p. 29.

[22] *The Travels of Sir John Mandeville*, trans. C. W. R. D. Moseley (Harmondsworth: Penguin, 1983), pp. 136–7. Mandeville's account was based on other sources, which was why he fell into disrepute. Marco Polo has a similar account which suggests that he did not visit the islands: *The Travels*, trans. R. E. Latham (Harmondsworth: Penguin, 1958), pp. 258–9. See also *Othello*, ed. Michael Neill (Oxford: Oxford University Press, 2006), p. 463; *Othello: A New Variorum Edition*, ed. Horace Howard Furness (New York: Dover, 1963, rpt of 1886), pp. 56–7.

[23] The general comments recorded in English annotations suggest that this was the case: Hamlin, *Montaigne's English Journey*, p. 89.

[24] On the last point see Daniel J. Vitkus and Nabil I. Matar, eds, *Piracy, Slavery, and Redemption: Barbary Captivity Narratives from Early Modern England* (New York: Columbia University Press, 2001).

[25] *Othello*, ed. Honigmann, p. 144.

[26] *Narrative and Dramatic Sources*, VII, p. 242. Cinthio passes rapidly over the courtship of the Moor and Disdemona, stating that, despite the opposition of her family who wish her to marry another man, she falls in love with him 'impelled not by female appetite but by the Moor's good qualities', and he, 'vanquished by the Lady's beauty and noble mind, likewise was enamoured of her'.

[27] For further comment on Shakespeare's scepticism of eyewitness accounts of events see Atsuhiko Hirota, 'History and Historiography', in Smith, ed., *Worlds of Shakespeare, Vol. II*, pp. 579–86, at p. 581.

I do not like the office.
But, sith I am entered in this cause so far,
Pricked to't by foolish honesty and love,
I will go on. I lay with Cassio lately
And being troubled with a raging tooth
I could not sleep. There are a kind of men
So loose of soul that in their sleeps will mutter
Their affairs—one of this kind is Cassio.
In sleep I heard him say 'Sweet Desdemona,
Let us be wary, let us hide our loves;'
And then, sir, would he gripe and wring my hand,
Cry 'O sweet creature!' and then kiss me hard
As if he plucked up kisses by the roots
That grew upon my lips, then lay his leg o'er my thigh,
And sigh, and kiss, and then cry 'Cursed fate
That gave thee to the Moor!' (3.3.413–28)

The speech is a vital dramatic crux, sealing Desdemona's fate as Othello, acting like a jealous monarch who has absolute power over the law, is determined to carry out her execution.

Iago's testimony needs to be read against Othello's before the council: the latter seals the legitimacy of their marriage, the former its end and her death. We know that—or, perhaps we think that we know that?—Iago is lying but he has not only timed the delivery of the speech to perfection, convincing his general of his wife's sustained infidelity after unsettling him with a series of disturbing hints and suggestions, but he has also produced an account that is even more credible and convincing than that of Othello before the council. Where Othello skilfully recycled some of the powerful clichés of travellers' tales, Iago reproduces Othello's worst fears in graphic form. The truth of Othello's speech cannot be validated; Iago's looks as if it can be, which leads to his asking Cassio about Bianca while Othello watches. The careful selection of details serves brilliantly to validate Iago's account: the toothache; the general wisdom that some men are 'loose of soul' and confess to their transgressions when unconscious; the reported speech; and the desire for physical pleasure that cannot be constrained within reasonable grounds. It is hard not to imagine the Duke responding that this speech would have persuaded him to kill his wife too.

The description of Cassio's apparent passion for Desdemona bears a striking resemblance to accounts of unbridled lust in contemporary murder pamphlets.[28] The involuntary crying out of the lover's name which has fatal consequences was also a common plot motif in such works and was staged in *Arden of Faversham* (1592), a play attributed to Shakespeare at various times.[29] Iago constructs his

---

[28] Hill, 'Bloudy Tygrisses', pp. 76–105; Frances E. Dolan, 'Home-Rebels and House-Traitors: Murderous Wives in Early Modern England', *YJLH* 4 (1992), 1–30, pp. 8–9.

[29] Anon., *Arden of Faversham*, ed. Martin White (London: Methuen, 1984), I.65–70; *Othello*, ed. Honigmann, pp. 73–4, 236; Emma Smith, *The Making of Shakespeare's First Folio* (Oxford: Bodleian Library, 2015), p. 13. Shakespeare's involvement is advocated in *The New Oxford Shakespeare:*

speech with admirable care. He opens with the claim that he is reluctant to speak at all, a lie which appears to validate his honesty.[30] Iago follows Quintilian in attempting to make his audience experience the scene he wishes to recreate, emotionally manipulating them to follow his logic, using the rhetorical technique, Enargia.[31] As Quintilian asserts, in forensic oratory 'Emotion is justifiably combined with Proofs of each fact'.[32] And Iago obeys the rules for a skilful forensic orator using concrete details to bring a case to life more vividly.[33] He succeeds, proving Quintilian's fear that rhetoric can be used for malign ends and demonstrating that a bad man can be a good orator.[34]

The plot of *Othello* hinges on apparently honest testimonies that are lies, forcing the audience to worry about what they really do and do not know. It is easy enough to realize that Iago is lying, but this does not help us navigate through the moral and epistemological mazes that the play so carefully establishes. Othello has already lied, but his testimony has been validated by his wife, and then by the council, suggesting that powerful oratory invariably wins the day. Iago's speech may not work on a theatre audience but it is easy for such an audience to see why it would work on Othello, or on many in his state of mind.[35]

II

Othello is a literary work saturated in a culture of lying. The play has been used to describe a particular way of failing to distinguish between truth and lies in forensic psychology. Paul Ekman coined the term the 'Othello error' to describe 'how *preconceptions* can bias a lie catcher's judgements'. According to Ekman, Othello 'is tortured by his belief that Desdemona lies', which leads him to interpret her nervousness and panic when he interrogates her 'in a way that will confirm what he least wants to be so, in a way that is most painful to him'.[36] The problem is that by this stage of the plot Othello is so steeped in lying and so exposed to lies that he cannot easily distinguish between them or, indeed, between truth and falsehood per se. Moreover, and in line with English beliefs about Italian behaviour based on reading courtesy books and political treatises, he thinks that lying is a way of life in the city where he has made his home but is always conscious of being a stranger.[37]

The Complete Works, Modern Critical Edition, ed. Gary Taylor, John Jowett, Terri Bourus, and Gabriel Egan (Oxford: Oxford University Press, 2016), pp. 117–81.

[30] William Empson, 'Honest in *Othello*', in *The Structure of Complex Words* (London: Chatto & Windus, 1952), pp. 218–49, at p. 220; Paul A. Jorgensen, 'Honesty in *Othello*', SP 47 (1950), 557–67, at pp. 563–7.

[31] Richards, *Rhetoric*, p. 111.   [32] Quintilian, *Institutes*, 6.1.5; Richards, *Rhetoric*, p. 44.

[33] Quintilian, *Institutes*, 5.11.   [34] Quintilian, *Institutes*, 2.15.

[35] My reading challenges a long-standing tradition which casts Othello as especially gullible, or credulous: for comment see Ania Loomba, *Gender, Race, Renaissance Drama* (Manchester: Manchester University Press, 1989), p. 52. I am grateful to Chloe Porter for advice on this point.

[36] Ekman, *Telling Lies*, p. 171 (emphasis in original).

[37] Hadfield, *Literature, Travel, and Colonial Writing*, pp. 226–42.

And the play suggests that he is right. Cassio, who is a reasonably honest and honourable character, proud of the reputation that he loses after the tavern scene, nevertheless thinks nothing of misleading the besotted Bianca, just as he lied to Iago about his knowledge of Othello and Desdemona's marriage.[38] This blindspot enables Iago to delude Othello about Desdemona, as well as supporting his judgement that Venetian women habitually deceive their husbands and that what the eye does not see is assumed not to exist: 'In Venice they do let God see the pranks / They dare not show their husbands; their best conscience / Is not to leave't undone, but keep't unknown' (3.3.205–7). Immediately before he gives Bianca the handkerchief that Othello gave Desdemona, Cassio lies to Bianca, a lie that is of little consequence to him, but of great matter to her:

Bianca: Save you, friend Cassio!
Cassio: What make you from home?
How is't with you, my most fair Bianca?
I' faith, sweet love, I was coming to your house.
Bianca: And I was going to your lodging, Cassio.
What, keep a week away? seven days and nights?
Eight score eight hours? and lovers' absent hours
More tedious than the dial eight score times?
O weary reckoning!
Cassio: Pardon me, Bianca,
I have this while with leaden thoughts been pressed,
But I shall in a more continuate time
Strike off this score of absence. Sweet Bianca,
      [Giving her Desdemona's handkerchief]
Take me this work out. (4.1.168–79)

We know from Cassio's earlier exchange with Iago that he is prepared to trifle with Bianca knowing that she cares for him more than he cares for her, so that when he claims that he was coming to her house he is lying, as he is when he pretends that he has been overwhelmed with 'leaden thoughts'. To compensate he gives her the handkerchief—a notorious plot device, as Iago could not have known that Cassio would do this—which enables Iago to further confirm Desdemona's guilt.[39] Cassio undoubtedly imagines that his lies are small and they do not affect his reputation: Bianca clearly has a different understanding of his conscious deceptions and his neglect helps to define who she is, a courtesan, not a fiancée or a wife.[40] More

---

[38] Empson, 'Honest in *Othello*', p. 222.

[39] Thomas Rymer, *A Short View of Tragedy* (London, 1695), p. 135; Michael C. Andrews, 'Honest Othello: The Handkerchief Once More', *SEL* 13 (1973), 273–84, at p. 284. On the symbolic importance of the handkerchief see Lynda E. Boose, 'Othello's Handkerchief: "The Recognizance and Pledge of Love"', *ELR* 5 (1975), 360–74.

[40] See Jyotsna G. Singh, 'The Interventions of History: Narratives of Sexuality', in Dympna Callaghan, Lorraine Helms, and Jyotsna G. Singh, *The Weyward Sisters: Shakespeare and Feminist Politics* (Oxford: Blackwell, 1994), pp. 7–58, at pp. 47–50; Alison Findlay, *Women in Shakespeare: A Dictionary* (London: Black, 2014), pp. 39–40.

significantly, we witness that the major lies are only possible because characters are prepared to articulate the smaller ones.

The handkerchief dominates the action of the fourth Act of the play. Cassio's demand/request that Bianca copy the pattern of the embroidered cloth echoes Emilia's words—'I'll have the work ta'en out' (3.3.300)—when she picks it up after Desdemona drops it. Emilia's action in keeping the handkerchief which her 'wayward husband' (296) had frequently urged her to steal includes her in the circle of deceit, dishonesty, and lying, especially as she notes his transgressive nature without asking why he might want it or deciding to return the handkerchief to its owner. Bianca is the only person who behaves innocently and honestly about the handkerchief but her understandable, albeit misplaced, accusation that this is 'some minx's token' (4.1.152) only serves to thicken Iago's plot. Both women are drawn into the circles of deception through the motif of copying, acting to supplement the plots initiated by men, perhaps a reminder that lies, especially in this play, might seem innocent but never are.

The handkerchief provides Iago with the opportunity to confirm Othello's suspicion that Desdemona is unfaithful because he realizes that 'Trifles light as air / Are to the jealous confirmations strong / As proofs of holy writ' (3.3.325–7), emphasizing the close interaction between the plot of *Othello*, legal processes, and the act of confession. In early modern England the ability to make an absolute distinction between truth and falsehood was both necessary and impossible in a culture defined by religious faith and public reputation.[41]

Convinced that Desedemona, rather than Iago, has given the handkerchief to Cassio, Othello provides Iago with the opportunity to give him 'ocular proof' (3.3.363) of her adultery. As a prelude to her murder Othello lies once more, transforming his role as a traveller to distant lands by representing himself as an exotic figure whose superstitious faith in magic is alien to the modernity of Europe:

> That handkerchief
> Did an Egyptian to my mother give,
> She was a charmer, and could almost read
> The thoughts of people. She told her, while she kept it,
> 'Twould make her amiable and subdue my father
> Entirely to her love; but if she lost it
> Or made gift of it, my father's eye
> Should hold her loathed and his spirits should hunt
> After new fancies. She, dying, gave it me
> And bid me, when my fate would have me wive,
> To give it her. I did so, and—take heed on't!
> Make it a darling like your precious eye!—
> To lose't or give't away were such perdition

[41] On public reputation in *Othello* see Jardine, *Reading Shakespeare Historically*, pp. 19–34. Julia Reinhard Lupton recognizes the ways in which the play engages with Pauline issues of faith, truthfulness, and inclusion/exclusion: 'Paul Shakespeare: Exegetical Exercises', in Elizabeth Williamson and Jane Hwang Degenhardt, eds, *Religion and Drama in Early Modern England: The Performance of Religion on the Renaissance Stage* (Farnham: Ashgate, 2013), pp. 209–31, at pp. 230–1.

As nothing else could match.
Desdemona: Is't possible?
Othello: 'Tis true, there's magic in the web of it:
A sibyl, that had numbered in the world
The sun to course two hundred compasses,
In her prophetic fury sewed the work;
The worms were hallowed that did breed the silk,
And it was dyed in mummy, which the skilful
Conserved of maidens' hearts. (3.4.57–77)

Othello weaves a skilful tale designed to prey on Desdemona's fears of the strange and unfathomable man she has married. The speech reminds us of the trial scene with Brabantio's judgement that his daughter had inexplicably fallen in love 'with what she feared to look on' (1.3.99); his allegation that only 'spells and medicines bought of mountebanks' (62) could have won her heart; and Desdemona's explanation that she could see into Othello's soul, rather than simply looking at his face. In doing so Othello shows that he understands only too well the culture of Venice where he has made his home as an alien and knows how to exploit the fears of its inhabitants, which were obvious enough in that earlier scene. Presumably what an audience should realize is that having told one particular, relatively innocent, lie at the start of the play, Othello can exploit the same knowledge to tell a much more dangerous one—which will help convince him that murdering his wife is justified because it will provide irrefutable proof of her guilt. In doing so *Othello* shows us just how problematic it can be to tell lies in order to produce the truth, and what a chain of unintended consequences can be set off as a result.

The handkerchief plot is in Cinthio's original story, but not the elaborate explanation that Othello provides.[42] The claim that a furious sibyl had the handkerchief woven can no more be true than Othello's statement that he had seen men whose heads grow beneath their shoulders. Sibyls were mythical women, mainly from the Mediterranean including North Africa (there was a Libyan sibyl), who had the gift of prophecy, furious because they had been abandoned in love and because they had the gift of eternal life but not eternal youth.[43] They provided riddles which foretold the future, an art inextricably bound up with truth-telling and lying, as Macbeth discovers when he realizes that the witches' prophecies consist of 'lies like truth'.[44] Othello calls on the sibylline figure and her art as a means to help him uncover the truth but finds that his lie destroys him as well as his wife. The handkerchief does help uncover the truth when Emilia reveals that she took it and gave it to her husband, but not in time to save Desdemona, a sign of the perilously misleading nature of prophecies which may reveal the truth but only in destructive ways at odds with the desire of those who rely on them (they have the same effect as lies even when they are true).[45]

[42] *Narrative and Dramatic Sources*, VII, p. 249.
[43] Jessica L. Malay, *Prophecy and Sibyline Imagery in the Renaissance: Shakespeare's Sibyls* (Abingdon: Routledge, 2010), pp. 4–6; Lemprière, p. 627.
[44] Shakespeare, *Macbeth*, 5.5.43.   [45] Malay, *Prophecy and Sibyline Imagery*, pp. 115–16.

The use of Egyptian mummy to dye the handkerchief holds out the promise of its immortality and the consequent fear that the curse will last forever if it is lost, supplementing and reinforcing the power of the sibyl. References to mummies and mummification were relatively common in early modern culture, especially on the stage, sometimes used, as here, to represent the dark supernatural mysteries of pagan North Africa.[46] The description of the silkworms as 'hallowed' suggests not merely the significance of silk in the luxury economy of early modern Europe, but the superstitious reverence of relics, a common Protestant attack on the Catholic Church and its concentration on the material at the expense of the spiritual.[47] The same, of course, is true of 'maidens' hearts', a disturbing compound noun that conjures up images of human sacrifice, vestal virgins, nunneries, and the sacred heart.[48]

As with Othello's speech to the Venetian council, we have no way of knowing how much—if any—of this is true. Having stated that the Sibyl gave the handkerchief to his mother, Othello then claims that the handkerchief is 'an antique token / My father gave to my mother' (5.2.214–15) just before he realizes that Desdemona is innocent, which suggests that he is not telling the truth but testing her in an inquisitorial manner designed to demonstrate her guilt rather than giving her a chance to prove her innocence.[49] We cannot know whether Othello is telling the truth when he states that his mother gave him the handkerchief when she was dying; whether he believes that it has any power to a beloved's affections; whether, if lost, it transforms love into hatred; nor whether its supposed powers can be transferred from one couple to another. A language of religious and legal truth is provided with no possibility of verification other than Othello's claim that ''Tis true', when Desdemona asks, with what is surely incredulity rather than cross-examination, 'Is't possible?' That the folio has Desdemona ask 'Is't true?' and Othello reply 'Most veritable' is an indication of the significance—and futility—of the legal language used in this exchange.[50] In Othello's mind what he witnesses later is enough to prove his suspicions and he can state with conviction to Emilia that the dead Desdemona is 'like a liar gone to burning hell' (5.2.127), echoing Revelation 21:8, 'all liars shall haue their part in the lake, which burneth with fire & brimstone, which is the second death' (Geneva translation).[51] The statement is riddling in its ambiguity in that Desdemona is 'like a liar', but surely not in the way that Othello imagines. Furthermore, it is not obvious, as the complex tradition of Christian theology recounted throughout this book demonstrates, that all liars are condemned to suffer everlasting torment.

---

[46] Philip Schwyzer, *Archaeologies of English Renaissance Literature* (Oxford: Oxford University Press, 2007), p. 165.

[47] On 'hallowed' see Shell, *Oral Culture*, pp. 46, 89. On relics see King, ed., *Voices*, pp. 60–5. On silk, see Braudel, *Civilisation and Capitalism*, III, pp. 217–18.

[48] On heart imagery and religion see Gregory Kneidel, 'Hard Hearts and Scandal', in Mary Arshagouni Papazian, ed., *The Sacred and Profane in English Renaissance Literature* (Newark: University of Delaware Press, 2008), pp. 236–52.

[49] Andrews, 'Honest Othello', pp. 273–4.   [50] *Othello*, ed. Furness, 3.4.90–1 (p. 222).

[51] See Harriet C. Frazier, '"Like a Liar Gone to Burning Hell": Shakespeare and Dying Declarations', *CD* 19 (1985), 166–80, at p. 174.

But in one way, at least, Othello is right that Desdemona is a liar. Her final words to Emilia are in answer to the question 'who hath done this deed' (121–2), the standard question that a murder trial would attempt to answer. However, Desdemona transforms the nature of the crime with what seems to be a well-intentioned lie, 'Nobody. I myself' (123). The significance of these words cannot be overestimated. Desdemona stands in pointed contrast to the epitaph that William Camden recorded in *Remains*, published just after *Othello* was probably first performed, based on that of Augustine ('Misericordia Domini inter pontem & fontem' (God's mercy can be found between bridge and stream)), of 'A Gentleman falling off his Horse, brake his neck':

> My friend judge not me,
> Thou seest I judge not thee:
> Betwixt the stirrup and the ground,
> Mercy I askt, mercy I found.[52]

The fate of the fortunate gentleman showed that there was always hope for those who could repent, however badly they might have behaved throughout their lives. Desdemona, on the other hand, risks her soul in lying about the nature of her death, *felo de se* (self-slaughter), and her posthumous reputation, although it is her husband who actually commits suicide. The reason she lies is not stated but as Desdemona asks to be commended to her 'kind lord' (123) she would appear to be lying to protect Othello's reputation, an action that recalls the disgrace of Cassio and his loss of reputation in the opening Act of the play, the event which began Iago's lethal plot.[53] But in doing so has she violated her conscience? Or confirmed her virtue? Put another way, does her lie remind us of the one told by the Hebrew midwives, that of Jacob to Isaac, or something far more mendacious?[54] Or, Adam's hiding from God after he and Eve had eaten the fruit of the tree of knowledge, a moment of panic inspired by his uxorious love for his wife (Genesis 3:10–12)?[55] The

---

[52] William Camden, *Remains Concerning Britain* (London: EP Publishing, 1974), p. 420.

[53] This lie has been characterized as Desdemona's third: see Mary Beth Rose, *The Expense of Spirit: Love and Sexuality in English Renaissance Drama* (Ithaca, NY: Cornell University Press, 1988), pp. 144, 152–3. On reputation and the link between Cassio and Othello see Joel B. Altman, *The Improbability of Othello: Rhetorical Anthropology and Shakespearean Selfhood* (Chicago: University of Chicago Press, 2010), pp. 74–5.

[54] Desdemona's lie has certain parallels to the opening story of Boccaccio's *Decameron*, which Shakespeare might have known. An unrepentant old sinner, Signor Ciappelletto, falling mortally ill in the house of two Lombardy merchants, agrees to deliver a false confession to a friar so that he can be buried in sacred ground and save his hosts from social embarrassment, and is posthumously revered as a saint: Giovanni Boccaccio, *The Decameron*, trans. G. H. McWilliam (Harmondsworth: Penguin, 1972), pp. 24–37 (introduction, pp. cxix–cxxii). On Shakespeare's possible knowledge of *The Decameron* see Herbert G. Wright, 'How Did Shakespeare Come to Know the "Decameron"?', *MLR* 50 (1955), 45–8; Gillespie, *Shakespeare's Books*, pp. 53–60. I am grateful to Duncan Fraser for suggesting the possible link between the stories.

[55] See, for example, Calvin, *Commentaries*, I, pp. 162–4; Josipovici, *Book of God*, p. 194. The tradition of Adam's uxorious love for Eve was more carefully developed in Milton's *Paradise Lost*: see Neil Forsyth, 'Milton's Corrupt Bible', in Kevin Killeen, Helen Smith, and Rachel Judith Willie, eds, *The Oxford Handbook of the Bible in Early Modern England, c. 1530–1700* (Oxford: Oxford University Press, 2015), pp. 209–23, at p. 214.

audience might have remembered Sir Edward Coke's warning to Father Garnet that the time before death was no time for equivocation.[56]

Fortunately, Iago's plot is uncovered, Desdemona's lie recedes in significance— as it has done ever since—and the truth behind her murder comes to light. Iago is the most successful and diligent liar in the Shakespeare canon.[57] When he is exposed there can be no doubt about the nature of his crimes:

> *Emilia*: But did you ever tell him she was false?
> *Iago*: I did.
> *Emilia*: You told a lie, an odious, damned lie!
> Upon my soul, a lie, a wicked lie!
> She false with Cassio? Did you say with Cassio? (5.2.174–8)

Given the serious nature of the accusation, the repetition of the word 'lie' four times in two lines, the most concentrated example in Shakespeare, this is an extraordinary dramatic moment. *Othello* is a play replete with damaging public allegations which need to be resolved one way or another. Othello is accused of bewitching and kidnapping Desdemona; Cassio is publicly shamed as watch for being drunk in dereliction of duty; Desdemona is publicly accused of being a whore by her husband; and, now, Emilia, not needing to wait for proof, is able to accuse her husband of lying about Desdemona's infidelity in front of witnesses.[58]

Such accusations were both striking and relatively rare in early modern English life, culture, and literature, given the significance of reputation, the easy and frequent recourse to the ecclesiastical courts to resolve disputes between neighbours, the penalties for slander, and, above all, the grave public shame of being labelled a liar.[59] Courts tended to award punitively high damages for slander and refuse to grant retrials or reconsider the level of awards made to successful plaintiffs, which further decreased the appetite for such legal disputes.[60] Emilia's accusation, therefore, is a strikingly dramatic moment on the early modern English stage. Like Richard Rich, Iago is defined as a liar.

We never learn why he tells such lies. In Cinthio's story the Ensign has 'the most scoundrelly nature in the world' and 'the basest of minds', but, being 'of handsome presence' and verbally adept, 'he so cloaked the vileness hidden in his heart with high sounding and noble words, and by his manner, that he showed himself in the likeness of a Hector or an Achilles'.[61] However, his plot does have a real motive beyond his wickedness, because he falls 'ardently in love with Disdemona, and bent all his thoughts to see if he could manage to enjoy her'.[62] In contrast, Iago has no superficial reason for his actions, although he has some strange suspicion that Othello

---

[56] See Frazier, 'Like a Liar Gone to Burning Hell', p. 168.

[57] Inga-Stina Ewbank, *Shakespeare's Liars* (London: British Academy, 1984).

[58] On the public accusations in the play see Jardine, *Reading Shakespeare Historically*, p. 26.

[59] On slander see Sokol and Sokol, *Shakespeare's Legal Language*, pp. 207–12; Gowing, *Domestic Dangers*, pp. 119–25. For specific cases see F. G. Emmison, *Elizabethan Life: Home, Work and Land* (Chelmsford: Essex County Council, 1976), pp. 151, 232, 234, 309.

[60] R. H. Helmholz, 'Damages in Actions for Slander at Common Law', *LQR* 103 (1987), 624–38.

[61] *Narrative and Dramatic Sources*, VII, p. 243.

[62] *Narrative and Dramatic Sources*, VII, p. 244.

may have cuckolded him: 'For that I do suspect the lusty Moor / Hath leaped into my seat, the thought whereof / Doth like a poisonous mineral gnaw my inwards / And nothing can content my soul / Till I am evened with him, wife for wife' (2.1.293–7). No evidence exists elsewhere in the text, and, as A. D. Nuttall has argued, in speculating that Othello has cuckolded him 'he has decided consciously to treat a story that could be false as if it were true'.[63] Perhaps this means that Iago is lying to himself, suggesting either that he has the vestiges of a conscience, however twisted, that he has not yet managed to suppress, or that he is so wicked that he cannot be honest even when alone and thinking aloud: or, maybe, he is the liar, described in Augustine and Bacon, who simply acts for his own pleasure.[64] For Michael Neill these lines exhibit a 'parallel fantasy' of Iago supplanting Cassio in Desdemona's bed, which enables Iago to retreat 'into the reassuringly objective language of moral accounting'.[65] It may be, however, that they reveal just how far Iago's habitual lying corrodes his conscience and his moral identity.

Iago's desire to lie may not have an origin but it does have a context, one that enables his plot to drive the action of the play and succeed in its terrible purpose. The lies told by the other characters—in particular, Othello, Cassio, Emilia, and Desdemona—establish a society in which lying is expected and tolerated, and it is only when lying leads to murder that it has to be stopped. Until Iago threatens to stab Emilia immediately after she reveals his crimes (5.2.221–2) he does not actually do anything other than lie, orchestrating those around him as they commit different crimes, serious (Cassio's failure as the watch) and petty (Emilia's stealing the handkerchief because she thinks it will please her husband).[66] His crimes are very much like those of most traitors in the period, words rather than actual deeds.

Iago's actions constantly remind the audience of the deadly religious conflict that was engulfing Europe after the Reformation. When Othello is finally convinced of Desdemona's guilt he swears an oath to Iago that he will never change his mind and that her fate is decided whatever happens:

Never, Iago. Like to the Pontic sea
Whose icy current and compulsive course
Ne'er keeps retiring ebb but keeps due on
To the Propontic and the Hellespont:
Even so my bloody thoughts, with violent pace,
Shall ne'er look back, ne'er ebb to humble love
Till that a capable and wide revenge
Swallow them up. Now, by yond marble heaven,
In the due reverence of a sacred vow
I here engage my words. (3.3.456–65)

---

[63] Nuttall, *Shakespeare the Thinker*, p. 282.   [64] See above, pp. 15, 27.

[65] Michael Neill, *Putting History to the Question: Power, Politics, and Society in English Renaissance Drama* (New York: Columbia University Press, 2000), p. 220.

[66] The stage direction, e.g. '[Iago tries to stab Emilia]' (ed. Honigmann, p. 326), is an editorial addition not in the quarto or folio, but Gratiano's line, 'Fie! Your sword upon a woman?' (222) makes his action clear.

Othello's 'sacred vow' of revenge appears at once Christian and pagan and so becomes a parody of the oaths that had to be sworn by both Catholics and Protestants to the monarch and the Pope, which invariably came into conflict whenever any pressure was applied to the promise in question.[67] Iago asks Othello whether his mind might change (455), which was what happened to many who had to swear such oaths, assuming they planned to keep them in the first place. Iago then swears to be loyal 'To wronged Othello's service' (470), a riddling promise that is clearly false if read connecting Othello to 'service' but true if linking him to 'wronged', the suppressed statement, a form of mental reservation by Iago, being that it is Iago who is causing the wrong, not Desdemona. Othello asks Iago to find 'some swift means of death / For the fair devil' (480–1), having forgotten that the Devil is the father of lies and that these will invariably appear disguised as truths.[68] Iago's response, 'I am your own forever' (482), functions not just to show how Othello has managed to damn himself through his misplaced faith in his 'honest' ensign, but also represents what many Christians thought confessional opponents were doing in swearing oaths of loyalty to their false churches.

When Othello accuses Desdemona of being a strumpet she denies his charge as she is a 'Christian' (4.2.84), a religious promise that either looks back to the time before the Reformation; believes that faith within Christendom is of the same nature; or a future when unity will return. The audience would realize that her words, especially on stage in England in the early 1600s, pointed to a current state of separation and division with Christians divided rather than united. Othello murders Desdemona in a horrible parody of a church service, specifically the last rites, exhorting her to make a last confession in order to absolve her soul of the sin of perjury:

> *Othello*:   Sweet soul, take heed,
> Take heed of perjury. Thou art on thy deathbed.
> *Desdemona:* I! but not yet to die!
> *Othello*:   Yes, presently.
> Therefore confess thee freely of thy sin,
> For to deny each article with oath
> Cannot remove nor choke the strong conception
> That I do groan withal. Thou art to die.
> *Desdemona*: Then Lord have mercy on me.
> *Othello*:   I say amen. (5.2.50–8)[69]

---

[67] In other contexts the reverence which ancient societies had for oaths was cited as 'conclusive proof of a natural law of respect for oaths': John Spurr, 'A Profane History of Early Modern Oaths', *TRHS* 11 (2001), 37–63, p. 41.

[68] For comment see Frances A. Shirley, *Swearing and Perjury in Shakespeare's Plays* (London: Allen and Unwin, 1979), pp. 119–20.

[69] On deathbed rites and confession see Ralph Houlbrooke, *Death, Religion, and the Family in England, 1480–1750* (Oxford: Oxford University Press, 1998), pp. 147–82. See also Appelbaum, *Terrorism*, pp. 180–1.

Othello has established himself as Desdemona's judge and her confessor, able to weigh her guilt, take her life, and provide her with absolution. Confident that he has seen through her guilty lies—her protestations of innocence only increasing his certainty that he is right—he adopts a complementary position in relation to Iago, the one bound in service to the other. However, it is the trusty sword of truth which is being wielded by the father of lies.

Iago plays the role of the Devil in the play, but who is he?[70] While the main characters have obvious Italian names, Iago's name is Spanish, the equivalent of the English James.[71] The name links him to the patron saint of Spain, St James, famous as the 'Moor-killer', commemorated throughout Spain, his name enshrined in Santiago de Compostela, which was the second largest pilgrimage site after Rome in Europe, long popular enough with pilgrims to warrant its own guidebook.[72] The name also links Iago to the newly installed King of England, who had signed the Treaty of London on 1 August 1604 to end the Anglo-Spanish War, exactly four months before the first known performance of the play (1 November).[73] The Act was vital to James's sense of himself as a triumphant Roman emperor inaugurating years of peace and plenty, even though the security it provided Britain was 'inconclusive'.[74]

The political landscape in the British Isles changed dramatically after the Gunpowder Plot, but it is important to note that the language and style of *Othello* bear many resemblances to those of *Macbeth*, the play most associated with the failed coup and subsequent moral panic.[75] Both plays create the illusion of insoluble anxiety that justifies constant paranoia. In *Macbeth* it is almost impossible to separate good kings from bad, true prophecy from false, and rational humans from savage beasts, all complementing the culture of distrust and deliberate falsehood that pervades the earlier play.[76] Both place heavy emphasis on 'equivocation', as a structural principle of the dramatic language, and at significant points in each play.[77] At the conclusion of the trial scene, the Duke delivers his judgement in rhyme, a striking

[70] For discussion of Iago as a vice figure or devil see Peter Holland, 'Resources of Characterization in *Othello*', *Sh. Sur.* 41 (1989), 119–32, p. 128. Comparisons of Iago to a devil are commonplace: see, for example, William Hazlitt, *Liber Amoris and Dramatic Criticisms* (London: Peter Nevill, 1948), p. 215; Virginia Mason Vaughan, *Othello: A Contextual History* (Cambridge: Cambridge University Press, 1994), p. 139.

[71] Barbara Everett, '"Spanish" Othello: The Making of Shakespeare's Moor', in Catherine M. S. Alexander and Stanley Wells, eds, *Shakespeare and Race* (Cambridge: Cambridge University Press, 2000), pp. 64–81, at pp. 67–8.

[72] Everett, '"Spanish" Othello', p. 67; Ohler, *Medieval Traveller*, pp. 184–98.

[73] Roger Lockyer, *James VI and I* (London: Longman, 1998), pp. 127, 138; Lockyer, *Early Stuarts*, pp. 12–13.

[74] Richard Wilson, *Secret Shakespeare: Studies in Theatre, Religion and Resistance* (Manchester: Manchester University Press, 2004), p. 160; Patterson, *James VI and I*, pp. 32–4.

[75] John Kerrigan notes that although *Macbeth* is the play in which it is assumed that 'equivocation destabilizes language', a 'fascination with casuistry . . . goes back to the earlier plays' (*Shakespeare's Binding Language*, p. 7).

[76] Andreas Höfele, *Stage, Stake, and Scaffold: Humans and Animals in Shakespeare's Theatre* (Oxford: Oxford University Press, 2011), pp. 51–67.

[77] Georgia Brown, 'Defining Nature Through Monstrosity in *Othello* and *Macbeth*', in Ivo Kamps, Thomas Hallock, and Karen L. Raber, eds, *Early Modern Ecostudies* (Basingstoke: Palgrave Macmillan, 2008), pp. 55–76, at p. 58.

contrast to the previous two hundred lines which have been delivered in blank verse, as well as the subsequent lines about military strategy which are in prose, especially as the Duke signals the significance of his words through a half line:

> Let me speak like yourself, and lay a sentence
> Which as a grise or step may help these lovers
> Into your favour.
> When remedies are past the griefs are ended
> By seeing the worst, which late on hopes depended.
> To mourn a mischief that is past and gone
> Is the next way to draw new mischief on.
> What cannot be preserved when fortune takes,
> Patience her injury a mockery makes.
> The robbed that smiles steals something from the thief,
> He robs himself that spends a bootless grief. (1.3.200–10)[78]

On the one hand the lines are empty commonplaces which can be found in every work on grief and consolation, resembling Polonius's bricolage of clichés passed off as wisdom and good advice in *Hamlet*.[79] On the other, they resonate throughout the play, reflecting, in haunting ways, on Othello's actions as he is surely someone who 'robs himself' as well as others, through a 'bootless grief', but not in the ways that the Duke's words are intended. Innocent expressions of comfort can become ambiguous and fraught with sinister significance in a paranoid world. It is also possible that the Duke's sentiments serve to further Othello's murderous actions when considered alongside Iago's representation of Venetian women as loose and careless in their sexual behaviour, his words also sounding like a commonplace, one that places Othello outside the circle of knowledge: 'In Venice they do let God see the pranks / They dare not show their husbands; their best conscience / Is not to leave't undone, but keep't unknown' (3.3.205–7).[80] In such a context the Duke's advice would seem to be that the cuckolded husband lessens his pain if he grins and bears his fate, advice that is as likely to inspire quite contrary behaviour.

Brabantio's reply is two lines longer than the Duke's short speech, his rhymes exposing the complacency of the Duke's sentiments:

> So let the Turk of Cyprus us beguile,
> We lose it not so long as we can smile;
> He bears the sentence well that nothing bears
> But the free comfort which from thence he hears.

---

[78] The folio has a different line arrangement and omits the last words, 'Let me speake like your selfe: / And lay a sentence, / Which as a grise, or step may helpe these Louers', but the quarto provides a more logical text.

[79] G. W. Pigman, III, *Grief and English Renaissance Elegy* (Cambridge: Cambridge University Press, 1985), p. 11; Stillman, *Philip Sidney*, p. 55.

[80] Andreas Mahler, 'Writing Venice: Paradoxical Signification as Connotational Feature', in Manfred Pfister and Barbara Schaff, eds, *Venetian Views, Venetian Blinds: English Fantasies of Venice* (Amsterdam: Rodopi, 1999), pp. 29–44, at pp. 31–2; Ania Loomba, *Shakespeare, Race, and Colonialism* (Oxford: Oxford University Press, 2002), p. 99.

But he bears both the sentence and the sorrow
That, to pay grief, must of poor patience borrow.
These sentences, to sugar, or to gall,
Being strong on both sides, are equivocal.
But words are words; I never yet did hear
That the bruised heart was pierced through the ear. (1.3.211–20)

Brabantio corrects the Duke by pointing out that what he imagines is a straight-forward choice is really finely balanced. In performing this verbal manoeuvre Brabantio makes an ambiguous sentiment far more nuanced, problematic, and reversible, undercutting his own last lines that words are just words and cannot pierce the wounded heart, which might be taken as the antithesis of the action of a play which shows that an apparently happy marriage can be undone all too easily by a sustained verbal assault.

Brabantio's opening lines are bitterly ironic, reminding the Duke of the threat of the Ottomans, which he refers to in the next line, as he beseeches the Duke to turn to matters of state (221). They also look forward to Othello's self-representation as 'a malignant and turbanned Turk' (5.2.351) in his final speech.[81] Smiling in the face of danger will not remove its threat. The next line seems at first to suggest that it is better to tolerate nothing before the second half of the couplet qualifies the statement, indicating that the advice proffered by the Duke is effectively useless even if it has to be obeyed. These lines are complicated: they look like a common-place but resist straightforward interpretation. They seem to mean that if the addressee has to suffer nothing more than the words of the Duke then things have not worked out as badly as they might have done. The next line then qualifies this optimistic outcome with what appears to be the reverse situation: if the addressee has to suffer in silence as well as heed the Duke's wisdom then he will have to use all his patience to withstand the grief caused. This looks like the familiar practice of arguing *in utramque partem*, but, in reality, the two apparent opposites are really the same. Either Brabantio accepts the Duke's 'wisdom' because it has no real effect on his actual feelings, or he accepts it and hides his real suffering. In neither case do the Duke's words have any bearing on reality or power to comfort him—they are either irrelevant or mistaken. The penultimate couplet further suggests that a real choice is being made through the distinction between sugar and gall, an apparent paradox derived from theories of the confusing nature of human sensory perception, and yet another commonplace.[82] The use of the word 'equivocal', the only example in the play, should alert us to the significance of this exchange which separates words and actions in a context where it is made clear that words—such as the wedding vows of Othello and Desdemona—undoubtedly have a major impact on human activity.

[81] David Scott Kastan, *A Will to Believe: Shakespeare and Religion* (Oxford: Oxford University Press, 2014), p. 108.
[82] Herman Roodenburg, 'Introduction: Entering the Sensory Worlds of the Renaissance', in Herman Roodenburg, ed., *A Cultural History of the Senses in the Renaissance* (London: Bloomsbury, 2014), pp. 1–17, at pp. 5–6.

In terms of legal judgements the word could mean 'different significations equally appropriate or plausible', as the *OED*, following William Fulbeck, notes.[83] However, Fulbeck is being critical of common law lawyers who are not clear enough in their judgements which 'should be certaine, and without ambiguous or equivocall tearmes', not recognizing an insoluble dilemma.[84] The word has been glossed in editions of *Othello* as 'equally appropriate', but surely the truth is that Brabantio's words, although apparently uttered in defence of the law, are more an acknowledgement that he, although close to the centre of power, had little option but to obey a judgement that he felt, rightly or wrongly, to be unjust.[85] Furthermore, the speech is also a recognition that many in England felt at odds with the law's pronouncements, including the prominent Catholic lawyer and legal historian Edmund Plowden (1518–85); were eager to challenge its rulings; and adapted their language, like Brabantio, in order to evade its reach.[86] Some would do so in order to escape persecution; others to enable them to actively oppose the regime.

Equivocation lies at the heart of *Othello*, just as it does in *Macbeth*. Shakespeare suggests that equivocation is permitted—even encouraged—in Venice's legal institutions, used to secure an uneasy short-term truce with each side manipulating language in calculating ways to accommodate the other at the cost of the clarity and precision that William Fulbeck recommended for anyone wishing to practise law in contemporary England. Whether Venice should be read as a version of England or an exotic society is a tantalizing question posed for Shakespeare's audience, as it was in Jonson's *Volpone*.[87] When used to secure what many will regard as a desirable outcome, such as the marriage of Othello and Desdemona, this ambiguity seems benign enough. But when used with malice, as we witness throughout the play, equivocation is a destructive force, the user's language functioning in the same way as words uttered with malice in a treasonable cause, as the statutes stated.

Iago, a mysterious man with a Spanish name in an Italian society, is, on the one hand, an obvious outsider. On the other, however, no one is trusted more by the other characters in the play: Othello places his faith in him as an intimate confidant, even as he promotes Cassio above him, eventually pledging his loyalty to Iago in the grim ceremony of oath-exchange at the end of the handkerchief scene. Desdemona trusts him, as does Cassio. Roderigo, recognizing that Iago is prepared to be sly and underhand, trusts him to press his suit for money, and Emilia is prepared to pilfer Desdemona's handkerchief for her husband to win his favour and good temper. Iago's soliloquies, as has long been noted by critics, serve to increase his mystery rather than reveal his inner self and motivations: James Hirsch has pointed out that Othello demands that Iago show him his thoughts

---

[83] *OED* 'equivocal', n. and adj., 2a.

[84] William Fulbeck, *A Parallele or Conference of the Ciuil Law, the Canon Law, and the Common Law of this Realme of England* (London, 1601), p. 68.

[85] *Othello*, ed. Honigmann, p. 148; *Othello*, ed. Neill, p. 228. Sanders (New Cambridge); Ridley (Arden 2); Furness (Variorum); and Pechter (Norton), do not provide a gloss.

[86] On Plowden see the *ODNB* entry.

[87] Maus, 'Proof', p. 41. On Jonson see above, p. 97–100.

(3.3.118), but 'the play demonstrates that one can never have direct access to the thought of another'.[88]

Lines such as

When devils will the blackest sins put on
They do suggest at first with heavenly shows
As I do now. (2.3.346–8)

cannot but remind audiences, as Richard Wilson argues, of the common perception of the Jesuits, represented in polemical assaults from Meredith Hanmer onwards, and fuelled by more recent fear about the pernicious effects of the practice of equivocation.[89] The connection would have been secured by Iago's last exchange:

Othello: Will you, I pray, demand that demi-devil
Why he hath ensnared my soul and body?
Iago: Demand me nothing. What you know, you know.
From this time forth I never will speak word.
Lodovico: What, not to pray?
Gratiano: Torments will ope your lips. (5.2.298–303)

Othello's question imitates Protestant fears of what militant Catholicism would do to the unwary and gullible soul: his suicide might be seen to complete the story.[90] Moreover, it confirms Iago's self-representation as a disguised devil, leading people to damnation. Othello uses the word 'pray', a polite mode of request, which suggests he assumes that prayer is now beyond him, a suspicion confirmed when Lodovico asks Iago whether he will open his lips to pray, activating the pun in the earlier line. Iago has succeeded in damning Othello and has either damned himself in the process, or is already damned as a devil. 'What you know, you know', is yet another case of a proverb or commonplace stated that serves to confuse and unsettle rather than confirm a pre-existing and generally agreed truth.[91] Read one way it is a tautology, acknowledging that everybody has some knowledge that can be quantified. Read another, especially for anyone who knew Montaigne's essay 'An Apology for Raymond Sebond', the statement is false and presumptuous: no one knows what they know and even choosing to play with a pet cat brings with it the uncertainty that we cannot know what the cat is thinking and who is really in control of the game.[92] The lines also recall Iago's cynical statement early in the

[88] James Hirsch, *Shakespeare and the History of Soliloquies* (Madison: Fairleigh Dickinson University Press, 2003), p. 29.
[89] Wilson, *Secret Shakespeare*, p. 166.
[90] Derek Cohen, 'Othello's Suicide', *UTQ* 62 (1993), 323–33.
[91] Tilley, *Proverbs*, K178 (p. 363); *Othello*, ed. Neill, p. 393.
[92] Michel de Montaigne, *An Apology for Raymond Sebond*, trans. M. A. Screech (Harmondsworth: Penguin, 1987), p. 17. On Shakespeare and Montaigne see Gillespie, *Shakespeare's Books*, pp. 347–8; Mack, *Montaigne and Shakespeare*, pp. 161–5. There is no equivalent moment in *Gli Hecatommithi*: the Ensign returns to his own country where he accuses another man of plotting to murder a nobleman and is then tortured so horribly as the authorities try to compare his story with that of the accused that his organs rupture and he dies miserably at home after his release from prison (*Narrative and Dramatic Sources*, VII, p. 252).

handkerchief scene, 'My lord, you know I love you' (3.3.119), which questions the state of Othello's knowledge rather than confirming Iago's loyalty. That line parodies Peter's declaration of loyalty to Jesus, 'thou knowest that I love thee' (John 21:15 (Geneva translation)): now, such knowledge is exposed as a lie.[93] The audience cannot know whether Iago is a devil whose manipulations are reaching fruition or a desperate figure whose plots have finally run out as his attempt to stab his wife when she reveals his scheme suggests (222). His echoing of biblical verses for malign purposes indicates that he is acting like the father of lies because, as Antonio asserted in *The Merchant of Venice*, 'The devil can cite Scripture for his purpose.'[94] The threat that torments will succeed in unlocking the mystery of Iago is a pointed reminder of the frequent recourse to torture which had been undertaken against the Jesuits in particular in the previous two decades, despite the frequent protestations that English law did not permit the physical abuse of prisoners.[95]

Iago is associated with the Jesuits and their invariably grim fate in England: certainly Edmund Campion, one of the first missionaries sent to England, had no doubt how his life was likely to end when he was summoned from his happy scholarly existence in Prague in 1579 before the mission was seriously underway.[96] But it would be foolish to assume that he stands for the Jesuits, or that he can tell us much about Shakespeare's view about Catholicism, or about the ethics of lying. Rather, *Othello* registers in an acute and challenging manner the ways in which various forms of lying characterized public life in England in the reign of Elizabeth, continuing into the early years of James's kingship. The play represents people lying in small, apparently insignificant ways, and telling lies that are obviously mortal sins which will have a terrible impact on others. Lies are told for reasons of courtesy and politeness; to prevent embarrassment; thoughtlessly, often out of carelessness; for self-interest; maliciously, to harm others; and for no apparent motive. They are told about possessions; about reputation and social standing; about moral behaviour; about personal loyalty; about sexual behaviour; and as witness or testimony to serious events which did not actually take place despite the claims under oath of the speaker. At the end of the play lying has become so endemic in Venetian society that the appeal to torture as a means of establishing the truth seems desperate and doomed to failure. The audience would undoubtedly have known of the practice of

[93] Beatrix Busse, *Vocative Constructions in the Language of Shakespeare* (Amsterdam: Benjamins, 2006), pp. 376–7.

[94] William Shakespeare, *The Merchant of Venice*, ed. John Drakakis (London: Black, 2010), 1.3.94 (p. 213). Iago's final statement could be read as an adaptation of such verses as Jesus's riposte to the woman who accuses him of being a puppet: 'Ye worship that which ye know not: we worship that which we know' (John 4:22 (Geneva translation)).

[95] Hanson, 'Torture and Truth', p. 53; Edward Peters, *Torture* (Oxford: Blackwell, 1985), pp. 79–80; Alford, *Watchers*, pp. 96–8; Kilroy, *Campion: A Scholarly Life*, ch. 8. Only in the seventeenth century as the law of proof was transformed throughout Europe did the use of torture significantly decline as a component of judicial procedures: see John H. Langbein, *Torture and the Law of Proof* (Chicago: University of Chicago Press, 1976), pp. 45–69.

[96] Kilroy, *Campion: A Scholarly Life*, pp. 131–2.

showing victims the instruments of torture as a means of eliciting a confession without having to use them.[97] Even so, Iago remains silent on stage.

Iago is the most subtle, sophisticated, and dedicated liar in the play, a very devil in his brilliant tactics and strategies in deceiving others, exactly as contemporary Protestant propaganda claimed their most astute Catholic opponents were, telling lies to hide other lies.[98] He lies directly through the invention of false testimony, which then leads to further imagined scenarios which sound as if they are true, as when he asks if Othello 'Would . . . grossly gape on? / Behold her topped?' (3.3.398–9). He lies through sins of omission and silence, which the vigorous Church of England apologist Matthew Sutcliffe saw as a hallmark of Jesuit deception, as 'by their owne silence [they] proue themselues to be traitors'.[99] Iago never seeks to correct the universal belief that he is 'honest', cultivating apparently honest behaviour—plain speaking, the seemingly careless and compulsive use of profanity—which he knows will mislead others. He uses a stolen object to create deceptive impressions with obviously malicious intent. Most insidiously, building on his reputation for honesty, he cunningly echoes what others say, so that words lose their semantic charge through the echo, as though there were an ambiguity about their meaning when really there is none in common usage:

> *Othello*: I'll not endure it. Would I were satisfied!
> *Iago*: I see, sir, you are eaten up with passion.
> I do repent me that I put it to you.
> You would be satisfied?
> *Othello*: Would? Nay, I will!
> *Iago*: And may—but how? How satisfied, my lord? (3.3.393–7)

Both speakers know what they mean by 'satisfied', but Iago exploits the sexual ambiguity in order to inflame Othello and diminish his ability to think rationally.[100] The first repetition of 'satisfied' instils some doubt in Othello's mind through Iago's use of the conditional, as though there were an ambiguity at work through the ordinary course of the conversation whereas he has just introduced it. Othello returns to the imperative ('will'), which enables Iago to wrest the initiative back through the introduction of a qualifying modal auxiliary ('may') which signals possibility rather than certainty. The speakers interact at cross purposes: Othello wants to know if his wife is unfaithful; Iago wants to know how he wants to know, countering the question of knowledge with an image of Desdemona captured *in flagrante delicto*. We witness equivocation in action, a speaker insisting on ambivalence and doubt when really there is none, knowing exactly what he is doing in the process.

---

[97] Maus, *Inwardness*, p. 81.
[98] See, for example, Morton, *Exact Discoverie*, p. 43. More generally see Cavanagh, *Language and Politics*, pp. 31–5.
[99] Sutcliffe, *Challenge*, p. 224. On Sutcliffe (1549/50–1629) see the *ODNB* entry.
[100] For Othello's usage see *OED*, 'satisfy', vb., 7a; Partridge, *Bawdy*, p. 231.

Iago's lies do not always look like lies; at least, not all would satisfy the academic criteria of the debates between philosophers and theologians from the Church Fathers onwards. But his overall strategy is to produce an illusion for malign purposes and most of his speech acts are directly or indirectly in line with William Perkins's simple definition of lying: 'Lying is when a man spekaeth otherwise then the trueth is, with a purpose to deceive.' Desdemona is not having an affair with Cassio, as he claims, a charge that Iago knowingly fosters to cause her death. *Othello* provides no answers to the problem of truth and lying, explaining to the audience how lying might be prevented or limited; why certain types of lies might be tolerated or even encouraged as a means of discouraging more serious lies; or whether lying is really a central facet of human behaviour. It is one of the great clichés of criticism of *Othello* that it often seems like a comedy that becomes a tragedy, the tension mounting unbearably as the deceptions, duplicities, and falsehoods grow ever more serious until a line is eventually crossed.[101] The Venetians imagine that some lies happen in the course of everyday life but do not believe that someone in their midst is proliferating more destructive falsehoods. If everyone told the truth except Iago he might be more readily exposed; he might succeed even more easily. If everyone was conscious that everyone else lied then Venetian society might be more horrible but more secure. What the audience witnesses is a story of lying when the people on stage think they understand the world around them, the limits of their knowledge, and the boundaries between truth and falsehood, but are deluded, a fable for a time of acute paranoia.[102]

It would be hard, and, I think, misleading, to argue that conceptions of lying had altered fundamentally between the trial of Anne Boleyn and the failed *coup d'état* of the Gunpowder Plot. But, of course, even if there was no revolution, conceptions of truth and falsehood were not exactly the same in 1600 as they were in 1530. Things change and any roughly equivalent period might well exhibit similar levels of transformation in the common understanding of fundamental values. Perhaps, thinking of English/British history, we might point to the seventy years or so between the Seven Years War (1756–63) and the First Reform Bill (1832); the invention of dynamite (c.1867) and the end of the Second World War (1945); or, even, the end of the era of Winston Churchill (1874–1965) and today. But I am a little sceptical. The conception of lying changed after 1530 because of the Reformation and the increased emphasis on the conscience of the individual cast adrift from an obvious institutional framework, a transformation that may have had a religious cause but which was not a development which could be confined to religion alone. It was not really new vocabularies of truth/falsehood and lying that emerged (although words such as '*sprezzatura*/recklessness' emerged, 'equivocation' took on a new significance, and there was the revival of classical rhetorical terms), but a greater range of possible scenarios, so that what could scarcely be articulated

---

[101] Stephen Rogers, 'Othello: Comedy in Reverse', *SQ* 24 (1973), 210–20; Victor Strandberg, 'The Comedy of *Othello*', *The McNeese Review* 19 (1968), 3–15; Susan Snyder, *Shakespeare: A Wayward Journey* (Newark: University of Delaware Press, 2002), pp. 29–45.
[102] Baldwin Smith, *Treason in Tudor England*, p. 36; Maus, 'Proof', p. 36.

in the wake of the Act of Supremacy had become part of the intellectual furniture by the time that Shakespeare wrote *Othello*. Lying, in short, had become more central to the imagination. The various answers given to the question of the moral behaviour of the Hebrew midwives or Jacob when he pretended to be his hairier brother, Esau, probably remained identical, but the ways in which they were given, and the contexts in which that question was asked were slightly, albeit significantly, different.

Bibliography

PRIMARY SOURCES

Manuscript

Abbot, George, 'James I of England: Narrative of the divorce between Lord Essex and his wife in 1613, written by Archbishop Abbot', BL Sloane MS 3828.

Garnet, Henry, 'A Treatise of Equivocation', Bodleian MS Laud Misc. 655.

Printed

Abbot, George, *Explicatio Sex Illustram Quaestionum: De Mendacio, De Circumcisione Et Baptismo, De Astrologia, De Praesentia In Cultu Idololatrico, De Fuga In Persequutione Et Peste, An Deus Sit Author Peccati* (Frankfurt, 1616).

Abbot, George, *The Case of Impotency as Debated in England: in that remarkable trial an. 1613* (London, 1715).

Agrippa, Henricus Cornelius, *Of the Vanitie and Uncertaintie of Artes and Sciences*, trans. Jan Sanford (London, 1569).

Allen, William, *A true, sincere and modest defence, of English Catholiques that suffer for their faith both at home and abrode* (Rouen, 1584).

Anon., *An Advertisment and Defence for Trueth Against Her Backbiters, and Specially Against The Whispering Fauourers, and Colourers of Campions* (London, 1581).

Anon., *A Particular Declaration Or Testimony Of The Undutifull and Traiterous Affection Borne Against Her Maiestie By Edmund Campion Iesuite* (London, 1582).

Anon., *Atto della Giustitia d'Inghilterra* (London, 1584).

Anon., *Essempio D'Vna Lettera Mandata D'Inghilterra A Don Bernadino Di Mendozza Ambasciatore in Francia per lo Re di Spagna* (London, 1588).

Anon., *A Myraculous, and Monstrous, but yet most true, and certayne discourse, of a woman (now to be seene in London) of the age of threescore yeares, or there abouts, in the midst of whose fore-head (by the wonderfull worke of God) there groweth out a crooked horne, of foure ynches long* (London, 1588).

Anon., *The Fearefull Example of God Showed on Perjured Person* (London, 1591).

Anon., *The Manner of the Death and Execution of Arnold Cosbie, for Murthering the Lord Boorke* (London, 1591).

Anon., *The Most Horrible and Tragicall Murther of the Right Honorable, the Vertuous and Valerous Gentleman, Iohn Lord Bourgh* (London, 1591).

Anon., *Sundrye Strange and Inhumaine Murthers, lately committed the first of a father that hired a man to kill three of his children neere to Ashford in Kent, the second of Master Page of Plymouth, murthered by the consent of his owne wife* (London, 1591).

Anon., *Newes from Scotland, declaring the damnable life and death of Doctor Fian a notable sorcerer, who was burned at Edenbrough in Ianuary last. 1591* (London, 1592?).

Anon., *A Most Horrible & Detestable Murther committed by a bloudie minded man vpon his ovvne vvife and most strangely reuealed by his childe that was vnder fiue yeares of age* (London, 1595).

Anon., *A Libell of Spanish Lies* (London, 1596).

Anon., *A Most Strange and Wonderfull Herring taken on the 26. day of Nouember 1597, neere vnto Drenton sometime the old and chiefe cittie of the kingdome of Norway. Hauing on the one side the picture of two armed men fighting, and on the other most strange characters, as in *the picture is here expressed. First printed in Dutch at Roterdam by Ian van Doetecam. And now translated into English* (London, 1598).

Anon., *The Manner of the Cruell Outragious Murther of William Storre* (London, 1603).

Anon., *The Divell of the Vault, or, The Vnmasking of Murther in a briefe declaration of the Cacolicke-complotted Treason, lately discouerd* (London, 1606).

Anon., *The Horrible Murther of A Young Boy of three yeres of age* (London, 1606).

Anon., *The Most Cruell and Bloudy Murther Committed by an Inkeepers Wife, called Annis Dell, and her Sonne George Dell, Foure yeeres since* (London, 1606).

Anon., *A Spectacle for Vsurers and Succers of Poore Folkes Bloud, Whereby they may see, Gods iust dislike and reuenge, vpon their vncharitable and Vnciuill oppression, with a horrible murther committed by a young man, that hanged his owne Mother in August last* (London, 1606).

Anon., *A True and Perfect Relation of the Whole Proceedings Against the Late Most Barbarous Traitor, Garnet, A Iesuite, and His Confederats* (London, 1606).

Anon., *Mistress Turners Repentance, Who, About the Poisoning of That Ho: Knight Sir Thomas Overbury, was executed the fourteenth of November, last* (London, 1615).

Anon., *Mistress Turners Teares, for the Murder of Sir Thomas Ouerbury* (London, 1615).

Anon., *A True Report and Exact Description of a Mighty Sea-Monster or Whale, cast vpon Langarshore ouer against Harwich in Essex, this present moneth of Februarie 1617* (London, 1617).

Anon., *Campian Englished. Or a translation of the ten reasons in which E. Campian insisted in his challenge, to the universities of Oxford and Cambridge. By a priest of the catholicke and Roman church* (Rouen?, 1632).

Anon., *Truth Brought To Light By Time*, in *Somers Tracts*, ed. Walter Scott (1809), pp. 304–63.

Anon., *Certain Sermons Appointed by the Queen's Majesty To be Declared and Read By All Parsons, Vicars, and Curates, Every Sunday and Holiday in Their Churches; And By her Grace's Advice Perused and Overseen For The Better Understanding Of The Simple People* (1574) (Cambridge: Parker, 1850).

Anon., *A Chronicle of King Henry VIII of England, Being a Contemporary Record of Some of the Principal Events of the Reigns of Henry VIII and Edward VI. Written in Spanish by an Unknown Hand* [*The Spanish Chronicle*], ed. Martin A. Sharp Hume (London: George Bell & Sons, 1889).

Anon., *Vindiciae, Contra Tyrannos, or Concerning the Legitimate Power of a Prince over the People, and of the People over a Prince*, ed. George Garnett (Cambridge: Cambridge University Press, 1994).

Anon., *The Book of Common Prayer: The Texts of 1549, 1559, and 1662*, ed. Brian Cummings (Oxford: Oxford University Press, 2011).

Aristotle, *The Art of Rhetoric*, trans. John Henry Freese (London: Heinemann, 1926).

Aristotle, *The Politics*, ed. and trans. Ernest Baker (Oxford: Oxford University Press, 1946).

Aristotle, *The Nicomachean Ethics*, trans. David Ross (Oxford: Oxford University Press, 1980).

Aristotle, *Poetics*, ed. and trans. Malcolm Heath (Harmondsworth: Penguin, 1996).

Aristotle, *The Art of Rhetoric*, trans. Anon. (London: Collins, 2012).

Ascham, Roger, *The Scholemaster* (London, 1570).

Aske, James, *Elizabetha Triumphans Conteyning the Dammed Practizes, that the diuelish popes of Rome haue vsed euer sithence her Highnesse first comming to the Crowne* (London, 1588).

Aubrey, John, *Brief Lives with An Apparatus for the Lives of our English Mathematical Writers*, ed. Kate Bennett, 2 vols (Oxford: Oxford University Press, 2015).

Augustine, *Treatises on Various Subjects*, ed. Roy J. Deferrari (Washington, DC: CUA Press, 1952).

Augustine, *Confessions*, trans. R. S. Pine-Coffin (Harmondsworth: Penguin, 1961).

Augustine, *City of God*, trans. Henry Bettenson (Harmondsworth: Penguin, 1984).

Augustine, 'On Lying', trans. H. Browne (http://www.newadvent.org/fathers/1312.htm).

Augustine, 'To Consentius, Against Lying', trans. H. Browne (http://www.newadvent.org/fathers/1313.htm).

Awdely, John, *The Fraternity of Vacabondes* (London, 1575).

Bacon, Francis, *The Oxford Francis Bacon, Vol. XV: The Essayes or Counsels, Civill and Morall*, ed. Michael Kiernan (Oxford: Clarendon Press, 1985).

Bacon, Lady Anne, *An Apology or Answer in Defence of the Church of England*, ed. Patricia Demers (London: MHRA, 2015).

Baker, Sir John, and S. F. C. Milsom, eds, *Sources of English Legal History: Private Law to 1750* (Oxford: Oxford University Press, 2010).

Baldwin, William, *A Treatise of Morall Phylosophie, contaynyng the sayinges of the wyse. Gathered and Englyshed* (London, 1547).

Baldwin, William, *Beware the Cat: the First English Novel*, ed. William A. Ringler, Jr, and William Flachmann (San Marino: Huntington Library, 1988).

Bale, John, *The Pageant of Popes, contayninge the lyues of all the bishops of Rome, from the beginninge of them to the yeare of grace 1555* (London, 1574).

Barlow, William, *An Answer to a Catholike English-man* (London, 1609).

Bateman, Stephen, *Batman Uppon Bartholome* (London, 1582).

Bicknoll, Edmund, *A Sword Against Swearing* (London, 1579).

Boccaccio, Giovanni, *The Decameron*, trans. G. H. McWilliam (Harmondsworth: Penguin, 1972).

Bodin, Jean, *The Six Bookes of a Common-weale*, trans. Richard Knolles (London, 1606).

Bracton, Henry de, *On the Laws and Customs of England*, trans. Samuel E. Thorne, 4 vols (Cambridge, MA: Harvard University Press, 1977).

Breton, Nicholas, *The Scholler and the Souldier, A Discipline Pithily Passed Betweene Them, The One Defending Learning, The Other Martiall Discipline*, in *The Wil of Wit, Wits Will, or Wils Wit, Chuse you whether Containing Fiue Discourses, The Effects Whereof Follow* (London, 1597).

Breton, Nicholas, *The Court and Country, or A Briefe Discourse Dialogue-wise Set Downe Betweene a Courtier and a Country-man Contayning the Manner and Condition of their Liues, with many delectable and pithy sayings worthy obseruation* (London, 1618).

Brewer, Thomas, *The Bloudy Mother, or The Most Inhumane Murthers, committed by Iane Hattersley vpon diuers infants* (London, 1610).

Bryskett, Lodowick, *A Discourse of Ciuill Life containing the ethike part of morall philosophie. Fit for the instructing of a gentleman in the course of a vertuous life* (London, 1606).

Buchanan, George, *Ane Detectioun of the Duinges of Marie Quene of Scottes* (London, 1571).

Bühler, Curt F., ed., *The Dicts and Sayings of the Philosophers: The Translations Made by Stephen Scrope, William Worcester and an Anonymous Translator* (London: EETS, 1941).

Bullein, William, *A Dialogue Against the Fever Pestilence*, ed. Mark W. Bullein and A. H. Bullein (London: EETS, 1888).

Bullinger, Heinrich, *Two Epystles, one of Heinrich Bullinger, another of Jhon Calvin whether it be lawfull for a Chrysten man to communycate or be pertaker of the masse of the papysts, wythout offendyng God and hys neyghboure* (London, 1544).

Caesar, Julius, *The Eyght Bookes of Caius Iulius Cæsar Conteyning his Martiall Exploytes in the Realme of Gallia and the countries bordering vppon the same*, trans. Arthur Golding (London, 1565).

Calvin, Jean, *What a Faithfull Man, Whiche is Instructe in the Worde of God, Ought to do, Dwellinge Amongest the Papistes* (London, 1548).

Calvin, Jean, *A Very Profitable Treatise made by M. Ihon Caluyne, declarynge what great profit might come to al christendome, yf there were a regester made of all sainctes bodies and other reliques*, trans. Stephen Wythers (London, 1561).

Calvin, Jean, *Three French Treatises*, ed. Francis M. Higman (London: Athlone, 1970).

Camden, William, *Remains Concerning Britain* (London: EP Publishing, 1974).

Campbell, Lily B., ed., *The Mirror for Magistrates* (Cambridge: Cambridge University Press, 1938).

Campion, Edmund, *Rationes Decem: Quibus Fretus, Certamen Aduersarius Obtultit in Causa Fidei* (Henley-on-Thomas, 1581).

Carles, Lancelot de, 'Poème sur la mort d'Anne Boleyn', in Georges Ascoli, ed., *La Grande-Bretagne devant l'opinion française, depuis la Guerre de Cent Ans jusqu'à la fin du XVIe siècle* (Paris: Gamber, 1927), pp. 231–73.

Casa, Giovanni della, *Galateo of Maister John Della Casa. Or rather, a treatise of manners*, trans. Robert Peterson (London, 1576).

Casa, Giovanni della, *Galateo* (Milan: Rizzoli, 1950).

Casa, Giovanni della, *Galateo, or, The Rules of Polite Behaviour*, trans. M. F. Rusnak (Chicago: University of Chicago Press, 2013).

Cassian, John, *The Conferences*, trans. Boniface Ramsey (Mahwah, NJ: Newman Press, 1997).

Castiglione, Baldesar, *The Courtyer of Count Baldessar Castilio*, trans. Thomas Hoby (London, 1561).

Catullus, *The Poems of Catullus*, trans. Peter Whigham (Harmondsworth: Penguin, 1966).

Cavendish, George, *The Life of Cardinal Wolsey*, ed. Samuel Weller Singer (London, 1827).

Cawdrey, Robert, *A Treasurie or Storehouse of Similies: Both Pleasaunt, delightfull, and Profitable, for all estates of men in generall* (London, 1600).

Charke, William, *An Answere to a Seditious Pamphlet Lately Cast Abroade by a Jesuite, with a Discouerie of that Blasphemous Sect* (London, 1580).

Chaucer, Geoffrey, *The Riverside Chaucer*, ed. Larry D. Benson et al. (Oxford: Oxford University Press, 1988, rpt of 1987).

Chettle, Henry, and Robert Greene, *Greene's Groatsworth of Wit: Bought with a Million of Repentance* (1592), ed. D. Allen Carroll (Binghampton, NY: MRTS, 1994).

Chrysostom, Saint John, *Six Books on the Priesthood*, trans. W. R. W. Stevens and T. P. Brandram, in Saint Chrysostom, *On the Priesthood; Ascetic Treatises; Select Homilies and Letters; Homilies on the Statues* (Edinburgh: T. & T. Clark, 1996), pp. 33–83.

Churchyard, Thomas, *A Musicall Consort of Heauenly Harmonie (compounded out of manie parts of musicke) called Churchyards Charitie* (London, 1595).

Cicero, *Murder Trials*, trans. Michael Grant (New York: Dorset Press, 1975).

Cicero, *On Duties*, ed. M. T. Griffin and E. M. Atkins (Cambridge: Cambridge University Press, 1991).

Cicero, *On the Commonwealth and On the Laws*, ed. James E. G. Zetzel (Cambridge: Cambridge University Press, 1999).

Clifford, Henry, *The Life of Jane Dormer, Duchess of Ferrara*, ed. E. E. Estcourt and Joseph Stevenson (London: Burns & Oates, 1887).

Closse, George, *The Parricide Papist, or Cut-throate Catholicke A tragicall discourse of a murther lately committed at Padstow in the countie of Cornewall by a professed papist, killing his owne father, and afterwardes himselfe, in zeale of his popish religion* (London, 1606).

Cockburn, J. S., ed., *Calendar of the Assize Records: Hertfordshire Indictments, James I* (London: HMSO, 1975).

Coignet, Mathieu [Martin], *A Politique Discourse upon Trueth and Lying An instruction to princes to keepe their faith and promise: containing the summe of Christian and morall philosophie, and the duetie of a good man in sundrie politique discourses vpon the trueth and lying*, trans. Edward Hoby (London, 1586).

Constantyne, George, 'A Memorial from George Constantyne to Thomas, Lord Cromwell', ed. Thomas Amyot, *Archaeologia* 23 (1831), 50–78.

Copley, Anthony, A Fig for Fortune: *A Catholic Response to* The Faerie Queene, ed. Susannah Brietz Monta (Manchester: Manchester University Press, 2016).

Cornwallis, William, *Essayes* (London, 1600).

Cox, Leonard, *The Arte or Crafte of Rhetoryke* (London, 1530).

Cox, Leonard, *The Paraphrase of Erasmus Roterdame vpon the epistle of saint Paule vnto his discyple Titus* (London, 1534).

Dante, *Inferno*, trans. John D. Sinclair (Oxford: Oxford University Press, 1961).

De Vocht, Henry, ed., *Humanistica Lovaniensia: Acta Thomae Mori: History of the Reports of His Trial and Death with an Unedited Contemporary Narrative* (Louvain: Publications of the Institute for Economics of the University, 1947).

Dekker, Thomas, *The Wonderfull Yeare, Wherein is shewed the Picture of London, Lying Sicke of the Plague* (1603).

Dekker, Thomas, *The Seuen Deadly Sinnes of London Drawne in Seuen Seuerall Coaches, Through the Seuen Seuerall Gates of the Citie Bringing the Plague with them* (London, 1606).

Dekker, Thomas, *The Whore of Babylon* (London, 1607).

Dekker, Thomas, *The Ravens Almanacke* (London, 1609).

Donne, John, *Ignatius His Conclaue* (London, 1611).

Donne, John, *Selected Prose*, ed. Neil Rhodes (Harmondsworth: Penguin, 1987).

Donne, John, *Pseudo-Martyr*, ed. Anthony Raspa (Montreal and Kingston: McGill-Queen's University Press, 1993).

Edwards, David, ed., *Campaign Journals of the Elizabethan Irish Wars* (Dublin: IMC, 2014).

Elizabeth I, *Collected Works*, ed. Leah S. Marcus, Janel Mueller, and Mary Beth Rose (Chicago: University of Chicago Press, 2000).

Elyot, George, *A Very True Report of the Apprehension and Taking of That Arch Papist Edmond Campion* (London, 1581).

Erasmus, Desiderius, *Here Folowith a Scorneful Image or Monstrus Shape of a Maruelous Strange Fygure Called, Sileni Alcibiadis Presentyng Ye State [and] Condicio[n] of this Present World*, trans. Anon. (London, 1543).

Erasmus, Desiderius, *Praise of Folly*, trans. John Wilson (New York: Dover, 2003).

Erasmus, Desiderius, and Martin Luther, *Luther and Erasmus: Free Will and Salvation*, ed. Ernest Gordon Rupp and Philip Saville Watson (Westminster: John Knox Press, 1969).

Ford, John, *The Collected Works of John Ford, Volume I*, ed. Gilles Monsarrat, Brian Vickers, and R. J. C. Watt (Oxford: Clarendon Press, 2012).

Formey, Jean-Henri-Samuel, *An Ecclesiastical History: From the Birth of Christ, to the Present Time*, 2 vols (London, 1766).

Foxe, John, *Acts and Monuments of the Church* (London, 1563) ('John Foxe's Acts and Monuments Online').

Fulbeck, William, *A Parallele or Conference of the Ciuil Law, the Canon Law, and the Common Law of this Realme of England* (London, 1601).

Fuller, Thomas, *The Worthies of England*, ed. John Freeman (New York: Barnes and Noble, 1952).

Gardiner, Samuel, *Doomes-Day Booke: or, An Alarum for Atheistes, A Watchword for Worldlinges, A Caueat for Christians* (London, 1606).

Garnet, Henry, *A Treatise of Equivocation*, ed. David Jardine (London: Longman, 1851).

Garzoni, Tomasso, *The Hospitall of Incurable Fooles*, trans. Edward Blount or Thomas Nashe (London, 1600).

Gentillet, Innocent, *A Discourse Vpon the Meanes of Wel Governing and Maintaining in Good Peace, a Kingdome, or Other Principalitie*, trans. Simon Patericke (London, 1602).

Geoffrey of Monmouth, *The History of the Kings of Britain*, trans. Lewis Thorpe (Harmondsworth: Penguin, 1966).

Gerard, John, *The History of the Catholics Under James I: Father Gerard's Narrative of the Gunpowder Plot*, ed. John Morris (London: Longmans, 1871).

Greenblatt, Stephen, and Peter G. Platt, eds, *Shakespeare's Montaigne: The Florio Translation of the Essays: A Selection* (New York: New York Review of Books, 2014).

Gribaldi, Matteo, *A Notable and Marueilous Epistle Concerning the Terrible Judgemente of God, upon hym that forsweare of men, denieth Christ* (London, 1550).

Guazzo, Stefano, *The Ciuile Conuersation*, trans. George Pettie (London, 1581).

Guevara, Antonio de, *A Dispraise of the Life of a Courtier, and a Commendacion of the Life of the Labouryng Man*, trans. Francis Bryan (London, 1548).

Hanmer, Meredith, *The Great Brag and Challenge of M. Champion A Iesuite* (London, 1581).

Harington, Sir John, *A Brief Apology of Poetry* (1591), in Gavin Alexander, ed., *Sidney's 'The Defence of Poetry' and Selected Renaissance Literary Criticism* (Harmondsworth: Penguin, 2004), pp. 260–73.

Harington, Sir John, *The Epigrams of Sir John Harington*, ed. Gerard Kilroy (Farnham: Ashgate, 2009).

Harpsfield, Nicholas, *The Life and Death of Sr Thomas Moore, knight*, ed. E. V. Hitchcock (Oxford: Oxford University Press, 1936), EETS, original ser., 186 (1932).

Hartley, T. E., ed., *Proceedings in the Parliaments of Elizabeth I, Vol. III: 1593–1601* (Leicester: Leicester University Press, 1995).

Harvey, Gabriel, *Letter-Book of Gabriel Harvey, 1573–1580*, ed. Edward John Long Scott (London: Camden Society, 1884).

Harvey, Gabriel, *Fovre Letters and Certaine Sonnets* (1592), ed. G. B. Harrison (Edinburgh: Edinburgh University Press, 1966).

Helmholz, R. H., ed., *Select Cases on Defamation to 1600* (London: Selden Society, 1985).

Herbert, George, *The English Poems of George Herbert*, ed. Helen Wilcox (Cambridge: Cambridge University Press, 2007).

Herodotus, *The Histories*, trans. Aubrey de Sélincourt and A. R. Burn (Harmondsworth: Penguin, 1972).

Hitchcock, Robert, *A Pollitique Platt for the Honour of the Prince, the greate profite of the publique state, relief of the poore, preseruation of the riche, reformation of roges and idle persones, and the wealthe of thousandes that knowes not howe to liue* (London, 1580).

Holmes, Peter, ed., *Elizabethan Casuistry* (London: CRS, 1981).

Hooper, John, *Whether Christian Faith Maye Be Kepte Secret in the Heart, Without Confession Therof Openly to the Worlde as Occasion Shal Serve* (London, 1553).

Howard, Henry, Earl of Surrey, *Poems*, ed. Emrys Jones (Oxford: Clarendon Press, 1964).

Hughes, Charles, ed., *Shakespeare's Europe: Chapter of Fynes Moryson's Itinerary* (London: Sherratt & Hughes, 1903).

James VI and I, *Triplici Nodo, Triplex Cuneus. Or, An Apologie for the Oath of Allegiance* in *Political Writings*, ed. Johann P. Sommerville (Cambridge: Cambridge University Press, 1994), pp. 85–13.

Jerome, *Commentary on Galatians*, ed. Andrew Cain (Washington, DC: The Catholic University of America Press, 1964).

Jerome, *Homilies: I (1–59 On The Psalms)*, trans. Sister Marie Liguori Eward (Washington, DC: The Catholic University of America Press, 1964).

Jones, Richard, *The Booke of Honor and Armes* (London, 1590).

Judges, A. V., ed., *The Elizabethan Underworld: A Collection of Tudor and Early Stuart Tracts and Ballads telling of the lives and misdoings of vagabonds, thieves, rogues, and cozeners, and giving some account of the operation of the criminal law* (London: Routledge, 1930).

Kant, Immanuel, 'On a Supposed Right to Lie from Altruistic Motives', (http://www.unc.edu/courses/2009spring/plcy/240/001/Kant.pdf).

Kermode, Lloyd Edward, ed., *Three Renaissance Usury Plays* (Manchester: Manchester University Press, 2009).

Kerrigan, John, ed., *Motives of Woe: Shakespeare and 'Female Complaint': A Critical Anthology* (Oxford: Clarendon Press, 1990).

Keymer, John, *John Keymors Observation Made Upon the Dutch Fishing about the year 1601 demonstrating that there is more wealth raised out of herrings and other fish in His Majesties seas by the neighbouring nations in one year, then the King of Spain hath from the Indies* (London, 1664).

King, John, *Lectures Upon Ionas* (London, 1599).

King, John N., ed., *Voices of the English Reformation: A Sourcebook* (Philadelphia: University of Pennsylvania Press, 2004).

Kinney, Arthur F., ed., *Rogues, Vagabonds, and Sturdy Beggars: A New Gallery of Tudor and Early Stuart Rogue Literature Exposing the Lives, Times, and Cozening Tricks of the Elizabethan Underworld* (Amherst: University of Massachusetts Press, 1973).

Knowles, James, ed., *The Roaring Girl and Other City Comedies* (Oxford: Oxford University Press, 2001).

Knox, Vicesimus, ed., *Elegant Epistles: Being a Copious Collection of Familiar and Amusing Letters* (Dublin, 1790).

Kyd, Thomas [?], *The Trueth of the Most Wicked and Secret Murthering of Iohn Brewen, goldsmith of London committed by his owne wife* (London, 1592).

Kyd, Thomas, *The Spanish Tragedy*, ed. Philip Edwards (Manchester: Manchester University Press, 1977, rpt of 1959).

Las Casas, Bartolomé de, *A Short Account of the Destruction of the Indies*, trans. Nigel Griffin (Harmondsworth: Penguin, 1992).

Latimer, William, 'William Latymer's Chronickille of Anne Bulleyne', ed. Maria Dowling, *Camden Miscellany* 30 (1990), pp. 23–65.

Lewkenor, Lewis, *A Discourse of the Usage of the English Fugitives, by the Spaniard* (London, 1595).

The Lisle Letters, ed. Muriel St. Clare Byrne, 6 vols (Chicago: University of Chicago Press, 1981).

Livy, *The Romane Historie*, trans. Philemon Holland (London, 1600).

Lupton, Thomas, *Siuqila. Too Good, to be true . . . Herein is Shewed by waye of dialogue, the wonderful maners of the people of Mauqsun, with other talke not friuolous* (London, 1580).

Lupton, Thomas, *The Second Part and Knitting vp of the Boke Entituled Too Good to be True Wherin is Continued the Discourse of the Wonderfull Lawes, Commendable Customes, [and] Strange Manners of the People of Mauqsun* (London, 1581).

Lupton, Thomas, *The Christian against the Iesuite* (London, 1582).

Luther, Martin, *Martin Luther: Selections from His Writings*, ed. John Dillenberger (New York: Anchor Books, 1961).

Machiavelli, Niccolò, *The Prince*, ed. Quentin Skinner and Russell Price (Cambridge: Cambridge University Press, 1988).

Mandeville, Sir John, *The Travels of Sir John Mandeville*, trans. C. W. R. D. Moseley (Harmondsworth: Penguin, 1983).

Manningham, John, *The Diary of John Manningham of the Middle Temple, 1602–3*, ed. Robert Parker Sorlien (Hanover: University Press of New England, 1976).

March, John, *Actions For Slaunder, or, A Methodicall Collection Under Certain Grounds and Heads of What Words Are Actionable in the Law* (London, 1647).

Marlowe, Christopher, *Tamburlaine*, ed. J. W. Harper (London: Black, 1971).

Marlowe, Christopher, *The Jew of Malta*, ed. N. W. Bawcutt (Manchester: Manchester University Press, 1978).

Marston, John, and Others, *The Insatiate Countess*, ed. Giorgio Melchiri (Manchester: Manchester University Press, 1984).

The Martin Marprelate Tracts: A Modernised and Annotated Edition, ed. Joseph L. Black (Cambridge: Cambridge University Press, 2008).

Martin, Randall, ed., *Women and Murder in Early Modern News Pamphlets and Broadside Ballads, 1573–1697* (Farnham: Ashgate, 2005).

Mason, Henry, *The New Art of Lying, Covered by Jesuits Under the Vale of Equivocation* (London, 1624).

Miola, Robert S., ed., *Early Modern Catholicism: An Anthology of Primary Sources* (Oxford: Oxford University Press, 2007).

Montaigne, Michel de, *The Essayes of Michael, Lord of Montaigne*, trans. John Florio (London, 1603), 3 vols (London: Everyman, 1910).

Montaigne, Michel de, *An Apology for Raymond Sebond*, trans. M. A. Screech (Harmondsworth: Penguin, 1987).

Montaigne, Michel de, *The Complete Works*, trans. Donald M. Frame (New York: Knopf, 2003).

More, John, *Three Godly and Fruitfull Sermons* (London, 1594).

More, Thomas, *A Frutefull, and Pleasaunt Worke of the Beste State of a Publyque weale, and of the Newe Yle called Utopia*, trans. Ralph Robinson (London, 1551).

More, Thomas, *The Correspondence of Sir Thomas More*, ed. Elizabeth Frances Rogers (Princeton: Princeton University Press, 1947).

More, Thomas, *The History of King Richard III and Selections for the English and Latin Poems*, ed. Richard S. Sylvester (New Haven: Yale University Press, 1976).

More, Thomas, *Utopia*, ed. George M. Logan and Robert M. Adams (Cambridge: Cambridge University Press, 1989).

Morice, James, *A Briefe Treatise of Oathes Exacted by Ordinaries and Ecclesiastical Iudges* (London, 1590).

Morton, Thomas, *An Exact Discoverie of Romish Doctrine in the Case of Conspiracie and Rebellion by Pregnant Obseruations* (London, 1605).

Moryson, Fynes, *An Itinerary Containing His Ten Yeeres Travell* (1617), 4 vols (Glasgow: MacLehose, 1907).

Munday, Anthony, *A Discouerie of Edmund Campion, and his confederates* (London, 1581).

Munday, Anthony, *A Breefe Aunswer Made Unto Two Seditious Pamphlets . . . Contayning a Defence of Edmund Campion* (London, 1582).

Munday, Anthony, *The English Roman Life*, ed. Philip J. Ayres (Oxford: Clarendon Press, 1980).

N., T., *A Pleasant Dialogue Betweene a Lady called Listra, and a Pilgrim Concerning the Gouernment and Commonweale of the Great Prouince of Crangalor* (London, 1579).

Nenna, Giovanni Battista, *Nennio, or A Treatise of Nobility Wherein is Discoursed What True Nobilitie is, with such qualities as are required in a perfect gentleman*, trans. William Jones (London, 1595).

Nowell, Alexander, and William Day, *A True Report of the Disputation or Rather Priuate Conference had in the Tower of London, with Ed. Campion Iesuite, the last of August. 1581* (London, 1583).

Ochino, Bernardino, *A Tragoedie or Dialoge of the Vniuste Vsurped Primacie of the Bishop of Rome, and of all the iust abolishyng of the same*, trans. John Ponet (London, 1549).

Overbury, Thomas, *Sir Thomas Overbury his Wife. With additions of New Characters, and many other wittie conceits never before printed* (London, 1614).

Ovid, *Metamorphoses*, trans. Mary M. Innes (Harmondsworth: Penguin, 1955).

Palmer, Thomas, *An Essay of the Meanes How to Make our Trauailes, into Forraine Countries, the more Profitable and Honourable* (London, 1606).

Paris, Matthew, *English History*, trans. J. A. Giles, 3 vols (London: Bohn, 1852–4).

Parsons, Robert, *A Conference About The Next Succession of the Crowne of Ingland* (London, 1594).

Peacham, Henry, *The Garden of Eloquence* (London, 1593).

Peele, George [?], *The Troublesome Reign of King John*, ed. Charles R. Forker (Manchester: Manchester University Press, 2011).

Perkins, William, *A Direction for the Government of the Tongue According To Gods Word* (London, 1593).

Perkins, William, *A Christian and Plaine Treatise of the Manner and Order of Predestination and of the Largenes of Gods Grace* (London, 1606).

Pico della Mirandola, *Oration on the Dignity of Man*, in Ernst Cassirer, Paul Oskar Kristeller, and John Herman Randall, Jr, eds, *The Renaissance Philosophy of Man* (Chicago: University of Chicago Press, 1948), pp. 215–54.

Plato, *Apology*, in *The Last Days of Socrates*, trans. Hugh Tredennick (Harmondsworth: Penguin, 1954), pp. 43–76.

Plato, *The Republic*, trans. Desmond Lee (rev. edn, Harmondsworth: Penguin, 1974).

Plutarch, *The Philosophie, commonlie called, The Morals*, trans. Philemon Holland (London, 1603).

Polo, Marco, *The Travels*, trans. R. E. Latham (Harmondsworth: Penguin, 1958).

Ponet, John, *A Defence for Mariage of Priestes by Scripture and Aunciente Wryters* (London, 1549).

Pricket, Robert, *The Iesuits Miracles, Or New Popish Wonders* (London, 1607).

Puttenham, George, *The Arte of English Poesie*, ed. Gladys Doidge Willcock and Alice Walker (Cambridge: Cambridge University Press, 1970, rpt of 1936).

Rabelais, François, *Gargantua and Pantagruel*, trans. J. M. Cohen (Harmondsworth: Penguin, 1955).

Ralegh, Sir Walter, *The History of the World* (London, 1617).

Ralegh, Sir Walter, *The Poems of Sir Walter Ralegh: A Historical Edition*, ed. Michael Rudick (Tempe, AZ: MRTS, 1999).

Reynoldes, Richard, *A Booke Called the Foundacion of Rhetoricke* (London, 1563).

Rhodes, Neil, with Gordon Kendal and Louise Wilson, *English Renaissance Translation Theory* (London: MHRA, 2013).

Roper, William, *The Life of Sir Thomas More*, in R. S. Sylvester and D. P. Harding, eds, *Two Early Tudor Lives* (New Haven: Yale University Press, 1962).

Rowland, Samuel, *Letting of Humors Blood in the Head-Vaine* (London, 1607).

Russell, D. A., and M. Winterbottom, eds, *Classical Literary Criticism* (Oxford: Oxford University Press, 1989).

Rymer, Thomas, *A Short View of Tragedy* (London, 1695).

Saint German, Christopher, *Hereafter Foloweth A Dyalogue in Englysshe, Betwyxt A Doctoure Of Dyuynyte, And A Student In The Lawes of Englande* (London, 1530).

Sander, Nicholas, *Rise and Growth of the Anglican Schism*, ed. David Lewis and Edward Rishton (London: Burns & Oates, 1877).

Saviolo, Vincento, *Vincentio Sauiolo His Practise In Two Bookes* (London, 1595).

Scott, William, *The Model of Poesie*, ed. Gavin Alexander (Cambridge: Cambridge University Press, 2013).

Seneca, Lucius Annaeus, *The Ninth Tragedie of Lucius Anneus Seneca called Octauia. Translated out of Latine into English, by T.N. [Thomas North] student in Cambridge* (London, 1566).

Shakespeare, William, *The New Oxford Shakespeare: The Complete Works, Modern Critical Edition*, ed. Gary Taylor, John Jowett, Terri Bourus, and Gabriel Egan (Oxford: Oxford University Press, 2016).

Shakespeare, William, *As You Like It*, ed. Agnes Latham (London: Methuen, 1975).

Shakespeare, William, *Hamlet*, ed. Harold Jenkins (London: Routledge, 1982).

Shakespeare, William, *King Henry VI, Part 3*, ed. John D. Cox and Eric Rasmussen (London: Thomson, 2001).

Shakespeare, William, *Macbeth*, ed. Nicholas Brooke (Oxford: Oxford University Press, 1990).

Shakespeare, William, *The Merchant of Venice*, ed. John Drakakis (London: Black, 2010).

Shakespeare, William, *A Midsummer Night's Dream*, ed. Harold F. Brooks (London: Methuen, 1979).

Shakespeare, William, *Othello*, ed. M. R. Ridley (London: Methuen, 1958).

Shakespeare, William, *Othello: A New Variorum Edition*, ed. Horace Howard Furness (New York: Dover, 1963, rpt of 1886).

Shakespeare, William, *Othello*, ed. Norman Sanders (Cambridge: Cambridge University Press, 1984).

Shakespeare, William, *Othello*, ed. E. A. J. Honigmann (London: Nelson, 1997).

Shakespeare, William, *Othello*, ed. Edmund Pechter (New York: Norton, 2004).

Shakespeare, William, *Othello*, ed. Michael Neill (Oxford: Oxford University Press, 2006).

Shakespeare, William, *King Richard III*, ed. James R. Siemon (London: Black, 2009).

Shakespeare, William, *Romeo and Juliet*, ed. Brian Gibbons (London: Methuen, 1980).

Shakespeare, William, *Shakespeare's Sonnets*, ed. Katherine Duncan-Jones (London: Thompson, 1997).

Shakespeare, William, *Titus Andronicus*, ed. Jonathan Bate (London: Routledge, 1995).

Shakespeare, William, *Othello*, ed. E. A. J. Honigmann, with a new introduction by Ayanna Thompson (London: Bloomsbury, 2016).

Sherry, Richard, *A Treatise of Schemes and Tropes very profytable for the better vnderstanding of good authors, gathered out of the best grammarians [and] oratours* (London, 1550).

Sidney, Sir Philip, *A Defence of Poetry*, ed. J. A. Van Dorsten (Oxford: Oxford University Press, 1973).

Sidney, Sir Philip, *An Apology for Poetry*, ed. Geoffrey Shepherd, rev. and expanded by R. W. Maslen (Manchester: Manchester University Press, 2002).

Sidney, Sir Philip, *The Correspondence of Sir Philip Sidney*, ed. Roger Kuin, 2 vols (Oxford: Oxford University Press, 2012).

Skelton, John, *The Complete English Poems*, ed. John Scattergood (Harmondsworth: Penguin, 1983).

Smith, Henry, *The Trumpet of the Soule, Sounding to Judgement* (London, 1591).

Southwell, Robert, *The Poems of Robert Southwell*, ed. James H. McDonald and Nancy Pollard Brown (Oxford: Clarendon Press, 1967).

Spenser, Edmund, *The Shorter Poems*, ed. Richard A. McCabe (Harmondsworth: Penguin, 1999).

Spenser, Edmund, *The Faerie Queene*, ed. A. C. Hamilton (Harlow: Longman, 2001).

Stubbes, Philip, *The Anatomie of Abuses*, ed. Margaret Jane Kidnie (Tempe, AZ: RETS, 2002).

Sutcliffe, Matthew, *A Challenge Concerning the Romish Church, her Doctrine & Practises* (London, 1602).

Tanner, J. R., ed., *Tudor Constitutional Documents, A. D. 1485–1603, with an Historical Commentary* (Cambridge: Cambridge University Press, 1930).

Tawney, R. H., and Eileen Powers, eds, *Tudor Economic Documents*, 3 vols (London: Longman, 1924).

Tesimond, Oswald, *The Gunpowder Plot: The Narrative of Oswald Tesimond alias Greenway* (London: Folio Society, 1973).

Thomas, Vivien, and William Tydeman, eds, *Christopher Marlowe: The Plays and Their Sources* (London: Routledge, 1994).

Thomas, William, *The Works of William Thomas, clerk of the privy council in the year 1549*, ed. Abraham D'Aubant (London, 1774).

Tillotson, John, 'Sermon Twenty Two: The Lawfulness and Obligation of Oaths', in *The Works of the Most Reverend Dr. John Tillotson* (London, 1720), pp. 209–19.

Topsell, Edward, *Historie of Serpents, Or The second Booke of Liuing Creatures* (London, 1608).

Tottel, Richard, *Songes and Sonettes, written by the ryght honourable Lorde Henry Howard late Earle of Surrey, and other* (London, 1557) (Menston: Scolar, 1970).

Tottel, Richard, *Tottel's Miscellany*, ed. Hyder Edward Rollins, 2 vols (Cambridge, MA: Harvard University Press, 1965, rpt of 1928).

Tottel, Richard, *Tottel's Miscellany: Songs and Sonnets of Henry Howard, Earl of Surrey, Sir Thomas Wyatt and Others*, ed. Amanda Holton and Tom McFaul (Harmondsworth: Penguin, 2011).

Tyndale, William, *An Exposicion Upon The V. VI. VII. Chapters of Mathewe* (Antwerp?, 1533?).

Tyndale, William, *An Answer to Sir Thomas More's Dialogue*, ed. Henry Walter (Cambridge: Parker Society, 1850).

Tyndale, William, *The Obedience of a Christian Man*, ed. David Daniell (Harmondsworth: Penguin, 2000).

Tyndale, William, *New Testament*, ed. Priscilla Martin (Ware: Wordsworth, 2002).

Vaughan, William, *The Spirit of Detraction, Coniured and Conuicted in Seuen Circles* (London, 1611).

Vermigli, Pietro Martire, *The Common Places of . . . Doctor Peter Martyr diuided into foure principall parts*, trans. Anthony Marten (London, 1583).

Vickers, Brian, 'Some Reflections on the Rhetoric Textbook', in Peter Mack, ed., *Renaissance Rhetoric* (Basingstoke: Macmillan, 1994), pp. 81–103.

Vickers, Brian, ed., *English Renaissance Literary Criticism* (Oxford: Oxford University Press, 1999).

Vienne-Guerrin, Nathalie, ed., *The Unruly Tongue in Early Modern England: Three Treatises* (Madison: Farleigh Dickinson University Press, 2012).

Vitkus, Daniel J., and Nabil I. Matar, eds, *Piracy, Slavery, and Redemption: Barbary Captivity Narratives from Early Modern England* (New York: Columbia University Press, 2001).

Vitruvius, *On Architecture*, trans. Robert Schofield (Harmondsworth: Penguin, 2009).

Webbe, William, *A Discourse of English Poetry*, ed. Sonia Hernández-Santano (Cambridge: MHRA, 2016).

Webster, John, *The Works of John Webster: An Old-Spelling Critical Edition*, ed. David Gunby, David Carnegie, Antony Hammond, and Doreen Delvecchio, 2 vols (Cambridge: Cambridge University Press, 1995).

Weldon, Anthony, *The Court and Character of King James* (London, 1650).

White, T. H., *The Bestiary: A Book of Beasts* (New York: Putnam, 1954).

Wilson, Arthur, *The History of Great Britain, being the Life and Reign of King James I* (London, 1653).

Wilson, Thomas, *The Arte of Rhetorique* (London, 1560).

Wilson, Thomas, *A Discourse upon Usury*, ed. R. H. Tawney (London: Bell, 1925).

Woodes, Nathaniel, *The Conflict of Conscience* (London, 1581).

Woodes, Nathaniel, *The Conflict of Conscience*, ed. Herbert Davies (Oxford: Malone Society, 1952).

Wotton, Sir Henry, *The Life and Letters of Sir Henry Wotton*, ed. Logan Pearsall Smith, 2 vols (Oxford: Clarendon Press, 1907).

Wriothesley, Charles, *A Chronicle of England during the Reigns of the Tudors, from A.D. 1485 to 1559, by Charles Wriothesley*, ed. W. D. Hamilton, 2 vols (London: Camden Society, 1875–7).

Wyatt, George, 'Some Particulars of the Life of Queen Anne Boleigne', in Cavendish, *Life of Cardinal Wolsey*, pp. 421–49.

Wyatt, Thomas, *Collected Poems*, ed. Joost Daalder (Oxford: Oxford University Press, 1975).

Wydeville [Woodville], Anthony, *The Dictes or Sayengis of the Philosophers* (London, 1477).

SECONDARY SOURCES

Ackerman, Alan, *Just Words: Lillian Hellman, Mary McCarthy, and the Failure of Public Conversation in America* (New Haven: Yale University Press, 2011).

Ackroyd, Peter, *The Life of Thomas More* (London: Vintage, 1999).

Adams, Caroline, 'Elizabeth I's Progresses into Sussex', in Matthew Dimmock, Andrew Hadfield, and Paul Quinn, eds, *Art, Literature and Religion in Early Modern Sussex* (Farnham; Ashgate, 2014), pp. 15–40.

Adamson, Sylvia, Gavin Alexander, and Katrin Ettenhuber, eds, *Renaissance Figures of Speech* (Cambridge: Cambridge University Press, 2007).

Aers, David, and Sarah Beckwith, 'The Eucharist', in Brian Cummings and James Simpson, eds, *Cultural Reformations: Medieval and Renaissance in Literary History* (Oxford: Oxford University Press, 2010).

Ahnert, Ruth, *The Rise of Prison Literature in the Sixteenth Century* (Cambridge: Cambridge University Press, 2013).

Alexander, Gavin, *Writing after Sidney: The Literary Response to Sir Philip Sidney, 1586–1640* (Oxford: Oxford University Press, 2006).

Alford, Stephen, *The Early Elizabethan Polity: William Cecil and the British Succession Crisis, 1558–1569* (Cambridge: Cambridge University Press, 1998).

Alford, Stephen, *Burghley: William Cecil at the Court of Elizabeth I* (New Haven: Yale University Press, 2008).

Alford, Stephen, *The Watchers: A Secret History of the Reign of Elizabeth I* (London: Penguin, 2012).

Allison, A. F., 'John Gerard and the Gunpowder Plot', *RH* 5 (1959), 43–63.

Altman, Joel B., *The Tudor Play of Mind: Rhetorical Inquiry and the Development of Elizabethan Drama* (Berkeley: University of California Press, 1978).

Altman, Joel B., *The Improbability of Othello: Rhetorical Anthropology and Shakespearean Selfhood* (Chicago: University of Chicago Press, 2010).

Altman, Shanyn, '"An Anxious Entangling and Perplexing of Consciences": John Donne and Catholic Recusant Mendacity', in *EJES: Mendacity in Early Modern Literature and Culture*, ed. Ingo Berensmeyer and Andrew Hadfield, 19 (2015), 176–88.

Amis, Martin, *Money: A Suicide Note* (London: Vintage, 2011, first published 1984).

Andreani, Angela, 'Between Theological Debate and Political Subversion: Meredith Hanmer's Confutation of Edmund Campion's *Letter to the Privy Council*', *Aevum* 3 (2016), 557–73.

Andrew, Edward G., *Conscience and its Critics: Protestant Conscience, Enlightenment Reason, and Modern Subjectivity* (Toronto: Toronto University Press, 2001).

Andrews, Michael C., 'Honest Othello: The Handkerchief Once More', *SEL* 13 (1973), 273–84.

Anglo, Sydney, *Machiavelli—the First Century: Studies in Enthusiasm, Hostility, and Irrelevance* (Oxford: Oxford University Press, 2005).

Anon., 'Perjury: The Forgotten Offense', *JCLC* 65 (1974), 361–72.

Anon., *The Van Doetecum Family: 1554–1606* (Rotterdam, Netherlands: Sound & Vision Interactive, 1998).

Anon., 'The History of Parliament' (http://www.historyofparliamentonline.org/volume/1604-1629/member/coningsby-sir-ralph-1555-1616).

Anon., 'House of Commons Information Office: Some Traditions and Customs of the House', p. 5 (http://www.parliament.uk/documents/commons-information-office/g07.pdf).

Anon., 'The Peerage' (http://www.thepeerage.com/p13766.htm).

Appelbaum, Robert, *Terrorism Before the Letter: Mythography and Political Violence in England, Scotland, and France, 1559–1642* (Oxford: Oxford University Press, 2015).

Archer, Harriet, and Andrew Hadfield, eds, A Mirror for Magistrates *in Context: Literature, History and Politics before the Age of Shakespeare* (Cambridge: Cambridge University Press, 2016).

Arendt, Hannah, 'Lying in Politics' in *Crises of the Republic* (Harmondsworth: Penguin, 1973), pp. 9–42.

Ariès, Philippe, *The Hour of Our Death*, trans. Helen Weaver (New York: Knopf, 1981).

Ashworth, E. J., 'Traditional Logic', in Schmitt and Skinner, eds, *Cambridge History of Renaissance Philosophy*, pp. 143–72.

Aston, Margaret, *England's Iconoclasts, Volume I: Laws Against Images* (Oxford: Clarendon Press, 1988).

Atkin, Graham, 'Raleigh, Spenser, and Elizabeth: Acts of Friendship in *The Faerie Queene*, Book IV', in Julian Lethbridge, ed., *Edmund Spenser: New and Renewed Directions* (Madison: Fairleigh Dickinson University Press, 2006), pp. 195–213.

Austen, Gillian, *George Gascoigne* (Woodbridge: Brewer, 2008).

Austin, J. L., *How to Do Things with Words*, ed. J. O. Urmson and Marina Sbisà (Oxford: Oxford University Press, 1976).

Backus, Irena, *Life Writing in Reformation Europe: Lives of Reformers by Friends, Disciples and Foes* (Farnham: Ashgate, 2008).

Baines, Paul, and Pat Rogers, *Edmund Curll, Bookseller* (Oxford: Oxford University Press, 2007).

Bainton, Roland H., 'The Immoralities of the Patriarchs According to the Exegesis of the Late Middle Ages and of the Reformation', *HTR* 33 (1990), 39–49.

Baker, Sir John, *The Oxford History of the Laws of England, Volume VI: 1483–1558* (Oxford: Oxford University Press, 2003).

Baker House, Seymour, '"the field is won": An Introduction to the Tower Works', in A. D. Cousins and Damian Grace, eds, *A Companion to Thomas More* (Madison: Farleigh Dickinson Press, 2009), pp. 225–42.

Bald, R. C., *John Donne: A Life* (Oxford: Clarendon Press, 1970).

Baldwin, T. W., *William Shakespere's Small Latine and Lesse Greeke* (Illinois: University of Illinois Press, 1944).

Baldwin Smith, Lacey, 'English Treason Trials and Confessions in the Sixteenth Century', *JHI* 15 (1954), 471–98.

Baldwin Smith, Lacey, *Treason in Tudor England: Politics and Paranoia* (London: Pimlico, 2006, rpt of 1986).

Barkan, Leonard, 'Making Pictures Speak: Renaissance Art, Elizabethan Literature, Modern Scholarship', *RQ* 48 (1995), 326–51.

Barker, S. K., 'International News Pamphlets', in Andy Kesson and Emma Smith, eds, *The Elizabethan Top Ten: Defining Print Popularity in Early Modern England* (Farnham: Ashgate, 2013), pp. 145–56.

Barnard, F. M., *Reason and Self-Enactment in History and Politics: Themes and Voices of Modernity* (Montreal: McGill-Queen's Press, 2006).

Barnes, J. A., *A Pack of Lies: Towards a Sociology of Lying* (Cambridge: Cambridge University Press, 1994).

Barnett, S. J., 'Where Was Your Church Before Luther? Claims for Antiquity of Protestantism Examined', *CH* 68 (1999), 14–41.

Barrell, John, *Imagining the King's Death: Figurative Treason, Fantasies of Regicide, 1793–1796* (Oxford: Oxford University Press, 2000).

Bartels, Emily C., *Spectacles of Strangeness: Imperialism, Alienation, and Marlowe* (Philadelphia: University of Pennsylvania Press, 1993).

Bartlett, Robert, *Trial by Fire and Water: The Medieval Judicial Ordeal* (Oxford: Clarendon Press, 1986).

Baseotto, Paola, *'Disdeining Life, Desiring Leaue To Die': Spenser and the Psychology of Despair* (Stuttgart: Ibidem-Verlag, 2008).

Bate, Jonathan, and Dora Thornton, *Staging the World: Shakespeare* (London: British Museum, 2012).

Bates, Catherine, *The Rhetoric of Courtship in Elizabethan Language and Literature* (Cambridge: Cambridge University Press, 1992).

Baumeister, Roy F., 'Lying to Yourself: The Enigma of Self-Deception', in Lewis and Saarni, eds, *Lying and Deception*, pp. 166–83.

Baumer, Franklin Le Van, *The Early Tudor Theory of Kingship* (New Haven: Yale University Press, 1940).

Behrend-Martínez, Edward J., *Unfit for Marriage: Impotent Spouses on Trial in the Basque Region of Spain, 1650–1750* (Reno: University of Nevada Press, 2007).

Beier, A. L., *Masterless Men: The Vagrancy Problem in England, 1560–1640* (London: Methuen, 1985).

Bell, Rudolph M., *How to Do It: Guides to Good Living for Renaissance Italians* (Chicago: University of Chicago Press, 2000).

Bellamy, John, *The Tudor Law of Treason: An Introduction* (London: Routledge, 1979).

Bellany, Alastair, 'Mistress Turner's Deadly Sins: Sartorial Transgression, Court Scandal, and Politics in Early Stuart England', *HLQ* 58 (1995), 179–210.

Bellany, Alastair, *The Politics of Court Scandal in Early Modern England: News Culture and the Overbury Affair, 1603–1660* (Cambridge: Cambridge University Press, 2002).

Bennett, Kristen Abbott, 'Red Herrings and the "Stench of Fish": Subverting "Praise" in Thomas Nashe's Lenten Stuffe', *R. & R.* 37 (2014), 87–110.

Bennett, R. E., 'Sir William Cornwallis's Use of Montaigne', *PMLA* 48 (1933), 1080–9.

Benson, Pamela Joseph, *Invention of the Renaissance Woman: The Challenge of Female Independence in the Literature and Thought of Italy and England* (University Park, PA: Penn State University Press, 1992).

Bentley, Lionel, 'Identity and the Law', in Walker and Leedham-Green, eds, *Identity*, pp. 26–58.

Berger, Harry, Jr, *Revisionary Play: Studies in the Spenserian Dynamic* (Berkeley: University of California Press, 1988).

Bernard, G. W., 'The Fall of Anne Boleyn', *EHR* 106 (1991), 584–610.

Bernard, G. W., 'The Fall of Anne Boleyn: A Rejoinder', *EHR* 107 (1992), 665–74.

Bernard, G. W., *Anne Boleyn: Fatal Attractions* (New Haven: Yale University Press, 2010).

Berry, Philippa, *Of Chastity and Power: Elizabethan Literature and the Unmarried Queen* (London: Routledge, 1989).

Berry, Philippa, 'Disjointed Times, and Half-Remembered Truths in Shakespearean Tragedy', in Richard Dutton and Jean E. Howard, eds, *A Companion to Shakespeare's Works*, 4 vols (Oxford: Blackwell, 2003), pp. 95–107.

Bertolet, Anna Riehl, 'The "blindnesse of the flesh" in Nathaniel Woodes' *The Conflict of Conscience*', in Betteridge and Walker, eds, *Oxford Handbook of Tudor Drama*, pp. 144–60.

Betteridge, Thomas, *Literature and Politics in the English Reformation* (Manchester: Manchester University Press, 2004).

Betteridge, Thomas, 'William Tyndale and Religious Debate', *JMEMS* 40 (2010), 439–61.

Betteridge, Thomas, and Thomas Freeman, eds, *Henry VIII and History* (Farnham: Ashgate, 2012).

Betteridge, Thomas, and Susannah Lipscombe, eds, *Henry VIII and the Court: Art, Politics and Performance* (Farnham: Ashgate, 2013).

Betteridge, Thomas, and Greg Walker, eds, *The Oxford Handbook of Tudor Drama* (Oxford: Oxford University Press, 2012).

Bevington, David, *From Mankind to Marlowe: Growth of Structure in the Popular Drama of Tudor England* (Cambridge, MA: Harvard University Press, 1962).

Bevington, David, 'Christopher Marlowe's *Doctor Faustus* and Nathaniel Woode's *The Conflict of Conscience*', in Pincombe and Shrank, eds, *Oxford Handbook of Tudor Literature*, pp. 704–17.

Blake, N. F., *Caxton and his World* (London: Andre Deutsch, 1969).

Blatt, Thora Balslev, *The Plays of John Bale: A Study of Ideas, Technique and Style* (Copenhagen: G. E. C. Gad, 1968).

Bly, Mary, *Queer Virgins and Virgin Queans on the Early Modern Stage* (Oxford: Oxford University Press, 2000).

Boicu, Dragoș, 'Marian Devotion as a Form of Legitimization of the Imperial Authority', *RESS* 6 (2014), 102–20.

Bok, Sissela, *Lying: Moral Choices in Public and Private Life* (Hassocks: Harvester Press, 1978).

Bok, Sissela, *Secrets: Concealment and Revelation* (Oxford: Oxford University Press, 1986).

Bolt, Roelf, *The Encyclopaedia of Liars and Deceivers* (London: Reaktion, 2014).

Boose, Lynda E., 'Othello's Handkerchief: "The Recognizance and Pledge of Love"', *ELR* 5 (1975), 360–74.

Bordo, Susan, *The Creation of Anne Boleyn: A New Look at England's Most Notorious Queen* (New York: Houghton, Mifflin, Harcourt, 2014).

Borot, Luc, 'Early Journalism in Sixteenth- and Seventeenth-Century England: The Interface between Literature and "Popular Culture"', *YSPSR* 9 (1998), 41–58.

Bossy, John, *The English Catholic Community, 1570–1850* (London: Darton, Longman & Todd, 1975).

Bossy, John, 'Moral Arithmetic: Seven Sins into Ten Commandments', in Leites, ed., *Conscience and Casuistry*, pp. 214–34.

Boswell, Jackson Campbell, *Dante's Fame in England: References in Printed British Books, 1477–1640* (Newark: University of Delaware Press, 1999).

Bosworth-Toller, Anglo-Saxon Dictionary (http://bosworth.ff.cuni.cz/054878).

Botelho, Keith M., *Renaissance Earwitnesses: Rumor and Early Modern Masculinity* (Basingstoke: Palgrave Macmillan, 2009).

Bowers, Terence N., 'The Production and Communication of Knowledge in William Baldwin's *Beware the Cat*: Toward a Typographic Culture', *Criticism* 33 (1991), 1–29.

Boyer, Allen D., *Sir Edward Coke and the Elizabethan Age* (Stanford: Stanford University Press, 2003).

Bradford, Alan T., 'Stuart Absolutism and the "Utility" of Tacitus', *HLQ* 45 (1983), 127–55.

Bradford, Ernle, *The Great Siege: Malta 1565* (Harmondsworth: Penguin, 1964).

Brancher, Dominique, '"When the Tongue Slips it Tells the Truth": Tricks and Truths of the Renaissance Lapsus', *RS* 30 (2016), 39–56.

Braudel, Fernand, *Civilisation and Capitalism, 15th–18th Century*, 3 vols, trans. Siân Reynolds (London: Collins, 1986, rpt of 1981).

Braun, Harald and Edward Vallance, eds, *Contexts of Conscience in Early Modern Europe, 1500–1700* (Basingstoke: Palgrave Macmillan, 2004).

Braund, Susanna, 'Complaint, Epigram, and Satire', in Patrick Cheney and Philip Hardie, eds, *The Oxford History of Classical Reception in English Literature, 1558–1660* (Oxford: Oxford University Press, 2015), pp. 345–72.

Brigden, Susan, *London and the Reformation* (Oxford: Clarendon Press, 1989).

Brigden, Susan, *Thomas Wyatt: The Heart's Forest* (London: Faber, 2012).

Brigden, Susan, 'Henry VIII and the Crusade Against England', in Betteridge and Lipscombe, eds, *Henry VIII and the Court*, pp. 215–34.

Briggs, Julia, 'Marlowe's *Massacre at Paris*: A Reconsideration', *RES*, ns, 34 (1983), 257–78.

Brook, V. K., *Whitgift and the English Church* (London: English Universities Press, 1957).

Brooke, Christopher, *Europe in the Central Middle Ages, 962–1154* (2nd edn, London: Longman, 1987).

Brooke, John, and Ian Maclean, eds, *Heterodoxy in Early Modern Science and Religion* (Oxford: Oxford University Press, 2005).

Brooks, Christopher W., *Law, Politics and Society in Early Modern England* (Cambridge: Cambridge University Press, 2008).

Brooks-Davies, Douglas, *Spenser's* Faerie Queene: *A Critical Commentary on Books I and II* (Manchester: Manchester University Press, 1977).

Brotton, Jerry, *The Renaissance Bazaar: From the Silk Road to Michelangelo* (Oxford: Oxford University Press, 2002).

Brown, Georgia, 'Defining Nature Through Monstrosity in *Othello* and *Macbeth*', in Ivo Kamps, Thomas Hallock, and Karen L. Raber, eds, *Early Modern Ecostudies* (Basingstoke: Palgrave Macmillan, 2008), pp. 55–76.

Bruhn, Karen, 'Reforming Saint Peter: Protestant Constructions of Saint Peter the Apostle in Early Modern England', 33 *C16J* (2002), 33–49.

Brundage, James A., 'Impotence, Frigidity, and Marital Nullity in the Decretists and the Early Decretalists', in P. Linehan, ed., *Proceedings of the Seventh International Conference on Medieval Canon Law* (Vatican City: Biblioteca Apostolica Vaticana, 1988), pp. 407–23.

Brundage, James A., *Medieval Canon Law* (London: Longman, 1995).

Bühler, Curt F., 'A Survival from the Middle Ages: William Baldwin's *Use of the Dictes and Sayings*', *Speculum* 23 (1948), 76–80.

Burgess, Glenn, *Absolute Monarchy and the Stuart Constitution* (New Haven: Yale University Press, 1996).

Burke, Peter, 'Tacitism', in T. A. Dorey, ed., *Tacitus* (London: Routledge, 1969), pp. 149–71.

Burke, Peter, *The Fortunes of the Courtier* (Cambridge: Polity, 1995).

Burke, Peter, *What is Cultural History?* (Cambridge: Polity, 2004).

Burns, J. H., with Mark Goldie, eds, *The Cambridge History of Political Thought, 1450–1700* (Cambridge: Cambridge University Press, 1991).

Burrow, Colin, *Epic Romance: Homer to Milton* (Oxford: Clarendon Press, 1993).

Burrow, Colin, 'Ben Jonson', in Claude Rawson, ed., *The Cambridge Companion to English Poets* (Cambridge: Cambridge University Press, 2011), pp. 122–39.

Bushnell, Rebecca W., *Tragedies of Tyrants: Political Thought and Theater in the English Renaissance* (Ithaca, NY: Cornell University Press, 1990).

Bushnell, Rebecca W., *A Culture of Teaching: Early Modern Humanism in Theory and Practice* (Ithaca, NY: Cornell University Press, 1996).

Busse, Beatrix, *Vocative Constructions in the Language of Shakespeare* (Amsterdam: Benjamins, 2006).

Butterworth, Emily, and Hugh Roberts, 'Introduction: Gossip and Nonsense in Renaissance France and England', *RS* 30 (2016), 8–16.

Byron, Brian, 'The Fourth Count of the Indictment of St. Thomas More', *Moreana* 10 (1966), 33–46.

Camden, Carroll, Jr, 'Elizabethan Almanacs and Prognostications', *The Library*, 4th series, 12 (1931), 83–108.

Cameron, Euan, *The European Reformation* (Oxford: Oxford University Press, 1991).

Campbell, Gordon, and Thomas N. Corns, *John Milton: Life, Work, and Thought* (Oxford: Oxford University Press, 2008).

Capp, Bernard, *When Gossips Meet: Women, Family, and Neighbourhood in Early Modern England* (Oxford: Oxford University Press, 2003).

Caraman, Philip, *Henry Garnet, 1555–1606, and the Gunpowder Plot* (London; Longmans, 1964).

Carr, E. H., *What is History?* (Harmondsworth: Penguin, 1964).

Carroll, Stuart, *Blood and Violence in Early Modern France* (Oxford: Oxford University Press, 2006).

Carson, Thomas L., *Lying and Deception: Theory and Practice* (Oxford: Oxford University Press, 2010).

Castor, Helen, *She-Wolves: The Women Who Ruled England Before Elizabeth* (London: Faber, 2011).

Cavanagh, Dermot, *Language and Politics in the Sixteenth-Century History Play* (Basingstoke: Palgrave Macmillan, 2003).

Cavanagh, Dermot, 'Modes of Satire', in Andrew Hadfield, ed., *The Oxford Handbook of English Prose, 1500–1640* (Oxford: Oxford University Press, 2013), pp. 380–95.

Challis, C. E., *The Tudor Coinage* (Manchester: Manchester University Press, 1978).

Chambers, R. W., *Thomas More* (Harmondsworth: Penguin, 1963, rpt of 1935).

Charlton, Kenneth, *Education in Renaissance England* (London: Routledge, 1975).

Chaudhuri, Supriya, 'Being True to Yourself: Lying in *Hamlet*', in Panja, ed., *Shakespeare and the Art of Lying*, pp. 59–76.

Cheney, Patrick, *Marlowe's Counterfeit Profession: Ovid, Spenser, Counter-Nationhood* (Toronto: University of Toronto Press, 1997).

Cheney, Patrick, ed., *The Cambridge Companion to Christopher Marlowe* (Cambridge: Cambridge University Press, 2004).

Chilton, Paul, 'Humanism and War in the Work of Rabelais and Montaigne', in J. R. Mulryne and Margaret Shewring, eds, *War, Literaure and the Arts in Sixteenth-Century Europe* (Basingstoke: Macmillan, 1989), pp. 119–43.

Chisholm, Roderick M., and Thomas D. Fehan, 'The Intent to Deceive', *The Journal of Philosophy* 74 (1977), 143–59.

Clark, Sandra, *Women and Crime in the Street Literature of Early Modern England* (Basingstoke: Palgrave Macmillan, 2003).

Clark, Sandra, *Renaissance Drama* (Cambridge: Polity, 2007).

Clark, Stuart, *Vanities of the Eye: Vision in Early Modern European Culture* (Oxford: Oxford University Press, 2007).

Coady, C. A. J., *Testimony: A Philosophical Study* (Oxford: Clarendon Press, 1992).

Cohen, Derek, 'Othello's Suicide', *UTQ* 62 (1993), 323–33.

Cohen, Jeffrey J., 'Postcolonialism', in Steve Ellis, ed., *Chaucer: An Oxford Guide* (Oxford: Oxford University Press, 2005), pp. 448–62.

Colclough, David, 'Talking to the Animals: Persuasion, Counsel, and their Discontents in *Julius Caesar*', in David Armitage, Conal Condren, and Andrew Fitzmaurice, eds, *Shakespeare and Early Modern Political Thought* (Cambridge: Cambridge University Press, 2009), pp. 217–33.

Coldiron, A. E. B., 'Form[e]s of Transnationhood: The Case of John Wolfe's Trilingual *Courtier*', *RS* 29 (2015), 103–24.

Coldiron, A. E. B., *Printers without Borders: Translation and Textuality in the Renaissance* (Cambridge: Cambridge University Press, 2015).

Coleman, James, 'Montaigne and the Wars of Religion', in Keith Cameron, ed., *Montaigne and His Age* (Exeter: University of Exeter Press, 1981), pp. 107–20.

Coles, Kimberly Anne, 'The Matter of Belief in John Donne's *Holy Sonnets*', *RQ* 68 (2015), 899–931.

Collinson, Patrick, *The Elizabethan Puritan Movement* (Oxford: Clarendon Press, 1967).

Collinson, Patrick, 'England and International Calvinism, 1558–1640', in Prestwich, ed., *International Calvinism*, pp. 197–223.

Collinson, Patrick, 'Ecclesiastical Vitriol: Religious Satire in the 1590s and the Invention of Puritanism', in Guy, ed., *Reign of Elizabeth I*, pp. 150–70.

Collinson, Patrick, 'Truth, Lies and Fiction in Sixteenth-century Protestant Historiography', in Donald R. Kelley and David Harris Sacks, eds, *The Historical Imagination in Early Modern Britain: History, Rhetoric and Fiction, 1500–1800* (Cambridge: Cambridge University Press, 1997), pp. 37–68.

Collinson, Patrick, *Elizabethans* (London: Hambledon, 2003).

Collinson, Patrick, *Richard Bancroft and Elizabethan Anti-Puritanism* (Cambridge: Cambridge University Press, 2013).

Contamine, Philippe, *War in the Middle Ages*, trans. Michael Jones (Oxford: Blackwell, 1984).

Cooper, John P. D., *Propaganda and the Tudor State: Political Culture in the Westcountry* (Oxford: Clarendon Press, 2003).

Cox-Johnson, Ann, 'Lambeth Palace Library, 1610–1664', *TCBS* 11 (1954–8), 105–26.

Crawford, Julie, *Marvelous Protestantism: Monstrous Births in Post-Reformation England* (Baltimore: Johns Hopkins University Press, 2005).

Crawforth, Hannah, Sarah Dustagheer, and Jennifer Young, *Shakespeare in London* (London: Bloomsbury, 2015).

Cressy, David, *Education in Tudor and Stuart England* (London: Arnold, 1975).

Cressy, David, *Literacy and the Social Order: Reading and Writing in Tudor and Stuart England* (Cambridge: Cambridge University Press, 1980).

Cressy, David, *Birth, Marriage, and Death: Ritual, Religion, and the Life-Cycle in Tudor and Stuart England* (Oxford: Oxford University Press, 1997).

Cressy, David, *Agnes Bowker's Cat: Travesties and Transgressions in Tudor and Stuart England* (Oxford: Oxford University Press, 2000).

Cressy, David, *Dangerous Talk: Scandalous, Seditious, and Treasonable Speech in Pre-Modern England* (Oxford: Oxford University Press, 2010).

Crewe, Jonathan V., *Unredeemed Rhetoric: Thomas Nashe and the Scandal of Authorship* (Baltimore: Johns Hopkins University Press, 1982).

Crockett, William R., 'Holy Communion', in Stephen Sykes and John Booty, eds, *The Study of Anglicanism* (London: SPCK, 1988), pp. 272–84.

Crompton, Samuel Willard, *The Printing Press: Transforming Power of Technology* (New York: Infobase, 2004).

Cross, Claire, *Church and People: England 1450–1660* (2nd edn, Oxford: Blackwell, 1999).

Cummings, Brian, *The Literary Culture of the Reformation: Grammar and Grace* (Oxford: Oxford University Press, 2002).

Cummings, Brian, 'Images in Books: Foxe *Eikonoklastes*', in Tara Hamling and Richard L. Williams, eds, *Art Re-Formed: Re-assessing the Impact of the Reformation on the Visual Arts* (Newcastle: Cambridge Scholars Press, 2007), pp. 183–200.

Cummings, Brian, 'Conscience and the Law in Thomas More', *RS* 23 (2009), 463–85.

Cummings, Brian, *Mortal Thoughts: Religion, Secularity, and Identity in Shakespeare and Early Modern Culture* (Oxford: Oxford University Press, 2013).

Cummings, Brian, 'Encyclopedic Erasmus', *RS* 28 (2014), 183–204.

Cummings, Robert ed., *Edmund Spenser: The Critical Heritage* (London: Routledge, 1971).

Cummings, Robert, 'Classical Moralists and Philosophers', in Gordon Braden, Robert Cummings, and Stuart Gillespie, eds, *The Oxford History of Literary Translation in English, Vol. 2: 1550–1660* (Oxford: Oxford University Press, 2010), pp. 371–89.

Cunningham, Andrew, and Ole Peter Grell, *The Four Horsemen of the Apocalypse: Religion, War, Famine and Death in Reformation Europe* (Cambridge: Cambridge University Press, 2000).

Cunningham, Lawrence S., *An Introduction to Catholicism* (Cambridge: Cambridge University Press, 2009).

Curthoys, Ann, and John Docker, *Is History Fiction?* (Ann Arbor: University of Michigan Press, 2005).

Curtius, E. R., *European Literature and the Latin Middle Ages*, trans. Willard R. Trask (Princeton: Princeton University Press, 1983, rpt of 1953).

Daniell, David, *William Tyndale: A Biography* (New Haven: Yale University Press, 1994).

Danner, Bruce, *Edmund Spenser's War on Lord Burghley* (Basingstoke: Palgrave Macmillan, 2011).

Davis, Natalie Zemon, *The Return of Martin Guerre* (Cambridge, MA: Harvard University Press, 1984).

Davis, Natalie Zemon, *Fiction in the Archives: Pardon Tales and their Tellers in Sixteenth Century France* (Stanford: Stanford University Press, 1987).

Dawley, Powel Mills, *John Whitgift and the Reformation* (London: Black, 1955).

De Grazia, Margreta, Hamlet *Without Hamlet* (Cambridge: Cambridge University Press, 2007).

Dean, David M., 'Parliament, Privy Council, and Local Politics in Elizabethan England: The Yarmouth–Lowestoft Fishing Dispute', *Albion* 22 (1990), 39–64.

Deneef, A. Leigh, *Spenser and the Motives of Metaphor* (Durham, NC: Duke University Press, 1982).

Denery II, Dallas G., *The Devil Wins: A History of Lying from the Garden of Eden to the Enlightenment* (Princeton: Princeton University Press, 2014).

Derrett, J. Duncan M., 'The "New" Document on Thomas More's Trial', *Moreana* 3 (1964), 5–22.

Derrett, J. Duncan M., 'The Trial of Sir Thomas More', *EHR* 79 (1964), 449–77.

Derrett, J. Duncan M., 'More's Silence and His Trial', *Moreana* 22 (1985), 87–8.

Derrida, Jacques, *Without Alibi*, ed. and trans. Peggy Kamuf (Stanford: Stanford University Press, 2002).

Devereux, E. J., 'Empty Tuns and Unfruitful Grafts: Richard Grafton's Historical Publications', *The Sixteenth Century Journal* 21 (1990), 33–56.

Devlin, Christopher, *The Life of Robert Southwell: Poet and Martyr* (London: Longmans, 1956).

Dewald, Jonathan, *The European Nobility, 1400–1800* (Cambridge: Cambridge University Press, 1996).

Dickens, A. G., *Lollards and Protestants in the Diocese of York, 1509–1558* (London: Hambledon, 1982, rpt of 1959).

Dillon, Anne, *The Construction of Martyrdom in the English Catholic Community, 1535–1603* (Farnham: Ashgate, 2002).

Dimmock, Matthew, *New Turkes: Dramatizing Islam and the Ottomans in Early Modern England* (Farnham: Ashgate, 2005).

Dimmock, Matthew, *Mythologies of the Prophet Muhammad in Early Modern English Culture* (Cambridge: Cambridge University Press, 2013).

Dobin, Howard, *Merlin's Disciples: Prophecy, Poetry, and Power in Renaissance England* (Stanford: Stanford University Press, 1990).

Doe, Norman, *Fundamental Authority in Late Medieval English Law* (Cambridge: Cambridge University Press, 1990).

Dolan, Frances E., 'Home-Rebels and House-Traitors: Murderous Wives in Early Modern England', *YJLH* 4 (1992), 1–30.

Dolan, Frances E., 'Re-reading Rape in *The Changeling*', *JEMCS* 11 (2011), 4–29.

Dolan, Frances E., *True Relations: Reading, Literature, and Evidence in Seventeenth-Century England* (Philadelphia: University of Pennsylvania Press, 2013).

Dominik, William, and Jon Hall, eds, *A Companion to Roman Rhetoric* (Oxford: Wiley-Blackwell, 2010).

Donaldson, Ian, *Ben Jonson: A Life* (Oxford: Oxford University Press, 2011).

Donaldson, Peter S., *Machiavelli and Mystery of State* (Cambridge: Cambridge University Press, 1992).

Doran, Susan, '"Revenge her most foul and unnatural murder": The Impact of Mary Staurt's Execution on Anglo-Scottish Relations', *History* 85 (2000), 589–612.

Duffy, Eamon, *The Stripping of the Altars: Traditional Religion in England, 1400–1580* (New Haven: Yale University Press, 1992).

Duffy, Eamon, *Fires of Faith: Catholic England Under Mary Tudor* (New Haven: Yale University Press, 2009).

Dugan, John, 'Modern Critical Approaches to Roman Rhetoric', in Dominik and Hall, eds, *Companion to Roman Rhetoric*, pp. 9–22.

Duke, Alastair, *The Reformation and Revolt in the Low Countries* (London: Black, 2003).

Duncan-Jones, Katherine, *Sir Philip Sidney, Courtier Poet* (London: Hamish Hamilton, 1991).

Duncan-Jones, Katherine, *Ungentle Shakespeare: Scenes from his Life* (London: Arden, 2001).

Dutton, Richard, '*Volpone*: Venice in London, London in Venice', in Andrew Hiscock, ed., *Mighty Europe 1400–1700: Writing an Early Modern Continent* (Frankfurt: Peter Lang, 2007), pp. 133–51.

Dutton, Richard, *Ben Jonson,* Volpone, *and the Gunpowder Plot* (Cambridge: Cambridge University Press, 2008).

Eccles, Mark, 'Jonson and the Spies', *RES* 13 (1937), 385–97.

Eden, Kathy, *Friends Hold All Things in Common: Tradition, Intellectual Property, and the Adages of Erasmus* (New Haven: Yale University Press, 2001).

Edson, Gary, *Mysticism and Alchemy through the Ages: The Quest for Transformation* (Jefferson, NC: McFarland, 2012).

Ehrman, Bart D., *Forgery and Counter-forgery: The Use of Literary Deceit in Early Christian Polemics* (Oxford: Oxford University Press, 2013).

Eire, Carlos M. N., 'Calvin and Nicodemism: A Reappraisal', *C16J* 10 (1979), 44–69.

Eire, Carlos M. N., *War Against the Idols: The Reformation of Worship from Erasmus to Calvin* (Cambridge: Cambridge University Press, 1986).

Ekman, Paul, *Telling Lies: Clues to Deceit in the Marketplace, Politics, and Marriage* (rev. edn, New York: Norton, 2001).

Elias, Norbert, *The Civilizing Process: Sociogenetic and Psychogenetic Investigations*, trans. Edmund Jephcott (rev. edn, Oxford: Blackwell, 1994).

Eliav-Feldon, Miriam, *Renaissance Impostors and Proofs of Identity* (Basingstoke: Palgrave Macmillan, 2012).

Elliott, Dyan, *Spiritual Marriage: Sexual Abstinence in Medieval Wedlock* (Princeton: Princeton University Press, 1995).

Elton, G. R., *Reformation Europe, 1517–1559* (London: Collins, 1963).

Elton, G. R., *Policy and Police: The Enforcement of the Reformation in the Age of Thomas Cromwell* (Cambridge: Cambridge University Press, 1972).

Emlyn-Jones, Chris, 'True and Lying Tales in *The Odyssey*', *GR* 33 (1986), 1–10.

Emmison, F. G., *Elizabethan Life: Home, Work and Land* (Chelmsford: Essex County Council, 1976).

Empson, William, 'Honest in *Othello*', in *The Structure of Complex Words* (London: Chatto & Windus, 1952), pp. 218–49.

Empson, William, *Seven Types of Ambiguity* (Harmondsworth: Penguin, 1961, rpt of 1930).

Ennis, Lambert, 'Anthony Nixon: Jacobean Plagiarist and Hack', *HLQ* 4 (1940), 377–401.

Enterline, Lynne, *Shakespeare's Schoolroom: Rhetoric, Discipline, Emotion* (Philadelphia: University of Pennsylvania Press, 2102).

Erne, Lukas, *Beyond the Spanish Tragedy: A Study of the Works of Thomas Kyd* (Manchester: Manchester University Press, 2001).

Escobedo, Andrew, *Nationalism and Historical Loss in Renaissance England: Foxe, Dee, Spenser, Milton* (Ithaca, NY: Cornell University Press, 2004).

Ettenhuber, Katrin, 'Hyperbole: Exceeding Similitude', in Adamson et al., eds, *Renaissance Figures of Speech*, pp. 197–216.

Ettenhuber, Katrin, *Donne's Augustine: Renaissance Cultures of Interpretation* (Oxford: Oxford University Press, 2011).

Evans, G. R., 'John Donne and the Augustinian Paradox of Sin', *RES* 33 (1982), 1–22.

Evans, G. R., *Problems of Authority in the Reformation Debates* (Cambridge: Cambridge University Press, 1992).

Evenden, Elizabeth, *Patents, Pictures and Patronage: John Day and the Tudor Book Trade* (Aldershot: Ashgate, 2008).

Evenden, Elizabeth, and Thomas S. Freeman, *Religion and the Book in Early Modern England: The Making of John Foxe's 'Book of Martyrs'* (Cambridge: Cambridge University Press, 2011).

Everett, Barbara, '"Spanish" Othello: The Making of Shakespeare's Moor', in Catherine M. S. Alexander and Stanley Wells, eds, *Shakespeare and Race* (Cambridge: Cambridge University Press, 2000), pp. 64–81.

Ewbank, Inga-Stina, *Shakespeare's Liars* (London: British Academy, 1984).

Fairfield, Leslie P., *John Bale: Mythmaker of the English Reformation* (Indiana: Purdue University Press, 1976).

Farey, Peter, 'A Deception in Deptford: Christopher Marlowe's Alleged Death' (http://www.rey.prestel.co.uk/add1.htm) (accessed 23 October 2015).

Ferguson, Arthur B., *The Articulate Citizen and the English Renaissance* (Durham, NC: Duke University Press, 1965).

Findlay, Alison, *Women in Shakespeare: A Dictionary* (London: Black, 2014).

Fisher, G. W., *Annals of Shrewsbury School* (London: Methuen, 1899).

Fitzmaurice, Andrew, *Humanism and America: An Intellectual History of English Colonisation, 1500–1625* (Cambridge: Cambridge University Press, 2003).

Fitzpatrick, Joan, *Shakespeare and the Language of Food: A Dictionary* (London: Bloomsbury, 2010).

Fletcher, Anthony, *Tudor Rebellions* (London: Longman, 1983).

Fletcher, Catherine, 'Performing Henry VIII at the Court of Rome', in Betteridge and Lipscombe, eds, *Henry VIII and the Court*, pp. 179–94.

Flynn, Dennis, *John Donne and the Ancient Catholic Nobility* (Bloomington: Indiana University Press, 1995).

Forsyth, Neil, 'Milton's Corrupt Bible', in Kevin Killeen, Helen Smith, and Rachel Judith Willie, eds, *The Oxford Handbook of the Bible in Early Modern England, c. 1530–1700* (Oxford: Oxford University Press, 2015), pp. 209–23.

Foster, Brett, 'Harry's Peregrinations: An Italianate Defence of Henry VIII', in Betteridge and Freeman, eds, *Henry VIII and History*, pp. 21–50.

Foucault, Michel, *Discipline and Punish: The Birth of the Prison*, trans. Alan Sheridan (Harmondsworth: Penguin, 1977).

Fox, Adam, *Oral and Literate Culture in England, 1500–1700* (Oxford: Oxford University Press, 2000).

Fox, Alistair, *Thomas More: History and Providence* (Oxford: Blackwell, 1982).

Fox, Alistair, and John Guy, *Reassessing the Henrician Age: Humanism, Politics and Reform, 1500–1550* (Oxford: Blackwell, 1986).

Foyster, Elizabeth A., 'Silent Witnesses? Children and the Breakdown of Domestic and Social Order in Early Modern England', in Anthony Fletcher and Stephen Hussey, eds, *Childhood in Question: Children, Parents and the State* (Manchester: Manchester University Press, 1999), pp. 57–73.

Fradenburg, Louise O., 'Criticism, Anti-Semitism, and the Prioress's Tale', in Kathryn L. Lynch, ed., *Chaucer's Cultural Geography* (London: Routledge, 2002), pp. 174–92.

Frantzen, Allen J., 'Bede and Bawdy Bale: Gregory the Great, Angels and the "Angli"', in Allen J. Frantzen and John D. Niles, eds, *Anglo-Saxonism and the Construction of Social Identity* (Gainsville: University Press of Florida, 1997), pp. 17–39.

Fraser, Antonia, *The Gunpowder Plot: Terror and Faith in 1605* (London: Weidenfeld & Nicolson, 1996).

Frazier, Harriet C., '"Like a Liar Gone to Burning Hell": Shakespeare and Dying Declarations', *CD* 19 (1985), 166–80.

Freeman, Arthur, 'Marlowe, Kyd, and the Dutch Church Libel', *ELR* 3 (1973), 44–52.

Freeman, Arthur, and Janet Ing Freeman, *John Payne Collier: Scholarship and Forgery in the Nineteenth Century*, 2 vols (New Haven: Yale University Press, 2004).

Freeman, Thomas S., 'Hands Defiled with Blood: Henry VIII in Foxe's "Book of Martyrs"', in Betteridge and Freeman, eds, *Henry VIII and History*, pp. 87–118.

Freer, Coburn, 'Lies and Lying in *The Jew of Malta*', in Kenneth Friedenreich and Roma Gill, eds, *'A Poet and a Filthy Play-maker': New Essays on Christopher Marlowe* (New York: AMS Press, 1988), pp. 143–67.

Freud, Sigmund, *The Psychopathology of Everyday Life*, trans. Alan Tyson (Harmondsworth: Penguin, 1975).

Frisch, Andrea, 'Montaigne and the Ethics of Memory', *L'Esprit Créateur* 46 (2006), 23–31.

Fuller, Lon L., *Legal Fictions* (Stanford: Stanford University Press, 1967).

Galbraith, Stephen, '"English" Black-Letter Type and Spenser's *Shepheardes Calender*', *Sp. St.* 23 (2008), 13–40.

Gallagher, Lowell, *Medusa's Gaze: Casuistry and Conscience in the Renaissance* (Stanford: Stanford University Press, 1991).

Galletti, Sara, 'Rubens's *Life of Maria de' Medici*: Dissimulation and the Politics of Art in Early Seventeenth-Century France', *RQ* 67 (2014), 878–916.

Gardiner, S. R., *History of England from the Accession of James I to the Outbreak of the Civil War, 1603–1642*, 10 vols (London: Longman, 1883–4).

Gaskill, Malcolm, *Crime and Mentalities in Early Modern England* (Cambridge: Cambridge University Press, 2003).

Giamatti, A. Bartlett, *Play of Double Senses: Spenser's Faerie Queene* (New York: Norton, 1975).

Gibbons, Katy, *English Catholic Exiles in Late Sixteenth-Century Paris* (Woodbridge: Boydell and Brewer, 2011).

Gibbs, Philip, *King's Favourite: The Love Story of Robert Carr and Lady Essex* (London: Hutchinson, 1909).

Gill, J. S., 'How Hermes Trismegistus Was Introduced to Renaissance England: The Influences of Caxton and Ficino's "Argumentum" on Baldwin and Palfreyman', *JWCI* 47 (1984), 222–5.

Gillespie, Stuart, *Shakespeare's Books: A Dictionary of Shakespeare's Sources* (London: Athlone, 2000).

Gillies, John, *Shakespeare and the Geography of Difference* (Cambridge: Cambridge University Press, 1994).

Gless, Darryl J., *Measure for Measure, the Law and the Convent* (Princeton: Princeton University Press, 1979).

Goffen, Rona, 'Renaissance Dreams', *RQ* 40 (1987), 682–706.

Goldberg, Jonathan, *Endlesse Worke: Spenser and the Structures of Discourse* (Baltimore: Johns Hopkins University Press, 1981).

Göller, Karl Heinz, 'Sir Hugh of Lincoln—From History to Nursery Rhyme', in Franz Link, ed., *Jewish Life and Suffering as Mirrored in English and American Literature* (Paderborn: F. Schöningh, 1987), pp. 17–32.

Gordon, Michael D., 'The Invention of a Common Law Crime: Perjury and the Elizabethan Courts', *AJLH* 24 (1980), 145–70.

Gordon, Michael D., 'The Perjury Statute of 1563: A Case History of Confusion', *PAPS* 124 (1980), 438–54.

Gowing, Laura, *Domestic Dangers: Women, Words, and Sex in Early Modern London* (Oxford: Clarendon Press, 1998).

Grabes, Herbert, *The Mutable Glass: Mirror-Imagery in Titles and Texts of the Middle Ages and English Renaissance* (Cambridge: Cambridge University Press, 1982).

Grafton, Anthony, 'The Availability of Ancient Works', in Schmitt and Skinner, eds, *Cambridge History of Renaissance Philosophy*, pp. 767–91.

Gray, Jonathan Michael, 'Vows, Oaths, and the Propagation of a Subversive Discourse', *C16J* 41 (2010), 731–56.

Gray, Jonathan Michael, *Oaths and the English Reformation* (Cambridge: Cambridge University Press, 2013).

Graziani, René, 'Philip II's Impressa and Spenser's Souldan', *JWCI* 27 (1964), 322–4.

Green, Jeffrey Martin, 'Montaigne's Critique of Cicero', *JHI* 36 (1975), 595–612.

Green, Jonathan, Research Fragments (http://researchfragments.blogspot.co.uk/search?q= herring).

Green, Stuart P., *Lying, Cheating, and Stealing: A Moral Theory of White-Collar Crime* (Oxford: Oxford University Press, 2006).

Greenberg, Adam Eric, Paul Smeets, and Lilia Zhurakhovska, 'Lying, Guilt and Shame' (https://www.aeaweb.org/aea/2015conference/program/retrieve.php?pdfid=135).

Greenblatt, Stephen, *Sir Walter Raleigh: The Renaissance Man and His Roles* (New Haven: Yale University Press, 1973).

Greenblatt, Stephen, *Renaissance Self-Fashioning: From More to Shakespeare* (Chicago: University of Chicago Press, 1980).

Greenblatt, Stephen, *Marvelous Possessions: The Wonder of the New World* (Oxford: Oxford University Press, 1991).

Gregory, Brad S., 'Tyndale and More, in Life and in Death', *Reformation* 8 (2003), 173–97.

Grell, Ole Peter, and Bob Scribner, eds, *Tolerance and Intolerance in the European Reformation* (Cambridge: Cambridge University Press, 1996).

Gresham, Stephen, 'William Baldwin: Literary Voice of the Reign of Edward VI', *HLQ* 44 (1981), 101–16.

Griffiths, Paul, *Youth and Authority: Formative Experiences in England, 1560–1640* (Oxford: Clarendon Press, 1996).

Griffiths, Paul J., *Lying: An Augustinian Theology of Duplicity* (Grand Rapids, MI: Brazos Press, 2004).

Grogan, Jane, *The Persian Empire in English Renaissance Writing, 1549–1622* (Basingstoke: Palgrave Macmillan, 2014).

Gunther, Karl, *Reformation Unbound: Protestant Visions of Reform in England, 1525–1590* (Cambridge: Cambridge University Press, 2014).

Guy, John A., *The Cardinal's Court: The Impact of Thomas Wolsey in Star Chamber* (Harvester: Hassocks, 1977).

Guy, John A., 'Henry VIII and the Praemunire Manoeuvres of 1530–1531', *EHR* 97 (1982), 481–503.

Guy, John A., 'Thomas More and Christopher St. German: The Battle of the Books', in Fox and Guy, *Reassessing*, pp. 95–120.

Guy, John A., 'Scripture as Authority: Problems of Interpretation in the 1530s', in Fox and Guy, *Reassessing*, pp. 188–220.

Guy, John A., *Tudor England* (Oxford: Oxford University Press, 1988).

Guy, John A., ed., *The Reign of Elizabeth I: Court and Culture in the Last Decade* (Cambridge: Cambridge University Press, 1995).

Guy, John A., 'Introduction: The 1590s: The Second Reign of Elizabeth I?', in Guy, ed., *Reign of Elizabeth I*, pp. 1–19.

Guy, John A., *'My Heart is My Own': The Life of Mary Queen of Scots* (London: HarperCollins, 2004).

Guy-Bray, Stephen, Joan Pong Linton, and Steve Mentz, eds, *The Age of Thomas Nashe: Text, Bodies and Trespasses of Authorship in Early Modern England* (Farnham: Ashgate, 2013).

Hadfield, Andrew, *Literature, Politics and National Identity: Reformation to Renaissance* (Cambridge: Cambridge University Press, 1994).

Hadfield, Andrew, *Spenser's Irish Experience: Wilde Fruyt and Salvage Soyl* (Oxford: Clarendon Press, 1997).

Hadfield, Andrew, *Literature, Travel, and Colonial Writing in the English Renaissance, 1545–1625* (Oxford: Oxford University Press, 1998).

Hadfield, Andrew, ed., *Amazons, Savages, and Machiavels: An Anthology of Travel and Colonial Writing, 1550–1650* (Oxford: Oxford University Press, 2001).

Hadfield, Andrew, *Shakespeare and Republicanism* (Cambridge: Cambridge University Press, 2005).

Hadfield, Andrew, 'Foresters, Ploughmen and Shepherds: Versions of Tudor Pastoral', in Pincombe and Shrank, eds, *Oxford Handbook of Tudor Literature*, pp. 537–53.

Hadfield, Andrew, 'Prose Fiction', in Michael Hattaway, ed., *A New Companion to English Renaissance Literature and Culture* (Oxford: Wiley, 2010), II, pp. 423–36.

Hadfield, Andrew, 'Spenser and Religion—Yet Again', *SEL* 51 (2011), 21–46.

Hadfield, Andrew, *Edmund Spenser: A Life* (Oxford: Oxford University Press, 2012).

Hadfield, Andrew, 'News of the Sussex Dragon', *Reformation* 17 (2012), 99–113.

Hadfield, Andrew, *'The Summoning of Everyman'*, in Betteridge and Walker, eds, *Oxford Handbook of Tudor Drama*, pp. 93–108.

Hadfield, Andrew, 'War Poetry and Counsel in Early Modern Ireland', in Valerie McGowan-Doyle and Brendan Kane, eds, *Elizabeth I and Ireland* (Cambridge: Cambridge University Press, 2014), pp. 239–60.

Hadfield, Andrew, 'Grimalkin and Other Shakespearean Celts', *YSPSR* 25 (2015), 55–76.

Hadfield, Andrew, 'A Red Herring?', *ELR* 45 (2015), 231–54.

Hadfield, Andrew, 'Renaissance England's Views of Rome', *BSRS* vol. xxxii, 2 (Oct. 2015), 9–12.

Hadfield, Andrew, review of Dallas G. Denery II, *The Devil Wins: A History of Lying From The Garden of Eden to the Enlightenment*, *TP* 29 (2015), 773–80.

Haigh, Christopher, 'The Continuity of Catholicism in the English Reformation', in Christopher Haigh, ed., *The English Reformation Revised* (Cambridge: Cambridge University Press, 1987), pp. 176–208.

Hale, John R., *Machiavelli and Renaissance Italy* (Harmondsworth: Penguin, 1972).

Hale, John R., *The Civilization of Europe in the Renaissance* (London: HarperCollins, 1993).

Halley, Janet E., 'Equivocation and the Legal Conflict over Religious Identity in Early Modern England', *YJLH* 3 (2013), 33–52.

Halliwell, James Orchard, *The Nursery Rhymes of England, Chiefly Collected from Oral Tradition* (London: Bodley Head, 1970, rpt of 1842).

Hamilton, Alastair, *The Family of Love* (Cambridge: James Clark, 1981).

Hamilton, Donna B., 'Richard Verstegan's *A Restitution of Decayed Intelligence* (1605): A Catholic Antiquarian Replies to John Foxe, Thomas Cooper, and Jean Bodin', *Prose Studies* 22 (1999), 1–38.

Hamilton, Donna B., *Anthony Munday and the Catholics, 1560–1633* (Farnham: Ashgate, 2005).

Hamlin, William M., *Montaigne's English Journey: Reading the Essays in Shakespeare's Day* (Oxford: Oxford University Press, 2013).

Hamrick, Stephen, '*Tottel's Miscellany* and the English Reformation', *Criticism* 44 (2004), 329–61.

Hanson, Elizabeth, 'Torture and Truth in Renaissance England', *Representations* 34 (1991), 53–84.

Happé, Peter, ed., *Tudor Interludes* (Harmondsworth: Penguin, 1972).

Hardison, O. B., Jr, 'The Two Voices of Sidney's *Apology for Poetry*', *ELR* 2 (1972), 83–99.

Harris, Brian, *Passion, Poison, and Power: The Mysterious Death of Sir Thomas Overbury* (London: Wildy, Simmonds & Hill, 2010).

Harvey, Irene E., *Labyrinths of Exemplarity: At the Limits of Deconstruction* (Albany, NY: SUNY Press, 2012).

Haugaard, William P., *Elizabeth and the English Reformation: The Struggle for a Stable Settlement of Religion* (Cambridge: Cambridge University Press, 1968).

Hazlitt, William, *Liber Amoris and Dramatic Criticisms* (London: Peter Nevill, 1948).

Heal, Felicity, *Reformation in Britain and Ireland* (Oxford: Oxford University Press, 2003).

Heal, Felicity, 'Readership and Reception', in Paulina Kewes, Ian Archer, and Felicity Heal, eds, *The Oxford Handbook of Holinshed's* Chronicles (Oxford: Oxford University Press, 2013), pp. 355–72.

Healy, Margaret, *Fictions of Disease: Bodies, Plagues and Politics* (Basingstoke: Macmillan, 2001).

Hecht, Jamey, 'Limitations of Textuality in Thomas More's Confutation of Tyndale's Answer', *SCJ* 26 (1995), 823–8.

Helgerson, Richard, *The Elizabethan Prodigals* (Berkeley: University of California Press, 1976).

Helmholz, R. H., *Marriage Litigation in Medieval England* (Cambridge: Cambridge University Press, 1975).

Helmholz, R. H., 'Damages in Actions for Slander at Common Law', *LQR* 103 (1987), 624–38.

Helmholz, R. H., 'Natural Law and the Trial of Thomas More', in Kelly et al., eds, *Thomas More's Trial by Jury*, pp. 53–70.

Herman, Peter C., *Squitter-wits and Muse-haters: Sidney, Spenser, Milton, and Renaissance Antipoetic Sentiment* (Detroit: Wayne State University Press, 1996).

Herrup, Cynthia B., *A House in Gross Disorder: Sex, Law and the 2nd. Earl of Castlehaven* (New York: Oxford University Press, 1999).

Highley, Christopher, 'Richard Verstegan's Book of Martyrs', in Highley and King, eds, *Foxe and His World*, pp. 183–97.

Highley, Christopher, *Catholics Writing the Nation in Early Modern Britain and Ireland* (Oxford: Oxford University Press, 2008).

Highley, Christopher, and John N. King, eds, *John Foxe and His World* (Aldershot: Ashgate, 2002).

Higman, François, *Calvin*, trans. Philip Maret (London: Collins, 1963).

Hill, Christopher, *Milton and the English Revolution* (London: Faber, 1977).

Hill, Tracey, *Anthony Munday and Civic Culture: Theatre, History and Power in Early Modern London, 1580–1633* (Manchester: Manchester University Press, 2004).

Hillman, Richard, *Shakespeare, Marlowe and the Politics of France* (Basingstoke: Palgrave, 2002).

Hirsch, James, *Shakespeare and the History of Soliloquies* (Madison: Fairleigh Dickinson University Press, 2003).

Hiscock, Andrew, 'Blabbing Leaves of Betraying Paper: Configuring the Past in George Gascoignes's *The Adventures of Master F. J.*, Thomas Nashe's *The Unfortunate Traveller* and Thomas Deloney's *Jack of Newbury*', *English* 52 (2003), 1–20.

Hoak, Dale, 'Booby, Baby or Classical Monster? Henry VIII in the Writings of G. R. Elton and J. J. Scarisbrick', in Betteridge and Freeman, eds, *Henry VIII and History*, pp. 241–59.

Hoenselaars, Ton, *Images of Englishmen and Foreigners in the Drama of Shakespeare and His Contemporaries* (Cranbury, NJ: Associated University Presses, 1992).

Höfele, Andreas, *Stage, Stake, and Scaffold: Humans and Animals in Shakespeare's Theatre* (Oxford: Oxford University Press, 2011).

Holderness, Graham, *Shakespeare and Venice* (Farnham: Ashgate, 2013).

Holland, Peter, 'Resources of Characterization in *Othello*', *Sh. Sur.* 41 (1989), 119–32.

Holland, Peter, '"The Interpretation of Dreams" in the Renaissance', in Peter Brown, ed., *Reading Dreams: The Interpretation of Dreams from Chaucer to Shakespeare* (Oxford: Oxford University Press, 1999), pp. 125–46.

Hollander, John, *Melodious Guile: Fictive Pattern in Poetic Language* (New Haven: Yale University Press, 1990).

Holm, Poul, 'The Bohuslen Herring: Interlude to Dutch Supremacy in the European Fish Market, 1556–1589', in L. M. Akveld, F. Broeze, F. S. Gaastra, G. Jackson, and W. M. F. Morzer Bruyns, eds, *In Het Kielzog Maritiem-Historische Studies aangeboden aan Jaap R. Bruijn, bij zijn vertrek als hoogleraar zeegeschiedenis aan de Universiteit Leiden* (Amsterdam: De Bataafsche Leeuw, 2003), pp. 182–8.

Holmes, Peter, *Resistance and Compromise: The Political Thought of the Elizabethan Catholics* (Cambridge: Cambridge University Press, 1982).

Hoppe, Harry R., 'John Wolfe, Printer and Publisher', *The Library*, 4th series, 14 (1933), 241–89.

Horodowich, Elizabeth, 'Venetians in America: Nicolò Zen and the Virtual Exploration of the New World', *RQ* 67 (2014), 841–77.

Hotson, Howard, *Paradise Postponed: Johann Heinrich Alsted and the Birth of Calvinist Millenarianism* (Dordrecht: Springer, 2000).

Hotson, Howard, *Commonplace Learning: Ramism and its German Ramifications, 1543–1630* (Oxford: Oxford University Press, 2007).

Houlbrooke, Ralph, *Death, Religion, and the Family in England, 1480–1750* (Oxford: Oxford University Press, 1998).

Houliston, Victor, 'An Apology for Donne's *Pseudo-Martyr*', *RES*, ns, 57 (2006), 474–86.

Houliston, Victor, 'Fallen Prince and Pretender of the Faith: Henry VIII as Seen by Sander and Persons', in Betteridge and Freeman, eds, *Henry VIII and History*, pp. 119–34.

Houliston, Victor, 'Filling in the Blanks: Catholic Hopes for the English Succession', *YSPSR* 25 (2015), 77–104.

Howard, Jean E., 'Renaissance Antitheatricality and the Politics of Gender and Rank in *Much Ado About Nothing*', in Jean E. Howard and Marion O'Connor, eds, *Shakespeare Reproduced: The Text in History and Ideology* (London: Routledge, 1987), pp. 163–87.

Howard, Jean E., *Theater of a City: The Places of London Comedy, 1598–1642* (Philadelphia: University of Pennsylvania Press, 2011).

Howell, Roger, *Sir Philip Sidney: The Shepherd Knight* (London: Hutchinson, 1968).

Hubbard, G. R., 'Possible Evidence for the Date of Tamburlaine', *PMLA* 3 (1918), 436–43.

Hulme, Peter, *Colonial Encounters: Europe and the Native Caribbean, 1492–1797* (London: Methuen, 1986).

Hulme, Peter, 'Introduction: The Cannibal Scene', in Francis Barker, Peter Hulme, and Margaret Iversen, eds, *Cannibalism and the Colonial World* (Cambridge: Cambridge University Press, 1998), pp. 1–38.

Hume, Anthea, *Edmund Spenser: Protestant Poet* (Cambridge: Cambridge University Press, 1984).

Hunt, Alice, 'Marian Political Allegory: John Heywood's *The Spider and the Fly*', in Pincombe and Shrank, eds, *Oxford Handbook of Tudor Literature*, pp. 337–55.

Hunt, Arnold, *The Art of Hearing: English Preachers and their Audiences, 1590–1640* (Cambridge: Cambridge University Press, 2010).

Hunter, G. K., 'The Theology of Marlowe's The Jew of Malta', *JWCI* 27 (1964), 211–40.

Hutson, Lorna, *Thomas Nashe in Context* (Oxford: Clarendon Press, 1989).

Hutson, Lorna, 'Fortunate Travelers: Reading for the Plot in Sixteenth-Century England', *Representations* 41 (1993), 83–103.

Hutson, Lorna, *The Invention of Suspicion: Law and Mimesis in Shakespeare and Renaissance Drama* (Oxford: Oxford University Press, 2007). ·

Huyssen, Andreas, 'Introduction: World Cultures, World Cities', in Andreas Huyssen, ed., *Other Cities, Other Worlds: Urban Imaginaries in a Globalizing Age* (Durham, NC: Duke University Press, 2008), pp. 1–23.

Ibbotson, Michael, 'Sixteenth-Century Contract Law: Slade's Case in Context', *OJLS* 4 (1984), 295–317.

Iliffe, Rob, 'Lying Wonders and Juggling Tricks: Religion, Nature, and Imposture in Early Modern England', in James E. Force and David S. Katz, eds, *Everything Connects: In Conference with Richard Popkin, Essays in his Honour* (Leiden: Brill, 1999), pp. 183–209.

Innes, Brian, *Fakes and Forgeries: The True Crime Stories of History's Greatest Deceptions: The Criminals, the Scams, and the Victims* (London: Reader's Digest, 2005).

Ives, E. W., 'Faction at the Court of Henry VIII: The Fall of Anne Boleyn', *History* 57 (1972), 169–88.

Ives, E. W., 'The Fall of Anne Boleyn Reconsidered', *EHR* 107 (1992), 651–64.

Ives, E. W., *The Life and Death of Anne Boleyn* (Oxford: Blackwell, 2004).

Ives, E. W., *The Reformation Experience: Living Through the Turbulent Sixteenth Century* (Oxford: Lion, 2012).

Janin, Hunt, *Medieval Justice: Cases and Laws in France, England, and Germany: 500–1500* (Jefferson, NC: McFarland, 2004).

Jansen, Katherine, Joanna Drell, and Frances Andrews, eds, *Medieval Italy: Texts in Translation* (Philadelphia: University of Pennsylvania Press, 2010).

Jardine, Lisa, 'The Place of Dialectic Teaching in Sixteenth-Century Cambridge', *SR* 21 (1974), 31–62.

Jardine, Lisa, 'Humanist Logic', in Schmitt and Skinner, eds, *Cambridge History of Renaissance Philosophy*, pp. 173–98.

Jardine, Lisa, *Reading Shakespeare Historically* (London: Routledge, 1996).

Javitch, Daniel, *Poetry and Courtliness in Renaissance England* (Princeton: Princeton University Press, 1978).

Jenkins, James Travis, *The Herring and the Herring Fisheries* (London: P. S. King and Son, 1927).

Jewell, Helen M., *Education in Early Modern England* (Basingstoke: Palgrave, 1998).

Johnson, Gerald D., 'John Trundle and the Book-Trade, 1603–1626', *SB* 39 (1986), 178–99.

Johnson, Lynn Staley, The Shepheardes Calender: *An Introduction* (University Park: Penn State University Press, 1990).

Johnston, Mark D., 'The Treatment of Speech in Medieval Ethical and Courtesy Literature', *Rhetorica* 4 (1986), 21–46.

Johnstone, Nathan, *The Devil and Demonism in Early Modern England* (Cambridge: Cambridge University Press, 2006).

Jones, Emrys, *The Origins of Shakespeare* (Oxford: Clarendon Press, 1977).

Jones, Howard, *Master Tully: Cicero in Tudor England* (Nieuwkoop: De Graaf Publishers, 1998).

Jones, Norman, *The English Reformation: Religion and Cultural Adaptation* (Oxford: Blackwell, 2002).

Jones, Norman, *Governing by Virtue: Lord Burghley and the Management of Elizabethan England* (Oxford: Oxford University Press, 2015).

Jonsen, Albert R., and Stephen Toulmin, *The Abuse of Casuistry: A History of Moral Reasoning* (Berkeley: University of California Press, 1988).

Jordanova, Ludmilla, *History in Practice* (2nd edn, London: Arnold, 2006).

Jorgensen, Paul A., 'Honesty in *Othello*', *SP* 47 (1950), 557–67.

Josipovici, Gabriel, *The Book of God: A Response to the Bible* (New Haven: Yale University Press, 1988).

Jost, Walter, and Wendy Olmsted, eds, *A Companion to Rhetoric and Rhetorical Criticism* (Oxford: Blackwell, 2004).

Jouanna, Jacques, *Greek Medicine from Hippocrates to Galen: Selected Papers* (Leiden: Brill, 2012).

Jowitt, Claire, 'Hakluyt's Legacy: Armchair Travel in English Renaissance Drama', in Daniel Carey and Claire Jowitt, eds, *Richard Hakluyt and Travel Writing in Early Modern Europe* (Farnham: Ashgate, 2012), pp. 295–306.

Kahn, Coppélia, 'Reading Faces in *Hamlet*', in Panja, ed., *Shakespeare and the Art of Lying*, pp. 37–58.

Kahn, Victoria, 'Reading Machiavelli: Innocent Gentillet's *Discourse on Method*', *PT* 22 (1994), 539–60.

Kane, Bronach, *Impotence and Virginity in the Late Medieval Ecclesiastical Court of York* (York: University of York, 2008), Borthwick Paper No. 114.

Kaplan, M. Lindsay, *The Culture of Slander in Early Modern England* (Cambridge: Cambridge University Press, 1997).

Karlin, Louis, 'More's Dialogue Concerning Heresies and the Idea of the Church', *More Studies* 3 (2008), 32–40.

Kastan, David Scott, *A Will to Believe: Shakespeare and Religion* (Oxford: Oxford University Press, 2014).

Katz, David S., *The Jews in the History of England, 1485–1850* (Oxford: Oxford University Press, 1994).

Kelly, Erin E., '*Conflict of Conscience* and Sixteenth-Century Religious Drama', *ELR* 44 (2014), 388–419.

Kelly, Henry Ansgar, 'A Procedural Review of Thomas More's Trial', in Kelly, Karlin, and Wegemer, eds, *Thomas More's Trial by Jury*, pp. 1–52.

Kelly, Henry Ansgar, Louis W. Karlin, and Gerard B. Wegemer, eds, *Thomas More's Trial by Jury: A Procedural and Legal Review with a Collection of Documents* (Woodbridge: Boydell, 2011).

Kendall, R. T., *Calvin and English Calvinism to 1649* (Oxford: Oxford University Press, 1979).

Kenny, Anthony, 'Antony Munday in Rome', *RH* 6 (1962), 158–62.

Kernan, Alvin, *The Cankered Muse: Satire of the English Renaissance* (New Haven: Yale University Press, 1959).

Kerr, Philip, ed., *The Penguin Book of Lies* (Harmondsworth: Penguin, 1990).

Kerrigan, John, *Shakespeare's Binding Language* (Oxford: Oxford University Press, 2016).

Kesselring, K. J., 'A Draft of the 1531 "Acte for Poysoning"', *EHR* 116 (2001), 894–9.

Kesselring, K. J., *Mercy and Authority in the Tudor State* (Cambridge: Cambridge University Press, 2003).

Kesselring, K. J., *The Northern Rebellion of 1569: Faith, Politics, and Protest in Elizabethan England* (Basingstoke: Palgrave Macmillan, 2007).

Kesson, Andy, *John Lyly and Early Modern Authorship* (Manchester: Manchester University Press, 2014).

Kewes, Paulina, ed., *Plagiarism in Early Modern England* (Basingstoke: Palgrave Macmillan, 2003).

Kilday, Anne-Marie, *A History of Infanticide in Britain, c.1600 to the Present* (Basingstoke: Palgrave Macmillan, 2013).

Kilroy, Gerard, *Edmund Campion: Memory and Transcription* (Farnham: Ashgate, 2005).

Kilroy, Gerard, *Edmund Campion: A Scholarly Life* (Farnham: Ashgate, 2015).

King, John N., *English Reformation Literature: The Tudor Origins of the Protestant Tradition* (Princeton: Princeton University Press, 1982).

King, John N., *Spenser's Poetry and the Reformation Tradition* (Princeton: Princeton University Press, 1990).

King, John N., '"The Light of Printing": William Tyndale, John Day, and Early Modern Print Culture', *RQ* 54 (2001), 52–85.

King, John N., *Foxe's 'Book of Martyrs' and Early Modern Print Culture* (Cambridge: Cambridge University Press, 2006).

Kingdon, Robert M., *Myths about the St. Bartholomew's Day Massacres, 1572–1576* (Cambridge, MA: Harvard University Press, 1988).

Kinney, Arthur F., 'Continental Poetics', in Jost and Olmsted, eds, *Companion to Rhetoric and Rhetorical Criticism*, pp. 80–95.

Kirk, Kenneth E., *Conscience and Its Problems: An Introduction to Casuistry* (London: Longmans, 1927).

Kirkpatrick, Robin, *The European Renaissance 1400–1600* (London: Routledge, 2014).

Kitch, Aaron, *Political Economy and the States of Literature in Early Modern England* (Farnham: Ashgate, 2009).

Kittsteiner, H. D., 'Kant and Casuistry', in Leites, ed., *Conscience and Casuistry*, pp. 185–213.

Klein, Bernhard, *Maps and the Writing of Space in Early Modern England and Ireland* (Basingstoke: Palgrave, 2001).

Kneidel, Gregory, 'Hard Hearts and Scandal', in Mary Arshagouni Papazian, ed., *The Sacred and Profane in English Renaissance Literature* (Newark: University of Delaware Press, 2008), pp. 236–52.

Knellwolf King, Christa, *Faustus and the Promises of the New Science, C. 1580–1730: From the Chapbooks to Harlequin Faustus* (Farnham: Ashgate, 2008).

Knowles, Ronald, *Shakespeare's Arguments with History* (Basingstoke: Palgrave, 2001).

Kocher, Paul H., 'François Hotman and Marlowe's *The Massacre at Paris*', *PMLA* 56 (1941), 349–68.

Kolb, Robert, 'The Influence of Luther's Galatians Commentary of 1535 on Later Sixteenth-Century Lutheran Commentaries on Galatians', *Archiv für Reformationsgeschichte* 84 (1993), 156–84.

Korhonen, Anu, 'The Witch in the Alehouse: Imaginary Encounters in Cultural History', in Jan Kusber, Mechthild Dreyer, Jörg Rogge, and Andreas Hütig, eds, *Historische Kulturwissenschaften: Positionen, Praktiken und Perspektiven* (Bielefeld: Transcript Verlag, 2010), pp. 181–205.

Korsgaard, Christine, 'The Right to Lie: Kant on Dealing with Evil', *Philosophy and Public Affairs* 15 (1986), 325–49.

Krantz, Susan E., 'Thomas Dekker's Political Commentary in *The Whore of Babylon*', *SEL* 35 (1995), 271–91.

Kraye, Jill, 'Moral Philosophy', in Schmitt and Skinner, eds, *Cambridge History of Renaissance Philosophy*, pp. 303–86.

Krostenko, B. A., 'Text and Context in the Roman Forum: The Case of Cicero's *First Catilinarian*', in Jost and Olmsted, eds, *Companion to Rhetoric and Rhetorical Criticism*, pp. 38–57.

Künne, Wolfgang, 'On Liars, "Liars", and Harmless Self-Reference', in Anne Reboul, ed., *Mind, Values, and Metaphysics: Philosophical Essays in Honor of Kevin Mulligan* (New York: Springer, 2014), pp. 355–431.

Kurlansky, Mark, *Cod: A Biography of the Fish that Changed the World* (London: Vintage, 1999).

La Rocca, John J., 'James I and his Catholic Subjects, 1606–1612: Some Financial Implications', *RH* 18 (1987), 251–62.

Lake, Peter, *Moderate Puritans and the Elizabethan Church* (Cambridge: Cambridge University Press, 1982).

Lake, Peter, 'Calvinism and the English Church 1570–1635', *P. & P.* 114 (1987), 32–76.

Lake, Peter, 'Anti-Popery: The Structure of a Prejudice', in Richard Cust and Ann Hughes, eds, *Conflict in Early Stuart England: Studies in Religion and Politics, 1603–1642* (Harlow: Longman, 1989), pp. 72–106.

Lake, Peter, 'Religion and Cheap Print', in Raymond, ed., *Oxford History of Popular Print Culture*, pp. 217–41.

Lake, Peter, *Bad Queen Bess? Libels, Secret Histories, and the Politics of Publicity in the Reign of Queen Elizabeth I* (Oxford: Oxford University Press, 2016).

Lake, Peter, and Michael Questier, 'Puritans, Papists, and the "Public Sphere": The Edmund Campion Affair in Context', *JMH* 72 (2000), 587–627.

Lake, Peter, with Michael Questier, *The Antichrist's Lewd Hat: Protestants, Papists and Players in Post-Reformation England* (New Haven: Yale University Press, 2002).

Lander, Jesse M., *Inventing Polemic: Religion, Print, and Literary Culture in Early Modern England* (Cambridge: Cambridge University Press, 2006).

Landreth, David, 'Wit Without Money in Nashe', in Guy-Bray, Linton, and Mentz, eds, *The Age of Thomas Nashe*, pp. 135–52.

Langbein, John H., *Prosecuting Crime in the Renaissance: England, Germany, France* (Cambridge, MA: Harvard University Press, 1974).

Langbein, John H., *Torture and the Law of Proof* (Chicago: University of Chicago Press, 1976).

Langley, Eric, *Narcissism and Suicide in Shakespeare and his Contemporaries* (Oxford: Oxford University Press, 2009).

Lawrence, Jason, *'Who the devil taught thee so much Italian?': Italian Language Learning and Literary Imitation in Early Modern England* (Manchester: Manchester University Press, 2005).

Lehmberg, Stanford E., *The Reformation Parliament, 1529–1536* (Cambridge: Cambridge University Press, 1970).

Leites, Edmund, ed., *Conscience and Casuistry in Early Modern Europe* (Cambridge: Cambridge University Press, 1988).

Lemon, Rebecca, *Treason by Words: Literature, Law, and Rebellion in Shakespeare's England* (Ithaca, NY: Cornell University Press, 2006).

Lerer, Seth, 'Aesop, Authorship, and the Aesthetic Imagination', *JMEMS* 37 (2007), 579–94.

Leslie, Ian, *Born Liars: Why We Can't Live Without Deceit* (London: Quercus, 2011).

Letts, Malcolm, 'Of Lying Travellers', *CR* 96 (1920), 95–100.

Letts, Malcolm, *Sir John Mandeville: The Man and his Book* (London: Batchworth, 1949).

Levine, Timothy R., ed., *Encyclopedia of Deception* (New York: Sage, 2014).

Levy, Fritz, 'The Decorum of News', in Joad Raymond, ed., *News, Newspapers and Society in Early Modern Britain* (London: Frank Cass, 1999), pp. 12–38.

Lewis, C. S., *English Literature in the Sixteenth Century Excluding Drama* (Oxford: Oxford University Press, 1973, rpt of 1954).

Lewis, Michael, 'The Development of Deception', in Lewis and Saarni, eds, *Lying and Deception*, pp. 90–105.

Lewis, Michael, and Carolyn Saarni, eds, *Lying and Deception in Everyday Life* (New York: Guilford Press, 1993).

Lewis, Michael, and Carolyn Saarni, 'Deceit and Illusion in Human Affairs', in Lewis and Saarni, eds, *Lying and Deception*, pp. 1–29.

Lievsay, John Leon, *Stefano Guazzo and the English Renaissance, 1575–1675* (Chapel Hill: University of North Carolina Press, 1961).

Linden, Stanton J., *Dark Hieroglipicks: Alchemy in English Literature from Chaucer to the Restoration* (Lexington: University Press of Kentucky, 1996).

Lindley, David, 'Embarrassing Ben: The Masques for Frances Howard', *ELR* 16 (1986), 434–59.

Lindley, David, *The Trials of Frances Howard: Fact and Fiction at the Court of King James* (London: Routledge, 1993).

Linton, Joan Pong, 'Counterfeiting Sovereignty, Mocking Mastery: Trickster Poetics and the Critique of Romance in Nashe's *Unfortunate Traveller*', in Naomi Conn Liebler, ed.,

Early Modern Prose Fiction: The Cultural Politics of Reading (London: Routledge, 2007), pp. 130–47.

Littlewood, Ian, *Sultry Climates: Travel and Sex Since the Grand Tour* (London: John Murray, 2001).

Loach, Jennifer, *Edward VI*, ed. George Bernard and Penry Williams (New Haven: Yale University Press, 1999).

Loades, David, *The Reign of Mary Tudor: Politics, Government and Religion in England 1553–58* (2nd edn, Harlow: Longman, 1991).

Loades, David, 'The Early Reception', 'John Foxe's Acts and Monuments Online' (http://www.johnfoxe.org/index.php?realm=more&gototype=modern&type=essay&book=essay7) (accessed 18 August 2015).

Loar, Carol, '"Under Felt Hats and Worsted Stockings": The Uses of Conscience in Early Modern English Coroners' Inquests', *C16J* 41 (2010), 393–414.

Lockyer, Roger, *The Early Stuarts: A Political History of England, 1603–1642* (London: Longman, 1989).

Lockyer, Roger, *James VI and I* (London: Longman, 1998).

Loewenstein, David, *Treacherous Faith: The Specter of Heresy in Early Modern English Literature and Culture* (Oxford: Oxford University Press, 2013).

Lohr, Charles H., 'Metaphysics', in Schmitt and Skinner, eds, *Cambridge History of Renaissance Philosophy*, pp. 537–638.

Loomba, Ania, *Gender, Race, Renaissance Drama* (Manchester: Manchester University Press, 1989).

Loomba, Ania, *Shakespeare, Race, and Colonialism* (Oxford: Oxford University Press, 2002).

Loomie, Albert J., S.J., *The Spanish Elizabethans: The English Exiles at the Court of Philip II* (New York: Fordham University Press, 1963).

López, Jorge Fernández, 'Quintilian as Rhetorician and Teacher', in Dominik and Hall, eds, *Companion to Roman Rhetoric*, pp. 307–22.

Loury, Glenn C., 'Self-Censorship in Public Discourse: A Theory of "Political Correctness" and Related Phenomena', *Rationality and Society* 6 (1994), 428–61.

Loxley, James, *The Complete Critical Guide to Ben Jonson* (London: Routledge, 2002).

Luborsky, Ruth Samson, and Elizabeth Morley Ingram, *A Guide to English Illustrated Books, 1536–1603*, 2 vols (Tempe, AZ: MRTS, 1998).

Lucas, Scott, *A Mirror for Magistrates and the Politics of the English Reformation* (Amherst: University of Massachusetts Press, 2009).

Lunney, Ruth, *Marlowe and the Popular Tradition: Innovation in the English Drama before 1595* (Manchester: Manchester University Press, 2002).

Lupton, Julia Reinhard, '*The Jew of Malta*', in Cheney, ed., *Cambridge Companion to Marlowe*, pp. 144–57.

Lupton, Julia Reinhard, 'Paul Shakespeare: Exegetical Exercises', in Elizabeth Williamson and Jane Hwang Degenhardt, eds, *Religion and Drama in Early Modern England: The Performance of Religion on the Renaissance Stage* (Farnham: Ashgate, 2013), pp. 209–31.

McCabe, Richard A., 'The Masks of Duessa: Spenser, Mary Queen of Scots, and James VI', *ELR* 17 (1987), 224–42.

McCabe, Richard A., *Incest, Drama, and Nature's Law 1550–1700* (Cambridge: Cambridge University Press, 1993).

MacCaffrey, Wallace, *The Shaping of the Elizabethan Regime* (London: Cape, 1969).

McCanles, Michael, 'Paradox in Donne', *SR* 13 (1966), 266–87.

McCoog, Thomas M., *'And Touching Our Society': Fashioning Jesuit Identity in Elizabethan England* (Toronto: PIMS, 2013).

MacCulloch, Diarmaid, *Thomas Cranmer: A Life* (New Haven: Yale University Press, 1996).

MacCulloch, Diarmaid, 'Archbishop Cranmer: Concord and Tolerance in a Changing Church', in Grell and Scribner, eds, *Tolerance and Intolerance*, pp. 199–215.

MacCulloch, Diarmaid, *Reformation: Europe's House Divided, 1490–1700* (London: Penguin, 2004).

McDiarmid, John F., ' "To Content God Quietlie": The Troubles of Sir John Cheke under Queen Mary', in Elizabeth Evenden and Vivienne Westbrook, eds, *Catholic Renewal and Protestant Resistance in Marian England* (Farnham: Ashgate, 2015), pp. 185–27.

McGinn, Donald J., *Thomas Nashe* (Boston: Twayne, 1981).

MacGrath, Patrick, 'The Bloody Question Reconsidered', *RH* 20 (1991), 415–35.

MacIntyre, Alasdair, 'Truthfulness, Lies, and Moral Philosophers: What Can We Learn from Mill and Kant?', *Tanner Lectures on Human Values*, pp. 309–69 (Princeton University) (tannerlectures.utah.edu/_documents/a-to-z/m/macintyre_1994.pdf).

Mack, Peter, *Elizabethan Rhetoric: Theory and Practice* (Cambridge: Cambridge University Press, 2002).

Mack, Peter, *Reading and Rhetoric in Montaigne and Shakespeare* (London: Black, 2010).

Mack, Peter, *A History of Renaissance Rhetoric, 1380–1620* (Oxford: Oxford University Press, 2011).

Mackay, James, *In My End is My Beginning: A Life of Mary Queen of Scots* (Edinburgh: Mainstream, 1999).

McLane, Paul E., *Spenser's Shepheardes Calender: A Study in Elizabethan Allegory* (Notre Dame: University of Notre Dame Press, 1961).

McLaren, Anne C., *Political Culture in the Reign of Elizabeth I: Queen and Commonwealth, 1558–1585* (Cambridge: Cambridge University Press, 1999).

Maclean, Ian, *Interpretation and Meaning in the Renaissance: The Case of Law* (Cambridge: Cambridge University Press, 1992).

McMahon, Vanessa, *Murder in Shakespeare's England* (London: Black, 2006).

McPherson, David C., *Shakespeare, Jonson and the Myth of Venice* (Newark: University of Delaware Press, 1990).

McShane, Angela, 'Material Culture and "Political Drinking" in Seventeenth-Century England', in Withington and McShane, eds, *Cultures of Intoxication*, pp. 247–76.

Maghenzani, Simone, 'The Protestant Reformation in Counter-Reformation Italy, c.1550–1660: An Overview of New Evidence', *CH* 83 (2014), 571–89.

Mahler, Andreas, 'Writing Venice: Paradoxical Signification as Connotational Feature', in Manfred Pfister and Barbara Schaff, eds, *Venetian Views, Venetian Blinds: English Fantasies of Venice* (Amsterdam: Rodopi, 1999), pp. 29–44.

Malay, Jessica L., *Prophecy and Sibyline Imagery in the Renaissance: Shakespeare's Sibyls* (Abingdon: Routledge, 2010).

Maley, Willy, ' "And bloody England into England gone": Empire, Monarchy, and Nation in *King John*', in Willy Maley and Margaret Tudeau-Clayton, eds, *This England, that Shakespeare: New Angles on Englishness and the Bard* (Farnham: Ashgate, 2010), pp. 49–61.

Mallette, Richard, *Spenser and the Discourses of Reformation England* (Lincoln: University of Nebraska Press, 1997).

Malloch, A. E., 'John Donne and the Casuists', *SEL* 2 (1962), 57–76.

Malloch, A. E., 'Father Henry Garnet's Treatise of Equivocation', *RH* 15 (1981), 387–95.

Manley, Lawrence, *Literature and Culture in Early Modern London* (Cambridge: Cambridge University Press, 1995).

Marius, Richard, *Thomas More: A Biography* (New Haven: Yale University Press, 1984).

Marsh, Christopher W., *The Family of Love in English Society, 1550–1630* (Cambridge: Cambridge University Press, 1994).

Marshall, Herbert, and Mildred Stock, *Ira Aldridge: The Negro Tragedian* (Carbondale: Southern Illinois University Press, 1968).

Martin, Randall, *Women, Murder, and Equity in Early Modern England* (Abingdon: Routledge, 2007).

Martz, Louis L., *The Poetry of Meditation: A Study in English Religious Literature of the Seventeenth Century* (rev. edn, New Haven: Yale University Press, 1962).

Martz, Louis L., *Thomas More: The Search for the Inner Man* (New Haven: Yale University Press, 1990).

Maslen, Robert W., *Elizabethan Fictions: Espionage, Counter-Espionage, and the Duplicity of Fiction in Early Elizabethan Prose Narratives* (Oxford: Clarendon Press, 1997).

Maslen, Robert W., 'William Baldwin and the Politics of Pseudo-Philosophy in Tudor Prose Fiction', *SP* 97 (2000), 29–60.

Maslen, Robert W., 'The Healing Dialogues of Doctor Bullein', *YES* 38 (2008), 119–35.

Mattingly, Garrett, *Renaissance Diplomacy* (Harmondsworth: Penguin, 1964, rpt of 1955).

Matz, Robert, *Defending Literature in Early Modern England: Renaissance Literary Theory in Social Context* (Cambridge: Cambridge University Press, 2000).

Maule, Jeremy, 'Donne and the Words of the Law', in David Colclough, ed., *John Donne's Professional Lives* (Woodbridge: Brewer, 2003), pp. 19–36.

Maus, Katharine Eisaman, 'Proof and Consequences: Inwardness and its Exposure in the English Renaissance', *Representations* 34 (1991), 29–52.

Maus, Katharine Eisaman, *Inwardness and Theater in the English Renaissance* (Chicago: University of Chicago Press, 1995).

Mayer, Jean-Christoph, ed., *Representing France and the French in Early Modern English Drama* (Newark: University of Delaware Press, 2008).

Mazella, David, *The Making of Modern Cynicism* (Charlottesville: University of Virginia Press, 2007).

Mears, Natalie, *Queenship and Political Discourse in the Elizabethan Realms* (Cambridge: Cambridge University Press, 2005).

Mendes, Maria, 'Hamlet's Ordeals', *Law and Hum.* 8 (2014), 269–89.

Mentz, Steve, *Romance for Sale in Early Modern England: The Rise of Prose Fiction* (Aldershot: Ashgate, 2006).

Merback, Mitchell B., 'Nobody Dares: Freedom, Dissent, Self-Knowing, and Other Possibilities in Sebald Beham's *Impossible*', *RQ* 63 (2010), 1037–105.

Merritt, J. F., ed., *Imagining Early Modern London: Perceptions and Portrayals of the City from Stow to Strype, 1598–1720* (Cambridge: Cambridge University Press, 2001).

Metcalf, Peter, *They Lie, We Lie: Getting On with Anthropology* (London: Routledge, 2002).

Milner, Matthew, *The Senses and the English Reformation* (Farnham: Ashgate, 2013).

Mitchell, A. R., 'The European Fisheries in Early Modern Europe', in E. E. Rich and C. H. Wilson, eds, *The Cambridge Economic History of Europe, Volume 5: The Economic Organization of Early Modern Europe* (Cambridge: Cambridge University Press, 1977), pp. 133–84.

Mitchell, Robert W., 'Animals as Liars: The Human Face of Nonhuman Duplicity', in Lewis and Saarni, eds, *Lying and Deception*, pp. 59–89.

Moller, Herbert, 'The Accelerated Development of Youth: Beard Growth as a Biological Marker', *CSSH* 29 (1987), 748–62.

Monta, Susannah Brietz, *Martyrdom and Literature in Early Modern England* (Cambridge: Cambridge University Press, 2005).

Monter, William, 'Heresy Executions in Reformation Europe, 1520–1565', in Grell and Sribner, eds, *Tolerance and Intolerance*, pp. 48–64.

Moran, Richard, 'Getting Told and Being Believed', *PI* 5 (2005), 1–29.

Morey, Adrian, *The Catholic Subjects of Elizabeth I* (London: George Allen and Unwin, 1978).

Morris, Stephen, 'Political Correctness', *JPE* 109 (2001), 231–65.

Moseley, Charles W. R. D., '"Whet-stone Leasings of Old *Maundeulie*: Reading the *Travels* in Early Modern England', in Ladan Niayesh, ed., *A Knight's Legacy: Mandeville and Mandevillian Lore in Early Modern England* (Manchester: Manchester University Press, 2011), pp. 28–50.

Moss, Ann, *Printed Commonplace-Books and the Structuring of Renaissance Thought* (Oxford: Clarendon Press, 1996).

Moss, Ann, 'Literary Imitation in the Sixteenth Century: Writers and Readers, Latin and French', in Norton, ed., *Cambridge History of Literary Criticism, Vol. III*, pp. 107–18.

Mosse, George L., *The Holy Pretence: A Study in Christianity and Reason of State from William Perkins to John Winthrop* (New York: Howard Fertig, 1968, rpt of 1957).

Moul, Victoria, *Jonson, Horace and the Classical Tradition* (Cambridge: Cambridge University Press, 2010).

Mousley, Andrew, 'Self, State, and Seventeenth-Century News', *The Seventeenth Century* 6 (1991), 149–68.

Mukherji, Subha, *Law and Representation in Early Modern Drama* (Cambridge: Cambridge University Press, 2006).

Muldrew, Craig, *The Economy of Obligation: The Culture of Credit and Social Relations in Early Modern England* (Basingstoke: Palgrave, 1998).

Munslow, Alan, and Robert A. Rosenstone, eds, *Experiments in Rethinking History* (London: Routledge, 2004).

Murphy, Emilie K. M., 'Musical Self-Fashioning and the "Theatre of Death" in Late Elizabethan and Jacobean England', *RS* 30 (2016), 410–30.

Murphy, Virginia, 'The Literature and Propaganda of Henry VIII's First Divorce', in Diarmaid MacCulloch, ed., *The Reign of Henry VIII: Politics, Policy and Piety* (Basingstoke: Palgrave, 1995), pp. 135–58.

Murray, Jacqueline, 'On the Origins and Role of "Wise Women" in Causes for Annulment on the Grounds of Male Impotence', *Journal of Medieval History* 16 (1990), 235–49.

Murray, Molly, *The Poetics of Conversion in Early Modern English Literature: Verse and Change from Donne to Dryden* (Cambridge: Cambridge University Press, 2009).

Myers, Jason A., 'Law, Lies and Letter Writing: An Analysis of Jerome and Augustine on the Antioch Incident (Galations 2: 11–14)', *SJT* 66 (2013), 127–39.

Najemy, John M., *A History of Florence, 1200–1575* (Oxford: Blackwell, 2006).

Najemy, John M., 'Machiavelli and History', *RQ* 67 (2014), 1131–64.

Neill, Michael, *Putting History to the Question: Power, Politics, and Society in English Renaissance Drama* (New York: Columbia University Press, 2000).

Nelson, Alan H., *Monstrous Adversity: The Life of Edward de Vere, 17th Earl of Oxford* (Liverpool: Liverpool University Press, 2003).

Newcomb, Lori Humphrey, 'A Looking Glass for Readers: Cheap Print and the Senses of Repentance', in Kirk Melinikoff and Edward Gieskes, eds, *Writing Robert Greene: Essays on England's First Notorious Professional Writer* (Aldershot: Ashgate, 2008), pp. 133–56.

Nicholl, Charles, *A Cup of News: The Life of Thomas Nashe* (London: Routledge, 1984).

Nicholl, Charles, *The Reckoning: The Murder of Christopher Marlowe* (London: Picador, 1993, rpt of 1992).

Nicholls, David, 'The Political Theology of John Donne', *TS* 49 (1988), 45–66.

Nicholls, Mark, *Investigating Gunpowder Plot* (Manchester: Manchester University Press, 1991).

Nicholls, Mark, 'Treason's Reward: The Punishment of Conspirators in the Bye Plot of 1603', *HJ* 38 (1995), 821–42.

Nicholls, Mark, and Penry Williams, *Sir Walter Raleigh in Life and Legend* (London: Continuum, 2011).

Nicholson, Catherine, *Uncommon Tongues: Eloquence and Eccentricity in the English Renaissance* (Philadelphia: University of Pennsylvania Press, 2014).

Nievergelt, Marco, *Allegorical Quests: From Deguiville to Spenser* (Woodbridge: D. S. Brewer, 2012).

Nohrnberg, James, *The Analogy of* The Faerie Queene (Princeton: Princeton University Press, 1976).

Nolan, John S., *Sir John Norreys and the Elizabethan Military World* (Exeter: University of Exeter Press, 1997).

North, Marcy L., 'Anonymity's Subject: James I and the Debate over the Oath of Allegiance', *NLH* 33 (2002), 215–33.

Norton, David, *A History of the Bible as Literature, Volume 1: From Antiquity to 1700* (Cambridge: Cambridge University Press, 1993).

Norton, Glyn P. , ed., *The Cambridge History of Literary Criticism, Vol. III: The Renaissance* (Cambridge: Cambridge University Press, 1999).

Nuttall, A. D., *A New Mimesis: Shakespeare and the Representation of Reality* (London: Methuen, 1983).

Nuttall, A. D., *Shakespeare the Thinker* (New Haven: Yale University Press, 2007).

Oakley, Francis, 'Christian Obedience and Authority, 1520–1550', in Burns and Goldie, eds, *Cambridge History of Political Thought*, pp. 160–92.

Oakley-Brown, Liz, *Ovid and the Cultural Politics of Translation in Early Modern England* (Aldershot: Ashgate, 2006).

Oberman, Heiko A., 'Containing Chaos in Early Modern Europe', in Grell and Scribner, eds, *Tolerance and Intolerance*, pp. 13–31.

Oborne, Peter, *The Rise of Political Lying* (London: Simon & Schuster, 2005).

O'Callaghan, Michelle, *The English Wits: Literature and Sociability in Early Modern England* (Cambridge: Cambridge University Press, 2007).

Ohler, Norbert, *The Medieval Traveller*, trans. Caroline Hillier (Woodbridge: Boydell, 1989).

Olsen, V. N., *John Foxe and the Elizabethan Church* (Berkeley: University of California Press, 1973).

Olson, Greta, *Criminals as Animals from Shakespeare to Lombroso* (Berlin: Walter de Gruyter, 2014).

Opie, Iona, and Peter Opie, *The Oxford Dictionary of Nursery Rhymes* (rev. edn, Oxford: Oxford University Press, 1997).

O'Reilly, Gregory W., 'England Limits the Right to Silence and Moves towards an Inquisitorial System of Justice', *JCLC* 85 (1994), 402–52.

Orlin, Lena Cowen, 'A Case for Anecdotalism in Women's History: The Witness Who Spoke When the Cock Crowed', *ELR* 31 (2001), 52–77.

Orlin, Lena Cowen, *Locating Privacy in Tudor London* (Oxford: Oxford University Press, 2007).

Orr, D. Alan, *Treason and the State: Law, Politics and Ideology in the English Civil War* (Cambridge: Cambridge University Press, 2002).

O'Sullivan, Orlaith, ed., *The Bible as Book: The Reformation* (London: British Library/Oak Knoll Press, 2000).

Overall, M. A., 'The Exploitation of Francesco Spiera', *C16J* 26 (1995), 619–37.

Padelford, Frederick M., 'Spenser and the Theology of Calvin', *MP* 12 (1914), 1–18.

Pagden, Anthony, *The Fall of Natural Man: The American Indian and the Origins of Comparative Ethnology* (Cambridge: Cambridge University Press, 1986).

Palmer, Patricia, *The Severed Head and the Grafted Tongue: Literature, Translation and Violence in Early Modern Ireland* (Cambridge: Cambridge University Press, 2014).

Palmieri, John J., and Theodore A. Stern, 'Lies in the Doctor–Patient Relationship', *The Primary Care Companion to the Journal of Clinical Psychiatry* 11 (2009), 163–8.

Panja, Shormishtha, ed., *Shakespeare and the Art of Lying* (Hyderabad: Orient BlackSwan, 2013).

Panja, Shormishtha, 'Introduction', in Panja, ed., *Shakespeare and the Art of Lying*, pp. 1–13.

Papazian, Mary Arshagouni, *John Donne and the Protestant Reformation: New Perspectives* (Detroit: Wayne State University Press, 2003).

Parish, Helen L., *Clerical Marriage and the English Reformation: Precedent, Policy and Practice* (Farnham: Ashgate, 2000).

Parish, Helen L., '"Monks, Miracles and Magic": The Medieval Church in English Reformation Polemic', *Reformation* 8 (2003), 117–42.

Parish, Helen L., *Monks, Miracles and Magic: Reformation Representations of the Medieval Church* (London: Routledge, 2005).

Parker, Geoffrey, *The Army of Flanders and the Spanish Road, 1567–1659* (Cambridge: Cambridge University Press, 1972).

Parker, Patricia, *Inescapable Romance: Studies in the Poetics of a Mode* (Princeton: Princeton University Press, 1979).

Partner, Peter, *Renaissance Rome, 1500–1559: A Portrait of a Society* (Berkeley: University of California Press, 1976).

Pask, Kevin, *The Emergence of the English Author: Scripting the Life of the Poet in Early Modern England* (Cambridge: Cambridge University Press, 1996).

Patterson, Annabel, *Fables of Power: Aesopian Writing and Political History* (Durham, NC: Duke University Press, 1991).

Patterson, W. B., *King James VI and I and the Reunion of Christendom* (Cambridge: Cambridge University Press, 1997).

Paul, Joanne, 'The Use of *Kairos* in Renaissance Political Philosophy', *RQ* 67 (2014), 43–78.

Paul, Joanne, 'The Best Counsellors are Dead: Counsel and Shakespeare's *Hamlet*', *RQ* 30 (2016), 646–65.

Paulson, Bo, *Dutch Herring: An Environmental History, C. 1600–1860* (Amsterdam: Aksant, 2008).

Peltonen, Markku, *The Duel in Early Modern England: Civility, Politeness and Honour* (Cambridge: Cambridge University Press, 2003).

Perry, Curtis, *The Making of Jacobean Culture* (Cambridge: Cambridge University Press, 1997).

Perry, Curtis, *Literature and Favoritism in Early Modern England* (Cambridge: Cambridge University Press, 2006).

Peters, Edward, *Torture* (Oxford: Blackwell, 1985).

Petrina, Alessandra, *Machiavelli in the British Isles: Two Early Modern Translations of* The Prince (Farnham: Ashgate, 2009).

Pettegree, Andrew, *Marian Protestantism: Six Studies* (Aldershot: Scolar, 1996).

Pettegree, Andrew, 'The Politics of Toleration in the Free Netherlands', in Grell and Scribner, eds, *Tolerance and Intolerance*, pp. 182–98.

Pettegree, Andrew, 'The Spread of Calvin's Thought', in Donald McGinn, ed., *The Cambridge Companion to Calvin* (Cambridge: Cambridge University Press, 2004), pp. 207–24.

Pettegree, Andrew, *Reformation and the Culture of Persuasion* (Cambridge: Cambridge University Press, 2005).

Pettegree, Andrew, *The Invention of News: How the World Came to Know about Itself* (New Haven: Yale University Press, 2014).

Phillips, James Emerson, *Images of a Queen: Mary Stuart in Sixteenth-Century Literature* (Berkeley: University of California Press, 1964).

Phillips, Joshua, *English Fictions of Communal Identity, 1485–1603* (Farnham: Ashgate, 2010).

Pigman, G. W., III, *Grief and English Renaissance Elegy* (Cambridge: Cambridge University Press, 1985).

Pilarz, Scott, '"Campion Dead Bites with his Friends' Teeth": Representations of an Early Modern Catholic Martyr', in Highley and King, eds, *Foxe and His World*, pp. 216–31.

Pincombe, Mike, 'Tragic and Untragic Bodies in *The Mirror for Magistrates*', in Archer and Hadfield, eds, Mirror for Magistrates *in Context*.

Pincombe, Mike, and Cathy Shrank, eds, *The Oxford Handbook of Tudor Literature, 1485–1603* (Oxford: Oxford University Press, 2009).

Pineas, Rainer, 'Thomas More's Use of Humor as a Weapon of Religious Controversy', *SP* 58 (1961), 97–114.

Pineas, Rainer, 'More Versus Tyndale: A Study of Controversial Technique', *MLQ* 24 (1963), 144–50.

Pineas, Rainer, 'William Tyndale: Controversialist', *SP* 60 (1963), 117–32.

Plaidy, Jean, *The Murder in the Tower: The Story of Frances, Countess of Essex* (New York: Random House, 2012, rpt of 1964).

Plett, Heinrich F., *Rhetoric and Renaissance Culture* (Berlin: Walter de Gruyter, 2004).

Plomer, Henry R., and Tom Peete Cross, *The Life and Correspondence of Lodowick Bryskett* (Illinois: University of Illinois Press, 1927).

Pocock, J. G. A., *The Machiavellian Moment: Florentine Political Thought and the Atlantic Republican Tradition* (Princeton: Princeton University Press, 1975).

Poole, Adrian, 'Identity of Meaning', in Walker and Leedham-Green, eds, *Identity*, pp. 9–25.

Poovey, Mary, *A History of the Modern Fact: Problems of Knowledge in the Sciences of Wealth and Society* (Chicago: University of Chicago Press, 1998).

Popkin, Richard H., *The History of Scepticism from Erasmus to Descartes* (rev. edn, Assen: Van Gorcum, 1960).

Popper, Nicholas, 'An Ocean of Lies: The Problem of Historical Evidence in the Sixteenth Century', *HLQ* 74 (2011), 375–400.

Prescott, Anne Lake, *Imagining Rabelais in Renaissance England* (New Haven: Yale University Press, 1998).

Prescott, Anne Lake, 'Menippean Donne', in Shami, Flynn, and Hester, eds, *Handbook of Donne*, pp. 158–79.

Prestwich, Mena, ed., *International Calvinism, 1541–1715* (Oxford: Clarendon Press, 1985).

Pritchard, Alan, *English Biography in the Seventeenth Century: A Critical Survey* (Toronto: University of Toronto Press, 2005).

Pritchard, Arnold, *Catholic Loyalism in Elizabethan England* (London: Scolar Press, 1979).

Questier, Michael C., 'Loyalty, Religion and State Power in Early Modern England: English Romanism and the Jacobean Oath of Allegiance', *HJ* 40 (1997), 311–29.

Questier, Michael C., 'Elizabeth and the Catholics', in Ethan H. Shagan, ed., *Catholics and the 'Protestant Nation': Religious Politics and Identity in Early Modern England* (Manchester: Manchester University Press, 2005).

Questier, Michael C., *Catholicism and Community in Early Modern England: Politics, Aristocratic Patronage and Religion, c.1550–1640* (Cambridge: Cambridge University Press, 2006).

Quint, David, *Montaigne and the Quality of Mercy: Ethical and Political Themes in the 'Essais'* (Princeton: Princeton University Press, 1998).

Quint, David, 'Archimago and Amoret: The Poem and its Doubles', in Patrick Cheney and Lauren Silberman, eds, *Worldmaking Spenser: Explorations in the Early Modern Age* (Lexington: University Press of Kentucky, 2000), pp. 32–42.

Raab, Felix, *The English Face of Machiavelli: A Changing Interpretation, 1500–1700* (London: Routledge, 1965).

Raffield, Paul, 'The Trials of Shakespeare: Courtroom Drama and Early Modern English Law', *Law & Hum.* 8 (2014), 53–76.

Rambuss, Richard, *Spenser's Secret Career* (Cambridge: Cambridge University Press, 1993).

Rattner, A., 'Convicted but Innocent: Wrongful Conviction and the Criminal Justice System', *LHB* 12 (1988), 283–93.

Raymond, Joad, *Pamphlets and Pamphleteering in Early Modern Britian* (Cambridge: Cambridge University Press, 2003).

Raymond, Joad, ed., *The Oxford History of Popular Print Culture, Vol. 1: Cheap Print in Britain and Ireland to 1660* (Oxford: Oxford University Press, 2011).

Redmond, Michael J., *Shakespeare, Politics, and Italy: Intertextuality on the Jacobean Stage* (Farnham: Ashgate, 2009).

Relihan, Constance C., *Fashioning Authority: The Development of Elizabethan Novelistic Discourse* (Ohio: Kent State University Press, 1994).

Renner, Bernd, 'From *Satura* to *Satyre*: François Rabelais and the Renaissance Appropriation of a Genre', *RQ* 67 (2014), 377–424.

Reynolds, E. E., *The Trial of St. Thomas More* (London: Burns & Oates, 1964).

Rhodes, Neil, *Elizabethan Grotesque* (London: Routledge, 1980).

Rhodes, Neil, *Shakespeare and the Origins of English* (Oxford: Oxford University Press, 2004).

Rhodes, Neil, 'Orality, Print and Popular Culture: Thomas Nashe and Marshall McLuhan', in Matthew Dimmock and Andrew Hadfield, eds, *Literature and Popular Culture in Early Modern England* (Aldershot: Ashgate, 2009), pp. 29–44.

Ribner, Irving, 'Marlowe and Machiavelli', *CL* 6 (1954), 348–56.

Rich, Adrienne, 'Women and Honour: Some Notes on Lying', in *On Lies, Secrets, and Silence: Selected Prose, 1966–1978* (New York: Norton, 1979), pp. 185–94.

Richards, Jennifer, 'Assumed Simplicity and the Critique of Nobility: Or, How Castiglione Read Cicero', *RQ* 54 (2001), 460–86.

Richards, Jennifer, *Rhetoric and Courtliness in Early Modern Literature* (Cambridge: Cambridge University Press, 2003).

Richards, Jennifer, *Rhetoric* (Abingdon: Routledge, 2008).

Richards, Jennifer, 'Health, Intoxication, and Civil Conversation in Renaissance England', in Phil Withington and Angela McShane, eds, *Cultures of Intoxication: P. & P. Supplement* 9 (2014), 168–86.

Richards, Jennifer, 'Reading and Listening to William Baldwin', in Archer and Hadfield, eds, Mirror for Magistrates *in Context*.

Rickman, Johanna, *Love, Lust, and License in Early Modern England: Illicit Sex and the Nobility* (Farnham: Ashgate, 2008).

Ricoeur, Paul, *History and Truth*, trans. Charles A. Kelbley (2nd edn, Chicago: Northwestern University Press, 1965).

Riddell, James A., and Stanley Stewart, *Jonson's Spenser: Evidence and Historical Criticism* (Pittsburgh: Duquesne University Press, 1995).

Ridolfi, Roberto, *The Life of Niccolò Machiavelli*, trans. Cecil Grayson (London: Routledge, 1963).

Riggs, David, *Ben Jonson: A Life* (Cambridge, MA: Harvard University Press, 1989).

Riley, Gillian, 'Food in Painting', in Fabio Parasecoli and Peter Scholliers, eds, *A Cultural History of Food*, 6 vols (London: Bloomsbury, 2013), III, pp. 171–82.

Rives, James B., '*Germania*', in Victoria Emma Pagán, ed., *A Companion to Tacitus* (Oxford: Blackwell, 2012), pp. 45–61.

Roberts, Jeanne Addison, 'Marriage and Divorce in 1613: Elizabeth Cary, Frances Howard and Others', in Laurie E. Maguire and Thomas L. Berger, eds, *Textual Formations and Reformations* (Cranbury, NJ: Associated University Press, 1998), pp. 161–78.

Robertson, D. W., Jr, 'Chaucerian Tragedy', *ELH* 19 (1952), 1–37.

Robinson, Benedict Scott, 'John Foxe and the Anglo-Saxons', in Highley and King, eds, *Foxe and His World*, pp. 54–72.

Robinson, Marsha S., 'Doctors, Silly Poor Women, and Rebel Whores: The Gendering of Conscience in Foxe's *Acts and Monuments*', in Highley and King, eds, *Foxe and His World*, pp. 235–48.

Roe, John, *Shakespeare and Machiavelli* (Woodbridge: Brewer, 2002).

Rogers, Stephen, 'Othello: Comedy in Reverse', *SQ* 24 (1973), 210–20.

Roodenburg, Herman, 'Introduction: Entering the Sensory Worlds of the Renaissance', in Herman Roodenburg, ed., *A Cultural History of the Senses in the Renaissance* (London: Bloomsbury, 2014), pp. 1–17.

Rose, Elliot, *Cases of Conscience: Alternatives Open to Recusants and Puritans Under Elizabeth I and James I* (Cambridge: Cambridge University Press, 1975).

Rose, Mary Beth, *The Expense of Spirit: Love and Sexuality in English Renaissance Drama* (Ithaca, NY: Cornell University Press, 1988).

Rosenberg, Eleanor, *Leicester, Patron of Letters* (New York: Columbia University Press, 1955).

Ross, Charles, 'Avoiding the Issue of Fraud: 4, 5 Philip & Mary c.8 (the Heiress Protection Statute), Portia, and Desdemona', in Constance Jordan and Karen Cunningham, eds, *The Law in Shakespeare* (Basingstoke: Palgrave Macmillan, 2007), pp. 91–108.

Rowe, Dorothy, *Why We Lie: The Source of Our Disasters* (London: Fourth Estate, 2011).

Rowse, A. L., *Simon Forman: Sex and Society in Shakespeare's Age* (London: Weidenfeld and Nicolson, 1974).

Rubin, Miri, *Gentile Tales: The Narrative Assault on Late Medieval Jews* (New Haven: Yale University Press, 1999).

Ruff, Julius R., *Violence in Early Modern Europe, 1500–1800* (Cambridge: Cambridge University Press, 2001).

Ryan, Clarence J., 'The Jacobean Oath of Allegiance and English Lay Catholics', *CHR* 28 (1942), 159–83.

Ryrie, Alec, 'Divine Kingship and Royal Theology in Henry VIII's Reformation', *Reformation* 7 (2002), 49–77.

Ryrie, Alec, *The Gospel and Henry VIII: Evangelicals in the Early English Reformation* (Cambridge: Cambridge University Press, 2003).

Ryrie, Alec, *The Age of Reformation: The Tudor and Stewart Realms, 1485–1603* (Harlow: Pearson, 2009).

Ryrie, Alec, *Being Protestant in Reformation Britain* (Oxford: Oxford University Press, 2013).

Sandler, Florence, '*The Faerie Queene*: An Elizabethan Apocalypse', in C. A. Patrides and Joseph Wittreich, eds, *The Apocalypse in English Renaissance Thought and Literature* (Manchester: Manchester University Press, 1984), pp. 148–74.

Santinello, Giovanni, *Models of the History of Philosophy: From its Origins in the Renaissance to the 'Historia Philosophica'* (Dordrecht: Kluwer, 1993).

Saul, Jennifer, *Lying, Misleading, and What is Not Said: An Exploration in Philosophy of Language and in Ethics* (Oxford: Oxford University Press, 2012).

Scarisbrick, J. J., *Henry VIII* (London: Methuen, 1988, rpt of 1981).

Schauer, Margery S., and Frederick Schauer, 'Law as the Engine of State: The Trial of Anne Boleyn', *William & Mary Law Review* 22 (1980), 49–84.

Schmitt, Charles B., and Quentin Skinner, eds, *The Cambridge History of Renaissance Philosophy* (Cambridge: Cambridge University Press, 1988).

Schramm, Jan-Melissa, *Testimony and Advocacy in Victorian Law, Literature, and Theology* (Cambridge: Cambridge University Press, 2000).

Schwyzer, Philip, *Archaeologies of English Renaissance Literature* (Oxford: Oxford University Press, 2007).

Scofield, Cora L., *A Study of the Court of Star Chamber* (Chicago: University of Chicago Press, 1900).

Scribner, R. W., *Popular Culture and Popular Movements in Reformation Germany* (London: A. C. Black, 1987).

Serjeantson, R. W., 'Testimony and Proof in Early-Modern England', *SHPS* 30 (1999), 195–236.

Serjeantson, R. W., Testimony', in Adamson, Alexander, and Ettenhuber, eds, *Renaissance Figures of Speech*, pp. 180–94.

Sessions, W. A., *Henry Howard, the Poet Earl of Surrey: A Life* (Oxford: Oxford University Press, 1999).

Sgroi, R. C. L., 'Piscatorial Politics Revisited: The Language of Economic Debate and the Evolution of Fishing Policy in Elizabethan England', *Albion* 35 (2003), 1–24.

Shagan, Ethan H., *Popular Politics and the English Reformation* (Cambridge: Cambridge University Press, 2003).

Shami, Jeanne, Dennis Flynn, and M. Thomas Hester, eds, *The Oxford Handbook of John Donne* (Oxford: Oxford University Press, 2011).

Shapin, Steven, *A Social History of Truth: Civility and Science in Seventeenth-Century England* (Chicago: University of Chicago Press, 1994).

Shapiro, Barbara J., *A Culture of Fact: England, 1550–1720* (Ithaca, NY: Cornell University Press, 2000).

Shapiro, James, *Shakespeare and the Jews* (Columbia: Columbia University Press, 1996).

Shapiro, James, *1606: William Shakespeare and the Year of Lear* (London: Faber, 2015).

Sharpe, J. A., '"Last Dying Speeches": Religion, Ideology and Public Execution in Seventeenth-Century England', *P. & P.* 107 (May 1985), 144–67.

Sharpe, J. A., *Crime and the Law in English Satirical Prints, 1600–1832* (Cambridge: Chadwyck-Healey, 1986).

Sharpe, Kevin, *Selling the Tudor Monarchy: Authority and Image in Sixteenth-Century England* (New Haven: Yale University Press, 2009).

Shell, Alison, *Catholicism, Controversy and the English Literary Imagination, 1558–1660* (Cambridge: Cambridge University Press, 1999).

Shell, Alison, *Oral Culture and Catholicism in Early Modern England* (Cambridge: Cambridge University Press, 2007).

Sherman, William H., *Used Books: Marking Readers in Renaissance England* (Philadelphia: University of Pennsylvania Press, 2010).

Shiffrin, Seana Valentine, *Speech Matters: On Lying, Morality, and the Law* (Princeton: Princeton University Press, 2014).

Shirley, Frances A., *Swearing and Perjury in Shakespeare's Plays* (London: Allen and Unwin, 1979).

Shrank, Cathy, *Writing the Nation in Reformation England, 1530–1580* (Oxford: Oxford University Press, 2004).

Shrank, Cathy, 'Manuscript, Authenticity and "evident proofs" against the Scottish Queen', in A. S. G. Edwards, ed., *Tudor Manuscripts 1485–1603* (English Manuscript Studies, 1100–1700, vol. 15) (London: British Library, 2010), pp. 198–218.

Shrank, Cathy, '"This fatall Medea," "this Clytemnestra": Reading and the Detection of Mary Queen of Scots', *HLQ* 73 (2010), 523–41.

Shuger, Debora Kuller, *Habits of Thought in the English Renaissance: Religion, Politics, and the Dominant Culture* (Berkeley: University of California Press, 1990).

Shuger, Debora Kuller, 'Sins of the Tongue', *Slate Magazine*, 15 Sept. 1999.

Simon, Joan, *Education and Society in Tudor England* (Cambridge: Cambridge University Press, 1979).

Simpson, James, 'Rhetoric, Conscience, and the Playful Positions of Sir Thomas More', in Pincombe and Shrank, eds, *Oxford Handbook of Tudor Literature*, pp. 121–36.

Simpson, James, 'The Psalms and Threat in Sixteenth-Century English Culture', *RS* 29 (2015), 576–94.

Sinfield, Alan, *Literature in Protestant England, 1560–1660* (New York: Barnes and Noble, 1983).

Singh, Jyotsna G., 'The Interventions of History: Narratives of Sexuality', in Dympna Callaghan, Lorraine Helms, and Jyotsna G. Singh, *The Weyward Sisters: Shakespeare and Feminist Politics* (Oxford: Blackwell, 1994), pp. 7–58.

Singh, Jyotsna G., ed., *A Companion to the Global Renaissance: English Literature and Culture in the Era of Expansion* (Oxford: Blackwell, 2009).

Skinner, Quentin, *The Foundations of Modern Political Thought*, 2 vols (Cambridge: Cambridge University Press, 1978).

Skinner, Quentin, *Machiavelli* (Oxford: Oxford University Press, 1981).

Skinner, Quentin, 'Political Philosophy', in Schmitt and Skinner, eds, *Cambridge History of Renaissance Philosophy*, pp. 389–452.

Skinner, Quentin, *Visions of Politics*, 3 vols (Cambridge: Cambridge University Press, 2002).

Skinner, Quentin, *Forensic Shakespeare* (Oxford: Oxford University Press, 2014).

Smith, David Chan, *Sir Edward Coke and the Reformation of the Laws: Religion, Politics and Jurisprudence, 1578–1616* (Cambridge: Cambridge University Press, 2014).

Smith, Emma, *The Making of Shakespeare's First Folio* (Oxford: Bodleian Library, 2015).

Smith, Rosalind, *Sonnets and the English Woman Writer, 1560–1621: The Politics of Absence* (Basingstoke: Palgrave Macmillan, 2005).

Smuts, Malcolm, 'Court-Centred Politics and the Uses of Roman Histories, c.1590–1630', in Kevin Sharpe and Peter Lake, eds, *Culture and Politics in Early Stuart England* (Basingstoke: Macmillan, 1994), pp. 21–44.

Smylie, Mike, *Herring: A History of the Silver Darlings* (Stroud: The History Press, 2004).

Snyder, Jon R., *Dissimulation and the Culture of Secrecy in Early Modern Europe* (Berkeley: University of California Press, 2009).

Snyder, Susan, *Shakespeare: A Wayward Journey* (Newark: University of Delaware Press, 2002).

Sobecki, Sebastian, '"A Man of Curious Enquiry": John Peyton's Grand Tour to Central Europe and Robert Cecil's Intelligence Network, 1596–1601', *RS* 29 (2015), 394–410.

Sokol, B. J., and Mary Sokol, *Shakespeare's Legal Language: A Dictionary* (London: Athlone, 2000).

Sommerville, Johann P., 'The "New Art of Lying": Equivocation, Mental Reservation, and Casuistry', in Leites, ed., *Conscience and Casuistry*, pp. 159–84.

Sonnino, Lee A., *A Handbook to Sixteenth-Century Rhetoric* (London: Routledge, 1968).

Southgate, Beverley, *Postmodernism in History: Fear or Freedom?* (London: Routledge, 2003).

Spade, Paul Vincent, 'Synonymy and Equivocation in Ockham's Mental Language', *JHP* 18 (1980), 9–22.

Spiegel, Gabrielle M., ed., *Practicing History: New Directions in Historical Writing after the Linguistic Turn* (London: Routledge, 2005).

Spufford, Margaret, *Small Books and Pleasant Histories: Popular Fiction and its Readership in Seventeenth-Century England* (Cambridge: Cambridge University Press, 1981).

Spurr, John, 'A Profane History of Early Modern Oaths', *TRHS* 11 (2001), 37–63.

Spurr, John, '"The Strongest Bond of Conscience": Oaths and the Limits of Tolerance in Early Modern England', in Braun and Vallance, eds, *Contexts of Conscience*, pp. 151–65.

Stacy, William R., 'Richard Roose and the Use of Parliamentary Attainder in the Reign of Henry VIII', *HJ* 29 (1986), 1–15.

Staines, John D., *The Tragic Histories of Mary Queen of Scots, 1560–1690* (Aldershot: Ashgate, 2009).

Stamatakis, Chris, *Sir Thomas Wyatt and the Rhetoric of Rewriting: Turning the Word* (Oxford: Oxford University Press, 2012).

Starkey, David, *Six Wives: The Queens of Henry VIII* (London: Vintage, 2004).

Stauffer, Richard, 'Calvin', in Prestwich, ed., *International Calvinism*, pp. 15–38.

Stead, Jennifer, '"Bowers of Bliss": The Banquet Setting', in C. Anne Wilson, ed., *'Banquetting stuffe': The Fare and Social Background of the Tudor and Stuart Banquet* (Edinburgh: Edinburgh University Press, 1991), 115–57.

Stegner, Paul D., *Confession and Memory in Early Modern English Literature: Penitential Remains* (Basingstoke: Palgrave Macmillan, 2015).

Stenner, Rachel, 'The Act of Penning in William Baldwin's *Beware the Cat*', *RS* 30 (2016), 334–49.

Stephanson, Raymond, 'The Epistemological Challenge of Nashe's The Unfortunate Traveller', *SEL* 23 (1983), 21–36.

Stern, Tiffany, *Making Shakespeare: From Stage to Page* (London: Routledge, 2004).

Stewart, Alan, *Close Readers: Humanism and Sodomy in Early Modern England* (Princeton: Princeton University Press, 1997).

Stewart, Alan, *Philip Sidney: A Double Life* (London: Chatto & Windus, 2000).

Stewart, Alan, *Shakespeare's Letters* (Oxford: Oxford University Press, 2008).

Stillman, Robert E., *Philip Sidney and the Poetics of Renaissance Cosmopolitanism* (Farnham: Ashgate, 2013).

Stone, Bernard Gert, *Morality: Its Nature and Justification* (Oxford: Oxford University Press, 1998).

Stone, Lawrence, *The Crisis of the Aristocracy, 1558–1641* (Oxford: Clarendon Press, 1979, rpt of 1967).

Story Donno, Elizabeth, 'Old Mouse-Eaten Records: History in Sidney's *Apology*', *SP* 72 (1975), 275–98.

Stoye, John, *English Travellers Abroad, 1604–1667* (rev. edn, New Haven: Yale University Press, 1989).

Strandberg, Victor, 'The Comedy of *Othello*', *The McNeese Review* 19 (1968), 3–15.

Strauss, Walter L., *The German Single-Leaf Woodcut, 1550–1600*, 3 vols (New York: Abaris, 1975).

Streete, Adrian, *Protestantism and Drama in Early Modern England* (Cambridge: Cambridge University Press, 2009).

Strohm, Paul, *Conscience: A Very Short Introduction* (Oxford: Oxford University Press, 2011).

Sullivan, Ceri, *The Rhetoric of Conscience in Donne, Herbert, and Vaughan* (Oxford: Oxford University Press, 2008).

Summit, Jennifer, 'Monuments and Ruins: Spenser and the Problem of the English Library', *ELH* 70 (2003), 1–34.

Syme, Holger Schott, *Theatre and Testimony in Shakespeare's England: A Culture of Mediation* (Cambridge: Cambridge University Press, 2012).

Tadmor, Naomi, *The Social Universe of the English Bible: Scripture, Society, and Culture in Early Modern England* (Cambridge: Cambridge University Press, 2010).

Tarlow, Sarah, *Ritual, Belief and the Dead in Early Modern Britain and Ireland* (Cambridge: Cambridge University Press, 2011).

Thomas, Catherine E., 'Toxic Encounters: Poisoning in Early Modern English Literature and Culture', *LC* 9 (2012), 48–55.

Thomas, Keith, 'Cases of Conscience in Seventeenth-Century England', in John Morrill, Paul Slack, and Daniel Woolf, eds, *Public Duty and Private Conscience in Seventeenth-Century England: Essays Presented to G. E. Aylmer* (Oxford: Clarendon Press, 1993), pp. 29–56.

Thomas, Keith, *The Ends of Life: Roads to Fulfilment in Early Modern England* (Oxford: Oxford University Press, 2009).

Thomson, Philip, *The Grotesque* (London: Methuen, 1972).

Tilmouth, Christopher, *Passion's Triumph over Reason: A History of the Moral Imagination from Spenser to Rochester* (Oxford: Oxford University Press, 2007).

Tittler, Robert, 'The English Fishing Industry in the Sixteenth Century: The Case of Great Yarmouth', *Albion* 9 (1977), 40–60.

Tonkin, Humphrey, *Spenser's Courteous Pastoral: Book VI of* The Faerie Queene (Oxford: Oxford University Press, 1972).

Tonkin, Humphrey, *The Faerie Queene* (New York: Unwin, 1989).

Trim, D. J. B., 'The Art of War: Martial Poetics from Henry Howard to Philip Sidney', in Pincombe and Shrank, eds, *Oxford Handbook of Tudor Literature*, pp. 587–605.

Trimpi, Wesley, 'Sir Philip Sidney's *An Apology for Poetry*', in Norton, ed., *Cambridge History of Literary Criticism, Vol. III*, pp. 187–98.

Turner, Henry S., 'Nashe's Red Herring: Epistemologies of the Commodity in *Lenten Stuffe* (1599)', *ELH* 68 (2001), 529–61.

Turner Wright, Celeste, 'Young Anthony Munday Again', *SP* 56 (1959), 150–68.

Tutino, Stefania, 'Notes on Machiavelli and Ignatius Loyola in John Donne's *Ignatius his Conclave* and *Pseudo-Martyr*', *EHR* 99 (2004), 1308–21.

Tutino, Stefania, *Law and Conscience: Catholicism in Early Modern England, 1570–1625* (Farnham: Ashgate, 2007).

Tutino, Stefania, 'Thomas Preston and English Catholic Loyalism: Elements of an International Affair', *C16J* 41 (2010), 91–109.

Tyacke, Nicholas, *Anti-Calvinists: The Rise of English Armenianism, c.1590–1640* (Oxford: Clarendon Press, 1987).

Tyacke, Nicholas, ed., *England's Long Reformation, 1500–1800* (London: Routledge, 1998).

Usher, R. G., 'James I and Sir Edward Coke', *EHR* 18 (1903), 664–75.

Utz, Richard, 'The Medieval Myth of Jewish Ritual Murder: Toward a History of Reception', *YWM* 14 (2000), 24–46.

Van Es, Bart, *Shakespeare in Company* (Oxford: Oxford University Press, 2013).

Vance, John N., 'Gross Anatomies: Mapping Matter and Literary Form in Thomas Nashe and Andreas Vesalius', in Guy-Bray, Linton, and Mentz, eds, *The Age of Thomas Nashe*, pp. 115–31.

Vaughan, Virginia Mason, *Othello: A Contextual History* (Cambridge: Cambridge University Press, 1994).

Vickers, Brian, *In Defence of Rhetoric* (Oxford: Clarendon Press, 1988).

Vinnicombe, Carolyn, 'Recusancy and Regicide: The Flawed Strategy of the Jesuit Mission in Elizabethan England', *Penn History Review* 19 (2012), 25–43.

Visser, Arnoud S. Q., *Reading Augustine in the Reformation: The Flexibility of Intellectual Authority in Europe, 1500–1620* (Oxford: Oxford University Press, 2011).

Wabuda, Susan, 'Equivocation and Recantation During the English Reformation: The "Subtle Shadows" of Dr. Edward Crome', *JEH* 44 (1993), 224–42.

Wabuda, Susan, *Preaching During the English Reformation* (Cambridge: Cambridge University Press, 2002).

Wagner, John A., 'Baldwin, William', in Wagner and Schmid, eds, *Encyclopedia of Tudor England*, pp. 86–8.

Wagner, John A., and Susan Walters Schmid, eds, *Encyclopedia of Tudor England*, 3 vols (Santa Barbara: ABC-Clio, 2012).

Walker, Garthine, *Crime, Gender and Social Order in Early Modern England* (Cambridge: Cambridge University Press, 2003).

Walker, Giselle, and Elisabeth Leedham-Green, eds, *Identity* (Cambridge: Cambridge University Press, 2010).

Walker, Greg, 'Saint or Schemer? The 1527 Heresy Trial of Thomas Bilney Reconsidered', in *Persuasive Fictions: Faction, Faith and Political Culture in the Reign of Henry VIII* (Aldershot: Scolar Press, 1996), pp. 143–65.

Walker, Greg, *The Politics of Performance in Early Renaissance Drama* (Cambridge: Cambridge University Press, 1998).

Walker, Greg, 'Rethinking the Fall of Anne Boleyn', *HJ* 45 (2002), 1–29.

Walker, Greg, *Writing Under Tyranny: English Literature and the Henrician Reformation* (Oxford: Oxford University Press, 2005).

Wallis, Patrick, 'Consumption, Retailing, and Medicine in Early-Modern London', *Ec.HR* 61 (2008), 26–53.

Walsham, Alexandra, *Church Papists: Catholicism, Conformity and Confessional Polemic in Early Modern England* (Woodbridge: Boydell and Brewer, 1993).

Walsham, Alexandra, *Providence in Early Modern England* (Oxford: Oxford University Press, 1999).

Walsham, Alexandra, *The Reformation of the Landscape: Religion, Identity, and Memory in Early Modern Britain and Ireland* (Oxford: Oxford University Press, 2011).

Walsham, Alexandra, 'Cultures of Coexistence in Early Modern England: History, Literature and Religious Toleration', *The Seventeenth Century* 28 (2013), 115–37.

Walsham, Alexandra, *Catholic Reformation in Protestant Britain* (Farnham: Ashgate, 2014).

Ward, John O., 'Cicero and Quintilian', in Norton, ed., *Cambridge History of Literary Criticism, Vol. III*, pp. 77–87.

Warner, Marina, *Alone of All Her Sex: The Myth and the Cult of the Virgin Mary* (Oxford: Oxford University Press, 2013).

Warnicke, Reitha M., 'The Fall of Anne Boleyn: A Reassessment', *History* 70 (1985), 1–15.

Warnicke, Reitha M., *The Rise and Fall of Anne Boleyn: Family Politics at the Court of Henry VIII* (Cambridge: Cambridge University Press, 1989).

Warnicke, Reitha M., 'The Fall of Anne Boleyn Revisited', *EHR* 108 (1993), 653–65.

Warren, W. L., *King John* (2nd edn, London: Eyre Methuen, 1978).

Waswo, Richard, *Language and Meaning in the Renaissance* (Princeton: Princeton University Press, 1987).

Watt, Tessa, *Cheap Print and Popular Piety, 1550–1640* (Cambridge: Cambridge University Press, 1993).

Waugh, Evelyn, *Edmund Campion: Scholar, Priest, Hero, and Martyr* (Oxford: Oxford University Press, 1980, rpt of 1935).

Weatherby, Harold L., *Mirrors of Celestial Grace: Patristic Theology in Spenser's Allegory* (Toronto: University of Toronto Press, 1994).

Webster, T. B. L., *The Tragedies of Euripides* (London: Methuen, 1967).

Weiner, Andrew D., *Sir Philip Sidney and the Poetics of Protestantism: A Study of Contexts* (Minneapolis: University of Minnesota Press, 1978).

Weinrich, Harald, *The Linguistics of Lying and Other Essays*, trans. Jane K. Brown and Marshall Brown (Seattle: University of Washington Press, 2005).

Wells, Stanley, 'Allusions to Shakespeare to 1642', in Paul Edmondson and Stanley Wells, eds, *Shakespeare Beyond Doubt: Evidence, Argument, Controversy* (Cambridge: Cambridge University Press, 2013), pp. 73–87.

Wells, Stanley, *Great Shakespeare Actors: Burbage to Branagh* (Oxford: Oxford University Press, 2015).

Welsby, Paul A., *George Abbot: The Unwanted Archbishop, 1562–1633* (London: SPCK, 1962).

Wernham, R. B., *After the Armada: Elizabethan England and the Struggle for Western Europe, 1588–1595* (Oxford: Oxford University Press, 1984).

Werrell, Ralph S., *The Theology of William Tyndale* (Cambridge: James Clark, 2006).

Whigham, Frank, *Seizures of the Will in Early Modern English Drama* (Cambridge: Cambridge University Press, 1996).

Whitaker, Virgil K., *The Religious Basis of Spenser's Thought* (Stanford: Stanford University Press, 1950).

White, Paul Whitfield, 'Marlowe and the Politics of Religion', in Patrick Cheney, ed., *The Cambridge Companion to Christopher Marlowe* (Cambridge: Cambridge University Press, 2004), pp. 70–89.

White, R. S., *Natural Law in English Renaissance Literature* (Cambridge: Cambridge University Press, 1996).

Wilders, John, *The Lost Garden: A View of Shakespeare's English and Roman History Plays* (London: Macmillan, 1978).

Williams, Arnold, *Flower on a Lowly Stalk: The Sixth Book of* The Faerie Queene (East Lansing: Michigan State University Press, 1967).

Williams, Bernard, *Truth and Truthfulness* (Princeton: Princeton University Press, 2002).

Bibliography

Williams, Raymond, *Modern Tragedy* (London: Verso, 1979, rpt of 1966).

Williams, Richard, '"Libels and Payntinges": Elizabethan Catholics and the International Campaign of Visual Propaganda', in Highley and King, eds, *Foxe and His World*, pp. 198–215.

Williams, Rowan, 'The Martyrdom of Thomas Cranmer: Sermon at Service to Commemorate the 450th Anniversary' Tuesday 21st March 2006 (http://rowanwilliams.archbishopofcanterbury.org/articles.php/1599/the-martyrdom-of-thomas-cranmer-sermon-at-service-to-commemorate-the-450th-anniversary).

Willson, David Harris, *King James VI and I* (London: Cape, 1956).

Wilson, C. Anne, *The Book of Marmalade* (Totnes: Prospect Books, 1999).

Wilson, F. P., 'Some English Mock-Prognostications', *The Library*, 4th series, 19 (1939), 6–43.

Wilson, Luke, *Theaters of Intention: Drama and the Law in Early Modern England* (Stanford: Stanford University Press, 2000).

Wilson, Richard, *Secret Shakespeare: Studies in Theatre, Religion and Resistance* (Manchester: Manchester University Press, 2004).

Wine, Celesta, 'Nathaniel Wood's *Conflict of Conscience*', *PMLA* 50 (1935), 661–78.

Wine, Celesta, 'Nathaniel Woodes: Author of the Morality Play *The Conflict of Conscience*', *RES* 15 (1939), 458–63.

Wiseman, Susan J., *Writing Metamorphosis in the English Renaissance: 1550–1700* (Cambridge: Cambridge University Press, 2014).

Withington, Phil, 'Introduction: Cultures of Intoxication', in Withington and McShane, eds, *Cultures of Intoxication*, pp. 9–33.

Withington, Phil, and Angela McShane, eds, *Cultures of Intoxication* (Oxford: Oxford University Press, 2014).

Witmore, Michael, *Pretty Creatures: Children and Fiction in the English Renaissance* (Ithaca, NY: Cornell University Press, 2007).

Womersley, David, 'Sir Henry Saville's Translation of Tacitus and the Political Interpretation of Elizabethan Texts', *RES* 42 (1991), 313–42.

Womersley, David, *Divinity and State* (Oxford: Oxford University Press, 2010).

Wood, Andy, *The 1549 Rebellions and the Making of Early Modern England* (Cambridge: Cambridge University Press, 2007).

Wood, Frederik T., 'The Comic Elements in the English Mystery Plays', *Neophilologus* 25 (1940), 39–48.

Wood, Thomas, *English Casuistical Divinity During the Seventeenth Century with Special Reference to Jeremy Taylor* (London: SPCK, 1952).

Woodcock, Matthew, '1603', in Raymond, ed., *Oxford History of Popular Print Culture*, pp. 578–89.

Woodcock, Matthew, *Thomas Churchyard: Pen, Sword, and Ego* (Oxford: Oxford University Press, 2016).

Woods, Gillian, *Shakespeare's Unreformed Fictions* (Oxford: Oxford University Press, 2013).

Wootton, David, 'John Donne's Religion of Love', in Brooke and Maclean, eds, *Heterodoxy in Early Modern Science and Religion*, pp. 31–80.

Worden, Blair, 'Ben Jonson among the Historians', in Peter Lake and Kevin Sharpe, eds, *Culture and Politics in Early Stuart England* (Basingstoke: Macmillan, 1994), pp. 67–89.

Worden, Blair, 'Politics in *Catiline*: Jonson and His Sources', in Martin Butler, ed., *Re-Presenting Ben Jonson: Text, History, Performance* (Basingstoke: Macmillan, 1999), pp. 152–73.

Wormald, Jenny, *Mary Queen of Scots: A Study in Failure* (London: Collins & Brown, 1991).

Wright, Herbert G., 'How Did Shakespeare Come to Know the "Decameron"?', *MLR* 50 (1955), 45–8.

Yates, Frances A., *The Art of Memory* (Harmondsworth: Penguin, 1966).

Yates, Frances A., *Astrea: The Imperial Theme in the Sixteenth Century* (London: Routledge, 1975).

Zagorin, Perez, *Ways of Lying: Dissimulation and Conformity in Early Modern Europe* (Cambridge, MA: Harvard University Press, 1990).

Zagorin, Perez, 'The Historical Significance of Lying and Dissimulation', *Social Research* 63 (1996), 863–912.

Zaller, Robert, *The Discourse of Legitimacy in Early Modern England* (Stanford: Stanford University Press, 2007).

Zarnowiecki, Matthew, *Fair Copies: Reproducing the English Lyric from Tottel to Shakespeare* (Toronto: Toronto University Press, 2014).

Zembaty, Jane S., 'Plato's *Republic* and Greek Morality on Lying', *JHP* 26 (1988), 517–45.

Zembaty, Jane S., 'Aristotle on Lying', *JHP* 31 (1993), 7–29.

Zizek, Slavov, 'What Rumsfeld Doesn't Know That He Knows About Abu Ghraib', 'In These Times', 21 May 2004 (http://www.lacan.com/zizekrumsfeld.htm).

Zurcher, Andrew, *Edmund Spenser's 'The Faerie Queene': A Reading Guide* (Edinburgh: Edinburgh University Press, 2011).

Theses

Altman, Shanyn, 'John Donne and Martyrdom', PhD thesis, University of Sussex, 2017.

Ashton, Anne M., 'Interpreting Breast Iconography in Italian Art, 1250–1600', PhD thesis, University of St Andrews, 2006.

Bouldin, Elizabeth, '"Dying Men's Wordes": Treason, Heresy, and Scaffold Performances in Sixteenth-Century England', MA thesis, North Carolina State University, 2005.

Buckley, Victoria Jane, 'Patterns of Mischief: The Impact of the Gunpowder Plot on the Jacobean Stage 1605-16', PhD thesis, University of Sussex, 2012.

Campbell, Philip, 'The Canon Law of the Henry VIII Divorce Case', senior thesis, Social Studies Department, Madonna University, Livonia, MI, 2009.

Foster, Andrew W., 'A Biography of Archbishop Richard Neile (1562–1640)', DPhil thesis, University of Oxford, 1978.

Fraser, Duncan, 'An Annotated Edition of Lordling Barry's *Ram Alley*', PhD thesis, University of Sussex, 2013.

Gaudet, Paul M., 'William Baldwin's *A Treatise of Moral Philosophy* (1564): A Variorum Edition with Introduction', PhD dissertation, Princeton University, 1972.

Hill, Alexandra Nicole, '"Bloudy Tygrisses": Murderous Women in Early Modern English Drama and Popular Literature', PhD thesis, University of Central Florida Orlando, Florida, 2009.

Quinn, Paul, 'Anti-Papistry and the English Stage, 1580–1642', PhD thesis, University of Sussex, 2006.

Schmid, Susan Walter, 'Anne Boleyn, Lancelot de Carle, and the Uses of Documentary Evidence', PhD thesis, Arizona State University, 2009.

Vince, Máté, 'From "Aequivocatio" to the "Jesuitical Equivocation": The Changing Concepts of Ambiguity in Early Modern England', PhD thesis, University of Warwick, 2013.

Index

362

Index

Index